Statecraft 2.0

BRIDGING THE GAP

Statecraft 2.0

What America Needs to Lead in a Multipolar World

DENNIS ROSS

OXFORD
UNIVERSITY PRESS

OXFORD
UNIVERSITY PRESS

Oxford University Press is a department of the University of Oxford.
It furthers the University's objective of excellence in research, scholarship,
and education by publishing worldwide. Oxford is a registered trade mark of
Oxford University Press in the UK and in certain other countries.

Published in the United States of America by Oxford University Press
198 Madison Avenue, New York, NY 10016, United States of America.

Library of Congress Cataloging-in-Publication Data

Names: Ross, Dennis, author.
Title: Statecraft 2.0 : what America needs to survive in a multipolar world / Dennis Ross.
Description: New York : Oxford University Press, 2025. | Series: Bridging the gap
| Includes bibliographical references and index.
Identifiers: LCCN 2024038581 (print) | LCCN 2024038582 (ebook) |
ISBN 9780197698921 (paperback) | ISBN 9780197698914 (hardback) |
ISBN 9780197698938 (epub) | ISBN 9780197698952
Subjects: LCSH: United States—Foreign relations—21st century. |
World politics—1989- | Multipolarity (International relations)
Classification: LCC JZ1480 .R675 2025 (print) | LCC JZ1480 (ebook) |
DDC 327.73009/05—dc23/eng/20241228
LC record available at https://lccn.loc.gov/2024038581
LC ebook record available at https://lccn.loc.gov/2024038582

DOI: 10.1093/oso/9780197698914.001.0001

Paperback printed by Integrated Books International, United States of America
Hardback printed by Bridgeport National Bindery, Inc., United States of America

The manufacturer's authorised representative in the EU for product safety is Oxford University Press España S.A. of El Parque Empresarial
San Fernando de Henares, Avenida de Castilla, 2 – 28830 Madrid (www.oup.es/en or product.safety@oup.com). OUP España S.A. also acts as
importer into Spain of products made by the manufacturer.

Contents

Preface

I learned a great deal about statecraft by being a policy practitioner for several decades in the Pentagon, the National Security Council staff at the White House and in a senior position at the State Department. In that latter position, I helped a master of statecraft, Secretary of State James Baker, as he orchestrated all of America's tools in producing German unification in NATO and then mobilizing and sustaining a broad coalition to deal with Saddam Hussein's invasion and occupation of Kuwait. As such, I was ready when asked to be the American negotiator on the Arab-Israeli conflict during the Clinton Administration. I understood how to manage whole of government efforts to use all of the administration's means to try to achieve the president's goals. As I watched the George W. Bush Administration conduct its foreign policies during its first term, I became increasingly convinced that its policies were failing because of how it was conducting statecraft. I decided to draft a book on statecraft and did so in 2005-2006. Among other things, I argued at the time that criticism of the Bush administration's policies for eschewing multilateralism was largely misplaced. Bush did not dismiss the value of multilateralism even on Iraq, where his administration focused on developing a "coalition of the willing." Bush produced partners, especially from what his Secretary of Defense Donald Rumsfeld called "new Europe."

Moreover, Bush's policies toward North Korea and Iran were also largely driven by working with others—though the policy approach on each went through a phase in his first term where, because of splits between the State and Defense departments and parts of the White House, there was more of an emphasis on unilateralism. My critique of Bush's policies had little to do with his employment of multilateralism—which is, after all, a means and not an objective—and much more about how poorly I thought multilateralism was applied.

Had I written that book later, in 2007–2008, I would have been less critical. Bush's policy approach as his second term unfolded became much better. The formulation of policy followed a more rigorous process, and his national security team worked well together. Issues were thoroughly debated, and fact-driven assessments—more than ideological ones—shaped the policy.

In reality, my criticism of Bush's policies was quite different from most of the critiques, which seemed to argue that if his foreign policy had just been guided by more collaborative diplomatic efforts, everything would have been fine. Too often his critics acted as if collaboration was an end in itself—but it never is. Collaboration needs to be tied to specific objectives—for example, working with those whose means can help us practically or tangibly achieve our goals or sharpen them or help us legitimize the objectives we seek to achieve.

In other words, there was a confusion of means and ends in too much of the criticism of Bush's policies, particularly on what was portrayed as his willingness to forgo working multilaterally and preferring to go it alone. In fact, Bush did not necessarily seek to act more unilaterally than most of his predecessors. The criticism also missed the point. When one contemplates a multilateral or unilateral approach, one is thinking of the means or the tools the United States needs to employ to achieve its interests in the world. One is or should be thinking of how to define one's purposes, make assessments about what one can and must do, and then go about implementing one's choices. All this is what I believed that Bush's critics missed.

In other words, I felt what was missing from the discussion of Bush's foreign policy was an understanding of statecraft. It was statecraft that I thought Bush, especially in the first term, did badly. What is statecraft? It is the use of assets or resources and tools (economic, military, intelligence, diplomatic—private and public) that a state has to pursue its interests and to affect the behavior of others, whether friendly or hostile. It involves making sound assessments and understanding where and on what issues the state is being challenged and can counter a threat or create a potential opportunity or take advantage of one. Statecraft requires good judgment in the definition of one's interests and a recognition of how to exercise hard military or soft economic power to provide security and promote the well-being of one's citizens.

As I wrote in the first book, statecraft is as old as conflict between nations or states and the desire to avoid or prevent it. Plato wrote about statecraft. Machiavelli theorized about it. And Bismarck practiced it, never losing sight of his objectives and recognizing that his objectives should never exceed his capabilities.

Statecraft is more difficult than ever in a world of rapid change, and with fewer national boundaries; more actors (states, and non-state actors such as religious groups and terrorist organizations); more diffuse power; continuing ethnic or intercommunal conflicts; and new kinds of challenges in national security, such as climate change, pandemics, and cyber threats. Nearly 30 years ago, Gordon Craig and Alexander George, two of the more thoughtful observers of diplomatic history, suggested that "adaptation to accelerated change has become the major problem of modern statecraft, testing the ingenuity and fortitude of those charged with the responsibility both for devising means and controlling international violence and for maintaining the security of their own countries."[1]

They were surely right, but the world has changed since they wrote their thoughtful treatise on statecraft. And it has changed in the two decades since I wrote my first book on this topic. There is a different political, military, and economic landscape internationally than when I was writing in 2005 and 2006. The United States is no longer the uber-power; the world is no longer unipolar. America is challenged from without and from within. And statecraft done well has become even more important as a result. US policymakers need to practice it far more effectively if they are to sustain domestic support for the US approach to the world.

It is because the international landscape has changed so much—and the challenges the United States faces from without and within are so different—that the structure of this book is different from my first book on statecraft. Now I feel compelled to explain how the world has changed—and how the United States is much more challenged than ever before. The rules-based system that the United States has championed is under fundamental assault, and I explain that in Chapter 1. I then go on to explain why in such circumstances one needs to use political tools and practice statecraft better. And yet, as I show, US politicians rarely do what is most basic to good statecraft: marry objectives and means. I show that this mistake is not the preserve of either party. Republican and Democratic presidents alike have both failed to match their objectives and means—and I illustrate this in Chapter 2 with a discussion of more contemporary examples of Barack Obama in Libya, Donald Trump in Iran, and Joe Biden in Afghanistan.

I analyze the reasons policymakers so often have a problem defining the right objective, and then in Chapter 3 I explain that if they are to develop sustainable policies, they have to shape objectives and use means that match American traditions in foreign policy. The United States has a tradition of unilateralism which grows out of the US self-image of being exceptional. But that self-image, that ethos, also accepts that the United States needs to make its weight felt in the service of what is good and right. After going through debates over what the role of the United States in the world needs to be (Chapter 4), I offer my own model to describe how and why the United States can, and indeed must, continue to play a leadership role internationally.

Chapter 5 to Chapter 9 examine historical cases of US statecraft. The aim in looking closely at cases of statecraft done well and badly is to distill lessons so that they can be applied to contemporary threats and challenges the United States faces on the world stage (Chapter 10). And I proceed to do that in chapters on China (Chapter 11), Iran (Chapter 12), and the Israeli–Palestinian conflict (Chapter 13). China is a global challenge, Iran a regional one, and the Israeli–Palestinian conflict is exploited by Iran in the region and by China and others seeking to use it to isolate not just Israel but the United States as well. All these conflicts pose daunting challenges that require the smart use of all political tools, including how policymakers frame the issues and their objectives, how they attract or mobilize partners and use leverage to protect their interests and counter threats.

I tie all the elements of good statecraft together in Chapter 14, and close the book with illustrations of how smart statecraft might be applied to non-traditional national security challenges like climate change, pandemics, and cyber threats. Given the reality that the United States has less relative power, it is essential that policymakers know how to use that power more effectively.

Acknowledgments

No book is ever the product of a single person, and this book would surely not have been possible without the help and support of many people. First, one of the great pleasures and benefits of being at the Washington Institute for Near East Policy is that its director, Robert Satloff, has created an environment that promotes serious analysis and scholarship—and gives the staff the support they need to write books. Rob has led the Washington Institute for thirty years, always with vision and a commitment to thinking through the most important policy challenges. I am lucky to have him as a colleague and a friend.

I also want to thank Jay Bernstein and Moses Libitzky—who have served as presidents of the Washington Institute during the time when I wrote this book. They have both been very strong supporters of my work and I am extremely appreciative of their support and friendship.

In addition to Rob, Jay, and Moses, I have held countless conversations with colleagues at the Institute and also at Georgetown University's Center for Jewish Civilization where I teach that affected my thinking and, no doubt, benefitted me as I conceptualized how to approach this book.

From a very practical standpoint, there are two assistants that I have had—Bennett Neuhoff and Cleary Waldo—who played a pivotal role in helping me produce this book. Both have served as my assistants, responsible not only for research but also providing my administrative support—no small task. Both have handled the administrative role superbly, and both handled the research role brilliantly. They came up with sources and offered insights that were of immeasurable help. Bennett was there at the creation of this book, and he really helped me get it launched. When Bennett left to take a job in government, Cleary stepped in and never missed a beat. Her work has been consistently outstanding— constantly raising questions I needed to consider or identifying new works which I needed to review. In Cleary's case, she also has worked tirelessly on the tedium of the book production process, from making sure the footnotes are correct, to fact-checking, and even helping to design the book cover. One thing I know for sure: both Bennett and Cleary are extremely talented, and whether in government or in academia, they will make their mark.

I was fortunate also to talk to and interview a number of people whose views benefitted me a great deal. The following took the time for discussions on parts of the book, and I am most appreciative that they did so. Tom Donilon, Daniel Douek, Fred Hof, David Petraeus, Norm Roule, Karim Sadjadpour, David Satterfield, Andrew Tabler, Ray Takeyh, and Robert Zoellick were generous with their time and their insights.

I must also thank David McBride at Oxford University Press. He was a believer in this book from the very beginning, and it was a true pleasure to work with him. Thanks also to Sarah Ebel at Oxford for always being responsive and who helped ensure the process went smoothly and on schedule. I also want to thank Hemalatha Ravivarman who oversaw the publication process and was also very responsive and committed to keeping us on schedule. I also owe thanks to Amron Lehte of Wild Clover Books who did the indexing for the book; it was done well and even ahead of schedule! Thanks, also to my long-time agent, Esther Newberg who has always been there for me.

Last, but certainly not least, I want to thank my wife Debbie. When I write books, I get fully absorbed, and she has the patience and the wit to tolerate my preoccupation. I have been so lucky to have her as my lifelong partner.

Chapter 1
Statecraft in a World of Disorder

Vladimir Putin shook the world with his decision to invade Ukraine. While Putin assumed that Ukraine would collapse quickly and he would rewrite the security architecture of Europe on his terms, he clearly miscalculated. Good statecraft, as we will see, depends heavily on good assessments, and Putin's belief system—not reality or facts—drove his assessment. That is a prescription for bad statecraft, and bad statecraft nearly always produces terrible results for those conducting it.

At the time of this writing, it is too soon to know fully what the consequences will be for Putin. Given his control of all the instrumentalities of power and loyalists in the key security institutions, he may well survive in power. But there can be little doubt that because of his egregious miscalculation, Russia is paying a terrible price in terms of military losses, economic decline, brain drain, and the diminution of whatever soft power it had. Strategically, it will emerge from this conflict a diminished power.

Moreover, rather than reshaping the security architecture in Europe along his preferred lines, Putin has altered, perhaps fundamentally, the security approach of the Europeans. He wanted to weaken and divide NATO but instead has revitalized it. He wanted to see NATO forces move farther away from the Russian borders but instead they are closer, with much larger strike forces. He wanted others in NATO to begin to adopt postures closer to the neutrality of Finland and Sweden; instead, Finland and Sweden jettisoned their historic neutrality and became members of NATO.

Putin, priding himself on his expertise on Germany, believed that Germany's reaction to the Russian invasion of Ukraine would be more rhetorical than real given German commercial interests and dependency on Russian energy. He never believed they would increase their defense spending threefold, cancel the Nord Stream 2 pipeline, provide arms to Ukraine, and seek to wean itself off Russian energy resources. Putin was convinced that Germany's (and Europe's) commercial interests would always trump its security concerns.

Statecraft 2.0. Second Edition. Dennis Ross, Oxford University Press. © Oxford University Press (2025).
DOI: 10.1093/oso/9780197698914.003.0001

For now, it is clear that Putin could not have been more wrong. Time will tell how enduring these changes in Europe will be. But Putin's invasion of Ukraine was a seismic event on the world stage. The war that Putin unleashed in Europe, with its targeting of cities and civilians, was something most Europeans and Americans deemed to be unthinkable in the twenty-first century. Regrettably, it has proven all too thinkable for Putin, but his relentless war on Ukraine and its civilian population and infrastructure has served as a wake-up call in Europe and the United States.

For President Biden, it gave great new impetus and a sense of urgency to produce what he had called for from the outset of his presidency: the restoration of a rules-based international order. In many respects, this call was a reaction to Donald Trump. Trump had walked away from the Paris Climate Accord, the Trans-Pacific Partnership, and the Joint Comprehensive Plan of Action (JCPOA, also known as the Iran nuclear deal). He ended American support for some UN agencies, including the United Nations Relief and Works Agency (UNRWA) —a body that provides material support and funds food and schools for Palestinian refugees in Gaza, the West Bank, Jordan, Lebanon, and Syria. And he refused to appoint new members of the Appellate Body of the World Trade Organization—the body that serves as referees in trade disputes internationally. This broader rejection of multilateralism did not stand in isolation but was a natural complement to Trump's disparaging of America's key alliances, even raising questions about whether he would remain in NATO.[1]

This was all anathema to Joe Biden. In his 36 years in the US Senate, he spent time with America's allies; he was a committed internationalist. He believed it was best for the United States not to go it alone, but that if it wanted others to play their part they needed to see that America was actually prepared to lead. So, in foreign policy, his first order of business as president was to re-establish US standing internationally and US commitment to its alliance system and multilateral institutions. He understood that the United States largely led the construction of this network of institutions and allies as a means for helping to manage international relations, minimize conflict, counter transnational threats, and promote prosperity. He was not just determined to restore US commitment to these institutions and partnerships but also to having the United States again assume a position of global leadership. Without America resuming its leading role globally, he believed—particularly at the time of growing threats from authoritarianism—the world would become far more dangerous.

Note what he had to say on February 4, 2021, two weeks into his presidency: "As I said in my inaugural address, we will repair our alliances and engage with the world once again, not to meet yesterday's challenges but today's and tomorrow's. American leadership must meet this new moment of advancing authoritarianism, including the growing ambitions of China to rival the United States and the determination of Russia to damage and disrupt our democracy."[2]

The challenges, the dangers from China and from Russia, threatened the very norms that made preserving peace and stability possible internationally. His remarks to the UN General Assembly on September 21, 2021, spelled out his belief in the importance of upholding these norms and the US role in doing so:

> We'll continue to uphold the longstanding rules and norms that have formed the development of nations around the world ... The United States will compete and will compete vigorously, and lead with our values and our strength. We'll stand up for our allies and our friends and oppose attempts by stronger countries to dominate weaker ones, whether through territory by force, economic coercion, technological exploitation, or disinformation.[3]

Here was Biden making a clarion call for a rules-based system to ensure that might did not make right. His posture was clear. But four years of Donald Trump, following eight years of Barack Obama, in which the United States seemed to be retrenching, made America's allies and friends doubt whether the United States was willing, or even able, to play a leading role. Worse, many feared that Trump could return and weren't certain they could count on the durability of Biden's path. And, that path itself seemed less compelling, even dubious, given the Biden administration's chaotic and mishandled withdrawal from Afghanistan.[4] Fairly or not, America's allies and friends saw a bungled withdrawal in which many in Afghanistan—both Afghans and partners who had forces there—felt that the United States had left them high and dry.

While President Biden took pride in the ability of the US military to carry out an evacuation of remarkable scale very quickly and in chaotic circumstances, the enduring images of the US withdrawal were families begging to get onto planes and being turned away, and an individual falling from the sky, unable to secure himself in the wheel well of one of the US transport aircrafts. In the midst of these tragedies, the terrorist group known as Islamic

State-Khorasan carried out a horrific attack that killed 13 US servicemen and over 90 Afghans.[5] These were hardly images of American strength—and it was not only US friends who took note of this but adversaries as well. Would Putin have gone ahead with his invasion of Ukraine had the United States not withdrawn from Afghanistan the way it did? Maybe he still would have done it, but it is hard to believe that the US failures in Afghanistan had no effect on him.[6]

It certainly had a catalyzing effect on the Biden administration. Using intelligence, it was active in advance of Putin's invasion both trying to deter the Russians and preparing US allies for a collective response. While Biden may have failed to deter Putin, he clearly succeeded in mobilizing a response from NATO that many pundits deemed unlikely.[7]

And how did Biden and Secretary of State Antony Blinken explain what the administration was doing and why it was doing it? In his press conference at the NATO Summit in late June 2022, Biden remarked:

> Before the war started ... I indicated to Putin [that] his action would cause a worldwide response, bringing together democratic allies and partners from the Atlantic and the Pacific to focus on the challenges that matter to our future and to defend the rules-based order against the challenges, including from China.[8]

Earlier in the spring when President Biden went to Poland after Putin's invasion of Ukraine, he proclaimed that, "We emerged anew in the great battle for freedom: a battle between democracy and autocracy, between liberty and repression, between a rules-based order and one governed by brute force."[9] On several occasions, Secretary Blinken also stressed the invasion's implications for the current world order.[10] Blinken believed that "Russia's aggression against Ukraine is not only an aggression against the Ukrainian people but an aggression against the basic principles of the world order." Without a strong and unified response to this aggression, we would be left with a world order where "might makes right."[11]

Biden and Blinken saw the rules-based order as preventing the international landscape from becoming one characterized by the law of the jungle. For them, the rules-based order built on respect for sovereignty and human rights was morally necessary, as it necessarily protected America's values and interests. Blinken explained when and what produced it: "After two world wars, countries came together around the United Nations to try to make sure that the world would never go to war again. And out of that grew a commitment to having some basic ... rules about how countries would relate to one another: respect for sovereignty, for independence, for territorial integrity, for human rights and the universal declaration of human rights, which, along with the United Nations charter, are the foundations of this rules-based order."[12]

This is the order that the Biden administration wanted to defend and reform. In Blinken's words, this order and the principles on which it is based "have allowed us, with lots of imperfections, to make sure that there wasn't another global conflict, that countries help preserve peace, stability."[13]

What are the imperfections that mean the rules-based order needs reforming? No doubt, Biden and Blinken had in mind the ills of globalization and the inequalities it gave rise to. For all the prosperity that lifted more than a billion people out of poverty internationally, globalization (and the rules-based order that made it possible) also produced yawning gaps between rich and poor and increasing struggles for the middle class.[14] Biden's slogan "Build Back Better" was applied not only to domestic realities but also to what the administration sought internationally as well—and for good reason.

The failings of globalization brought about a surge in populism, virulent nationalism, and the rejection of the other. Yes, these constitute a threat to globalization and to a rules-based order. But even before the surge in populism and the emergence of populist leaders, the order was being threatened. In fact, it is fair to say that the order has been under assault and its norms challenged by Russia, China, and others for some time.

The Faltering Rules-Based International Order

Challenges to the rules-based order did not begin with Putin's invasion of Ukraine. Nor did they emerge from Donald Trump's walk-away from multilateral agreements or institutions, or from his distaste for alliances and the obligations that come with them. Vladimir Putin signaled his unhappiness with the structure of international relations in his February 2007 speech at the Munich Security Conference. He challenged the concept of "a unipolar world."[15]

The outcome of the Cold War, with the United States as the victor, lent credence to the idea that the world was neither bipolar nor multipolar but unipolar. So did several other factors:

- the currency given to the argument about the "end of history,"[16] at least in terms of which ideology had won and the absence of an ongoing ideological struggle;
- the general perception that the United States dwarfed all other powers not only in economic but also military terms;
- and the readiness of the United States to use its hard power to shape political outcomes designed, in theory, to promote US values and interests.

At Munich, Putin in the presence of European leaders and a number of senior American officials, including the US Secretary of Defense Robert Gates, challenged the very idea of a unipolar world: "What is a unipolar world? It is a world in which there is one master, one sovereign." He went on to explain that the world neither should nor could be unipolar, saying, "I consider that the unipolar model is not only unacceptable but also impossible in today's world." It was impossible because there were other nations and the "economic potential of new centers of global economic growth [would] inevitably be converted into political influence and will strengthen multipolarity."[17] But it was also unacceptable because Russia had interests and rights, and those would not be denied. No one could impose on Russia, and Putin left no doubt that it was the United States that was trying to impose on others: "One state, of course, first and foremost the United States, has overstepped its national borders in every way. This is visible in the economic, political, cultural, and education policies it imposes on other nations."[18]

No doubt, Putin was reacting to America's war in Iraq and its policy of regime change. On this, he had support from many in his European audience. If there were rules, the United States was the one breaking them. For Putin, it was not just of recent vintage but included a series of actions, including the US-led use of force in Kosovo not sanctioned or authorized by the UN; the "color" revolutions in Ukraine and Georgia; and NATO's expansion eastward to Russia's borders. The latter threatened Russia. Moreover, according to Putin, NATO's expansion broke the promises made when a unified Germany was permitted to become part of NATO.[a]

---

[a] I will address the issue of whether the United States made promises about no NATO expansion in Chapter 5. While there was a promise not to put non-German NATO forces into the territory of

Putin's speech was essentially calling out the behavior of the United States, its betrayal of promises. Was it a case of what is good for the goose is good for the gander, and, therefore, Russia could act similarly? Perhaps, because in 2008 Putin invaded Georgia and, in a game plan he has subsequently repeated in Ukraine, recognized two breakaway republics—Abkhazia and Ossetia. Here was a case of changing a border by force. It was a blatant rejection of one of the fundamental norms of the rules-based order, yet it drew a very mild response from Western countries.

But it was not only Russia that was acting in a way to challenge the ongoing viability of the rules-based order—or more precisely the US-led rules-based order. China, too, was acting as if the rules did not apply to it. Its military expansion in the South China Sea, involving aggressive exercises and the construction of artificial islands, began during President Barack Obama's first term, and reflected the Chinese decision simply to impose its sovereignty on the 90 percent of the area it claimed. This is an area rich in resources, especially untapped oil and gas, and one where $3.4 trillion dollars of sea-borne trade passes each year.[19] The area also has many other claimants, including the Philippines, Indonesia, Malaysia, and Vietnam.

The Philippines, after a number of incidents of Chinese harassment of its fishing boats and oil rigs, brought suit in The Hague against China's construction of artificial islands in Philippine economic zone—as well as Chinese warships chasing Philippine vessels away from the area. After reviewing all the evidence, the international tribunal overwhelmingly found in favor of the Philippines.

The tribunal condemned China's land reclamation projects, saying they caused "severe harm to the coral reef environment and violated its obligation to protect fragile ecosystems and the habitat of depleted, threatened, or endangered species."[20]

But its criticism was not limited to the environmental damage that China was causing. The tribunal found that China violated sovereign rights of the Philippines in its exclusive economic zone by interfering with Philippine fishing and oil exploration. More fundamentally, the UN body concluded that "there was no legal basis for China to claim historic rights to resources in

---

the former German Democratic Republic (GDR), there was no American promise made about not extending NATO eastward because at the time the Warsaw Pact had not yet collapsed. However, Secretary General of NATO Manfred Woerner did make a public statement—coordinated with the Bush 41st administration—in which he said, "the fact that we are ready not to place a NATO army outside of German territory gives the Soviet Union a firm security guarantee." Putin cited this statement in his Munich speech.

the sea areas falling within the '9-dash line.'"[21],[b] Here was the core of China's claims, and the international tribunal rejected them.

What was China's response? It acted as if the tribunal's finding did not exist and had no meaning or weight. President Xi Jinping said the ruling would not affect China's "territorial sovereignty and marine rights." In other words, the Chinese would not respect the decision of this UN body, and its actions violating the finding would continue unabated in the South China Sea.

Much like with the Russian invasion of Georgia, there was no consequence for China's rejection of the tribunal's finding. Other actions both before and after The Hague tribunal's decision against China signaled a similar disdain for the norms that the United States believed should define international relations. Russia's invasion of Crimea in 2015 was another blatant example; Russia used force to dismember Ukraine—a member state of the UN—and absorb Crimea into the Russian Federation.

That Putin sent in "little green men," Russian military forces that had no identifying insignia, suggested he was uncertain about whether his military foray would trigger a tough response by the United States and its allies. He was preserving deniability in case there was such a reaction, permitting him to withdraw with little loss of face. None, however, was forthcoming, and Putin was soon no longer denying the Russian military intervention or the readiness to absorb Crimea.[c]

Once again, the reaction to Putin's action was limited. Not only were Western sanctions against Russia relatively mild, but India, Brazil and South Africa—3/5 of the BRICS countries at the time—refused to condemn much less criticize the Russian move, hardly a sign that broadly acceptable international norms were being threatened. Even before seizing Crimea, Putin promoted a separatist movement in eastern Ukraine, arming the separatists, providing general logistic support, and even moving in actual Russian forces to help them seize and hold territory. Initially, he denied that Russian forces were involved, later acknowledging only that Russia's military personnel had gone there on their holiday.

What motivated Putin to act was the removal from office of then-president of Ukraine, Viktor Yanukovich, in February 2014. Yanukovich, under great

---

[b] The nine-dash line is how China defines its territorial claims over disputed waters in the South China Sea.

[c] Putin would arrange a referendum in Crimea to create the veneer of legitimacy for the absorption of Crimea into Russia.

pressure from Putin, rejected the Ukrainian-European Association Agreement; in response, the Ukrainian public exploded in mass protests, taking over Maidan Square, and leading the Parliament to remove Yanukovich from office. Putin, seeing Ukraine pulled into the Western orbit, fostered the separatist movement and then seized Crimea. This was Putin's sphere of influence, and he would show the cost of seeking to limit it.

While Putin may not have intended it, Malaysia Airlines Flight 17—a flight originating in Amsterdam and going to Kuala Lumpur—was shot down over eastern Ukraine on July 17, 2014. All people on board (285 passengers and 15 crew members) were killed; general outrage internationally could not move Russia to cooperate with the investigation that was led by the Dutch Safety Board. The Russians denied that they or the separatists were responsible for the Russian-made surface-to-air missile that shot the civilian airliner down.[22,d]

Once again, outrage was one thing; imposing any price was another, and there was no real consequence for Russia. If there was no price for something as blatant as shooting down a commercial airliner owned by a country with no connection to the conflict, one might ask whether there were any norms that bound or limited behavior internationally.

Syrian President Bashar al Assad's use of chemical weapons in his war against his own people suggested there were not. Assad's behavior was another stark reminder that boundaries on acceptable behavior were disappearing and the US-led rules-based order no longer imposed limits or commanded respect. Peter Juul, seeing globalization as the outgrowth of the US-led rules-based order, traces its breakdown to an earlier point. He argues that the financial meltdown of 2008 discredited the main pillar of globalization: the free flow of finance around the world.[23] That it was American investment houses using financial instruments—bundling secondary mortgages that were not secure—that produced the collapse only raised further doubts about the United States, and provoked challenges to the rules-based order it had shaped and led.

Earlier I quoted Secretary Blinken's reference to the period after World War II in which countries came together to have some basic understandings, principles, and rules about how states should relate to one another as a way of avoiding war and managing international relations. Before becoming

---

[d] However, the Dutch Safety Board investigation found that the 53rd Anti-Aircraft Missile Brigade of the Russian Federation was responsible for the launch of the missile that brought Flight 17 down.

secretary of state, Antony Blinken in an article with Robert Kagan explained this point more fully: "after World War II, when America stayed engaged, built strong alliances with fellow democracies, and shaped the rules, norms and institutions for relations among nations, we produced unprecedented global prosperity, democracy and security from which Americans benefitted more than anyone."[24]

Blinken and Kagan were not just advocating for American engagement, they were speaking about the need to preserve what they saw as the foundations of the liberal rules-based international order. That order, led by the United States and based on the UN, the World Bank and International Monetary Fund, and America's democratic allies, took root in the years after World War II and the advent of the Cold War—and for Blinken and Kagan, it produced 70 years of unprecedented security and prosperity.

Yes, the United States did forge these institutions in the 1940s and early 1950s. But can we really say that America forged a rules-based order at that time? Or that a US-dominated liberal order emerged at that time? I do not think so.

The Cold War Order, Its Demise, and the Rise of a US-Driven One

The Cold War itself pitted the US-led bloc against the Soviet bloc. The balance of terror had a great deal to do with the absence of war between the two powers, especially given the fear of escalation to nuclear war. Mutual Assured Destruction (MAD) produced a recognition of the danger of direct conflict and the need not to let competition get out of hand.

The Soviet leadership accepted the logic of the balance of nuclear terror, and, especially after the Cuban Missile Crisis, became more open to managing US competition to avoid the danger of a nuclear war. At no time, however, did the Soviets accept the US-led rules-based order. For Moscow, that order was a reflection of America's containment of Soviet power. It was part of the struggle for dominance.

Soviet policy aimed to break it, undermine us, and extend the USSR's reach. Stalin rejected the Marshall Plan and divided Europe. His successors created the Warsaw Pact opposite NATO. They crushed the revolt in Hungary in 1956 and did the same later to the Czech "spring" in 1968.

From supporting Castro in Cuba and so-called national liberation movements throughout the third world, to providing arms and false intelligence to Egypt which set in motion the events that produced the Arab-Israeli War of 1967, the Soviet Union was competing with the United States and seeking to counter both its power and its vision of the world. The Soviet Union provided weapons and military support to insinuate itself in different regimes and foster a dependency. It used the KGB to support terrorist groups, including those who carried out the kidnapping and murder of Israeli athletes at the Munich Olympics. And it adopted the Brezhnev Doctrine—meaning any country that had become part of the Soviet/communist bloc could not leave it, and the Soviets had the right to prevent such a departure or reverse it if it had taken place. The intervention in Afghanistan was a reflection of the Brezhnev Doctrine application not simply in Eastern Europe but in the third world.

But Afghanistan was also a turning point. The costs were high, and the failings of the Soviet system were becoming more obvious. It could not keep up with the surge in defense spending of the Reagan administration. Its sclerotic leadership was incapable of preventing the ongoing decline within the Soviet Union. Leonid Brezhnev grew old and increasingly infirm at the end of his rule. His successors—Konstantin Chernenko and Yuri Andropov—each lasted only a year before dying in office. Both seemed symptomatic of a political system that was infirm and was losing even a semblance of legitimacy, with an ideology embraced only by those whose power depended on it.

After the succession of old, sick leaders, Mikhail Gorbachev, from the younger generation, emerged as the General Secretary of the Communist Party. He was determined to reform the system and show it could be vital and productive. He sought to end costly foreign policy adventures and revitalize domestic economic development with glasnost (openness) and perestroika (reconstruction).

He wanted partnership with the United States and the West in general, believing they could assist the internal transformation of the Soviet Union. He was not trying to revolutionize the USSR, but reform it. In a private discussion with Secretary of State James Baker, Soviet Minister of Foreign Affairs Eduard Shevardnadze poignantly explained why he and Gorbachev were so determined to transform the Soviet Union: "We can build a rocket, but we cannot produce a safe hypodermic needle." He went on to bemoan the way the Soviet Union lagged behind the West in terms of meeting the basic health and economic needs of its people. It could not transform the country and meet its domestic needs without producing a different relationship with the United States.[e]

Gorbachev and Shevardnadze were not seeking détente. This was not the Nixon–Kissinger concept of managing US competition in a nuclear-armed world—at a time of what they perceived as American decline because of Vietnam. It was not Brezhnev's view that détente would make it safe for the Soviets to gain power internationally at the expense of the United States. No, Shevardnadze and Gorbachev saw adventures on the outside as threatening the means and the potential for modernization and reform on the inside. "New thinking" in foreign policy meant ending competition in the third world and not financing the military pursuits of traditional Soviet clients. (Syrian President Hafez al Assad discovered during a trip to Moscow in 1987 that Gorbachev would not finance or materially support his aim of strategic parity with Israel.) It also meant no more interventions in Eastern Europe to save regimes that resisted change and faced upheaval.

Once it became clear that the Soviet Union would not save leaders like Walter Ulbricht in the German Democratic Republic, those leaders were not going to survive for long. Mass demonstrations swept old leaders away, but reformist replacements could not contain the desire to have what Western Europeans had. In Germany, it did not take long before the symbol of the Cold War and the division of Europe—the Wall and the broader Iron Curtain—were swept away.

Gorbachev may not have faced the same public groundswell reflecting rejection of regimes imposed from the outside, but he faced the need for change and a system that was resistant to it. Too many state and party officials who owed their power and privilege to the existing system resisted his efforts at reform. Many in the broad security establishment saw the United States through the prism of threat and rivalry—and perceived Gorbachev as surrendering Soviet power and acquiescing in the face of an American agenda. They had a hard time stomaching the loss of Germany. They saw him conceding too much on both strategic and conventional arms control. They hated his joining the United States in opposing Saddam Hussein's absorption of Kuwait. For them, Iraq was the most important client state

---

[e] This conversation took place on the plane traveling from Washington DC to Jackson Hole, Wyoming for a ministerial meeting in September 1989. Only Baker, Shevardnadze, Sergei Tarasenko (Shevardnadze's closest aide), and I were in the cabin and took part in the conversation.

the Soviets had in the Middle East. It was unthinkable that the Soviet Union would collaborate with the United States in threatening it, and in promoting American power at their expense.

I witnessed these attitudes very directly. Baker and Shevardnadze held a ministerial meeting in Irkutsk; before the meetings concluded on August 2, 1990, Saddam Hussein invaded Kuwait.[f] Baker would proceed to fly to Mongolia on a previously scheduled trip. I, however, flew back to Moscow on Shevardnadze's plane ostensibly to hold policy-planning talks with Tarasenko. Needless to say, these were overtaken by events, and on the plane with Shevardnadze I suggested that no one would believe that our public commitments to partnership would have any real meaning if, in this case of overt aggression, we failed jointly to condemn it and commit ourselves to reversing it. If we truly were beginning a new era, together, we had to demonstrate it in response to this blatant act of aggression. Shevardnadze and Tarasenko agreed.

Upon getting to Moscow, I drafted a joint US-Soviet statement that Tarasenko accepted.[g] It condemned Saddam's invasion, called for imposing an arms embargo on Iraq, threatened sanctions, and signaled that our two countries were prepared to do more if Saddam did not withdraw from Kuwait.

When I called the National Security Advisor Brent Scowcroft to get White House clearance for the statement and its content—and read him the draft that Tarasenko had accepted—he remarked, "now, I know the Cold War has ended." Baker had approved the idea of a joint statement but told me that his return from Mongolia required it to be significant in terms of demonstrating how far the US-Soviet relationship had come.

Gorbachev and Shevardnadze might have been ready for the transformation of our relationship, but many of those in the Soviet national security establishment—Foreign Ministry, Defense Ministry, KGB—were not, and Tarasenko soon faced their heated opposition. They rejected the draft and sought to denude the statement of all of its content: not only did they reject the arms embargo and any mention of sanctions, but they were not

---

[f] On the first day of the ministerial, Baker informed Shevardnadze that US intelligence suggested that Saddam was about to invade Kuwait. Shevardnadze doubted it, saying Saddam was a "thug but he was not crazy." Still, he said he would check and after doing so, Shevardnadze came back assuring Baker that there would be no invasion just posturing. When Saddam did invade the next day, Tarasenko told me that Shevardnadze felt blind-sided, misled, and embarrassed.

[g] Peter Hauslohner of my staff suggested a joint statement that Baker and Shevardnadze would publicly issue together.

willing even to use the word "condemn" in response to Iraq and its invasion. Tarasenko was caught between my insistence that it was better not to have a statement if it was empty of any real content, and his colleagues in the national security establishment who actually wanted the statement to say nothing against Saddam and Iraq.

In the end, Shevardnadze made a decision on his own authority to override all the objections and preserve much of the content of my original draft. When Baker arrived, Shevardnadze explained that he had to overcome the old thinkers, caught in the traditional Soviet era dogma—he only asked of Baker that he commit to not surprising Gorbachev or him by using force any time soon. Baker assured him, provided there was no need to save American citizens in either Iraq or Kuwait.

While Gorbachev engendered deep opposition among the national security establishment for pivoting away from traditional Soviet clients and investing far less in extending Soviet reach, his ability to transform Soviet foreign policy depended ultimately on his success in domestic policy. Had he shown that his policy was working and that he was delivering the goods domestically, he would have built his authority. But he could not show that, as his efforts at reform proved hard to implement.

One indication of how much resistance he faced and how little control over the process of implementation he had—and how little transparency there was—was revealed by a startling admission Gorbachev made to Baker and me.[h] During one meeting in 1991 where we discussed what was happening on the domestic front, Gorbachev acknowledged that his government could not account for what had happened to tens of billions of dollars which had come from the Germans and Europeans not only to cover the costs of relocation of Soviet forces out of Germany and to launch a massive housing construction program but also to help overhaul the economy. There was nothing to show for the money and no one could account for where it went. At a time when there was a debate on the US side about doing more to help Gorbachev with financial assistance, this revelation undercut those policymakers who were arguing that the United States needed to provide a big infusion of aid to help Gorbachev succeed.

A few months later, not long after the failed coup against Gorbachev in August of 1991, I was again in Moscow with Baker. We saw Gorbachev in his

---

[h] I would accompany Baker to his private meetings with Gorbachev. The only people present were Gorbachev, his interpreter Pavel Palazhchenko, Baker, and me.

office, but we also saw the man who had blunted the coup and saved Gorbachev, Boris Yeltsin. In writing Baker's night note to President Bush after our meetings with each of them—and with the heads of other republics—I wrote that it might have been only a few weeks since our last trip to Moscow, but it felt like we had come to a different country. Gorbachev's weakness and dependence on Yeltsin were unmistakable—and Yeltsin was very clear: the Russian Republic, which he presided over, would soon establish its independence from the Soviet Union. With other heads of the various republics, we heard the same message, and it was clear that the USSR would soon no longer exist.

The demise of the Soviet Union would be followed by an economic collapse in Russia, accompanied by a nearly complete breakdown of law and order. Everything that defined the Soviet Union seemed lost. Crime was rampant. Unemployment soared. The concept of post-traumatic stress syndrome (PTSD) is not applied to countries and their populations, and yet the Russian population following the collapse of the Soviet Union— what Vladimir Putin calls the "worst geopolitical tragedy of the twentieth century"—surely seems to have suffered from PTSD.

Gone was their image of being a super-power. They seemed more like a super-pauper. They lost their stature, their sense of identity, and the respect and fear that they had commanded on the world stage. Putin would draw lessons from the loss of order. For him, it was not just the chaos but the weakness it both reflected and ensured that had to be reversed. In his book *First Person*, he explained that the Soviet Union collapsed because it was suffering a "paralysis of power."[25] Later, in justifying his "special military operation" in Ukraine, he repeated this phrase, declaring that the demise of the USSR "has shown us that the paralysis of power ... is the first step toward complete degradation and oblivion."[26]

Restoring Russian power and the internal order that enabled it became a mission for Putin. He blamed the United States for contributing to this weakness and disorder because of the role that consultants from the United States and other Western countries (like Jeffrey Sachs and Andres Aslund) played in convincing Yeltsin and his chief economic aides, Yegor Gaidar and Boris Fyodorov, that "shock therapy" was needed to transform the Russian economy.

Whatever the theory of shock therapy, the way it was implemented led to state enterprises collapsing, with few places for their employees to go; it imposed terrible austerity on the Russian public, even as there was little or no safety net. It produced privatization that largely fed corruption and a sell-off of state assets at bargain basement prices. It essentially gave away natural resources to those either in the former party or state structure or to those connected to the nomenklatura (key administrative positions in the Soviet bureaucracy). This was the time when the oligarchs emerged, gaining control over oil, steel, copper, timber, and other resource-based companies.

Putin resented the collapse even as he learned how to exploit it. He also resented what he perceived to be America's exploitation of Russian weakness, especially the decision to expand NATO eastward during the Clinton administration. Yeltsin would win a second term, but his heart condition and excessive drinking increasingly incapacitated him, leading to his resignation on December 31, 1999. Yeltsin had made Putin his prime minister in his second term, and upon his resignation he appointed Putin president.

It was the collapse and weakness of the Soviet Union—the country that had been the other super-power—that truly ended the Cold War and created the reality that it was no longer a bipolar world. When combined with the first Gulf War in 1991, in which American diplomacy mobilized an international coalition and the US military expelled the Iraqi forces from Kuwait, the Soviet collapse left the United States as the only global power. The United States was the uber-power—and the world seemingly was unipolar. When President George H. W. Bush explained why the United States had to reverse the Iraqi aggression, he did so on the basis that this was necessary to secure "a new world order."

There was no US-led rules-based order during the Cold War years. But following the demise of the Soviet Union and the US application of force to reverse Saddam Hussein's aggression and absorption of Kuwait—what he called Iraq's 19th province—there was such an order.

When Joe Biden talked of a rules-based order, he was thinking—consciously or not—of what had existed in the 1990s and following 9/11. True, the alliances and the multilateral institutions that made up the structure of the rules-based system Biden was seeking had been created in the late 1940s, but US rules did not really begin to apply until the end of the Cold War in the 1990s. At that time, Russia was too weak to challenge us. And China was still bent on modernization in which it sought to take advantage of the rules-based system the United States led. Globalization and the free flow of capital, an integral part of the US-led rules-based system, produced great investment in China and allowed it to grow economically at a phenomenal rate.

In his 2005 book *The Opportunity*, Richard Haass argued that there were no longer any great power struggles or competition—and that created a moment, an opportunity, to promote greater stability internationally, to resolve conflicts, to promote peace-making and to foster economic progress globally.[27] That world no longer exists, and yet, for good reasons, the Biden administration wanted to restore a rules-based system.

Constraints on American Power

In the world of today, the United States has competitors. America is far more constrained in trying to impose the rules as it sees them. The 1990s were unique because American power really did dwarf that of others. Just as significantly, potential competitors of the United States focused far more on their internal needs. They were not inclined to challenge America.

But it is different today. For Putin, there is the desire for payback for exploiting Russian weakness, but there is also a legacy of the United States and others not responding when he tested the limits, and he came to understand that he could get away with doing so. From Georgia to Crimea to Syria, Putin saw that he could manage the reaction of the United States and its allies and expand Russian power and influence. Perhaps as importantly, his ability to deliver order and economic stability domestically, while also restoring the image of Russia as a power on the world stage with unmistakable stature and respect, allowed him to tap the wellsprings of Russian nationalism. He reminded the Russian public what they had lost, and he had recaptured.

So much of Putin's hold on the Russian nationalist psyche depends on his standing up to plots against Russia led by the United States. Of course, he controls the media, minimizes discordant voices, and feeds a constant stream of news and images of the threats that Russia faces and he resists. Opposition to the United States—while also appearing an equal to it—is very much a part of Putin's Russia and requires him to continually challenge US power and the rules it seeks to impose.

For his part, President Xi Jinping of China sees Russia as an essential partner in countering the US effort to impose its values and rules. For him, those values and rules are designed to constrain what China does on the inside, and limit and prevent it from getting its full measure of power and influence on the world stage.

In the Cold War, the United States faced a nuclear military threat and Russian use of its power to compete with America and build relationships with third-world nationalist/authoritarian leaders to limit the reach of US-led rules. Today, the challenge is far more formidable because unlike Russia, China is also a global economic competitor—one that threatens to surpass us.[28],[i]

China has become the largest manufacturing hub internationally and the world's biggest exporter of goods. Its trade relationships create leverage. Its Belt and Road Initiative has provided more than a trillion dollars in Chinese-led infrastructure projects which deepen relationships with oil-rich countries—Saudi Arabia and the UAE—and also foster debt and dependency with oil-poor countries, including Pakistan, Malaysia, Kenya, Uganda, Bolivia, and Peru.[29] Moreover, Chinese investments and economic support come with no strings attached on human rights, climate change, or reducing corruption.

If this were not enough of a challenge, China is also insinuating itself in the UN institutional structure and creating its own multilateral institutions to counter and constrain US power. Today, Chinese nationals head four of the 15 specialized agencies of the UN: the Food and Agriculture Organization, the International Telecommunications Union, the International Civil Aviation Organization, and the UN Industrial Development Organization. Even where Chinese nationals are not in the lead, China exerts its influence on the heads of the agencies. Recall how Tedros Adhanom Ghebreyesus, Director General of the World Health Organization, not only acceded to Chinese wishes to limit any systematic investigation into the origins of COVID, but even lauded Chinese cooperation in sharing information about the virus when it was still clearly withholding it. If the United States and its allies once dominated the specialized agencies of the UN system—one of the structural underpinnings of the rules-based order the way the United States defined it—that is simply no longer the case.

Moreover, China and Russia have been setting up alternative, competing multilateral structures. Some are Chinese-led, others Russian-led. In terms of financing infrastructure, the Chinese created the Asian Infrastructure Investment Bank as an alternative to the Asian Development Bank—a

---

[i] According to estimates from the IMF World Outlook, there is one measure in which China has already passed us. Its 2022 projection was that China will account for 18.8 percent of the world's GDP based on purchasing power parity, with the United States accounting for only 15.8 percent. Twenty years ago, China was at only 8.1 percent and the United States was at 19.8 percent. Still as we will see in Chapter 11, there are many other indicators that show China is not close to surpassing the United States.

multilateral institution the United States and its allies had established. China's bank has made great strides in providing financing for its Belt and Road Initiative throughout Asia. China's reach structurally and financially extends into Africa and Latin America—and in Latin America, the Chinese have built a regional grouping called China- CELAC (CELAC stands for the Community of Latin America and Caribbean States).

Other structures with China and Russia in the lead are more oriented toward security: the Shanghai Cooperation Organization (SCO) promotes cooperation among security services and conducts exercises. Initially, it had countries from Central Asia joining China and Russia; but since its inception, both India and Pakistan were added and, more recently, Iran's status is being upgraded from observer to full member. Similarly, the Russians created the Collective Security Treaty Organization, based in Moscow and including Armenia, Belarus, Kazakhstan, Kyrgyzstan, Russia, and Tajikistan—and under its aegis, the Russians sent troops into Kazakhstan to help quell domestic upheaval.

The aim of these and other multilateral organizations is to create alternative or parallel structures of extra-regional governance. All of them can be seen as an extension of Russian and Chinese power.

However, it is not only the power of Russia and China—and their efforts to develop alternative multilateral structures—that limits America's rules and definition of order on the world stage. There are regional powers as well and they, too, are determined to upend regional orders and challenge US interests.

Iran is a good case in point. Its nuclear program represents in the eyes of its neighbors, especially Israel, a threat—one that could trigger a pre-emptive strike against the totality of the Iranian nuclear infrastructure and a war with Iran. Conversely, if there is no Israeli or American military action against the Iranian nuclear program and diplomacy fails to stop Iran from becoming a nuclear-weapons state (or one that is a turnkey away from that capability), Saudi Arabia has already declared it too will match what Iran has.[30] Turkey and Egypt will soon follow, and Iran with nuclear weapons will almost certainly spell the end of the nuclear non-proliferation treaty—perhaps the most successful arms-control treaty of the Cold War and post-Cold War eras.

But it is not only Iran's nuclear program that threatens the region; Iran directly and indirectly threatens international waterways like the Strait of Hormuz and the Bab el Mandeb. It bears responsibility for producing and provoking wars in the region with its support for Shia militias and resistance Sunni groups like Hamas; it is Iranian money, arms, and training that has helped to turn groups like Hezbollah and Hamas into militaries. Would Hamas have carried out its onslaught against Israel on October 7, triggering a terrible war in Gaza and Hezbollah attacks against Israel, without Iranian material support–support that included helping both Hezbollah and Hamas build weapons production facilities and depots? Would the Houthis have been able to fire more than a thousand rockets and drones into Saudi Arabia before a ceasefire in April 2022 or continue to disrupt shipping in the Red Sea with their attacks without the Iranians? Iran's Shia proxies don't only threaten neighboring states, they also paralyze the governments and states where they reside, whether it is Lebanon and Iraq. While Iran may prefer to act through proxies, it has also demonstrated it will use force directly: for example, it launched cruise missiles and drones against Abqaiq, the largest oil processing facility in Saudi Arabia in 2019 and fired ballistic missiles and drones against Israel in 2024. (And, of course, now the Iranians are contributing to conflict outside the region by becoming a military supplier of drones and missiles to Russia.)

Threats in Europe from Russia, threats in the Indo-Pacific from China, threats from Iran throughout the Middle East and beyond, and threats from North Korea against South Korea and Japan, all remind us of those who increasingly challenge America. The United States cannot deal with all these threats alone.

There are limits to US power, and these challenges do not occur in a vacuum. The United States does not just face constraints on the outside. It also faces them domestically. The high costs of the US wars in Iraq and Afghanistan—and the dubious results—have understandably soured much of the American public on the use of US force abroad. Combined with the financial meltdown in 2008, there has been new questioning of elites and a surge of populism. The Republican Party, even before Trump, had a populist, anti-elite, anti-government element. The "Tea Party" gave expression to those sentiments. It promoted the polarization of US politics. Newt Gingrich, as Speaker of the House during the Clinton presidency, shut down the government. Republican obstructionism during Clinton's time, and the impeachment of Bill Clinton, fed polarization, but also created incentives for Democrats to create payback as developments in Iraq during the Bush 43rd presidency turned increasingly negative.

The absence of weapons of mass destruction, the deeply sectarian and brutal nature of the war within Iraq, and the very high cost of a war of choice—not necessity—added to disillusionment about US involvement not just in the Middle East but more generally. The US-led war in Iraq did not cause domestic American polarization, but it certainly deepened it. Consensus on the US role internationally also became a victim of polarization and of US overuse of military force for purposes that seemed hard to justify or explain.

The result, unlike in the decade after the end of the Cold War, is that the United States is far more constrained today internationally and domestically than it was during the time when the country was unmistakably the dominant power internationally—and could apply that power. Critics of the American use of power refer to that period as one of US hegemony. Dominance or hegemony are terms that no longer fit the reality of US power.

And yet, during the Biden presidency, America was led by a president who believed that the United States needed to play a leading role internationally in countering threats to a rules-based order. For Biden, without a rules-based order, autocracies would gain, US interests and values would suffer, and the world would become a far more dangerous place.

Biden was guided, correctly, by the belief that when the United States seemingly withdraws or retrenches, it creates vacuums. Nature abhors a vacuum, and the international landscape does as well. Wherever the United States withdraws, others are quick to fill-in—and those forces are rarely moderate, stabilizing ones. They are certainly not committed to a rules-based order that the United States and its allies favor.

Without such an order, without boundaries for what happens internationally, it is hard to see how it will be possible to mobilize the collective actions to deal with the great challenges of our time: blunting the growth of autocracy, saving the earth from climate change, coping with the next pandemic, and managing the disruptive effects of the pace of technology.

In a world where the United States is more constrained, it needs to be able to use the tools of statecraft far more effectively. In fact, the greater the constraints, the more US policymakers must be able to employ all the tools in their toolkit for promoting US interests and values. Put simply, in a world where power is more diffused, the United States is far less dominant, others are not inclined to acquiesce to it, and domestic support is not a given, America must be able to take the maximum advantage of all its tools—and that means good statecraft is more important than ever. In reality, US politicians no longer have the luxury of exercising it badly. In Chapter 2, I will turn to a discussion of statecraft and the difficulty of conducting it well.

Chapter 2

Statecraft, Its Meaning, and Why It Is Often Done Poorly

Statecraft is not simply another way of referring to diplomacy. While including all diplomatic procedures, it is much more than only exercising diplomacy. Some define statecraft generally as the "art of conducting state affairs."[1] Others describe it more specifically as the "organized actions governments take to change the external environment in general or the policies and actions of other states in particular to achieve the objectives that have been set by policymakers."[2]

As a former policymaker, I would describe statecraft as knowing how best to integrate and use every asset or military, diplomatic, intelligence, media, economic, organizational, and psychological tool policymakers possess (or can manipulate) to meet their objectives. Statecraft involves exercising leverage to influence others—those who are already friendly and share policymakers' purposes, and those who do not. But statecraft requires more than simply orchestrating all the resources directly or indirectly at one's disposal. It requires putting one's means into a broader context of goals and capabilities.

Statecraft starts with understanding one's role and broad purposes. It requires a definition of objectives that are desirable, even ambitious, but also tied to an appreciation of what is possible. Strategies and tactics must be fashioned that create a match—not a mismatch—between aims and the means available for acting on those aims. As such, statecraft puts a premium on being able to assess an existing or emerging threat wisely. Such assessments must evaluate the nature of the danger, its likelihood of materializing, its possible consequences, and its timing, as well as which other actors have the capabilities to be helpful in countering it. Often those who are not our allies may have the greatest leverage on a potential adversary, and statecraft involves determining and then employing the most effective means to bring those who are not our friends to exercise their influence constructively.

Statecraft 2.0. Second Edition. Dennis Ross, Oxford University Press. © Oxford University Press (2025).
DOI: 10.1093/oso/9780197698914.003.0002

Consider, for example, that China and Xi Jinping had more leverage on Putin than anyone else when it came to Ukraine. Had the Chinese been willing, they could have put real pressure on Russia to stop the war. Leaving aside their impact on Russia's political isolation, the Chinese could have dramatically increased the economic pressure on Russia by threatening to reinforce American and European sanctions. However, given Xi Jinping's priority of limiting the weight and "rules" of the United States internationally, he was not likely to be responsive to the US pressure. Had the United States been able to get others who matter to the Chinese to go to them, and had the United States made clear the Chinese would pay a price for their support of Putin, it might have made a difference. What, for example, might have happened if the United States could have gotten the Saudi Crown Prince to go to Xi Jinping and say the war had to stop to prevent rising food prices from de-stabilizing Egypt, Jordan, Tunisia, and Lebanon—and this was a matter of grave concern to Saudi Arabia? If nothing else, the Chinese, given Xi's clear desire to extend what he calls the "strategic partnership" with Saudi Arabia, might have had more of an interest in showing responsiveness to the Kingdom and creating greater distance from Putin.[a]

To be sure, statecraft is not only about countering or fending off threats, but also about taking advantage of opportunities to alter the landscape and make the world safer and more responsive to one's interests or goals. Richard Nixon and Henry Kissinger understood that an opening to China could be strategically beneficial, creating leverage vis-à-vis the Soviet Union and giving the Chinese a new stake in economic cooperation and stability regionally and internationally. Recognizing a strategic opening is certainly one requirement of statecraft. Being able to marshal the wherewithal to act on an opening and exploit it, in the final analysis, is one of the better measures of effective statecraft. Similarly, missing opportunities or squandering them may be one of the better measures of statecraft poorly executed.

Chester Crocker, a scholar and former policy practitioner, describes smart statecraft as "what you get when wits, wallets, and muscle pull together so that leverage in all its forms is harnessed to a realistic action plan or political strategy that can be set in motion by agile diplomacy. Smart statecraft does not dispense with hard power, it uses hard power intelligently, recognizing

---

[a] For the first two weeks of the war, there were Chinese voices making this very case. Given the Biden administration's impulse to keep Mohammad bin Salman at arm's length, this was not something the administration was likely to pursue at least in the early stages of the war.

the limits as well as the potential of purely military power, and integrating it into an over-arching strategy."[3]

Implicit in Dr. Crocker's words is that soft power is also crucially important. No one has done more to identify soft power, or the power of attraction, than Joseph Nye. As Nye has said, soft power influences others by attraction rather than coercion or payment.[4]

Attraction is the key word here. When others are attracted to you, they seek association with you. They embrace your objectives. Soft power creates great advantages at minimal cost. Nye observes that a state's soft power stems from three sources: its culture, its political values, and its policies. In this connection, the United States has held an attraction for others because of the universal appeal of its culture (blue jeans, movies, and Coca-Cola), its values (human rights and democracy), and its policies (accounting for the interests of others and responding to humanitarian calamities).[5]

Perhaps, the strongest factor in attraction is the image and reality of success. The United States is an extraordinary success story in terms of leading the world in technology, finances, science, medicine, education, military prowess, and broadly speaking political stability. What has weakened the US soft power has been the country's missteps on the outside (e.g., the war in Iraq) and its increasing dysfunction on the inside. Donald Trump has added to the damage by fostering greater polarization and seemingly pursuing a policy largely devoid of values. Suddenly, the United States seemed to stand for little and was not prepared to stand by allies.

China saw an opening to present itself as an alternative to us. Aside from trying to act as if it was a good global citizen in contrast to Trump (recall Xi Jinping's speech to Davos in 2017), China today seeks to present itself as a more successful model than the United States.[6] For a time, it tried to use its approach to COVID as proof of its superiority to the United States in terms of managing the virus with many fewer deaths and in its ability to restore its economy much more quickly. Whatever success China may have had early on, COVID has become not just a much harder sell for the Chinese, but it now appears as a liability. Over time, the image of Chinese success on COVID began to wane even before the signs of civic anger and unrest emerged around the country over the strict lockdown protocols. Its vaccine has been far less effective than the mRNA vaccines developed in the United States. Moreover, its so-called 'Zero-COVID' policy produced draconian lockdowns which slowed economic growth dramatically,[7] limited the development of greater immunities to COVID and its variants, imposed terrible hardships on the Chinese public, and finally proved to be so unpopular in China that it triggered unprecedented national protests—not simply local ones—against the government's policies.[8,b]

This is not to say that China has no appeal to regimes with little interest in democracy. Saudi Arabia wants to modernize without democratizing. But even in a place like Saudi Arabia, where the China model of modernization without democratic rights might seem to be attractive, China's appeal is limited. Yes, the Saudis see real value in their commercial relationship with China. However, when I speak to leading members of the government—or those who are well-to-do and part of the Saudi elite about their view of China and the United States, their response is typically, "Where do you think we send our kids for education and where do we park our money? America."

Moreover, even as the Saudis increasingly question reliability of the United States, they know they cannot count on China for security. Whatever their doubts, they still see no alternative to the United States–and those doubts, incidentally, seem to have eroded with the Saudis over the last year seeking a formal defense treaty with America.

Even if the United States is more constrained internationally, this country remains the leading global power—both because of its hard and soft power. Nonetheless, since its comparative advantages have declined internationally and it faces a more dubious public, the United States needs to be able to conduct statecraft more effectively. Regrettably, the track-record of Republican and Democratic administrations alike has generally been poor when it comes to practicing statecraft.

Why Have Administrations So Often Failed to Conduct Statecraft Well?

The most basic criterion for good statecraft is to marry objectives and means. That might seem obvious. Indeed, why adopt any policy in which there is a gap between the objectives and the means one has or can mobilize to achieve them? And yet, in viewing American foreign policy over many administrations, marrying objectives and means often seems the exception rather than the rule.

---

[b] Lockdowns have made it hard to get basic necessities like food or access to healthcare, triggering protests in a number of cities. Moreover, complaints on social media in China about the lockdowns have been widespread.

In my earlier book on statecraft, I focused very heavily on the failings of the George W. Bush administration in exercising statecraft, especially in its first term. The administration's failure to marry objectives and means often stemmed from its faulty assessments—too often letting its ideology, rather than reality, guide its assessments. In that book, I referred to the Bush administration's faith-based, not fact-based, assessments.

The war in Iraq vividly demonstrated that the administration saw what it wanted to see, not what it needed to see. Its aspirations guided its objectives, and the ideology of those who dominated the policy blinded them to the realities in Iraq—and precluded even holding an internal debate over the risks and costs of going to war. Policy was not thrashed out because there was no process for doing so. In Bush's second term, especially with the personnel changes, policy became more systematic and the internal ideological wars that characterized the first term ended. Secretary of State Condoleezza Rice, Secretary of Defense Robert Gates, and National Security Advisor Stephen Hadley collaborated closely. In his role at the White House, Hadley presided over a systematic policy process.[9] No longer did differences turn into pitched battles. Even on Iraq, a new policy approach that did a far better job of connecting aims and means became possible.[c]

While I may have singled out the Bush 43rd administration for its inability to marry objectives and means, it, unfortunately, does not stand alone in this respect. Nor was the Bush administration the only one to make poor assessments which led to terrible consequences. Both well before and after George W. Bush, there has been no shortage of examples of poor assessments producing decisions with calamitous results. Much has been written about the failings of American decision-making in both the Korean and Vietnam wars. My purpose here is simply to draw attention to how misguided the assessments were in both cases.

Consider, for example, the Truman administration's misreading of the Chinese during the Korean War and the decision to continue the US-led offensive past the 38th parallel in order to unify the Korean Peninsula. True, the North Koreans had invaded the south, attacking across the 38th parallel, the border between the north and south. And General Douglas MacArthur led UN military forces (which were predominately American) in a successful counterattack that forced the North Korean Army to retreat

---

[c] The "surge" in 2007 followed a careful review of the options that the United States had, and the recognition that Sunni Awakening Councils represented an effective Iraqi partner.

back to the north. While President Truman would ultimately fire General MacArthur for insubordination, he authorized the offensive across the 38th parallel, even though the Chinese warned that they would not tolerate UN forces moving toward the Yalu River (their border with North Korea). Those warnings were misread by the Truman administration at great cost.[d]

Hans Morgenthau would later describe the great mistake of the Korean War not being the initial intervention but changing the US objective from defending South Korea to liberating the North. For Morgenthau, the United States moved from a military goal to a political one that was beyond the country's capability.[10]

The Vietnam War, too, was driven by fundamentally flawed assumptions and poor assessments. The Eisenhower, Kennedy, and Johnson administrations acted on the assumption that communism was monolithic and that the Containment Doctrine meant its spread must be countered everywhere. But the Sino-Soviet split demonstrated there was no monolithic movement, meaning there was no need to be "containing" it in Southeast Asia. No doubt because policymakers in these administrations misread the North Vietnamese as part of an aggressive, expanding international communism, they were incapable of understanding that the North Vietnamese could also be nationalists—and ultimately had more credibility and the will to fight than those with whom the United States partnered in the South.

The Johnson administration, in particular, misread the Vietnamese landscape, producing a military strategy that had US forces take areas of the countryside at great cost, only to withdraw from them not long afterward. Similarly, the pacification effort, supposedly with the aim of winning hearts and minds, had the opposite effect and yielded more enemies than allies. President Johnson thought he could remake Vietnam, failing to see what his most serious critic in the Senate, J. William Fulbright, saw. Fulbright trenchantly questioned "the ability of the United States ... to create stability where there is chaos, the will to fight where there is defeatism, democracy where there is no tradition of it, and honest government where corruption is a way of life."[11] Fulbright could also have been describing how the United States approached Iraq as well as Afghanistan—failing to understand what

---

[d] MacArthur actually wanted to fight and defeat the Chinese, but Truman did not, believing the bigger threat was the Soviets moving against Europe. The Korean War would turn into a stalemate, with American forces suffering over 40,000 dead and 100,000 wounded. And the outcome was to re-establish the 38th parallel as the border.

it was dealing with and trying to do social engineering not only of the Iraqi and Afghani militaries but also of their societies.

Not surprisingly, poor assessments leading to gaps between objectives and means have also characterized the administrations after Bush 43rd. The Obama, Trump, and Biden administrations have all misread realities and failed to learn lessons. Before turning to a discussion of examples of how and why each of these administrations failed to marry objectives and means, it is worth noting that while misreading or misunderstanding the reality on the ground can lead to ignoring the risks of action, it can also produce excessive caution and inability to see the costs of inaction. That was definitely President Obama's mistake.

Obama and Syria and Libya

The Obama administration's approach to Syria vividly demonstrates the costs of inaction. With over 600,000 dead, half the prewar population displaced, a refugee crisis that unsettled Europe, chemical weapons used, the country and its economy devastated, and a power vacuum that invited outside intervention, the costs were very high. So high that in 2016, Obama admitted that if it had not been for Iraq, his approach to Syria might have been different.[12]

The point is not just that context matters in influencing the decisions leaders make. That is a given. The point is that Obama equated Syria and Iraq, and he believed any intervention would produce the same disastrous results. Leaving aside the obvious fallacy that not all interventions are the same and need not require large numbers of US ground troops, Obama neglected to think about the obvious differences between the two cases. In Iraq, the United States intervened with large forces and produced regime change. In Syria, the uprising and threat to the Assad regime came from within. Yes, foreign forces would be drawn in; but in Syria, it was the Assad regime itself that produced a domestic uprising.[e]

There is irony in the Obama administration's policy of avoidance in Syria and its intervention in Libya. I say "irony" because it was the lessons of Iraq—ones wrongly learned—that led to the administration's objective of avoidance in Syria, and yet those lessons are certainly lacking in the case

---

[e] In Chapter 9, I will explore the Syrian case in-depth.

of Libya. Robert Gates takes note of this irony, wondering how the Obama administration could support intervention in Libya, produce regime change, and have no plan for who or what would replace Qadhafi. Gates notes that Obama replicated the mistakes of the Bush administration in Iraq, failing to learn from them. Just like in Iraq, Gates argues, the United States failed to plan for an international role to re-establish order and a working government.[13]

While Obama has called Libya the worst mistake of his presidency, he believed at the time that he had learned the lessons of the Bush administration. It is true that unlike during Bush, there were extensive internal deliberations on how to respond to the uprisings against the Qadhafi regime and his increasingly brutal efforts to put them down. Inter-agency meetings took place daily to discuss options in Libya as challenges to Qadhafi's rule spread throughout the country and his rhetoric about exterminating the opposition became more extreme.

It is important to remember the context: Mohammed Bouazizi, a fruit and vegetable vendor in Tunisia, set himself on fire in protest of being denied the right to sell his produce because he lacked a permit. His act of self-immolation, his protest, literally unleashed pent up frustration throughout the Middle East in response to capricious and corrupt rule—with publics losing their fear and sweeping away first the Tunisian and then the Egyptian leaders. What happened in Tunisia and Egypt soon spread to Libya; within the Obama administration, the United States focused very much on how to manage the change.

Obama, initially, was optimistic. He saw people power in the public squares sweeping away entrenched leaders largely through peaceful protest. Obama saw this as alternative model to al Qaeda's prescription for change. Here were peaceful mass demonstrations, not violence and terror and the killing of innocents, leading to Presidents Ben Ali in Tunisia and Mubarak in Egypt being forced out of power. The militaries they had built up to preserve themselves in power would not do their bidding against the Tunisian and Egyptian publics.

Obama would often join our daily inter-agency meetings in the Situation Room at the White House. The aim in Tunisia and Egypt was to try to ensure that protests that swept away leaders could be channeled into mechanisms for writing constitutions, setting up the bases for elections, organizing political parties and NGOs, and helping the economies as the transitions unfolded. But the focus in Libya had to be different because Qadhafi was waging war on his public—or at least on those who were opposing him.

The inter-agency process produced sanctions, the freezing of Libyan assets in the United States, engagement with and recognition of a transitional Libyan authority, and the development of the Friends of Libya coalition—and adoption by the UN Security Council of an arms embargo on Libya. But as the Qadhafi threats escalated and the British and French leaders, David Cameron and Nicolas Sarkozy, made clear they would militarily intervene even if the United States would not, Obama convened a meeting in the Situation Room to consider our options. There were those—Vice President Biden and Secretary Gates—who opposed US intervention. Gates argued that the United States had no vital interests at stake and should neither assume responsibility for a no-fly zone nor commit any American forces.[14] Biden supported the Gates argument, saying that the United States did not need to be involved in another Middle Eastern conflict.

Secretary of State Hillary Clinton was in Europe at this point and took part in the discussion via secure link. She chose not to directly argue for or against an intervention; instead, she said we should be under no illusions: the French and the British were going to act militarily, and we needed to think about the consequences of them doing so without the United States. Did we want to shape their actions or be unable to influence them? And were we so sure they might not start something they could not finish?

The back-benchers in this meeting—Samantha Power and myself, both senior members of the National Security Council staff, and Antony Blinken, Biden's national security advisor—were called on by Obama to speak. Samantha focused on the humanitarian consequences of not stopping Qadhafi: his forces were moving toward Benghazi after taking Misrata, and Power cited reports of those forces going through the hospital in Misrata and killing everyone. Qadhafi was, she reminded President Obama, declaring that he would exterminate the opposition like "rats." And there was nothing to stop Qadhafi's forces from getting to Benghazi, a much larger city than Misrata, and carrying out a massacre. Speaking with great passion, she said the United States had the means to stop him, and we could not stand aside and do nothing as a human catastrophe unfolded.

I went next and took issue with Robert Gates's argument that the United States had no vital national interests in what was happening in Libya. I pointed out that the United States did have vital interests in Egypt and that a massacre in Benghazi—certain to happen if the United States did not stop it—would trigger a mass refugee flow from Libya into Egypt. That was the last thing Egypt needed as it was going through a transition—a transition that was going to be difficult enough politically and economically without the burden of tens of thousands of Libyan refugees streaming across Egypt's western border. I added that no one in the room questioned whether the United States had vital interests in the Middle East, and everyone in the region would be watching how and whether America would respond to Qadhafi. I concluded by saying it was an illusion to think that a non-response—one that would permit a humanitarian slaughter in Benghazi—would not affect how the United States was seen and the choices that regional actors would subsequently make.

Antony Blinken followed me and essentially combined Samantha's argument for a humanitarian intervention and mine that American interests in the region also required the United States to stop Qadhafi's forces from getting to Benghazi. Notably, he directly challenged his boss's position.

Obama recessed the meeting telling us he would make a decision and we should plan to reassemble later that evening. He would subsequently inform Tom Donilon, the national security advisor, and Gates of his decision—and Donilon informed us. In essence, Obama decided that the United States would intervene but not unilaterally; the country would use its unique capabilities—ones the British and French lacked—to destroy the Libyan air defense capabilities. The US military would act for 10–14 days, taking out what could threaten the aircraft of US NATO partners; from that point, the NATO forces would take the lead with the United States in the background providing intelligence and logistic support. Before the US military would launch its air-to-ground missions—defeating Libyan air defense and hitting Qadhafi forces as they moved toward Benghazi—Obama wanted a UN Security Council resolution authorizing the US action, and a commitment from Arab partners to call for such an intervention (with at least some being part of the military coalition).[15]

Susan Rice, the US ambassador to the UN, would intensively work to produce an "all necessary measures" resolution to protect Libyan civilians, especially in the Benghazi area. In advance of the UN's action, Secretary of State Clinton worked with a number of Arab foreign ministers to produce a resolution at the Arab League calling for the UN Security Council to impose a no-fly zone to protect Libyan civilians—language that was adopted in the UNSC Resolution 1973.[f]

President Obama believed he was acting on the lessons of Iraq. He was bounding American military involvement, making sure it would be limited in time and scope. The United States was acting with broad international and regional support given the resolutions of both the UN Security Council and the Arab League. The United States was not acting unilaterally but in a broad coalition that included the country's NATO allies and Arab militaries from the UAE and Qatar. Unlike the Bush administration, Obama satisfied himself thinking that the United States had a patina of international legitimacy.

Still, it all went badly. The problem was not the initial military intervention—although the British, French, Danish, and other NATO allies needed much more US military support than what the Obama administration understood. The problem was that the aim declared by the United States was to save the Libyan civilian population, when in reality it was inevitably going to become regime change. The United States might stop Qadhafi from getting to Benghazi, but he was not going away; and anywhere he faced opposition, he would seek to exterminate it. Moreover, the longer the United States engaged militarily to stop him, the more the US military acted around the country to defeat his forces, the less America could accept an outcome in which he was still there.

While there were some efforts to negotiate a peaceful outcome in which there would be a hand-over of power and a departure of Qadhafi—both Tony Blair, who was then a representative of the Quartet (the US, the EU, Russia, and the UN), and President Jacob Zuma of South Africa reached out to Qadhafi—they were unavailing. In neither instance did the Obama administration have much confidence that such outreach would or could work. Thus, the objective morphed from merely protecting Libyan civilians to regime change.

For those of us who had argued for intervention, there was an assumption from the outset that Qadhafi would have to go because he would not reconcile himself to opposition or anything less than total control. To be fair, there was planning for a post-Qadhafi Libya.

---

[f] The resolution was adopted with 10 votes for and 5 abstentions. Both the Russians and Chinese abstained, with President Medvedev in Russia responding to President Obama's appeal not to block a resolution that was about saving Libyan civilians.

There was intensive work with the Libyan National Transitional Council (NTC)—a group of Libyans who constituted a developing government in exile. The Friends of Libya, also known as the Libyan Contact Group, was shaped largely by the United States and its European allies; together with NTC, Libyan Contact Group focused on developing a governing structure to assume responsibility for the day after Qadhafi. The work included recognizing the NTC as a government in exile so the frozen assets could be turned over to it; preparing a constitution and elections for an interim government; setting up planning structures and the ability to deliver services; building a judicial structure; shaping financial governance and promoting economic growth—all of this with the Obama administration intimately involved. In fact, the administration developed 30 non-military programs to support this effort.[16]

But there was one glaring omission in all this work: creating security on the ground was not part of the effort. US and allied militaries operated from the air. Those fighting Qadhafi on the ground were a variety of militias, largely tribal, from different parts of the country. They had little in common, and there was essentially no coordination between them. Military support was flowing to them from different sources, including Qatar and the UAE, who backed different militias. And the Transitional Libyan Council was largely disconnected from the militias.

How could there be governance without security? How could there be order without security? It is not as if these questions were not asked. But in bounding US involvement, President Obama mandated that there would be no American "boots on the ground." He would avoid another Iraq by not permitting any US ground forces into Libya. The United States would discuss with its allies the creation of a multi-national force to provide security, integrate the militias into one military, create police forces, control all the Qadhafi weapons, and prevent them from proliferating outside the country. But if the United States was not prepared to provide a contingent of forces, it could not get others to do so.[8]

Given the relatively small size of the militias, I found out—in informal discussions with my colleagues in the Joint Staff and several senior military officers, including the vice chair of the Joint Chiefs of Staff—that our leading military officers believed an international force of 20,000 could fill the void and provide security until an integrated Libyan military could be

---

[8] The United States did provide limited assistance to locate stockpiles of chemical weapons.

established and function. To attract others, we collectively felt that 5,000 American troops would be necessary.[h]

Of course, there was no guarantee that such a force could work or that its mission could be achieved within a set time. In Bosnia, for example, the peace-keeping force for implementing the peace agreement is still there. While clearly a risk, look at what has transpired without such a force: continuing chaos, ongoing fighting, competing governments in Tripoli and Benghazi, governance largely failing in a state with oil resources and a relatively small population.

By not providing for security, the Obama administration failed to understand the most basic lesson of Iraq. Ironically—in thinking he was avoiding another Iraq—President Obama, by ruling out any US forces on the ground, guaranteed in Libya, just like in Iraq, the creation of a vacuum after regime change. Here was an example of not just failing to match objectives and means. In this case, the means became the ends.

Yes, means can and should inform objectives. Means by definition are not ends. When the means become the ends, they create an inevitable distortion, and you collectively lose sight of what you are trying to achieve. Put simply, if the means become the objective, one needs to rethink the objective. If the objective is not important enough to justify certain means, one should keep the objective far more limited. In retrospect, those of us who argued for the original intervention needed to spell out to President Obama what he needed to take into consideration:

- regime change and a responsibility to ensure no vacuum afterward;
- the means the United States and its allies would have to employ to ensure security;
- the kind of forces that would be required to establish security and to preserve stability in the transition;
- which of US allies and partners could and would contribute military or police forces and what the division of labor would look like.

To make President Obama consider all of that, especially in the context of Iraq and Afghanistan, would have been a tall order. But here again we see

---

[h] Our informal discussions were advanced enough that we discussed who could make up the forces and felt a Muslim presence was necessary. In this connection, we felt a Turkish military contribution would be essential. It is worth recalling that as part of the Bosnian settlement, the United States contributed 20,000 forces out of the 60,000 NATO-led Implementation Force (IFOR).

the importance of being able to think through the costs of inaction, not just the cost of action—or in this case, the cost of limiting US involvement to the point that the United States guaranteed a vacuum in the aftermath of Qadhafi's demise. Admittedly, the costs of action are often more immediate and tangible than the costs of inaction.

In this connection, President Obama would consistently ask the question, "Where does this end?" He was right to ask it. But the corollary question also needed to be asked: "What happens if we don't act?"

Ultimately, Libya is a textbook example of not marrying objectives and means. We can also see such examples in the Trump and Biden administrations.

Trump and Iran

Trump's "maximum pressure" policy toward Iran was another classic case of a misguided assessment. The assumption in the administration—certainly reflecting the Trump mindset—was that squeezing the Iranians economically would either force them to concede much more on their nuclear program or trigger such upheaval at home that the regime might collapse.

Trump's worldview was almost exclusively shaped by economic factors, and he seems to have projected his perceptions onto others—assuming that tough economic pressures on the one hand and promises of great economic payoffs on the other would permit him to score great foreign policy successes where his predecessors had failed. Recall his pitch to Kim Jong Un of North Korea: a slick video of enormous growth potential, including condos on the beach. Similarly, tariffs on adversaries (China) and tariffs on allies (the Europeans) were natural tools for Trump—and "trade wars were easy to win."[17] So it was no leap for him to believe that tougher economic sanctions would force the Iranians to come to the table and seek a deal.

While his first secretary of state Rex Tillerson, his first secretary of defense James Mattis, and his second national security advisor H. R. McMaster all advised him not to pull out of the nuclear deal with Iran, known as the Joint Comprehensive Plan of Action (the JCPOA), he did it anyway. He would re-impose sanctions and toughen them. By withdrawing from the JCPOA, Trump isolated us, not the Iranians, not appreciating that political isolation of Iran was a form of pressure. He failed to use the leverage that his threat of withdrawing created on European allies of the United States—they were clearly willing to pay something to keep the United States in the deal.

British, French, and German leaders all reached out to Trump to try to persuade him to stay in the deal, authorizing negotiations with the administration to try to address its concerns. The administration pressed for a number of things, including lifting the sunset provisions. The Europeans agreed to everything except lifting those provisions, saying sunsets represented the core of the deal. But they agreed that the sunset provisions would have to be extended or modified before 2030, when they lapsed. French President Emmanuel Macron would go so far as to publicly declare that a follow-on agreement to the JCPOA would need to be negotiated to correct the sunset provisions.[i]

Of course, it was not only the failure of the Trump administration to exploit its leverage on its Euroepan partners if the administration wanted to strengthen the JCPOA or build pressure effectively on Iran for a follow-on agreement to overcome the deal's flaws. It was also the inability of the administration to think through what the Iranians might do after the United States withdrew. Indeed, the Trump administration had no plan for what to do if the Iranians began to dramatically expand their nuclear program—or began to execute their own policy of maximum pressure against US friends and interests in the region. The Iranians would do both after Trump, at the urging of his second secretary of state Mike Pompeo and his first national security advisor John Bolton, revoked in May 2019 the waivers that had allowed eight countries to buy oil from Iran. It was the revocation of the waivers, one year after Trump withdrew from the JCPOA, that limited Iranian oil exports to, at one point, less than 100,000 barrels a day–something that truly did impose a far greater squeeze on Iran's economy.

As if to say, "if we cannot export our oil, we will call into question whether others can do so," the Iranians, using frogmen, attached limpet mines to four oil tankers, disabling them. There were several more attacks on oil tankers in the Gulf of Oman. In addition, the Houthi missile attacks on the Saudi Arabia ratcheted up dramatically. Three months later, in September 2019, the Iranians, from their own territory, carried out a direct attack on the most

---

[i] Brian Hook, the administration's point person on Iran, negotiated for four months with his European counterparts, and by his own admission much progress was made in those discussions. But when Trump was asked about why he withdrew from the JCPOA when the Europeans had addressed his administration's concerns in talks with Brian Hook, Trump said he did not know Hook.

important Saudi oil processing facility—Abqaiq—using drones and cruise missiles.[18] Trump's reaction to the attacks on tankers was to say that the United States did not get its oil from the Persian Gulf, so others should take the lead on securing it—and that the attack on Abqaiq was an attack on Saudi Arabia, not America.[19]

While the Trump administration would begin to provide more weapons to the Saudis and join those allied naval forces who took the lead in acting to safeguard shipping in the Persian Gulf, the administration clearly signaled that its maximum pressure campaign was limited to economic tools. When the Iranians shot down a US drone, President Trump chose not to retaliate—making it clear that only if Americans were killed would there be military retaliation. Yes, Trump would authorize the targeted killing of Qassem Soleimani, the head of the Qods Force of the Iranian Revolutionary Guard in January of 2020. Trump was, however, very careful not to retaliate further when the Iranians carried out their own military reaction against the al Asad base in Iraq, where there was a significant American military presence. The onslaught of missiles left many American forces injured but none died, and Trump authorized no further military action.

Trump might well have been wise to do so. The larger point, however, is once again that there was a big mismatch between the objectives and means employed to pursue the Trump administration's Iran policy. Secretary of State Mike Pompeo would lay out 12 conditions that Iran would have to meet for the United States to change its approach to the Islamic Republic.[20] Pompeo's conditions would have effectively meant the end of the Islamic Republic—something Ali Khamenei, the Supreme Leader of Iran, has always believed is the aim of the United States. The Pompeo conditions were surely desirable, but the secretary of state offered nothing beyond sanctions as the means America had to achieve them.

Here again, we see an impulse to establish ambitious objectives, but these objectives were completely divorced from the means the United States had to achieve them. Were they meant to be purely rhetorical? Was the aim simply to create measures or standards that the Iranians would have to meet? How would this affect others who the United States wanted to join it in isolating the Iranians? The problem is that US allies and others saw the conditions—and therefore US objective—as being unachievable. Little thought seems to have been given to the impact of adopting a posture that US allies would find largely divorced from reality—or at least one that seemed designed to force the regime to fundamentally change all its behavior toward the outside world and also toward its public.

It is certainly defensible to condition a change in US approach to Iran on the Iranian regime accepting that it can no longer do such things as threatening its neighbors; or using Shia militia proxies as leverage against different regimes; or supporting terrorist groups with arms, moneys, and training; or continuing its human rights abuses of its own citizens. From a statecraft perspective, one would still want to see a strategy—even a long-term one—that spelled out how one would go about achieving these aims through a calibrated approach with different means available.

The problem is that it was not Trump's approach. Just as he wanted a deal with North Korea, he wanted a deal with the Iranians. Trump was ready to go along with a four-point document prepared by President Macron of France, which outlined three very general commitments that Iran would agree to make: refrain from aggression, not acquire nuclear weapons, and negotiate a long-term framework for regional security. For its part, the United States would agree to lift sanctions. President Rouhani of Iran insisted that the United States first lift all sanctions before Iran would take any steps—and Trump (under pressure from his national security advisor and secretary of state) rejected that. Remarkably, however, Trump was willing to accept the four-part document, even though the Iranian commitments were all rhetorical and general while the lifting of sanctions was tangible and specific, and some would be lifted once the Iranians initiated the dialogue. (At the time, there were officials in the administration who told me that they were relieved that Rouhani rescued them from accepting the Macron initiative—a proposition they saw as a trap.)

Shortly thereafter, at the G-7 meeting in 2019, Macron raised—and Trump accepted—that Iran would be given a 15-billion-dollar credit line if it would come back into the JCPOA. Trump also was anxious for Macron to work out a phone call for him with Rouhani. In all these instances, it was the Iranians who rejected the outreach, not Trump. The point is not that Trump was wrong to pursue or be open to any of these initiatives. On the contrary, he may well have been right to do so.

The point is that Trump's objective was a deal, while that of his senior advisors was regime change. It is hard to match objectives and means when an administration seemingly has two different and competing objectives. This may also explain why Brian Hook could tout the success of the administration's approach to Iran, even as Iran was becoming more aggressive in the region and advancing its nuclear program by no longer respecting the limits of the JCPOA.[21,j]

Biden and Afghanistan

The Biden administration, too, has had a decidedly mixed record on matching objectives and means. In withdrawing from Afghanistan, President Biden was surely right that the United States could not walk away from the deal that the Trump administration made with the Taliban. To do so, and not to withdraw, would surely have produced a determined Taliban campaign to show how much the US forces would pay in blood for not living up to the deal. But Biden's decision to withdraw was also based on what he repeatedly said: that this withdrawal would not look like the United States leaving Vietnam, with people hanging from helicopters.

Regrettably, the withdrawal from Afghanistan created imagery even worse than Vietnam. The chaotic withdrawal seemingly left allies and Afghan partners high and dry. It sent a terrible signal to friends and foes about the reliability of the United States and seemed to show US weakness.

It was not only that the assessment of the administration was fundamentally flawed; so was the decision-making process that led to it. That President Biden overruled the military's desire to keep a force of roughly 3,000 in Afghanistan was legitimate. What was not is that he then let Secretary of Defense Lloyd Austin and Chairman of the Joint Chiefs of Staff General Mark Milley devise a plan that made the safe withdrawal of the US forces essentially the only objective of the United States. Yes, there was a need to get the US forces out safely, and yes, the way to reduce their vulnerability as their numbers dwindled was to withdraw stealthily. But the US military stealth withdrawal and non-coordination with the Afghan forces increased *their* vulnerability and led to a fundamentally illogical approach in which the United States was withdrawing the military before it withdrew civilians.

The military defined a very narrow objective that ignored that the United States had other objectives as it left Afghanistan. The United States had an interest to get out in a way that did not look like the US military were fleeing

---

j For Hook, the fact that Iran was forced to reduce the material assistance it was providing Hezbollah—requiring Hezbollah to find other sources of revenue—was proof that the administration's policy of economic pressure was working. That Iran was ratcheting up conflicts in the area and accelerating its nuclear program seemed to matter less because the long-term aim was weakening the regime. But that was not Trump's aim.

or leaving Afghanistan as the regime was collapsing. Similarly, the United States had a commitment to all those Afghans who worked with the US military and were spread throughout the country—and, therefore, had to be safeguarded and able to leave with the US military personnel. The same was true for American allies who had forces on the ground and felt an obligation to those who had worked with them.

The plan created by the Joint Chiefs of Staff seemed to take no account of these other objectives. They may well have rationalized their plan based on intelligence assessments that the Afghan regime would not collapse and would last at least six months.[22] But how capable would the regime and the Afghan military be in securing the government and also all Afghans who had worked with the US military and felt the need to leave when they left? How much of the Afghan military fit the category of those who felt they must also evacuate with their families as the US military withdrew? That the US military put the safety of its forces first was understandable, but the policy process required assessing this plan against other objectives—and there was no serious questioning of the plan. According to media reports—and to what one senior administration person told me—Jake Sullivan raised a question about the plan in one meeting with Austin and Milley, but he did not persist with his questioning. Nor did he or Antony Blinken press their concerns with President Biden.

Maybe they were convinced that he was determined to withdraw and was not inclined to listen. But clearly, they too bought the assessments that there was time and there would not be immediate collapse of the Afghan military and the regime. While this surely was an intelligence failure, it was also more than that. Why weren't the other objectives raised, much less addressed? The military's plan for evacuation should have been challenged on many bases, including the following questions:

- How would the plan provide for those Afghans to whom the United States owed a commitment, who needed to be evacuated from the country but were not in Kabul?
- How, given this plan, would the US military be able to provide for the security of those they needed to evacuate from the country if the United States had already withdrawn its forces?
- How would the plan meet the needs of NATO allies of the United States who also felt the need to get Afghans working with them out of the country?

- How would the plan, and its call for the early departure of the US military from the Bagram Air Base, affect mindsets of the Afghan military and the Taliban?

It is interesting that the Biden administration seemed focused on getting US forces out but still being able to say that the United States would be able to carry out an anti-terror mission once the US military was out of Afghanistan. Implicitly, the administration was acknowledging that Afghanistan without at least a limited US military presence could again become a haven for terrorist groups that could threaten the United States and its interests. President Biden was at pains to say that "over the horizon presence" of the United States in the Middle East would permit the US military to strike at terrorist groups in Afghanistan and remain secure without having to remain in the country.[k]

As important as that objective might be, it was a reminder that the administration did expect that the Taliban would, in time, end up taking over in Afghanistan. It was a matter of time. Within the administration, a groupthink developed that US withdrawal would go smoothly and there would be a decent interval before a likely Taliban take-over. Groupthink always dismisses any considerations outside the group assumptions.[l] And, in this case, the other near-term objectives that the United States had beyond getting its forces out safely were simply not addressed. If the Trump administration failed in its Iran policy because it had two conflicting objectives, the Biden administration failed because it seemed blind to what else it needed to be able to do as the US military withdrew its forces. In both administrations, statecraft failed because the objectives were either unclear or they were simply incomplete. Either way, there was no marriage of objectives and means.

To its credit, the Biden administration acted differently in the run-up to Putin's invasion of Ukraine. The administration seemed to think things through much more systematically. Its objective was clear and discreet, and it used an effective set of means to mobilize others. For example, Biden conveyed to Putin that Russia would pay a very high price in terms of unifying NATO and in terms of far-reaching sanctions that would be imposed.

---

[k] The killing of Ayman Zawahiri in Kabul in 2022 seemed to validate Biden's point.
[l] Proof of the groupthink about how smoothly the withdrawal would go: President Biden, Secretary of State Blinken, National Security Advisor Sullivan, and a number of key deputies all planned to be on vacation at the time the withdrawal of US military forces was to be completed in August, ahead of schedule.

His administration backed up the threats by releasing intelligence to show it knew that Russia was planning to invade and using that to mobilize NATO allies to agree on tough sanctions if Putin went ahead with the invasion. Putin could not frame the issue because the United States did so.

Unfortunately, the Biden administration still failed in its objective of deterrence because it could not make its threats sufficiently convincing. Its well-orchestrated and intensive diplomatic efforts were not sufficient to deter Putin—in no small part because he had seen a pattern of soft US and Western responses to his actions starting with Georgia over the years. Moreover, he thought he would win very quickly, create a fait accompli, and the world would simply adjust to the new reality.

Putin was profoundly wrong. His miscalculations—and his belief that his gains would be dramatic while US threats would not be sustained—meant he was unlikely to be deterred. But the United States also miscalculated. The US offer to evacuate Vladimir Zelensky indicated that the Biden administration shared the Russian assessment that the Ukrainians would collapse quickly, and that Moscow would take over in Kyiv. While Putin's miscalculations meant deterrence was an objective that was unlikely to be achieved, how might the possibility of war termination have been affected if the United States had not shared Putin's assessment of a lightning collapse of the Kyiv regime?

How different might things have been if the United States had understood that the Russian military machine was largely hollow, bereft logistically, with terrible command problems, and the morale of its forces profoundly weak in the face of a determined Ukrainian fighting force. Had the Biden administration understood that the Ukrainians could muster an effective, highly motivated force and the Russians could not, the United States could have provided heavier weapons much earlier. That would have raised the cost to the Russians and Putin from the outset.[m]

Had the US assessments been better and the US provision of weapons been adjusted accordingly, the leverage on Putin and his interest in looking for a way out might have been possible earlier in the war. Of course, there is no guarantee of this because Putin's assessments were faith-based, not fact-based. Still, Putin was not entirely indifferent to the realities on the

---

[m] Putin's implied threats of nuclear weapon usage have put limits on what the United States was prepared to do to support Ukraine. But the fact is that the United States supplied HIMARS and other effective artillery only months into the conflict and those weapons proved very effective in raising the costs to the Russians and also facilitated Ukraine going on the offensive.

ground—note the withdrawals from Kyiv, Kharkiv, and Kherson—and he also recognized certain limits: he never attacked any of the supply lines of weapons coming from any NATO countries.

We cannot know if better assessments on the US part might have affected the ability to end the Russian war in Ukraine. But we certainly know now that the United States was terribly wrong in its assessment about what would happen once the Russians invaded.

Wrong Assessments and the Mismatch of Objectives and Means

Are wrong assessments the reason it is so difficult to marry objectives and means? They are certainly one factor. Assessments need to be thought of along a number of dimensions. First, do we have a good understanding of larger geopolitical realities and concepts for dealing with them? As I noted on Vietnam, applying the US concept of containment made little sense in Southeast Asia. Second, from a less conceptual and more tactical standpoint, do we understand the situation on the ground? Do we have a good appreciation of who and what we are dealing with? From Vietnam to Iraq, American misjudgments and poor understandings of the realities the United States was facing are hard to exaggerate, and obviously shaped what turned out to be misguided objectives. Third, there is the issue of our ideological predisposition or inclinations, and how often they drive poor assessments. Unquestionably, ideological inclinations played a major, even decisive, role in Iraq. Everything that drove the Bush 43rd administration to invade and remove Saddam Hussein was an ideological mindset—a mindset that created a prism through which all intelligence was perceived.

We are reminded again that context matters. After 9/11, Bush and the key players around him understandably were riveted on making sure that the worst did not happen—that the worst weapons must not get into the worst hands. There was, of course, also the legacy of how the first Gulf War ended; in the minds of many of the key players around Bush, there was the shared belief that they let Saddam Hussein off the hook and allowed him to decimate the Shia who rose up against him. Apart from guilt about that, the key players around Bush harbored a view that Saddam Hussein was a threat who was determined to possess weapons of mass destruction, and the United States had the means to prevent that.

Of course, ideology and its impact on shaping poor assessments is not unique to the United States. Vladimir Putin completely miscalculated on Ukraine. His deep-seated beliefs that Ukraine is not a real country shaped his assessment of what would happen when Russia invaded. (Obviously, other factors contributed as well; some were part of Putin's ideological mindset and some not. His mindset about the role of Russian power and his belief in restoring countries once part of its orbit into Russia again was one element, but so was his assumption that the United States and others would not sustain any real pressure on Russia. On that, there was a track record that informed his judgments.)

Politics and political considerations or pressures also contribute to the mismatch of objectives and means. At times, US presidents adopt objectives because of pressures—even though those objectives might not be achievable, or at least not thought through in a way to determine whether their means (or those they could mobilize) could fulfill them. When President Obama announced that Bashar al-Assad had lost his legitimacy and could not remain in power, he was driven largely by public pressures to do something about Assad's killings of increasing numbers of Syrians. Similarly, media pressures to respond to what was happening in Syria led Obama to declare his redline on the use of chemical weapons by the Syrian regime in a press conference.[23]

Obama was not unique in responding to political pressures or perceived political needs in adopting objectives quite independent of whether the United States had the means or the will to achieve them. So much of Lyndon Johnson's approach to Vietnam was his perception of what had destroyed the Truman presidency—ironically, not a tremendously costly war in Korea which should have made Johnson chary of getting into a land war in Asia, but rather the imagery that Truman had lost China. For Johnson, US politics dictated that one could not look soft on communism. He had to stand up to the communist threat, and he was doing so in Vietnam and preventing a set of dominos from falling.

It should be no surprise that political factors will influence what presidents decide and lead to the adoption of misguided objectives. Presidents may also be driven by something else: their own belief that they can do things because they will it. To say it takes an enormous ego—and will—to run for the US presidency is an understatement. Because this is an extremely difficult job, it takes extraordinary self-belief to feel you can do it—and that, of course, says nothing about the sheer will it takes to run for the office given the rigors and demands of doing so. As such, presidents often adopt objectives out of self-belief.

Franklin Delano Roosevelt felt he could charm Joseph Stalin and reassure him. Bill Clinton once told me after a meeting with Syrian leader Hafez al-Assad that he knew how to deal with him and could convince him of what would be necessary to achieve peace.[n]

US presidents often tend to personalize objectives and their ability to achieve them. Not surprisingly, that can produce objectives that do not relate well to means. Of course, other factors also contribute to the adoption of objectives that ultimately are not feasible. At times, initial success expands the belief of what can be achieved and leads to a change in objectives. The United States led an international intervention in Somalia to address a famine caused by a conflict of warlords in the last year of the Bush 41st administration. Those warlords agreed to a ceasefire to permit the massive delivery of food, and the mission—largely involving the establishment of corridors for delivering food—was very successful in the spring and summer of 1992. But President Bush in December 1992, the last month of his presidency, convinced the UN to expand the mission to protect aid workers, and he sent 25,000 US combat forces to lead the UN troops there.

What seemed logical soon transformed the mission into one in which the United States was fighting one of the militias and the warlord who dominated Mogadishu, Muhammed Farah Aydid. A humanitarian mission became a more political one for what seemed like understandable reasons. In the process, however, the United States became enmeshed in a conflict for which it had little appetite. The Battle for Mogadishu would produce the infamous Blackhawk Down incident, the dragging of the bodies of US Marines through the streets of the city, and the US military withdrawal from Somalia.[o]

In the case of Somalia, one could argue that initial success did not lead the United States to think through the consequences of expanding the objective.

---

[n] After meeting Assad in Damascus in October 1994, President Clinton told me that he knew what drove Assad. He had dealt with politicians like him in Arkansas who found it difficult to do anything, and he knew what it would take to move him. I told him, "Mr. President, you never dealt with anyone like him in Arkansas. This is a guy who had close to 20,000 people killed in the city of Hama to wipe out the Muslim Brotherhood—there was no one in Arkansas like that." I did not persuade him.

[o] President Clinton inherited the mission and did not alter it. But with 28 other countries contributing forces to the UN mission, he drew US forces down to 1,200, without altering the objective that had expanded and involved fighting the Aydid militia. He would withdraw the remainder of US forces after the deaths of 18 US Marines.

One other factor that contributes to the mismatch of objectives and means is not defining objectives well. Too often, objectives are adopted at a level of generality because of the pressure of either business or political considerations. The latter often produce what I refer to as "motherhood objectives," or "apple pie objectives"—so vague and amorphous that they function more as slogans than as actionable goals. An example of such a vague objective would be broadly "preserving freedom," with no definition of what that means.

In Vietnam or in Iraq, American objective was democratization, because that is what the United States stands for. The realities in both Vietnam and Iraq made that mission impossible. However, US self-image requires objectives that meet the standard worthy of this country or what it perceives itself to be.

Today in the United States, there is a debate over what this country's role in the world should be. No approach to the application of American statecraft is going to be sustainable if it is divorced from the American self-image and the traditions that shape it. To that, we will now turn.

Chapter 3

America's Self-Image, Traditions, and Role in the World

No US president can conduct foreign policy without regard to America's self-image and (what I like to call) its ethos. Similarly, statecraft done well is not just about a narrow approach to marrying objectives and means. Indeed, creating and implementing a sustainable policy will depend on being able to strike a chord with the American people. A policy that seems to go against what the United States stands for will inevitably face resistance.

Henry Kissinger's approach to détente with the Soviet Union produced opposition from Democrats and Republicans alike because it dealt with the Soviets as if it was a normal power with whom the United States could do business. Ronald Reagan was not speaking only for himself when he made it clear that the Soviet Union was an "evil empire," not a normal power. By doing business with it, Kissinger was perceived to be taking morality out of US foreign policy. The adoption of the Jackson–Vanik amendment to the Trade Act of 1974 was a direct assault on détente because it imposed a limit on trade with the Soviet Union unless it stopped restricting Jewish emigration and permitted other human rights. The amendment was designed to take away one of Kissinger's tools (namely, trade as an inducement) for trying to alter Soviet behavior because the supporters of Jackson–Vanik in the Congress believed that Kissinger was too willing to give the Soviets a pass on human rights. For them, Kissinger's détente seemed shaped solely by a focus on interests to the exclusion of American values. (Kissinger's critics, most notably Democratic Senator Henry Jackson, accused Kissinger of pursuing a policy of "moral disarmament." Kissinger responded at one point by saying that "the preservation of human life and society are moral values too.")[1]

It is, of course, possible to pursue a policy that puts greater emphasis on America's interests than on its values. But to sustain such a policy will not be easy. It requires preparing the ground with the public, and a major effort at educating it on why American interests are at stake and why the United States must take certain steps to protect and promote them. The greater the

Statecraft 2.0. Second Edition. Dennis Ross, Oxford University Press. © Oxford University Press (2025). DOI: 10.1093/oso/9780197698914.003.0003

threat, the easier the task of explaining to the public what the United States must do. Still, constant explanations of what America is doing are almost certain to be required.

Policies that the public can relate to because they seem to reflect who Americans are and how they have traditionally seen themselves will be far simpler to sustain. By definition, conducting good statecraft requires a good understanding of self-image and ethos. If nothing else, such an understanding can help US policy-makers mobilize the means domestically to carry out their policies, maintain them, and achieve the objectives America has set.

The US Image of Exceptionalism

Deeply engrained in the American psyche is a belief in exceptionalism. Americans have long believed that the United States embodies a unique set of values that stand out and set America apart. Walter McDougall points out that America's Founding Fathers and the clergy, publicists and other opinion leaders at the time perceived that the "new nation was a distillation of virtues latent in the civilization they left behind but susceptible of realization only in America." America was for them "a holy land."[2] As early as 1630, Massachusetts Governor John Winthrop would speak of this land as a City upon a Hill with the eyes of all people upon us—words that Ronald Reagan would often recall.[3]

America was a land of abundance where civil and religious freedom was permitted—unlike the lands from which the colonists had come. A land rich in resources, with great expanse, safely removed from potential enemies and providing its people liberty, must surely reflect the hand of God. This theme of providence placing special favor upon the United States is the essence of America's perceived exceptionalism. Preachers in the eighteenth and nineteenth centuries would say that "God has still greater blessings in store for this vine which his own right hand hath planted," and "the Lord shall have made his America Israel 'high above all nations which he hath made.'"[4] In other words, America was the new Israel, its people chosen in a new promised land.

Different US presidents would echo this belief that America was chosen and was carrying out God's will. Note Woodrow Wilson's words: "I believe that God planted in us the vision of liberty ... I cannot be deprived of the hope that we are chosen, and prominently chosen, to show the way to the nations of the world how they shall walk in the paths of liberty."[5]

Wilson made this statement as part of his explanation for why the United States had to enter World War I in 1917. Ironically, this view that America was chosen, that it was exceptional, that it was selfless, that it embodied values that were God-given, and that all peoples aspire to, was shared by presidents who saw themselves as having a responsibility to export these values to others. Woodrow Wilson and George W. Bush took this responsibility seriously and were determined to impose our values on others. Thomas Jefferson and Barack Obama saw things differently: rather than attempt to impose American values on others, the United States should serve as a model that others could emulate.

For much of his presidency, Barack Obama did not speak of America's exceptionalism. His hesitancy to speak of it until 2014 probably reflected his desire to draw clear distinctions from Bush and his sensitivity to charges of American arrogance. However, understanding that exceptionalism is an essential part of the American identity, he clearly came to believe that he needed to explain his policies by embracing it. Speaking at West Point on May 28, 2014, Obama said: "I believe in American exceptionalism with every fiber of my being."[6] However, once Obama began to speak of the exceptionalism, he also tied it to the need to perfect the American "experiment" at home so it could serve as an example for others. In this way, Obama shared much in common not just with Jefferson but with the Founding Fathers more generally. As Walter McDougall observed, "American Exceptionalism as our founders conceived it was defined by what America was at home. Foreign policy existed to defend, not define, what America was."[7]

As such, American exceptionalism, for much of the history of the United States, was not a vehicle for trying to export or impose the American model on others. Americans were not crusaders. Indeed, for those like John Quincy Adams, that would risk actually changing who Americans were. In a speech on July 4, 1821, he spelled this out in vivid terms:

America does not go abroad in search of monsters to destroy. She is the well-wisher to the freedom and independence of all. She is the champion only of her own. She will recommend the general cause by the countenance of her voice, and the benignant sympathy of her example. She well knows that by once enlisting under the banners other than her own, were they even the banners of foreign independence, she would involve herself beyond the power of extrication, in all the wars of interest and intrigue, of individual avarice, envy, and ambition, which assumed the colors and usurped the standards of freedom ... She might become the dictatress of the world. She would be no longer the ruler of her own spirit.[8]

This did not mean that the United States did not intervene. Jefferson would send the US Navy and Marines to Tripoli to stop the Barbary pirates from attacking US shipping. But intervention was not about exporting American values, it was about protecting America's interests against threats and attacks. The Founding Fathers worried about investing too much power in the federal government—power that could usurp individual rights. Hence, their focus on separation of powers. Foreign policy powers were essential for protecting from foreign threats, but needed to be limited so that those powers did not threaten liberty at home. The same would apply to building and maintaining armed forces. Yes, they were necessary, but they too could not be allowed to pose a threat to the liberty and the rights of American citizens.

Of course, liberty had to have an economic underpinning as well. Without prosperity and wealth generation, it could not be sustainable. In the eyes of America's founders, political and economic freedoms were inextricably linked—and trade was an essential part of developing the economy and generating revenues. As Robert Zoellick writes, "From the earliest days of independence, Americans viewed trade as an expression of liberty ... After all, the American Revolution arose out of protests against London's controls and taxes on trade. London and other centers of empire had extended trade through conquest and maintained domination through imperial monopolies. Americans wanted to end Europe's attempts to possess their wealth through exclusive arrangements."[9]

Free trade was, thus, an essential pillar of America's approach to the world from its earliest days. Initially, American farmers needed markets; later American industries needed them. Making sure other countries did not block America's access to trade and investment guided much of the US approach to foreign policy. In the first year of independence, John Adams would draft the Treaty Plan of 1776, with national treatment representing its core principle: "US merchants and ships would receive the same standing in foreign countries as their own domestic merchants and ships."[10] Thomas Jefferson opposed restrictions on trade, making clear such restrictions served private not public interests and explicitly saying, "I think all the world would gain by setting commerce at perfect liberty."[11] Later, John Hay's Open Door policy toward China, and the American intervention in response to the Boxer Rebellion at the turn of the twentieth century, was driven by the objective of making sure that no other country had economic rights, privileges, or access denied to America.

Liberty—politically and economically—was the guiding principle for the United States from its founding. Protecting it, guarding against encroachments on it, ensuring that there would be neither domestic nor foreign threats to it was the preoccupation of America's early leaders. Not surprisingly, liberty also meant being free of foreign entanglements or obligations. The United States needed to be free to engage in commerce with whom it wanted, but that did not mean having special relations with anyone. That could bind America in ways that ultimately limited the country's liberty. In his farewell address, George Washington warned against having special ties with or unending hostility toward any other country, saying that "nothing is more essential than that permanent, inveterate antipathies against particular nations and passionate attachments for others should be excluded."[12]

Washington was not ruling out understandings with foreign countries but, as he would declare, "The great rule of conduct for us in regard to foreign nations is, in extending our commercial relations to have with them as little political connection as possible. So far as we have already formed engagements let them be fulfilled with perfect good faith. Here let us stop."[13] He saw alliances as folly and favored neutrality. He asked, "Why forgo the advantages of so peculiar a situation? Why quit our own to stand upon foreign ground? Why, by interweaving our destiny with that of any part of Europe, entangle our peace and prosperity in toils of European ambition, rivalship, interest, humor or caprice?"

It was Jefferson who would call for no foreign entanglements. But it was Washington who set the tone and provided the logic for it in his farewell address in 1796. The United States would avoid alliances; it would not be embroiled in European conflicts; it would keep the Europeans out of the Western Hemisphere so they could not bring those conflicts closer to US borders; it would be neutral to provide options to its people—especially until America could become stronger both economically and militarily. Neutrality meant freedom of action, not isolation. In the words of one historian, the Founding Fathers defined neutrality as "the perfect independence of the United States; not isolation from the great affairs of the world."[14]

America could not be isolated from the world because trade, commerce, and capital from foreign investment were so central to its economic growth. Since isolation was not an option, neutrality meant being free to act on its own. Neutrality in practice meant that the United States could always act unilaterally. In other words, exceptionalism—because of the American virtues—argued for unilateralism. In truth, the United States was never isolationist; it was unilateralist. Being unilateralist did not mean only avoiding alliances; it also meant being unencumbered. It meant that the United States could use its military forces abroad when the country deemed it necessary—typically to protect or extend US trading rights and interests. As Walter Russell Mead points out, the United States was interventionist throughout the nineteenth century to serve its commercial interests. From countering the Barbary privates, to Commodore Perry's opening up Japan, to intervention in Korea in 1871, to the response to the Boxer Rebellion, there was little hesitancy to use US forces abroad. Americans were exceptional, they had this right; in parallel, the United States, given providential favor, had a "Manifest Destiny" to expand its dominion across the North American continent.[15]

Again, America's image of being exceptional justified unilateralism. And the conduct of American foreign policy until Wilson's time reflected it. In fact, Wilson's efforts to promote collective security after the war ran against the grain of the unilateralist tradition. He used his belief in America's exceptionalism to justify the country's involvement in the war—after his slogan in the 1916 presidential election was "He Kept Us Out of War". For Wilson, the exceptionalism—America's having been chosen—justified America's need to fight this war to end all wars.

But would he truly have changed his earlier posture on the war in which he declared that "the United States must be neutral in fact as well as in name" if it had not been for the resumption of unlimited German U-boat attacks against all shipping, including American shipping in early 1917? The sinking of US merchant and passenger ships—and the deaths of Americans—was a direct threat. The interception of the Zimmermann telegram, in which the Germans proposed a military alliance with Mexico and promised the return of former Mexican territories consisting of Texas, Arizona, and New Mexico if America entered the war, further crystallized the threat that Germany posed to the United States. It is not clear that any US president could have withstood the pressure to enter the war at that point.

For Wilson, however, the war had to have a higher purpose. It had to reflect who Americans were. And, in light of the terrible nature of this particular war with its horrific losses, the United States would join it not to return the world to the prewar status quo in which European powers and their empires competed with one another, but to extend US values to others and bring self-determination to colonial peoples. Wilson's 14 Points would change the nature of the world. Only such a result could justify what Wilson understood meant ending US neutrality and joining the war on the side of the Entente—effectively no longer "steering clear of European embroilments."

The American intervention in the war did not contradict either the US image of exceptionalism or the related tradition of neutrality and unilateralism. Wilson was on safe footing here. But in adopting collective security after the war, he was not. On this, he was directly countering that tradition. He sought to explain it in terms of American higher purpose, but the Senate would reject the Treaty of Versailles and the leading role of the United States in the League of Nations because it would make America responsible for others and limit US freedom of action. Wilson was trying to transform international relations and preserve peace by making the United States a leader in actively preserving peace on the world stage. That had never been the American role or self-image. Henry Cabot Lodge, Republican Majority Leader in the Senate, would present 14 reservations to the Treaty—an answer to Wilson's 14 Points, on which Wilson was not prepared to compromise. In essence, Lodge's reservations were all about ensuring that no one could impose on the United States obligations or raise questions about its policies. In the reservations, Lodge spelled out that the United States would assume no responsibility for ensuring the territorial integrity or the independence of any other state nor would it submit itself to arbitration or to questions by the Council of the League on its long-established policies, like the Monroe Doctrine. Moreover, it was only the United States that could decide if its responsibilities had been fulfilled, and only the United States would make decisions on its security, or any issues related to its domestic jurisdiction.[16]

Lodge was not against America acting internationally, or even being a part of the League of Nations, provided it could do so based on terms defined exclusively by the United States and without any binding obligations. America might be exceptional, but it was still not a crusading nation. The cost of World War I was a strong argument against becoming crusaders since American forces had suffered many casualties: nearly 53,000 combat deaths and roughly 202,000 wounded. While the losses might have paled in comparison to the European deaths, they were still daunting. At the same time, the war also devastated the economies of European countries, while it left the United States strong economically and financially powerful, being a creditor nation for the first time.

In these circumstances, the United States would not withdraw from the world; it would simply limit its responsibilities. The Harding administration wanted "normalcy" at home and abroad. The use of force was out of the question. But American diplomacy would still be active. The term "relentless diplomacy," used by Antony Blinken in 2021 to explain how the Biden administration would conduct its foreign policy, might aptly describe the approach of Charles Evans Hughes, the secretary of state in the Harding administration. In the aftermath of the rejection by the US Senate of the Treaty of Versailles, Hughes understood the constraints within which he had to operate but also found much space for creative diplomatic initiatives. He would organize the Washington Conference and, using soft power and the power to frame issues, he would effectively produce real arms control and an approach to regional security in Asia.

In the Washington Conference, Hughes saw competition in naval forces as increasing the potential for conflict. As Robert Zoellick points out, battleships "were the strategic weapons of the age (similar to bombers and missiles of a later era.)"[17] Hughes, recognizing the public mood not only in the United States but internationally about the dangers and terrible costs of war, seized the initiative in launching the conference with his proposal to reduce the weapons that made conflict more likely and more costly. The British, the French, the Italians, and the Japanese at this point, given their own public realities, felt the need to respond favorably. Hughes's initiative would lead to a treaty that would limit the number of capital ships in US, British, French, Italian, and Japanese fleets for 10 years. The number of ships in each fleet and their tonnage allowed reflected ratios that were worked out in the negotiations and affected not only the size of naval forces but also the rate of modernization. The US Senate, which had rejected the Treaty of Versailles, would ratify the Five-Power Naval Limitation Treaty in March 1922—a treaty that was perceived as reducing the risk of war and defense expenditures.

Other arms-control agreements and declarations, including a ban on poison gases—one of the scourges of World War I—would in time emerge from the discussions launched by the Washington Conference. Similarly, the conference would also lead to a four-power treaty among the Americans, the

British, the French, and the Japanese also to last for 10 years. The treaty pledged to respect each other's rights in the Pacific, and to consult with one another in the event of disagreements, controversies, or aggressive actions. The four-party accord would replace the Anglo–Japanese treaty—which Hughes saw as limiting US interests and actually risking conflict. Unlike Wilson, Hughes would consult closely with Senator Lodge and bring him into the negotiations. Lodge would justify support for the treaty saying that it "substituted a four-power agreement to talk for a two-power agreement to fight."[18] Lodge would orchestrate the Senate's favorable vote for the treaty. Interestingly, to be able to do so still required from Lodge adopting a reservation which stated that the treaty involved "no commitment to armed force, no alliance, no obligation to join any defense."[19]

In all the agreements that Hughes would produce, including those involving China, there were no enforcement mechanisms. Hughes counted on moral and public suasion. This worked in producing the arms control and regional security agreements, but it could not sustain them as conditions changed. In a world of economic autarky, protectionism, and surging nationalisms, the readiness to cooperate and not build up forces disappeared in the 1930s, and the effort that President Hoover made to extend the agreements from the Washington Conference failed. Moral suasion not backed by the threat of force and the ability to impose tangible costs will always have its limits.

Hughes understood that he could not wield threats. The consensus on not being involved again in a foreign war meant the threat of force was off the table. It is not difficult to see parallels with the environment that the Biden administration inherited. The "endless wars" in the Middle East meant that Biden, too, could not easily employ the threat of military or non-economic coercion. Just as Hughes believed that the United States needed to be active diplomatically, so did Biden and his secretary of state. Similarly, Biden too had to be careful about assuming new security responsibilities or obligations.

There were, of course, big differences between the Harding and Biden administrations in foreign policy. For one thing, Biden was socialized by a very different US role in the world. He was a believer in all the post–World War II institutions that the United States forged to prevent occurrence of war. He accepted multilateral institutions in which the United States played a major role, the alliance structure the United States shaped, and the broader American responsibilities to lead in the world. There was no such tradition when Harding became president—just the opposite. Moreover, Harding was in many respects a reaction to Wilson's crusade to remake the world in America's image and based on its values.[a]

But the similarities in terms of American hesitancy in the aftermath of wars being fought are striking. The great reluctance to employ, much less speak about or brandish, force as an instrument of statecraft is very much the same. Neither in the post–World War I decade nor in the Biden administration was American foreign policy characterized by withdrawing from the world, but its use of statecraft had to take account of the reality that there was no public support for the use of force. Intervention was inherently seen as potentially involving the United States in wars and commitments to others—and here the tradition of avoiding such obligations again expressed itself.

That would affect the Biden administration's relationships with the Gulf Arab states, especially the United Arab Emirates and Saudi Arabia. Both would question whether they could count on the United States as they faced greater threats from Iran—and would perceive that the United States was withdrawing from the region. The great irony is that the numbers of US forces in the region, 35,000–40,000, remained largely unchanged. There was no measurable withdrawal of US forces. But the perception in the region, one shared by Israel and the Gulf Arab States alike, was that the United States would not use force, especially against the Iranians. While their common perceptions of the US hesitancy raised their collective doubts about America and drew these Arab states closer to Israel, it also made them less responsive to American requests and interests. The Saudis, even after President Biden visited the Kingdom in the summer of 2022—at some domestic political cost—rejected the administration's request to postpone oil production cuts in October of that year. Those cuts raised gasoline prices, added to inflationary pressures, helped the Russians with more oil revenue even as Putin brandished nuclear threats, and damaged Biden politically. And, yet the Saudis said no to the administration.[b]

---

[a] That Wilson could emphasize liberty, freedom, and self-determination for the peoples in European colonies and yet hold profoundly racist attitudes is to say, at the very least, ironic.

[b] What made the Saudi decision all the more striking is that while they claimed they made the decision purely out of concern that oil prices would collapse without a reduction in output, they rejected a US proposal to address that concern. The Biden administration proposed delaying the production cut by a month, and should prices drop, the United States would refill the US strategic petroleum reserve to keep demand up and prevent prices from falling too much. In fact, the oil prices did drop, seemingly proving that the Saudi arguments about the oil market and the importance of stabilizing it were correct.

Less trust in the United States also meant that America had less leverage with the Saudis, which was reflected in the behavior of the Emiratis as well. In their case, the president of the United Arab Emirates, Mohammad bin Zayed (popularly known as MbZ), felt that there was a moment in which the United States was particularly found wanting in terms of its commitment to the security of the United Arab Emirates. The Houthis in Yemen launched missiles and drones against civilian targets in the Emirates on January 17, 2022. Three people were killed, and a fuel tank near the airport was set on fire. The physical destruction may not have been extensive, but MbZ perceived this attack as crossing a threshold and posing a unique threat to the Emirates, particularly because their economy depended on their being a regional haven of safety and security. He counted on the United States responding quickly to help shore up Emirate defenses against such attacks and to bolster Emirate deterrence—and, as I was told by Yousef al Otaiba, the long-serving Emirate ambassador to the United States, MbZ was shaken by what he saw as the very slow and limited American response. MbZ would go so far as to tell a former US official he had long known that he "made a mistake 30 years ago," when he had made his choice and "bet on a relationship depending on the United States."[c]

MbZ's disquiet and his distrust was manifested in his insistence that verbal assurances from the United States were not sufficient; he needed formal security commitments—but the Biden administration was reluctant to make a formal commitment to come to defense of the United Arab Emirates. Ultimately, while MbZ was not prepared to walk away from the United States, he was prepared to hedge his bets—canceling the procurement of the US stealth F-35 fighter jet in favor of less sophisticated French fighters and even visiting Vladimir Putin at a time when political isolation of Putin was the Biden administration's policy.[20]

The perception of American hesitancy, readiness to withdraw from the region magnified by the way the Biden administration left Afghanistan, and reluctance to take on commitments, all reflected a reality that the "forever wars" had created. The mood of the US public was clear and meant—at least until Putin invaded Ukraine—that America would be reluctant to intervene, much less even threaten the use of force. It is not just that the American posture seemed to harken back to earlier periods like that after World War I.

---

[c] This former official told me about the conversation, and it was echoed in my talks with senior Israeli officials who also passed on similar comments to me.

It is that the US role in the world was being questioned domestically. Perhaps that should have come as no surprise given the terrible costs of the wars in Iraq and Afghanistan and their dubious results. But perhaps the questioning also reflected something deeper about the American traditions in foreign policy. Until after World War II, the United States sought neither world leadership nor to assume obligations and alliances abroad.

Following World War II, the US posture changed fundamentally. Suddenly, the United States made the decision to lead and was able to forge a domestic consensus to do so. America's self-image would justify this, but in no small part because of the perception of threat. Before turning to a discussion in Chapter 4 of the current debate over America's role in the world and how it reflects different aspects of American traditions, it is worth briefly recapping how much the United States changed in its worldview and sense of responsibilities in the post–World War II era.

How and Why America Became a Leader of Institutions and Alliances

In the 1930s, the United States manifested its worst unilateralist impulses. It would adopt the Smoot–Hawley Tariff Act of 1930 that imposed tariffs on thousands of goods and agricultural items to protect American businesses and farmers—yielding reciprocal tariffs in the process. It devastated trade and undercut commerce. As a result, protectionism deepened the Great Depression even as it reflected a reaction to it. Here, unilateralist instincts trumped the tradition of free trade.

But the populist and nationalist sentiments that produced protectionism expressed themselves even before the Great Depression, and they were not limited only to economics. The Johnson–Reed Act of 1924 sought to preserve the ethnic, demographic make-up of the United States by completely excluding immigrants from Asia and limiting visas provided to those coming from other countries to 2 percent of the number of that nationality living in the United States. The rise of Nazism and the desperation of those trying to escape it brought no amendments or adjustments to the Johnson–Reed Act. America's borders remained largely closed to Jewish refugees and others, producing especially unconscionable rejections of entry for German Jewry who had few other places to go.[21,d]

---

d One of the most notorious instances was the denial to 900 Jews, coming on board the ship MS St. Louis, entry to Miami in June 1939. All 900 were forced to return to Europe.

No political movement more clearly embodied the belief in unilateralism and nativist instincts in the 1930s than America First. The movement's leaders and organizers were motivated principally by their desire to keep the United States out of the gathering storm in Europe. Although some of its leaders like Charles Lindbergh had sympathies for the Germans, their main motivation was to keep America out of the looming war, believing that the United States could ultimately remain aloof and not be affected by the war's outcome. Even if some people in the State Department seemed to reflect these attitudes and were mostly concerned about not causing problems with the Germans, President Franklin Delano Roosevelt understood the dangers of being an island in a hostile world.[e]

Roosevelt understood the stakes even as he had to contend with the continuing mood of the American public and the Congress. With war having already begun in Europe in 1940, the Selective Training and Service Act (the draft) passed by only one vote in the House of Representatives. Sounding like Wilson in 1916, Roosevelt proclaimed during his presidential campaign in 1940, "I have said this before, but I shall say it again and again and again; your boys are not going to be sent into any foreign wars."[22] Still, Roosevelt understood the dangers of Hitler defeating the British and spoke of the United States being the "great arsenal of democracy." In July 1940, when the British lost 10 destroyers in 11 days to the German Navy and Churchill requested assistance, Roosevelt approved the provision of 50 destroyers to the British in return for 99-year leases of British bases in the Caribbean and Newfoundland. This would be a forerunner of the Lend-Lease Act adopted in March of 1941, after only two months of debate in the Congress. Roosevelt would describe the act as one that would allow America to provide supplies to any country whose security was vital to the defense of the United States.

President Roosevelt was not just linking America's security to the provision of assistance to others. He was saying that these were countries vital to the US defense. America might still not have been prepared to go to war for others, but it was not a great leap to see the United States forging alliances. By declaring that America would be the arsenal of democracy, Roosevelt was certainly also signaling his intent to have the United States play a larger role internationally—but at that stage, it was to help defeat the Nazis. After the Japanese attack on Pearl Harbor and the German declaration of war against the United States, Roosevelt saw himself leading a wartime alliance.

---

[e] For State Department attitudes toward Germany in the 1930s, see Erik Larson's *In the Garden of the Beasts*.

Even before the United States entered into the war, Roosevelt and Churchill issued the Atlantic Charter. For Churchill, the charter was designed to bind the Americans to the British; for Roosevelt, it was designed to lay out the principles that should guide the world after the war. The United States was not yet in that war, but the principles reflected America's higher purposes and its desire to move the world in the direction of its vision. Roosevelt's vision was much like Wilson's, and the principles embodied in the charter called for free exchanges of trade, self-determination, disarmament, and collective security.

Collective security may have run against the American tradition of unilateralism, but Roosevelt, like Wilson, could not see an alternative to it. Moreover, another terrible world war demonstrated that the United States could not stand aloof, and a different approach was required. Roosevelt believed he could bring the American people along, no doubt, in part because of the unprecedented nature of his presidency and his ability to connect with the American public. Moreover, he felt he had learned the lessons of Wilson's failure both domestically and internationally. Domestically, unlike Wilson, he would work with the Republicans, and there was good reason to believe that could be successful.[f] Internationally, Roosevelt reasoned that the League of Nations had failed because it lacked an enforcement mechanism. He would solve that problem by creating the Four Policemen: the Americans, the British, the Soviets, and the Chinese. They would assume the responsibility for enforcing the will of what would be the United Nations. Roosevelt believed that the wartime alignment could be maintained in peacetime, and their collective interest in preserving the peace would prevail.

Of course, Roosevelt saw himself as the critical agent for making this work. He had enormous confidence in his own abilities and was convinced he could manage the four leaders so that the Four Policemen concept would work. In reality, he was focused almost exclusively on Stalin because he believed that Churchill and Chang Kai Shek had little choice but to go along with the United States. This helps to explain why Roosevelt would side so openly with Stalin against Churchill in the meetings in Tehran and Yalta. In doing so, he felt he would win Stalin's confidence, build a relationship

---

[f] There was an internationalist wing of the Republican Party and a more extreme unilateralist wing. In the Senate, Arthur Vandenberg represented the former and Robert Taft the latter. Thomas Dewey, the New York governor who would win the Republican nomination for the presidency in 1944 and 1948, aligned with the internationalists and openly clashed with Taft.

with him, and reassure him to the point where Stalin would get comfortable enough to support this approach and play the role. Whereas Churchill saw the world through the lens of sheer power and understood that power is what mattered to Stalin, Roosevelt did not.

Reflecting traditional American attitudes, Roosevelt rejected what Churchill favored: a "balance of power" approach to the world. He thought that the United States would create the world anew, and that he could get Stalin, responsible for killing millions with forced collectivization and the great purges, to go along. He called Stalin "Uncle Joe" and described in a private note to Francis Perkins, his secretary of labor, how, by making the relations personal with Stalin, "The ice was broken and we talked like men and brothers."[23] Roosevelt would report to the American public after the Tehran meeting with Churchill and Stalin that he got along fine "with Marshal Stalin. He is a man who combines a tremendous, relentless determination with a stalwart good humor. I believe he is truly representative of the heart and soul of the Russian people, and I believe that we are going to get along very well with him and the Russian people—very well indeed."[24]

Yes, this was still wartime, and presenting Stalin—our wartime ally—favorably might be understandable for domestic consumption. But as Roosevelt's note to Perkins indicates, he believed this and was not just saying it for political reasons. In truth, he needed to believe it if collective security was to work—and he was convinced that collective security must define the world and the place of the United States in it after the war. In his presentation to the Congress after meeting Stalin and Churchill in Yalta in February 1945, Roosevelt was enthusiastic about the agreements that the three leaders had reached. Those agreements, he declared, "ought to spell the end of the system of unilateral action, the exclusive alliances, the spheres of influence, the balances of power, and all the other expedients that have been tried for centuries—and have always failed. We propose to substitute for all these, a universal organization in which all peace-loving Nations will finally have a chance to join."[25]

Here was Roosevelt's case for the United Nations. In his mind, it would help to create a permanent structure of peace. That structure also required a multinational economic dimension. Roosevelt and those around him like Secretary of State Cordell Hull understood how protectionism and monetary policies had contributed to the Great Depression—and created the conditions that helped to produce the war. Hull would say that Americans "learned that a prohibitive protected tariff is a gun that recoils upon ourselves."[26] Fundamentally, the administration operated on the premise that the United States could not recover economically if the world did not recover economically. But that required a set of agreed-upon rules to guide monetary, developmental, and commercial policies. The administration would bring together 730 delegates from 44 countries at Bretton Woods in July 1944. At the end of three weeks, the delegates reached an agreement that created a set of rules, institutions, and procedures to regulate the international monetary system. The Bretton Woods agreement established the International Monetary Fund (IMF) and the International Bank for Reconstruction and Development (IBRD), which would later become known as the World Bank. In 1946, the General Agreement on Tariffs and Trade (GATT) emerged with the aim of promoting international trade by reducing or eliminating trade barriers.[g]

Shortly after the Bretton Woods agreement was forged at the end of July, another conference was held at Dumbarton Oaks. The conference at Dumbarton Oaks was all about reaching an agreement on the principles for establishing what would become the United Nations. By the fall of 1944, the multinational structure of the postwar era was taking shape. Roosevelt was setting in motion his postwar vision and its multinational nature. (The founding document of the United Nations, its charter, would be adopted in San Francisco two months after Roosevelt's death in June 1945.)

One could argue that Roosevelt's response to the war reflected the understanding that America could not stand apart; it could not retain complete freedom of action; it needed to embed itself in international institutions to avoid yet another terrible global war. Even if that meant that the United States could no longer hue to the unilateralist tradition, America would not have to give up its basic values. On the contrary, American values were shaping the guiding principles of these international institutions. The United Nations Charter embraced American values. Similarly, the Bretton Woods system was guided by American traditions and the commitment to avoiding discriminatory trading practices, keeping markets open, and preventing the granting of special privileges and access to some and not others.

In other words, while unilateralism was de-emphasized for the sake of broader international comity, the structure being established was consistent with American values and other traditions. What did not change during Roosevelt's time was the unwillingness of the United States to assume

---

[g] In 1995, the GATT was absorbed into the World Trade Organization, which extended it.

obligations to others and forge alliances outside of the UN system to deal with security threats. Roosevelt hoped that the UN and the Four Policemen would resolve that. And, in the immediate aftermath of the war, there was little interest in looking at the Soviet Union and Stalin through a different lens. Roosevelt's vision held sway, especially as the desire to demobilize US forces and have them return home was understandably strong.[27,h]

But this vision, reflecting American values and hopes, was not sustainable because it was based on a perception of Stalin and the Soviet Union that never fit reality. Roosevelt never grasped what drove Stalin, neither his determination to expand the border to the west (for both offensive and defensive reasons) nor his paranoia about the consequences of lacking complete control domestically. Had he lived longer, Roosevelt would have soon discovered that Stalin would have exploited all efforts to reassure him. He would have seen that Yalta was a dead letter, and wherever Soviet forces reached, the Soviets would impose regimes there. The so-called Wise Men around Truman would see all of this as well as the realities in Europe—and both would contribute to changing the American mindset and convincing Truman and those around him that the United States must assume a wholly different posture internationally than it had ever held.

The conditions in Europe were far worse than the administration or the Congress had understood, and the British were also no longer capable of sustaining either a presence or the role they had had prior to the war. Two weeks after Roosevelt's death, John J. McCloy, then assistant secretary of war, wrote a memo to President Truman about his just-completed trip to Europe, reporting that, "There is a complete economic, social, and political collapse in Central Europe, the extent of which is unparalleled in history (unless one goes back to the collapse of the Roman Empire)."[28] Throughout the remainder of 1945, the realities on the ground became more desperate in Europe. At the same time, the Soviet behavior in Eastern Europe became more egregious, and Stalin rejected cooperation on atomic energy.

By late 1945 and early 1946, there was a recognition within the Truman administration that something needed to be done to rescue the situation in Europe and to counter the Soviets. Initially, this impulse faced resistance from liberal New Dealers like Eleanor Roosevelt and Vice

[h] In May 1945, the United States had 12.3 million people in the armed forces, and 1.5 million 14 months later. Bear in mind, the press coverage of Stalin and the Soviet Union was very sympathetic during the war, especially given the profound suffering and losses inflicted on the Soviets by the Nazis.

President Henry Wallace. Both still believed in Roosevelt's approach to the Soviets and opposed cooperation with the Europeans against the Russians, convinced that it would provoke Stalin and his insecurities. Senator Robert Taft did not share their concerns about Stalin's insecurities, but he was not buying that America's security and well-being depended on engagement with and rescue of Europe—or cooperation with the Europeans. He was a determined, unreconstructed unilateralist and saw only folly in getting more involved either in Europe or in opposing the Soviets. For different reasons, then, the left and the right shared an opposition to a more assertive policy toward Europe—and there was no domestic political base to support deeper engagement.

But this would begin to change in 1946. On March 6, 1946, Winston Churchill would give a speech in Fulton, Missouri. He put what was happening internationally in perspective, speaking of "poverty and privation which are in many cases the prevailing anxiety." But there was another source of anxiety that was exacerbating the dangers—and, as Churchill pointed out, it was the reality of the Soviets imposing facts in Europe:

> From Stettin in the Baltic to Trieste in the Adriatic, an iron curtain has descended across the continent. Behind that line all the capitals of the ancient states of Central and Eastern Europe, Warsaw, Berlin, Prague, Vienna, Budapest, Belgrade, Bucharest, and Sofia, all these famous cities and the populations around them lie in what I must call the Soviet sphere, and all are subject ... not only to Soviet influence but to a very high and, in many cases, increasing measure of control from Moscow.[29]

It was not as if Churchill was addressing the danger out of the blue. A month before Churchill spoke, Stalin had predicted an inevitable clash between the communist and capitalist powers.[30] The descending Iron Curtain represented one Soviet threat, but there were others: Russia was pressuring Turkey domestically and on access to the straits; it was violating its agreement to withdraw its forces from northern Iran; it was supporting insurgency in Greece; and it was promoting the communist parties in France and Italy amid widespread labor unrest. By 1947, European countries, west and east, seemed in desperate economic straits, and the Soviets seemed poised to exploit them and expand further west. In this setting, on February 21, 1947, the British ambassador in Washington informed the State Department that his government was broke and in five weeks would stop assistance to

Greece and Turkey.[31] For Secretary of State George Marshall, the unmistakable consequence would mean the Soviets would fill the vacuum in the Eastern Mediterranean unless the United States acted to prevent this.

The Truman Doctrine emerged as the result. President Truman invited Arthur Vandenberg and the Republican leaders to the White House to enlist their support for this new-found assumption of American responsibility. In the White House meeting, Under-Secretary of State Dean Acheson made the case to Vandenberg and his colleagues, later writing, "This was my crisis. For a week, I had nurtured it. These Congressmen had no conception of what challenged them; it was my task to bring it home." He would tell them that if the Soviets broke through in the Eastern Mediterranean, they would be able to spread throughout the Middle East, Africa, and southern Europe. In his words, "The Soviet Union was playing one of the greatest gambles in history at minimal cost," and it was up to the United States "to break up the play." Vandenberg responded by saying to President Truman, "Mr. President, if you will say that to the Congress and the country, I will support you and I believe that most of the members will do the same."[32]

Truman would speak to a joint session of Congress on March 12, 1947, and make the case in very stark terms:

> At the present moment in world history nearly every nation must choose between alternative ways of life. The choice too often is not a free one. Our way of life is based upon the will of the majority, and is distinguished by free institutions, representative government, free elections, guarantees of individual liberty, freedom of speech and religion, and freedom from political oppression. The second way of life is based upon the will of a minority forcibly imposed upon the majority ... The free peoples of the world look to us for support in maintaining their freedoms. If we falter in our leadership, we may endanger the peace of the world—and we shall surely endanger the welfare of this Nation. Great responsibilities have been placed on us by the swift movement of events. I am confident the Congress will face these responsibilities squarely.[33]

The choice was stark and the stakes very high, and the Senate would endorse Truman's call to action. The Marshall Plan, the vast American aid plan that rebuilt Europe, would soon follow. While Henry Wallace would call it the "Martial Plan," and Robert Taft would describe it as a socialist blueprint, they were in the minority. Stalin would reject the American offer to take part in the Marshall Plan, and the coup in Czechoslovakia in February 1948 would ensure the adoption of the plan by overwhelming numbers in the Congress. The Czech coup extinguished any sense of possibility with the Soviet Union—even for those who still harbored hopes for it. NATO would soon be developed, and America was now the leader of alliances and was no longer governed by what then Secretary of State Cordell Hull had proudly described in 1936 as a policy of "peace, commerce, and honest friendship with all nations, entangling alliances with none."[34]

That was the American tradition from Washington and Jefferson's time. But that tradition was also married to a self-image of exceptionalism—of deep virtue, selflessness, and the embodiment of moral principles that were universal. The sense of threat, combined with America's moral principles, justified the adoption of a revolutionary departure of American foreign policy. The United States now assumed great responsibilities in the world, and those guided American foreign policy for more than 70 years after World War II. But the "overreach" of Iraq and Afghanistan have produced a debate about what America's role in the world should be.

No approach to statecraft can be successful if it is not informed by that role. By definition, the role should shape how America defines or contemplates acceptable objectives. So how should it think about that role? In Chapter 4, I will turn to a discussion of what I will call the different schools of thought about what America's role in the world should be—and conclude with my own proposed approach taking account of American traditions and self-image.

Chapter 4

Different Schools of Thought about America's Role in the World

It should be no surprise that there continues to be a debate about what America's role in the world should be. Two terrible wars, in Iraq and Afghanistan, were bound to foster debate about how and why the United States got into them and what lessons need to be learned about America's posture internationally. Barack Obama and Donald Trump might have been poles apart in attitude, but they both seemed to favor a posture of retrenchment internationally from America's overseas obligations. They cast their arguments differently, with Obama speaking of power having a new meaning in the twenty-first century and Trump emphasizing that no one was any longer going to get a free ride.

Beyond the rhetoric, there were very different premises guiding the two presidents. Both may have felt that the United States was stretched too thin— and even too quick to use force—but their starting points were different. Obama was an internationalist; he favored engagement and even having the United States act as an agenda setter. I would hear him say in the Oval Office and the Situation Room that if the United States did not set the agenda, no one would. But for all his belief in engagement, he was a minimalist. America's role needed to be limited, force needed truly to be a last resort, avoidance in conflicts was the best option and always less costly than engagement. Trump's posture was different. It was all about transactions. Ideology and values made no difference for him. Trump had a penchant for authoritarian leaders and no real use for alliances. There were no particular values that mattered to him other than, seemingly, making money in the transactions—and from that standpoint he had a set of instincts and a slogan for how he approached all other states: America First. Regardless of whether he knew the origins of the slogan and the movement in the 1930s, his attitudes were consistent with it. He was a unilateralist through and through.

Statecraft 2.0. Second Edition. Dennis Ross, Oxford University Press. © Oxford University Press (2025).
DOI: 10.1093/oso/9780197698914.003.0004

As outlined in Chapter 3, his instincts fit at least one of the traditions in America's approach to the world. It is ironic that Trump was not about American exceptionalism or purity. Quite the contrary: in one interview where Trump was expressing his respect for Vladimir Putin, his interviewer, Bill O'Reilly, said, "Putin is a killer"—and Trump responded with, "There are a lot of killers. We have a lot of killers. Well, you think our country is so innocent."[1] But if Trump was not about American exceptionalism, his posture of America First struck a chord with a segment of the American public at least in part because it was rooted in the American tradition.

The point is that there is not only one tradition that reflects American attitudes toward the outside world and America's place in it. Walter McDougall identified eight traditions, all of which reflect the belief in American exceptionalism. But he drew a distinction between what he called the "old testament" and the "new testament" traditions. For McDougall, the distinction between the first four "old testament" and the latter "new testament" traditions is that the former are generally passive toward the outside world and the latter are progressively more active in seeing America's responsibility to remake it.[2] McDougall observed that there were gradations and basic distinctions between the traditions—and that American foreign policy could swing widely between them. Because McDougall believed that all of these traditions are very much consistent with the American self-image—indeed, they all reflect it—different US presidents are attracted to different traditions. The context does much to explain why some presidents are attracted to particular traditions and not others. Written during the Clinton administration, McDougall noted three periods when America had presidents—McKinley, Wilson, and Clinton—who were prone to great activism in exporting American values and trying to remake the world. (According to his criteria, George W. Bush would surely also have qualified for what McDougall referred to as "global meliorism.")[3]

Walter Russell Mead, too, wrote about America's self-image and its impact on the role of the United States internationally, but rather than speak of traditions, Mead spoke of different schools. He identified four schools that describe different approaches to America's role in the world: Jefferson's, Hamilton's, Jackson's, and Wilson's. Throughout the US history, different leaders have embraced and reflected these schools or tendencies. For example, Jefferson believed very much in American values and their compelling nature—meaning that these values stood on their own, and the morals of a nation should be the same as morals of an individual. Hamilton accepted American virtue but also believed in the centrality of the federal government, the role of power internationally, and the need of the United States to create balance with those who could be a threat to the country. Jackson was a populist who would react to threats but cared little about other states. And Wilson wanted to remake the world on the basis of America's universal truths.[4]

While there is some overlap between McDougall and Mead, the main value for my purpose is that both explain that the image of American exceptionalism is very strong and yet can rationalize very different postures in the world. As long as one is mindful of the US self-image, it is possible to strike a chord with the American public—and clearly in the current debate over what America's role in the world should be there are a range of arguments about which posture serves American interests. There are those who put the premium on American interests, and others who emphasize values. I see some as connecting better with the American traditions and self-image than others—but all reflect the influence that the context has on them. In summary, I identify five different schools of thought in what has emerged over the last few years as the debate on the US role in the world:

1) America First
2) Progressives/Restrainers
3) Spheres of Influence
4) Realists/Balance of Power
5) Liberal Internationalists

To be sure, there is some overlap between the groups and some of those within the groups. The instincts of those who believe that American foreign military presence is the cause of conflict want to pull US forces back from nearly everywhere. Those who believe in spheres of influence may not think that the United States needs to withdraw everywhere, but they definitely favor leaving areas that should be recognized as Russian or Chinese spheres of influence. And some categories (e.g., progressive) may actually embody a range of attitudes—even if they share the point of departure on the need for an American retrenchment and the scaling back of US ambitions.[5] As I go through each of these schools or tendencies, I will point out how well I believe the school does or does not connect to the American self-image.

America First

Donald Trump made his slogan America First a point of pride. It was not merely a political slogan: it was a statement about how the United States would approach the world, and how at long last, it would elevate American interests over those of others. He explained in his inaugural address that he was ending the era in which others were allowed to take advantage of the United States: "For many decades we've enriched foreign industry at the expense of American industry. Subsidized the armies of other countries while allowing for the very sad depletion of our military. We've defended other nation's borders while refusing to defend our own ... We've made other countries rich while the wealth, strength, and confidence of our country has disappeared over the horizon. From this moment on, it's going to be America First."[6]

America First meant that the United States would do what it wanted without constraints. Alliances were a drag. NATO was "obsolete" and "irrelevant." Obviously, Trump looked at threats as if no alliances were necessary—even though his administration would produce a national security strategy that identified a great power competition with Russia and China as central. To accommodate Trump's unilateralist instincts, the national security strategy spoke of the need to modernize America's alliances and make sure everyone paid their fair share.

But there was a deeper issue with Trump and America First. It was a rejection of globalism and the idea of a liberal international order. It was not just that alliances were an encumbrance; so, too, were multilateral institutions. In Trump's second speech to the United Nations General Assembly, he declared: "America is governed by Americans. We reject the ideology of globalism, and we embrace the doctrine of patriotism."[7] A year later at the UN, he again repeated this theme, asserting, "The future does not belong to globalists. The future belongs to patriots. The future belongs to sovereign and independent nations."[8]

If there was a Trump ideology, it was an ideology of sovereignty. It was the nation-state, not international or multinational organizations, that was the locus of decision-making. No other body would impose on the United States or deny it its freedom of action—this is what America owed to its citizens, and this principle would guide US foreign policy. Moreover, this was the best way for all countries to act. As Trump would say to the UN General Assembly, "In foreign affairs, we are renewing this founding principle of sovereignty. Our government's first duty is to its people, to our citizens—to serve their needs, to ensure their safety, to preserve their rights, and to defend their values. I will always put America first, just like you, as the leaders of your countries will always, and should always, put your country first. All responsible leaders have an obligation to serve their own citizens, and the nation-state remains the best vehicle for elevating the human condition."[9]

Here was a counterpoint to globalization and institutions designed to produce collective norms and common responsibilities. Here was an approach that emphasized unilateralism not just for the United States but for all others as well. Again, while Trump may not have focused on the conceptual underpinnings of his emphasis on sovereignty and unilateralism, there were those who served in the Trump administration who did. Michael Anton would serve as a speech writer for President Trump and would later pen an article entitled "The Trump Doctrine."[10] He would explain that at the core of the Trump Doctrine was sovereignty and nationalism, and that was a good thing because countries "putting their own interests first was the way of the world, an inexpugnable part of human nature." The sooner everybody recognized this, the better it would be internationally: "Let's all put our own countries first, and be candid about it, and recognize that it's nothing to be ashamed of. Putting our interests first will make us all safer and more prosperous."[11]

In other words, if everyone adopted a nationalist approach, the world would be safer because it was unnatural to try to impose global norms, and countries would inevitably resist them. Anton was drawing his intellectual inspiration from the work of Yarom Hazony—and his book *The Virtue of Nationalism*.[12] In fact, a number of themes in Trump's speeches appear drawn directly from Hazony's work. For example, Trump explained that, "The essential divide that runs all around the world and throughout history ... is the divide between those whose thirst for control deludes them into thinking they are destined to rule over others and those people and nations who want only to rule themselves."[13]

Hazony, too, divided the world into these two categories, describing them as imperialism and nationalism—with imperialism or traditional empires denying states the right to rule themselves and imposing on them an external "political regime."[14] Nationalism, on the other hand, can create a world that is governed best and most peacefully because the best is possible only "when nations are able to chart their own independent course, cultivating their own traditions and pursuing their own interests without interference."[15] (Trump consistently echoed these words and the sentiments behind them.) Hazony went so far as to argue that nation-states were the only political units in which freedom and democracy ever developed and lasted. Trump emphasized this point as well: "Sovereign and independent nations are the only vehicle where freedom has ever survived, democracy has ever endured, or peace has ever prospered."[16]

Anton, citing Hazony, explained that the imperialism of the past is being played out today with globalization: "while traditional empires may have gone out of fashion, globalization has taken its place as the imperialism of our time. Globalization represents an attempt to do through peaceful means—the creation of transnational institutions, the erosion border, and the homogenization of intellectual, cultural, and economic products— what the Romans ... achieved through arms."[17] America had gone astray by embracing globalization and by promoting liberal internationalism— something that led to absorbing immense costs as America fought "dumb wars to spread the liberal international gospel to soil where it won't grow or at least hasn't yet; [and] military campaigns the United States can't even end, much less win."[18]

For Anton and Trump, the United States had no interest in globalization, liberal internationalism, or democracy promotion. In Anton's words, America's vital interests never meant "the imposition of democracy."[19] From this standpoint, America First shared much in common with the Progressive/Restrainers who also believed that the United States was guilty of overreach—and that overreach has cost America a great deal. Unlike the Restrainers, however, advocates of America First want little or nothing to do with multinational organizations and institutions. And that is, in my opinion, one of the fundamental failings of the America First school of thought.

We are living in a world of challenges and threats that respect no borders. COVID was a reminder that while a collective approach is simply desirable on some issues, it is essential on others. The cost of largely unilateral approaches on COVID was enormous—and it was measured in deaths, profound economic losses, and the inability to staunch the virus once there was a vaccine because the vaccine was not available to much of the world. The result was the emergence of variants like Delta and Omicron. There should have been much more collaboration to ensure the production of enough vaccines and the means to transmit them globally to increase the probability of preempting the emergence of variants which perpetuated the pandemic.

There is no way a unilateral approach to a pandemic can succeed. Do not look only at the Trump administration and its American First approach. Look at China and the failure of its approach on COVID: it would not use the mRNA vaccines that were far more effective than the Chinese vaccine; it thought it could impose complete closures and shut down COVID even as it shut down its economy and imposed terrible hardships on its public.[20] The shutdowns not only helped ensure hardships but also prevented the buildup of immunities to the virus.

Climate change is like pandemics: there are no unilateral answers for it. Trump and other supporters of America First seemed to believe that the United States could close itself off from the world, as if climate and pathogens can be stopped at the border. These, of course, are not the only transnational threats. Countering proliferation of weapons of mass destruction and fighting terrorism are far more likely to succeed if there are collective approaches with shared intelligence, denial of safe havens, joint actions, collective sanctions, etc. Fortunately, there were people working for Trump who understood the importance of fostering alliances and collective actions, especially when it came to fighting terror.[a]

America First might operate divorced from the reality that there are many issues that do not respect borders, but it is a school of thought that definitely appeals to the American instinct to be able to operate internationally without constraint or being tied down by others. While true, it has at least one other major failing. By showing little interest in values or in contributing to the global commons, Trump and other supporters of America First denied the United States its soft power. Soft power cannot substitute for hard power, but when America is at its best in terms of standing for higher purposes, it is a pole of attraction. Its objectives are more naturally embraced by others, and US leverage organically grows internationally as a result. The Pew polls demonstrated how the image of America and its appeal declined during the Trump presidency.[21] Of course, the effort to export and impose American values directly, including by regime change during the George W. Bush presidency, also resulted in the loss of American soft power. Ironically, with the Bush presidency, America's overuse of hard power damaged its soft power. The problem was the lack of restraint; this realization is what animates Progressives/Restrainers.

---

[a] James Jeffrey was named the envoy for Syria who worked on countering ISIS, and few American diplomats have been better at forging allied approaches.

Progressives/Restrainers

Progressives share one common theme with America First: passionate opposition to American overreach and involvement in wars in places in which they believe the United States has no interests. Neither school want the United States involved in the so-called endless wars of the Middle East. Politicians on opposite ends of the political spectrum like Bernie Sanders and Rand Paul might agree on very little, but they both agree that the United States has had an overly militarized foreign policy, and it has fought wars that it had no business fighting. Both believe that the United States needs to pull its forces back from overseas bases. And while they disagree on how to redirect US resources, they both want what they would describe as far less American adventurism abroad. Rand Paul is not a Progressive, but he does favor restraint internationally.[22] Unlike Progressives, he is not a globalist who believes in international responses to challenges. Progressives are globalist in their orientation, with a strong preference for the role of international law. Nothing could be more of an anathema to someone like Paul (or Trump and America First) than international law—the essence of multilateralism and a key constraint on sovereignty.

That said, Rand Paul is more of a Restrainer than America First supporters. While he would not share the values of a Bernie Sanders, the two of them can find a home for their views at the Quincy Institute for Responsible Statecraft. Its ethos is restraint. It favors peace and a strong predisposition against the use of force—and since it has been funded by both the Koch Brothers and George Soros, it really does include those on the far ends of the political spectrum. Its stated purpose is "to promote a positive, non-partisan vision of foreign policy and critique ideologies and interests that have mired the United States in counterproductive and endless wars that make the world less secure."[23]

Restraint and retrenchment define the way Progressives and the Quincy Institute approach US foreign policy. What drives them is a deep belief that American power has been misused—and it has been misused with terrible consequences because of the American self-image of exceptionalism. Just as Trump and his version of America First does not embrace American exceptionalism, neither do Progressives and Restrainers. On the contrary, it is this image, in their eyes, that has led the United States astray. Andrew Bacevich, a co-founder of the Quincy Institute, is a historian.[b] He is a leading

---

[b] He also happens to be a graduate of West Point who served in the military between 1969 and 1992. He fought in both Vietnam and the first Gulf War.

conceptualizer of the Restrainers school, and he argues that America's sense of exceptionalism has driven it to seek global primacy—a posture that has led to "serial misuse of military power." It is this self-image that must be jettisoned. In his words, "Only if Americans abandon their fealty to the idea of American Exceptionalism and the militarism that sustained it, might it be possible to conclude that the wars in Vietnam and Afghanistan served some faintly useful purpose."[24]

For Bacevich and other Restrainers, America's quest for global primacy led to the over-militarization of US foreign policy, especially because America's primacy (or what some call its hegemony or dominance) was "achieved largely ... through the use or threatened use of military power."[25] As Stephen Wertheim argues, "Dominance, assumed to ensure peace, in fact, guarantees war. To get serious about stopping endless war, American leaders must do what they most resist: end America's commitment to armed supremacy and embrace a world of pluralism and peace."[26] Wertheim echoes all Restrainers when he explains that the United States can do that by withdrawing its forces from around the globe: "the United States can proudly bring home many of its soldiers currently serving in 800 bases ringing the globe, leaving small forces to protect commercial sea lanes. It can reorient its military, prioritizing deterrence and defense over power projection."[27]

This withdrawal of forces globally will, according to Restrainers, yield very important benefits. For one thing, it will reduce America's impulse to use force. In Wertheim's words, "Shrinking the military's footprint will deprive presidents of the temptation to answer every problem with a violent solution. It will enable genuine engagement in the world, making diplomacy more effective, not less."[28] Moreover, the withdrawal of forces will actually reduce the probability of conflict. Restrainers, especially as reflected in writings of the Quincy Institute, believe that American forward military presence and exercises are provocative and make the Russians, the Chinese, the Iranians, and the North Koreans feel threatened, provoking responses from them and increasing the risk of war. Ann Wright, writing for the Quincy Institute, took particular aim at naval exercises that the United States conducted with its Asian allies and a number of NATO countries in the Pacific, saying that the "RIMPAC military war exercises have dangerous intended and unintended consequences that put the Pacific region at ever increasing risk of military confrontation and destruction."[29] For Restrainers, it is American forward presence and provocations, not the imperial ambitions or aggressive intentions or covetous desire to control natural resources that are responsible for conflicts. According to Rand Paul, the United States would not face threats from the Middle East if it did not have forces in the region.[30]

Wertheim spoke for many Restrainers when he said that decades of unilateral American actions yielded the reality that "it is US military power that threatens international law and order."[31] Stephen Walt went even further, saying: "Using American power to remake the world has led to illegal wars, excessive government secrecy, targeted killings, the death of thousands of innocent foreign civilians, and repeated violations of US and international law."[32] Put simply, for Restrainers, the United States has acted much more as a rogue state than those countries different American administrations have identified as malign actors.

To be sure, Ukraine has caused problems for the Progressive/Restrainer worldview. As Vladimir Putin acts to recreate an imperial Russian past, one would think that it would be difficult to blame American overreach or forward presence as the cause of the war. But many Restrainers do not buy this argument. For example, Jeffrey Sachs, a prominent Progressive, blames the conflict on those who pushed expansion of NATO and the "neoconservatives" who did so much to provoke Russia's invasion of Ukraine.[33] Similarly, a non-Progressive but a leading Restrainer John Mearsheimer, too, placed the blame on those who pushed NATO expansion and put the Russians in the corner as a result.[34]

Other Restrainers are less concerned with who is to blame for the war and focus more on the need to end it. Their accent is on emphasizing the need for diplomacy and peace. Fair enough, but this inevitably downplays the issue of Russian aggression and tends to lead to pressure on the Ukrainians, not the Russians, to concede to make peace possible. The moral equivalence that is embodied in the writings of those at the Quincy Institute led to fissures and the resignations of two prominent senior fellows at the institute, Joseph Cirincione and (ret.) Major General Paul Eaton. Cirincione, former head of the Ploughshares Fund, in explaining his resignation as Distinguished Non-Resident Fellow at the Quincy Institute, said, "you cannot find a word on the website or an analysis about the horror or the crimes that Russia is doing. If the United States were doing this, there would be a river of posts denouncing that behavior."[35] He said that for months he had tried to change the posture of the institute which "cast blame on the US and NATO for a war driven entirely by Russian President Vladimir Putin." In response, Lora Lumpe, the CEO of the Quincy Institute, explained, "Joe has made it clear that he disagrees with the priority that staff experts have put on reaching a diplomatic resolution to end this war; we have heard Joe's concerns, but believe that any US policy that risks significant escalation, including bringing the United States into the war with a nuclear-armed Russia, should be avoided."[36]

For Progressives, avoiding war is their lodestar. Their premise has been that it is American overreach, driven by America's need for primacy, that is the principal cause of conflict. Necessarily some have to blame the United States for the war in Ukraine, but that strains the bounds of credulity and appears to make them apologists for Russia. This reflects the deeper problem with Restrainers: their desire to avoid war and escalation gives those determined to coerce their neighbors the assurance that they have little to fear from making threats and even following through on them. Quite the contrary, it gives them an incentive to make threats, believing they either can get away with them or will be able to force concessions to avoid conflict. Restrainers never portray bad or aggressive actors for what they are, and it is not just the Russians in Ukraine—a portrayal that ultimately a Progressive like Joseph Cirincione could not stomach. Iran in the Middle East is presented largely as acting defensively. In the Quincy Institute's new paradigm for the Middle East, Paul Pillar, Andrew Bacevich, and others make the case for American withdrawal from the region. They accept the need to prevent a regional hegemon from emerging but say that can be achieved by relying on regional actors to check one another. They argue that the United States must stop classifying some actors as "good" and others "bad." There are no moral distinctions.[37]

One of Restrainers' weaknesses is that values, a basic element of the American self-image, are not considered a part of this image. Progressives might argue that is not true for them; it is worth noting that while all Progressives believe in restraint and retrenchment, not all Restrainers are progressive. As noted above, Rand Paul is a Restrainer, but not a Progressive, just as Joseph Cirincione is a Progressive even as he believes in restraint in foreign policy. There will be a continuing struggle among Progressives and Restrainers over this issue of drawing moral distinctions but also over American national interests—especially in the era of great power rivalry, where the behavior of Russia and China will make it inevitable to decide what is right and wrong. To his credit, Stephen Wertheim has acknowledged that there is a challenge for those who favor a progressive foreign policy to reconcile their belief in restraint and retrenchment with the threats that may come from the Russians and the Chinese. He says that while Progressives "prefer to speak the language of values," they must not "shy away from talking about the national interest."[38] That dialogue will work, he suggests, because as competition with the Russians and the Chinese exposes America to larger risks and costs, "it will be essential to show why overreach would harm the people whom US foreign policy is supposed to serve, and why a principled and restrained approach would make them safer. A hardheaded progressivism is not a concession to right-wing nationalism but the antidote to it, robbing demagogues of the specter of a naïve, anti-American 'globalism' to decry."[39] Maybe, but I believe that Progressives will find it difficult to strike this balance and preserve credibility in the process.

Spheres of Influence

It should come as no surprise that those favoring the Spheres of Influence approach do so because they see it being a more realistic, less costly, and less risky posture than trying to preserve the liberal rules-based international order—an order that depends in their eyes on continuing US dominance. In a world of competing powers, American dominance is simply not sustainable or even possible—or so this school believes. Given that, the United States has little choice but to adjust its behavior. The post–Cold War world produced, in Graham Allison's words, a "unipolar moment, not a unipolar era."[40] Neither the Russians nor the Chinese would simply acquiesce for long in unmistakable American supremacy: the price of the United States trying to impose it was simply too high. For Allison, that need not be a problem, and recognizing spheres of influence can be stabilizing—indeed, it has been in the past.

Allison makes the point that it was the balance of terror and the resulting recognition by the United States of the Soviet sphere in Eastern Europe that kept the cold peace of the Cold War era. Throughout the Cold War, the United States accepted limits and did not challenge the Soviets in the bloc. Dwight Eisenhower did not challenge the Soviets during the uprising in Hungary in 1956. Lyndon Johnson did not come to the aid of the Czechs during the Prague Spring of 1968. The risk of nuclear war dictated that the United States respect the Soviet sphere of influence.

However, the collapse of the Soviet Union seemed to change everything. As Allison observes, "In the heady aftermath of the Cold War ... US policymakers had ceased to recognize spheres of influence—the ability of other powers to demand deference from other states in their own regions or exert predominant control there—not because the concept had become obsolete. Rather, the entire world had become the de facto American sphere."[41]

For Allison and others like Peter Beinart, American hegemony was bound to recede in the face of China and Russia acting to assert and promote their interests, especially in the regions close to them. These countries would not let the United States impose on them, and they had the power to prevent America from doing so. Beinart, like Allison, embraces the need for recognizing the spheres of other competing powers. He points out that the United States historically acted to prevent any single power from coming to dominate either Europe or Asia or the oil fields of the Persian Gulf, fearing that, "If an enemy consolidated control over these power centers, it might stop the United States from trading across the Atlantic and Pacific or deny it access to oil, either of which would wreck America's economy."[42] But preventing the emergence of another hegemon in Europe, Asia, or the Persian Gulf did not require denying the Soviets a sphere of influence in Eastern Europe. And the United States did not do that.

But, according to Beinart, that changed after the collapse of the Soviet Union; "in keeping with its general post–Cold War reluctance to grant competitors a sphere of influence," the United States "has tried to extend its power right up to the borders of Russia and China. That risks sparking conflict in places that the Russian and Chinese governments consider crucial to their security but the American people do not consider crucial to theirs."[43]

For both Allison and Beinart, recognizing spheres of influence is simply prudent. It reflects reality, and the behavior of both Russia and China should come as no surprise. "Traditionally," Allsion observes, "great powers have demanded a degree of deference from lesser powers on their borders and in adjacent areas, and they have expected other great powers to respect that fact. Recent actions by China and Russia in their respective neighborhoods are just the most recent examples of that tradition."[44]

In essence, both Allison and Beinart argue that spheres of influence are inevitable and that, by accepting and recognizing them, one can use them as a mechanism for avoiding conflict and promoting stability in a world of competing great powers. Those who believe in the Spheres of Influence approach, much like America First and Restrainers, do not embrace American exceptionalism. Fundamentally, they think that exceptionalism produces unnecessary adventures and leads to overreach. They share the view that it is not America's role to remake the world or even to assume that alliances are enduring or should necessarily be based on shared values. Note Allison's observation: "Alliances are not forever. Historically, when conditions have changed, particularly when a focal enemy has disappeared or balances of power have shifted dramatically, so, too, have other relationships among nations."[45]

The first three schools of thought I have identified place a premium on defining American interests narrowly, with values decidedly secondary. Instead, immediate need and costs—and avoiding unnecessary risks—are what guide America First supporters, Restrainers, and Spheres of Influence advocates.

Sphere of Influence advocates see this approach as fitting the realities of a world where the United States has lost its dominance and the Russians and, especially the Chinese, are dissatisfied powers who are seeking to change the rules of the game. Aside from essentially dismissing values and the self-image that the majority of Americans still believe in, the Spheres of Influence school has at least two flaws.

First, it assumes that the spheres will be static, and that the Russians and the Chinese will be satisfied with America's recognition of their area of dominance. Perhaps if what was driving the Russians and the Chinese (and maybe also regional states like Iran) was purely insecurity, those who favor this conceptual approach to foreign policy would be right. But can one really assume that only defensive impulses motivate the Russians and the Chinese? Vladimir Putin has cited approvingly Peter the Great's war on Sweden as driven by the need to reclaim areas that had once been part of Russia.[46] And President Xi of China is clearly motivated by having China achieve leadership globally as something reflecting the country's rights and destiny.[47] In other words, why would one assume that the boundaries of the sphere will remain static? Why assume that the Russians and the Chinese will not seek to expand the sphere—and that this expansion itself will not become a source of friction?

Second, what about the countries that fall within these spheres of influence? Russia has demonstrated that it is not just the foreign policy of states like Ukraine that it cares about; it wants to dictate Kyiv's domestic policies as well. In addition to the moral question of whether we should accept such domination, there is also the practical question: What are other countries, especially global leaders like the United States, supposed to do when those who in live in such states rebel against the Russians or the Chinese? True, in the Cold War, the United States essentially accepted that the Russians would put down any domestic dissent. Beinart makes the case that America has little choice but to accept such outcomes because it does not have the means to defend these countries. As he wrote, "If the United States could actually defend Ukraine, Georgia, or Taiwan, perhaps then the horror of war of might be worth it. But America cannot at least at a price that the American people are willing to pay. Morally, therefore, America better serves these countries by helping them reach the best possible accommodation with their great power neighbors rather than encouraging their defiance with promises America can't keep."[48]

To be fair to Beinart, he wrote these words before the war in Ukraine. Still, his basic views have not changed; Beinart and Restrainers, with whom he has much in common, favor the position of supporting an end to the war and inevitable Ukrainian concessions. Ultimately, there will probably need to be mutual concessions to end the war, but the spirit of the Spheres of Influence school is to tilt toward the will of the Russians. For Sphere of Influence advocates, it is too costly and dangerous to do otherwise. But they lack a good answer for whether the sphere can really be static and stable and what happens when those countries and peoples in the sphere are not willing to acquiesce. The former means the United States still have to be willing to impose limits and make clear the costs of trying to push out the boundaries of the sphere. And the latter will challenge American values and self-image.

Realists/Balance of Power

This school might seem to encompass all those who claim to be realists. John Mearsheimer and Stephen Walt are two academics who define themselves as realists. They see the world through the lens of interests, not values, which they see as distorting and producing overreach. They believe force should only be used in those circumstances where the United States is directly threatened. They recognize that a hostile power coming to dominate either Europe or Asia could be threatening to American national interests, but they also believe that US allies need to carry the bulk of the responsibility for their own defense. They argue for off-shore balancing, meaning that the United States does not need large forces abroad and can intervene, if necessary, when those who might affect American interests are threatened. And yet I described Mearsheimer and Walt as Restrainers and have not put them in the Realists/Balance of Power category—and for good reason. In Walt's case, he has written the manifesto for Restrainers for the Quincy Institute.[49] As for Mearsheimer, he has been outspoken in making the case that the United States put Russia in the corner and should have understood that Russia would feel obliged to invade Ukraine.[50]

Moreover, they take a decidedly negative view of Israel, decrying the Israeli lobby for using its influence to get administrations to pursue foreign policies in the Middle East that they claim serve Israel's interests, not America's. Their views of Israel are revealing about their basic approach and show what separates them from those who actually defined the Realism school—like Hans Morgenthau, its intellectual godfather, and his most important disciple, Henry Kissinger.[51,c]

Apart from wildly exaggerating the actual influence of the lobby on US policy toward the region, their view of Israel demonstrates how narrowly these authors define American interests. It also shows how they see values as potentially distracting America from the appropriate focus on its interests. For them, Israel is a liability not an asset given how much they believe it costs the United States in its relationships with the Arabs. Shared values, the historic foundation of the US-Israeli relationship, should not, in their eyes, blind us to what is important.[d]

Hans Morgenthau and Henry Kissinger took a very different view of Israel, and their attitudes provide greater insight into the Realist school and what is important for its proponents. Both saw support for Israel as matching America's interests and values. Both emphasized that interests should guide policy, but they did not dismiss values. Kissinger understood how values contributed to America's soft power—and drew on his own experience in this regard: "Having found a haven from Nazi tyranny in the United States, I had personally experienced what our nation meant to the rest of the world, especially the persecuted and disadvantaged."[52]

Both of these men were Jewish refugees from Nazi Germany, and it is hard to see how that could not have colored their views toward Israel. And

---

c I have written elsewhere how misguided their view of the lobby's impact on different administration policies is (see *Doomed to Succeed*; see also my "Foreign Policy" piece criticizing their book on Israel lobby). Among other things, I point out that every time an American president felt that US interests were at stake, they prevailed over the opposition to the lobby: Carter's F-15 sales to Saudi Arabia, Reagan's AWACs sale to the Saudis, George H. W. Bush withholding loan guarantees to Israel, Barack Obama and the Iran nuclear deal (JCPOA).

d Of course, they also argue that Israel's occupation of Palestinians means that it does not really share American values either. In *Doomed to Succeed*, I show how many Arab leaders did not allow US support for Israel to affect their relationship with America because their main priority was survival and security, and they looked to the United States to provide that.

yet, Morgenthau was actually negative in his views of Israel prior to the 1967 war, seeing it as a state that might not be self-sustainable. But the 1967 war changed that and had a profound effect on Morgenthau. He would later speak of feeling pride in Israel that "was based in part on a military victory but also upon the type of military victory. I mean the triumphant way in which Israel overcame all its surrounding enemies. It was a kind of biblical victory. You could imagine the cohorts of God fighting the battle of the Jews."[53]

For his part, Kissinger was supportive of Israel but at times was also critical of the Jewish state. When he was frustrated in his first attempt to negotiate a second pull-back of Israeli forces in the Sinai in 1975, he called for a "reassessment" of America's relationship with Israel—very publicly consulting with prominent critics of Israel. That said, Kissinger—both in government and later out of it—was clearly a strong supporter of Israel.[54] As secretary of state, consider the scope of the commitments and assurances he made to Israel to produce the Sinai II agreement in September 1975— ranging from budgetary support ($2 billion), to promising F-16 aircraft in principle, to assuring that the United States would not present any initiative on peace without first consulting with Israel, and to committing not to deal with the Palestine Liberation Organization (PLO) unless three conditions were met, including recognition of Israel.[55] (Had Walt and Mearsheimer ever commented on this set of commitments to Israel in 1975, they would have seen it as tying America's hands and granting Israel too much control over US policy.)

Kissinger, however, believed that his commitments were necessary to get the agreement and that it served US interests. He felt that this agreement cemented the relationship with Sadat and built a basis for peace. Beyond this, he felt that a strong and secure Israel promoted American interests in the Middle East, enhancing deterrence and also forcing the Arabs to come to the United States if they wanted to recover land lost to Israel or affect Israel's behavior. A closer relationship between Washington and Jerusalem increased American leverage on Israel. Anwar Sadat, in explaining why he made peace with Israel, said that "America held 99% of the cards" if he was to get his land back. Kissinger saw the merits of demonstrating that the relationship between the United States and Israel provided influence, but he also was motivated, at least in part, by the fact that Israel was a democracy and was deserving of US support as a result. By contrast, Walt and Mearsheimer saw Israel as complicating America's interests with the Arabs—and believed that it was the Arabs in terms of their numbers and their oil that should define US interests. (No doubt, the international backlash against Israel over the death and destruction of its war in Gaza in response to Hamas' onslaught of October 7, 2023 would be cited by Walt and Mearsheimer now about the costs of association and support for Israel–and they would not be entirely wrong.)

Kissinger and Morgenthau, however, evaluated interests (and reality, costs, and benefits) differently from Walt and Mearsheimer. They could be hardheaded in terms of defining America's interests and how the United States could enhance its power to protect its interests or counter threats to them. But the world was not a laboratory where interests were necessarily black and white. The United States had an interest in those with whom it assumed commitments and shared values—even if it came at some cost to America and the US was not benefiting economically or in some more narrow concrete sense.

The concept of credibility, of course, also mattered greatly to Kissinger. He was not an off-shore balancer. He understood that being off-shore might not be a sufficient source of reassurance. It might raise questions in the minds of those to whom the United States had commitments about whether America actually would intervene when they might truly need it. And if countries, especially in the Middle East, had doubts about the United States, they would begin to hedge bets and accommodate those who threatened them.

Walt and Mearsheimer seemingly ignored that the mere act of withdrawing forces because the United States does not want to be drawn into conflicts or believe its presence is too costly will raise doubts for allies and partners about how willing and prepared America is to come to their defense if they are threatened. During the Biden administration, both Saudis and Emiratis began to hedge their bets, especially with the Chinese.[56] Among other things, Saudi leaders told me that the administration's withdrawal of Patriot missiles from the Kingdom when they were being attacked by Houthi rockets from Yemen critically affected Riyadh's view of American reliability. Ironically, this withdrawal took place because the Pentagon decided that the United States needed these missiles more in the Indo-Pacific theater, but it ultimately contributed to Chinese encroachment in the Middle East, which in turn has necessitated greater effort by Washington to maintain its status as partner of choice for regional states like Saudi Arabia.[e]

---

[e] This decision fit perfectly with the Walt–Mearsheimer playbook. The irony is that if one believed that the relationship with Saudi Arabia was critical to American interests in the Middle East and beyond, it would be clear that this was not a wise step to take.

For the genuine Realists, power is the defining element of international relations. Nothing is more elemental than its pursuit. As Morgenthau wrote, "International politics, like all politics, is a struggle for power. Whatever the ultimate aims of international politics, power is always the immediate aim."[57] Israel mattered to both Morgenthau and Kissinger because its character meant it would always strategically align with the United States in the competition for power in the region, even if Jerusalem and Washington are not always in lock-step either on more tactical details of best methods and means to pursue it. The fact that Israel has the strongest forces in the region only added to its importance to the United States. Its recent decimation of the leadership and militaries of Hezbollah and Hamas has clearly weakened Iran's so-called "Axis of Resistance," and shifted the regional balance of power more in favor of America and its partners. Assuming that Israel is open to a political outcome that permits the creation of new realities in Lebanon and Gaza, this more favorable balance of power in the conflict-laden Middle East would lend credence to the Morgenthau and Kissinger view of Israel's importance for the United States.

Morgenthau explained that conflict was an inseparable part of human nature. Violence was an ever-present threat and sometimes a necessary tool, with man being "as good as he can be in an evil world."[58] Solutionism was inherently impossible. The pursuit of national interest and "the struggle for power [are] universal in time and space and [are] undeniable fact[s] of experience." While the readiness to use military force was necessary, "the armed forces," Morgenthau wrote, "are an instrument for war; foreign policy is an instrument of peace." He observed that "no domination can last that is founded upon nothing but military force." And, although he did not use the term, he showed his intuitive understanding of the importance of soft power, declaring that "all foreign policy is a struggle for the minds of man."[59]

Power remained the crucible of international relations, and for Morgenthau there was but one means for curbing humans' unalterable lust for it: the balance of power. Force must offset force and create a balance. In an anarchic world, the balance of power was "necessary" as an "essential and stabilizing factor."[60] It was the only thing that could create a condition for peace. It was, he explained, "the very law of life."[61]

Foreign policy conducted in a democracy did create special pressures and constraints on the diplomat who might feel the need, given the balance of power, to pursue some policies that might run counter to popular attitudes or instincts. But the United States, he noted, had a special character and self-image, and US policy could not operate in opposition to it. "America," he said, "addresses itself to all the nations of the world." Its ideal of equality and freedom has global relevance, for "if we fail, the nations of the world will look elsewhere for models of social engagement and political institutions to emulate and we will be alone in a hostile world."[62]

Here we see the contrast with Walt and Mearsheimer. For them, values are incidental and do not shape what countries do—the good of a state on the world stage, in their eyes, is best served by addressing only their narrow interests and not worrying about standing for something or having a higher purpose. Morgenthau and Kissinger, however, the true Realists, took this higher purpose into account—even as they both wanted the maximum flexibility to pursue balance of power policies. Wanting to stand for something was important for America, but it must not let moral claims guide policy lest we deal in absolutes. While a higher purpose was important to consider for Morgenthau and Kissinger, overemphasis of moral claims would only limit the options of the United States and drive it to overreach. Morgenthau was a fierce critic of Vietnam, saying he had "always warned against the foolish and improvident use of power."[63] While Kissinger felt that the impact on America's credibility necessitated that the United States not simply withdraw from Vietnam, lest others lose their faith in US commitments or staying power, he was not indifferent to the risk of the United States becoming the world's policeman.

To avoid the risk of becoming stretched too far in terms of commitments, Kissinger believed that the application of US power had to be guided by an understanding of American national interest. In Kissinger's words, if America's approach to the world was not guided by national interest, the result would be "an undifferentiated globalism and confusion about our purposes."[64] This was a prescription for excessive interventionism that was neither wise nor sustainable.

Balance was needed. Melvin Leffler would later write about the George W. Bush administration, explaining that its policies produced mistaken and costly interventions because they were driven exclusively by values—and interests needed to discipline values.[65] Like Morgenthau and Kissinger, Leffler was not saying that there is no place for values in US foreign policy. Rather he was saying that national interest needs to inform how and in what ways the United States operationalizes its values, promotes democracy, and considers whether to intervene for humanitarian reasons.

Here was the Realist credo: power and national interest guide the international reality. Balance of power is necessary to give others a reason to respect some basic rules and operate within limits; it is a means to mitigate the anarchy realists believe is intrinsic to the international system. The balance of power could not eliminate or prevent conflict—that was inevitable given the clash of interests between states. But it could limit conflict, even as it reduced the incentive for war.

In a world of competing powers, the balance of power was the only way to ensure stability. Others would not acquiesce in American dominance or supremacy, so the United States needed to shape a balance of power that supported its interests and those of US allies and partners. As Kissinger would write, the new shape of international politics with competing great powers meant that "for the first time, the United States [could] neither withdraw from the world nor dominate it."[66]

What separates the Realist/Balance of Power school from America First is not the belief in national interest, but rather the former's conviction that the United States must be prepared to use force and have partners as the country "balances" or counters its adversaries. Also, unlike both America First and Restrainers, the Realist/Balance of Power school does not believe in retrenchment. Superficially, Realists seem to have much in common with the Spheres of Influence school; there certainly is a readiness to see, as Kissinger would often note, that America's adversaries have interests too. He would recognize those and even try to come to some understandings to shape America's competition and make it peaceful. But that would not extend to letting the clock turn back and permitting the Russians to restore its domination of Eastern Europe, or China to do the same to the countries on its periphery. (On the war in Ukraine, Kissinger observed early on that there might have to be a territorial adjustment to end the conflict, but he was not for surrendering it to Russia and letting the Russians dictate its future.)

The Realist view might place the highest priority on American interests, but it does not dispense with values. Still, when there was tension between the two, interests would dominate—and, as Kissinger found as secretary of state, that prioritization clashed with the American self-image and generated much criticism of his policies. Liberal Internationalists, by contrast, advocate for courses of action which reflect the American self-image, placing a greater emphasis on values.

Liberal Internationalists

Only the Realist/Balance of Power and the Liberal Internationalist schools believe in the continuing role for American global power and inveigh against American retrenchment. Liberal Internationalists believe in the importance of the US role globally and argue that America's power must underpin an international order based on multilateral institutions and alliances.

In Chapter 1, I showed that President Biden and Secretary of State Antony Blinken have been believers in the rules-based international order. Blinken made the case for it when he was out of government, and his speeches as secretary of state have explained why it is so important to preserve a rules-based order against those who seek to undermine the basic norms that are so necessary to preserve it. Supporting Ukraine in the face of Russia's invasion was justified by both President Biden and Secretary Blinken on the grounds that the rules-based international order is at stake in this fight.

Again, as we saw in Chapter 1, the liberal international order that Biden and Blinken sought to preserve is one that encourages peaceful, predictable, and cooperative behavior among states consistent with a set of principles and democratic values: respect for sovereignty, inviolability of borders, peaceful change, the free flow of capital and trade, freedom of expression, protection of human rights, and the rule of law. Yes, they have sought adjustments to fix some of the excesses of globalization and inequalities it produced with regard to the movement of capital and trade, but these principles and values are the hallmark of Liberal Internationalists. Indeed, unlike the Realist/Balance of Power schools, Liberal Internationalists tend to prioritize values over interests.

To be sure, Biden and Blinken are not theorists. They are policymakers, and their belief in liberal internationalism shaped their policies. They are mindful of the need for limits, but liberal internationalism reflects their worldview. There are those who intellectually make the case for liberal internationalism and its manifestation: a liberal, rules-based order that has the United States as its linchpin.

John Ikenberry and Robert Kagan may be the most prolific of liberal internationalism's academic advocates, but they are certainly not alone. Ash Jain and Matthew Kroenig write about the state of the international order, focused very much on creating new mechanisms that join all democracies in preserving and adapting it.[67] All advocates of liberal internationalism essentially argue that the retrenchers do not understand the consequences of the United States not leading the order, and they make the case that there is no acceptable alternative to American leadership. Kagan acknowledges that the liberal rules-based order has flaws and can never work perfectly, but he also argues: "The enduring truth about the liberal world order is that, like Churchill's comment about democracy, it is the worst system—except for all others."[68]

Ikenberry, in particular, challenges not just retrenchers but also the Realist school. He understands that Realists believe that anarchy is the fundamental condition of international relations and that cooperation among states pursuing their national interests will rarely define their behavior. But he takes issue with that conclusion, saying, "Liberal internationalists do not deny that states pursue their own interests, often through competitive means, but they believe that the anarchy of that competition can be limited. States, starting with the liberal democracies, can use institutions as building blocks for cooperation and for the pursuit of joint gains."[69] According to Realists, the balance of power naturally limits anarchy in the international system; liberal internationalists, on the other hand, contend that institutions can be built with the express purpose of limiting that same anarchy.

Cooperation is an essential element of the liberal order, but power is too. Strong, aggressive, illiberal states can challenge the order and make weaker states feel vulnerable. But if those weaker states know that rules and institutions can protect them, and that the leading state in the liberal order will act "within an agreed-upon set of rules and institutions and not use its power to coerce" them, they will see great benefit in supporting it.[70]

Of course, as both Ikenberry and Kagan point out, the United States has not always observed the rules. Vietnam, Kosovo, and Iraq are examples where, as Kagan points out, the United States acted as if the rules-based system was designed to support its interests alone. And yet, none of the members of the liberal order, even if critical of America's actions, chose to leave it. Yes, Kagan says, the United States acted as a hegemon, but Europeans and Asians accepted it: "The order held together because the other members regarded American hegemony ... as relatively benign and superior to the alternative."[71] Ikenberry, while acknowledging American violation of the rules at times, points out that "the overall logic of the order gives many countries around the world, particularly the liberal democracies, incentives to join with rather than balance against the United States."[72] He cites an additional reason for this. American strategy across the decades sought:

> to build an international order that would be open, friendly and stable: open in the sense that trade and exchange were possible across regions; friendly in the sense that none of these regions would be dominated by a rival illiberal great power that sought to close off its sphere of influence to the outside world; and stable in the sense that the post-imperial order would be anchored in a set of multilateral rules and institutions that would give it some broad legitimacy, the capacity to adapt to change, and the staying power to persist well into the future.[73]

The attraction of the United States to others and the critical role it plays in preserving the order, especially in Europe and East Asia, has led many countries, in Ikenberry's words, "to worry more about being abandoned by the United States than being dominated by it."[74] Here we also see the counterpoint to those who seek American retrenchment. Forward American presence in terms of deployments and bases provides US partners "not just with security but also greater certainty about the US commitment."[75]

Of course, there is the question of whether the United States can sustain its role as the power that holds the liberal, rules-based international order together. It is precisely because of American overreach that there is a debate about America's role in the world. It is why Restrainers want the United States to retrench; why the Spheres of Influence supporters want the United States to recognize and accept Russian and Chinese dominance in their neighborhoods; and why quasi-Realists like Walt and Mearsheimer want off-shore balancing and for US allies to bear much more of the burden of their own defense. Their collective impulses are understandable given the costs of wars in Iraq and Afghanistan, which were either ill-considered or conducted with no realistic goals or real understanding of the landscape. And yet, representatives of all of these schools of thought collectively fail to appreciate what the world would look like if the United States withdrew the way they want. They act as if the resulting vacuums would not be filled by the worst forces, and as if US allies and friends wound not feel the need to accommodate those who would threaten them in the aftermath of America's withdrawal.

These schools of thought generally also fail to understand that there is an American self-image of selflessness on the world stage that still permeates an important part of the public. True, there is an isolationist tradition of wanting little to do with the rest of world, but that impulse—though also deeply rooted in part of America's "exceptional" ethos—tends not to be the dominant one in the American public. To be sure, the context can affect that—and after multiple costly, drawn-out wars with unsatisfactory con-clusions, the impulse to be hesitant, especially about the use of force, is understandable. Even with the experiences of those wars, however, Amer-ican engagement with the rest of the world remains largely supported. Most Americans strongly agree with President Biden's support for Ukraine, provided it does not lead to direct conflict between the US and Russia.[76]

In other words, America First, Restrainers, and Spheres of Influence are schools of thought that ultimately fail to meet either the American self-image or US needs internationally. With regard to these two factors, Realists/Balance of Power and Liberal Internationalists have both strengths and weaknesses. The former too often run afoul of American values, as Henry Kissinger did in his role of secretary of state. The latter have prob-lems with knowing when, where, and how to intervene, as well as how to get allies and partners to contribute more to their own defense.

Perhaps Liberal Internationalists have learned the lesson of overreach. Certainly, at one level, they may be able to persuade US allies and partners that without their contributing more to their own defense, it will be harder for the United States to sustain the role they want. The fear of Trump's return may provide a real strong motivation for US allies to do more. The Russian invasion of Ukraine also signaled to the Europeans that power matters, the threats are real, and their commercial interests cannot always dominate.

Similarly, on the use of force and intervention, the United States needs to be guided by a number of considerations. First, does America have a credible local partner that is prepared and willing to fight on its own? In defeating ISIS territorially, the United States had a local partner that did the fighting on the ground, the Syrian Democratic Forces (SDF).[f] In rooting out ISIS from its hold on Raqqa, its self-declared capital, the SDF lost more than 11,000 of its fighters, while the United States lost six. America's role was to provide air power, spotting for artillery, weaponry, as well as logistic and intelligence support. To Ukraine, the United States has provided an array of advanced weaponry, some training, and financial assistance. Both against ISIS and in Ukraine, there is a form of American intervention, but the US military is not

---

[f] The SDF is largely but not exclusively Kurdish.

leading the fighting, and in each case, there is a partner that is willing and determined to fight on its own.

This leads to a second point. Intervention cannot and should not be reduced to a binary choice: either the United States puts tens of thousands of its forces on the ground, or it does nothing. There are many additional options in between these two extremes. America can decide its role and the character of its intervention based on its stakes, the consequences of inaction, the needs of US regional partners, and the degree to which US local partners demonstrate their credibility and readiness to fight. (In the Middle East, the United States should have learned that it is a mistake to intervene with large ground forces.)

All this means that America can avoid overreach and interventions that inevitably make the United States less able to act and produce more domestic ire from such schools of thought as America First, Restrainers, and Spheres of Influence.

Conclusion

So where do I come out on the Realist/Balance of Power and Liberal Internationalist schools? I see the logic and the limits of both. That is why I would combine them—essentially creating a hybrid model. Realists use interests to temper where the United States might be involved and to limit the potential to become the world's policemen. Liberal Internationalists are right to give weight to American values—indeed, reminding the world that the United States stands for something that matters. It separates the United States from those who do not. It is an essential part of US soft power. Standing for a set of values also contributes to America's competitive advantages internationally, particularly as it makes it easier to identify with the United States and not with America's illiberal competitors.

But there are times when America's interests are more important and have to predominate. Take the relationship with Saudi Arabia. With the Saudis, America's interests were decisive even for a president like Jimmy Carter, for whom human rights were a guiding principle. His fear of another oil embargo led him not to make human rights an issue with the Saudis. Carter needed not to go that far: the United States does not need to dispense with its human rights concerns and can and should raise them with the Saudis. Washington must do so, however, in a way that does not hector the Saudis or put them overly on the defensive even as it makes clear there will be limits in our relationship if they do not operate within certain limits when it comes to human rights.

In reality, both the US and Saudi Arabia have a mutual stake in having a good relationship, and that mutual stake will not go away any time soon. For the Saudis, whatever their doubts about the United States, they know that no one else can provide for their security or come to their rescue when needed, as evidenced by the fact that their efforts to pursue a defense treaty with the United States persisted even amid regional turmoil after the October 7th attacks. For the United States as well, the Saudis remain important for a number of reasons. First, as America transitions away from fossil fuels (which will take 20–30 years), it needs a stable oil market to manage the transition and avoid great economic disruptions, and the Saudis are critical for that. Second, like the United States, the Saudis are not interested in upending the regional and international orders; they favor their preservation. Thus, Riyadh is essential for coalitions in the region and beyond as the United States must counter threats from Iran and engage in longer-term competition with China and Russia over time. Third, because the Saudi domestic transformation has made modernization—not Wahhabism—the source of state legitimacy, the United States has a profound interest in the success of their efforts—something that also makes the Kingdom a crucial partner in countering radical Islamist ideologies. That, by the way, is both an interest and a value, and one that is only more important in a post-October 7th Middle East.[8] In short, Saudi well-being, stability, and security are important to the United States; America's relationship with the Saudis and American commitments to them need to reflect that.

In essence, America's approach needs to combine elements of both the Realist and Liberal Internationalist schools. That means the United States needs a balance between its interests and values. America needs a rule of reason, understanding that sometimes either its interests or values must take precedence, but neither should be ignored entirely when the other is necessarily prioritized. With the exception of Donald Trump, most presidents do try to strike a balance of sorts between the two, with some tilting toward interests and others toward values. The problem is less that they tilt in one direction more than the other; the problem is the lack of explanation for what they are doing and why. Because the American self-image is one of

---

[8] A successful Saudi Arabia could at long last create a successful model of development that Arab states have never had and that has been the source of appeal of radical ideologies from Nasser's Arab nationalism to al-Qaeda's Islamism.

a selfless United States, presidents must do more to explain why America's interests sometimes require them to give values lesser weight—like, for example, with the Saudis.

One thing is for sure: the United States must retain its leading role if there are to be norms internationally that reflect its values. But that is simply not possible without American hard power. Hard power without soft power will always have its limits. But soft power without hard power will generate less attraction not only because others will feel they cannot count on America, but also because they will believe that the United States simply does not understand the threats or realities they face.

That certainly was the effect when President Obama stated that those who thought that the Russians and the Iranians were gaining in Syria did not understand power in the twenty-first century. To America's partners in the Middle East—who face directly and daily Iran's aggressive efforts to redefine the regional order and gain hegemony—the president signaled a lack of understanding of the realities of the region. To them, there was no doubt that hard power mattered greatly and only its exercise would deter the Iranians.

Applying the hybrid model, one that combines the Realist and Liberal Internationalist schools, will mean continuing to emphasize values even as US policymakers explain that sometimes America's interests must take precedence. If this explanation is provided, no apology will be necessary. It is important to recognize that the hybrid model is also based on being willing to use America's hard power oftentimes to reinforce its soft power. The combination of both can enhance deterrence—and the combination of both also simply reflects who Americans are. In fact, America remains the strongest global power because of its economic, financial, military, technological, medical, educational, cyber, informational, entrepreneurial, cultural, and ethnic diversity strengths. But the United States is not dominant the way it was in the immediate post–Cold War period. The United States now has competitors, and it has to use all its tools more effectively—something that will also help preserve the domestic support needed to sustain America's role.

Once again, we come back to the need for good, smart statecraft. While I have given past examples of not marrying objectives and means, it is important to go beyond that and actually develop a framework or structural guide for conducting statecraft. With that in mind, I want to explore in depth examples of good and bad statecraft. What do the good and bad examples have in common? What key lessons can be distilled? What do those lessons tell us about the best practices in the carrying out effective statecraft? To that, I will now turn.

There is no better way to grasp statecraft done well or not so well than to look at a number of historical examples. I have chosen a number of cases in which I was either directly involved or in a position to talk to key decision-makers and, thus, have a good understanding of what was driving the American decisions at the time. I have also chosen these particular cases because the decision-makers believed the stakes were high. High stakes provide a good measure of the effectiveness of statecraft because different administrations believed that a great deal was riding on the achievement of their objectives. To understand each case, I will offer an overview of what happened, why US policymakers developed the objectives they did, the obstacles they faced, and the means used to overcome these challenges.

Chapter 5
German Unification in NATO

It is safe to say that almost no one initially thought it conceivable that Germany could be unified and integrated into NATO. Bartholomew Sparrow, Brent Scowcroft's biographer, observed that few outside the leadership of the Bush administration thought it was even desirable: "In early 1989, it would have been hard to find a single prominent journalist or political leader who favored the creation of a single, unified Germany."[1]

Many did not favor it because most leaders in Europe, officials in the State Department, and pundits in the Washington chattering class were convinced that the Soviet leadership could never accept such an outcome. And yet, the application of effective statecraft made it happen.

Background and Context

Nothing more clearly embodied the Cold War than the division of Germany into Western and Eastern nations. The division took on a life of its own, and the so-called Four Powers at the time—the United States, the Soviet Union, France, and the United Kingdom—assumed rights and responsibilities at the conclusion of World War II as a result of their victory. The victorious powers became the supreme authority over Germany, and their inability to come to an agreement on a final peace treaty or on the fate of a reconstituted political authority in Germany led in time to the creation of two states.

In reality, the Soviets, the British, and the French—having paid such a horrific price in wars with Germany—feared the revival of German power in Europe and had little interest in any early reconstitution of a united German state. American attitudes were shaped less by history and more by the fear of Soviet power spreading west into Germany. Successive American administrations thus pressed the British and that French to accept the need for prosperity in the US zone of control in Germany, and for the advent of self-government. This, in turn, created the basis for the establishment of the Federal Republic of Germany (West Germany). Berlin remained

Statecraft 2.0. Second Edition. Dennis Ross, Oxford University Press. © Oxford University Press (2025). DOI: 10.1093/oso/9780197698914.003.0005

under the direct control of the Four Powers; in effect, the Federal Republic had the legal status of an interim state whose "final structure and borders" would be determined in an eventual peace settlement.[2] The Soviets, having subsequently set up a state in the area they occupied, argued that Germany as a country had ceased to exist and that it had been replaced by two states: the Federal Republic (West Germany) and the German Democratic Republic (GDR, or East Germany). The position of the United States, Britain, and France, as embodied in their 1952 treaty with the Federal Republic, was that international conditions precluded the reunification of Germany. Until a peace settlement could be negotiated, the Four Powers would retain their rights and responsibilities, and the final borders of the German state would remain unresolved. The presumption of the treaty was that "Signatory States [would] cooperate to achieve, by peaceful means, their common aim of a reunified Germany enjoying a liberal-democratic constitution, like that of the Federal Republic, and integrated within the European community."[3]

While reunification (to be achieved through all-German elections) might have been the stated goal, no one acted to promote it. On the contrary, the division of Germany came to be an accepted fact. American policymakers, more sympathetic than any of the other Four Powers to the Germans, nonetheless came to see the German question as "secondary to the overall management of the U.S. relationship with the Soviet Union."[4] In time, West German leaders also adapted to this reality. Even Helmut Kohl, who more than other West German leaders maintained a public commitment to resolving the German question, dismissed the idea that Soviet leader Mikhail Gorbachev might offer unity to Germany at some point, saying as late as October 1988: "I do not write futuristic novels ... What you ask now, that is in the realm of fantasy."[5]

And yet the fantastic became quite real, and in short order. Gorbachev introduced "new thinking" in 1986, and by 1988 there were profound stirrings in Poland and Hungary testing the limits of Soviet control and tolerance for increasing independence in Eastern European countries.[a] By the summer of 1989, a reformist leadership in Hungary set in motion a train of events that led to the Berlin Wall coming down in November. When Hungary opened its border with Austria, essentially lifting the Iron Curtain there,

---

[a] Gorbachev believed that perestroika (restructuring) was necessary not only in the Soviet Union, but also in the countries of the Warsaw Pact. While not envisioning that they would leave the alliance or reject socialism, he also made clear that political decisions for Poland and Hungary should be made in Warsaw and Budapest, not Moscow.

East Germans began streaming into Hungary in order to get to Austria and flee to the West. Initially, the Hungarian government would not allow the East Germans to cross the Austrian border, but it was also unwilling to force them to return home. Soon Hungary let them cross into Austria, triggering a virtual hemorrhage of East Germans seeking asylum. Even as the East German government blocked direct transit to Hungary, other routes were exploited, and soon swelling numbers of other asylum-seeking East Germans camped out in the West German embassy in Prague. Fearing contagion to their own population, the Czech government worked out a deal with the help of the West German foreign minister, Hans-Dietrich Genscher, in which the asylum-seekers were allowed to go to West Germany after returning first to East Germany. (The East Germans accepted this deal, hoping to end the embarrassing image of large numbers of asylum-seekers prior to the celebrations planned for the fortieth anniversary of the state.)

Rather than staunching the flow of East Germans trying to get out of their own country, however, the deal gave the mass exodus new impetus. And at this point, the Kohl-led government of West Germany began to drop all pretenses of working with the East German government and seeking only legal, controlled emigration. Though the Soviets began to issue warnings to the West German government of the danger of not respecting "postwar realities," Gorbachev was not prepared to countenance a draconian violent crackdown in East Germany. At that point, only such a crackdown might have blunted daily demonstrations demanding change. Erich Honecker, the aging East German leader, knowing he could not get Soviet backing for such a crackdown, hesitated and was removed from power in mid-October of 1989, barely a week after Gorbachev had visited the German Democratic Republic (GDR) for the fortieth-anniversary celebrations. The reformers who took Honecker's place sought to end the crisis in East Germany by promising a new course. With repression no longer an option, pent-up frustrations gave way to continuing demonstrations: 500,000 people turned out on the streets on November 4.

Hoping to demonstrate responsiveness and gain popularity, the reformist government eased restrictions on foreign travel, but they did not intend to go so far as to remove the exit visa requirement. Nonetheless, on the night of November 9, Günter Schabowski, one of the new reformist leaders, gave a rambling press conference and, near the end of it, read the text of a new travel law that had just been approved by the Central Committee: "Requests for private trips abroad may be submitted from now on even in the absence of special prerequisites."[6]

Rumors quickly spread that all restrictions had been lifted, and huge crowds almost immediately assembled at the Berlin Wall. The guards simply gave way, opening the wall, and crowds poured into West Berlin. The next day—November 10—was a day of euphoria in Berlin, a city undivided for the first time in four decades. The unthinkable was now thinkable. The wall came down figuratively and then literally on the night of November 9–10, 1989; by September 12, 1990, there was a ceremony in which a unified Germanywas formally reconstituted and the rights and responsibilities of the Four Powers ended.

How did German unification happen with Soviet opposition and with low expectations from nearly every quarter? As late as October 25, 1989, the American embassy in Bonn (West Germany) was reporting to decision-makers in Washington that "virtually no one believes reunification is the first order of business on the German–German agenda."[7] Only three days before the wall came down, Mikhail Gorbachev told his ambassador in East Germany, "Our people will never forgive us if we lose the GDR."[8] Yet, less than two weeks later it was unquestionably on the agenda, and the Bush 41st administration fashioned a strategy to make sure that a reunified Germany would be a member of the NATO alliance.

The Bush Administration Makes German Reunification in NATO Its Objective

If it had been up to the State Department, the United States would not have embraced the integration of a unified Germany into NATO as a goal. The State bureaucracy was conditioned to think that unification would create instability, and that the notion had few supporters even in the two Germanies. When Robert Zoellick, politically appointed counselor and confidant of the new secretary of state James Baker, asked a visiting West German general in early 1989 about German attitudes toward reunification, Roz Ridgway, who was then assistant secretary of state for European affairs, rebuked him, saying that unification was "the subject that all Americans are interested in and no German cares about."[9] The embassy cable from October 25 signaled a similar hesitancy even when the march toward reunification had clearly begun.

President Bush and his senior advisors saw it differently. As early as May 1989—well before the wall had come down—the president said in an interview that he would "love to see" Germany reunified.[10] The president and those around him believed that the new Soviet glasnost (openness) would lead to a far-reaching transformation in Europe and that no such transformation would be complete without the reunification of Germany. The Cold War began there, and it would end there. In the words of Robert Zoellick, an architect of the policy, "President Bush, Secretary Baker, and National Security Advisor Brent Scowcroft and their colleagues recognized that their decisions would shape Europe for decades to come ... The U.S. aim was to unify Europe in peace and freedom, while seeking to avoid a 'Versailles victory' that invited its own destruction."[11]

The analogy to the Treaty of Versailles is critical for understanding how Bush's advisors applied statecraft to German reunification: Germany could not be singled out for special treatment, and there could be no "restrictions on German sovereignty" as a price of the country's unity. In Zoellick's words, "any limits imposed from the outside would create the potential for future grievances"—just as they had after the Treaty of Versailles, when the Allies required reparations that bankrupted Weimar Germany and set the stage for the Nazi accession to power.[12]

At the same time, Germany's history of violent conquest could not be ignored. The president and his advisors believed that if Germany was not embedded in NATO, it would be a source of danger. If neutral, it would seek security by gaining its own nuclear capability, which would put Europe on a nuclear hair trigger and cause the nuclear nonproliferation regime to unravel as other states capable of developing nuclear weapons chose to do so. How could the United States ensure this would not happen and that Germany would be unified and in NATO?

Three considerations guided US policymakers. First, if the American side identified from the beginning with German aspirations and coordinated literally every step together with German leaders, they would not opt to remain neutral and make a separate agreement with the Soviets. Second, to win the confidence of others and lessen their fears of a German revival, Germany should be embedded in European institutions. And third, to ensure that Europe, during a period of transition, did not become a source of global instability, America needed to be wedded to Europe. For Bush, Baker, and Scowcroft, "America was now and should remain a 'European power.' It should remain so 'as long as Europeans want that.'"[13]

Ironically, it was the political leadership of the administration (not the mid- or working-level foreign affairs specialists) who had the broader, more historic perception of the far-reaching changes in Europe and tried to position the United States in advance of them. The most senior American officials read Chancellor Kohl correctly and succeeded in winning his trust. Kohl saw almost instinctive US support, came to count on it, and saw the United States removing the numerous obstacles to unification.

Obstacles to Achieving the Bush Administration's Objective

From the outset, the Soviets, the British, and the French were opposed to, or at least decidedly unenthusiastic about, the German reunification. For the Soviets, the division of Germany symbolized that Germany could never again threaten the Russian people. For the British and the French, a unified Germany brought back terrifying memories of German domination, and they worried that London's and Paris' respective weights in Europe would be diminished. While they might have favored an end to the Cold War and to the division of Europe, they believed it should occur only gradually and in stages.

The British and French preferred stability, and they saw Mikhail Gorbachev as a Soviet leader in whom the West had a very high stake because he would make cooperation, not conflict and confrontation, a new reality. Margaret Thatcher and François Mitterrand, the British and French leaders, believed that German unification in NATO would be a political disaster for Gorbachev and would look like an unmistakable defeat, thus destabilizing Europe as well as the USSR.

Bob Blackwell, the national intelligence officer for the Soviet Union in the CIA, shared this concern and wrote that "if it were to appear that Soviet troops were being forced to retreat from the GDR, he [Gorbachev] had 'lost' Germany, and the security environment for the USSR was now more threatening, the domestic fallout—when combined with other complaints—could pose a threat to his position. Gorbachev at least has to have one eye on this contingency."[14]

Gorbachev apparently did. In late November 1989, he told Mitterrand that the day Germany unified, "a Soviet marshal will be sitting in my chair."[15] When movement toward unification began to gain momentum, he bluntly responded to a question about Soviet attitudes toward a united Germany being in NATO: "We cannot agree to that. It is absolutely ruled out."[16]

Some of Gorbachev's harsher public statements came after high-level meetings with either President Bush or Secretary Baker in which the actual discussions, even while reflecting Soviet disquiet over unification, were far more measured. Clearly, Gorbachev was under domestic internal pressure, and for understandable reasons.

No matter how you sliced it, the Soviet Union seemed to be losing. As Vadim Zagladin, Gorbachev's advisor, said, "There used to be two Germanys—one was ours and one was yours. Now there will be one and you want it to be yours."[17] But this was only part of the story. The Soviet position in Eastern Europe was unraveling, and there were increasing challenges emerging within the Soviet Union as Lithuania was pressing for independence. Everywhere Gorbachev looked, perestroika was causing problems, not providing salvation. In such circumstances, he could hardly appear to be acquiescing in a defeat of historical proportions—the removal of one of the major vestiges of the Soviet victory in the Great Patriotic War (as Russians refer to World War II) and its incorporation into the alliance that was arrayed against the USSR.

Moreover, Gorbachev knew he had leverage. He had nearly 400,000 troops in the GDR, a fact that could not be wished away by Washington. Also, the hesitancy toward German unification of other European powers was being publicly expressed, and given the historic posture of the opposition Social Democrats in favor of reaching out to the Soviet Union, Gorbachev had good reason to believe he could play on the German fear of the Soviet opposition to unification. Beyond this, his own direct conversations and communications with Thatcher and Mitterrand made clear that he knew where the British and the French stood on unification. Thatcher told Gorbachev that "although NATO had traditionally made statements supporting Germany's aspiration to be reunited, in practice we were rather apprehensive."[18] Mitterrand was dubious, saying, "Reunification poses so many problems that I shall make up my mind as events occur."[19]

In reality, Thatcher was afraid (as she warned President Bush) that Germany would be "the Japan of Europe, but worse than Japan." She (and Mitterrand too) even worried that "the Germans will get in peace what Hitler couldn't get in war."[20]

Thatcher urged President Bush to focus on democratizing the GDR, not reunification. After Helmut Kohl unveiled a 10-point plan for unification, Thatcher's foreign minister Douglas Hurd said, "I believe that there is a need for an eleventh point which says that nothing will be done to destroy the balance and stability of Europe or create anxiety in the minds of people who have a right to be worried."[21]

In Germany, such fears were bound to resonate domestically. The Social Democratic opposition was particularly sensitive to the anxieties of the neighbors and the Soviets. But it was not just the opposition; Foreign Minister Genscher was also uneasy. In fact, after Soviet foreign minister Eduard Shevardnadze publicly posed seven, obviously negative, questions about reunification, Genscher approvingly cited responses that the newspaper *Bild Zeitung* offered to the Shevardnadze queries—responses that called on Germany to consider abolishing NATO and the Warsaw Pact or reducing the American presence in Germany to a "symbolic contingent."[22] Genscher's ministry was convinced that the Soviets could not accept full NATO membership for a united Germany, and Genscher shared the view of Thatcher and Mitterrand that it was not in America and Europe's collective "interest to defy Gorbachev if success meant the reformer's downfall and the end of perestroika."[23]

If Soviet, British, and French concerns were not enough, the Poles were also uneasy over the issue of Germany's eastern border. The Poles worried a newly reunified Germany, integrated into NATO, would make claims on areas on Poland's western border which had been annexed from Germany after the war. Warsaw certainly added to the obstacles the Bush administration faced as it was trying to achieve its objective.

The Means to Overcome the Obstacles

The obstacles to successful German reunification and integration into NATO were formidable; but even in such circumstances, those who seize the initiative can shape the reality. The Bush administration was poised to do so and had a partner in Helmut Kohl.

Seizing the initiative, however, requires more than just anticipation. It also requires a clear objective that reflects a good reading of the situation and of all the players. And it requires the ability to get out in front on the issue and force others to respond to your formulations and actions.

The day after Helmut Kohl presented his 10-point plan—the plan that would create unification in the form of a federation following a period of confederation—Secretary Baker laid out four principles to guide the approach to unification. The four principles had been drafted by Francis Fukuyama, who was my deputy on the Policy Planning Staff in the State Department. They were: (1) Self-determination for the Germans must be pursued without prejudice to its outcome. No particular vision of unity should be endorsed or excluded; (2) Unification should occur in the context of Germany's continued commitment to NATO, to an increasingly integrated European Community, and with due regard for the legal role and responsibilities of the Allied [Four] powers; (3) Unification should be gradual and peaceful; (4) The inviolability of borders must be respected as stated in the Helsinki Final Act.

This formulation was important and savvy from several standpoints. It addressed the perceived causes of potential instability: timing, pace, and the inviolability of borders. It also addressed, at least implicitly, a role for the Soviets as one of the Four Powers, by referring to their "legal role and responsibilities." It did so before anyone else could shape a definitive response to what Kohl had called for and was announced ahead of President Bush's summit with Gorbachev in Malta, which was extremely important to Gorbachev and one he had no interest in ruining. (Two days after the Malta Summit with Gorbachev, President Bush, with an eye to cementing the four principles as guidelines for unification, repeated them with a slight modification in a speech to a summit of NATO leaders in Brussels.) By framing the issue, the administration provided the basis for how to resolve the unification question and also began a necessary conditioning process for transforming attitudes.

But the administration was not just framing the issue for leaders and senior officials in private. German unification was a very public issue. East Germans essentially rallied around unification and made it a public movement. History made unification a matter of concern for other publics in Europe and the Soviet Union. And no leaders could be indifferent to public concerns or interests. As such, transforming attitudes was an obvious key to overcoming the psychological obstacles to German unification in NATO; reformers' words and actions had to be able to reach out and influence different publics.

Public diplomacy was a crucial tool for identifying with aspirations in Germany, addressing concerns elsewhere, and pointing the way to resolution. Framing was involved, but so was presenting new ways to think about the changes taking place in Europe, particularly in Germany—ways that highlighted new, hopeful possibilities while also taking account of concerns about security and freedom. That was the meaning of Secretary Baker's speech in Berlin, 10 days after the Malta Summit, in which he offered a new architecture for Europe. Baker called for NATO to become more of a political and less of a security alliance, and for new forms of cooperation to make European (East–West) integration a new reality. Later in February, the same logic drove Baker to issue a high-profile public statement to explain the mechanism that had been privately hammered out to manage the unification process. The process, called "Two Plus Four,"(meaning the two Germanies plus the four powers) was designed in part to show Germans the practical means for making unification real, and to assure the Soviets that they would have a place at the table and that any outcome would be shaped by their participation and input.

"Framing" and "public diplomacy" represented one set of tools for overcoming the obstacles. Necessary but not sufficient, they were a complement to the forms of personal and private diplomacy that were required to orchestrate every move with the Germans, manage the hesitancy of the British and the French, and bring the Soviets along to see that their needs would be addressed, particularly as they joined a train that they would not be able to stop.

The diplomatic efforts at the highest levels of the administration were remarkable for their extensive, intensive, and time-consuming nature. The president and the secretary of state conducted a highly personal diplomacy that involved an extraordinary number of face-to-face meetings with other leaders. Phone calls were certainly made, especially in the interim between meetings or to brief other leaders on the meetings that had just taken place with their fellow leaders. This was especially true with both Kohl and Gorbachev. Following a meeting with one, President Bush would place a call to brief the other on where things now stood. These were not perfunctory phone calls; they were highly substantive and were designed to move the process along or address rumors or undo a false impression that might otherwise become rooted and create problems. Though these calls, and meetings at lower levels, were an essential part of the diplomacy, there can be no doubt that the face-to-face meetings at the president's and secretary's level were the heart of the effort.

To give an idea of the scope and intensity of the personal diplomacy of the president and the secretary of state, it is worth noting that President Bush met Chancellor Kohl in either strictly bilateral settings or on the margins of broader multilateral events nine times over a period of roughly one year. (Four of those meetings were in only bilateral settings.) He saw

Prime Minister Thatcher eight times during the same period, and three of those meetings were for exclusively bilateral purposes. He also saw President Mitterrand eight times at many of the same multilateral events, and had two meetings set exclusively for their bilateral discussions. With Gorbachev, he held two high-profile summit meetings during this period.

Baker's meetings were far more numerous, totaling close to 30 separate encounters with each of his German, British, French, and Soviet counterparts—many on the margins of multilateral events during this same time period. Of course, in many cases he visited their capitals for meetings, or they visited Washington. When he visited foreign capitals, he would see not only the foreign minister but also the president or prime minister—and, of course, he would have opportunities to speak publicly in each locale.

I cite the number of meetings—which was extraordinary and certainly has no parallel with any other administration—only to give an indication of the scope of what was involved, but it was the quality of the meetings, and what was accomplished in them, that mattered most. Because the United States was operating on the premise of identifying with the German aspirations even as America managed the fears of the other parties, both the president and the secretary put a premium on coordinating closely with the Germans before dealing with others.

The president's private meetings with Kohl did much not only to win the confidence of the German chancellor but also to bring him along on core questions. Their discussions in Germany in May 1989 (prior to a speech the president made in Kohl's home province) began a process in which President Bush showed his personal sympathy for unification and German aspirations. Their December 3, 1989 meeting in Brussels, which immediately followed the president's December 2-3 Malta summit with Gorbachev,) deepened Kohl's appreciation for Bush's conditioning efforts with the Soviet leader, whose negative remarks had triggered similarly negative comments from Thatcher and Mitterrand at the summit. Finally, inviting Kohl to Camp David in February 1990—the first time a German chancellor had ever been a guest there—was critical for solidifying the Two Plus Four negotiating process (involving the two Germanies plus the United States, Russia, France, and the United Kingdom), and for gaining an unmistakable commitment from the chancellor that unification must take place with the new Germany a full member of NATO.

Meanwhile, within the administration, the one thing the American side feared Gorbachev might do was to offer support for unification conditioned on Germany's strict neutrality. Bush, Baker, and their closest aides all believed neutrality would produce an enduring source of instability and competition between the blocs. Kohl came to understand this American concern but was also convinced that it would take the United States working with Gorbachev—with inducements and reassurance—to get him to go along. Even then, Kohl argued that only directly with Bush could Gorbachev concede on NATO.[24]

In fact, the American–German consultation on the approach to the Soviets was open, candid, and remarkably close. When Baker went to Moscow to see Shevardnadze and Gorbachev in the middle of February 1990, the United States informed the Germans prior to Baker's arrival about what he planned to do and say. With Kohl scheduled to see Gorbachev immediately after our visit, I drafted (before we left Moscow) a detailed letter from Baker to Kohl that summarized what had transpired in the meeting: the key arguments Gorbachev used against unification; Baker's rebuttal; his explanation of why Germany in NATO was in Soviet interests and why a neutral Germany that might feel the need for its own nuclear deterrent was not; and, finally, our suggestions for how Kohl should handle his meeting with Gorbachev both in terms of tone and substance. Kohl later told President Bush that hearing from Baker prior to seeing Gorbachev had been extraordinarily helpful.

While Bush lobbied Kohl, Baker was working on each of his counterparts—Genscher, Hurd, Dumas, and Shevardnadze. Baker used his meetings and phone calls with Hurd and Dumas to mitigate Thatcher's and Mitterrand's opposition. Mitterrand was keen to transform the European Community into the European Union, creating real integration that would allay French fears of German unification. In his eyes, a European Union, with a common currency and common policies, would create a European Germany, not a German-dominated Europe. Here, too, Baker and Bush emphasized their support for European integration, provided Germany was a full member of NATO. As a result, Mitterrand's earlier apprehensions gave way to active support for the American posture on unification in NATO, leaving Thatcher largely isolated. While not happy, she dropped her active opposition.

The Soviets were understandably the most important obstacle, and they required a special effort. The challenge was to balance two conflicting needs: winning Gorbachev's and Shevardnadze's confidence by showing that their concerns about unification would be addressed, while also leaving no doubt that it would be futile and counterproductive to try to prevent unification. Too much emphasis on one part of the equation would undermine the other.

Baker worked intensively to balance these messages for the Soviets. From February to August 1990, Baker saw Shevardnadze nearly every other week at some venue around the world. Of course, a full array of issues—ranging from arms control to bilateral economic relations to the internal changes taking place in the Soviet Union and Eastern Europe—was on the table. But German unification was a centerpiece of nearly every discussion. Bush saw Gorbachev less often but made a point of keeping in regular contact by phone. Bush called Gorbachev after seeing Kohl to brief him on the discussion; at another point, he called him to explain the US initiative to put a ceiling on the numbers of American and Soviet conventional forces in Europe. And his outreach paid off, with Gorbachev telling Bush during the president's call to describe his conversations with Kohl at Camp David, "That is twice [you have called me], and I am in debt. I will have to draw some conclusions from this."[25]

The conclusion Gorbachev drew was that Bush and Baker were committed to helping him make perestroika succeed. This was Gorbachev's highest priority, and he staked everything on it. He was convinced that this could not be achieved without moral support and enormous economic assistance from the West.

Not surprisingly, he had initially worried that President Bush might see the changes taking place in the Soviet Union and Eastern Europe as a sign of weakness that could be exploited. But at the Malta Summit, Bush began by presenting 20 different initiatives on US–Soviet relations, including new proposals for arms control and economic cooperation. Gorbachev responded by saying that he had been looking for tangible expressions of US support—and now he saw it. Bush made a point then (and in subsequent meetings with Gorbachev) to emphasize how he had deliberately understated the US response to the fall of the Berlin Wall—drawing some domestic US criticism for it—so as not to "complicate your life." And Gorbachev said he had noted that and appreciated it.[26,b]

Similarly, in his much more extensive meetings with Gorbachev and Shevardnadze, Baker dealt at length with Soviet fears. In Moscow, Shevardnadze once arrived to a meeting with Baker directly from a Central Committee

---

[b] I was in this meeting, and I could see how Gorbachev's whole demeanor changed as Bush presented his initiatives and they had this exchange.

meeting in which he and Gorbachev had come under personal attack for "weakening" the Soviet Union and bringing great "joy" to Soviet enemies. Baker listened sympathetically and, on this and other occasions, asked about steps the United States could take to help them counter the criticism even as he also reminded him of the importance of standing up to the hardliners.

But Baker was not just offering sympathy and advice. He was also working hard to persuade, explaining why it was important not to single out the Germans or to appear to be trying to deny them their aspirations; why a neutral Germany would feel the need to guarantee its security by having its own nuclear weapons—a result that no Soviet or American leader could want; why the institutions in Europe should be transformed to take account of new realities; and why NATO, in these new circumstances, would not be a threat to the Soviet Union.

Sympathy and persuasion, while important, would likely have fallen on deaf ears if they had not also been accompanied by a serious effort to respond to Soviet needs. And here Baker went to great lengths both to be responsive and to show Gorbachev and Shevardnadze how the United States was being responsive: (1) The United States proposed and produced the mechanism, Two Plus Four, which gave Gorbachev an "explanation," permitting him to show that nothing was being decided without the Soviets or being imposed on them, and that they had a hand in shaping the outcome of unification. (2) The United States put together a package of nine assurances that addressed Soviet concerns on security, political, and economic issues in Europe and Germany. On Germany, specifically, this included both a commitment to have no non-German NATO forces deploy to the former GDR territory and a financial commitment to cover the cost of both of withdrawal of Soviet forces and to build massive new housing for them and their families in the Soviet Union. (3) The United States worked with the Germans to convey a promise from them on the ceiling of forces they would maintain even prior to the round of conventional arms talks in which these limits would be adopted as part of a broader reduction of forces in Central Europe. (4) The United States announced a trade agreement at a time when Gorbachev desperately needed one. With the Soviet economy declining, Gorbachev was convinced the trade deal would provide a significant economic boost, one that was essential both practically and psychologically.

More than anything else, Shevardnadze told Baker that Gorbachev must be able to show his critics that Germany, the United States, and NATO were no longer threats to the Soviet Union. In July of 1990, when the

Communist Party Congress would be held, Gorbachev would need to be able to show that the European landscape had been transformed and that German unification in NATO could not become a new danger to the USSR.

With that in mind, the administration at the most senior levels formulated a declaration for the NATO Summit that would be held in parallel with the Communist Party Congress. President Bush decided to share the draft declaration only with other NATO leaders on the eve of the summit and to have Secretary Baker work on the draft at the summit itself. It would not be in the hands of bureaucrats, and Baker told his NATO counterparts, "We do not need to water down this document. It would be a mistake. We have one shot at this. These are different times. This is not business as usual."[27] Accordingly, the declaration was written in direct political language—not security or bureaucratic jargon. It pronounced a new pathway for NATO and Europe, making nuclear weapons "truly weapons of last resort," eliminating US nuclear artillery; proposing a new, less offensive military strategy; offering further cuts in conventional weapons; inviting the members of the Warsaw Pact to open liaison missions in NATO; and unveiling a declaratory commitment to nonaggression that invited the Warsaw Pact to reciprocate. Years of policy were being reversed in recognition of Gorbachev's needs. To make sure the declaration was produced intact, President Bush had raised the stakes by making leaders responsible for finalizing it and by having his secretary of state preside over the process for adopting it.

Proclaimed during the Party Congress, the declaration had the desired effect of undermining Gorbachev's challengers who were charging that Gorbachev, by surrendering a huge asset in the GDR, was increasing the danger that an aggressive and hostile NATO would now pose to the USSR. Shevardnadze told Baker that the new NATO doctrine exposed Gorbachev's critics, robbing them of their main argument, and he added, "Without the declaration, it would have been a very difficult thing for us to take our decisions on Germany ... you compare what we're saying to you and to Kohl now with our Berlin document, it's like day and night. Really it is heaven and earth."[28]

The Berlin document that Shevardnadze referred to was actually a speech he made at a ministerial meeting of the Two Plus Four on June 22, 1990 (the forty-ninth anniversary of the German invasion of the Soviet Union). In it, he retreated from understandings on unification that had been reached over the preceding three weeks: a Soviet agreement to respect German sovereignty upon unification, and Soviet acknowledgment that Germany was free to choose which, if any, alliance it wanted to join. In Berlin,

Shevardnadze declared the opposite: the Four Power rights would remain even after unification, and for a five-year transition period Germany would remain split between NATO and the Warsaw Pact, with the alliance issue remaining open after that.

How was it possible to manage the situation, given such a reversal? By using one other mechanism or tool that was critical to maintaining and lubricating the high-level personal diplomacy of the president and the secretary—special back channels. In this case, my relationship with Sergei Tarasenko—Shevardnadze's chief assistant and confidant—proved indispensable. Normally, I would coordinate with Tarasenko before the leaders' or secretaries' meetings to avoid surprises or to find out where there were problems that would have to be managed; in this case we had not had the opportunity to do so. When I rushed to see Tarasenko after the Berlin speech to find out what had happened, he explained that Shevardnadze had been forced to present a Politburo-drafted statement, and that he and Gorbachev would act on the previous understandings as long as the United States was tough in response to this statement and could deliver clearly on the changed nature of NATO by the time of the Party Congress.

On this and other occasions, the back channel with Tarasenko made it possible to understand a Soviet move and how US or German responses might affect the maneuverings in Moscow; it allowed all sides to explain what they could and could not do; and it also permitted them to design the words and actions that each of the sides could use to help the other, knowing when the timing was right to take a new step or respond to a challenge. There were other back channels with the Germans—Robert Blackwill, at the National Security Council, worked discreetly with Horst Teltschik, Chancellor Kohl's national security advisor, while Robert Zoellick built a very close relationship with Frank Elbe, Hans-Dietrich Genscher's right-hand man. (At certain junctures, the US side would put Tarasenko and Elbe together to try to ameliorate German–Soviet problems and prepare for crucial meetings.)

The back channels enabled everyone involved to prevent misunderstandings, to manage them when they occurred, and to condition attitudes of decision-makers in private. Without the back channels, the trust that was required to manage the process would have been far more difficult to achieve.

Of course, the ability to build trust also depended on the character of the personal diplomacy conducted by the US president and his secretary, who were each active in solving problems that emerged at different points.

President Bush secretly mediated the German–Polish problems on their border, problems created by Kohl's hesitancy stemming from political considerations ahead of Germany's election. To defuse the issue, President Bush called Kohl prior to Polish prime minister Tadeusz Mazowiecki's visit to the White House and worked out language on the border issue that Kohl would discreetly commit to, and that Bush would privately show Mazowiecki, with the American assurance that this language would be incorporated into a German–Polish treaty after unification. Mazowiecki accepted Bush's assurance.[c]

Before concluding the case of German unification in NATO, there is one other point worth clarifying, and it relates to how statecraft was conducted there and the promises or assurances that were offered to Gorbachev to make it easier for him to accept the transition. In Chapter 1, I cited Putin's argument that Europeans and the United States betrayed the promise, made at the time of German unification, not to expand NATO to the east.[29] While it is true that Baker promised that NATO forces would not be placed into East Germany—and specifically into the areas that the Soviet military was leaving—he made no promise about no expansion elsewhere.[30] I was with him when he promised Gorbachev, speaking only in the context of German unification, that there "would be no extension of NATO's jurisdiction for forces of NATO one inch to the east." This was not east as it related to areas outside of Germany or to Eastern Europe. Putin may seek to take this out of context, but recall the timing of this promise: in the spring of 1990 the Warsaw Pact had not yet collapsed. Baker was talking only about Germany, and in the final treaty that unified Germany, foreign troops were barred from being deployed to what had been East Germany. German forces that were part of NATO could deploy there only in 1994—the point at which Soviet troops had to be out of the former GDR territory.

The issue of NATO expansion into Eastern Europe was not even something contemplated at the time. The Soviet Union had not collapsed, and the United States was not thinking about weakening it. Baker's promise was tied to German unification and Soviet force withdrawals from the territory that would now be part of the new Germany. Later, the Clinton administration would make the decision to expand NATO because Eastern European countries had withdrawn from the Warsaw Pact, and it had literally evaporated.

---

[c] Baker, too, quietly worked to defuse the crisis over Lithuania's declaration of independence, getting Gorbachev to open a dialogue in return for the Lithuanians "freezing" their declaration.

Eastern European publics wanted to be part of the West, and these governments sought to join the Western alliance. For some, especially in Poland, there was a fear of a Soviet/Russian resurgence—but in the 1990s, within the Clinton administration, that seemed hard to imagine.

Conclusion

American statecraft in producing German unification in NATO was successful for multiple reasons: the Bush administration at the highest levels anticipated the issue and put it in the larger context of sweeping changes in the landscape of Europe; it developed a clear objective and forged deep trust with the main driver in the process, the German chancellor; it moved quickly to gain control of the agenda and it framed the issue for all to deal with; it used public diplomacy not to shape US image abroad but to reinforce how the United States framed the problem by appealing to different European publics in terms they could understand; it reflected the enormous time and the energy the president and the secretary of state spent in personal diplomacy with their counterparts; it used back channels to underpin and smooth the personal diplomacy and to avoid misunderstandings; it developed a mechanism (Two Plus Four) to steer the unification issue and create a basis for resolving the legal and political problems; and it managed those parties most likely to be able to derail the process (principally the Soviets) by combining responsiveness and firmness, and ensuring that Gorbachev and Shevardnadze had a public and private "explanation" for the process and the outcome.

Notwithstanding this concerted and deliberate effort, the process of German unification relied on good fortune and luck, too. While the administration certainly read Gorbachev well and, as in all good statecraft, developed and used its leverage effectively, Gorbachev was indecisive and failed to use Soviet leverage to force the United States to change or modify its objectives. He made tough statements from time to time, but he assumed that the British and the French would do more to oppose unification and certainly would not give a unified Germany full membership in NATO. He overestimated their readiness to resist the American president and slow the diplomatic onslaught that the United States created. And he was reluctant to create a crisis with the United States or Germany because his priority was perestroika, and he needed American and German support.

Luck and timing are often a part of dealing effectively with any issue. The more effectively leaders position themselves, the more effectively they anticipate events and read circumstances, the more likely they will be to take advantage of moments, and the "luckier" they may be. And here, knowing when to act may be as important as how one chooses to act. In other words, timing is critical. Maybe the best way to capture the meaning of timing is with an apt analogy: timing is to statecraft what location is to real estate. Seizing moments is critical. By definition, moments of opportunity do not last and can easily be lost. The very concept of a window of opportunity is bound by time; fail to act, and the window closes.

Nowhere was this truth more clearly revealed than in the case of German unification. The critical Soviet Communist Party Congress and NATO Summit came in July 1990. On August 2, Iraq invaded and seized Kuwait. Had the invasion come on May 1, would the president of the United States and his secretary of state have been able to devote the time, effort, energy, and resources to German unification? There can be little doubt about the answer to this question. As it happened, the pursuit of unification and the trust that was developed with Gorbachev and Shevardnadze strengthened America's hand in dealing with what has become known as the first Gulf War. Before turning to that case and its contrasts with the lead-up to the war with Iraq in 2003, let me first discuss another European case: the collapse of Yugoslavia, the war in Bosnia, and that war's resolution.

Chapter 6
Bosnia: Finally Getting it Right

During the Cold War, Yugoslavia was a unique Communist country in Europe. It did not share a border with the Soviet Union; it fought Nazi occupation during World War II, led by a partisan Josip Broz Tito, who subsequently became its leader; and it was not liberated by the Soviet army. Tito broke with Stalin after the war, unwilling to be simply a tool of the Soviet leader. As the leader of Yugoslavia, Tito was a fierce nationalist, determined to keep Yugoslavia unified as one country and free of Soviet domination. While his strongman and strong-arm rule might have held Yugoslavia's diverse ethnic groups together in their respective republics, the pressures for disintegration grew in the decade following Tito's death in 1980.

Serb nationalism, in particular, became an increasingly potent force and was used by Slobodan Milošević to build his power and his following in Serbia. His language invoking Greater Serbia incited passions among Serbs who had historically felt victimized, and it played on the fears and the separatist impulses of the Croats, Slovenians, and Bosnian Muslims. But his actions were not limited only to orations; using the Yugoslav National Army (a force that came to be dominated by the Serbs), he began to arm ethnic Serbs and form large paramilitary forces, especially in the Serbian parts of Croatia and Bosnia. By the early 1990, there were frequent skirmishes in Croatia and a strong independence movement in Slovenia.

Independence in Slovenia could not be viewed in isolation; in the Bush administration, there was a recognition that if Slovenia declared itself independent, it would trigger other cascading developments: Croatia would likely follow suit; Serbia would undoubtedly try to separate the Serb part of Croatia and join it to Serbia and act to do the same in Bosnia. For its part, Croatia might also seek to take the part of Bosnia dominated ethnically by Croats. In short, the Yugoslav experts in the administration understood that Slovenia's declaration of independence would set in motion not just the unraveling of Yugoslavia but also a widening civil conflict. And yet in the early 1990 when visiting Belgrade, Deputy Secretary of State Lawrence Eagleburger, in commenting on how the United States would respond to

Statecraft 2.0. Second Edition. Dennis Ross, Oxford University Press. © Oxford University Press (2025). DOI: 10.1093/oso/9780197698914.003.0006

a Slovenian declaration of independence, said that while the United States hoped Slovenia would not leave the federation, America would not do anything to force it to reverse its policy.[1]

No one in the administration was more aware of the likely consequences of Slovenia declaring independence than Larry Eagleburger. Earlier in his career, he had served as America's ambassador to Belgrade. He understood well what might happen, but was dubious that much could be done either to persuade the Slovenians not to proceed or to prevent the inevitable events that would lead to conflict as a result. Moreover, he was convinced that intervening in this conflict was a mistake, believing that it was a civil war which the United States could affect only at great cost. Given Eagleburger's expertise on Yugoslavia, his views carried special weight within the administration.

To be fair to Eagleburger, he was not operating in a vacuum. He was well aware that the unfolding drama in Yugoslavia was more a sideshow for the US president and the secretary of state than a main event. Their preoccupation was managing the transition in the Soviet Union and ending the Cold War; they focused on Gorbachev and how to respond to his needs even while they were working with the states of Eastern Europe newly freed from the Soviet grip. They looked to develop a new security architecture to shape a world no longer governed by the realities of the Cold War.

Perhaps the disintegration of Yugoslavia, with the potential for civil war, ethnic cleansing, refugee flows, and even the spread of conflict, should have been seen by the administration as a threat to the institutions they hoped to construct in the new Europe. However, this presupposed a full appreciation of how costly the war in Yugoslavia would become. While Deputy Secretary Eagleburger believed the situation was bad and was going to get worse, he and the administration's decision-makers viewed the conflict as localized. It might have tragic consequences for the Bosnians in particular, but the war was unlikely to spread and engage America's broader stakes in Europe. In light of America's other priorities, it was not worth the investment.

Secretary Baker shared the view that, unlike in the Persian Gulf, US vital national interests were not at stake. He later wrote, "The Yugoslav conflict had the potential to be intractable, but it was nonetheless a regional dispute. Milošević had Saddam's appetite, but Serbia did not have Iraq's capabilities or ability to affect America's vital interests, such as access to energy supplies. The greater threat to American interests at the time lay in the increasingly dicey situation in Moscow, and we preferred to maintain our focus on that challenge."[2] So America's focus remained elsewhere as Yugoslavia moved toward disintegration and then, in 1991, devolved quickly into conflict.

Limited Objectives, Many Obstacles

"Avoidance" is the term that best describes the Bush administration's objective as it faced the disintegration of Yugoslavia and the emergence of separate states. In fact, the Bush administration's response to the breakup of Yugoslavia and the war in Bosnia was shaped by its perception of the costs of American involvement—and those convinced President Bush and Secretary of State Baker to stay on the sidelines of the conflict. Aside from rhetorical support for efforts to stop the fighting, there was no real stomach for a serious intervention, even one that was only diplomatic. Five factors drove the Bush administration's objectives and approach to Bosnia.

First, as Secretary Baker indicated, the United States had other priorities. The Soviet Union, America's main preoccupation and rival for more than 40 years, was going through a transition. Its leader, who sought partnership with the United States, was under increasing threat, and the country itself appeared on the verge of unraveling. With thousands of nuclear weapons in Soviet arsenals, it was understandable that President Bush and Secretary Baker would be focused on the USSR. It was the "dicey situation in Moscow," with its "global ramifications" that constituted a greater threat than Yugoslavia's disintegration.[3] Besides the concern of what would happen in the Soviet Union, there was also the sense of possibility in the Middle East after the Gulf War; as Baker would later say, "in the summer of 1991, we were already consumed by the Middle East peace process and close to getting the parties to the table."[4]

Second, the administration's leaders felt that Yugoslavia was a European problem and should be handled by the Europeans. With the Cold War ending, the Europeans were looking to solidify a separate identity and to assume clear responsibilities on the Continent at a time when plans for European integration (known as "EC-92") were in the offing and presaged the transformation of the European Community (EC) into the European Union (EU). European ministers were very open about this identity and responsibility. Jacques Poos, foreign minister of Luxembourg, spoke on behalf of the EC when he said about Yugoslavia, "This is the hour of Europe; it is not the hour of America."[5] If European leaders were anxious to demonstrate their capacity through the existing EC mechanisms to handle problems, the Bush admin-istration was only too happy to let them deal with the Yugoslav crisis. John Shalikashvili, who served as chair of the Joint Chiefs of Staff following his stint as the American four-star general commanding NATO, later described this reality very clearly: "We forget this now, but everywhere you went in Europe in 1991 and 1992 there was this enormous optimism about what the new Europe could do ... The Europeans would handle this one, they were saying, and the Americans, who had just finished the Gulf war and were play-ing out their role as the overseer in the end of the Soviet empire, were only too glad to accommodate them."[6]

Third, the administration feared that to prevent Yugoslavia's disintegra-tion and conflict would take a military intervention, and for Larry Eagle-burger and Colin Powell, Shalikashvili's predecessor as chair of the Joint Chiefs of Staff, it looked like Vietnam all over again. Each feared that the United States would be dragged into an ethnically driven conflict that would know no end, that would inflict high casualties on US forces, and that the American public and political leaders would tire of very quickly.[7] While there were some in the military, such as Chief of Staff of the Air Force Mer-rill McPeak, who believed that American air power could make quick work of the Serbs as they escalated the conflict in 1991, they were in the minor-ity. Powell, especially, viewed airstrikes as the first step on a slippery slope toward a quagmire. The last thing he wanted after the first Gulf War, which seemed to have ended the Vietnam syndrome, was to be sucked into a messy civil war again. As he wrote in a *New York Times* op-ed in 1992, "You bet I get nervous when so-called experts suggest that all we need is a little surgical bombing or a limited attack. When the desired result isn't obtained, a new set of experts then comes forward with talk of a little escalation. History has not been kind to this approach."[8]

Fourth, the administration's leaders had been going full bore, moving seamlessly from one crisis to the next since the onset of the Yugoslav conflict. When Larry Eagleburger was in Yugoslavia in February 1990, the presi-dent, Jim Baker, and their teams were in the midst of working intensively on German unification (which I discussed in Chapter 5). The high point of that German unification process passed just prior to Saddam's invasion of Kuwait, which kept them all absorbed until the spring of 1991, when the internal pressures and economic/political challenges experienced by Gorbachev became far more acute. When the Serbian siege of Dubrovnik occurred in the beginning of October 1991, Secretary Baker was consumed with the aftermath of the failed coup against Gorbachev and with putting together the Madrid peace conference. In short, it was not only other preoccupations that precluded involvement in the unfolding Yugoslav disaster—it was also fatigue. Taking on a conflict that was seen as largely localized, as someone else's problem, and too hard in any case, was simply more than the Bush administration—whose leaders were already emotionally and intellectually drained—was ready to contemplate.

Fifth, there were also domestic political realities. By 1992, with his poll numbers dropping in no small part because he seemed interested only in foreign policy and not domestic needs, the last thing President Bush needed was to look like he was going to go to war over another distant problem.

The Bush Administration's Limited Means

Notwithstanding the many factors limiting the Bush administration's involvement in Bosnia, it did make a belated effort to stem the violent breakup of Yugoslavia. As violence grew in 1991, and efforts by the EC to mediate the conflict yielded little, Secretary Baker made a one-day trip to Belgrade to see if it was possible to forestall the impending scenario of unilateral declarations of independence and the almost certain civil war that would ensue. In what amounted to a shuttle in one building, he met with the leaders of each of the republics and encountered strange fatalism from some of his interlocutors and outright lying from others—such as Milošević, who denied arming paramilitary Serb forces and fomenting ethnic conflict. While Baker pleaded to avoid unilateral actions and warned Milošević of the consequences of promoting violence, there were no teeth in the warnings.

One day's commitment to discussions was unlikely to have much effect on any of the leaders, and it did not. Still, it was not too late to prevent Milošević's ethnic cleansing, even though he was becoming increasingly brazen in spelling out his intentions. During the same month of Baker's visit, Milošević had lunch with the EC ambassadors and told them that if Yugoslavia broke up, he would carve out a new Serbia. He explained that he cared little about Slovenia but he would add the Serb-populated areas of Bosnia, Croatia (especially Krajina), and Montenegro to a Greater Serbia.[9] Milošević undoubtedly was testing what the likely response would be to taking territories from his neighbors as Yugoslavia dissolved, and he soon found out that egregious actions on the part of the Serbs would provoke little reaction.

In early October 1991, Serb forces imposed a siege and inflicted a prolonged artillery and naval bombardment on Dubrovnik. It was a signal event, a test for Milošević to see what he could get away with before facing an international reaction. Though Dubrovnik did not present a difficult military problem, with Serb artillery and naval guns highly vulnerable, there was no Western military reaction. Soon, a more cruel and brutal Serbian assault against the Croat city of Vukovar set in motion a deepening pattern of ethnic cleansing.

As violence between Serbs and Croats worsened in 1991, the UN Security Council adopted a resolution calling for an end to the conflict and imposing an arms embargo on all parties in Yugoslavia—a response that put the aggressor and victim in the same category. When the UN negotiators worked out a cease-fire in Croatia in early 1992, with Krajina under Serbian control, the Yugoslav National Army moved its armor and artillery forces from Croatia to Bosnia. While Croatia was not landlocked and could get arms, the same was not true for the Bosnian Muslims—who remained largely at the mercy of both Serbs and Croats.

When the Slovenian and Croatian declarations of independence came in 1992, with the encouragement of the Germans and the Italians, the conflict widened. By late spring, the signs of ethnic cleansing became more apparent and more gruesome, especially in Bosnia. With the systematic bombings of the Bosnian capital, Sarajevo, and the exposure by journalists of Serb-created concentration camps, the killings of all Muslim males in some Bosnian villages, and the expulsion of Muslims in others, the Bush administration supported efforts by the UN to rein in the Serbs, impose economic sanctions on them, and provide some protection and humanitarian assistance to the Bosnians. But the UN forces that were sent were small in number (12,000 in all), and their mandate was weak and very limited. The so-called UN protection force (UNPROFOR) offered little protection in practice, and the US military remained deeply averse to any involvement in Bosnia. By late 1992, the Serb irregulars and the Bosnian Serb army that Milošević had created had seized a great deal of Bosnian territory and forced 750,000 Muslims from their homes.

With the atrocities no longer hidden from public view, and shocking pictures of the concentration camps appearing in the summer of 1992, presidential candidate Bill Clinton denounced the Bush administration for standing by and doing little in the face of gross human rights violations and Serb aggression. He called for a change in policy, and supported air strikes against Serbs and an end to the arms embargo against the Bosnian Muslims, the main victims at this juncture of Serb aggression.

In effect, Clinton as the presidential candidate was calling for a policy of "lift and strike": lift the arms embargo that had been voted by the UN Security Council but punished the weak Bosnians far more than the arms-laden Serbs, and strike the Serb forces using significant air power. However, not only did the Bush administration and the US military oppose such a policy, but also US allies—particularly the British, the French, and the Dutch, who made up the bulk of UNPROFOR—were dead set against any such posture. Their forces were on the ground and were too small to protect the Muslims, and unfortunately too weak even to protect themselves from retribution by Serb forces.

Nonetheless, after the 1992 election, Secretary of State Lawrence Eagleburger sought to get the Bush administration to adopt the lift-and-strike policy and was authorized to sound out the Europeans on the idea. They rejected it, but there was one final warning—this time one that implied real coercion—before President Bush left office. In what became known as the Christmas warning, President Bush, in a message to Milošević, warned that, "In the event of conflict in Kosovo caused by Serbian action, the United States will be prepared to employ military force against Serbians in Kosovo and in Serbia proper."[10] Kosovo, an enclave along the Albanian border with a population that was 90 percent Albanian and 10 percent Serb, had deep historic meaning to the Serbs. It was the place where in 1389 Serbs had committed suicide rather than surrender to the Turks. It was where Milošević had played on the Serbian sense of injustice to build his own following around the Serb nationalist calling. But it was also a place that could easily trigger a war with Albania and a broader conflict in the Balkans as a whole.

Here the Bush administration drew a clear red line. Had such a warning been made over Bosnia, Milošević might have contained his ambitions and spared his people and the Muslims enormous pain and suffering. Instead, the Clinton administration inherited the Kosovo warning and a Bosnia that was increasingly controlled by Serb forces with atrocities and ethnic cleansing continuing against the Muslims.

It also inherited the so-called Vance–Owen plan for ending the conflict in Bosnia. Former Secretary of State Cyrus Vance and former British Foreign Secretary David Owen were UN envoys who made an effort to negotiate an end to the fighting. They put together a plan that would have created 10 cantons in Bosnia: three with a Serb majority, two with a Croat majority, three with a Muslim majority, one mixed Croat–Muslim, and a special canton for Sarajevo. The Bush administration had quietly supported the plan, seeing it as the best possible solution available and one likely to stop the bloodshed at a time when no one was prepared to take tough measures against the Serbs.

In the end, avoidance was clearly the objective; as a result, the administration supported the efforts of others to stop the fighting, even as it minimized its own involvement. The administration left the heavy lifting to the international community, which was similarly disinclined to protect Bosnia. The Christmas warning indicated that had the Bush administration viewed Bosnia in a different light, perhaps a different outcome could have occurred. But since it did not perceive Bosnia as a serious problem—or at least one in which the United States did not have serious stakes—there was no political will to intervene. As such, the Bush administration behaved uncharacteristically in this case, lacked effective statecraft, and left the cleanup to the next administration.

The Clinton Administration's Approach: New Objective, Similar Means

The new Clinton administration, however, did not like the Vance–Owen plan. For Clinton and those around him, the plan legitimized Serb gains made through a genocidal policy. While the administration was unwilling to attack the plan publicly, its coolness to it was unmistakable, and when the State Department spokesman, Richard Boucher, refused to comment on whether the Vance–Owen plan ratified ethnic cleansing, Owen later wrote that the no-comment answer was the equivalent of rubbing "salt in the wound."[11]

But if the president and his team wanted to change the policy, they failed to devise a plan for achieving the objective of ending the fighting in Bosnia. Confronting many of the same obstacles or constraints that their predecessors had faced, the Clinton administration lacked the will to act effectively in the Balkans. Implementing any kind of change on the ground would have required a pronounced diplomatic initiative to organize European allies of the United States behind such action, willingness to deploy America's own military assets into the theater of conflict, and bureaucratic unity within the administration to implement decisions. From 1993 to 1995, the Clinton policy toward Bosnia contained none of these components at a level necessary to counter the increasingly deadly civil war in that country.

The US military was against getting involved; America's allies, who had troops on the ground, opposed the lifting of the arms embargo, fearing that their forces would bear the brunt of more severe fighting in escalating confrontation. An American call for greater military pressure against the Serbs rang hollow, as the new administration was not prepared to put its forces at risk, and the European forces were the ones exposed to the expected Serb retaliation. America's allies were open to a shift in policy only if the United States was prepared to assume the military burden and cost.

It might have been one thing to talk about such a shift in the campaign; it was another to implement it in office. Rather than launch a new policy, the Clinton administration launched a review of US policy in the Balkans. The review took three months and reflected the old divisions within the new administration. Some, most notably at the State Department and at the National Security Council, saw the stakes in moral and national security terms of allowing Bosnian Serb ethnic cleansing to go unchecked, and favored using force against the Serbs. Others, most notably the military, led by Chair of the Joint Chiefs Colin Powell, opposed any use of force, citing the likelihood of a quagmire. At the end of the review, the conclusion appeared to embrace the policy that Clinton had supported as the presidential candidate: namely, lift and strike. Lift the arms embargo and provide Bosnian Muslims the arms to defend themselves; and using air power, strike decisively at Bosnian Serb and Serbian forces and infrastructure as necessary.

However, this posture was essentially a slogan—more rhetorical than real. Indeed, in May 1993, Secretary of State Christopher went to Europe to sound out the Europeans on lift and strike. The operative words are *sound out*; he went to consult and try to persuade, not to present a policy that the United States was prepared to implement, particularly if it meant any US military involvement. Perhaps if he had gone to inform the allies of America's new approach and how it intended to carry this approach out, the reaction might have been different. But if he was asking and not telling, then the answers were bound to be starkly negative, and they were. At every stop starting in London, Secretary Christopher heard clear rejections of lift and strike. Lifting the embargo would require revoking a Security Council resolution, and an increased flow of arms would only lead to an escalation in fighting that the British, the French, and the Dutch feared would ensnare their troops already on the ground. Adding air strikes against Serbs to that mix would only ensure Serb retaliation against the international contingent in Bosnia. If the United States wanted to shift the policy, it would have to take the lead with its own military forces being exposed to the consequences.

Secretary Christopher returned, declaring to President Clinton that lift and strike as a policy could be implemented only if the president was prepared to insist on it with the allies and enforce it with American forces. But at this stage of his administration, the president had other priorities. It was his domestic agenda that mattered—"it's the economy, stupid" was the refrain that had elected Clinton—and he was not about to squander his political capital on an issue in which he faced the very clear opposition of the US military and of Chair of the Joint Chiefs of Staff Colin Powell. Powell, the hero of the first Gulf War, was in his last year as chair and he, not Clinton, had stature on national security issues.

If anything, Clinton's reluctance to invest political capital on Bosnia—notwithstanding his posture during the presidential campaign—made Christopher even more reluctant to press for greater US involvement. Instead, after Christopher's European trip, the policy became one of containment of the conflict, even as the rhetoric remained tough toward the Serbs.

Limited Objective, Limited Means

Unfortunately, Serb aggression against Bosnian Muslims continued, with sieges and bombardment of Muslim cities and towns. The administration's options remained very constrained. Unwilling to risk alliance cohesion for the sake of Bosnia, hamstrung by the Pentagon's opposition to any role for US forces, stung by the imagery of Black Hawk Down in Somalia and the inglorious American withdrawal of forces, and constrained by the president's increased hesitancy to invest in Bosnia, the administration looked for ways to increase leverage on Serbia at a low cost.

One mechanism for doing so was the forging of a Croat–Muslim federation, and the administration succeeded in facilitating such a union in 1994. In the words of Secretary of State Christopher, "The two sides needed to turn their energies against the stronger and more threatening adversary, the Bosnian Serbs."[12] The federation was designed to create common cause between Croats and Muslims, both of whom had lost or were losing ground to Serb offensives, but the Croatian president's dislike of the Muslims made this a difficult basis on which to build leverage against the Serbs. Nonetheless, it did make a difference over time as Franjo Tudjman, the president of Croatia, permitted arms to reach the Muslims—of course, with the Croats keeping some of them for themselves. Later in 1995, with the Bihać pocket in Bosnia surrounded by the Serbs and with a slaughter of Muslims in the offing, the Muslims and Croats forged a common front. They fought against the Serbs, with the Croats, in particular, taking advantage of the Serbs' being overextended, and began to turn the tide of battle on the ground.

The administration sought to build leverage in other ways as well. In an effort to improve coordination and present a more united front against Serbia, the administration created a new forum called the Contact Group. It consisted of the United States, the United Kingdom, France, Germany, and the Russians. If nothing else, the messages to Milošević and the Serbs would be more in sync and would include the Serbs' traditional friends and protectors, the Russians. By July 1994, the Contact Group developed a peace plan, with a detailed map that placed 51 percent of Bosnia under the Croat–Muslim federation and 49 percent for the Bosnian Serbs. The Muslims and Croats accepted the plan—after all, they would be recovering roughly 20 percent of the territory that had been lost—and the Serbs rejected it. Nonetheless, the plan remained a focal point of Contact Group efforts.

In addition to forging the Croat–Muslim federation and the Contact Group, the administration also sought to pressure the Serbs through at least limited use of air power. While not being able to persuade the Europeans to accept the policy of lift and strike, the administration did win support for NATO air strikes in response to Serb threats against the six Muslim enclaves in Bosnia that had been designated as safe areas by UNPROFOR. There was a price, however: in order to support the US proposal, the Europeans required the creation of a dual-key arrangement whereby both NATO and the UN had to sign off on when, where, and how such air strikes would occur before they could be authorized. In reality, dual-keys became an inhibitor, not a facilitator, of air strikes, as the UN machinery was rarely willing to go along with the proposed strikes. Even when they were agreed upon—as in the case of Serb threats and the shelling of Bihać, one of the safe areas, in November 1994—the air strikes were so limited as to be described as "pinpricks."

If it was not the difficulty of reaching agreement in NATO and with the UN high command, it was the concern about triggering retaliation against the British, the French, or the Dutch forces that limited the application of air power even when air strikes might have been approved in response to Serb threats. By 1995, the fear of Serb retaliation was replaced by the fear of the Serbs taking UNPROFOR troops as hostages—which the Serbs did in the spring of 1995 when air strikes against Serb ammunition dumps and weapons were authorized in response to renewed Bosnian Serb shelling of Sarajevo. The Serbs seized more than 350 UN peacekeepers and chained them to ammo dumps and bridges—possible targets of the air strikes. Rather than being frightened by very limited air strikes, which basically signaled how little the international forces were prepared to do, the Serbs began to turn the UN peacekeepers into human shields to protect what they valued from any such attacks. That ended the air strikes, since protecting UN forces became more important than protecting the Bosnians and made the safe areas safe only for Serb attacks.

As the humiliation of UN forces became more pronounced, the frustration within the administration became more acute. When Jacques Chirac, the new president of France, declared that the humiliation of French forces was unacceptable, there was pressure from the French to increase the number of troops on the ground—at least to be able to protect themselves. Chirac's insistence at the G-7 meeting that a new policy must be implemented in Bosnia helped to foster a new look at options within the Clinton administration.

Both Warren Christopher and National Security Advisor Tony Lake began looking at alternatives built around not pulling the UN forces out but rather securing them, and tying a more secure presence to a push for a comprehensive diplomatic solution in Bosnia. Lake, in particular, generated options for producing an endgame diplomatically.

Any serious diplomatic effort to solve the Bosnian problem, however, required having serious leverage on the Serbs, and that was still missing. But that was about to change, as the Serbs overplayed their hand and the Croats began effectively using their military forces for the first time.

More Ambitious Objective, More Ambitious Means

President Clinton's frustration had grown with a policy that left the United States appearing weak and irresolute; in response to his increasing anger over the choices he was being left with, the administration began to wrestle with possible ways to change what Secretary Christopher described as the "problem from hell."

Coincident with the administration exploring new options, on July 6, 1995, the Serbs launched a brutal new assault—on Srebrenica, a "safe area" protected by a Dutch contingent of UNPROFOR, and on its population of 40,000 Muslims. As the onslaught worsened, the Dutch forces initially watched, and then fled. NATO belatedly bombed a few Serb sites, but it was too little and too late. By July 11, the Serbs had seized Srebrenica, and five days later they had killed 7,000 Muslim men and boys. Not satisfied with having absorbed Srebrenica, the Serbs seemed poised to go after two other supposedly protected areas—Žpa and Goražde.

Srebrenica was too much to swallow. The Pentagon's civil and military leaders—Secretary William Perry and Chair of the Joint Chiefs John Shalikashvili—both saw the massacre as a decisive turning point. Now each felt that for the United States and NATO not to respond would put the alliance and America's standing in the world at risk. For Shalikashvili, the moral fabric of the West and NATO was literally at stake. If the United States was reluctant to act before because its actions might have torn NATO apart, now Shalikashvili feared that America's failure to respond would threaten NATO's future. Perry saw the challenge in similar terms, saying, "The issue was not taking [UN] peace-keepers hostage, the issue was taking the whole policy of the international community hostage."[13] Previously, it was the Pentagon's leadership that resisted more aggressive policies in Bosnia; now they were prepared to take the lead in creating new rules, with Perry saying that the answer to a threat to Goražde or any other safe area must not be pinpricks but a "massive air campaign."

John Major called a conference to respond to the shock of Srebrenica, and the Clinton administration prepared the ground for a new approach militarily, with President Clinton telling French president Chirac that any attack on the safe areas should be met by a sustained air campaign designed to "cripple" the Serb military capability. The London conference, with some arm-twisting by the administration still required, produced a new consensus on what became known as the "Goražde rules": any Serb attacks against the safe areas would be met by sustained and decisive use of air power throughout Bosnia. To facilitate such responses, the dual-key system would be modified by removing civilian UN officials from the decision-making process.[14]

Although ironing out how the Goražde rules would work in practice still proved difficult, involving a 13-hour meeting of the NATO foreign ministers to nail down the specifics, a clear threshold had been crossed. Srebrenica in this sense triggered a profound change in how Serb aggression would be dealt with by the United States and its allies. Two other factors combined to transform the realities in Bosnia fundamentally.

First, the fortunes of the war changed dramatically on the ground. The Serbs not only overplayed their hand before the world, finally going too far and triggering a response, but they were also overstretched with their forces. When the Croats came to the defense of Bihać on July 25, they made quick work of the Bosnian Serb forces. Soon thereafter, the Croats launched an offensive against the Bosnian Serb forces in Krajina, the Croatian area taken by the Serbs in 1991; even though the State Department had urged the Croats not to widen the war, the latter soon successfully forced the Serb forces and civilians to flee Krajina. By early August, "for the first time in the four-year Balkan conflict, the Serbs had suffered a significant military defeat."[15] Suddenly, the balance of forces on the ground had changed.

Second, the administration also decided to go for a diplomatic solution to the conflict. Almost simultaneously with the Croat offensive, the administration considered certain "endgame" papers for bringing the conflict to a conclusion. The president saw an opening and believed, in his words, that we needed to "bust our ass to get a settlement in the next few months ... We've got to exhaust every alternative, roll every die, take risks ... If we let this moment slip away, we are history."[16]

From July to August 1995, the dynamics in Bosnia were transformed. Instead of the Muslims being on the brink of defeat in Bihać, with other safe areas about to fall and with talk increasing of having to withdraw UNPRO-FOR in humiliation, suddenly the Serbs were on the run, losing territory; the West for the first time was ready to threaten the meaningful use of force; and the Clinton administration was about to present a comprehensive plan for settling the conflict.

Not only did the administration formulate a seven-point plan for ending the conflict, but National Security Advisor Tony Lake took an interagency delegation with him to Europe to present the plan. Unlike Christopher, Lake was not going to consult on the virtue of the plan; he was going to inform Europeans of what the United States had decided and how it would proceed. Like James Baker during the first Gulf War, Lake would ask in private for their support of a plan that would go ahead whether or not European countries were prepared to go along with the United States.

This time the European leaders, given four years of warfare, with 300,000 deaths and 1.2 million refugees, were ready to admit that they could not deal with Bosnia and were ready to follow the American lead. Everywhere the Lake team went they found strong support for a plan that drew on the Contact Group's 51:49 solution: a unified Bosnian state with two autonomous entities involving the Croat–Muslim federation and the Bosnian Serbs who had a special relationship with Serbia; and a readiness to end the sanctions regime against Serbia and produce a broad economic reconstruction plan as part of a diplomatic settlement.

Moreover, for the first time, embedded in the plan was a serious combination of carrots and sticks to be employed with all sides. If the Muslims cooperated and the Serbs blocked an agreement, the embargo on arms to the Muslims would be lifted and the Serbs would face massive air strikes in support of the Muslims; if the Muslims did not negotiate in good faith and the Serbs did, there would be a lift and leave policy—namely, there would be a lifting of the embargo and sanctions against the Serbs, no training or arms for the Muslims, and no air strikes against the Serbs.

This new American policy had to be implemented. Richard Holbrooke, assistant secretary of state for European affairs, was chosen to carry out the American commitment to its new policy. He had long called for a serious US intervention to stop Serb aggression, the atrocities, and the war itself. Now he would lead a small team to do so. He launched a series of shuttle missions to make an all-out effort to end the war.

Means to a Diplomatic End: The Holbrooke Shuttles

During the first of his shuttles, his team could not fly to Sarajevo, given the siege, and had to travel on the winding, narrow Mt. Igman Road to get there. In trying to maneuver around a truck on the narrow mountain road, the French armored personnel carrier in which a number of the team members were riding went over the side of the road and rolled down a cliff. Ambassador Robert Frasure, Deputy Assistant Secretary of Defense for European Affairs Joseph Kruzel, and US Air Force colonel Nelson Drew were killed in the accident. The loss of three key members of the team—representing the

State Department, the National Security Council staff, and the Pentagon—
redoubled the sense of mission and obligation to finish what the team had
started.

Holbrooke embodied the president's attitude of pulling out all the stops
in trying to forge an agreement that would end the war. The first shuttle
mission was geared toward probing each side's intentions and interests. The
second mission would be designed to outline the broad parameters of a settlement. It was preceded by a Bosnian Serb mortar attack on Sarajevo that
killed 37 people. Holbrooke understood that he would have no credibility
with either the Muslims or the Serbs if the "Goražde rules" were not implemented. President Clinton agreed, giving the command that "we have to hit
them [the Bosnian Serbs] hard."[17]

To avoid the hostage-taking of the past, 92 UN troops were withdrawn
from Goražde, and a massive bombing campaign started before the Holbrooke team arrived in Belgrade. Though Holbrooke expected Milošević to
be tough in their meeting, the Serb leader surprised the team by providing
them with a letter signed by the seven members of the Bosnian Serb leadership and by the patriarch of the Serb Orthodox Church agreeing to join
a negotiating delegation in which Milošević would have the final word. In
addition, Milošević agreed in the meeting to the 51:49 ratio for Bosnia as
the basis for negotiations. For one year, Milošević had resisted representing the Bosnian Serbs and the 51:49 ratio—yet now, under the pressure of
intensive bombing of the Bosnian Serbs, he was showing how responsive he
could be. Only two hours into the meeting did Milošević ask for a bombing halt to help the negotiations; Holbrooke responded that the shelling of
Sarajevo must first stop and that the Bosnian Serb guns must be withdrawn
from around the city.

Holbrooke used the second shuttle mission to get an agreement on a general legal and political framework for Bosnia. He proposed that the three
foreign ministers—Serb, Muslim, and Croatian—meet within a week in
Geneva to endorse this framework, and succeeded in getting them to do
so. It took nonstop talks to make sure everybody would show up, and there
were crises up to the last minute; yet on September 8, 1995, the three foreign
ministers came and signed what became known as the Geneva Principles:
Bosnia would be one state with shared power between the Croat–Muslim
federation and the Serbs; there would be free elections, human rights standards, binding arbitration of disputes, and parallel special relations with
neighbors.

All this had been agreed in the context of a massive bombing campaign against the Bosnian Serbs. Coercion unmistakably worked, and Holbrooke was a master of knowing how to employ it. When the Bosnian Serbs subsequently betrayed their promises to pull artillery back from Sarajevo as part of the bombing pause Holbrooke had been working to negotiate, he pushed to resume the intensive bombing—and still pulled off the agreement on the Geneva Principles.

The third shuttle mission began with increasing pressure from within NATO and from the Russians to stop the bombing campaign. Both had objected to the use of American Tomahawks, with the Russians particularly angered over what they saw as coordination between the Croat–Muslim ground offensive against the Bosnian Serbs and the Tomahawk attacks against Bosnian Serb infrastructure. NATO allies were also upset over targets being struck that they felt went beyond those that had been agreed upon. Within the Pentagon, the US military was also saying that it was running out of the "Option Two" targets that had been agreed upon, and they favored a bombing halt. Holbrooke and his team did not want to bring the bombing to an end but understood that, given the circumstances, it might be difficult to sustain. At the outset of the third shuttle mission, therefore, they knew they might have to see what they could get from Milošević in exchange for a suspension of the bombing.

Once again, the team was pleasantly surprised to see that if the bombing stopped, Milošević was ready to produce an end to the siege of Sarajevo by the Bosnian Serb forces. He asked Holbrooke and his team to meet the Bosnian Serb leaders and, after difficult discussions, they accepted an American plan in which they stopped all their offensive operations around Sarajevo, began to relocate their heavy weapons, allowed road access to Sarajevo, and permitted the opening of the city's airport for humanitarian missions—all in return for a halt to the bombing.

The Muslim leadership, believing that they were on the brink of decisive military victories, were not happy over the bombing halt. But even though the bombing was halted, the ground offensive led by the Croats continued. The Holbrooke team saw value in not stopping it prematurely, particularly because it was changing the realities on the ground and making the eventual negotiations on the map easier to conduct. Washington might favor an end to the Croat offensive, but Holbrooke and his team did not. They would press for restraint only at a juncture when the Croats and Muslims might turn on each other; otherwise, Holbrooke was reluctant to surrender leverage on the Serbs, and at one point he even urged Croatian president Tudjman to take more towns in order to have land to give away once the negotiations commenced.[18] As Holbrooke would later say, "For me, the success of the Croatian (and later, in similar circumstances, the Bosnian–Croat Federation) offensive was a classic illustration of the fact that the shape of the diplomatic landscape will usually reflect the balance of forces on the ground."[19]

As part of this same shuttle mission, Holbrooke and the team negotiated "further agreed principles" that fleshed out the Geneva Principles and were concluded in a second meeting of foreign ministers in New York. Much like the run-up to the Geneva meeting, this too came down to the last minute. The question whether the Bosnian elections had to be direct and whether the office of the presidency would have "exclusively" foreign policy powers created a crisis, requiring nonstop negotiations not only in New York but also in Belgrade and Sarajevo. When Sacirbey, the Muslim foreign minister, appeared to back out of an agreement at the last moment, Secretary Christopher told him that if he did not relent and go along with the original understanding, President Clinton would announce the failure of the New York meeting and blame the Muslim government for it. With that, the further agreed principles were adopted by the three foreign ministers on September 26, 1995. In what became known as the "New York Principles," the powers of the joint presidency, the parliament, and the constitutional court were agreed upon.

Two days later, Holbrooke and his team set out on their fourth shuttle mission to the Balkans in six weeks. The purpose of this mission was to get an agreement, set a firm date for a peace conference, and produce a ceasefire throughout Bosnia. Milošević had already indicated that he wanted to come to a summit and was ready to deal; he had indicated as much by leaning on the Bosnian Serbs, pushing them to give up the siege of Sarajevo, and recognizing Bosnia as an independent state. Milošević wanted an end to the sanctions on Serbia and wanted to be accepted internationally. Croation president Tudjman was also keen for an agreement, having gained back most of the territory that mattered to the Croats and now beginning to see the Bosnian Serbs regrouping militarily. Only the Muslims were resistant; their leadership was divided and feared that any settlement might be a trick.

The peace conference was designed to have all the leaders and their delegations co-located and to conduct proximity talks, with the Holbrooke team acting as the principal go-between. Holbrooke wanted the talks to take place in the United States so that the American side would be able to control the setting, agenda, and course of the talks. Dictating the process would, in Holbrooke's eyes, give the United States more leverage to make the nego- tiations succeed. Holbrooke faced a nearly united opposition to this plan from President Clinton's top advisors, who all feared that an American venue for the talks would magnify the costs of failure if they did not work. How- ever, Holbrooke's argument soon carried the day within the administration, with the help and advice of Deputy Secretary of State Strobe Talbott and Tom Donilon, Secretary Christopher's chief of staff, on how best to craft his points. Concerns over European sensitivities about having the United States running everything resulted in instructions that Holbrooke work with the Contact Group on follow-up meetings or ceremonies to be conducted in a European capital. And, of course, the Contact Group would have a team at the site of the negotiations.

Holbrooke also wanted to be able to announce the cease-fire at the same time that he announced the peace conference. The Muslims, who were the most hesitant about accepting the cease-fire and the peace conference, laid down stiff conditions for the cease-fire: restored utilities to Sarajevo, demilitarized Banja Luka, and road access to Goražde. In addition, Alia Izetbegovič, the president of Bosnia, wanted ten more days before a cease- fire would go into effect. Holbrooke used both the Croats and the Serbs to pressure the Muslims, and also exerted his own pressure, reminding Izetbegovič of the risks he was running by letting the fighting continue too long, warning, "If you continue the war, you will be shooting craps with your nation's destiny."[20]

Finally, Izetbegovič agreed that if the gas lines to Sarajevo were function- ing and there was an open road to Goražde, he would accept a cease-fire in five days, and he wanted Miloševič commitment to this. Holbrooke went to Belgrade but left two members of his team in Sarajevo. As Holbrooke worked to get Miloševič acceptance, he had an open phone line to Izetbegovič to be sure the president of Bosnia would not change his mind, and one to Wash- ington for consultations; and over a period of three hours an agreement was reached on the cease-fire.

With that in hand, Holbrooke then worked the agreement on the announcement of the peace conference. This was October 5. The cease-fire was agreed to take hold on October 11, and the conference would begin two weeks later.

Peacemaking in Action: The Dayton Conference

Prior to the beginning of the peace conference, intensive work was needed on several fronts. First, Holbrooke directed that a full-draft peace treaty be completed. He had had a small team in the State Department begin drafting in September on all legal questions, but now he had them working on a framework agreement and seven annexes that addressed disengagement and the cessation of hostilities, constitutional structure, arbitration, human rights, refugees and displaced persons, national monuments, and implementation. By October 15, they had put together at least the first cut of such a draft agreement. Soon thereafter, three annexes were added on the elections, public corporations, and NATO's implementation forces (IFOR) for carrying out any agreement that was concluded.

Second, discussions on IFOR needed to be conducted, and were complicated not only by different views within the administration on how extensive the role and missions of the forces might be, but also by the Russian desire to take part but not in a capacity subordinate to NATO.

Holbrooke's team took a maximal view on what would be required for the forces in terms of assisting refugee return, providing security for the elections, arresting war criminals, ensuring freedom of movement, and the like. In the Pentagon, fear of mission creep (the expansion of a project or mission beyond its original goals) led to a minimalist preference. The minimalists wanted to be only peacekeepers; the maximalists were far more geared toward state-building. General Shalikashvili eventually offered a compromise that would grant IFOR the "authority" to work in all such areas but not the "obligation" to do so—giving the forces great discretion on the scope of the mission. As for dealing with the Russians, this was managed by both Deputy Secretary of State Strobe Talbott on a general level—helping to ensure that Bosnia would neither spoil more general US–Russian relations nor subvert the reformers in Russia—and on the military level by Secretary of Defense Perry. Though it took time, Perry was eventually able—working with Russian defense minister Pavel Grachev—to finesse the participation of the Russian forces in a way that had the local Russian commander answering to the American general in charge of IFOR and not technically to NATO. (The former was acceptable to the Russians; the latter was not.)

Third, the Holbrooke team worked with the Europeans on all implementation issues—civil and military—while also trying to condition the different Balkan parties on what would happen once the peace conference convened.

In the last and shortest shuttle mission prior to the conference, Holbrooke brought Carl Bildt of the EU and Russian foreign minister Igor Ivanov to meetings that started in Belgrade, where Holbrooke announced that the peace conference would take place at Wright-Patterson Air Force Base in Dayton, Ohio.

Throughout this period, the American effort effectively required managing three parallel sets of negotiations involving the Balkan parties, the NATO allies, and the Russians. All this was done while also preparing the choreography of a major peace conference.

The peace conference represented a roll of the dice. Holbrooke saw it in "all or nothing" terms, understanding that it was essential to build the sense of what was at stake for all those involved. Ending the war would require a very clear awareness on the part of Milošević, Tudjman, and Izetbegović of not just what they could gain by success but what they would be certain to lose by failure. Ultimately, the conference succeeded.

It went through different phases, with the first week designed to build some basis for progress by formalizing the federation agreement between the Croats and Muslims while also working out the one territorial issue that mattered to President Tudjman of Croatia—Eastern Slavonia, which was solely a Serbia–Croatia issue. In the first week, there was no movement on the core issues of the map or the constitution. Progress was very painful and slow throughout the second week—with most of the work being done by the American team shuttling between the sides after direct meetings of the parties proved to be counterproductive. Divisions within the Bosnian team were paralyzing them, and most of the movement tended to be driven by Milošević, who was anxious to reach agreement.

On the key issue of control over Sarajevo, it was Milošević who broke the stalemate, on the sixteenth day, by simply conceding the issue to the Muslims, telling them that after three years of shelling by the cowardly Bosnian Serbs, the Muslims had "earned" the city. With Dayton hovering on the brink of failure on the twenty-second day, Milošević acted again. First, in conversations with Haris Silajdžić, he sought to resolve the key territorial stumbling block of getting the Bosnian Serb territory up to 49 percent. Then, when overcoming the differences on the status of the city Brčko became the only way to work out the territorial questions, he offered the compromise of arbitration by an international mediator to resolve the issue. He did not want Dayton to fail. He was ready for the conflict to end, and to gain the economic benefits that would result from that.

One of the factors that contributed to Milošević's concessions was Holbrooke's use not just of coercive means but also of positive inducements. Holbrooke wanted to suspend sanctions against Serbia at the beginning of the peace conference, believing that Milošević also needed to see the rewards at the right moment. While he faced opposition within the administration, Holbrooke read Milošević's desire for economic relief and manipulated it well.

On the last day of the conference, the Bosnian Muslims exasperated Secretary Christopher and Holbrooke as they appeared unable to take yes for an answer, putting at risk all they had achieved through the agreement that was available. In the final hour, as the United States grew frustrated with the Muslims, Christopher told Izetbegović that there were no more deadlines and the United States needed an answer immediately. Izetbegović reluctantly agreed, and the Bosnian war was over—at least on paper.

For a conflict that the United States had wanted no part of during the Bush administration, and for which it had shown reluctance to assume any military obligations during the Clinton administration, America now was prepared to commit 20,000 troops—one-third of the IFOR troops—to help implement the agreement that US leadership had produced.

Evaluating the Bosnia Case

The Bosnian case represents both ends of the spectrum in statecraft. During the Bush years, it was a conflict that was avoided. Fatigue from German unification and the first Gulf War reduced the inclination to be involved, and the president and his senior advisors rationalized America's non-involvement by convincing themselves that this was a conflict that Europe should manage. When ethnic cleansing became unmistakable, with the gruesome images of concentration camps in the summer of 1992, the administration supported the development and deployment of UNPROFOR; later, when Serb actions in Kosovo risked a possible expansion of the war, President Bush warned Milošević, but this came at the end of the administration.

For the Bush administration, this was the wrong war at the wrong time in the wrong place. Could more have been done to deter Milošević and his Greater Serbia ambitions? Almost certainly, but that would have required active involvement and readiness to use coercive diplomacy that Milošević would have believed credible. It was not in the cards for an administration that did not believe in the stakes and that seemed guided by an objective more of avoiding involvement than of solving the conflict.

But the Clinton administration arrived in January 1993 with a sense of outrage over what Serbia was doing. Ethnic cleansing was decried, Serb aggression was not to be tolerated, arming the Muslims was called for, and stopping a conflict in the heart of Europe was certainly seen as an important American national security interest. And yet it took until the summer of 1995—and the massacre in Srebrenica—to finally move the administration to transform the situation and produce the use of force and diplomacy to end the war.

What is remarkable about the period from August 1995 through the end of the Dayton negotiations is that in many ways it is a model of effective statecraft. The objective was finally defined in a clear way and with a strategy and the means to pursue it. The Clinton administration not only framed the objective in a way that generated support internationally, but also acted in a unified, disciplined fashion even when some differences remained internally. The marriage of force and diplomacy was carried out masterfully, particularly as the United States resisted alliance pressures to stop NATO's bombing of the Serb positions prematurely, and also held off the calls to seek a cease-fire before the realities on the ground had changed to a point where they served the prospects of a negotiated settlement. The diplomacy itself was intense and nonstop, with coordination taking place simultaneously with the Contact Group, the Europeans, the UN, the Russians, and the various Balkan parties (including within the Muslims, between the Croats and the Muslims, and with Milošević and the Bosnian Serbs). And a sequence for negotiations was developed and implemented, culminating in the marathon of Dayton.

Throughout the course of Holbrooke's involvement, coercive means were exploited to build leverage, inducements were employed to render rewards for good behavior, and communication channels were used to inform, explain, and assuage. More than anything else, the Holbrooke team worked constantly to deal with Muslim fears and internal divisions, intervened whenever potential fissures between the Croats and Muslims threatened to erupt, acted to build Milošević's interest in managing the Bosnian Serbs, and spent time briefing the Europeans when the potential for their resentment at the Americans running the show might have become a problem.

The assessment of the different parties, their stakes, and the incentives and disincentives that could be orchestrated to affect the parties was done well and often on the run, befitting an intensive effort. Could it have worked in 1995 without the Serb leader Slobodan Milošević wanting an end to Serbia's isolation and the sanctions, and international acceptability for himself? Probably not, but give credit to Richard Holbrooke and his team for reading Milošević correctly and for understanding the dynamics of the Bosnian Muslim leadership. And give credit to President Clinton for backing this all-out effort and for deciding to commit 20,000 American troops to implement the agreement.

What is unmistakably clear is that the administration succeeded in ending the war—the war that resulted in close to 100,000 people being killed and nearly two million displaced, the war that involved ethnic cleansing and war crimes. So, ending it was a main priority, first objective—and the statecraft that produced that outcome met the near-term objective. How did the statecraft do in terms of longer-term objectives? Here the answer is not as optimistic—assuming that there were the means to do better.

Richard Holbrooke set for himself a more ambitious and longer-term objective than only ending the war. Derek Chollet, who worked for Holbrooke, would later write that "Holbrooke's main objective was to end the war. But to him, a durable cease-fire was not enough. He worked to forge an agreement that would create a unified, democratic, multiethnic, and tolerant Bosnia. Holbrooke described his position as 'maximalist,' and as such, it elicited doubts within the US government and with allies, not to mention among the warring parties themselves."[21]

Holbrooke succeeded in creating principles that created a single state with a rotating presidency, courts, and dispute resolution mechanisms. But he strongly believed that the state would remain ethnically divided with little integration if those Serbs responsible for war crimes were not arrested. There needed to be accountability. That is why he pushed for the most expansive powers of IFOR so that the forces had the mission for actively pursuing and apprehending those responsible for war crimes. As noted above, the US military was not alone in resisting this mission. Peacekeeping was one thing, the pursuit of war criminals quite another. Neither US forces nor US allies wanted that mission, fearing it would embroil them in a continuing conflict with the Serbs in Bosnia. Shalikashvili's compromise was to create the authority to make arrests but not the mandate to do so.

Holbrooke's instinct was probably right. While over time there would be arrests (including the arrest of Radovan Karadzic in 2008)—thirteen years after the conclusion of the war—the ethnic lines had hardened in

Bosnia–Herzegovina by that time. For some critics of the Dayton Accords, the flaw was built into the accords themselves because they "ended the war by granting ethnically cleansed territory to those who had cleansed it and by proclaiming that Bosnia would be, as many Bosnian politicians have put it since, 'one country of three nations.'" The result, as Carol Schaeffer observed, was that everything was segregated, touching "nearly every aspect of Bosnian life—not just politics but schools and other public services."[22] Others, like Peter Lippman, have echoed that the Dayton Accords "rewarded the people who had divided the country, prosecuted the war, and left them and their political heirs in position to further their political, their wartime goals by other means."[23]

Carl Bildt's view of Dayton and its aftermath is more nuanced than the critics. He served as the first high representative for Bosnia–Herzegovina—a role designed to help oversee the civil administration of the Dayton Accords. He too says, "while we failed to reverse the ethnic division of the country— Sarajevo is more solidly Muslim than ever, Banja Luka is more solidly Serb than ever, and Mostar is as deeply divided as ever—we did prevent the physical division of the country. Today you pass the Inter-Entity Boundary Line and hardly notice where it is." The checkpoints are gone.[24]

While Bildt also acknowledges that "politics in the post-Dayton decades have, far too often, been little more than ethnic trench warfare," he does not believe that the accords could have been different to any meaningful extent. In his words, the "details could well have been different, but no fundamentally different deal was possible—and prolonging the war was neither politically nor morally defensible."[25]

Even the critics of Dayton acknowledge that it ended the war and the suffering. The aftermath might have been different with more accountability, but it is hard to fault the statecraft that produced it. And, with all the problems in Bosnia–Herzegovina—it is poor, it is ethnically divided, it is not developing economically, the Serbs are led by a nationalist with ties to Putin—it is remarkable that generally all three groups would probably vote for the Dayton Accords if they had the chance to do so again.[26,a]

Ultimately, the key to ensuring that the Dayton Accords did more than only end the war depended on creating accountability and ensuring that as much effort went into building the civil administration as has gone into

---

[a] While there are no current polls on attitudes of the groups toward Dayton, it is noteworthy that polling done 20 years after Dayton showed clear pluralities indicating they would support the Dayton Accords if a referendum was held on them.

ensuring security. That, of course, relates to the statecraft done afterward. The statecraft done before, the statecraft that produced Dayton, remains a remarkably good example of statecraft being done well.

Presidential leadership and involvement played a far greater role in the first Gulf War in 1991, but were managed very differently before and during the run-up to the Iraq War, in 2002–2003. That would change by the time of the surge in 2006–2008, when the Bush 43rd administration would more closely approximate the Bush 41st. To those cases, we will now turn.

Chapter 7
Undoing Iraqi Aggression in Kuwait

On August 2, 1990, Iraq invaded neighboring Kuwait and seized a country Iraqi leaders began referring to immediately as the "nineteenth province" of Iraq. The George H. W. Bush administration condemned the invasion and called for the immediate, unconditional withdrawal of Iraqi forces. It moved swiftly to get the UN Security Council to adopt a resolution in which the invasion was unanimously condemned; by Sunday, August 5, President Bush declared, "This will not stand—this aggression against Kuwait."

With that statement, the president was declaring that the United States, either on its own or with others, would act to ensure that the Iraqi seizure of Kuwait would be undone. At the time of the declaration, Secretary James Baker said to me, "I hope we can succeed diplomatically because the president has just committed us to war with Iraq if we can't." Baker knew his boss and understood the implications of Bush's declaration. That President Bush would make such a statement was remarkable: after all, the United States had no preexisting commitment to Kuwaiti security, and had done little before the invasion to signal any serious American interest in the fate of Kuwait.

Moreover, it was Iraq to whom the United States had drawn steadily closer once the Reagan administration had taken it off the terrorism list in 1982. President Reagan would restore diplomatic relations with Iraq in 1984, and the United States would increasingly tilt toward it, favoring Iraq in the war it launched against Iran. Even though Iraq had invaded Iran, the American view of the threat posed by the revolutionary mullahs ruling Iran (and American antipathy to Iran in the wake of the 1979–1981 hostage crisis) led the Reagan administration to support Iraq and its secular Ba'athist regime led by Saddam Hussein. Adopting the traditional realist posture that the "enemy of my enemy is my friend," Ronald Reagan—hardly a disciple of the realpolitik school of foreign policy—offered very tangible and meaningful support to Iraq. America provided the Iraqi regime with intelligence and TPQ-37 advanced radars, which had significant force-multiplying effects. And in 1987, when Iran was attacking oil tankers to cut off Iraq's oil revenues, the

Statecraft 2.0. Second Edition. Dennis Ross, Oxford University Press. © Oxford University Press (2025).
DOI: 10.1093/oso/9780197698914.003.0007

United States "reflagged" neutral tankers and protected them with US warships to prevent such a loss. In addition, the Reagan administration offered extensive credit guarantees to the Iraqi government to buy agricultural goods from the United States and maintained that program even after the United States began receiving reports that the Iraqis were misusing the credits to free up funds for military purchases. Remarkably, even Iraq's use of chemical weapons against the Iranians and Iraq's own Kurdish population did little to affect Iraq's relations with the United States.

With the end of the Iran–Iraq War in 1988, the policy of seeking to improve relations with Saddam Hussein continued, and the Bush administration embraced it in its first year—sending officials to see Saddam in Baghdad even as Secretary Baker would meet Iraq's foreign minister, Tariq Aziz, at the State Department. Only in 1990 did American efforts to improve ties with Iraq get put on hold—and only because Saddam began to pressure his neighbors to increase oil prices and to threaten to attack Israel with chemical weapons. In response to Iraq's increasingly bellicose posture against its neighbors, the Bush administration began a review of the agricultural credit program, which eventually led not to its revocation but to the suspension of a second tranche of $500 million dollars in credits. In May 1990, Saddam charged that Kuwait and the United Arab Emirates were guilty of direct aggression against Iraq and declared that if words had no impact, "something effective must be done."[1]

Throughout the spring and summer of 1990, America's Arab friends in the Middle East counseled restraint in the face of Iraq's threats, and the Bush administration did little. For the most part, the policy was being handled in the administration by second-tier officials at the time, and attention of the president and the most senior level remained riveted principally on German unification. Much like the Saudis, the Egyptians, and the Jordanians, those American officials felt that Saddam was posturing because of increasing economic troubles; even when the verbal threats became more pronounced and Iraq moved heavy concentrations of troops to the Kuwaiti border in the second half of July, Arab regimes and the US ambassador to Iraq assured the administration's leaders of Saddam Hussein's benign intentions. President Hosni Mubarak of Egypt, after seeing Saddam, declared on July 25, "I believe he … has no intention of attacking Kuwait or any other party." And on July 29, King Hussein of Jordan told President Bush in a phone call, "Nothing will happen."[2] As Robert Gates, then the deputy national security advisor, would later say, "The truth of the matter is, the people who knew it best, the leaders, who lived in the region, who knew the language, knew the culture, knew the history, were all ... saying nothing was going to happen."[3]

But they proved to be wrong, and the attack came four days after King Hussein assured the US president there would be no invasion. Not surprisingly, the attack transformed America's policy.

Why Was Bush's Objective to Reverse Iraqi Aggression?

The Iraqi seizure of Kuwait came as a shock. Even when Iraqi troops crossed the border, the initial assumption was that the action might be a limited land grab (perhaps of the Rumaila oil field) as a way of extracting economic concessions from the Kuwaitis. Though even a limited seizure of territory would have been deeply disturbing, few in the neighborhood or in the Bush administration foresaw the possibility of Iraq actually seizing all of Kuwait. Their assessments were guided by wrongheaded assumptions about Saddam Hussein.

The administration had to scramble in response. Certainly, the shock of the invasion affected the administration's mindset. But what shaped the adoption of its objective to reverse the invasion was the early recognition that far more was at stake than the future of Kuwait. Iraqi forces stood poised at the Kuwaiti–Saudi border, only 275 miles from the Saudi capital of Riyadh, and little prevented the Iraqi forces from advancing into the Kingdom. Suddenly, the specter of Iraq seizing Saudi northern oil fields, and the Saudi capital, conjured up the image that a hostile power could gain a stranglehold over the flow of oil from the Middle East, with potentially devastating consequences for the economies of the Western industrialized world. Preventing that outcome had long been defined as a fundamental US interest. Previously, the Soviets were seen as the prime threat; the Khomeini revolution in Iran indicated that such a threat could be more localized. And now Iraq's absorption of Kuwait could enable it to dominate the Gulf States, determine the flow of oil, and use its leverage on the oil supply to blackmail US allies and pursue its pan-Arab objectives in the region—including its anti-Israel agenda. The Iraq seizure of Kuwait thus posed an unmistakable threat to American interests in the Middle East.

For President Bush, it was not just the oil and America's vital interests in the Middle East that were at stake—as important as they might be. The president believed that Iraq's actions threatened the structure of international relations after the Cold War. With the fall of the Berlin Wall, one era had ended. Would this new one be governed by the rule of law or the law of the jungle? Would it be characterized by order or disorder? In James Baker's words, the president's instinctive sense from the beginning was that "this was no ordinary crisis, that it truly would become a hinge point of history," and how the United States responded would have a great influence on whether there would be a new world order—terminology that President Bush now began to use.[4]

This concern for shaping the post–Cold War world was *why* Iraq's aggression could not stand, and why it was so important *how* the United States undid Iraq's actions. President Bush was prepared, in his words, "to deal with this crisis unilaterally if necessary," but he did not want the United States doing it alone and making this a confrontation between America and Iraq.[5] Rather, for President Bush and Secretary Baker, it had to be the world against Saddam. There had to be a coalition that would signal that the world would not tolerate this kind of behavior. Indeed, for Bush and Baker, the United States needed to lead an international coalition to counter this aggression and undo the Iraqi occupation of Kuwait.

Consequently, President Bush, in his words, "wanted the United Nations involved as part of our first response." He was convinced, "Decisive UN action would be important in rallying international opposition to the invasion and reversing it."[6] Secretary Baker affirmed, "Almost by definition, the first stop for coalition building was the United Nations."[7]

Forging an international consensus would make America's action legitimate and define the ground rules of the era. It would show that aggression would not be permitted and that those who engaged in it would unmistakably lose.

While President Bush defined his objective in these terms, it was no simple task to fashion a strategy for achieving it. Deterrence of further Iraqi military thrusts, especially into Saudi Arabia, had to be the first order of business, and the development of a coalition to undo the aggression could not simply be mandated; it had to be nurtured and constructed. Practically speaking, it would take time to put military forces in place to counter the Iraqis, and the Saudis would have to accept the deployment of large American forces in the Kingdom—something they had always been loath to consider, fearing that admitting large numbers of "non-believers" to defend the "custodians" or protectors of the holy places might affect the very legitimacy of the royal family.

But deterring the Iraqis required getting American forces to the Kingdom, starting with tactical air wings that could be deployed quickly. And yet, King Fahd avoided giving an answer to President Bush when the latter initially raised the issue. Fahd deferred the discussion by saying he would work with the team that the president would send to Saudi Arabia. The King, Custodian of the Two Holy Mosques, understood the need for US forces and wanted Saddam defeated, but he was not only wary about the appearance of having to rely on non-believers, but also worried that once there, US forces might not leave. Here, the weight of the personal relationship that Bush had already established with King Fahd and Bush's personal credibility made all the difference. In that initial call, Bush, sensing Fahd's unease, told the King, "When we work out a plan, once we are there, we will stay until we are asked to leave. You have my solemn word on this."[8] Secretary of Defense Richard Cheney led the team that Bush had sent to see Fahd, and Cheney would later recount, "I could remember going to talk to King Fahd when I asked him for approval to deploy the force to Saudi Arabia. His basic response ... 'Okay, we'll do it. We'll do it because I trust George Bush and because I know when it's over with, you'll leave.'"[9]

Developing personal relationships is especially important in the Middle East—and is part of the art of statecraft when it comes to this region—and Bush's ability to reassure Fahd meant that the United States could begin to build the forces for deterrence. That was one thing. But being able to put together an international coalition would be quite another. Each phase required time. While the president's declaration that the Iraqi aggression would not stand was certainly stark, the early strategy of the administration (as outlined by the president and his senior advisors in the National Security Council meeting of August 4) was all about deterring Saddam even as the United States built up pressures on Iraq designed to make the occupation of Kuwait untenable. Coercive diplomacy, starting with political isolation and leading to economic sanctions, was designed to "make Saddam Hussein pay such a high price" that he would realize the need to withdraw from Kuwait. It was hoped that this would be sufficient, but the president understood that if isolation and sanctions failed, Saddam would have to be expelled by military force.[10]

The strategy depended on establishing an international consensus and a broad-based coalition. "Having decided on building a coalition," Secretary Baker said later, "we turned our attention to the practical and arduous task of actually putting one together and maintaining it throughout the crisis ...

In retrospect, I believe maintaining the coalition's solidarity was even more difficult than assembling it in the first place."[11]

What Obstacles Did the Administration Face?

The obstacles to achieving the objective established by the president were formidable. Some of them stemmed from a structural reality: influential countries such as the Soviet Union would find it difficult to be a part of a coalition designed to exert great pressure on Iraq, their principal client state in the Middle East. Other obstacles grew out of the inherent complexities in the process the administration sought to use to apply pressure on Iraq—namely, the adoption of resolutions in the UN Security Council. Even assuming that consensus *could* be developed among the five permanent members of the Council about escalating pressure on Iraq (certainly not a given by any means), the non-aligned bloc might balk over coercing a country in the developing world, and if nothing else, could prevent resolutions from appearing to have broad support.

Still other obstacles were bound to arise given the incremental nature of the strategy, which by definition meant that there would be different phases. Gaining support for political isolation would not necessarily be difficult. But getting it again for sanctions, and then for enforcement of these sanctions to inflict genuine penalties on Iraq, and finally again for the actual use of force to expel Iraq, was bound to be extremely challenging. Each of these phases would re-create opposition from those who were instinctively hesitant, opposition that would have to be managed and overcome.

If these structural obstacles were not sufficient, there were others that were certain to be daunting: employing sanctions that imposed an effective boycott against the Iraqi economy would damage those countries, such as Turkey and Egypt, whose economies depended on commercial ties and subsidized oil from Iraq. They would find it difficult to go along with embargoes if they were not compensated for what they were losing financially—and that "bill" would rise very quickly into billions of dollars. Who was going to provide that money to sustain the effectiveness of the embargoes on all Iraqi trade? Moreover, would the United States find it so easy to sustain the costs of America's own military buildup in the Gulf, particularly given the sudden turnabout in US policy toward Iraq that inevitably raised questions about how the United States could go from trying to improve relations with Iraq to coercing it?

In this sense, the economic costs would trigger political costs as well. Bear in mind that the administration had done little or no conditioning to change the public perception of Iraq. In addition, few looked at Kuwait as a country that was worth fighting for. So domestic opposition was yet another important obstacle the administration would have to contend with if it was to achieve its objective of forcing Iraq to disgorge Kuwait.

In retrospect, it appears that Saddam counted on creating a fait accompli to which the world would have to adjust. He apparently assumed that the international community would criticize but accept a reality that it could not undo. He expected that the Soviet Union, his longtime patron and supplier of the bulk of his heavy armaments, would block any meaningful pressures on him. He had strong ties to the Soviet military establishment, and the Soviets had a large military support presence in Iraq that he thought they would not jeopardize for the sake of the Americans. Similarly, Saddam probably also believed, with some justification, that the French, who had very large commercial interests in Iraq—and defense industries heavily dependent on large arms sales to the Iraqi military—would understand how much they had to lose by imposing any significant economic sanctions on his regime.

Saddam was right to see impediments—convinced the US would find it difficult to overcome the interests of these two permanent members of the Security Council, each with a veto. Beyond this, the Iraqi leadership apparently also was convinced, again with some justification, that Arab countries would find it difficult to sustain support for external pressure on Iraq. Joining with an outside power to try to impose on a brother Arab would conjure up all the imagery of a history of colonialism that the people of the region loathed—and local regimes would be fearful of domestic reactions as a result. To make Arab involvement in any international coalition against Iraq less likely, the Iraqis also sought early on to make this an Arab–Israeli, not a world-against-Iraq, issue. Seeing initial condemnations of the Iraq invasion even in the Arab world, Saddam offered a "peace plan" on August 12—ten days after the seizure of Kuwait—suggesting that he had invaded Kuwait for the Palestinians, and declaring that the issue of Kuwait could be discussed in the context of ending the Israeli occupation of the Palestinian territory. Later, Iraqi foreign minister Tariq Aziz began to say that if there were an attack against Iraq, it would retaliate by firing missiles at Israel, something that Iraqis assumed would trigger Israeli retaliation and make it impossible for Arabs to act in a way that made them appear to be siding with the Israelis.

Aziz told Secretary Baker at their meeting on January 9 in Geneva that the Arabs would defect from any coalition with the United States for essentially atavistic reasons: "Once a people enter battle and fire prevails and blood is spilled, then people go back to their origins and behave instinctively. If you were to attack an Arab state, you will be the enemy in many Arab countries."[12] Many American experts on the Arab world echoed Aziz's words in warning the Bush administration about the consequences of using force against Iraq. One such expert, Christine Helms, in a fall meeting with President Bush, declared that if the United States went to war against Iraq to oust it from Kuwait, "no American would be able to do business or set foot in the Arab world for the next twenty years."[13] It does not matter now whether such experts were profoundly wrong; what matters is what the administration had to contend with at the time in terms of real or perceived obstacles.

Even the framing of the issue was something that Saddam could potentially affect. He clearly understood that he had the tools and symbols to try to reframe the issue so that it was not Iraq against the world but rather Iraq confronting Israel. Turning this into an Arab–Israeli conflict could make it very difficult to sustain the coalition and to keep its Arab members.

One last set of obstacles to achieving the president's objective should also be noted. Within the administration, there were doubts at certain key junctures about going to the UN Security Council. The fear was that the Security Council might not agree to the resolutions the United States sought, and if the United States tried for them and failed, its ability to then use Article 51 of the UN Charter (the "self-defense" provision) to justify its use of force would be seriously undermined. But for a president who believed that unmistakable international backing for America's actions was important both for legitimizing its steps and for establishing a crucial precedent for shaping a new international order, gaining endorsement by the UN was necessary even if there were obstacles.

Similarly, gaining this endorsement but lacking congressional and popular backing at home would create questions about America's ability to sustain the policy it had adopted. And yet, when the administration in November 1990 (three months after the invasion) began to move from a deterrence-and-sanctions approach to dramatically building up US forces to give the United States the offensive capability to expel Iraq from Kuwait if necessary, leading figures in Congress, such as Senators Sam Nunn and Bob Kerrey—both centrist Democrats and credible on security issues—became openly critical of the policy. Moreover, polls at the time indicated that 47 percent of the US public felt that the administration was "too quick to get American military forces involved rather than seeking diplomatic solutions."[14] With Nunn holding hearings in which former military officials (such as retired admiral William J. Crowe Jr., Bush's first chair of the Joint Chiefs of Staff) argued against the use of force and for maintenance of a sanctions-only approach, the administration had a congressional problem, and ameliorating it was yet another obstacle to overcome.

The Means Used to Overcome the Obstacles

President Bush was very clear in establishing his objective and in his desire to have an international consensus for backing it. Effectively, the administration sought to "frame" the issue by building the international consensus around the objective of the intolerability of the Iraqi seizure of Kuwait and the need to see it reversed. Personal diplomacy was again employed very intensely and at very senior levels, much as with German unification. But in this case, the personal diplomacy, including the use of back channels, was geared toward putting together a broad coalition to demonstrate that Iraq was isolated; keeping key players on board as the process of ratcheting up pressure on Iraq unfolded; sustaining the coalition over time while managing problems as they emerged or could be anticipated; and agreeing on who would play what roles in the event of war—whether sending forces and/or financially supporting the effort.

While the UN Security Council remained the critical forum for expressing the international consensus—and President Bush was to call America's UN ambassador, Tom Pickering, shortly after the invasion to convene an emergency session of the Security Council—the real starting point for producing the coalition that the president sought was getting the Soviets on board. They might have been on the decline, but they were still a military super-power and Iraq's principal military patron.

Without the Soviets, there would be no clear international consensus. Soviet opposition to America's objective would provide protection and cover for Saddam Hussein; it would give Arab nationalists a reason to stay on the fence; and it would give the French an excuse to assume a posture midway between the United States and the Soviets. Conversely, a joint US–Soviet approach would make it impossible for the French to be softer on Iraq than the Soviets. Additionally, should the Soviets join the United States in opposing and pressuring Saddam, the realities at the UN would be transformed: a much stronger basis for agreement among the permanent five members would be created; the non-aligned, who, belying that description, typically voted with the Soviets, would be much more likely to support resolutions that the United States might now author.

No wonder President Bush thought that "Soviet help in particular was key, first because they had veto power in the Security Council, but also because they could complete Iraq's political isolation."[15] The United States, thus, moved quickly to forge a common approach with the Soviets. The first step—and America's first essential "means"—for overcoming the obstacles to the administration's objective was forging a joint statement with the Soviets in response to the Iraqi invasion.

At the time of the invasion (August 2, 1990), Secretary Baker was meeting with Foreign Minister Shevardnadze of the USSR in Irkutsk, Siberia, and I was with him.[16] When Baker reported to Shevardnadze on the morning of August 2 that the United States had intelligence reports suggesting an Iraqi invasion of Kuwait now appeared imminent, Shevardnadze doubted them. He said to Baker, Saddam Hussein is "a thug, but he is not stupid." Still, Shevardnadze instructed his aide Sergei Tarasenko to check and see what "our people" know. Tarasenko reported back shortly that the Soviet "system" believed that nothing would happen. Shevardnadze was plainly embarrassed when, less than two hours later, Baker told him that Iraqi forces had crossed into Kuwait; Shevardnadze was the foreign minister of a country with thousands of its citizens (military and civilians) on the ground in Iraq, and he was blindsided by his national security establishment, requiring the visiting American secretary of state to inform him of the Iraqi invasion.

Shevardnadze's embarrassment may well have contributed to his readiness to work with the United States in setting up a joint response initially. With Baker leaving Irkutsk for a scheduled trip to Mongolia, I had previously arranged with Sergei Tarasenko to fly back to Moscow on Shevardnadze's plane, so Sergei and I could hold policy planning talks. While we had felt that such talks would be useful, the real reason for holding them at the time was that I wanted to get home for the weekend and had planned the trip back to Moscow as an excuse to avoid going with Baker to Mongolia.

Regardless of my less-than-altruistic motivations, the joint US–Soviet statement grew out of my discussions with Shevardnadze and Tarasenko on the plane back to Moscow. Once there, Peter Hauslohner, a member of my staff, suggested that since we both condemned the invasion and understood its consequences, we should adopt a joint public posture and issue a joint statement. But I understood that such a statement, while useful for putting the Soviets on record with the United States and for "framing" the issue internationally, would have far greater impact if it was mutually announced at the political level. That would leave no doubt that this was a common policy and would send an extraordinary signal to the world. Such an announcement, of course, would require Baker to leave Mongolia and come to Moscow to stand with Shevardnadze and make the statement.

Naturally, before raising this idea with Tarasenko, I needed to know that Baker would come. I reached the secretary in Ulan Bator. He immediately understood the value of the statement and authorized me to pursue the idea with Tarasenko and Shevardnadze—with the proviso that the joint announcement must have enough "meat" in it to justify his unexpected presence in Moscow.

Over the next 24 hours, I rode an emotional roller coaster. Initially, I was on a high as both Tarasenko and then Shevardnadze agreed that it was an opportunity to show the world that the Cold War was over and that the United States and the USSR were no longer adversaries but rather partners in trying to develop a world of greater peace and stability. That, of course, required a joint statement that did more than merely condemn the Iraqi invasion; in addition, it had to call for an arms embargo on Iraq and further punitive measures if Iraq's withdrawal were not forthcoming. Our first draft reflected these points—and even implied a readiness to go beyond strictly economic sanctions and threaten military means if the Iraqis did not withdraw. The statement was written in blunt language, but Tarasenko was confident he would be able to get it approved. On this basis, I told Baker, and he made plans to come to Moscow; I also reached National Security Advisor Brent Scowcroft who was with President Bush, and he was surprised and pleased, believing this was very significant and telling me that "now he knew the Cold War was over."

There was only one problem: Tarasenko's confidence was misplaced. The Soviet bureaucracy fought back, seeing the draft as serving America's interest, damaging the client central to the Soviet position in the Middle East, and putting the Soviets on the ground in Iraq in potential danger—and the draft was completely emasculated. We went back and forth, with me threatening to tell Baker not to come and arguing that a weak statement devoid of actions would demonstrate to the world how little we could do together in response to the Iraqi aggression. In the end, Shevardnadze took it upon itself to overrule the Soviet traditionalist establishment and agree to a forceful statement, even acknowledging (as he stood with Baker and spoke to the assembled media) that deciding to make this joint announcement had been no simple undertaking: "Let me tell you that it was a rather difficult decision for us ... because of the long-standing relations that we have with Iraq. But despite all this ... we are being forced to take these steps ... because ... this aggression is inconsistent with the principles of new political thinking and, in fact, with the civilized relations between nations."[17]

Here was the Soviet foreign minister not only issuing a joint statement with his American counterpart but also publicly framing the issue the way the United States wanted the world to see it and respond to it. In private, he was determined to stick with us, but he did ask Baker to promise that the United States had no intention to use force anytime soon. Baker agreed, with the caveat that this assumed no American citizens were being threatened or harmed in Kuwait.

Why did Shevardnadze do it? He and Gorbachev believed that our relations (and international relations more generally) needed to reflect a new basis, and the secretary of state was going to make an unscheduled trip to Moscow to demonstrate this. Having seen how the German unification issue and the transformation of NATO were handled, Shevardnadze and Gorbachev trusted Bush and Baker. But that did not mean the United States was over the hump with the Soviets on how to respond to Iraq. Literally every subsequent decision point on Iraq had to be managed carefully, particularly because of Gorbachev's opposition to the use of force and because of the political backlash that increasingly began to brew in Moscow over the image and reality of declining Soviet power.

In this sense, managing the Soviets and keeping them in the coalition was an ongoing challenge. In late August, the Soviets opposed stopping an Iraqi oil tanker heading toward Aden, even though the Security Council had passed a resolution imposing a trade embargo on Iraq. Gorbachev felt that an additional UN resolution was necessary to authorize military enforcement of the embargo—and he wanted one more chance to try to get Saddam Hussein to withdraw before enforcing the embargo and adopting such a resolution. Other than Secretary Baker, all of the president's senior advisors wanted to stop the tanker, believing that the credibility of the embargo was at stake. But as Secretary Baker told President Bush, "We're going to be much worse off losing the Soviets than losing the ship," and the president gave Baker a few days to work the issue with the Soviets.[18] Baker did so. He spoke daily to Shevardnadze, seeking to affect the Soviet calculus by explaining not only the pressure he was under but also the importance of having the mandatory Security Council resolutions mean something. Baker used the phone conversations to move Shevardnadze and Gorbachev, and effectively put Gorbachev in a position in which his desire for delay became a test of Soviet abilities to change Saddam's behavior. Since they could not do that, the Soviets stayed in the coalition and supported the new resolution.

Later, in the fall, the political counterattacks and pressure within the Kremlin against Shevardnadze led Gorbachev to allow Yevgeny Primakov, a longtime Soviet Arabist with a close relationship to Saddam, to come to Washington to try to persuade the Bush administration to alter its approach away from pressure on Saddam to an engagement strategy in which Saddam might be given something in order to get him to withdraw. My back-channel relationship with Tarasenko, which had proven so instrumental during German unification, again was useful at this point and in the later stages, when the United States became primed to use force. At this juncture, Tarasenko sent me an extraordinary message through a secure channel, showing both desperation and the extent of his trust in this relationship:

Dennis,
Primakov is coming over Shevardnadze's opposition. He is against Saddam paying a price. He wants to reward him. His mission has been pushed on Gorbachev and if he succeeds, he will replace Shevardnadze as foreign minister and end everything we have been working for. He must be seen as failing and creating problems with the United States. This is a desperate situation.
     Sergei

Baker and I informed President Bush of this message, and it was agreed that I would see Primakov first and only then would he see Baker and then the president. I had known Primakov for some time, taking part in the Pugwash dialogues with him when I was an academic outside the government.[a]

His argument was that we could only avert a war if we gave Saddam "face-savers." Primakov said that Saddam would not back down without them—and I responded, saying that what Primakov called face-savers were actually rewards for Saddam's aggression and Bush would not go along and accept giving Saddam payoffs. I added that if Primakov thought I was

[a] The Pugwash dialogues largely involved academics and think-tank participants from the United States and the Soviet Union, and I met Primakov several times during the years 1984–1986 when I was at the University of California, Berkeley.

adopting a tough position on this, he would actually see that Bush's attitudes were much harder than mine. If anything, Bush came on even more strongly with Primakov than I had suggested—no doubt, because he genuinely felt that what Primakov was asking was wrong, but also because he was determined to show that Primakov had failed in his mission. Following the meeting, President Bush then sent Gorbachev a message, saying Primakov's approach would allow Saddam Hussein to show that aggression paid off and would undo the very principles that Bush and Gorbachev had agreed upon in their own joint statement issued in Helsinki in September 1990.[19]

Primakov and the traditional elements in the Soviet national security apparatus were stymied for the moment. But to move from sanction enforcement to a resolution that would authorize the use of force to expel Iraq was a big leap for Gorbachev. His "new thinking" was about de-militarizing international relations and promoting dialogue—backing the use of force seemed to negate his basic approach. Not surprisingly, it would take an intense lobbying effort by Baker and the president, reminiscent of that on German unification, to persuade Gorbachev. And, once again, Shevardnadze proved instrumental in bringing the Soviet leader around.

However, in this case, what did the trick was less the provision of rewards—although the United States would respond to urgent Soviet economic needs at one point—and more the readiness to bring the Soviets into US confidence and be responsive to Gorbachev on the crafting of the most important UN Security Council resolution. During a day in and around Moscow in which Baker would spend nearly 13 hours with Shevardnadze and then Gorbachev, explaining the need for a new resolution to authorize force against Iraq, Baker offered something previously unimaginable: a confidential military briefing by Lieutenant General Howard Graves to Shevardnadze on how the US military would fight the war if Iraq did not withdraw from Kuwait. Given the sensitivity of the subject, only Baker, Graves, and Shevardnadze were present, and both Tarasenko and I were asked to leave the room. Shevardnadze was so impressed by this demonstration of American readiness to treat the Soviets as partners that after Graves left the room and Sergei and I had returned, he asked Baker to delay his meeting with Gorbachev to give him some time to "lobby" Gorbachev on the importance of the resolution.

Later, upon listening to Gorbachev's concerns, Baker revised the language of the draft resolution to take account of Gorbachev's reluctance to mention "force" explicitly, and instead inserted language that would authorize the use of "all necessary means"—which legally meant the same thing. He also incorporated into the resolution a 45-day clock before the ultimatum in the resolution would be operative and "all necessary means" would be authorized. Baker did this to accommodate Gorbachev's concern about an ultimatum that ruled out one last effort at diplomacy. Gorbachev suggested that there be two resolutions: one with an ultimatum for withdrawal and a second one to then authorize force; Baker said that the second resolution would render the first one meaningless, but one resolution with a clock would address Gorbachev's concern.

Active, Intensive Diplomacy

The "all necessary means" Security Council resolution transformed the US posture from deterrence and containment of Iraq in Kuwait to one of being able, with international sanctions and backing, to expel Iraq from Kuwait. Even though the United States had successfully orchestrated the adoption of five Security Council resolutions at this point, Prime Minister Margaret Thatcher did not favor pursuing this one—and National Security Advisor Scowcroft and Defense Secretary Dick Cheney supported her view. They worried that the United States would not be able to garner a consensus on actually going to war without some crippling amendments; to try and fail would make it appear that America was using force over international opposition. Better simply to rely on the previous resolutions and Article 51 of the UN Charter. But as Secretary Baker said,

> I agreed with all of them that it would be extremely damaging to lose such a crucial vote. *It made no sense to try for the resolution unless we were certain the votes were there for approval.* I believed, however, that intensive diplomacy could enable us to obtain the necessary support. I argued that it could be done in such a way that we would never submit the issue to the Security Council for a vote unless we were certain we had sufficient commitments to know the ultimate result. In the end, the President agreed it was a risk worth pursuing.[20]

Though it took a special effort to produce this resolution, with Secretary Baker meeting either the leaders or leading officials of every sitting member of the Security Council, the diplomatic effort exemplified the unusual means that were employed from the outset to move the Security Council to adopt resolutions against Iraq. The administration operated at three different levels in managing the Security Council. Tom Pickering, the US ambassador to the United Nations, worked his counterparts in New York; in Washington, ambassadors from the countries on the Security Council were called in for meetings at the State Department; and in the foreign capitals of the countries on the Security Council, US ambassadors discussed every resolution with their host countries. The message was that each of these resolutions mattered and could affect every relationship of that country with the United States, and that there would be no "free" votes.

To reinforce the seriousness of American consultations, each resolution was drafted first in Washington and then shared with other capitals before negotiations in New York even took place. Little was left to chance on the resolutions, especially on the "all means necessary" one.

Baker had promised the president that the resolution would not be brought up if the United States did not have the votes; while Baker took an extended trip every month to see the Soviets, America's NATO allies, and the Saudis, the Egyptians, the Kuwaitis, and the Syrians to manage the coalition (and its Soviet, European, and Arab constituent parts) and to move it from one phase to another, it was his trips to see a senior representative of every sitting member of the Security Council that were the most arduous.

Starting on November 3, he spent 18 days traveling to 12 countries on three continents. In Baker's words, "I met personally with all my Security Council counterparts in an intricate process of cajoling, extracting, threatening, and occasionally buying votes. Such are the politics of diplomacy."[21]

With the Chinese, who were anxious to end the chill in relations with the United States after the breakdown triggered by the Tiananmen Square massacre in 1989, the question was whether there would be a senior-level visit to China by an American official. Even though Baker would meet every one of his Security Council counterparts, he met the Chinese foreign minister Qian Qichen in Egypt, not in China. Qian wanted a presidential visit in return for support for the resolution; Baker promised only a visit by the undersecretary of state to prepare for a visit by him the following year. The Chinese ultimately abstained, permitting passage of the resolution. With the Ivory Coast, Baker promised to explore G-7 debt forgiveness. With Malaysia, he made clear that bilateral relations with the United States would be seriously affected by a "no" vote.

Such were the means that Baker used to produce the necessary votes, and he succeeded in doing so.

Tin-Cup Trips and Personal Diplomacy

From early on in the crisis, the president and his senior advisors understood that sustaining support for the coalition and for sanctions on Iraq would be costly, not just politically but also financially. Countries such as Turkey, and Egypt in particular, would be exposed to extreme economic hardship for respecting the embargo. Turkey would have to close down the Iraq oil pipeline, an extremely expensive proposition for Turkey. To meet both US needs and the needs of those who could not sustain the embargo, Baker launched what came to be known as his tin-cup trips to raise money. He focused principally but not exclusively on the Saudis, the Kuwaitis, the Germans, and the Japanese; at this time, the latter two were prohibited by their constitutions from contributing any military forces.

Baker used his leverage effectively with these four, explaining that costs of this conflict would eventually be measured in blood, and it would not be possible for him to defend in Congress those countries that would gain immensely from the United States expelling Iraq if those countries were not paying their fair share. The logic was compelling, and Baker eventually collected $53.7 billion from these four countries and other allies, leaving the United States to absorb only $7.4 billion of the costs of the war.[22] Aid packages were put together for Turkey and Egypt and were also instrumental in building Gorbachev's stake in staying the course: privately at one point, Gorbachev asked Baker if he could ask the Saudis to provide a four-billion-dollar credit line to the Soviets to manage urgent economic needs. Baker did so, and the Saudis, understanding how critical the Soviets were to the coalition, agreed to help.

Much as in the German case, the intensity and scope of the personal diplomacy conducted by the president and the secretary of state were extraordinary. While President Bush held fewer face-to-face meetings than during the German unification process, he nonetheless met all the key leaders in the coalition (including Gorbachev twice), and his telephonic diplomacy earned him the nickname the "mad dialer."[23] From the outset of the conflict, he was on the phone, calling US ambassador at the UN to give him instructions or speaking to the Saudi king Fahd and Egyptian president Hosni Mubarak to make sure they would be responsive. These were not "check the box" calls; Bush sought to gain support or to reinforce the positions and confidence of those who might be wavering. And at certain key junctures, especially on the eve of the transition from air war to ground war, he held long phone conversations with Gorbachev and others.

For his part, Baker's travels were exhaustive and exhausting. Consider that after issuing the joint statement with Shevardnadze, he returned home to take part in a National Security Council meeting with the president and then turned around almost immediately and flew to Turkey to work out several understandings with Turkish prime minister Ozal. The United States required an agreement with Turkey over cutting the Iraq oil pipeline and using Turkish bases in the event of a war with Iraq. The meeting also provided the Turks the opportunity to outline what they needed to sustain these positions, and Baker agreed to consult on each step should additional pressure need to be brought to bear against Saddam Hussein. Next, Baker flew to Brussels to gain NATO endorsement of America's steps vis-à-vis Turkey—a NATO member—and put the alliance on record against Iraq.

Baker's subsequent trips, most of which involved going first to the Middle East and then to Moscow and back to Europe before returning home, focused on holding the coalition together even as he pursued difference purposes: first the tin-cup exercise; then the effort discreetly to explain to coalition members why the United States was moving from a deterrence-only posture militarily to one that would enable the United States to use force offensively if necessary—and the additional moneys and bases the American side would need for such an increase in forces; then the around-the-world effort to garner support for the "all necessary means" resolution; and finally, one last set of visits to Middle Eastern and NATO countries both before and after the meeting with Tariq Aziz in Geneva to hold the line and prevent any backsliding or division in the coalition in the days leading up to the end of the ultimatum period.

Between the trips and visits to Washington and the phone calls, holding the coalition together was a daily effort. The president and his most senior advisors were riveted on the Gulf crisis and in Richard Haas's words, "Everything else was secondary. The U.S. government, for better or worse, revolved around this set of issues."[24]

New ground could be broken for the sake of the coalition. In addition to the unprecedented focus on the Soviets as the core of the coalition, and getting the Saudis to accept a major US military presence in the Kingdom to deter and later defeat the Iraqi army, Baker also met with Syrian president Hafez al Assad in Damascus to enlist him as an active member of the coalition aligned against Saddam Hussein. While I had felt that there was no need to have the secretary of state travel to Damascus and give this kind of recognition to a leader whose country was on America's terrorism list, particularly when Assad's own enmity with Saddam would generate his support, the president and the secretary saw Syria's overt inclusion in the coalition as essential for gaining credibility in the Arab world. In retrospect, they were probably more insightful than I was: Assad brought Arab nationalist credentials to the coalition, making Saddam's isolation appear much more complete, even in the Arab world.

More than anything else, the readiness to reach out to Syria demonstrated the priority that the administration assigned to having a very broad-based coalition. Baker made Damascus a regular stop on his Middle Eastern trips in the run-up to the war; ironically, Israel was never a stop in advance of the war. The fear of Saddam's being able to exploit hostility to Israel and to make it harder for the Arab partners in the coalition to preserve their anti-Saddam position led to this anomalous situation.

That did not mean, however, that the administration was indifferent to Israeli concerns. It simply did not want Saddam to be able to transform the crisis into an Arab–Israeli imbroglio. But as part of the effort to keep the coalition intact, Baker used his trips starting in November to raise the threat of Iraq striking Israel if it came to war to oust Iraq from Kuwait. With the Saudis, the Egyptians, the Syrians, and others in the Middle East, he raised this contingency and elicited from the leaders of all those Arab states a commitment that they would stay in the coalition, provided Israel did not strike first but only retaliated after an Iraqi strike.

Notwithstanding the conditioning and preexisting commitments, when the Iraqis did launch Scud missiles against Israel on the second night of the war, the administration was convinced that the coalition might be jeopardized if Israel retaliated, particularly because an Israeli air strike would involve overflying one of its Arab neighbors—most likely Jordan. An Israeli military action would, in Brent Scowcroft's words, "change the entire calculus for the coalition."[25]

To prevent such an escalation, Baker and the president spoke to Prime Minister Yitzhak Shamir, and Secretary Cheney to Defense Minister Moshe

Arens, to persuade Israel not to strike back. Arens felt that Israel must retaliate for the credibility of its own deterrent; if it did not retaliate, it signaled that Israel could be pressured into not reacting even when attacked. Shamir was sensitive to this but also more understanding of the American entreaties not to transform the war and thus play into Saddam's hands. However, the administration offered more than only words to persuade the Israelis, both in terms of what it was willing to do for Israel and what it would withhold from it. The United States provided ongoing intelligence; accepted Israeli advice on targeting in Iraq; diverted US air and special operations forces to go after the Scuds in western Iraq and demonstrated that the United States could fly many more attack sorties than the Israelis could against possible Scud launch points; sent Patriot missiles immediately to Israel, which the United States believed were effective in shooting down the Scuds; created a new downlink to give the Israelis a few extra minutes of early warning on the firing of Scuds from western Iraq; sent to Israel the deputy secretary of state, Lawrence Eagleburger, and a team of senior officials as a sign of American support and to be sure Prime Minister Shamir held the line in the face of pressures from the Israeli military to respond.

What may have been more persuasive than anything else with Shamir was that the United States withheld the de-confliction codes from Israel. They were known as the IFF codes—the identification of friend and foe codes. Defense Minister Arens sought these because he understood that without them, if Israel sent aircraft to attack targets in Iraq, there was a great danger that either Israel might shoot down American aircraft or US planes might shoot down Israeli fighters/bombers. Baker, who spoke to Shamir almost every day during this period, was convinced that it was the withholding of the IFF codes that had more impact on the Israeli prime minister than anything else.

He might have been right because notwithstanding the American efforts to prevent them, there were 39 Iraqi Scud missiles that succeeded in hitting Israel, with that generation of Patriot missile proving not to be very effective against them. Fortunately, the material damage was relatively limited and, though the pressure on Prime Minister Shamir to retaliate from the Israeli military and Ministers Arens and Sharon was intense, Shamir held the line and Israel did not retaliate. The combination of intense engagement with him and the American assistance, reassurance, presence, and pressure seemingly did the trick.

Managing Domestic Realities and Going the Extra Mile

The administration was quick to frame the issue internationally and successful in producing the international consensus based on America's core objective. The administration's efforts to produce UN Security Council resolutions that isolated Iraq and then imposed sanctions on it also won public and congressional support. The focus of the administration's work was international, geared to forming and sustaining the coalition.

Congress was asked to do little, and no senior official in the administration made any effort throughout the first month after the Iraqi invasion to put what the United States was doing in the context of a larger explanation. Standing with Shevardnadze and offering a joint statement that condemned the Iraqis and called for countermeasures, and getting off a helicopter and declaring that this aggression would not stand—as the president did—signaled intent and resolve but did not offer a more detailed public explanation of what the United States was doing and why. The focus of the effort was on diplomacy—private, not public. Unlike with German unification, when the administration was highly conscious of public sentiments in Germany, the Soviet Union, and Europe, and felt a need to address those sentiments and try to shape them, the focus was different in this case. Here, the concern was to win the support of foreign governments with the assumption that the American public would follow.

Thus, the very first effort to craft a broader conceptual explanation for America's response to the Iraq invasion took place only in September of 1990, when Secretary Baker had to testify before the Senate Foreign Relations Committee. The secretary and the president were not giving speeches; they were working their counterparts to keep pressure on Saddam. The two efforts need not have been mutually exclusive, but in this case the effort to talk clearly, consistently, and coherently about America's response and its strategy for undoing the Iraqi aggression tended to be made mostly in private.

That did not become a problem until the United States sought to shift course from deterrence and sanctions to the possible use of force—and at that point the administration did not have a built-in reservoir of support domestically. On the contrary, it faced serious domestic opposition. When a bipartisan congressional delegation came to see President Bush on October 30—two days after Congress had adjourned for the midterm elections—Speaker of the House Tom Foley gave the president a letter signed by 81 Democratic congressmen that reflected deep concerns about reports that the "United States has shifted from a defensive to an offensive posture and that war may be imminent." The letter went on to say that the members believed "that the UN-sponsored embargo must be given every opportunity to work and that all multinational, non-military means of resolving the situation must be pursued."[26]

No doubt, that letter reflected the reality that public conditioning had been limited to this point. As President Bush later explained, "part of our problem was that so much was happening away from public view, and few people outside of the top echelon in the White House were paying attention to what was going on in Kuwait."[27] While certainly true, the problem was also that the administration was simply not giving a clear, coherent explanation to the public of what was at stake and why force might prove necessary. The problem became more acute when Secretary Baker, near the end of his global tour to drum up support for the "all necessary means" resolution, answered a press question about US stakes in the Gulf by saying, "jobs, jobs, jobs."

Why did Secretary Baker, probably the most attentive of any of the senior leaders in the Bush administration to the need for domestic and congressional support for the administration's policy, offer this rationale? Because, in his words,

> for weeks I'd been frustrated by the administration's collective inability to articulate a singular coherent, consistent rationale for the president's policy. Our public pronouncements had ranged from the principled to the esoteric. At times we talked of standing up to aggression and creating a new world order. At others we called Saddam the new Hitler and cited the threat to global stability from rising oil prices ... we had done a lousy job of explaining not only the fundamental economic ramifications of Iraq's aggression but also to the threat to global peace and stability ... and we were beginning to pay a political price at home as a result of our rhetorical confusion.[28]

Baker was, of course, correct, but his public response had made it appear that the United States had only narrow commercial reasons for going to war and putting American lives at risk. "Why not let sanctions play out?" was the response of a growing chorus of critics in Congress and in the punditry class. The answer that sanctions were not working and Saddam was simply digging in and fortifying his position in Kuwait was an appropriate response rhetorically but not politically.

Politically, given increased public doubts, it was important to gain a congressional resolution of support to go to war—or so Secretary Baker believed. Most of his senior colleagues—especially Defense Secretary Cheney—did not share his views. Much as they feared the risk of pursuing a Security Council resolution on "all necessary means" and failing, so too did they worry about the consequences of seeking and then losing a congressional vote on a resolution that backed going to war. President Bush sided with Baker, not because the president felt he lacked the legal authority to commit US forces to war. Rather, Bush understood that the war might prove to be costly, and that to launch it amid domestic opposition and without congressional blessing would make it very difficult to sustain the effort.

The administration ultimately succeeded in winning a congressional vote on the war by employing two basic means: first, it got the UN on record authorizing such a mission; and second, it proved that the United States had, in fact, exhausted every means available short of war for trying to get Saddam to withdraw from Kuwait.

With regard to the UN, the logic was essentially to build momentum for dealing with Congress's doubts by obtaining an international mandate for using force. In effect, the administration could then pose the question: Were members of Congress less willing to confront aggression than the UN was? Certainly, questions about the legitimacy of using force were bound to be fewer in Congress once the Security Council had adopted the "all necessary means" resolution. While this was undoubtedly true, both President Bush and Secretary Baker felt that something more was needed—some further demonstration of the lengths to which the administration had gone to use diplomatic means to produce Iraqi withdrawal. And, in fact, they acted to show that they had gone "the extra mile" the morning after the passage of the "all necessary means" resolution at the UN.

The president, Secretary Baker, and National Security Advisor Scowcroft met, and the president then went out and announced, on the morning of November 30, one last initiative to avert war: he invited Saddam Hussein to send his foreign minister to Washington, and he was offering to send Secretary Baker to Baghdad anytime between December 15 and January 15 for face-to-face discussions. This was a dramatic announcement that caught everyone by surprise, including senior staff. I was appalled, and told Baker so afterward, saying that this initiative was bound not only to be seen by US coalition partners as a sign of wavering on America's part, but even worse, it would give Saddam Hussein a perfect opportunity to render the 45-day clock and deadline in the Security Council resolution meaningless. After all, that clock ran out on January 15, and now Saddam merely had to accept the president's initiative by offering talks at or near the deadline.

After additional consideration and some pointed conversations with Saudi ambassador Bandar bin Sultan, the president withdrew the offer and dropped the idea of an exchange of visits, though Secretary Baker did meet Tariq Aziz in Geneva. Without getting into a discussion about some of the external consequences of the announcement, the point here is that America's domestic needs as perceived by the president and the secretary produced this going-the-extra-mile initiative. And to be fair to Bush and Baker, they were correct in terms of its impact. The president's announcement changed the dynamics in Congress, and while the vote on the subsequent resolution was close, the administration did gain a congressional resolution endorsing the use of force.

The president's initiative had one other salutary effect: it headed off other possible bad ideas in the final period leading up to the war. With a 45-day clock and the certainty of war if Saddam did not pull out of Kuwait by January 15, a wide variety of initiatives or intermediaries might well have leaped into the vacuum created during this period. But with the president's announcement and the expected direct US–Iraqi discussions, there was no vacuum to be filled. While some of his advisors might not have fully appreciated what the president was doing, he used his unique "means" to answer a genuine domestic problem and preempt potentially unhelpful international interventions.

Conclusion

Before Saddam Hussein invaded Kuwait, the Bush administration, at least at the highest levels, was consumed with managing German unification in NATO. It was certainly not sending the kind of signals that might have deterred the invasion; to be sure, given Saddam's enormous capacity for miscalculation, that might not have mattered. Some may argue that because it was not paying attention before, and because it defined its objectives basically as undoing Iraq's occupation of Kuwait and not as destroying the power of Saddam's predatory regime, the George H. W. Bush administration left problems that had to be attended to later—a view that many in the administration came to believe.

But Bush was quick to settle on a clear objective and to frame it in a way that was embraced internationally. He settled on a basic strategy for achieving the objective and built an international coalition for carrying it out. America's objectives once the war began remained Iraq's expulsion from Kuwait and not the destruction of Saddam Hussein's regime. This was the basis on which the international coalition had been constructed and maintained. Yes, the US military would destroy much of the infrastructure Saddam had developed for weapons of mass destruction during the war, and the international coalition would agree that the resolutions for a cease-fire should include inspections so Iraq would not be able to develop weapons of mass destruction and threaten its neighbors.

The essence of the objective, however, remained the same, and the determination to act on the basis of an international consensus guided the administration's policy. Its communications with those in the coalition were clear and ongoing. Problems were anticipated and dealt with using intensive personal diplomacy at the highest levels. Hand-holding when useful, pressure when necessary, and high-level attention at all times with the key members of the coalition were the norm, particularly when moving from one phase to the next.

Notwithstanding all the attention and effort, luck still played a part in developing and sustaining the coalition. Indeed, there can be little doubt that having Saddam Hussein as the adversary made achievement of the administration's objective easier. Would the coalition have remained intact had Saddam Hussein been smarter? Could he not have undone the coalition or at least made it difficult to launch the war if he had announced a partial withdrawal shortly before the January 15 deadline imposed in the "all necessary means" resolution? The administration constantly assumed he might do this and then declare readiness to withdraw further once negotiations commenced—and the United States tried to condition those coalition partners it thought most vulnerable to such an initiative. But the administration had little doubt about the impact such an initiative by Saddam would have had. And yet, Saddam never took any real conciliatory steps to create fissures within the coalition. Only by striking Israel did he try to drive a wedge in the coalition, and the United States managed that by getting the Israelis not to respond.

In truth, Saddam Hussein had it in his power to make it far more difficult for the Bush administration to achieve its objective. But being the master of miscalculation, he assumed he would win more by a war in which he believed he could hold his own and force the coalition eventually to give up the effort. Once again, we see a case of statecraft done well—perhaps with the exception of poor framing of US stakes and rationale for action domestically. But the ultimate success, measured in terms of an objective achieved, was made easier by good fortune or luck—in this case, the luck of having an adversary who could not use the leverage he had.

Perhaps the administration's agility in anticipating contingencies and conditioning its coalition partners to them would have permitted it to manage more adroit moves by Saddam Hussein. Certainly, President Bush's sensitivity to the coalition and its sustainability made this move likely.

So did his determination not to expand the objectives in Iraq. He felt that the United States had built the coalition on one basis and could not alter that basis as victory was in the coalition's grasp. Was Bush's reluctance to expand his objectives also driven by his desire not to have the coalition come apart as its mission was being completed? That was certainly a factor in his thinking. However, other considerations led him to resist the impulse either to go after Saddam Hussein or even crush the Republican Guard and make Saddam's regime more susceptible to being overthrown. First, the president and those immediately around him felt that if US forces went to Baghdad, they could trigger a long, messy war with an uncertain outcome. (Bush, in particular, had drawn lessons from the Israeli siege of Beirut in 1982, and was convinced that sending military forces into an Arab capital would be a colossal mistake.) Second, Bush and Baker worried about Iraq fragmenting and becoming both a source of greater instability in the Middle East and creating an opportunity for Iranian/Shia expansion into the Arabian Peninsula. Third, the leadership of the US military was dead set against continuing the war. They had a neat, clean victory and wanted nothing to detract from that or to prolong their presence in southern Iraq. This desire led to a profound reluctance to shoot down Iraqi helicopter gunships that effectively destroyed the Kurdish and Shia uprisings after the war, and after President Bush had called on the Iraqi people to unseat Saddam Hussein.

America's unwillingness to come to the aid of the Shia in particular, as they were being ruthlessly suppressed by Saddam after the war, certainly did cost the United States with Shia in Iraq and created conspiracy theories about American purposes in Iraq. For some, it makes the first Gulf War a case in which statecraft might have been exercised well during the run-up to the war itself but done poorly at the end, particularly because of the legacy that was left.

While some criticism may be warranted, especially for not at least stopping the Iraqi military from using its helicopters against the Shia and the Kurds, the larger question is whether the administration had the right objective for the first Gulf War. An essential part of statecraft is defining objectives and making them feasible and achievable. Inevitably, there could and should be questions raised about whether an objective responds only to near-term needs or is also shaping a longer-term future effectively. To the extent that the administration reversed Saddam's aggression and won international support for disarming his regime of its weapons of mass destruction, its definition of objectives responded not only to the near term. Whether more was achievable is debatable.

The president made a judgment call. All major foreign policy decisions come down to that. In cases when statecraft is done well, all factors are carefully considered. Sometimes, with the passage of time, judgments turn out to be wrong. So long as they reflect careful consideration, with thorough internal discussion, one cannot ask for more. In this case, the tools of the trade were skillfully employed, and the consideration of objectives—even at the end—was serious. It is not possible to say the same about the decision to go to war in Iraq in 2003.

Chapter 8
George W. Bush and the Iraq War: A Tale of Two Terms

If statecraft was done well in the run-up and conduct of the first Gulf War by the George H. W. Bush administration, the same cannot be said of his son's approach to the second Gulf War in Iraq. As I will show, unlike with his father's administration, the objective for going to war in 2003 was not clear; necessarily, the framing of America's purposes was inconsistent; the diplomacy was far too limited and not at the right levels; the assumptions guiding the administration's understanding of what it was getting into were largely divorced from reality; the administration was deeply divided, with those raising questions being excluded; and, remarkably, the United States went to war without ever really debating the pros and cons of doing so.

In short, it would have been hard to practice statecraft more poorly than the George W. Bush administration did in going to war in Iraq and managing the aftermath of this decision. That said, his decision to surge American forces late in his second term was preceded by a very different and far more systematic approach than his decision to go to war in 2003. Condoleezza Rice, Bush's national security advisor in the first term and secretary of state in the second, later offered a simple explanation for the change: George W. Bush "was a different president in 2006 than he was in 2003."[1] She was referring principally to his hands-on, questioning approach—not to his decisiveness. In fact, what we will see in this chapter is that George W. Bush, who referred to himself as "the decider" in the year after 9/11, was still the driver of the decision. The surge almost certainly would not have happened if not for his determination to change the strategy in Iraq that had been set by his secretary of defense, Donald Rumsfeld, and by George Casey, the commanding general of US forces in Iraq from June 2004 until February 2007.

Yes, there was a process that evolved and was driven by the White House, and it reflected serious analysis—and that analysis proved to be right even if it did not fully take into consideration developments on the ground that

Statecraft 2.0. Second Edition. Dennis Ross, Oxford University Press. © Oxford University Press (2025). DOI: 10.1093/oso/9780197698914.003.0008

in the end were pivotal for its success. David Satterfield, who was the deputy chief of mission in the US embassy in Iraq between 2004 and 2005 and then the State Department's lead official on Iraq afterward, would later say that Bush was right with the surge but for the wrong reasons.[2] Others, like former general David Petraeus, would dispute that assessment, believing that the surge was right both analytically and practically. While Satterfield and Petraeus might disagree on the assessment of the surge beforehand and the reasons for its success, they and others certainly agree that George W. Bush was decisive. In reality, both George H. W. Bush and George W. Bush were very decisive when it came to US policies that led to wars with Saddam Hussein 1991 and 2003—and to a change in strategy after the latter war had gone very wrong. The irony is that effective statecraft is unlikely in a circumstance where the president is not decisive. And yet, a president who does not use all the tools in his toolkit, has a poor assessment of the situation, falls victim to groupthink, and lacks a serious process for debating options is destined to produce bad statecraft even if he is decisive.

In this chapter, we will see that in the war in Iraq, George W. Bush was largely responsible for both bad statecraft with terrible consequences, at least up to the end of 2006, and then for much better statecraft in 2007–2008 with positive if not enduring results. Because going to war in Iraq was based on so little understanding of what the United States was getting into—which led to devastating consequences for Iraq, the region, America's standing in the world, and American public's readiness to support engagement in the Middle East—it makes sense to analyze how and why this happened in detail. It is important to explain why the gap between objectives and means was so great and outline all the statecraft failings. But that is not the whole story of the Bush 43rd administration and Iraq. And precisely because there was a better approach to statecraft toward the end of the administration, it is also important to explain why Bush decided by mid-2006 that the strategy had to change and how he went about adopting a path in which he invested a great deal to make sure that his objectives and means were connected.

Background and Context

In 1991, Saddam Hussein's seizure of Kuwait was undone, but America's conflict with Iraq did not end. Regime change was explicitly rejected as an objective by President George H. W. Bush, who resolved early on to stick to the terms of the international coalition he had helped to forge. There was agreement on expelling Iraq from Kuwait; however, there was no consensus on expelling Saddam Hussein from Iraq. President Bush encouraged Iraqis to remove Saddam Hussein, but he would not intervene when Shia in the south and Kurds in the north openly rebelled against Saddam's regime. Fear of mission creep and the disintegration of Iraq led the administration to stand aside and allow the Republican Guard forces (which had emerged largely unscathed from the war) to use their superior firepower to decimate the uprisings.

While President Bush had been determined not to redefine the mission to permit intervention internally in Iraq, he was not prepared to permit Iraq to threaten its neighbors or destabilize the region after the war. And here the administration was successful in also getting the UN Security Council to embrace two additional objectives.

First, the Iraqi army's assault against the Kurds in the north triggered a massive refugee flow to—and in some cases across—the Turkish border. Given its own delicate relationship with Turkey's Kurdish population, Turkey would not permit a massive influx of refugees. To prevent a humanitarian disaster, a protected area under UN control was established in the north, and most of the Kurdish refugees were able to return at least to this area. In time, the Kurdish zones were stabilized, rebuilt, and became largely autonomous from the rest of Iraq—with a no-fly zone for the Iraqi air force adding to the area's quasi-independence.

Second, the Security Council agreed that Iraq's capacity to develop or possess weapons of mass destruction (WMD) had to be eradicated. The council adopted an inspection and monitoring regime and mandated that economic sanctions could not be lifted until inspectors certified that all such capability had been destroyed. According to the terms of the cease-fire resolution 687, Iraq was to cooperate with the inspection regime and to furnish within 15 days all information in any way connected to its WMD programs, labs, or even scientists.

But Iraqi cooperation was not forthcoming. Instead, a pattern of partial, grudging responses began. Only under great pressure would the regime reluctantly respond and belatedly permit the inspectors to go to the facilities they sought to investigate. The Iraqi approach came to be described as one of "cheat and retreat." Iraqis would seek to block, inhibit, stall, and deceive the inspectors, making their work as hard as possible. Eventually, when the pressure grew and threats were made by the United States, the Iraqis would acquiesce to particular inspections. Notwithstanding the Iraqi-imposed impediments to their work, the inspectors succeeded in finding and subsequently destroying far more WMD-related material during the period between 1991 and 1998 than US forces did during the first Gulf War.

To be sure, Saddam remained unrepentant and continued to try to defy the international community. In 1993, he was responsible for an assassination plot to kill former president George H. W. Bush and the Kuwaiti emir during Bush's visit to Kuwait. President Clinton authorized a nighttime cruise missile attack against Iraqi intelligence headquarters in Baghdad in response. In 1994, Saddam again threatened Kuwait, requiring a buildup of US forces before he backed down. Several years later, in 1998, Saddam prevented inspectors for several months from monitoring sensitive sites, and the Clinton administration, following a number of warnings issued from the Security Council, was poised to carry out massive air strikes against Iraq in early November. Only a last-minute retreat in a letter from Saddam to Kofi Annan prevented the US air campaign at that time. Within a month, Saddam walked away from the promises he had made to the secretary-general. As a result, the United States carried out four days of intensive, far-reaching air and missile strikes that inflicted heavy damage on all suspected WMD targets and related military targets.

In response, Saddam refused to allow the reentry of inspectors and declared the end of the inspection regime. While that precluded any further inspections, it also prevented the lifting of economic sanctions on Iraq. The sanctions had imposed terrible costs on the Iraqi public, without staunching the flow of money Saddam used to maintain his omnipresent security system and the lavish lifestyle of his ruling clique.

The toll that sanctions took on the Iraqi population was very grim. The standard of living plummeted, health care deteriorated dramatically, and the country was generally impoverished. The suffering of the Iraqi public—the image Saddam sought to cultivate and exploit—increasingly raised questions about the costs of the sanction regime internationally. To sustain it, and to ease the impact on the Iraqi public, the Oil-for-Food program was developed at US instigation, adopted by the Security Council and managed by the UN. But corruption and Saddam's manipulation of the program helped to bolster him without doing much to change the image worldwide of Iraqi suffering.

Saddam's capacity to sustain the regime—while inflicting greater suffering on most Iraqis—helped to foster competing pressures in the international community and within the United States. Internationally, concern for the plight of the Iraqi people triggered increasing pressure to lift the sanctions. Domestically, there was a chorus of voices in the United States beginning to demand that it was time for regime change. Those lobbying for such a posture were driven by the fears that the mood internationally would make sanctions unsustainable and that once Saddam escaped the sanctions, he would again become a source of grave danger in the region. For domestic critics of the Clinton administration, this promised to produce the worst of all worlds: Saddam free of sanctions and free to accumulate the moneys necessary to feed his appetite for WMD.

In January 1998, the Project for a New American Century sent President Clinton a letter stating, "The current policy, which depends for its success upon the steadfastness of our coalition partners and the cooperation of Saddam Hussein, is dangerously inadequate." The letter emphasized the need for regime change, and its signers included Donald Rumsfeld, Paul Wolfowitz, and Richard Armitage—all of whom would come to have leading positions in the Bush administration that was to follow.[3]

This group played a pivotal lobbying role with Congress, which a few months later adopted the Iraqi Liberation Act. Regime change thus acquired a bipartisan character, even though little was done to act on it. But for those who would be around George W. Bush as he prepared to run for the presidency, there was a deep-seated preoccupation with Iraq and a shared perception that, in the words of Richard Perle, "the feebleness of the Clinton Administration" was appalling.[4]

The legacy of how the war ended, and the conviction that Saddam was an ongoing threat, certainly shaped the views of key Bush advisors such as Paul Wolfowitz. Did they shape Bush's views as a presidential candidate or did they simply reinforce what he already believed? It is difficult to answer this question with any certainty, but one thing is clear: during the presidential campaign, one of the very few foreign policy issues Governor Bush would address and often highlight was Iraq and Saddam Hussein. Following the election, when Bush met President Clinton at the White House on December 19, 2000, the outgoing president told Bush that it appeared from the campaign that the incoming president's national security priorities were missile defense and Iraq, and president-elect Bush acknowledged that this was correct.[5]

The New Bush Administration and Iraq

Upon becoming president, however, George W. Bush (and his White House staff) was not riveted on Iraq, and the initial policy was developed and managed largely by the State Department. "Smart sanctions" defined the policy, which was designed not to accelerate regime change but to make sanctions much more sustainable. The idea was to loosen the sanctions regime on non-military, non-dual-use technologies and allow much more trade and investment with Iraq. The logic: ease the dire economic situation in Iraq while still making it difficult for Saddam to develop WMD. In this way, Saddam would still be "in the box," but the pressure for lifting all the sanctions would dissipate—or so the theory went.

The September 11th attacks changed all this. The world was transformed for the Bush administration in terms of threats, priorities, preoccupations, and missions. Both Secretary of Defense Rumsfeld and Deputy Secretary Wolfowitz quickly focused on Saddam Hussein. Within hours of the attack, Rumsfeld wrote notes in which he contemplated attacking Saddam Hussein in response: "best info fast. Judge whether good enough [to] hit S.H. at same time."[6]

They were not alone: President Bush was also thinking of Saddam Hussein. On September 12, when he was in the Situation Room, he told his counterterrorism team, "See if Saddam did this. See if he's linked in any way." Richard Clarke replied by saying, "But, Mr. President, al Qaeda did this." The president responded, "I know, I know but ... see if Saddam was involved. Just look. I want to know any shred."[7]

Even though the president in the meeting on September 15 at Camp David with his national security team did not accept Wolfowitz's preference for making Iraq the focus of America's initial military response to 9/11—emphasizing instead that Afghanistan would be first—he did not take his eye off Iraq. At the end of the Camp David meeting, he privately asked the outgoing chair of the Joint Chiefs of Staff, Hugh Shelton, if it was a mistake to focus on al Qaeda and not Saddam.[8] On September 16, Bush told National Security Advisor Condoleezza Rice that he wanted plans drawn up if it turned out that Iraq was implicated in the 9/11 attacks; on September 17, he stated to his senior advisors, "I believe Iraq was involved."[9] And, as early as November 21, the president privately asked the secretary of defense, "What kind of a war plan do you have for Iraq? How do you feel about the war plan for Iraq?" After Rumsfeld expressed his concern about the state of war plans in general, President Bush—72 days after the destruction of the Twin Towers—told Donald Rumsfeld, "Let's get started on this. And get Tommy Franks looking at what it would take to protect America by removing Saddam Hussein if we have to."[10]

At a press conference on November 26, five days after asking Rumsfeld to get started on the war plan for Iraq, the president declared that Saddam Hussein needed to let inspectors back into Iraq to prove he was not developing WMD. When asked what the consequences would be if Saddam did not do so, Bush replied, "He'll find out." On December 28, 2001, General Tommy Franks, the head of Central Command, briefed the president at the president's ranch in Texas on the initial plans for Iraq; by February 2002, the president ordered General Franks to begin shifting troops from Afghanistan to the Gulf. [11] In March, President Bush joined a meeting that Condoleezza Rice was having with three senators. He left little doubt about his intentions: "Fuck Saddam. We're taking him out."[12]

While the president would say he had no war plans on his desk, he not only directed the preparation of war plans but also expected to go to war to remove Saddam Hussein a full year before the United States went to war. Richard Haass, then director of the policy planning staff in the State Department, described a meeting he had in June 2002 with Condoleezza Rice, then national security advisor, in which he began to raise some of the hard questions about going to war in Iraq, and she cut him off, saying, "Save your breath. The President has already decided what he's going to do on this."[13]

For Haass, the decision to go to war simply "happened," it was never actually made. Momentum built up behind the presumption of war and took on a life of its own. During the summer of 2002, unease about the drift toward war began to build outside of the administration. At a time when the administration seemed to assume that it had a blank check to do whatever it deemed necessary in the war on terror, and presumed that a war with Iraq could simply be mandated accordingly, questions began to percolate about the wisdom of such a war. But among many in Congress and the foreign policy cognoscenti, these questions remained largely inchoate until Brent

Scowcroft, the former national security advisor, wrote an article in *The Wall Street Journal* on August 15. In the article, entitled "Don't Attack Saddam," Scowcroft argued that there was "scant evidence to tie Saddam to terrorist organizations, and even less to the September 11 attacks." Besides observing that Saddam had little incentive to make common cause with al Qaeda— America's real target—Scowcroft asserted, "There is a virtual consensus in the world against an attack on Iraq at this time," and warned that "so long as that sentiment persists, it would require the U.S. to pursue a virtual go-it-alone strategy against Iraq, making any military operations correspondingly more difficult and expensive."[14]

For a variety of reasons, Scowcroft's article energized questioning about the administration's course on Iraq. First, it was August, there was a virtual news vacuum, and here was a story: the national security advisor to the George H. W. Bush, someone known to be very close to the former president and unlikely to adopt a position that George H. W. Bush would reject, was seemingly challenging the course on which President George W. Bush was launched. Second, the president and his advisors had offered little public explanation or justification for a path that seemed inexorably to be leading to the war with Iraq. Third, Scowcroft's argument created a focal point for others to embrace and yet not be accused of being soft on fighting terrorism or defending an indefensible figure such as Saddam Hussein— after all, Scowcroft had been the national security advisor to two Republican presidents.[15,a]

But it was not only those outside the administration who seized on Scowcroft's article. The leading official who had doubts about the march toward war with Iraq, Secretary of State Colin Powell, used it to marshal greater support for going through the UN to deal with the Iraqi threat. His argument effectively was that the United States would need bases, over-fight rights, and access if America believed that war was going to be necessary; if nothing else, Powell argued that the United States could not simply do it alone. If America was to gain what it needed from others in warfare, it was necessary, at least, to try for a diplomatic solution first, which meant going through the UN.[16]

While Bob Woodward reports that Powell called Scowcroft after the article appeared to thank him for providing the secretary "some running room"

---

[a] Todd S. Purdum and Patrick E. Tyler, "Top Republicans Break with Bush in Iraq Strategy," *The New York Times*, August 16, 2006, https://www.nytimes.com/2002/08/16/world/top-republicans-break-with-bush-on-iraq-strategy.html

to move on what was now his "opportunity," I know from my own conversations with Scowcroft that he spoke with Powell about their mutual misgivings about where the administration was headed on Iraq prior to writing the article, and Powell encouraged him to speak out.[17,b,c] Secretary Powell was trying to steer the president toward the UN, believing this might create an alternative to war by redirecting the United States more toward an international effort to restore inspectors in Iraq.

With the president slated to address the UN General Assembly on September 12, a year and a day after the 9/11 attacks, Powell was hoping to use the speech to focus on Iraq and the need for a new Security Council resolution. According to Bob Woodward, the president made the decision to make Iraq the focal point of his address to the UN the day after the Scowcroft article appeared. In doing so, Bush instructed Condoleezza Rice and his speechwriter Mike Gerson to "tell the UN that it's going to confront this problem or it's going to condemn itself to irrelevance."[18]

Vice President Cheney may not have been enthusiastic about going through the UN, but he certainly favored the idea of challenging it to be relevant if the president was going to speak there about Iraq. Cheney doubted that the UN could be a vehicle for dealing with Saddam Hussein, and feared that trying to get inspectors back into Iraq was potentially dangerous. As he said in a speech on August 26, 10 days after the president's instruction to Mike Gerson on his UN address, "A return of inspectors would provide no assurance whatsoever of his [Saddam Hussein's] compliance with UN resolutions. On the contrary, there is a great danger that it would provide false comfort that Saddam was somehow back in his box." And, for the vice president, there was "no doubt that Saddam Hussein now has weapons of mass destruction. There is no doubt he is amassing them to use against our friends, against our allies, and against us."[19]

Here was a call to action. The vice president was not just setting the stage for the president's challenge to the UN or trying to counter the secretary of state's preference for inspections as the way to contain Saddam. He was also responding to increased public questioning triggered by Scowcroft's article about the administration's policy toward Iraq. No one from the administration had countered the burgeoning view that Saddam was not the prime

---

[b] Scowcroft and I were in Aspen at the time, part of Aspen Strategy Group that was meeting then, and he told me of his discussion with Powell and why he had just written the article.

[c] I had conversations with Scowcroft in early August about what Powell was thinking and his seeking help from the outside from those who shared his concerns.

threat and, in any case, could be handled by putting the UN and inspectors on the case.

The vice president was mindful of the need to preserve a domestic base for America's actions, including his presumption—like the president's—that war would be necessary to remove Saddam Hussein as a threat. Even with the president slated to go to the UN, Vice President Cheney was instrumental in developing a political strategy that focused on getting a congressional resolution authorizing whatever means might be necessary for dealing with Saddam Hussein before getting a UN resolution. He wanted every member of Congress to be forced to go on record on where they stood on Saddam Hussein and his dangerous regime before the midterm elections in early November.

In fact, throughout the fall, it was the domestic strategy that was uppermost in the minds of the White House. Unlike in 1991, forging a domestic, not international, base of support required and received the greatest attention. A full-court press with congressional leaders began the day after Labor Day; the following day, two dozen senators from both parties were invited to the Pentagon for briefings on Iraq with the vice president, the secretary of defense, and George Tenet, the director of Central Intelligence. As one senior administration official said, the White House lobbying campaign with the Hill included "not-so-subtle mentions of the regrets experienced by those lawmakers ... who did not vote for the 1991 'use of force' resolution before the Persian Gulf war."[20]

The domestic strategy was built around getting a congressional resolution authorizing the president to use force to deal with the Iraqi threat, while the UN strategy was geared toward getting inspectors back into Iraq; if Iraq failed to comply with all the requirements, then force could be authorized. The president's speech to the UN did catalyze a great deal of activity, with the secretary of state in New York trying to strike quickly to develop a consensus on action to follow up on the president's call for showing that the UN could be relevant.

The two strategies could easily have meshed, with broad-based congressional support being a useful lever for American diplomats to use with the Security Council. But the strategies tended to diverge in terms of their objectives. With Congress, the administration was focused on the use of force to get rid of Saddam Hussein and his WMD. With the UN, the focus necessarily became disarmament, not regime change or even necessarily the use of force. The difference was significant insofar as the French, the Russians, and others on the Security Council saw the return of inspectors as a device to produce Iraq's disarmament.

Secretary Powell's initial flurry of activity—he held a dozen meetings with foreign ministers on September 13 at the UN—cemented the consensus for pressure on Iraq. But when Iraq, working with Kofi Annan, announced its readiness to have inspectors return, American efforts to produce a clear, unequivocal Security Council resolution quickly ran into difficulty. Neither the French nor the Russians were prepared for a strongly worded resolution that created an automatic trigger on the use of force if the Iraqis were not in compliance with the demands of a new resolution.

Following nearly two months of discussions, Secretary Powell succeeded in producing a unanimous Security Council resolution 1441, which mandated unconditional and unfettered access for inspectors and promised "serious consequences" if Iraq failed to comply. The "consequences" were, however, understood differently by France and the United States. The French, as their ambassador to the United Nations declared in his explanation of his vote on 1441, understood that this resolution created a "two-stage approach," and that noncompliance would lead "the Council [to] meet immediately to assess the seriousness of these violations ... [and] France welcomes the fact that ... all elements of automaticity have disappeared from the resolution."[21] By contrast, even though Powell made a critical concession to produce the resolution—namely that the Security Council would be convened to discuss what to do if Iraq rebuffed the inspectors or was shown to have illegal weapons—the American posture was that a failure to comply meant Saddam Hussein was once again in "material breach," and that that was sufficient to trigger the use of force.[22]

A month prior to the adoption of UN Security Council Resolution 1441, Congress voted to authorize the president to use force "as he determines to be necessary and appropriate" to defend the nation against "the continuing threat posed by Iraq." When it was clear that congressional authorization would be forthcoming, a senior White House official asserted, "Once Congress acts, that's final—that's all that has to happen in our system."[23] The point was that this is what was going to govern the president's behavior, not the resolution in the Security Council. The administration saw Security Council's actions as desirable but not necessary to allow the United States to use force.

When Security Council Resolution 1441 passed, it was hailed by the president: now the world must not, President Bush declared, "lapse into unproductive debates over whether specific instances of Iraqi noncompliance are serious ... If Iraq fails to fully comply, the United States and other nations will disarm Saddam Hussein."[24]

The president was clear, and the administration's efforts to seek support for military action, especially as it related to over-flight rights and access for US forces, became more pronounced. At the same time, America's buildup of forces in and around Iraq also became more visible. For the administration, all this activity simply underscored that Saddam had to comply or else; for others, it signaled an American intent not to give the new inspection regime a chance.

The difference in perception—or the "ambiguity," as Wolf Blitzer called it in an interview with Secretary Powell shortly after 1441 was adopted—came back to haunt the administration as it saw Saddam's initial response being one of noncompliance.[25] Iraq was given one month to provide a full accounting of its WMD capabilities and infrastructure, and no one—including the French and the Russians—believed the Iraqi report was responsive. But France and Russia felt that the inspectors had to be given a chance to go to Iraq and offer their findings.

And it was not only the French and the Russians; most members of the Security Council felt that UN weapons inspectors in Iraq must be given the time to complete their work, even "if it means delaying the onset of hostilities."[26] On January 20, at a Security Council meeting ostensibly held on terrorism, in Secretary Powell's presence, the French and German foreign ministers came out strongly against any early resort to force. Dominique de Villepin, the French foreign minister, who had specifically asked for the session on January 20 to be held at the ministerial level, went so far as to declare, "Nothing justifies envisioning military action."[27]

From seemingly driving the train at the Security Council and being in control of events, the United States looked increasingly to be in the minority. Even America's most important ally, British prime minister Tony Blair, who was under increasing domestic pressure not to rush to war, declared that the weapons inspectors must be given "time and space" to finish their work, and that the January 27 date for Hans Blix, the chief of the UN inspection team in Iraq, to report to the Council "shouldn't be regarded in any sense as a deadline."[28]

The American plan had, in fact, been to use Blix's report as the deadline for decision. Tony Blair's opposition made that impossible. To make matters worse, Blair now made clear to President Bush that the latter needed a second resolution at the Security Council to actually authorize the use of force. The fear expressed by Vice President Cheney that going to the UN could become a trap was now materializing. Nonetheless, President Bush, appreciating the importance of Blair and his domestic needs, agreed to go for a second resolution. Here again, however, French opposition proved particularly troublesome.

The French, particularly President Chirac and his foreign minister Villepin were far more active in framing the issue and lobbying for votes than the United States was. Chirac produced a trilateral statement with the Russian and German leaders, calling for "the substantial strengthening" of the "human and technical capabilities" of the weapons inspectors in Iraq.[29] The answer to the Iraqi WMD program was to have the inspectors do their job and carry out Iraqi disarmament—or, at least for the French, the Russians, and the Germans, to see that the inspectors were given enough time to do the job and to resort to force only when it became clear that Saddam Hussein would never permit them to do the job.

In response to Secretary Powell's presentation to the Security Council on February 5, Villepin, who was to travel to Africa to persuade key non-aligned members on the Security Council, declared, "If this approach fails and leads us to an impasse, we will not rule out any option, including, as a last resort, the use of force ... For now, the inspections regime, favored by Resolution 1441, must be strengthened, since it has not been completely explored ... Why go to war if there still exists some unused space in Resolution 1441?"[30]

To be sure, the administration made an effort to persuade the Security Council and others. Secretary Powell's presentation on February 5 to the council highlighted Iraq's continuing deception and presented evidence of ongoing Iraqi WMD programs. Powell and the administration were persuasive with what Secretary of Defense Donald Rumsfeld called "new Europe," the countries of Eastern Europe, and with a number of members of "old" Europe: the British, the Italians, the Spanish, the Portuguese, and the Danish. But with the exception of the British and the Spanish (and the Bulgarians), most of US supporters were not on the Security Council. Soon after the second resolution was introduced, it became clear that the American and British positions were in the minority. With the head of the International

Atomic Energy Agency, Mohamed ElBaradei, and chief UN inspector Hans Blix reporting that at least some progress was being made with the Iraqis, efforts to persuade several non-aligned members on the Security Council—including Mexico, Chile, Cameroon, and Guinea—became more difficult. These members began to insist they would support a second resolution only if it gave the inspectors more time and if it also included benchmarks on Iraqi performance or non-performance.

The administration was unwilling to go along with such a phased resolution, believing that new reasons for delay would be found—and the debating of noncompliance would rule out America's ability to use force. Even though the United States introduced the second resolution, and President Bush even proclaimed at one point that he wanted all members to "show their cards," America did not have the nine (out of 15) votes needed to pass a resolution, and therefore chose not to bring the resolution to a vote.

Unfortunately, having presented a second resolution, America's failure on it created the impression that the United States was going to war over the opposition of the UN Security Council. Nonetheless, President Bush believed that he had the legal basis needed to launch the war against a regime that had defied the international community since 1991. In speaking to the country on March 19, 2003, to announce the beginning of war, he explained, "Our nation enters this conflict reluctantly—yet our purpose is sure. The people of the United States and our friends and allies will not live at the mercy of an outlaw regime that threatens the peace with weapons of mass murder."[31]

The End of Major Combat Operations and Their Aftermath

The military campaign to take Baghdad and oust Saddam Hussein took three weeks. Cobra II, the military plan for the campaign, depended more on technology, high mobility, precision-guided weapons, and information dominance on the battlefield than on massive forces. Bypassing areas and not fully subduing them fit the plan of getting to Baghdad quickly and forcing a collapse of the regime. It was Secretary Rumsfeld's concept of warfare, reflecting what he saw as the revolution in military affairs. For Rumsfeld, technology and surprise made much more sense in this era than employing large forces. He pressed General Tommy Franks, the head of Central

Command, and Franks in turn pressed his senior officers, such as General David McKiernan, to reduce the number of forces used, keep their buildup time to a minimum, and not count on forces continuing to flow to Iraq once Saddam was ousted.

Anthony Zinni, a Marine Corps general, had been the previous head of Central Command. He developed a war plan for Iraq that provided for a minimum of 380,000 troops to stabilize the country, minimize chaos, subdue any remaining opposition, control all provinces in the country, and safeguard the borders. His plans were rejected in favor of a significantly smaller force. Rumsfeld had been determined to transform the military, its structure, and its approach to war fighting, and the military plan for Iraq reflected his thinking.[32]

At the time, Colin Powell argued that the forces were far too small to achieve the mission. Upon seeing the plan developed by General Tommy Franks, Zinni's successor at Central Command, Powell told Franks in September 2002 (six months before the invasion), "I've got problems with force size and support of that force, given the long lines of communications and supplies."[33] Thirteen months later, after the invasion and the occupation of Iraq, Powell would tell President Bush in October of 2003, "Petroleum is interesting. Electricity is interesting ... [but] Mr. President, none of this makes any difference unless there's security ... Security is all that counts right now."[34]

But Rumsfeld was running the show, and he rejected such thinking; Powell—the former general, chair of the Joint Chiefs of Staff, the hero of the first Gulf War, and the secretary of state—was sidelined and ignored on the question of force size and military strategy. Rumsfeld, however, was not only determined to dictate how the invasion would be conducted and with what forces. He was also determined to transform the concept of what to do after the end of major combat operations. In mid-February, one month before the war, Rumsfeld gave a speech entitled "Beyond Nation-Building"; in it, he described how the postwar reconstructions of the 1990s bred a culture of dependency and were, therefore, wrongheaded. The Bush administration would do things differently in Iraq, reflecting the minimalist approach of Afghanistan. Unlike in the Balkans, where US forces were tied down in a long-term commitment, the Americans would have a smaller presence and be "enablers"; they would limit their presence and assistance and "enable" the Iraqi people to shape their own future. The United States would not rebuild or reconstruct; it would not create a massive bureaucracy to run a country after warfare—as in Bosnia or Kosovo. Much like the use of massive force in military campaigns, the Balkans represented the "old" way of thinking about what needed to be done after a conflict.

As Lawrence Di Rita, Rumsfeld's spokesman, told Jay Garner—the retired general Rumsfeld selected to manage the period in Iraq after the "war"—the secretary was determined to avoid the mistakes that the State Department had made in the Balkans, and the United States would not be creating a long-term military or reconstruction effort. "DoD would be in charge, and this would be totally different than in the past ... We would be out very quickly."[35] (De Rita explained to Garner and his team, "All but twenty-five thousand soldiers will be out by the beginning of September.")[36] To reduce US troop level from more than 160,000 in April to 25,000 in four months suggested a very rapid withdrawal of forces.

Rumsfeld's insistence on limiting the number of troops available and on a rapid drawdown led Garner to tell General McKiernan, "There was no doubt we would win the war, but there can be doubt we will win the peace."[37] Unfortunately, Garner, who was replaced by L. Paul "Jerry" Bremer in May 2003 as the civilian running what became the Coalition Provisional Authority, proved to be far closer to predicting reality than his boss, Donald Rumsfeld.

Changing Objectives

The administration's goals in Iraq appeared straightforward. Regime change was clear; Saddam Hussein had to go. From the time President Bush gave instructions to Secretary Rumsfeld to develop the war plans for Iraq in November 2001, the purpose had been to remove Saddam Hussein.

On a number of occasions, including with visiting leaders, the president made the point publicly that Saddam Hussein represented a danger to the international community, had developed WMD in violation of UN Security Council resolutions, and had used them against his own people and his neighbors—and that after 9/11, the United States understood that it could not risk the danger of Saddam's giving such weapons to terrorists. America would not let him do that; and America would certainly not wait to be hit again. The logic of the post-9/11 world demanded that the United States remove such dangers before they were inflicted on Americans.

The president's new national security doctrine of "preemption" provided a conceptual rationale for such a policy.[38]

As President Bush was also keen to point out, removing Saddam Hussein's regime predated preemption as America's national security strategy. The policy of the Clinton administration toward Iraq had also been regime change—and President Bush often noted this as a way of suggesting that his determination to deal with Saddam was not a departure for American policy.

However, in August 2002, as questions began to be raised about the administration's seeming march to war, and President Bust decided to go to the UN for an additional resolution, the administration's objective began to morph into one of disarmament of Iraq. While the fear that terrorists might get their hands on WMD—and that Saddam Hussein might be the one to give them such capabilities—was certainly part of President Bush's continuing rationale for pressing for action against him, the focus for the UN was disarmament and not regime change.

This created an inevitable tension in terms of what the United States was saying and what it would be seeking. Tim Russert, the host of Meet the Press, raised the apparent contradiction with Vice President Cheney in an interview on the eve of the president's address to the United Nations General Assembly:

RUSSERT: If Saddam did let the inspectors in and they did have unfettered access, could you have disarmament without a regime change?

VICE PRESIDENT CHENEY: Boy, that's a tough one. I don't know. We'd have to see. I mean, that gets to be speculative, in terms of what kind of inspection regime and so forth.

RUSSERT: But what's your goal? Disarmament or regime change?

VICE PRESIDENT CHENEY: The president's made it clear that the goal of the United States is regime change. He said that on many occasions. With respect to the United Nations, clearly the UN has a vested interest in coming to grips with the fact of Saddam Hussein's refusal to comply with all those resolutions.

RUSSERT: So you don't think you can get disarmament without a regime change?

VICE PRESIDENT CHENEY: I didn't say that. I said the president's objective for the United States is still regime change. We have a separate set of concerns and priorities with the UN.[39]

Russert was to raise the same basic question again with Secretary of State Powell a month later on his show:

RUSSERT: So he [Saddam Hussein] can save himself, in effect, and remain in power?

SECRETARY POWELL: All we are interested in is getting rid of those weapons of mass destruction. We think the Iraqi people would be a lot better off with a different leader, a different regime, but the principal offense here are weapons of mass destruction, and that's what this resolution is working on."[40]

Here, Secretary Powell is describing regime change as something that would benefit the Iraqi people, but it is clearly secondary to the objective of eliminating Saddam's weapons capabilities. Leaving aside the obvious difference in tone and content between the secretary and the vice president, the two different objectives had very different implications in terms of US action. Regime change by definition required the use of force; disarmament did not. The objective shaped the means. The administration's confusion on objectives was likely to create confusion on means as well.

Of course, such confusion could have been avoided had there been a clear and agreed-upon sequence of steps. For example, disarmament through inspection and UN-run weapons destruction would be the initial objective, and only if this was frustrated by the Iraqis would the United States then produce disarmament through the use of external force—which presumably meant removing the Saddam Hussein regime as well. That certainly appears to be what Secretary Powell had in mind.

President Bush, however, appears to have had much more in mind. The president appears to have set his sights on goals that went well beyond only disarmament and even regime change. Regime change, in the president's eyes, would unleash much more far-reaching transformations in Iraq, internationally, and in the war on terrorism more generally. In a speech to the American Enterprise Institute one month before the war, President Bush declared that liberating Iraq would be part of a broader approach to democratizing the Middle East. Iraq, the president said, would become a democratic model for the region. The president's objective was to win the war on terrorism not only by military means but also by implanting democracy in the heart of the Middle East. When anger and alienation no longer existed in the Middle East because oppressive regimes were replaced by democratic ones, Jihadists would no longer find it so easy to recruit terrorists; in this way, removing Saddam not only would deal with the WMD threat but would also change the balance fundamentally in the Middle East and in the war on terrorism.

The goals were lofty and visionary. Within Iraq, there would be liberation, an end to tyranny, and the emergence of a society based on moderation, pluralism, and democracy. Outside Iraq, the removal of the regime would mean that Iraq was no longer a threat to its neighbors; a safe haven for terrorists would disappear; an object lesson for Iran and even North Korea would be created on the danger of going nuclear and resisting the United States; and the emergence of a new model of democracy in the midst of the Arab world would likely have a domino effect throughout the area. The president's optimistic view of what would be achieved by regime change even extended to the Israeli–Palestinian conflict. On the eve of the war, he told one group that the liberation of Iraq would produce peace between the Israelis and the Palestinians.[41]

These were the goals and expectations. Much later, in 2006, President Bush began to explain the difficulties the administration faced in achieving its objectives in Iraq by saying that no military plan survives contact with the enemy. It would have been far better had the administration seen the obstacles in 2003.

Obstacles to Achieving the Administration's Objectives

The obstacles the administration faced ranged from the absence of international support for its most important objective to the realities within Iraq itself. Leaving aside what it might face in Iraq, the first problem the Bush administration had to confront was opposition to the objective of regime change. There was consensus on forcing Iraq to live up to UN Security Council resolutions and disarming it as a consequence. But on the Security Council, very few of the countries were prepared to support regime change.

France and Russia were both against it, and France, in particular, was very energetic in mobilizing others to oppose regime change and the use of force. And here, the tension in objectives between disarmament and regime change was bound to make even an attempt at producing a sequenced approach problematic. After all, there were basically different mindsets as to what constituted giving the inspection process a fair chance. America's position was that Saddam was already in material breach of Security Council resolutions, and the first sign that he was resisting 1441 justified the use of force. The French and the Russians—and most of the members of the Security Council—took a different view. Patience was called for in their eyes, and represented a major problem for the administration in terms of the time and content of any inspections process. The ambiguity of 1441 only served to blur these differences and make a unified approach more difficult when subsequent negotiations took place.

But even if the administration had been prepared to be more patient, there was an additional problem with a sequenced approach: while France was willing to support the use of force for purposes of disarmament if it became unmistakable that the inspections could never work, it did not necessarily follow that such a use of force automatically meant regime change. In fact, though President Chirac was not convinced that force would ever prove necessary, even if it did, he still believed that, much as in 1991, force could be used against the WMD and not necessarily against the regime itself. In other words, it was possible to forcibly disarm Iraq of WMD without having to change the regime, which could be very messy and create untold consequences.[42]

Two factors also compounded America's readiness to work the UN process. President Bush was mindful of the political difficulties his father had faced, and was determined not to repeat them. Once he realized there might be a domestic problem in acting against Iraq, his administration focused a great deal of energy and effort on mobilizing domestic support for military action. That is why his approach in the fall of 2002 was geared to Congress first and to the Security Council second. Whereas his father sought to get a UN Security Council resolution to create a domestic base to support America's use of force, George W. Bush worried first about a congressional resolution and saw it as the base for action at the UN. But generating congressional authorization to use force against Iraq before achieving a Security Council resolution on inspections raised red flags at the UN on what the real purpose of the resolution was. While certainly generating greater pressure on the Security Council to produce a resolution on fostering disarmament through inspections, congressional authorization also produced even greater determination among members of the Security Council to give inspections a chance and not create a rush to war.

America's buildup of forces, however, left the United States with little interest in having a drawn-out process of inspections—or even a second resolution that might have given Saddam more time and create benchmarks on performance for the Security Council. Even if the forces involved were much smaller than in 1991 or than General Zinni had envisioned, they still would number roughly 160,000, and the administration was loath to leave them in the area for an extended period of time. (Ironically, in 1990, the United States had nearly 250,000 troops in the Gulf region by the end of October, and close to 500,000 by December. And yet, the George H. W. Bush administration would not launch the war until after the 45-day clock in the UN Security Council resolution expired on January 15, and there was no great pressure to use the force lest the United States not be able to sustain this large presence. Even with a significantly smaller force in the George W. Bush administration, that fear of not being able to keep US forces deployed in the area was paramount.)

To be sure, there were other force-related obstacles. Tommy Franks's war plan counted on a northern front, and that required being able to muster an invasion force from Turkey. But the newly elected government there, led by the Muslim party—the Justice and Development Party—was quick to join the chorus saying that a second Security Council resolution authorizing force was absolutely essential. The Turkish foreign minister, Yasar Yakis, not only emphasized that such a resolution was necessary from Turkey's standpoint, but also called attention to a more fundamental problem of public opposition to Turkey's playing the role envisioned for it: "If we are talking about the extensive presence of American forces in Turkey, we have difficulty in explaining this to Turkish public opinion. It may be difficult to see thousands of American forces being transported through the Turkish territory into Iraq or being stationed or deployed somewhere in Turkey and then carrying out strikes in Iraq."[43]

In addition to the international obstacles that the United States faced, there were, of course, the sectarian realities within Iraq itself. Saddam's rule had cemented the historical advantages for the Sunnis in Iraq, and probably generated one million people who depended on and benefited from his Ba'ath regime. Shias became more of an underclass during his rule and, after the 1991 uprising, had been subjected to even greater deprivation and brutality. Kurds faced Saddam's deliberate Arabization of areas that had traditionally been Kurdish, especially in the city of Kirkuk. Several consequences flowed from Saddam's sectarian policies: Sunnis, if Saddam lost power, would resist losing their dominance to a traditionally Shia under-class. The Shias, who were the numerical majority, would feel that they were finally entitled to receive their due within Iraq, and were bound to be on guard against Sunni efforts to claw back power. And the Kurds, who had enjoyed a protected status of nearly complete autonomy since the creation of the northern zone in 1991, would not simply retain a strong interest in preserving their quasi-independent status from the rest of Iraq, but would also be determined to undo the Arabization of Kirkuk and repatriate the Kurds who had been expelled.

Two last obstacles to achieving the administration's objectives should be noted. First, while the administration sought to make postwar Iraq a model for the rest of the region, this was bound to face problems. Shias were certain to emerge as the leaders of post-Saddam Iraq, given their strong numerical majority, and most of the Arab world is Sunni. Wouldn't others in the region find this a source of threat and not attraction? If so, that would undercut the credibility and appeal of Iraq as a model. Making Iraq non-sectarian and an economic success would, thus, be an imperative.

However, success in Iraq also depended on the administration's being able to draw on all its resources in a coherent, systematic fashion. Unfortu-nately, here there was another problem. The administration was plagued by poisonous relations that pitted the Defense Department and the vice pres-ident's office against the State Department and the CIA. The former saw the great evil of Saddam Hussein and believed deeply that his ouster would have a transformative impact on the region. The latter tended to see Iraq in terms of its divisive, "Balkan" character, retained great skepticism about the region's potential socially and culturally for democratic change, and favored stability over transformation as a result. Such an analytical divide might have fostered a creative tension that permitted a wider variety of problems to be anticipated and dealt with. But that assumed an ability to take each other's concerns seriously and respond to them. Instead, what emerged in the administration was the perception that those who were on the other side of the ideological divide were not to be trusted. Their concerns were not to be taken seriously, their motivations were suspect, and therefore the questions or problems they raised should not be considered.

This division reached absurd lengths. The Pentagon forbade officials from taking part in a simulation the CIA ran before the war on what would happen in Iraq when Saddam Hussein's regime fell—believing that the problems that would surface would give credibility to those who argued against going to war in the first place.[44] In addition, Tom Warrick, who ran the Future of Iraq Project at the State Department, was fluent in Arabic, and had great familiarity with Iraq, was kept off Jay Garner's team—notwithstanding Garner's strong desire to have him—because he was opposed by Secretary Rumsfeld and the vice president's office. And, even though a consortium of think tanks offered the administration a panel of experts to provide facts and options for postwar planning—and National Security Advisor Rice told them, "this is just what we need"—the effort was vetoed because it implied "nation-building," and that was an unacceptable doctrine in the White House and the Defense Department.[45,d]

Divisions within the administration were simply never resolved. The attitudes differed fundamentally on what was needed both to conduct the war and manage Iraq in the aftermath of Saddam's demise. As noted earlier, Secretary Powell raised deep concerns about insufficient troop size, and those concerns were simply dismissed and not addressed. Similarly, he directed his department to create multiple working groups to plan for what needed to be done in postwar Iraq, resulting in a thousand pages of analytical work in the Future of Iraq Project, and that was also ignored. It led Powell in his farewell meeting with President Bush to tell the president that the national security decision-making process—meaning, principally, the National Security Council process—was broken.[46]

Means Used to Overcome the Obstacles

The administration certainly recognized some of the obstacles and sought to deal with them. Secretary Powell made an effort at the Security Council to forge an international consensus on objectives. He worked hard to produce Resolution 1441 and did deliver a 15–0 vote in its favor. Along the way, he made approximately 150 phone calls between September 12 (the day of President Bush's speech at the UN) and November 10 (the day the resolution was adopted). Powell had countless meetings at the UN in New York and Washington. While he did not travel to capitals, he worked hard to produce the resolution, and succeeded. His success, however, did not bridge the differences on objectives; it simply masked them. Perhaps the secretary believed that the resolution would create a new reality. If so, he was bound

---

[d] The administration also ignored similar warnings from experts affiliated with the Army War College and the National Defense University.

to be disappointed. The French and the Russians interpreted his key concession to produce the resolution—namely, that the Security Council must be reconvened for a discussion if Iraq were found to be in noncompliance—as mandating that there could be no automatic resort to force. They felt confident that they were creating obstacles to the use of force, while the secretary believed that he was creating a path that would either obviate the need for force because Saddam would comply or justify it because he had not done so.

The secretary's judgment that the UN route provided his only real means to try to reconcile the difference in objectives was understandable. However, the only way the UN path could have succeeded is if the inspectors had immediately reported that Saddam Hussein had changed his behavior. Given Saddam's desire to preserve ambiguity about his WMD for deterrence purposes against Iran and for coercive purposes domestically, that, unfortunately, was never in the cards.

What about the means used to get a second resolution? After all, achieving a second resolution would have created a basis—backed by the Security Council—on which to use force against Iraq. Prime Minister Blair felt that a second resolution was essential, and even though the administration believed 1441 to be sufficient authorization and said so publicly, President Bush understood his partner's needs, and instructed that the United States make the public effort to secure a second resolution. The same basic technique used for the first resolution was applied. The secretary of state made numerous calls to his counterparts and also had meetings in Washington and at the UN in New York. In addition, the president telephoned those most recalcitrant, such as Presidents Putin and Chirac.

To try to persuade members of the Security Council—and the international public more generally—Secretary Powell, who was considered the most credible of administration leaders on the world stage, also made a detailed, televised presentation before the council, offering evidence that Saddam Hussein was continuing to develop his WMD programs and obstructing the work of the inspectors in defiance of Resolution 1441.[47,e]

---

e Ironically, according to the interrogation of captured Iraqi generals and officials, some of the evidence that Secretary Powell cited as proof of Iraqi efforts to hide their continuing WMD programs was, in fact, evidence of guidance given by Saddam to make sure that all traces of WMD residue were destroyed once and for all.

The secretary and his key aides also discussed in New York, or on the phone, different ways to accommodate concerns of countries such as Mexico and Chile, each of whom, if persuaded, might have swung enough votes to cross the threshold of having at least nine Security Council members supporting the resolution. Had that been the case, then either France or Russia would have had to veto the resolution; the French strategy, according to their ambassador to the UN, was to block the resolution, not veto it.

Additional efforts were made to gain international support; the administration won the support of most of the Eastern European countries to back military action in Iraq and to garner both limited logistic and in some cases small combatant force contributions to the effort. Statements of support were also orchestrated to show that the United States did have international backing for going to war.[48]

The administration also used offers of financial assistance to try to win support from those whose involvement was seen as critical. In the case of Turkey, the administration, trying to persuade the Turkish government to permit American forces to operate from and through the country, offered a sizable package of potential assistance: three billion dollars in aid, three billion dollars in financing, and promises to secure one billion dollars in free oil and access for Turkish companies to reconstruction contracts in both Iraq and Afghanistan.[49] With the Russians, there were also hints of inducements, at least with regard to Russian oil companies not losing out on the existing contracts they had to develop Iraqi oil fields—assuming, of course, that the Russians played ball on the second resolution. And with Chile, there was the suggestion that a Free Trade Agreement could be reached quickly.

Whether trying to forge an international consensus on objectives or to produce support or important backing of others, the administration made an effort politically and economically to demonstrate that it was not acting alone. The secretary of state worked the phones and the environs of the Security Council in New York. The deputy secretary of defense was sent to Turkey to win Turkish support, and the undersecretary of state for political affairs went to Moscow and Paris to gain Russian and French acquiescence. Though the president and the secretary took one trip to Russia, as we will see in discussing why the administration's efforts and the means employed failed, the level of the effort tended to be too low, lacked intensity, and had to overcome other policies that soured the atmosphere.

How did the administration deal with the obstacles related to the internal realities in Iraq and the consequences of warfare? It planned to deal with contingencies that it found most likely and dangerous. In a briefing at the White House on February 24, 2003, less than a month before the war, the interagency preparations for providing "humanitarian support in Iraq in the event of any military action" were outlined. The displacement of people, a breakdown in the distribution of food, and the destruction of oil wells and infrastructure were uppermost in the list of concerns. The need to ensure the quick provision of humanitarian supplies was a clear priority. Two guiding principles for shaping America's response to these contingencies were (1) to rely primarily on civilian relief agencies and (2) to ensure effective civil–military coordination.[50]

Representatives of several governmental agencies explained the nature of the planning to deal with the expected contingencies. What is unmistakably clear is that planning for contingencies was geared toward the disruptive humanitarian consequences of the war—perfectly sensible but not particularly related to sectarian realities and the consequences of the collapse of the regime and the power vacuum that might result from that.

To be sure, the administration was mindful of minimizing the human impact of the war and the disruption of services, and it tended to see its strategy as cutting off the head of the snake but leaving the body intact. In the words of Elliott Abrams, the lead briefer at the White House, on February 24, the military campaign would be designed to "minimize the displacement and the damage to the infrastructure and disruption of services."[51] The assumption was that with Saddam and his cronies gone, a new Iraq could rapidly emerge, provided the United States did limited damage to the infrastructure and the Iraqis had their oil intact to finance their recovery and reconstruction.

It was not unreasonable to worry about the contingencies that the administration considered and to develop the means to deal with them. It is interesting, however, that destruction of oil wells and refugee flows and displaced persons reflect contingencies seen in the first Gulf War, when Saddam set the Kuwaiti oil fields on fire and triggered a massive Kurdish refugee problem. While generals are often accused of preparing to fight the last war, it appears that Secretary Rumsfeld planned to fight a different war of "shock and awe," with much smaller forces, but prepared for the contingencies of the last war.

The fact that Saddam had set Kuwait's oil fields on fire but not his own was a distinction considered not to be important. The assumption was that if Saddam was going down, he would bring everything down with him. The problem was that Saddam thought he would survive, and he was not going to destroy the financial source of his power. Similarly, who were going to be the refugees of 2003? They would not be the Kurds, because those remained protected. Displaced people from fighting could certainly be created, but massive refugee flows were unlikely, particularly given the plan for the war, which was to move rapidly toward Baghdad and bypass areas without fully subduing them.

And here we see the gap in military and civilian planning. Notwithstanding the claim that there would be close civil–military coordination on relief, the military plan made that difficult, at least in the early going. The US military would be bypassing areas, not acting to control them. Relief agencies would not be able to get into Basra and other areas throughout southern Iraq because the military aim was to get to Baghdad quickly, not facilitate the entry and security of those providing relief in areas that US forces had already gone through on the way to the north.[52,f]

There were certainly other inconsistencies: one of the avowed purposes of the war was to deal with Iraq's WMD and ensure that they could not be given to or fall into the hands of terrorists. Yet the shock-and-awe plan did not provide for the forces necessary to find and control WMD sites or to control the borders in a way that would have prevented terrorists from either going to such sites or smuggling what they acquired out of the country.

Perhaps the reason this inconsistency did not figure highly in the minds of the administration planners is that the overriding objective was getting rid of Saddam. Get rid of Saddam, produce regime change, and everything would fall into place, not fall apart. That was the critical assumption, and it was based on a flawed assessment. Statecraft must start with assessments based on reality, and not on faith. If we are to understand the failures in Iraq, this is the starting point.

Understanding the Failures in Iraq

The greatest single failure in Iraq is related to the assessments. Certainly, the intelligence failure on WMD created a major problem; had the United States been able to display the WMD to the world, the region, and the Iraqi public,

---

[f] Jay Garner had counted on being able to move quickly into Basra but was told by General David McKiernan that there would be no forces available to help in that regard.

there would have been far greater acceptance of the legitimacy and importance of the US mission. With displays of truly awful biological toxins and weapons, who would have challenged the need or the merits of the mission? President Bush was sensitive to this, wanting there to be camera crews with forces who would seize the WMD to show the world what the US military was uncovering in Iraq.[53]

Ironically, however, the United States was lucky that there turned out to be no WMD, because the US military were so ill-equipped to control all the possible sites and to prevent terrorists from getting their hands on them.[54] And here, again, we see flawed planning and flawed assessments. It is not just that the assessment that the US military would be greeted as liberators proved to be wrong; the administration also failed to anticipate the chaos, the looting, and the complete breakdown of law and order.

Each of these latter events had a devastating impact on the nature of America's task in Iraq. The chaos and the looting made the challenge of reconstruction vastly more difficult. One estimate of the cost of the looting was $12 billion dollars, the equivalent of the revenues Iraq was projected to generate in the first year after the war.[55] Quite apart from the cost of repair, the materials lost and destroyed greatly complicated the task of providing electricity and reconstituting oil production, and further vitiated American credibility with the Iraqi people. After all, in a region in which conspiracy was like oxygen and breathed by everyone, Iraqis asked how the United States could remove the seemingly all-powerful and untouchable Saddam Hussein in three weeks and yet could not prevent looting or get the electricity resumed. The explanation inspired by conspiracy theories was that the United States did not want to restore order because Americans simply wanted to occupy Iraq.

Was looting something that was hard to imagine or prepare for? No, it was not: outside humanitarian groups that met with administration officials warned the administration about it. In the State Department's Future of Iraq Project, there were similar warnings. And when Jalal Talabani, who later became president of Iraq, came with other Iraqi opposition leaders to meet with Vice President Cheney and Secretary of Defense Rumsfeld in August 2002, he called attention to the danger of looting, observing that there were many poor people in Baghdad, and that if there was no authority in Baghdad, they would take the law into their own hands.[56]

Moreover, there were those both within the administration and outside who were focused on the need to establish law and order quickly. One official in the Justice Department proposed a plan that called for 5,000 international police advisors to be rushed to "Iraq to fill the law enforcement vacuum after the collapse of Saddam's government."[57] Robert Perito of the United States Institute for Peace briefed the Defense Policy Board on February 28, 2003, only weeks before the war, calling for a civilian constabulary to keep order, and telling the board that the United States would not be able "to rely on local authorities" to meet the needs of providing law and order, and that "prior experience indicates the regular Iraqi police will be unavailable, intimidated or unprepared to act in the chaotic postwar environment."[58]

But such warnings and proposals flew in the face of the administration's image of what would happen in Iraq after Saddam fell. Problems that America needed to deal with in Iraq were seen as largely humanitarian; without Saddam, Iraqis would no longer be oppressed and could assume their responsibilities, no longer impoverished and inhibited by a brutal dictator and his corrupt elite. Looting, disorder, lack of security, and insurgency were not part of the administration's assessment or planning. While the CIA did not warn of insurgency, its National Intelligence Council did warn that the "building of an Iraqi democracy would be a long, difficult, and probably turbulent process, with potential for backsliding into Iraq's tradition of authoritarianism."[59] After generations of being oppressed, it would not be easy to share power.

In the world of division and distrust in the administration, such warnings were interpreted as an indication of opposing the enterprise of liberating Iraq and bringing democracy to the country. For those who were driving the policy, and who were convinced of what would be achieved in Iraq, there was every reason not only to dismiss the doubters as wrongheaded but also to dismiss and ignore the problems they raised. Secretary Rumsfeld might speak of planning, but such planning was limited, came late in the process, and gave short shrift to the very problems that would plague the US military once they were in Iraq.

To make matters worse, once American troops were in Iraq, there was a continuing denial of what was happening on the ground. During the phase of major combat operations, the attacks of Fedayeen Saddam were not seen as a precursor of an insurgency that required dealing decisively with these forces and that demanded they not be allowed to melt away. Afterward, Secretary Rumsfeld denied that the US military were facing a guerrilla war, refused even to use the word "insurgents," and continued to refer to violent incidents as being the work of dead-enders who, by implication, could not amount to much.

Though an insurgency should have been anticipated—and was not—by the administration policymakers, there were those who foresaw it as a certainty. They saw Sunnis finding it difficult to accept losing their status of dominance in Iraq—the status they had enjoyed since Ottoman times. Those in the administration who understood this, suggested that rather than submit to the Shia, whom Sunnis saw as an underclass, the remnants of the regime would find sanctuary in the tribal areas of the Sunni triangle and fight an insurgency from there.[60] Had such warnings been heeded, the administration would have understood not only that it needed more forces, especially to pacify Anbar province (an area where the absence of forces made it easy for the insurgency to take root), but also that the United States needed to avoid any possibility of becoming a symbol of occupation in Iraq. Once America became such a symbol, the insurgency was bound to become far more sustainable.

Perhaps if the administration had seen that it would be facing an insurgency and needed to avoid the insurgents' acquiring legitimacy and sustainability, it would have understood the importance of having UN backing for the war. The United States did not need the Security Council backing to remove Saddam, but certainly needed it afterward. It was essential that the United States not become the administrator of Iraq after Saddam lest America be seen as an occupier. The United States needed a UN administrator or an international administrator (such as Carl Bildt) on the ground in Iraq, but not an American administrator. But the administration believed that this was America's victory and that America, not others who did not share America's vision—whether at the UN or in the State Department—would shape the post-Saddam Iraq.

The Defense Department planners who controlled the process did not foresee an insurgency; President Bush was an optimist, and those empowered in his first term on Iraq foresaw a rapid movement toward a model democracy, with the United States as its enablers. The administration would later create the Coalition Provisional Authority and remake Iraq: the United States would "de-Ba'athify" the system and disband the military—strategic blunders on par with the decision to have an American administrator guide post-Saddam Iraq to the Promised Land. The administration's assessments were shaped by an ideology, not by the realities of Iraq. The first task of statecraft is to have objectives that are clear and not confused. They can be ambitious, but they must fit the world as it is, not as we wish it might be; it takes well-grounded assessments to refine objectives and shape them so they fit reality.

Clearly, the Bush administration failed in the first task of statecraft. Unfortunately, it also failed in the second task: frame the objective in a way that gets others to accept its legitimacy. Colin Powell's effort to reframe the objective as "disarmament" was successful to a point. It might even have been successful in overcoming the gap between disarmament and regime change—the administration's real objective—if Powell could have persuaded his boss and his colleagues to give the inspection process enough time to make it appear credible to others on the Security Council, especially swing votes such as Mexico and Chile. In such circumstances, he might have been able to produce a second resolution at the UN that would still have won backing for the use of force.

But the failure on the second resolution, no doubt partly the result of the context in which the Bush administration was not willing to allow more time for the inspection process, also resulted from what can only be described as a failure on the third task of statecraft: effective use of diplomacy. The diplomatic effort made by the administration was extremely limited. Where was the high-level attention? Where was the intensity of the effort? Where was the constant working of issues and readiness to preempt problems or to reassure at critical moments? Where was the travel by the most senior officials to the critical foreign capitals to show the administration's concern for the political needs of others and give them an explanation with their publics?

This is not to say there was no effort, but rather that a limited number of phone calls by the president, and a secretary of state who made only one trip to Russia and China, are simply not sufficient in circumstances where the administration needed to convince others that it was seeking to do the right thing. The higher our stakes, the greater our effort should be. However, in this case, as the United States raised its stakes to get ready for the use of force, and as such use became even more controversial, the administration's effort varied little. Certainly, Secretary Powell did not travel or even match the number of phone calls he made in advance of gaining support for Resolution 1441. Perhaps he felt that such efforts could not pay off.

But with Turkey so critical to the United States having a northern front, how is it possible that the secretary of state would not visit that country? True, the deputy secretary of defense went and, true, the incoming

Turkish leader was invited to the White House and, true as well, a very significant package of assistance was offered. But the vote in the Turkish parliament went down by 3 votes out of 514 cast. Had a major public effort in Turkey been made by the United States, showing sensitivity to Turkish concerns, demonstrating publicly (not only privately) America's responsiveness to Turkish economic needs, giving interviews in Turkey to the electronic and print media, would the vote still have gone down?

Maybe the mood in Turkey would have ruled it out. However, when you barely lose in parliament with a relatively weak diplomatic effort, it is at least arguable that raising the profile of what the administration was doing and reaching out much more visibly to the Turkish public—and thereby strengthening the hand of those Turkish leaders arguing for responsiveness—might well have made the difference. To prove the point, contrast the effort of the Bush 43rd administration with that of the Bush 41st administration in the first Gulf War. In the six months leading up to the war, Secretary Baker made three trips himself to Turkey; the president called Turkish prime minister Ozal nearly 60 times—phone calls that became part of the public domain in Turkey, so that Ozal could speak credibly about his talks with his "friend" President Bush. Acting in this way with an ally builds their stake in being responsive, even on those issues that are difficult. In 2002–2003, the administration simply did not make an effort that either helped produce a new dynamic within Turkey or even raised the costs to the Turks of turning the United States down.[61]

Of course, the limited diplomacy cost the United States not only with Turkey. Secretary Powell seems to have believed that visits to capitals could not accomplish much more than meeting at the UN or talking on the phone with his counterparts. Phone calls have utility, especially if there is already a strong personal relationship. But face-to-face meetings with counterparts will always be critical in any negotiating process. Face to face, one can read the body language as well as the verbal responses; face to face, there is more opportunity to persuade or dissuade; over the phone, it is always easier to say no. Face to face, there always seems to be more time to explore the nature of differences and find ways to overcome or manage them; and face to face, there is a more natural tendency to do real strategizing: anticipating emerging problems, determining where someone in a possible coalition will need to be shored up, and comparing notes on who else may be helpful in persuading recalcitrant parties to come along.

While meetings in New York could have overcome the limitations of phone calls, they were bound to have some disadvantages. Almost by definition, the number of meetings with different foreign ministers is certain to limit the time for each. Of course, there is great value in having multilateral settings for meetings, because coordination can take place far more easily. It was not wrong for Secretary Powell to see the utility of operating at the UN. But such meetings could not take the place of going to capitals, where time, outreach, and context would have created more opportunity to achieve America's desired end.

Unfortunately, the administration's statecraft failings were not limited to confused objectives, disastrous assessments, misguided planning, weak diplomacy, and poor communication and framing of the issues. Perhaps the least understandable failing of its application of statecraft was in its approach to the second resolution at the UN. True, Tony Blair insisted on the need for a second resolution, but it is hard to imagine that Blair thought he would be better off with a very visible public failure in trying to produce it.

Contrast the administration's approach with Secretary of State James Baker's effort to produce the "all necessary means" resolution in 1990. Baker believed the resolution was necessary and yet was opposed in this by Prime Minister Thatcher and Secretary of Defense Cheney—both of whom argued that the United States had the necessary legal basis for war already and would undercut its position politically if the administration went for such a resolution and failed. Baker responded that he would not go for the resolution in public unless he was absolutely certain that he could produce it.

Baker explored the issue with the other members of the Security Council in private, determined not to go public until or unless he was certain he had the votes. In 2003, the Bush administration should have done the same—and Blair would certainly have been better off with an outcome in which the United States was not going to war after failing to win backing for a new UN resolution giving America the authority to do so.

In the end, the Bush 43rd administration's approach to going to war in Iraq and managing its aftermath stands as a model of how not to do statecraft. Could statecraft have been more effectively employed? Given the sectarian reality and the need to make sure there was no power vacuum after Saddam, Iraq was bound to be difficult. However, a realistic assessment of what the United States was getting into, a military plan with far more forces capable of dealing with the full array of missions, an understanding that existing institutions could not simply be dismantled, a Baker-type management of the

UN Security Council, and an international, rather than American, administration of Iraq, would have avoided many of the mistakes the George W. Bush administration made. The insurgency did not have to take on roots the way it did—and a focus on security could have certainly minimized, if not preempted, the sectarian war that emerged.

David Petraeus would later recount that as he led the 101st Airborne Division into Iraq, he saw that many of the assumptions that guided the administration going into the war were invalidated, first and foremost that the United States did not need larger forces to be able to provide stability in a post-Saddam Iraq.[62] Moreover, he observed not only that there was insufficient planning for the "Phase IV" operations for stabilizing Iraq following regime change, but that the planning done was focused overwhelmingly on humanitarian operations and not on the "establishment of wide area security, repairing critical infrastructure, re-establishing basic services and instituting governance—all issues that had been given inadequate attention by the planners and leaders at the most senior levels."[63]

While Rumsfeld dictated the shape of postwar planning and the creation of the Coalition Provisional Authority, he—as noted earlier—denied the reality that the US military were facing an insurgency. But that reality was finally understood by 2004 and began to guide the military's approach.

Background to the Surge

The Coalition Provisional Authority was established with General Jay Garner as its head on April 21, 2003—a month after the Bush administration launched its attack on Iraq. As noted above, Garner had grave doubts about the size of the forces going in and their ability to provide security that would be needed after Saddam. He also understood that one could not simply deconstruct the existing institutions, especially the military, not only for reasons of security and law and order but also given the reality of high unemployment. He sought to dismantle the elite Republican Guard—the backbone of Saddam's regime—but use the bulk of the military to help with reconstruction.

Garner's problem was that the Rumsfeld Strategy produced a power vacuum even as it generated little capability to deal with the looting and chaos that followed Saddam's fall. Garner's image was soon tainted by the terrible imagery of mass looting of infrastructure and of the symbols of the Iraqi heritage in the state museum; the complete breakdown of law and order; the inability to provide electricity; and the general absence of governance. Believing that General Garner was not up to the task, Rumsfeld convinced President Bush to replace him on May 11 with Ambassador Paul "Jerry" Bremer. As the Coalition Provisional Authority administrator, Bremer was determined to go in a different direction than Garner. Bremer issued his first directive on May 16 in which he disbanded the Ba'ath party and began a process of "de-Ba'athification." Bremer's second order, issued one week later, dismantled the Iraqi military, security, and intelligence infrastructure.

Bremer's decisions unfortunately deepened the disorder and the chaos and were driven by a central presumption: America's problem in Iraq was not a Sunni insurgency but the monumental task of cleansing the country of those who had brutalized it. America's main task was seen as proving to the Shia and the Kurds that the United States was not going to remove Saddam Hussein only to allow his henchmen to take over and empower a new Sunni regime.[64] These assumptions were not without some logic. Since at least initially the administration did not believe there would be a Sunni insurgency, there was a need to reassure the Shia majority and the Kurds that they would no longer be suppressed by a Sunni regime—and thus could participate in the development of the new Iraq. With the goal of the Coalition Provisional Authority being to dismantle itself and turn governance over to an interim Iraqi authority in one year, it was essential for these previously subjugated populations to see that this was truly a new day—as the United States made sure there could not be comeback for those who were part of the previous regime.

Unfortunately, there was an insurgency, and it was fed, at least in part, by an approach that seemed to completely disenfranchise the Sunnis. Too few forces in Anbar and Nineveh provinces gave the insurgency the chance to take root, and de-Ba'athification meant large numbers of Sunnis were suddenly unemployed.[65,g] Combined with the disbanding of the military, the de-Ba'athification order produced immediately 400,000 newly unemployed Iraqis, many of whom still possessed their military weapons.

Secretary Rumsfeld may have denied there was an insurgency, but General John Abizaid, who replaced Tommy Franks as the head of Central Command in June 2003, was quick to see it. With a background in the

---

g Being a Ba'ath party member was necessary to get a job in the civil service; even being a teacher required one to be a member of the party.

Middle East and fluent in Arabic, Abizaid came to his position with a belief that US forces would necessarily be a target. He would say at one point, "Foreign forces are always rejected in the Middle East. They're like a disease that enters the organism and then all the anti-bodies form and try to reject it."[66]

When General Casey assumed command of US forces in Iraq in the summer of 2004, he and Abizaid were of like mind. They felt the need to accelerate the transition from American forces to Iraqi forces. With a smaller American footprint, and with the emergence of Iraqi governance, the insurgency would lose its appeal—or so they believed. President Bush would describe US strategy as the Iraqi forces "stand up, we will stand down." The strategy thus became one of transition, with a belief that creating political and economic progress would create security.

And by that measure, there was considerable progress made in the years 2004–2005. The ground was prepared, and by June 2005, elections were held for a transitional National Assembly; a constitution was drafted and approved, and in December 2005, a parliamentary election was conducted with high turnout and with relatively limited violence. A new political reality was seemingly emerging in Iraq—one in which Iraqis would be assuming responsibility for their own governance. The assumption guiding US policy was that once the Iraqis had a stake in the new system and thus the United States was no longer seen as an occupier, the vast majority of Iraqis would view the insurgency principally as a threat, and those trying to stoke it would have neither credibility nor appeal.

Good in theory, perhaps, but what the approach ignored was the sectarian dimension of Iraqi politics and life in the post-Saddam reality. The presumption was that a new Iraqi national identity would emerge—in which the republic would not be shaped by sectarian but national politics. And with time that might well have been the case. But the new politics with elections actually favored the majority and those who were Shia. The new governance that was emerging gave power to those who had been oppressed by the Sunni minority—and Sunni Arabs saw little place for them in Iraq. The disbanding of the military and de-Ba'athification had penalized primarily the Sunnis, and the emerging political process was largely excluding them.

Into this mix, Abu Musab al-Zarqawi of al Qaeda in Iraq wrote a letter to Osama bin Laden and the al Qaeda leadership in which he made the case for targeting Shia. This, in his thinking, would produce a violent Shia reaction, and the resulting sectarian conflict would unite the Sunnis. The intelligence community got a hold of the letter, and the State Department would publish it in February 2004. In March 2004, Zarqawi's group carried out a series of bomb attacks on Shia celebrating the Ashura holiday, killing nearly 200 people. Following that, they launched a campaign of assassinations, bombings, and kidnapping of Shia civilians. Among the attacks was the bombing of a mosque in July 2004 in which 98 people were killed, and in August a suicide truck bomb targeted Shia workers, killing over 100.

Counter-terror raids by the new Iraqi military, which the US military was training, targeted Zarqawi's group, killing those connected with it but also innocent Sunni civilians.[67] Zarqawi's aim was to trigger a sectarian war, and the more Shia were killed and violence escalated, the closer he came to achieving this goal. Shia militias emerged—most notably Jaish al Mahdi, led by Moktada al Sadr—and launched their own attacks against Sunnis under the guise of protecting the Shia from those threatening them. But it was not only the Jaish al Mahdi militia operating outside the purview of the Iraqi government; it was also the new Shia-run Interior Ministry that was arresting and torturing Sunnis without much regard for whether or not they were part of al Qaeda or involved in attacks against the authority.

The security situation was deteriorating even as the Bush administration believed that political progress was being made. According to the strategy, the security was supposed to improve. Indeed, that was the core assumption underpinning the strategy. But as Condoleezza Rice would later say, "The Pentagon kept saying, from 2004 onward, well, when the politics straighten out then the security will straighten out. The politics were getting somewhat better, but the security situation wasn't straightening out."[68]

The destruction of the al-Askari Mosque—one of the most important Shia shrines in Iraq—in February 2006 hit the administration much the way the Tet Offensive hit the Johnson administration in Vietnam: it was a shock, and it prompted a recognition that a strategic reassessment was desperately needed. The security situation and level of violence were getting worse, and the situation was evolving in a way that the administration had neither expected nor predicted. The symbolism of the attack served as a wake-up call within the Bush administration. This was not just about a Sunni insurgency. There was a sectarian war taking place—and just as the administration was slow to recognize the insurgency, so too it had failed to fully comprehend that a sectarian conflict was intensifying. But the destruction of the al-Askari Mosque in Samarra was a turning point.

David Gordon, the head of the National Intelligence Council at the time, felt something fundamental was changing in Iraq. He would later say that he was concerned that "we were transitioning into something very different, that we were really transitioning into a civil war, and that was definitely the predominant view in the intelligence community."[69] For others, the symbolism of the destruction of the al-Askari Mosque, and the psychological effect it had, confirmed what they already suspected to be true: what the United States was dealing with in Iraq was more than just an insurgency. Douglas Lute, who was the director of operations for Central Command under General Abazaid from 2004 to 2006, would say, "I think maybe the genesis, the original genesis—that things were not going well, and maybe slipping out of control came with the bombing of the Samarra mosque in what was early, early 2006. I think by then it became increasingly clear that we weren't dealing only with a Sunni insurgency, but we are dealing with a combination of factors that were approaching the point of being overwhelming."[70]

Stephen Hadley saw this as an indication that the entire mission in Iraq was at risk, and something different needed to be done. President Bush would later recount how Hadley's views affected him: "When Hadley, whose judgment I trust a lot, came in and said, 'We're going to have to do something, it's falling apart,' that was a seminal moment. In other words, up to that point in time, we were hoping things would get better, and they weren't."[71]

From this point, the president began to ask harder questions of the military about the strategy, but Abizaid and Casey remained convinced that the major problem was the insurgency. After all, it was the Sunni Islamists that blew up the al-Askari Shrine. Rumsfeld had come around to support their position, in part because he remained anxious to draw down US forces, while Abizaid and Casey were even more convinced, in the words of Peter Mansoor, that withdrawing US forces from "Iraq's cities would help reduce violence. After the Samarra bombing, they failed to adjust their thinking on the issue."[72]

But questions about the war, its costs, its directions, its prospects which seemed increasingly dismal, and its effects on the region were growing in Congress. In March 2006, they would lead to the Congressionally mandated formation of the Iraq Study Group, to be headed by James Baker and Lee Hamilton.

The Iraq Study Group's mission was to investigate the war and its conduct and to make basic recommendations. The group's report certainly provided an outside impetus to change course in the war, but it was the growing doubts about the strategy within the administration itself, and especially at the White House, that would initially put pressure on Casey and Abizaid to alter the strategy and ultimately impose the surge over their opposition.

Casey and Abizaid still remained convinced they were on the right track by the late spring of 2006 because after the December elections and months of bargaining, Nouri al Maliki assumed the office of prime minister on May 20—meaning there was no longer an interim government but rather a legitimate, duly elected Iraqi one. Moreover, on June 8, US forces succeeded in killing Zarqawi. Casey, in the aftermath of these developments, opted for launching Operations Together Forward I and II to show that things were now moving in the right direction. Unfortunately, instead of demonstrating the success of the handover to Iraqi forces, these operations failed, seemingly proving the opposite—and the security situation continued to deteriorate. Fred Kagan of the American Enterprise Institute, who was part of a group of outside experts called in to discuss the war with President Bush, said that Together Forward "was absolutely a counterproductive operation that was driven by a, at this point I've got to say, pretty blind acceptance of our own theories of what was going, not enough in touch with what was actually going on."[73]

Casey had been driven not just by the belief that the way to defeat the insurgency was to get US forces out of the cities but also by the directives of Rumsfeld which were all about getting the Iraqis to take over. But he acknowledged with General Peter Pace, the chair of the Joint Chiefs of Staff, and also with Abizaid in July 2006, that he had changed his mind about how quickly the United States could reduce forces, telling Pace, "I don't see us as off-ramping here. This is a security situation that has not gone in the direction I thought it was going to go in."[74]

Reflecting his and President Bush's concerns, Hadley raised a question with Casey: "Is it part of the US and coalition security mission to stem increasing levels of sectarian-fueled violence?" According to Bob Woodward, this question weighed on Casey. He knew classic counter-insurgency strategy held that security of the population was the top priority, but he also understood that undertaking that task "would require more forces, and he was hesitant to ask for more because it was contrary to his overall strategy of preparing and training the Iraqis to take over."[75]

At the same time, Megan O'Sullivan, who had served in the Coalition Provisional Authority in Baghdad and had become responsible for Iraq policy at the White House, wrote a memo to Hadley on July 19, entitled

"Adjusting Our Security Strategy to the New Realities in Iraq."[76] In it, she pointed out that the "current focus on drawing down coalition troops is one of several factors suggesting that we are executing a plan based on assumptions that are no longer valid."[77] She suggested that it was the moment to determine whether the United States had "strategic options for filling any gaps between available US resources and what may be required to ensure long-term success in Iraq."[78]

In her memo, O'Sullivan was artfully suggesting that there was a need to explore the feasibility of expanding US forces in Iraq as opposed to drawing them down. Here is the first carefully articulated suggestion that a surge might be necessary. However, Peter Feaver, who worked with O'Sullivan on the National Security Council staff, later explained her real aim: she was actually trying to push the idea "of a thoroughgoing review ... but instead of launching it in a formal interagency way, she hit on the idea of teeing up the questions that had been the terms-of-reference questions for the review, giving those to the president to ask Casey directly."[79]

O'Sullivan would later describe this as asking hard questions in a private setting that would trigger re-thinking, noting that Hadley was "feeling really uncomfortable with where things are going, and the president's feeling really uncomfortable."[80] Hadley described the tough, provocative questions that O'Sullivan and her colleagues prepared for the president to ask in his secure video conference calls with Casey and US ambassador to Iraq, Zalmay Khalilzad, as designed to provoke them "to take a strategic relook." Hadley wanted them to be on board with the need for such a reassessment.[81]

While Hadley wanted them to see the need for such a "relook," he also decided by early September that a serious reconsideration of the options could not wait, and he directed the "Iraqi team" at the National Security Council to launch a private review. That group—consisting of O'Sullivan, Feaver, Kevin Bergner, and Brett McGurk—concluded that the existing strategy was based on flawed assumptions, and they began to shape an alternative based on increasing the forces with an eye toward providing security first and foremost in the cities.

Parallel to the National Security Council private internal review, two other reviews in the Pentagon and the State Department were also launched at this time. Peter Pace, after prodding from retired General Jack Keane—who told him the strategy was failing and he needed to do his job and not simply accept Casey and Abizaid's approach—established his own private review. Pace created what became known as the "Council of Colonels," who he charged with a ground-up strategy review, with all possible options to be considered. At the same time, Condoleezza Rice, who was deeply skeptical of the existing strategy and what it was costing the United States in the region and world, also pushed an internal review within the State Department.

At this time in September 2006, none of the reviews being conducted were known to those in the other departments. Hadley, adding to the parallel nature of the reviews, directed his deputy J. D. Crouch to ask Bill Luti on the National Security Council staff, a former Department of Defense official, "to put on his force planner hat and use his informal contacts at the Pentagon and design a surge. What would it look like? What would the—what forces would you need? How would you deploy the forces? And what would the surge look like? And could it succeed ... I wanted this to be completely independent."[82]

Luti's analysis showed that with an influx of five brigades, focused principally on Baghdad, a surge could work. O'Sullivan's team knew nothing about the request to Luti, but as Hadley observed, Luti's findings "validated where Megan and her team were going." He gave a copy of Luti's work to Chairman Pace and later to O'Sullivan. Only then did Hadley decide it was necessary to have a formal review process—one timed to be launched after the 2006 midterm elections, not wanting stories coming out that the administration was questioning the existing approach in Iraq and the strategy of Generals Casey and Abizaid.[83]

The formal interagency review process was launched in November, and its guidance "was to assess all available policy options."[84] It involved all the relevant departments and agencies, but it did not produce a consensus, especially with both the State Department and parts of the Pentagon skeptical about the surge. Secretary of State Rice doubted the surge would work; she believed that the sectarian conflict could not be resolved by the United States and would essentially have to burn itself out. Other than Pace, the chiefs felt that US forces were already strained to the limits—with morale an issue given the need for repeated deployments of US soldiers to Iraq—and grave doubts about where the additional forces for the surge would come from. Hadley, however, insisted that the president be presented with all the options, including the surge. And the president made the decision to adopt that option. He would announce the decision on January 7, 2007, and over the next six months the additional forces would be phased into Iraq—with a vastly new mission and a different pattern of deployment.

The surge was not just an increase of forces; it was guided by a counter-insurgency mission, meaning protection of the population was its top priority. The surge would be largely successful in dramatically reducing violence and ending the sectarian war and the ethnic cleansing that was producing hundreds of bodies every day in Baghdad. It transformed the security situation and the political realities in Iraq. At this point, let us turn to the statecraft employed in this decision and its implementation.

Objective

Was the objective clear? The aim was ambitious—protect the Iraqi population so it could sort out its internal differences peacefully and stabilize politically and economically. Nearly four years into the conflict, this objective was about fundamentally changing the course of the war and was driven by President Bush. David Satterfield believes that President Bush defined the objective for the surge: the United States is not going to lose this war. In Satterfield's words, the president "believed to his core that success was possible. He also believed to his core that it would be inexcusable and irresponsible, in a historical context, for him having invested this extraordinary amount of treasure, this extraordinary amount of lives, American and Iraqi, not to make one final push to see if success could be achieved."[85]

For Bush, defeat was not an option; hearing Hadley's concerns that the United States needed to change course lest everything fall apart, was a "seminal moment" for the president. Meghan O'Sullivan would cast the objective more prosaically and less dramatically than Satterfield, saying that the objective of the surge was "to help stabilize Iraq's security situation in order to enable Iraqis to resolve their disputes through political means."[86]

Bush may have driven the objective, but there were those working for him who were convinced that success was possible, and they felt they read the situation in Iraq better than US military leadership there. In other words, their assessment of the reality differed from that of Casey and Abizaid.

Meghan O'Sullivan observed that Casey and other military leaders continued to believe that the root of the violence was the American presence:

Even in October [2006], that was still the view that was coming to the White House most consistently, which was the only way to bring down levels of violence is to bring down levels of US forces ... I think I asked them just to say, 'Can you tell us how Iraqis react to you when you go into their neighborhoods or you leave them?' And, to my memory, every single one of the commanders said they welcomed us with open arms when they arrived and people begged them not to leave.[87]

O'Sullivan would continue to go to Iraq and pose questions to the local commanders, but given her time in the Coalition Provisional Authority, she had developed her own contacts with a range of Iraqis. Her assessment that a surge was needed and would work had become stronger during the course of 2006 and very much drove the review of her team at the National Security Council. It also influenced President Bush. At one point, "the president asked Meghan O'Sullivan ... how her friends in Baghdad were feeling. She replied that they have 'never been so scared' or pessimistic about their future. This moved the president ... If she was worried, the president was worried."[88]

Given her time in Iraq and her support for the effort, President Bush was predisposed to accept her assessment about what was now needed, and Hadley too became a believer in it—especially as the situation worsened and there was little sign that the military leadership in Iraq either grasped the situation, its causes, or the remedies for it.

But O'Sullivan's team, at least some of the Council of Colonels, and General David Petraeus—who had rewritten the army manual on counterinsurgency—were clearly on a different page than the US military leadership in Baghdad. They collectively shared the assessment of the realities on the ground and the means that would be needed to achieve the objective that the president had adopted.

Means

At one level, the means involved an increase of US forces, but the surge could not succeed in overcoming the "obstacles" to transforming the deteriorating situation and stabilizing Iraq with just more American military power. It would rely on other means, including both political and economic/reconstruction resources, as well.

Meghan O'Sullivan described the surge as reflecting a very different strategy—this was no longer about pushing a transition to Iraqi forces as the goal; rather, the new approach emphasized first and foremost ensuring security for the Iraqi population. However, this did not mean that the goal of strengthening the Iraqi army and increasing their responsibility for security had been abandoned. The surge was not just about providing additional American forces; it also was predicated on a commitment from Iraq's leadership to increase Iraq's military as well.[89] And it involved creating growth and economic possibility in key provinces—hence, there would be a doubling of the number of provincial reconstruction teams (PRTs). To ensure security for the PRTs, brigade combat teams would be embedded with them.

The role of the PRTs was twofold: build up the economies of local areas and identify moderate actors to support at the local level. This approach naturally complemented the emergence of the Sons of Iraq/the Sahwa (Awakening Councils) who were already fighting al-Qaeda in Iraq. They would be paid by the United States, and US forces would deploy with them— to that end, the US military increased its presence by 4,000 troops in Anbar province where the bulk of the fighting with al Qaeda was taking place.

The surge was accompanied by a change in commanders—Petraeus for Casey in February 2007 and Admiral William Fallon for Abizaid in March 2007—and a new ambassador, Ryan Crocker for Zalmay Khalilzad, also in March 2007. In addition, Robert Gates replaced Donald Rumsfeld as Secretary of Defense less than a month after the midterm elections. Not only would the means being applied change to fit the objective, but there would now be a new team on the ground responsible for its implementation—and this team were deep believers in the approach and worked very well together. They not only had the full backing of the president, but he had daily calls with them to make sure they had what they needed. This produced, in David Petraeus's words, "a whole of government effort" with rapid responses from every agency to requests Petraeus and Crocker would raise with President Bush. It also gave Bush constant insight into what was happening on the ground.[90]

Bush's hands-on effort extended to weekly secure video calls with Iraqi Prime Minister Nuri al Maliki. Bush understood that if there was not an Iraqi partner in the surge and its aims, there could not be success. There had to be Iraqi commitments to generate additional forces as part of the surge, and there needed also to be a readiness to adopt a national, not sectarian, approach to the use of force and governance. Bush was convinced that if he invested in Maliki and engaged with him, he could be that partner.

Bush's instinct was to focus on personal relations. In the Middle East, leaders often focus on the personal relations, and Bush's predisposition in this regard turned out to be an effective means with Maliki. Zalmay Khalilzad would say that the "most important thing to understand about Maliki ... was his near-existential fear of a Baathist coup ... He watched like a hawk as the United States built and reformed the Iraqi security forces, fearing that we were empowering individuals who would execute a coup."[91] Engaging Maliki the way Bush did on very much of a personal level may have been the only way to move him. Bush would later say that "in order to affect how another leader behaves, you have to court that person and have to befriend that person, and you can't do it by hectoring or lecture."[92] That would be his approach to Maliki, treating him as an equal and a partner, with the idea that the two of them "were 'in this together'—they would either succeed or fail together."[93]

Of course, notwithstanding his instincts, Bush still needed Maliki to act as a national leader if the surge had any hope of succeeding. His meeting with Maliki in Amman on November 30, 2006 proved to be pivotal in convincing him that Maliki would do his part and the surge could work. Without that assurance, Bush would have been uneasy about going ahead with the surge, notwithstanding his belief that defeat was not an option. As Stephen Hadley, Megan O'Sullivan, and Peter Feaver would later write, "President Bush believed that a public commitment from Maliki [that a surge would be carried out on a strictly non-sectarian basis] was in many ways a prerequisite for his own decision to authorize the surge ... Such a commitment would mean much more than simply putting Maliki on record; it would require him to do something courageous and irreversible: take on the political party of Moktada al Sadr that had been critical in making him prime minister."[94]

Maliki would, in fact, take on Sadr and his militia, responding to Bush who in the Amman meeting told him he was willing to commit tens of thousands of additional forces, provided Maliki did his part. Bush persuaded Maliki.

Although from this point on Bush was ready to act on the surge, he understood that his own military's leadership was not in favor of this plan, and he would need to bring them along. Hadley would work on Chairman Pace, sharing Luti's analysis with him, and Pace's own Council of Colonels review eventually convinced the chairman that the surge was the right thing to do. Hadley hoped that Pace and the formal review would similarly bring the other heads of the services, as well as Casey and Abizaid, on board.

But it did not. The Army and Marines were bearing the burden of having fought two wars starting in Afghanistan and then moving to Iraq, where the war had not gone according to expectations (or, rather, assumptions), and there was an unmistakable strain on the manpower of these services. Bush understood that the surge would be unpopular in Congress, and its critics would seize on any dissonance from the military.[h] So he knew that he needed to bring the military commanders around to "be on board with any decision he made."[95]

He went to meet the Joint Chiefs of Staff in "The Tank," the secure facility that the chiefs use in the Pentagon. Bush was meeting them on their turf. He faced real resistance from the heads of the Army and the Marines who argued that a surge "would 'break the force' and demoralize the troops and their families ... President Bush responded that while he understood the problem, what really broke a military force was losing a war—implying that without a surge, that is what would happen in Iraq. The chiefs suggested that the American people and the Congress would not support a surge. President Bush replied that managing the politics was his job, not theirs."[96]

That was not enough to persuade them, but Bush made a promise that reassured them. He promised that as part of the surge, he would make a request to Congress to increase the size of both the Army and Marine forces overall. Hadley, O'Sullivan, and Feaver point out that analysis had been done months earlier at the National Security Council that showed it was possible to increase the overall force size in a way that would help ease the strain caused by the surge in the short run.[97]

In many ways, Bush's confidence, decisiveness, and engagement helped to bring the military around—just as investing personally in Maliki moved the Iraqi leader to act in ways he had not done before and reduce his sectarian instincts at least as long as Bush was president. Presidents have considerable means that they can call on to overcome obstacles and achieve their objectives, but their own level of commitment and belief matters. In this case, Bush had analysis and reviews revealing that a surge was an effective option, and his own beliefs led him to persevere in the face of those who were skeptical or dubious.

Perhaps the biggest skeptic was his secretary of state, Condoleezza Rice. She saw the surge as a roll of the dice—the last card the United States could play—and worried and wondered what would happen if it failed. She doubted that the United States could make the difference in a sectarian war, she did not trust Maliki, she was worried about the toll the war was taking

[h] I was called to testify before the Senate Armed Services Committee after the surge was announced. I appeared on January 25, 2007 with General Keane, and while he was supportive of the surge, I was skeptical. I doubted that it could work if there was not more of an indication that Maliki could act as a national leader, not a Shia one.

on America's interests in the region and internationally—and she routinely expressed her skepticism. According to David Satterfield, at one point Bush had had enough and rebuked her, saying "I am sick and tired of your defeatist attitude."[98]

Satterfield would later recount that he and Rice were wrong and Bush was right—but that Bush was right for the wrong reasons. One could argue that the success of Bush's plan depended on luck. If it had not been for the Sons of Iraq rising to fight al Qaeda and for Moktada al Sadr retreating in the face of Maliki's directing the military to fight his militia, the surge, according to Satterfield, would not have succeeded, and he and Rice would have been proven correct.

Satterfield says that at the time, there was "no factual basis to believe the surge would produce a different result than the operations that preceded it." He says the tribal awakening took place because al Qaeda was threatening the very structure of the tribes, but that was not clearly visible yet. Sadr and his senior commanders saw the fight turning against them and decided not to resist, but that too was not something the administration understood at the time. Satterfield believes that without these two developments the surge would have failed.[99]

Hadley and O'Sullivan argue otherwise. They believe that Maliki's readiness to fight Sadr's militia was the result of the president's readiness to do the surge and of his persuasion. Moreover, they argue that the surge was not just focused on security for Baghdad, and point out that President Bush also ordered several battalions into Anbar province. "The Marine battalions were to link up with the Sunni tribes in Anbar province and provide them with training, equipment, operational planning, intelligence, and close air support. The Marines also offered assurances, backed by commitments from the Iraqi government, that when the fight was over, the Sunni tribes would not be abandoned by Baghdad."[100]

What may be true is that when the surge was first conceived and formulated, the two critical developments—the Sons of Iraq rising and Sadr's forces withdrawing—were not in evidence. That said, by the time the surge was implemented, they were—and the surge clearly helped to sustain these developments.

Aside from employing military, political, and economic means effectively—and taking advantage of the emergence of the Sons of Iraq and the end of the Jaish al Mahdi resistance—the administration used diplomacy to get Iraq's Sunni Arab neighbors to restore relations with Baghdad and offer support to it. This, too, demonstrated how the administration was going to bat for Maliki and the regime. At the same time, the United States created a carrot and stick approach to the Iranians in Iraq. David Petraeus describes how the US military arrested Qods Force operatives but he and Crocker also met with and talked to Iranian officials—making clear the United States would not tolerate the provision of weapons to Shia militias even as the discussions with Iranian officials indicated that the administration understood Iran had some legitimate concerns in Iraq.[101] What is also noteworthy is that the Iranians did not push back against US pressure—in fact, Petraeus explained that the Iranians were shocked by the arrests of their Qods Force officials and scaled back their actions as a result.

Conclusion

It is hard to avoid the conclusion that George W. Bush, at least with regard to Iraq, had two very different administrations. The statecraft of the first, which included invading Iraq and removing Saddam Hussein from power, was bad from almost every perspective or measure. The objectives and framing were at times confused and divorced from reality. The assessments of what the United States was getting into were poorly understood, and the administration excluded those who had the most expertise on Iraq. The military doctrine and forces deployed reflected Rumsfeld's theory about war in an era of hyper mobility, intense firepower, and the ability to fuse intelligence with operations better than ever before. This could produce shock and awe, but what about what would happen afterward? Nowhere in this process does one see Bush asking skeptical questions—indeed, there does not seem even to be a coherent process. Small wonder that the postwar phase was a disaster.

Bush in the second term, thus, had to overcome the disaster created by his administration's approach to the war. He probably still relied on the military's approach for too long, but he did begin to ask hard questions. He had a team at the White House and the State Department that began asking hard questions even in 2005, before the al-Askari Shrine was blown up. It did take Stephen Hadley and the Iraq team at the National Security Council to challenge the assumptions of the military command in Iraq—and the process of reviews took a long time to actually unfold—but it did take place.

The parallel reviews were each no-holds-barred. Yes, there was a presumption at the National Security Council about the need for more forces and for a new strategy focused on population protection, but its review, like the others, looked at everything. One could argue that had each department known about the other parallel reviews earlier, that process could have been integrated and been more efficient. Still, given how poor the prior assessments had been, and how key assumptions had not been challenged and simply taken as a given, the parallel reviews actually made it more likely that the internal discussions would be freer and more likely to reconsider everything. Ironically, when the review was finally formalized in November 2006, it did not produce consensus, but it did outline in detail the pros and cons of different options, including the surge.

The process might not have been perfect, but the statecraft surrounding the surge was sound. Once the new strategy was agreed upon, the objective and means were in sync. The framing of the surge and its aims were spelled out effectively. The forces fit the mission, and Bush used his leverage with Maliki smartly—and Petraeus and Crocker managed the follow-through and their leverage deftly as well. As it turned out, the timing of the surge was fortuitous with the emergence of the Sons of Iraq and with Jaish al Mahdi retreating. Was it just luck? Or was there an interaction with what the administration was now prepared to do? Maybe a little of both. In any case, the surge was successful in providing security, reducing violence, and creating much more political space within Iraq so disputes could be settled peacefully.

The surge certainly achieved its near-term objectives. By 2008, there was a 90-percent reduction in violence, al Qaeda in Iraq was largely defeated, the leading Iran-backed Shia militias were largely sidelined, and Iran's influence was greatly diminished.[102] How did the plan do in terms of intermediate and longer-term objectives?

In her transition memo for the incoming Obama administration, Meghan O'Sullivan wrote that much had been achieved, but the next 18 months would prove critical to Iraq's future—and her words proved to be prophetic.[103] She emphasized that the upcoming elections—initially, the provincial council elections that would take place almost immediately after Obama took office and then the national elections in March 2010—would help determine how things evolved over time. In her eyes, how the elections were conducted, their aftermath, the drawdown of American forces, the integration of the Sons of Iraq into the Iraqi security forces, and the follow-on negotiations to the Status of Forces Agreement would all go far in defining whether the surge would have an enduring successful effect.

To his credit, President Obama backed away from his campaign position of drawing down the US presence one brigade per month. He also designated then-Vice President Biden to work with Maliki—and the elections that O'Sullivan flagged did take place in an atmosphere that remained largely stable and secure. The national election also produced a multi-sectarian party, Iraqiya (Iraqi National Movement), which was headed by Iyad Allawi, a Sunni, and won the most votes. However, it could not cobble together enough votes to form the government. Still, Iraqiya's electoral success was a remarkable development—a truly national party won the most votes, drawing votes from all groups. It was the best indication that there was hope for an Iraqi government that could transcend sectarian politics. Unfortunately, the inability of Iraqiya to produce a majority in parliament to form a government led the Obama administration, after months of political stalemate, to back Nuri al Maliki again as prime minister, instead of Allawi. Could the administration have done more and used its leverage to broker a government with Allawi as the head? It is not clear. What is clear is that the United States and Iran ended up supporting Maliki again. Regrettably, the sectarian Maliki, whom Zalmay Khalilzad described as having an existential fear of a Sunni coup, returned as well. While Vice President Biden, not Obama, would deal with Maliki and tried to follow the Bush approach, the US military was drawing down, and its reduced presence seemed to add to Maliki's suspicion and paranoia about a coup. Maliki began to make changes in the security establishment and army even before the United States completed its withdrawal of all US forces by December 31, 2011—the date mandated by the Status of Forces Agreement (SOF) that the Bush administration had negotiated with the Iraqi government.

O'Sullivan points out that there was always a plan to renegotiate the SOF to enable an ongoing American presence—relatively small, advisory, counter-terror, but also a force that could be augmented if needed. This was, in fact, what the Obama administration sought to negotiate—and probably would have succeeded had it not been for the Arab Spring, which proved infectious as Arab publics lost their fear and demanded better governance and reform. In Iraq, it produced large demonstrations, and suddenly no Iraqi groups—including the Sunni politicians who most wanted the United States to stay—were prepared to vote for a new SOF that provided US forces immunity from prosecution (Obama's condition for keeping any forces in Iraq).

As a result, all US military forces were gone from Iraq by the deadline of December 31, 2011.

Hadley, O'Sullivan, and Feaver argue that a "continued US force presence—even a small one—would have provided the United States some continued influence over Maliki." They also point out that these US forces would have provided some additional military capability while giving the United States grounds to maintain pressure on Maliki—as it had been doing for years—to "refrain from politicizing Iraqi military appointments and intervening in operational decisions."[104] Hadley, O'Sullivan, and Feaver go on to argue that the withdrawal of US forces sent a message to the Iraqis that "we were no longer fully committed to their cause," and that message, in turn, boosted those who wanted Iraq to return to its old political ways, even as such a return ensured that there would be no "credible and forceful counterbalance" to Iran's influence.[105]

Whether the argument made by Hadley, O'Sullivan, and Feaver is correct or not, what is unmistakable is that Maliki replaced competent military leaders with Shia loyalists, did the same in the intelligence and security organs, and walked away from his promise to integrate the Sons of Iraq into the security services. In addition, he stopped the payment to the 100,000 Sons of Iraq whom the United States had been paying and he had committed to continue compensating. His governance was not just sectarian, it was also corrupt.

The political and economic dimensions of the surge—which were critical to its success—thus disappeared. The surge was well thought out, but clearly all of its dimensions needed to be sustained if it was to become institutionalized. In retrospect, the return of Maliki, instead of Allawi—and without a continuing American presence—meant that the surge could not produce longer-term success in Iraq. That, however, should not detract from the fact that the surge is an example of statecraft done well.

Chapter 9
Syria: A Debacle in Every Sense

At the time of writing this book, the conflict in Syria may have settled into a new status quo on the ground, with Bashar al-Assad still in power; with his regime having recaptured important parts of Syria it had lost, like Aleppo; with areas of Syria in the northwest, like Idlib, controlled by Turkish-backed Islamist groups; and with areas in the northeast—like Manbij, Kobane, and Raqqa—controlled by the Kurdish-led Syrian Democratic Forces. An American military contingent of about 900 is deployed largely to work with the Syrian Democratic Forces to prevent ISIS from re-emerging. And with Arab states increasingly arguing that isolation has not worked, most are now reconciling with Assad, and Syria's membership in the Arab League has been restored.

From that standpoint, Assad has won. He is still in power, which has always seemed his only concern. But his country has been devastated, its population has been impoverished, there are roughly six million people displaced in the country, he is dependent on the Russians and the Iranians, and the country needs at least $300 billion for reconstruction (which is not going to be forthcoming). With foreign presence and over 40 percent of the country not controlled by the regime, and with refugees not returning, one could argue that the Syrian conflict is not over. But the story of how it got to this point is worth telling in some detail. I will do a serious evaluation of the Obama administration's statecraft in Syria. As we will see, there was an unwillingness to use the means necessary to achieve the publicly stated objectives, in no small part because of the fear of the consequences of being sucked into another costly and messy conflict in the Middle East. The administration's assessments were poor and there was an inability to see the consequences of not acting at different points throughout the conflict.

Of course, context mattered; after Iraq, any US president would have been hesitant. The realities in Syria reinforced hesitancy. As Hillary Clinton would later write, Syria was a "wicked problem."[1] Wicked, because the challenges were unmistakable, and, unfortunately, all the options appeared to be bad. In this chapter, I will not pretend that the challenges the administration

Statecraft 2.0. Second Edition. Dennis Ross, Oxford University Press. © Oxford University Press (2025). DOI: 10.1093/oso/9780197698914.003.0009

confronted in the Syrian conflict were simple or easy to address. I will point out, however, that the Obama administration's approach ensured the worst of all possibilities—namely, a humanitarian disaster with a very high death toll; huge refugee flows which helped generate a populist, nationalist reaction in Europe; regional actors who, seeing that the United States would do little, competed with each other, compounded the fissures in the opposition, and deepened its dysfunction; Iranian and, increasingly, Russian intervention that grew more deadly as they saw little risk of any American response; and the emergence of extreme Islamists and ISIS who claimed to be protectors of the Sunnis from the Assad regime, which bombed and imposed starvation sieges on Sunni civilian-populated areas. ISIS went from being the "junior varsity" terrorists to being such a threat that President Obama would re-deploy several thousand troops to the region after running on a promise to bring America's troops home from Iraq.[2] While the Obama administration was never prepared to fight the Assad regime, it did feel obliged to fight ISIS and even effectively imposed a no-fly and no-drive zone in eastern Syria—something it rejected doing against the Assad regime even as Assad's forces relentlessly bombed Syrian civilians.

As I pointed out in Chapter 2, when there is a gap between objectives and means, it always produces bad statecraft. No case more vividly demonstrates the gap between publicly stated objectives and the means applied than the Obama administration's approach to Syria—and it is hard to find a case where the consequences of that gap proved to be so severe. How and why did it happen?

The Evolution of the War in Syria and of the Obama Administration's Approach

At the outset of the Obama administration, there was a strong impulse to demonstrate differences from the Bush policies, especially on the issue of engagement. The administration was prepared to talk to countries—engage countries—that Bush had sought to isolate. Syria fit in that category. Engagement, however, was not thought of as acquiescence to these states. Indeed, in the case of Iran, where I had a leading responsibility for shaping and implementing the policy, the animating idea was that the United States needed to demonstrate internationally that the source of the problem with Iran was its behavior, not America's unwillingness to talk to Tehran.

With Syria, the aim of engagement was to see if it was possible to alter Assad's approach to Iraq, Hezbollah, and Iran. During much of the Bush administration, the Assad regime had permitted jihadi fighters to enter Syria and move into Iraq to fight the United States. With Obama determined to wind down US presence in Iraq, the focus was on stabilizing the realities on the ground there, and the last thing the United States needed was for Assad to reactivate the flow of jihadis into Iraq. But Assad was also facilitating the movement of Iranian and Syrian weaponry to Hezbollah in Lebanon, and that too was something the administration wanted to end, particularly given the concern that this weaponry could trigger another war between Israel and Hezbollah.

Early on, US policymakers had interagency meetings to discuss how to define outreach to the Assad regime. It was decided that Jeffrey Feltman, the assistant secretary of state for the Near East Affairs Bureau, would go to Syria and express America's interest in gradually improving relations—a process in which there could be an incremental approach to lifting sanctions if President Assad would show he would prevent any movement of jihadis/radical Islamists through Syria to Iraq and cooperate in counter-terror activities.[a] Feltman was joined by Dan Shapiro from the National Security Council staff, and as a way of signaling that promises of sanctions relief could be real, they were authorized to allow Qatar to provide spare parts for Assad's presidential aircraft.

To be sure, Feltman explained that for there to be real relief and even the potential of economic help for a Syrian economy that was enjoying a limited opening, the administration would need to see that Syria was not promoting Hezbollah or providing (or facilitating) the transfer of weapons to it. Assad proclaimed innocence and denied any such support—even though both the Americans and the Israelis had very good intelligence on Iranian weapons being transferred to Hezbollah from and through Syria. Nonetheless, the administration pursued the engagement, and Assad indicated that he was ready to improve relations with the United States.

Feltman and Shapiro would be followed to Damascus by George Mitchell, the president's envoy for Arab–Israeli peace. Mitchell wanted to sound Assad out on what it would take to resume a track for negotiations between Syria and Israel, something that Mitchell would later authorize his deputy Fred Hof to pursue. But much like ensuring that Syria would not compound

---

[a] Early after 9/11, Assad had cooperated in counter-terror, but that did not last too long.

the problems in Iraq, Mitchell wanted to give Assad a stake in not creating problems for or pressure on the Palestinians.[b] That the administration was serious about seeing whether engagement could lead somewhere was demonstrated not only by nominating an ambassador to return to Syria, but also by raising the level of discussions with Assad. The administration sent William Burns, the under secretary of state, the number three position in the State Department, to see Assad. Burns would later write, "Before 2011, the Obama Administration tested with Assad whether some modest improvement in relations might be possible. Special Envoy George Mitchell had extensive discussions in Damascus ... and I visited Assad twice to gauge his seriousness about clamping down on cross-border support to extremists in Iraq and broader counterterrorism (CT) cooperation."[3] Assad signaled his readiness to work with the United States but, in fact, he made few tangible moves.

The outreach to Assad was not driven only by wanting to demonstrate a difference from Bush or by trying to give Assad an incentive not to contribute to problems in Iraq or with the Palestinians. It was also shaped by a perception that Assad was opening up Syria and wanted to make genuine economic progress—and his desire to develop and modernize the country, it was believed, could provide the United States an opening to offer him payoffs for changed behavior.

Assad had worked hard to foster an image of being a modernizer. He wanted to be seen as open, connected to the public, and building a new Syria. Pictures of him driving himself in Damascus, going out to dinner in cafés and restaurants with his wife Asma, were all part of a determined effort to make him appear approachable and very different from his father. His early efforts at reforms proved to be wanting, but liberalization of the banking sector and facilitation of outside investments had a real impact, especially in telecommunications, tourist-related infrastructure, and real estate. In fact, Assad did open the economy to the outside world, and the Syrian nominal GDP more than doubled between 2005 and 2010, from $28.9 billion to $60 billion.[4] Cities like Damascus and Aleppo reflected the change. Upscale neighborhoods and downtown areas emerged and seemed to fit the image that Assad was cultivating—and that Asma seemed to embody.

Asma al-Assad is from a Syrian Sunni family and had become an investment banker in London—chic, stylish, and very much the modern

---

[b] Assad made clear that he was open to resuming a Syrian–Israeli negotiating track but felt the negotiations needed to be concrete on issues like the border.

woman. In March 2011, *Vogue* did a story about her entitled "A Rose in the Desert," gushing over how she was trying to bring culture, the arts, and modern education to Syria.[5] She seemed not just a reflection of change but an attractive advocate of it. To a group of Arab alumni of Harvard, she said, "Our identity must become that of a learning regime ... opening ourselves to new perspectives ... adopting new skills."[6]

So there were actually hopes that a strategic change was possible. But the inequalities and the character of the regime kept intruding. Corruption remained high—with the members of the Assad clan and relatives like the Makloufs monopolizing broad sectors of the economy and requiring large payoffs for any investments from the outside. And the reality of Assad's alignments with Iran and Hezbollah remained unchanged. In fact, in the spring of 2010, the Obama administration determined that the Syrians were beginning to provide Hezbollah with Scud missiles—surface-to-surface missiles that could be used against the Israelis and that had a range far more than any projectiles that Hezbollah had at the time. These transfers carried the risk of conflict, with Israel not waiting to be hit by them. Since John Kerry (who was then a senator) was known to have built a relationship with Assad, President Obama decided that the administration should ask Kerry to go and convey a clear message to the Syrian president that these transfers were dangerous and would kill any prospect of an improvement in US–Syria relations. The president asked me to brief Kerry and go over his message to Assad, and I worked with Kerry and his key aide, Frank Lowenstein, on his talking points.

Kerry would report back, providing us with the transcript of their discussion. Once again, Assad played dumb on the Scud transfers, even arguing that if there were missiles going to Hezbollah, it was the work of smugglers. Kerry did not accept this and pushed back but their conversation then veered onto the content of a peace deal with Israel, with Kerry offering language that would require Syria to break with Iran and Hezbollah if Israel were to withdraw to the lines agreed upon on June 4, 1967. Kerry even returned to Washington with language that he said Assad accepted which stated that in the event of Israeli withdrawal, there would be a bilateral Israeli–Syrian relationship in which "neither side renders aid or comfort to any act of any other party, state, or non-state, threatening the security of the other."[7]

Kerry's visit may not have produced Assad's commitment on the Scuds, but it did appear to create an opening for a possible agreement between Syria and Israel that would not be based on the traditional concept of land for peace but rather on "land for strategic realignment"—meaning that Israel would withdraw from the Golan Heights and in return Syria would strategically end its alignment with Iran and Hezbollah. If realized, this would mean the end not just of Scuds to Hezbollah but the end of the Iranian land-bridge through Syria to Lebanon. In fact, Kerry's visit did lead the administration to pursue serious indirect negotiations between the Israelis and the Syrians. Fred Hof would go to see Assad, then join me in Israel to see Netanyahu and his team. This negotiation became more detailed and precise on the definition of Israeli withdrawal on the one hand, and Syrian obligations on the content of peace and its strategic reorientation on the other, than even during the 1999–2000 efforts, in which we had come close to an agreement. This effort would come to an end when, as I will outline later, Assad effectively declared war on the Syrian public in response to protests and demonstrations.

The "Arab Spring" and Daraa Triggers the Protests

On December 17, 2010, Mohammed Bouazizi, a fruit-seller in Tunisia, was once again denied a permit to sell his fruit without paying a bribe. This was the last straw in a series of humiliations that Bouazizi had experienced throughout his life. His anger and frustration led him to set himself on fire— but he did not just ignite himself; he set the whole Middle East on fire. This act of ultimate protest reflecting hopelessness resonated with publics in Middle Eastern countries who knew what it meant to be powerless, facing corrupt officials and dysfunctional governments that never addressed public needs while they enriched a small circle of those in and connected to power. By February 2011, the Tunisian and Egyptian presidents were swept away, Libya's leader Muammar Qadhafi was facing an uprising, and massive demonstrations were taking place in Iraq; Syria was not immune to the wave of protest sweeping the region.

Assad, who sought to present himself as a reformer, took notice of demonstrations sweeping the region in the weeks after Bouazizi immolated himself. But in an interview with *The Wall Street Journal* on January 31, 2011, Assad spoke of a "new era" in the region, and even acknowledged that Syria faced economic difficulties but contended that the country would remain stable because he was "closely linked to the beliefs of the people."[8] While Assad would, in fact, prove to be disconnected from the Syrian people, he was right about the economic difficulties. Yes, Syria's GDP had doubled between 2005 and 2010, but this improvement masked that poverty had become worse as drought hit the rural areas hard, the government offered no assistance, especially as investment shifted to the cities, and up to 1.5 million people (out of a total population of less than 24 million) were forced to migrate to urban areas big and small. There was no absorptive capacity in the cities, and shanty towns and slums emerged. Those living in these camps were both impoverished and disconnected from their social moorings. They were also overwhelmingly Sunni. Their poverty stood in sharp contrast to the signs of new wealth in cities like Aleppo and Damascus, where luxury apartments and high-rises were built. One sign that indicated the scope of the depression in farming, triggering this mass migration to the cities, was the precipitous decline in those working in Syria's agricultural sector. In 2001, agriculture made up 30 percent of the economy; by 2010, that number had dropped to 13.2 percent.[9] Such a dramatic decline would be difficult for most any country to grapple with, but it was especially hard in Syria, where economic opportunities in the cities did not await largely unskilled workers coming from rural, farming communities.

There was, thus, a fertile breeding ground for discontent, especially at a time when the demonstrations throughout the Middle East were spreading and providing an outlet for it. Initially, there were some small demonstrations in Damascus, less from the poor and socially dislocated, and more from those who wanted human rights activists to be released from jail. It was as if these initial demonstrations, which did not attract large crowds, were testing to see the limits of what Assad's regime would tolerate. The answer was "not much," as those who took part were arrested and in some cases beaten. But events in Daraa would change everything.

In the southwestern city of Daraa in late February 2011, a group of five boys, the youngest being 11 and the oldest being 16, spray-painted graffiti at their school saying "doctor, you are next" and "down with the regime." "Doctor" referred to Assad, who was trained as an ophthalmologist. These spray-painted slogans reflected the spirit of protests throughout the region, and these boys were acting out what they were seeing on Al Jazeera.

The local Mukhabarat, secret police, arrested those boys and more than a dozen others who knew what they had done. The parents had no access to them; worse, the boys were beaten and, in some cases, tortured. When the parents went to plead for their release with local officials, they were told that only the Mukhabarat could release them. The boys and their families were from the Abazeid clan in Daraa, and the male elders of the clan asked to meet with the local head of the Mukhabarat and plead for their release. Atef Najib, a cousin of Assad, was the local Mukhabarat chief, and he mocked and humiliated those who came to see him. While a number of versions circulate of what Najib told the group, one version, according to Sam Dagher, had Najib telling the group to "forget your children" and if you "want new children in their place, send your wives and we will impregnate them for you."[10]

Word of the offensive and humiliating treatment of the elders spread quickly and produced a planned demonstration at a mosque in Daraa on Friday, March 18. Several thousand gathered outside of the Omari mosque in Daraa, and snipers began to open fire on the crowd, resulting in a number of dead and wounded. The killings provoked demonstrations that spread far beyond Daraa, with protests the following week in Homs, Tartous, and neighborhoods near Damascus like Douma. Again, the demonstrations were met with a violent response. The videos from cell phones showing Mukhabarat forces firing at unarmed civilians went viral and helped spur protests and demonstrations more widely—protests that now began to erupt every Friday around the mosques where thousands would gather.

None of the demonstrations at this point were promoting regime change—the slogans centered on freedom, dignity, reform, and compensation for the families who had suffered losses from the regime's use of violence. Nonetheless, as the numbers of protestors killed and wounded grew, so did the anger of those protesting. In Daraa, one week after the initial March 18 demonstration, crowds of younger demonstrators went into the city's main square, knocked over the statue of Hafez al-Assad, father of Bashar al-Assad, and tore down a billboard of the current president. Dozens were gunned down.

Assad decided to address the Parliament on March 30, with expectations running high that he would be contrite, conciliatory, offer compensation to victims, and speak of reforms. Manaf Tlass, who would later defect, was at the time a general in the Syrian military and a longtime friend of Bashar al-Assad and the whole Assad family. He appealed to Assad to take a number of steps to defuse the tensions and the anger that was now fueling the demonstrations. To that end, he urged Assad to announce the arrest of Atef Najib and others in the Mukhabarat, make apologies and offer compensation to the victims of regime violence, and present new reforms as a way to regain support and give those demonstrating a reason to stop. According to Manaf, Assad assured him he would heed his advice and take these steps.[11]

Tlass was not alone in being told Assad would adopt a conciliatory posture and reach out to the public. John Kerry recounted how Syria's ambassador to the United States contacted him and told him that when Assad addressed the Parliament he would "engage in a reconciliation process for a reform agenda."[12]

But Assad did not do so; instead, he doubled down. While acknowledging there were some understandable grievances among the Syrian people, Assad's theme was that Israel and its allies were carrying out a conspiracy against Syria—as if the protests were being stage-managed from outside by an Israeli hand. Assad was not reaching out; he was justifying a crackdown by vowing to defeat this conspiracy. His address to parliament did not stem the emergence of wider protests, it provoked them. On April 1, after Friday prayers in Douma—10 miles from Damascus—thousands coming out of Friday prayers took to the streets and occupied the town's municipal square. In central Homs on the same day, large numbers went to the streets to chant in support of Daraa and demand the ouster of the local governor. In Latakia, protests resulted in the killings of dozens of demonstrators.

Maybe Assad thought briefly about a conciliating posture toward the protests, but a regime that was based on control and the omnipresent Mukhabarat was very unlikely to believe that anything except a tough response designed to instill fear would work. Indeed, for those closest to Assad like his brother Maher, other family members, and Ali Mamluk, who headed air force intelligence and was then serving as director of the National Security Bureau, any concessions would convey weakness, perpetuating the protests and giving demonstrators hope. The Assad clan believed that an iron fist, not concessions, would stop the protests—only a violent, heavy-handed approach would signal to the protestors that they could lose everything and be killed or arrested, with those arrested and in jail being subjected to a level of brutality that would leave them envying the dead.[13,c] For the Assad leadership, only a tough, unrelenting response would deter the protestors from coming out.

But Assad and his cronies were wrong, and 150,000 people filled the streets of Douma in response to the funerals being held for those killed

---

[c] Accounts of torture and beatings; of being crammed into cells where there was often no place to lay down or relieve themselves, and where the dead were frequently not removed; of being denied water and provided rancid food—all offer a vivid picture of what awaited those who were arrested. Pictures of emaciated victims that have a haunting similarity to images from the Holocaust were smuggled out of Syria by Cesar and presented to Congress; these images are shown and discussed in the 2023 documentary *Corridors of Power*, directed by Dror Moreh.

in the protests on April 1. It was this mass response to the funerals—this massive demonstration in Douma—that seemed to ignite the existing Friday demonstrations and add dramatically to the number of those involved. At this point, the demonstrations after Friday prayers began to take place throughout Syria. North, south, east, and west Syria saw protests every week, with the numbers growing of both people involved in demonstrations and those being killed by the regime.

The initial American public response showed an ambivalence. Secretary of State Clinton in a television interview on March 27 said, "There's a different leader in Syria now. Many members of Congress of both parties who have gone to Syria in recent months have said they think he is a reformer."[14] Granted, this was before Assad's speech to parliament on March 30 and the killings on April 1 in response to demonstrations. But it was after live fire was being used to respond to protests and after the numbers of demonstrators being killed were already rising. Why did she make this comment?

First, she was hoping that the image Assad cultivated generally and with visitors—that he was a reformer—might be used to get him to act in a way in which he lived up to how he wanted to be seen internationally. Second, she was fully aware of the discreet discussions the administration was conducting between Assad and Netanyahu, and the progress that Fred Hof and I believed was being made. Secretary Clinton hoped she might protect this effort and its promise—and that Assad would act in a way to help preserve it. Unfortunately, while her comments reflected the hope that the administration might still be able to work with him, his speech to the Parliament suggested that was an illusion.

As the month of April unfolded and the demonstrations spread, the administration's responses became tougher rhetorically and practically. Rhetorically, the administration stepped up its criticism of the regime, with President Obama on April 8 and again on April 22 calling for "this outrageous use of violence to end now," and urging Assad to "change course."[15] By the end of April, President Obama announced sanctions on a number of individuals, including Assad's brother Maher, Ali Mamluk, and others identified as being responsible for the killings. By May 19, in his speech given at the State Department on the need for reform in the Arab world—a response to the "Arab Spring"—Obama singled out Syria and Assad for special mention. His words were far tougher than any of his comments to date; he outlined a series of steps the regime needed to take, and declared that Assad had to make a choice:

The Syrian people have shown their courage in demanding a transition to democracy. President Assad now has a choice: He can lead or get out of the way. The Syrian government must stop shooting demonstrators and allow peaceful protests. It must release political prisoners and stop unlawful arrests. It must allow human rights monitors access to cities like Daraa and a serious dialogue to advance a democratic transition. Otherwise, President Assad will be challenged from within and will continue to be isolated abroad.[16]

Here was a forceful statement. Hillary Clinton would take it a step further on June 3, saying that Assad was about to lose his legitimacy. She would give a speech on July 11 in which she said that Assad was running out of time to change course and bluntly declared that "President Assad is not indispensable and we have absolutely nothing invested in him remaining in power."[17] Between June 3 and July 11, the demonstrations in Homs and Hama were estimated to be in the hundreds of thousands, with the demonstrators effectively declaring that they were taking over the squares—and in Hama with protestors declaring the city theirs. On July 1, to demonstrate support for what remained largely peaceful protests, the American and French ambassadors, Robert Ford and Eric Chevallier, went to Hama—literally being engulfed by the crowd. Many may have believed that the ambassadors' presence and show of support would give the regime pause and prevent an attack on the demonstrators who were now largely encamped in the squares. It would do so for a few weeks, but then there would be a full military assault on the square in Hama.[d]

It was not only the Obama administration that was turning away from Assad. President Nicolas Sarkozy of France, who had feted Assad and Asma only a few months before in Paris, condemned the response to protests, calling the situation in Syria "unacceptable." Both Turkey and Qatar, whose leaders had embraced Assad as a reformer, sent emissaries to persuade him to stop the killings—and true to his nature, Assad would promise responsiveness and then do the opposite. He would give a speech at Damascus University where on the one hand he promised to revoke the state of emergency and on the other referred to the protestors as germs.[18]

---

[d] Not long after Ambassador Ford's visit to the central square in Hama, a mob of regime toughs, the shabiha, attacked the American embassy, prompting the administration to pull Robert Ford out of the country.

The Turks, Qataris, and Saudis, even after he broke promises to them, still tried to persuade Assad to alter his course, with both the Qataris and the Saudis offering money. The emir of Qatar sent his son, Tamim bin Hamad al-Thani, to meet with Assad, and Tamim promised that the Qataris would turn the slums in Damascus into the "most prestigious neighborhoods" in the city if Assad would stop the killings and prevent "the situation from exploding further."[19] Assad assured him that the situation was not as bad as it was being portrayed.[20,e] King Abdullah of Saudi Arabia sent his son Abdulaziz bin Abdullah to see Assad three times, with the aim of getting him to stop the killings. Offers of financial aid were made, and in some cases delivered, while Assad would promise responsiveness but change nothing.

The brutality of the assaults and the torturing of those arrested were hard to fathom; clearly, the aim of the regime was to shock people into submission. Walid Jumblatt, the Lebanese Druze leader, sought to persuade Assad to calm the situation and to stop the excesses of his security forces. In particular, he drew attention to the killing (that took place in late April) of Hamza al-Khatib, a 13-year-old boy from Daraa. The boy was tortured and mutilated, with his body returned to his parents a month later with his penis cut off. Assad denied that there had been torture, saying that the body had decomposed in the morgue.

At the time, there were rumors that Assad might not be fully in control, and was not ordering the violence–either his brother Mahar or the Mukhabarat was responsible for it. But if Assad wanted to create some distance from the violence and signal he did not approve of it, especially given what Jumblatt raised in the meeting, he left little doubt that this was his policy, saying "I am in full control but I need people to fear me."[21]

By mid-July, the death toll was climbing: the UN reported that 1,900 protestors had been killed and more than 8,000 had been arrested.[22] While protests had been peaceful and largely remained so, military defections of (largely) Sunnis began to increase, with these defectors feeling the need to provide protection to the crowds who were protesting. Some units dominated by Sunnis refused to fire on protestors and were themselves executed by Mukhabarat officers—more and more of whom were now accompanying soldiers into the field.

And still the protests gained even greater momentum. In Homs and Hama, the number of those protesting was nearly 500,000. The numbers of

e Tamim became emir in 2013.

defecting soldiers increased, and they tended to focus at this point on providing protection from the regime to the largely Sunni-led protests. It was now that the tenor of the protests changed, with more and more calling for Assad to leave. The make-up of the opposition began to take a more sectarian direction, with more territories falling under their control. And now Local Coordinating Councils were established in areas that were no longer under regime control. Though largely in Sunni areas, these committees—at least in the early stages—were also mostly free of the Muslim Brotherhood and other Islamists.

With the advent of Ramadan in August of the same year (2011), those gathering for prayers grew in numbers. Ramadan may be a time of reflection and peace, but not for the Assad regime. Rather than backing off and adopting a live-and-let-live posture during Ramadan, the regime saw the mosques inspiring resistance and demonstrations, and it began attacking those emerging from prayers. For King Abdullah of Saudi Arabia, the killings of people emerging from prayer was simply too much to take. On August 8, the king ended his personal silence on Assad, withdrawing his ambassador and declaring that what was happening in Syria was abhorrent and unacceptable. He branded the Assad regime a "killing machine."[23]

As the news out of Syria got progressively worse, the political pressures on the administration and the president to adopt a tougher position toward Assad became much stronger.[f] President Obama felt it was time to say that Assad would need to leave but agreed that such a statement would have more weight if joined by the European Union and others, including Turkey. He would call the Turkish leader and make the case that the Turkey should echo America's statement on Assad or make its own, and Recep Tayyip Erdoğan asked President Obama to give him one last chance to persuade Assad to stop before declaring he must go.[g]

Why was Erdoğan hesitating? He had invested in Assad, was increasing trade and commerce with Syria; areas in southern Turkey and northern Syria were building a network of economic relations—and Erdoğan still believed it was possible to move Assad. Erdoğan told President Obama that

---

[f] On August 2, Senators Gillibrand, Kirk, and Lieberman introduced the Syria Sanctions Act of 2011, which aimed to penalize contributors, investors, and abettors of the Syrian energy sector. The next day, in a letter to the president, a group of 68 bipartisan senators urged a more punitive posture toward Syria, including full enforcement of the Syrian Accountability and Lebanese Sovereignty Restoration Act of 2003.

[g] I prepared the points for these calls, and the president agreed to Erdoğan's request for one last effort to move Assad before calling for his departure.

he would send his foreign minister, Ahmet Davutoglu, to see Assad with a list of tangible steps the latter must take (including no firing on civilians). If Assad once again betrayed his promises, Turkey would join America's call for him to leave. Once again, Assad promised to take all the steps Turkey was demanding; and once again, he took none of them. Erdoğan would say before aligning himself with President Obama's posture, "I've sent my foreign minister, and personally got in touch many times [with Assad], the last time three days ago on the phone. In spite of all this, civilians are still getting killed."[24]

With Erdoğan and the British, the French, and the Germans on board, President Obama issued the following statement on August 18, 2011: "We have consistently said President Assad must lead a democratic transition or get out of the way. He has not led. For the sake of the Syrian people, the time has come for President Assad to step aside." The others would make similar calls for Assad to leave following the president's statement. In backgrounders to the press, the administration made it clear that it was not talking about removing Assad by force, but it was, nonetheless, now publicly calling for Assad to depart.

Regional and International Efforts to End the Killings and Produce a Political Process in Syria

With the unrestrained use of force against Syrian civilians continuing, the Arab League sought to intervene and stop the killing. In early September, a few weeks after Obama called for Assad to step aside, Nabil El-Araby, the secretary-general of the Arab League, traveled to Damascus. He urged Assad to reform and later announced a deal in which the Syrian president pledged to stop the killings and pull his military forces back from the cities. Assad seemingly never hesitated to agree to what outside mediators asked of him. The problem was not getting his agreement, it was getting him to live up to his promises. Secretary-General El-Araby soon discovered that rather than pulling forces back, the Assad regime was intensifying its use of tanks against the cities.

Frustrated, El-Araby returned in late October with a list of demands that included a pull-back of Syrian tanks and heavy weapons from the cities, release of political prisoners, and the beginning of a dialogue with the opposition. On November 2, El-Araby announced that Assad had agreed to these terms; within days, El-Araby declared that the Syrian regime was violating the agreement.[25] El-Araby then threatened to suspend Syria's membership in the Arab League if the Syrian government did not respect the agreement, and by November 16, when Assad had not complied, the Syrians were suspended from the Arab League.[26]

Under pressure from the Russians, Assad agreed on December 12 to a slightly modified Arab League plan, this time with Arab monitors to enter Syria and monitor the events on the ground and implementation of the plan. The monitors arrived on December 22. They were small in number, unarmed, and with little experience of being in what amounted to a war zone. The aim of the Arab League plan was to stop the killing and launch a political process—and clearly the hope was that the presence of their monitors would act as a deterrent to the regime's continuing onslaught against civilians. But Assad's modus operandi was to agree, presuming this would relieve pressure, and then continue to try to crush the growing opposition. The Russians would periodically put pressure on him to respond to political initiatives but never imposed any penalties on him for not fulfilling his promises. Putin would later tell Obama that he had "no love" for Assad and that Moscow had "no real leverage with Damascus."[27]

The Arab League monitors, often blocked from being able to observe attacks or their aftermath and finding it increasingly dangerous to move around so they could report, pulled out in January 2012. Given the Syrian behavior, the Saudis said they would no longer pay for the mission, and the Arab League then went to the UN seeking its partnership to try to stop the bloodshed in Syria. The secretary-general agreed to a joint mission and appointed Kofi Annan as the joint special envoy of the UN and the Arab League in February.

Even before the Arab League initiative was launched, the Syrian opposition sought to organize itself and create a representative. The Syrian National Council had been formed back in October 2011. The idea was that it would be an umbrella organization, encompassing all those seeking the end of the Assad regime. In theory, the Local Coordinating Councils represented a grass-roots mechanism to plug into the Syrian National Council; in reality, their connection was tenuous. The Free Syrian Army had also emerged, made up essentially of defectors from the Syrian military, but it was also an organization more in name than in substance, with local elements tied to their home areas and only loosely tied together under a broad umbrella. With the formation of the Free Syrian Army, what initially had been demonstrations calling for reform had turned into a full-fledged revolt against the regime. There was, in the eyes of the collective opposition, no peace to be made with a regime that was slaughtering peaceful protestors.

In March 2012, Kofi Annan put together a six-point plan to end the conflict in Syria. The essence of the plan was withdrawal of Syrian forces from cities, permission for peaceful protest, access for humanitarian relief, free movement of journalists, and the beginning of a political transition that would address the aspirations and concerns of the Syrian people. The Russians, who had earlier vetoed a resolution condemning the Syrian regime's use of violence against its people, were prepared to support Annan's plan with a presidential statement from the UN Security Council. By definition, a statement did not possess the weight of a resolution, nor did it carry with it the potential for punitive action if Assad refused to accept and implement Annan's plan. But the Russians were on record supporting the aims of the plan—and they did lean on Assad to accept it. And, in accordance with the plan, the UN sent monitors to Syria.

Once again, Assad would accept the plan, and for a short while even limit the regime's violence. But, in the words of Hillary Clinton, Assad would take "no credible steps" to implement it.[28] After one month, Kofi Annan reported to the UN Security Council that the Syrian regime was responsible for "serious violations"; on May 25, videos emerged of regime thugs, the shabiha, carrying out a massacre in a village close to Homs. UN monitors went to the scene and confirmed that more than 100 villagers had been killed, including a large number of children. There was a similar attack in a village near Hama on June 6. At this point, the UN vehicles began to be attacked, and the UN monitoring mission was suspended.

During this period, the Free Syrian Army began "defensive" operations; Turkey, Qatar, and Saudi Arabia began to provide more arms and money to Syrian rebels. However, there was little, if any, coordination of the assistance they were giving. With violence becoming more widespread and Annan's plan little more than a piece of paper, he pushed to convene an Action Group for Syria. He wanted the Iranians to be there, but that was vetoed by the United States and the British; in the end, the foreign ministers of the United States, Russia, the United Kingdom, France, China, Japan, Turkey, Qatar, and Iraq convened in Geneva on June 30. Neither the Iranians nor the Saudis were invited. The final statement of the Geneva meeting was entitled "Principles and Guidelines on a Syrian-Led Transition," and it called for a

"Transitional Governing Body" to have "full executive powers" to include members of the government and the opposition on the basis of "mutual consent."[29]

The main debate at Geneva was not over the key principles of a cease-fire: pull-back of forces, access to humanitarian supplies, or a political transition. Rather, it was centered on the fundamental question whether Assad could remain. For the Russians, he had to be a part of the transition, and for the United States and others, he could not be. To produce an acceptable final statement encapsulating the plan, Secretary Clinton proposed the language of full executive powers and inclusion of government and opposition figures based on "mutual consent." Clinton believed that this formulation would ensure Assad's exclusion because, as she argued, there was no way members of the opposition would agree to Assad being part of a new government. Here was a plan based on a set of principles; it spelled out how the transitional government could be set up, what it would work toward, and it had the backing of the United States and Russia, and of important regional states. There was one problem: Sergey Lavrov, the Russian foreign minister, declared quickly that the plan did not require Assad to go. Hillary Clinton would declare the opposite. Kofi Annan, too, left no doubt as to where he stood on Assad staying or going by saying that the Syrian people who had fought so hard for their independence were not going to "select people with blood on their hands to lead them."[30]

Annan had hoped that the Geneva document would become a UN Security Council Resolution under Chapter VII—meaning that noncompliance would be met with punishment. But again, the Russians would block such a resolution, and Annan resigned in August 2012. This was not the only important development of that month.

Obama's Red Line on Chemical Weapons

In August, the Intelligence Community began to see indicators that the Syrian regime might be getting ready to move some of its chemical weapons (CW). It was not clear whether this might be preparation for using CW or to make the stockpile less vulnerable to seizure by the rebels. But it was on Obama's mind, and he chose to answer a question on Syria at a press conference to give what became known as his red line warning to Assad. Note his words:

I have, at this point, not ordered military engagement in the [Syrian] situation. But the point you made about chemical and biological weapons is
critical. That's an issue that doesn't just concern Syria; it concerns our close
allies in the region, including Israel. It concerns us. We cannot have a situation where chemical or biological weapons are falling into the hands of the
people. We have been very clear to the Assad regime, but also to other players on the ground, that a red line for us is we start seeing a whole bunch
of chemical weapons start moving around or being utilized. That would
change my calculus. That would change my equation.[31]

He then warned Assad of "enormous consequences." Obama's words left little doubt that if Assad violated this red line, the United States would act. The
beginning of his answer is noteworthy because Secretary Clinton, Defense
Secretary Panetta, and CIA Director David Petraeus had come to Obama
and recommended providing military assistance to the Syrian opposition—
and he had rejected their collective recommendation not long before this
press conference. He posed a question to them: when had the United States
backed an insurgency that could be considered a success? As Hillary Clinton recalls, it was a good question, "but Petraeus and I argued there was a
big difference between Qatar and Saudi Arabia dumping arms in the country and the United States training and equipping non-extremist forces. And,
getting control of that mess was a big part of our plan's rationale."[32]

I will discuss later whether Obama's approval, not rejection, of the Clinton, Panetta, and Petraeus's recommendation could have made a difference.
Here, two points are worth making: First, Obama's opening line probably
reflected his recent rejection of the plan presented to him—and his stick-
ing with that decision. But his answer—one that surprised his advisors, with
Leon Panetta later saying that "I didn't know it was coming"—was Obama's
way of explaining what it would take for him to change his mind: Assad
moving or using CW. No doubt, in giving this answer, President Obama
thought he was putting down a marker to deter Assad from the use of these
weapons.[33] Second, the plan he turned down was overt support; earlier
in the spring of 2012, he had approved a finding for covert action against
the Assad regime and in support of the rebels. Several former intelligence
officials briefed me on this finding. Plans were drawn up to act on it, but
here too, even though the president had approved the finding, he subsequently chose not to act on it. The fundamental point is that the president,

very hesitant to involve the United States in the situation in Syria, had gone on record laying out the conditions under which he would be compelled to act.

Of course, the red line implicitly gave Assad a pass on other weapons his regime was using against civilian-populated areas. While it is possible that the Obama red line gave Assad pause on using CW at this point, it gave him no reason to stop what he had begun to use at this time: a horrific, if primitive, weapon—the barrel bomb. Dropped from helicopters, these were oil barrels filled with TNT and packed with steel rods and shrapnel—weapons designed to tear bodies apart. They were often dropped on bakeries where people congregated to get bread, schools where they thought they might find refuge, and hospitals and clinics where the wounded were being treated. As the news and images of the effect of barrel bombs spread, Hillary Clinton explored with Turkey, in August 2012, the idea of a no-fly zone to prevent the Syrians from carrying out these attacks, at least in northern Syria. Turkey was open to it, but neither President Obama nor top US military officials were prepared to go along.[34]

But even as the regime was killing increasing numbers of Syrians in cities and towns, rebel forces grew and were seizing more territory, and the Syrian military was shrinking, racked by defections, desertions, and attrition. This reality may explain why Assad began to use CW. Ben Rhodes would write that the administration "received the first reports of small-scale chemical weapons use toward end of 2012."[35] That explains why on December 3, 2012, nearly five months after he put down his red line marker, Obama made the following statement: "I want to make it absolutely clear to Assad and those under his command. The world is watching. The use of chemical weapons is and would be totally unacceptable. And if you make the tragic mistake of using these weapons, there will be consequences, and you will be held accountable."[36]

Rhodes also notes that the Intelligence Community "was resistant to snap judgments, particularly after the experience of inaccurate statements made about weapons of mass destruction in Iraq before the 2003 invasion of Iraq." Meaning that even though the administration had reports of such usage, it was not prepared to call attention to them or to Syrian usage—notwithstanding the red line—in the absence of absolute certainty. It would be several months before the administration was prepared to confirm the Syrian use of CW; just prior to that confirmation, Tom Donilon, the national security advisor, asked me how I would recommend responding if it appeared likely that the Assad regime had used CW in limited attacks.[h]

I replied that the president's red line required a military response, irrespective of the size of attacks. A threshold had been crossed with their usage; if the administration did not carry out a tough, disproportionate response, Assad would think that the red line was not serious and he could do more. Donilon asked me what would be an appropriate, disproportionate response—I told him that the US should hit the units that used the CW and hit bases from which the helicopters dropping the barrel bombs operate." That would send a message that the United States would not only make those who fired the weapons pay a price, but also that the United States was prepared to do more to affect the regime's ability to kill Syrian civilians. Donilon asked me what I would think if the president chose not to respond with a military strike but said the Syrian use of CW crossed a threshold and therefore the United States would cross a threshold and now provide weapons to the opposition? I told him that I saw the logic, but the problem was that it was the administration's logic, not Assad's. If the United States was going to deter Assad, it had to affect his thinking and logic—not reflect only the thinking and logic of the administration.

Donilon was clearly trying to figure out the right response and at the same time convince President Obama. Obama chose the more minimal response; to keep it minimal, he himself did not even announce the decision. Instead, he had Ben Rhodes issue the statement that the United States would henceforth provide assistance to the opposition because Assad had crossed a threshold in using CW.[37]

Even after Rhodes's statement, delivery of small amounts of lethal equipment to Syrian opposition groups took months. The program, named Timber Sycamore, was based on a thorough vetting process, and as the provision of arms by the United States was minimal and very slow to arrive, the opposition groups were getting money and arms from a number of other sources. Throughout 2013, they continued to gain territory and carry out attacks on the capital. On August 7, the first day of the Eid marking the end of Ramadan, the opposition groups were able to fire salvos of rockets and mortars into the upscale Damascus neighborhood where Assad and his family lived. Was this the trigger for Assad deciding to launch a devastating sarin nerve gas attack

---

[h] I had left the administration in December 2011 but was running a back channel between Israelis and Palestinians for the administration, and Donilon would regularly call on me to consult on other issues.

on the Damascus suburb of Ghouta on August 21—an attack that would kill over 1,400 people, including 400 children? Or was it suffering more defeats on the ground and believing that a terrorizing CW attack that could kill so many so quickly could shock the opposition into drawing back? Or was it that he already believed he could get away with it, given America's minimalist response to earlier uses of CW—or some combination of all these factors?

Whatever the reason for Assad's decision to use sarin gas, it was an unmistakable challenge to President Obama's red line—and, at least initially, it appeared to provoke President Obama to consider a military response. Samantha Power, who had favored the use of force against Assad and had long been rebuffed in her arguments, recounts that she was shocked that the president had asked the Pentagon to draw up targets for military strikes. She had not expected the president to change his approach, but Obama, as she later wrote, "was enraged by Assad's attack. Rather than debating next steps with us, as he generally did, he made clear he had decided to punish Assad."[38]

Secretary of State John Kerry took the lead in making the case for a military response, laying out proof of the regime's responsibility: it was the only one who had sarin gas; the United States knew the launch points of the rockets carrying the weaponized sarin which were in regime-controlled areas; and the United States had intercepted communications between senior regime officials proving they did it. Kerry would give an impassioned speech laying out the case for military action:

> It matters that nearly a hundred years ago, in direct response to the utter horror and inhumanity of World War I, that the civilized world agreed that chemical weapons should never be used again. It matters because if we choose to live in a world where a thug and a murderer like Bashar al-Assad can gas thousands of his own people with impunity, even after the United States and our allies said no, and the world does nothing about it, there will be no end to ... the dangers from those others who believe they can do as they will.[39]

The administration was coordinating with the British and the French to carry out a set of strikes together. David Cameron, given the history and unpopularity of British involvement in Iraq, decided to seek a parliamentary endorsement of military strikes in response to Syria's use of CW in Ghouta, but the motion to approve in the House of Commons was defeated. This vote came the day before Kerry's speech from the State Department, suggesting that the United States was still on track to proceed. But the British defeat began to create doubts in President Obama's mind about the value of proceeding with military strikes without getting congressional endorsement as well. He worried that Assad could put hostages in the areas that the United States might strike, and that the strikes would have little effect on his CW stocks. And what if he used them again after the strikes? Would the United States be dragged into a conflict?

Obama did not raise these doubts with National Security Advisor Susan Rice, with Secretary of State John Kerry, or with Secretary of Defense Chuck Hagel—all of whom favored carrying out the strikes and emphasized the importance of doing so in a meeting held in the Situation Room at the White House on August 24, 2013. In Ben Rhodes's words, "The tone of the whole meeting suggested an imminent strike."[40] But after the meeting, Obama asked Denis McDonough, his chief of staff, to join him for a walk on the White House grounds. McDonough was the one senior official who was very hesitant about using force—having questioned the legal basis of military action and what would come next. Here was a sympathetic ear for Obama's own doubts. After their walk, Obama made up his mind to change the script and the prospect of immediate military action. The president would subsequently tell Rice, Kerry, and Hagel that he had decided to postpone any military strikes for now in favor of seeking congressional approval for any such action. He made clear that he wanted to share the responsibility—something for which there was no consensus on Capitol Hill.

The French, who had moved their forces into position to strike, were poised to act. President Obama called President Holland of France—a call in which Holland was expecting the go-decision on strikes. Instead, Obama told him there would be a delay, but the French foreign minister Laurent Fabius later said that he and President Holland had "interpreted the conversation to mean the military strikes were off the table."[41]

Expectations had been raised that the United States was about to strike, and yet, Ben Rhodes would later write that Obama was "testing Congress, public opinion, to see what the real maneuvering room was for his office when it came to intervention in Syria."[42] Was the red line also a test? It seemed to have been lost in the political realities here, but CW had been used, a red line had been crossed, and Assad had no particular reason to believe there was any great cost in using them again.

Immediately after Obama's announcement on August 31 that he was seeking congressional authorization prior to any military strikes, I received a call from a senior Israeli security official—Zohar Palti. I had known Zohar for years. Zohar was very concerned about Obama's decision that seemed to walk away from the red line. Being worried about the impact on the value and credibility of America's word, he started by saying that this was "a dark day for the United States and all its friends in the region." But he quickly pivoted to asking: Why not go to the Russians now and see if a joint initiative could be launched to remove the CW stocks from Syria? The pivot was seamless, without a pause, and made me wonder whether there had been an Israeli approach to Putin already.

While Obama's and Kerry's accounts are different about the genesis of the joint Russia–US effort to remove CW from Syria, they both make the point that the initial cryptic discussion was at the G-20 meeting in St. Petersburg on September 5–6, 2012, nearly a week after Obama's decision to go to Congress. Obama later said that he had pulled Putin aside and told him "that if he forced Assad to get rid of the chemical weapons, that would eliminate the need for us taking a military strike."[43] Kerry recounted it differently but implied that nothing had really happened until he said in a press conference in London on September 9 that Assad could avoid an American attack if he turned over all of Syria's CW. Immediately afterward, Sergei Lavrov reached out to Kerry urgently, saying that he and Putin had discussed this and would make a public statement taking up his "proposal." Kerry and Lavrov would agree on a framework for eliminating Syria's CW, and this framework would be adopted by a unanimous vote of the UN Security Council on September 27.

Whether or not the Israelis played a role in this, the joint initiative did succeed in getting over 90 percent of the CW stocks out of Syria.[i] It also seemed to show that diplomacy might lead somewhere. Here was a joint effort in which the international community dealt directly with Assad's regime, seemingly treating it as a partner, to fulfill the mission of CW removal. The Russians had applied pressure on Assad—who, after all, had denied having CW—to acknowledge the stockpiles, their locations, and chemical precursors, and to let outside specialists come in and arrange the movement of the weapons out of the country. This development created hope that a resumed diplomatic process could lead somewhere.

---

[i] Regrettably, these stocks did not include chlorine, which the Assad regime would later weaponize and use.

Geneva II, ISIS Emerges, and the Vienna Principles

Locating and arranging for the removal of the CW was a complicated pro-
cess, and it took the US and Russia about a year—from October 2013 to
September 2014—to complete it. That process involved both significant US-
Russia cooperation and collaboration with the Assad regime, and the United
States would push for a parallel political process based on the Geneva princi-
ples. Pressure to convene a conference grew in October 2013. In November,
Assad's regime announced its intention to attend a conference, but the
opposition was initially hesitant. At this point, the National Coalition for
Revolutionary and Opposition Forces had effectively absorbed the Syrian
National Council into what now constituted a broader coalition of forces, the
Syrian Opposition Coalition (SOC). While not dominant, Islamist groups
were now more prominent in this body. This broader coalition was reluctant to take part in the Geneva II Conference but was pressured by the
Saudis and Qataris—each of whom supported different groups within this
umbrella organization. The SOC would relent and vote to attend Geneva
II on November 11, but with two conditions for participating: the regime
would provide access to areas it was besieging, and it would release prisoners, especially women and children. Neither of these conditions were met by
the regime, yet the SOC's leadership body decided, again under pressure, to
attend.[j]

Geneva II would be convened in Montreux, Switzerland in late January
2014. The SOC delegation was willing to discuss confidence-building measures, but Assad's representatives led by Foreign Minister Walid al-Mualem
showed no interest in negotiations. Lakhdar Brahimi, who had become the
UN and Arab League special envoy on Syria after Kofi Annan resigned,
would say that the opposition was open to negotiating and was making an
attempt to do so. Brahimi would also make it clear in early 2014 that Assad's
representatives were stonewalling on every possible issue: no discussion of
transition, no openness to acting on creating humanitarian corridors for
relief, no release of prisoners, etc. A second round of discussions took place
on February 10–15, ending with Brahimi apologizing publicly "to the Syrian people for the conference's failure, stating that the regime had refused

---

[j] That this was highly controversial within the organization is indicated by 45 out of the 120 SOC
delegates voted against attending.

to countenance a transition government and that he would consult with the conference co-sponsors on how to move forward."[44]

Assad may have been in the process of surrendering most of his CW, but that was the limit of his acquiescence—and even that had been forced on him. In the meantime, the sieges and the use of barrel bombs continued. The assault on Sunnis was attracting more and more Islamists from the region, from Chechnya, from Europe, and even a small number from the United States to come and protect them. Yusuf al-Qaradawi, the radical Muslim Brotherhood preacher, had a huge international following among Sunnis that stemmed largely from meting out advice on a weekly religious call-in program. He used his platform in Qatar to issue extremist fatwas—most notably against Jews but also, among other things, to justify suicide bombings. Suicide is a sacrilege in Islam, but al-Qaradawi said that dying in the service of an operation to protect Islam was not suicide. He came to call on Muslims to go fight Bashar al-Assad, whom he decried was massacring Sunnis to serve the interests of Iran and the Shia, urging Sunnis to join the rebels in Syria.[45]

No one and nothing did more to promote the growth and recruitment of ISIS than Bashar al-Assad and the war in Syria. Secretary Kerry would say in a speech in January 2014 that Assad was "a one-man super magnet for terror."[46] Later, he would accurately describe the reality in which fighting "Assad in Syria had become a *cause célèbre* for aspiring jihadis from the region and Europe, abetted by some of our Sunni friends, who were glad to see angry young men fight the apostate Shia regime."[47,k]

ISIS began to build its presence as a result of the resistance against Assad throughout 2013. The opposition was able to seize Raqqa from the regime, and it was one of the first provinces to declare its independence from Assad. But the divisions within the opposition made it easier for ISIS to take Raqqa from the other groups. In January 2014, having seized Raqqa and continuing to expand, ISIS declared Raqqa the capital of its territory—the self-proclaimed Islamic State. Now there was the symbol of statehood and the naming of a new caliph—which for many fulfills a necessary step for uniting all Muslims. This added tremendously to ISIS's credibility and its appeal to recruits to come to Syria and protect Sunnis—and serve the

---

[k] Assad's regime was not a Shia regime, but an Alawi one; a distinction that the jihadis did not draw.

so-called Islamic State. Despite its advances, however, President Obama was not yet impressed: "If a junior varsity team puts on a Lakers uniform that doesn't make them Kobe Bryant."[48]

The fall of Mosul in Iraq in June 2014 would change Obama's view on the nature of the threat and dramatically build the standing of ISIS and the territory under its control. ISIS's takeover of Mosul was also a bonanza for the group in terms of money, huge stocks of military equipment, and religious credibility. The group's claims that God must be on its side had newfound resonance, especially with fewer than 1,000 ISIS fighters defeating an Iraqi military force that was allegedly 30,000 strong.[l]

Whereas in January 2014, ISIS was seen as the "junior varsity" of terrorists, by June they had become the primary threat. After the fall of Mosul, President Obama would announce $500 million to train and equip the opposition in Syria—but it was to fight ISIS, not Assad.

Of course, this was also serving Assad's purposes. He had tried from the outset to label those fighting his regime as terrorists—and the presence of the Islamic State in Syria suddenly lent some credence to his argument. Al-Qaeda groups like the al-Nusra Front were in the northeast near Idlib, and they were gaining relative to the groups that the United States had begun to back with lethal assistance.[49,m] ISIS and the groups like al-Qaeda focused on Assad as the enemy, giving them an advantage over those whom the United States was prepared to support who also saw Assad as the main threat to the Sunnis, not the Islamists.

Once Obama made the decision in August to authorize targeted airstrikes to help rescue the Yazidis in Iraq from ISIS, the administration was now using force against the so-called Islamic State, or what John Kerry and those in the area called Daesh.[n] The beheadings of American journalists James Foley (on August 19, 2014) and Steven Sotloff (on September 3, 2014), as

---

[l] Nuri al-Maliki, Iraq's prime minister, had hollowed out the military, firing Sunni and Shia officers identified with the United States, packing the military's leadership with Shia loyalists, and not fulfilling promises to absorb the Sons of Iraq or Sahwa (Awakening) movements into the military—the very Sunni forces that had fought and with US backing had defeated the Islamists in Iraq. The military under Maliki had become consumed by widespread corruption and led by officers who were rarely where the fighting was. The 30,000 figure was probably an exaggeration, with corrupt officers pocketing the money of ghost soldiers whom they added to the ranks but who did not actually exist. It is true that ISIS was outnumbered probably 20:1; the numbers, however, mattered little when soldiers with absentee officers simply walked away and gave Mosul to ISIS.

[m] By 2016, al-Nusra was the dominant group there, and it would seize weapons the United States had provided to a group fighting under the banner of the Free Syrian Army.

[n] This was an Arabic acronym formed from the English words "Islamic State in Iraq and Syria," but its meaning in Arabic was derogatory; Kerry would emphasize it and not give the group the credit of being "Islamic."

well as aid workers Peter Kassig (on November 16, 2014) and Kayla Mueller (in February 2015) only added to public outrage against ISIS and strengthened the rationale for fighting it. While the United States would organize a broad coalition of 60 nations to fight ISIS, Obama was now bombing in both Iraq and Syria. In Syria alone, from June 2014 to March 2016, the United States would carry out 3,401 air strikes against ISIS. The Syrians and the Russians would carry out air strikes against those they claimed were ISIS but, in fact, their actual bombings were against the rest of the opposition—and rarely did they strike ISIS targets. On the contrary, once ISIS seized the oil fields in Syria, the regime was actually buying its oil from them.[50]

In reality, Assad's regime was losing territory in the east to ISIS and in the northwest (including half of Aleppo) to opposition groups, and there were now inroads even into areas historically dominated by Alawis. While the Iranian and Hezbollah presence was becoming more important in helping the regime, it was not proving to be enough. By the summer of 2015, the position of Assad's regime throughout the country had weakened further. Vladimir Putin would decide to intervene militarily to rescue the regime, sending in Russian forces on September 30. As John Kerry would later write, "The Russians told us they were sending their military into Syria in a typical Russian manner—which is to say, they did not tell us at all."[51]

In his memoir, Kerry was candid enough to say that the Russians had "upped the ante to the degree that they knew we would not match."[52] He believed that whatever gains the opposition had made throughout the country would be difficult to maintain and, unfortunately, it could only expect a "bloody winter."[53] If, until then, Kerry had hoped that the administration might put pressure on Assad to negotiate, he understood that it would be far more difficult at that point. So, his focus shifted to producing a cease-fire, believing that the Russians might actually find that in their interest.

He was able to persuade Russian Foreign Minister Lavrov to go along with a new international group on Syria called the International Syrian Support Group; in time, this group would include 31 nations. Unlike the earlier efforts on Geneva I and II, this time Iran would be part of the group. And the convening of the group not in Geneva but in Vienna would include foreign ministers of Iran, Saudi Arabia, and others from the region. Once again, the Russians seemed to be supportive of a diplomatic initiative. This one would be built on the original Geneva principles from 2012, but it would develop them more and create a timetable for implementation. Two statements were issued by the group on October 30 and November 14, 2015, spelling out a process that would start with a cease-fire, followed by negotiations between the regime and the opposition with the aim of producing a constitution within six months, and elections within 18 months. Al-Nusra and ISIS were excluded from the process, but the other opposition groups would be represented in the negotiations.

These Vienna Principles were then turned into UN Security Council Resolution 2554, which was adopted on December 18, 2015. The starting point was a cease-fire, but the essence of the Geneva principles remained, meaning that everything was geared toward launching a political transition process. But the role or inclusion of Assad was again left vague. Did he have to leave? It was not clear, even if there was to be a transition from the current regime.

Talks began in January 2016 between the regime and the opposition with yet another UN and Arab League special representative, Staffan de Mistura. They stalemated quickly on producing a cease-fire, but Kerry and Lavrov met in Munich on February 11 and agreed to a cessation of hostilities that would begin on February 27. (Why the cessation of hostilities and not a cease-fire? The opposition felt that a cease-fire implied that they would be willing to give up the fight against Assad; hence, the cessation of hostilities was easier for them to accept. Why not have the cessation of hostilities begin immediately? Because Kerry and Lavrov believed that it would take time to line everyone up and get full agreement on implementing it.)

While the cessation of hostilities was not perfect, it initially reduced the level of violence dramatically. Even over the next three months, there was a notable decline in violence, which also permitted access for deliveries of humanitarian assistance. And by March 14, talks began on the political transition. The inherent problem with the cessation of hostilities was one big loophole: the exclusion of al-Nusra and ISIS-permitted attacks against them. But in the Idlib area in particular, al-Nusra and more moderate groups were commingled. Assad began to launch attacks, claiming they were against al-Nusra or ISIS but almost always also attacking other groups in the opposition who were part of the process. In response, these groups began to retaliate against the regime, and the violence began to escalate. Then, on April 19, the regime bombed a market in the town of Marat al-Numan in Idlib province and killed 37 people. The opposition was outraged and walked out of the political talks, and the cessation was a dead letter by May.

What is noteworthy is that during the period of relative calm, there were protests against Al-Nusra in the opposition-held areas against both Assad's regime and, in the northwest. That actually demonstrated that for a short period, the cessation had promise. Its breakdown showed that Assad's regime would never observe any agreement for long—and that it would face no repercussions for its violations.

This would become more pronounced by the fall of 2016. As the killings and starvation sieges became more pronounced, Kerry made one last approach to try to get a cease-fire working with the Russians. He felt it was essential to ground the Syrian Air Force. In his words, its continual bombing was the primary driver of refugees in and from Syria, and it made the opposition feel like "sitting ducks."[54] He met with Putin and Lavrov, and they were willing to keep the Syrian Air Force on the ground if the United States would set up a joint operations center with them to coordinate attacks against Daesh and al-Nusra. Secretary of Defense Ash Carter was against this plan, but Kerry saw little downside and, though not enthusiastic, Obama approved it. For 48 hours the effort seemed to be working, but a US airstrike targeting Daesh forces mistakenly hit a Syrian military unit and killed 62 Syrian soldiers. Assad used the attack as a pretext to hit a humanitarian convoy whose route had been agreed and coordinated, including with the Russians. Still, the Russians protected Assad at the UN Security Council, and Kerry then concluded that the game was over: "As I walked out of the Security Council chamber, I felt for the first time that we had arrived at the end of the road. If the Russians were going to speak from a script of alternative facts, negotiations had gone from improbable to impossible."[55]

The Russians would waste no time in increasing their bombing and obliterating eastern Aleppo from the air. This happened after the bombing and a siege in December 2016, with Hezbollah largely acting as the shock troops on the ground to take the remnants of the city. The Russians carried out nearly all of the bombing operations, using coordinates provided by the UN to target hospitals and clinics.[56] The eastern part of Aleppo was retaken by the regime; it recovered only rubble.

The Trump administration would end Timber Sycamore in July 2017, and President Trump would meet twice with Putin that year, reaching agreement on creating three de-escalation zones.[57] But the Russians and the Syrians used the agreements to shift forces to concentrate on each of these zones one at a time, subduing them after imposing sieges, denying humanitarian assistance, and then permitting fighters to evacuate to the north and Idlib, which remains to this day under the control of Islamists.

Estimates vary on how many Syrians were killed in the war. Civilian deaths alone total at least 350,000, and non-civilian deaths very likely total another 200,000.[58] The population of Syria at the outset of the war was roughly 23–24 million; refugees inside and outside the country now comprise essentially half of that population.[59] The devastation of cities and the economy, as well as a generation of children forced out of school and experiencing trauma, will shape Syria for the foreseeable future. The damage is unmistakable; let us now take a closer look at the statecraft of the Obama administration.

Objectives and Obstacles to Be Overcome

As I noted earlier, this is a textbook case of a huge gap between objectives and means. What were the objectives of the Obama administration? They evolved: initially, the goal was to get Assad, the self-proclaimed reformer, to act like a reformer. Stop the killing, release prisoners, and carry out reforms. Early on, Hillary Clinton did not want to give up hope that Assad might yet decide to follow the path of reform and peace-making. But violence increased, and in April 2011, President Obama exhorted Assad to lead the change necessary for the country or get out of the way. In May, the president presented that less as an American call and more as the choice that Assad needed to make: lead the transition in the country or step aside. By August, Assad's actions had rid him of his right to decide: he had lost his legitimacy, and he had to go.

While the Obama administration never fully walked away from the objective that Assad had to go, one begins to see an additional interim, short-term objective: get Assad to negotiate with the opposition. In June 2012, Hillary Clinton explained that she was pushing for a strong UN Security Council Resolution focusing on a peaceful political transition. She tried to convince the Russian foreign minister Lavrov not to oppose it, and he asked what would happen "if Assad refused to comply. Would it be a Libya-style intervention?" "No," she responded, "The plan was to use this resolution to pressure Assad to negotiate."[60]

John Kerry would later explain that he "hoped the opposition's progress combined with our military intervention against Daesh might finally force the regime back to the bargaining table."[61] Similarly, one official speaking to Sam Dagher in describing Washington's strategy said: "The idea was not to give them [the opposition] the means to win the battle; it was to give them the means to be more structured in order to show the regime that there was no military victory possible and a need to go to the negotiating table."[62]

One might ask the question: What was to be negotiated at the table? Derek Chollet, who held several senior positions in the White House, State Department, and Pentagon during the Obama administration, provides the answer and offers a more complete definition of the administration's objective in Syria. That objective, he wrote later, was a "managed transition"—a phrase that Obama would use only in 2015, "four years after he first said Assad had to go."[63] Chollet would explain that the best outcome "would be for Assad to leave as part of a negotiated settlement, in a way that would allow a transitional government to take hold and basic order to be preserved."[64]

In other words, the objective remained that Assad must go, but this needed to be carefully managed. Negotiations were thus a tactical objective—in reality a means—designed to have Assad leave not all at once, but rather as part of an agreed process and solution. But what would happen if he was not prepared to leave under any circumstances? What would happen if the opposition could simply not live with him given CW, barrel bombs, starvation sieges, and the number of people he was responsible for killing or torturing in prison? What would happen if the opposition was so fragmented that it could not negotiate—or if those who negotiated could not deliver? And how was the pursuit of the administration's objective affected by the emergence of ISIS?

Understanding these questions and developing answers for them had implications for the administration's objective and the means to be used to achieve it. But these questions also highlight many of the obstacles the administration was bound to face in trying to achieve its objective.

In reality, there was a range of different obstacles, including the character of the opposition and the difficulty of organizing it; the sectarian nature of Syria and enduring support for Assad among the Alawis, Christians, and other minorities; the very significant support he got from Iran and Russia; the competition among America's regional partners who were opposed to Assad; and the splits within the administration and the mindset of the president.

As Susan Rice would say, "The rebels were fractured and lacked a coherent, achievable agenda."[65] They were, and they did. The opposition was divided between secular and non-secular forces, and between insiders and outsiders. For understandable, practical reasons, the leaders of the organizations like the Syrian National Council needed to be those living outside of Syria. But fissures quickly developed between those living in exile and those who were in Syria and doing the fighting. The LCCs were on the inside but under-represented in the Syrian National Council; the council, and later the

SOC, had a hard time building their credibility with those doing the fighting because the council and SOC never succeeded in becoming the main conduit for providing the means (arms and money) to combat and resist the regime.

What is more, these organizations themselves lacked coherence and stability. To give just a small flavor of the divided nature of the opposition, it is worth noting that the largest organization designed to represent it constantly underwent leadership change. Burhan Ghalioun was the president of the Syrian National Council—the initial organization representing the opposition—at the outset, from 2011 to 2012. The Syrian National Council was then replaced and subsumed by the SOC, a much broader coalition, more representative of the Syria's ethnic make-up and including secular and more religious members alike. Ahmed Moaz al-Khatib, a moderate Sunni cleric would serve as its first president in 2012–2013 before resigning. Ahmad Jarba, Hodi al-Bakaa, Khaled Koja, Anas al-Abdeh, and Riad Seif successively served for a year each before resigning, followed by the return of Anas al-Abdeh. Constant turnover of leaders is hardly a sign of stability and coherence, but it was not the worse manifestation of the fragmentation. The number of armed groups or factions and local militias was at one point estimated to be roughly 1,000, with many of those tied to fighting in their local areas. The larger organized fighting groups alone included the following: the Free Syrian Army, formed in 2011; the Supreme Military Council of the Free Syrian Army, formed 2012; the Syrian Islamic Liberation Front, which emerged in 2012–2013; the Southern Front, formed in 2014; Jaysh al-Fateh (Army of Conquest), which emerged in 2015; and the National Army (Turkey-backed), which emerged in 2017.[66]

This list does not include Jabhat al-Nusra and ISIS—they were not part of the organized or recognized opposition, but these radical Islamists were fighting Assad's regime and, of course, also fighting the rest of the opposition and other rebel groups whom they saw as rivals and a threat. One of the great fears of the administration in providing arms was that the weapons would fall into the wrong hands. The experience of providing Stingers to the Mujahideen in Afghanistan and having them proliferate elsewhere was an ever-present argument for an abundance of caution that shaped the thinking of many in the administration.

What compounded the fragmentation of the opposition—and the proliferation of arms going to it—was the competition among the Saudis, the Qataris, and the Turks. They supported different groups with money and arms, with the Qataris and the Turks much more open to supporting groups affiliated with al-Nusra. The opposition may not have been coherent, but the support for groups competing within it exacerbated those differences, and made it hard to achieve any sort of coordinated approach—or even shared priorities. Moreover, the competition was in both directions: it was not just that the Saudis, the Qataris, and the Turks were often favoring different groups, but differing groups or militias were then competing to see who could get more—and not with the aim of sharing, but with the aim of becoming the preferred partner for these outside benefactors.

Similarly, both the limitation in the organizing power of the SOC and the frequent turnover of its leaders were also the result of the competition between the Saudis and the Qataris in particular. As John Phillips writes, Moab al-Khatib was a popular figure who might have been able to create real credibility for the SOC, but he and the SOC at that point were too tied to the Saudis, and that engendered opposition. Moreover, al-Khatib was willing to talk to some of Assad's backers—making him largely unacceptable to the Qataris. Much like in Libya, Qatar mostly gave to Islamist groups, believing that they were more determined and motivated fighters.[67]

For his part, Assad needed the opposition not to be moderate but to be Islamist; this served not just to foster the narrative that this is who he was fighting, but also to make the conflict a sectarian one. He released the radical Sunni Islamists from prison, he did little to fight these groups, and he played on the fears of Alawis and Christians that his survival was essential for their survival. This was not a hard sell because they were convinced that the radical Islamists would slaughter them.

I made this point to President Obama in a small group meeting that he convened to discuss Syria in early September 2011, a few weeks after he had said that Assad had to leave. At one point, the president said that he thought that Assad would be forced out much the way Hosni Mubarak had been forced to give up power in Egypt. In response, I explained that would not be the case; I said that Assad would turn this into a sectarian conflict because that was his only chance at survival. Releasing jihadis from his prisons was part of that strategy; Assad understood that the fears of the minorities in Syria were quite real and justified when it came to the radical Sunni Islamists.

That meant that Assad could count on significant support from within Syria. But he was also receiving critical support from outside. The support that the Iranians and the Russians provided him grew over time and constituted a major obstacle to the objective of having him leave—either by force or through a negotiated transition and exit. The Iranians were all in, with Qassem Soleimani, the leader of the Qods Forces, going to Syria in 2012 to organize militias and bring Shia militias from Iraq and as far away as Afghanistan to fight. Weapons, militias, and money were all coming from Iran to sustain the regime. In 2013 alone, the Iranians provided Assad with $4.6 billion in loans and continued to provide oil, as they had done all along.[68] The most important of all the militias, Hezbollah, would provide forces, including the shock troops for much of the fighting on the ground. The reason for this was that for the Iranians, Syria was part of their so-called axis of resistance, and in the words Saeed Jalili, an official close to Supreme Leader Ali Khamenei, "Iran won't allow under any circumstances the breakup of the axis of resistance, of which Syria is a fundamental part."[69]

But Syria was important for Vladimir Putin as well. After what had happened in Libya, Putin was not going to acquiesce to regime change if it seemed driven once again by the United States and its partners. On July 9, 2012, Putin spoke about how Russia could no longer be "passive observers and follow developments." He would add, "I am sure that many of you still have the tragic events in Libya before your eyes. We cannot allow a repeat of such scenarios in other countries—in Syria, for example."[70] Russia would up the ante of its support ahead of direct intervention in September 2015. That intervention fundamentally changed the balance of forces, especially because of the use of Russian air power.

Even before the Russian intervention, the Syrian Air Force and its attacks gave the regime an advantage for which the rebels had only limited answers. Not surprisingly, the introduction of Russian air power compounded the advantages of a regime that had lost a great deal of territory.

The administration was loath to give air defense capabilities to the opposition. There was the fear of repeating the Afghanistan experience and of getting drawn further into the conflict. The Iraq and Libya examples were fresh in the minds of the president and the Joint Chiefs of Staff. While he was still secretary of defense, Robert Gates would say that the United States did not need to get into another Middle Eastern conflict, a view shared by the national security advisor, Susan Rice. But this was not a view held by all in the administration: Hillary Clinton, newly appointed Secretary of Defense Leon Panetta, and Panetta's successor at the CIA, David Petraeus, all believed that only "having skin in the game" would yield the ability to shape events and affect the opposition, regional partners supporting the opposition, and even the Russians.[o]

But President Obama was against being drawn more into what he feared would be another Iraq (and Libya). He would turn down the plan that Clinton, Panetta, and Petraeus would present to him in August 2012 for vetting, training, and arming the opposition; he would not act on the secret finding that he had approved for a serious covert program until later, and even then would limit its application; and he would reject the idea of implementing a no-fly zone in all or even a part of Syria. So what were the means the United States used to try to overcome all the formidable obstacles to the achievement of its objective of a "managed transition?"[71,p]

The Means the United States Used Given the Dominant Mindset of the Administration

The means can be summarized quite easily: sanctions and diplomacy. The Obama administration began to sanction those around Assad and his family in 2011 and ratcheted up sanctions as the regime's violence against protestors became worse. Fred Hof, who would play a leading role in the State Department on Syria until his resignation in late 2012, would later describe his efforts after President Obama called for Assad to leave: "I had, in fact, taken the president's step-aside words as an order ... my near term focus was on tightening the economic noose around the neck of the Assad regime."[72] To that end, he traveled to Europe to work out an agreement with senior French, British, and German officials to boycott Syrian fuel oil—one of the most important sources of discretionary hard currency for Assad's regime. In Hof's words, this would have a limited effect on Europeans and the price of oil but a big effect on the regime.[73]

Hof was, of course, acting at the direction of the secretary of state, but tightening the economic noose was the favored approach of the administration for putting pressure on Assad to change course. It was constantly

---

[o] Words Hillary Clinton would use with me in February 2012.

[p] Derek Chollet would identify one other practical objective—namely, contain and mitigate. He said that it was never uttered. The administration believed that managed transition might take a long time or be difficult to achieve, so the United States would try to contain the conflict and mitigate its consequences, especially for Syria's neighbors. The United States led the world in providing humanitarian assistance, and also deployed Patriot batteries to Turkey and Jordan—all while increasing US military aid to Jordan.

searching for ways to increase the pressure on Assad but was limited by an unwillingness to use military means—either directly or indirectly. As Susan Rice would say, the administration "did consider and reconsider (again and again) many significant steps short of direct war against Assad. At the same time, we imposed what American and European sanctions we could; but absent UN Security Council authority, which Russia consistently blocked, comprehensive global sanctions were not achievable." Still, as she would add, "We provided $6 billion in humanitarian assistance to the victims of Syria's conflict and more to the neighboring states coping with the burden. We spent untold amounts of senior-level energy trying to negotiate with Russia, Syria, and other key players to try to end the conflict peacefully. At various points, we tried to exploit potential diplomatic openings, but none ever came to fruition."[74]

Hillary Clinton, and John Kerry in Obama's second term, would lead the diplomatic efforts to produce multilateral approaches to launch a political process and to provide aid to the opposition and especially to the refugees being displaced by Assad's war on his own people. Clinton did much to mobilize and organize a meeting of the Friends of the Syrian People in Tunisia in February 2012. She would help to orchestrate the meeting of what UN Secretary-General Ban Ki-moon would call the Action Group on Syria in Geneva—in which Kofi Annan's plan would be pushed and the Geneva principles would be adopted. Kerry would produce the Vienna Principles, which built on and refined the Geneva principles, and they would be incorporated into UN Security Council Resolution 2254.

Both Clinton and Kerry would seek to mobilize humanitarian assistance, with the United States leading the way in providing it. Together with European allies, the United States also provided security-related non-lethal assistance to the opposition's military leadership—such as it was. That assistance translated into things like vehicles, computers, communications tools, bullet-proof vests, and night-vision goggles; all of that was useful, but hardly likely to provide much protection. In the words of Samuel Dagher, "To average Syrians, the Western approach to defeating Bashar seemed cynical if not complicit with the regime that was murdering them day after day."[75]

Both Clinton and Kerry would become convinced that diplomacy could not succeed without being backed by force or coercion. Both felt the need to be able to impose a higher price on Assad for his ongoing behavior. Why, they argued, would he ever comply if he never bore any consequences for his noncompliance? Clinton, in particular, also believed that without leverage the United States could neither do more to organize the opposition nor get US partners who were providing arms to coordinate their efforts.

Even after I left the administration in December 2011, Secretary Clinton would ask to see me from time to time. She knew that I had pushed for a more coercive approach while I had been in the administration.[q]

In early February 2012, she asked me to come see her. I did not have to wait long to understand why she wanted the meeting when she asked, "Do you favor giving the Syrian opposition arms?" I said that I did, for several reasons: first, Assad was attacking his civilian population, and those trying to protect that population deserved the means to do so. Second, because the United States was not supplying arms and Assad was killing civilians, others had stepped in to provide weapons They were doing so, however, with no coordination, no conditions to make the opposition get its act together as the price for the getting the arms, and no readiness to promote only the moderates in the opposition. Third, by withholding arms, the United States denied itself leverage with the opposition and the Saudis, the Qataris, and the Turks; and it meant that the United States had little or no influence over who got the weapons and whether they received any effective training in their use. Fourth, the Russians and the Iranians needed to see that the United States would raise the costs to them, which would be the key to giving them an incentive to work out a political process in order to end the war. Last, I said, you can see that our current efforts are failing, more people are dying, the refugee numbers are exploding, the war is imposing devastating costs, and the secular opposition is weakening as the Muslim Brotherhood and the more extreme Islamists are getting arms and money. The current path offers no hope of shifting the direction of the war and its consequences, but we already see that it is radicalizing the opposition—and that will become more true, not less, if the United States continues to withhold arms. Arms are not a panacea, but in this case, not providing them only promises more disasters.

She was nodding in agreement as I ticked off the reasons, and she responded simply, "We aren't going to be able to influence the shape of things if we have no skin in the game." At this point, I sensed that she wanted

---

[q] Before I left my position as the senior person on the Middle East on the National Security Council staff, I had posed questions about how many dead in Syria it would take for the administration to do more. Why wouldn't the United States provide lethal assistance to the opposition given Assad's attacks on the cities and towns? Why, having implemented no-fly zones for so long in northern and southern Iraq, was it impossible to have a no-fly zone over at least a part of Syria, given Assad's use of his aircraft and the dropping of barrel bombs only on civilian areas?

to see me as part of her thinking through what arguments she could most effectively marshal to make the case for providing arms to the opposition. I asked if this was going to be a difficult sell, and she said yes, telling me there was not a lot of support for this in the administration in no small part because of "where the President's head is at." Much would happen over the next several months, including the failure of Kofi Annan's plan, the clear decline in America's leverage to affect what was happening in the opposition and the growth of more radical groups, and the president's decision first to approve a finding on covert action but then not to implement it. But by the summer, Clinton was working with David Petraeus on the vetting, training, and arming proposal. Petraeus would present the plan to President Obama with the support of both Clinton and Panetta.

President Obama was not persuaded, saying he felt that what the United States would provide would neither be enough to drive Assad from power nor be particularly meaningful given all the weapons already flowing into the country.[76] As noted earlier, Clinton and Petraeus argued that providing arms would offer the United States the means to organize the opposition and manage the arms going to it. Moreover, they said, "the goal was not to build up a force strong enough to defeat the regime. Rather the idea was to give us a partner on the ground to work with that could do enough to convince Assad and his backers that a military victory was impossible."[77]

The president rejected the plan, just as he would reject Secretary Kerry's later efforts to use force more directly to hold Assad accountable for violating the cessation of hostilities, attacking moderate rebel forces but sparing al-Nusra or ISIS, and blocking delivery of humanitarian assistance—even when corridors for delivery had been agreed upon. As Kerry would later write, "I never succeeded in persuading [Obama] to give me the tool I wanted most: greater leverage. Not boots on the ground or a large-scale operation; even a small strike on an appropriate target would send a message."[78] He would add that he "wasn't the only one calling for more forceful interventions. Samantha Power, ambassador to the UN, and to some extent CIA director John Brennan also believed the risks of inaction outweighed those of limited military force. But the Pentagon—and, more important, the president—remained as unconvinced as ever that overt military action to support the Syrian opposition, however limited, was worth pursuing."[79]

Neither Clinton nor Kerry could gain the leverage they needed to move the needle diplomatically. Both refer to the resistance of the Pentagon to limited military moves in support of the Syrian opposition or against Assad.

Clinton would speak of "our military brass" and its reluctance to get involved in Syria—and its penchant for making "consistently dire projections of the forces" that would be needed to do nearly anything in Syria.[80] The best indication of this was that in response to meetings we were having in the fall of 2011, and to the questions I kept posing about why we could not do more, President Obama asked Martin Dempsey, chairman of the Joint Chiefs of Staff, in November 2011 to provide some military options for possible interventions in Syria. The response drafted by the Joint Chiefs of Staff was clearly designed to reinforce the doubts President Obama had. In January 2012, Chairman Dempsey would present a series of slides at the White House in which he would show that it would take 70,000 US servicemen to impose a no-fly zone over Syria.[81] The military briefing also made clear that all options would be costly, and if the President were to go ahead and order action on any of these options, it would be impossible for the United States to act militarily against the Iranians if diplomacy failed to stop the Iranian nuclear program.

While US military leadership was not eager to be involved in Syria, it was the president who consistently made the decision not to act. To be fair, any president after Iraq would have been hesitant. Clinton suggests that this hesitancy should not have been surprising, especially for a president who "had been elected in large part because of his opposition to the war in Iraq and his promise to bring the troops home. Getting entangled in any way in another sectarian war in the Middle East was not what he had in mind when coming into office."[82]

No doubt, Clinton is right. (Clearly, Obama's experience in Libya also added to his hesitancy.) But this does not fully capture President Obama's thinking or mindset. The importance of reducing the use of US military power was clearly an important element of his worldview. In a press conference in March 2012, Obama said, "The notion that the way to solve every one of these problems is to deploy our military, that hasn't been true in the past and it won't be true now. We've got to think through the lens of what's going to be effective, but also what's critical for US security interests."[83]

That observation reflected not just America's bad experience in using force in the greater Middle East (in Iraq and Afghanistan), but also a more general belief that those who resorted to the use of military forces failed to grasp the meaning of power in the twenty-first century. In his discussions with Jeffrey Goldberg, he observed that Putin's actions in Crimea in 2014 and intervention in Syria in 2015 to preserve Russian control and influence came at great cost to Russia. Obama said that those who thought these interventions were a sign of strength "fundamentally misunderstand the nature of power in foreign affairs or in the world more generally. Real power means you can get what you want without having to resort to exerting violence."[84]

One can argue that if everyone else thinks that hard power matters, and acts accordingly, then it does. But that was not Obama's view. It was not just a different view of the meaning of power and the idea that the use of the military instrument often actually comes at the expense of America's power, it was also his view that greater involvement in the Middle East was a mistake—its "tribal" warfare could not be ended from the outside, and getting drawn into it distracted the United States from what was more important internationally, especially given developments in Asia. Goldberg concluded from his many conversations with Obama that the president had a number of

> dovetailing conclusions about the world, and America's role in it: The first is that the Middle East is no longer terribly important to American interests. The second is that even if the Middle East were surpassingly important, there would still be little that an American president could do to make it a better place. The third is that the innate American desire to fix the sorts of problems that manifest themselves most drastically in the Middle East inevitably leads to warfare, to the deaths of US soldiers and to the eventual hemorrhaging of US credibility and power. The fourth is that the world cannot afford to see the diminishment of US power.[85]

Given his worldview, his perspective on the use of force, and how he saw the Middle East, it should not be a surprise that President Obama would resist greater involvement in Syria and rationalize his decisions. His rejection of the Clinton–Panetta–Petraeus plan in the summer of 2012 did not, as I and many others believed, stem from concerns that the conflict in Syria would heat up during his re-election campaign. We believed that he would eventually authorize their plan after the election, but that was wrong—he really did not want any greater involvement in Syria. Note that after his re-election, the president justified his reluctance to provide lethal assistance by saying, "We have seen extremist elements insinuate themselves into the opposition, and one of the things that we have to be on guard about ... is that we're not indirectly putting arms in the hands of folks who would do Americans harm or do Israel harm."[86]

It is true that radical Islamists were becoming more and more important in the opposition, but that was increasingly the case because the United States was not providing arms to the more moderate elements. President Obama was much too smart to rationalize not strengthening the moderates by providing them means–nor use American leverage to get others to provide weapons and money only to moderates and not extremists–and then justify not helping the moderates because the extremists too strong. No, his hesitancy reflected his view of the world and Middle East region.

But one might ask, then: Why call for Assad to leave? Indeed, if the administration was prepared to apply only limited means to achieve that objective, why make that public call? Here, the explanation may relate to a poor understanding of the realities in Syria. Recall that President Obama said in the internal White House meeting just a few weeks after his call for Assad to leave that he expected him to go the way of Mubarak, meaning that his call would be organically realized by the Syrian people themselves.[87,r]

This seemed to be the conventional wisdom in the administration at the time—no doubt driven by the events in Tunisia, Egypt, and Libya. Ben Rhodes would say that the administration was counting on both the building internal pressures and international isolation to "cause the regime to crumble."[88] To that end, defections were encouraged in the army and the government. Sanctions were imposed on all those associated with the Assad family and the regime. The assets of the Assad family were frozen, and his wife, mother, sister, and sister-in-law were also banned from traveling to European Union member states. All during this time, the regime was increasingly losing territory to the opposition.

The belief, in short, was that the pressure on Assad's regime would lead him to look for a way out. Brett McGurk, who had a responsibility for organizing the fight against ISIS in the Obama administration, would later explain that the prevailing assumption (even as he also acknowledged that it turned out to be wrong) was "that he [Assad] wouldn't be able to withstand the pressure—the diplomatic isolation, the military pressure, the economic pressure—and eventually he would negotiate himself out of power. But it was a total misreading. We did not understand the dynamics of Syria, or Assad's readiness to hold onto power at all costs. Short of an invasion, he was not going anywhere."[89]

---

r Obama was not alone in that view—even seasoned Middle East observers, like Israeli defense minister Ehud Barak, were saying that they expected at the time that Assad would be gone in weeks.

Not everyone shared the prevailing assumption, however. The US ambassador to Syria, Robert Ford, did not believe that Assad was so vulnerable and was likely to fall or seek a way out. Ford was thus against making the public call for Assad to leave. He was convinced, like I was, that Assad had a staying power not only because of the support of the minorities and the Alawi dominance of the security services, but also because he would pay any price to survive and hold onto power. Sam Dagher basically captured the predominant assessment within the White House and much of the administration at that point when he wrote that Obama's approach was based on the assumption that the "regime derived its strength from the army, the government, and other institutions found in normal states, when, in fact, the underpinnings of this regime were the family and clan, more than 2 million Alawites, the mukhabarat system, the Hezbollah militia in Lebanon, and Iran."[90]

Fred Hof would also take issue with the conventional wisdom and the general assessments in the administration at the time. Hof would later recall how he argued that without meaningful military moves against Assad's regime, "there was, contrary to what Obama thought, a real possibility that Assad would survive."[91]

There was a strange duality to the position within the administration and the assessments coming out of the Intelligence Community. On the one hand, the president and those closest to him, like Ben Rhodes, were convinced that Assad's days were numbered—political and economic pressure would be sufficient to produce his fall from power. On the other hand, the Intelligence Community had little faith in the opposition and saw few moderates in it. While I was questioning the assumption that Assad would simply fall and argued that the United States needed to be doing what it could to help the moderate opposition, the Intelligence Community seemed reluctant to engage them.

I discovered this very directly. In December 2011, I left the administration but retained a consulting relationship with the White House. At the Washington Institute for Near East Policy, I would have two colleagues, Andrew Tabler and Jeffrey White, who were meeting with different members of the Syrian opposition in southern Turkey and in northern Syria. They were mapping out all the opposition groups and had identified natural partners for the administration to support. I conveyed this to Tom Donilon, and he told me that the CIA was saying that it was hard to identify anyone with whom the United States could work. I told him that this statement made no sense: "Tabler and White are meeting these groups that fit the bill and are compiling lists of those we could and should work with." When Tom conveyed my argument to the Intelligence Community, this all seemed to be news to them. Tabler then shared the lists with CIA analysts, but there was no apparent follow-up with the groups that Tabler and White had identified.

In January 2012, Tabler arranged for me to meet Farouq Habib, a 30-year-old lawyer who served on the Revolutionary Council of Homs. He was impressive, understood the importance of organizing, and had a clear vision of the importance of democratizing the new Syria. He said to me that "if Assad falls but the Muslim Brotherhood replaces him, then we lost the revolution." I asked him, "What do those whom you represent need to succeed?" He replied, "Practical support: we have little money, few if any arms, little communication means—and the Muslim Brothers are able to offer money and arms. How are we supposed to persuade people who are being attacked by the regime's security forces that they need to stick with us and not be drawn to the Muslim Brothers, when they can provide them arms and sustain them with money. Without the means, we can't compete, especially when the Muslim Brothers seem to have a lot of both money and arms." He plaintively told me that the Americans said publicly that they were providing non-lethal support—but "we don't see it, and when we reach out, we get no response." He concluded with me by saying that money to help sustain people and/or communications gear would help, even if the administration would not provide any arms. I would learn later that neither money nor communications equipment was ever provided to Habib's group.

This was not only my or Andrew Tabler's experience. Fred Hof had the responsibility of dealing with the opposition for the State Department. He would say, "There were times when I offered senior people the opportunity to meet with certain people and make their own assessment as to whether there was any there, there—and to the best of my knowledge, there was no follow up."[92]

How can one explain this? In the CIA's case, as one former official explained, there were two factors that account for this. First, there was a genuine belief at the Agency that many of those in the opposition who had been identified as moderates were simply not consequential and could have little effect. Second, some of those in the Agency who had responsibility for this area were dubious that there would be much support for the effort from the White House, and they were very reluctant to start building relationships with those on the ground and build expectations and make commitments that would not be met.

While that might explain the hesitancy to provide support to those in Syria that Tabler and White were identifying, it does not explain why the intelligence assessments also seemed to be off. Fred Hof has offered an explanation for what he considered to be a poor feel for what was going on inside Syria: "During the days when I would visit Damascus, I would also sit down with our local intelligence chief [and his folks] and I have to say I was underwhelmed by their analysis and the amount of knowledge they had about what was actually going on in the country. I don't think it was a great collection priority before the violence, and it was never upgraded once the violence started ... I didn't see evidence of any great overwhelming interest in what was going on. At the time, I thought maybe people were taking their cue from the President ... He wasn't all that interested, why should they dedicate the resources?"[93]

It would not be the first time that the posture of the White House would affect how the Intelligence Community approached an issue. Obviously, high presidential interest generates responsiveness from the Intelligence Community. Responsiveness need not shape intelligence that suits what the president wants to hear—as was the case during the first term of the Bush 43rd administration—but can reflect, as Hof suggests, the level of priority for gathering intelligence and the assets used to acquire as much hard information as possible. But it is hard to escape the conclusion that the level of interest—or in this case, the lack of interest—also affected the approach to acquiring intelligence. If the president did not want to be involved, why bother?

If that was the instinct in the Intelligence Community, it was bound to be reinforced by the president's approach to the covert program. As noted above, the initial finding for covert action was approved by President Obama in the spring of 2012. The finding was guided by the publicly stated objective that Bashar al-Assad must go—and the CIA came back with a set of recommendations for what it would take through a covert program to achieve this objective. In keeping with the finding and the recommendations to fulfill it, the Agency organized two meetings, the first in Istanbul in the spring of 2012 and the second in Jordan at the Dead Sea that summer. The meetings brought together the key Middle Eastern intelligence chiefs as well as Turkish, British, and French counterparts of the United States, and they developed a coordinated plan involving all these different actors, their capabilities, and a division of labor approach to achieving the goal.

But all this was based on what the United States would do. And before the second meeting, the United States was going to take its initial step of providing arms and ammunition to key groups actively fighting the regime—groups that, in the words of one of those involved in this effort, were not dominated by extremists. Another participant in this program said the airlift was set to go: the planes had been ordered 72 hours in advance but still required President Obama to give the final go-ahead. According to the participants I talked to, he simply chose not to give an answer at all—not a no, but simply no response in answer to the question, "Can we launch?" With no final approval, the flights were canceled at the last minute. The second meeting went ahead as scheduled, but without the American delivery of arms, the plan was effectively off the table. One of the senior Arab officials there said that the other participants would proceed on their own since the United States was unable to do so. Rather than a coordinated approach shaped and managed by the administration, there was a proliferation of arms going into Syria with no priority or coherence.[s]

To be fair, in 2013, after the use of CW, President Obama would go ahead with the Timber Sycamore covert program. It would turn out to be a disaster for multiple reasons: it would take months to get off the ground; the vetting process was very slow, even "torturous" in the words of one official; the arms provided were deliberately limited, and as another official told me, "we would train them but not allow them to keep the weapons;" the opposition would not be provided armor or anti-air systems which could have been effective against the Syrian military, and once the United States began to get more serious in providing arms, it insisted that those getting arms had to fight ISIS not Assad. One can imagine how the opposition felt about this condition: Assad was their enemy, who was killing Sunnis; ISIS would become a threat to many in the opposition, but only later.

Timber Sycamore was never able to lead to the fielding of a significant force. Even with all the vetting, or at least in part because of it, Secretary of Defense Ash Carter would acknowledge that the program could only field about 60 fighters. The failure of Timber Sycamore simply fortified Obama's instinct to keep America's involvement to a minimum. He never saw how the administration's hesitancy and its rules and limitations contributed to the demise of those the United States backed on the ground.

---

[s] This account is based on interviews with several former senior intelligence officers—all of whom were part of this program and all of whom requested not to be named. I had known and worked with all of them for years.

With the emergence of ISIS—and the beheadings of four American journalists and aid workers, which understandably made ISIS the incarnation
of evil for the American public—the US military would start launching air
strikes and special operations in Syria and Iraq. But America's target in Syria
was ISIS, not Assad. David Petraeus would later talk about the irony of the
Pentagon claiming that the dense Syrian air defense made the cost of imposing a no-fly zone too high—and yet when the United States developed a
military campaign to go after ISIS, a no-fly zone was imposed.[94] True, Assad
had no reason to activate his air defense when the US military was attacking
ISIS targets. But it is also the fact that Israel carried out countless air strikes
against Hezbollah, Iranian, and Syrian regime targets without being particularly constrained by the Syrian air defenses—and when Syrian air defense
radars *were* turned on and missiles were fired at Israeli aircraft, the Israelis
would destroy those missile batteries. The air defense network was not the
insuperable obstacle that US military leaders made it out to be.

What is more, the United States also found a local partner that was willing
to fight ISIS on the ground in Syria. The Syrian Democratic Forces made up
largely but not exclusively of Kurds, proved to be a highly credible partner
prepared to fight ISIS. It needed the means to do so, which included not
just weapons and munitions, but also intelligence and spotting for artillery
shelling. The administration gladly provided all this and air strikes, but the
Syrian Democratic Forces did the fighting on the ground. It rooted ISIS out
of the towns it had taken, including its self-declared capital, Raqqa. Here was
a local partner that was willing to fight and simply needed the means to do
so, and Obama made the decision to partner with them.

It is, of course, also true that the Russians and the Iranians had no reason
to resist the United States targeting ISIS, especially because it freed them
up to target the rest of the opposition to Assad. Still, from time to time the
United States would make mistakes with its targeting and hit Assad forces.
While Assad might have used it as an excuse not to observe the cessation of
hostilities or to shut down humanitarian corridors—which his forces rarely
respected in any case—it is, nonetheless, interesting that he never retaliated
against the United States, nor did the Iranians or the Russians seek to do
anything in response. No doubt, those decisions were dictated by simple
prudence, but it was a reminder that US forces created a certain reality that
others respected.

But this was a lesson that the Obama administration never applied
to dealing with Assad. The presumption against using force against the

regime—and the belief that America would be sucked into a quagmire—simply precluded it. Obama was hesitant about acting on the red line out of fear that the United States would not be taking out chemical weapons or their stockpiles in its attack, and Assad might afterward use them again. But even if that would have happened—then what? Would the United States have to strike again, and where would it stop? As Jeffrey Goldberg concluded from his talks with Obama, "The president had come to believe that he was walking into a trap—one laid both by allies and by adversaries and by the conventional expectations of what an American president is supposed to do."

In Obama's words, "dropping bombs on someone to prove you're willing to drop bombs on someone is just about the worst reason to use force."[95] He did not buy the argument that he needed to follow through on the red line threat and conduct the military strikes for the sake of America's credibility. And, his decision was a source of great pride to him, as he told Goldberg:

> I'm very proud of that moment. The overwhelming weight of conventional wisdom and the machinery of our national-security apparatus had gone fairly far. The perception was that my credibility was at stake, that America's credibility was at stake. And so for me to press the pause button at that moment, I knew, would cost me politically. And the fact that I was able to pull back from the immediate pressures and think through in my own mind what was in America's interest, not only with respect to Syria but also with respect to our democracy, was as tough a decision as I've made—and I believe ultimately it was the right decision to make.[96]

He would add that there is "a playbook in Washington that presidents are supposed to follow ... Where American is directly threatened, the playbook works. But the playbook can also be a trap that can lead to bad decisions."[97]

Obama and many in the administration believed that it was the right decision because the United States was ultimately able to get the vast majority of Syria's CW withdrawn without using force. Derek Chollet would later explain, "By October 2013, without a bomb being dropped, Assad's regime had admitted having a massive chemical weapons program it had never acknowledged, agreed to give it up, and submitted to a multinational coalition that removed and destroyed the deadly trove."[98] The criticism of the president's decision not to militarily enforce the red line and to portray it as a failure, Chollet argues, is misplaced and "reveals a deep—and misguided—conviction in Washington foreign policy circles that a policy must be perfectly articulated in order to be successful—that in this sense the means matter more than the ends. Far from a failure, the red line episode accomplished everything it set out to do—in fact, it surpassed expectations. But the fact that it appeared to occur haphazardly and in a scattered way was enough to brand it a failure." Indeed, Chollet goes on to argue that it has been "hard for the administration to claim the red line as a strategic success because of the improvised way it unfolded. And it's possible Obama could have achieved the same result through different means— means that might have generated a greater sense of American leadership. But that shouldn't cloud how we remember the chapter: In foreign policy, the end result matters more than the road one took to get there."[99]

For Chollet, much like Obama, the issue of credibility is decidedly secondary—especially because, as he points out, if the United States had acted militarily to preserve its credibility, "we would have delivered a less advantageous outcome for our overall security" because the United States would not have been able to remove the bulk of Syria's CW.[100]

Chollet's argument about removing over 90 percent of Syrian CW should not be dismissed; the removal was an important success. And it is not surprising that for the Obama administration in particular, this was seen as a great achievement because the administration's approach was guided in part by the fear that CW could fall into the hands of extremists, especially if there was a collapse of the Syrian state. Later, when writing to explain why the administration's approach to getting CW out was such a success, Chollet stated, "The rise of ISIS was terrifying enough; it would be exponentially more dangerous if it had had the chance to get its hands on hundreds of tons of Syrian chemical weapons."[101]

But there is a problem with Chollet's reasoning. The very weakness of the administration's response to the killing of 1,400 people with sarin gas in Ghouta, and the chilling images of dead children from the attack lined up on the ground, did, as I will note later, a great deal to help the rise of ISIS and its recruiting power.

The Chollet argument also overlooks that the administration *did* have other options for getting CW out even if it had carried out a set of limited military strikes. If, as Chollet and Rice believe, the Russians acted to lean on Assad so the United States would not use force, the US military certainly could have carried out limited strikes and then gone to Putin and made a cessation of strikes contingent on CW removal. That would have demonstrated that the administration acted on the red line and still allowed Putin to show that he managed the outcome. Yes, removing CW stocks was an achievement, but because Obama, Chollet, and others take a narrow view of the consequences of not acting militarily, they overlook or seriously underestimate the longer-term impact of setting a red line and then not acting on it. Unfortunately, there have been other consequences that we are still living with.

Credibility affects how others see the United States and whether it can be counted on. Lose that, and others—allies and friends as well as adversaries—draw conclusions about what they can and cannot do. In this case, the conclusions were varied, but all pointed in one direction: there were no circumstances in which the United States would act militarily against Assad—notwithstanding the president's rhetoric. That had implications for what happened in Syria, in the region, and beyond.

It is ironic that the last of Goldberg's conclusions about the Obama worldview was that Obama believed that "the world cannot afford to see the diminishment of US power." And, yet, failing to act on the red line had this very effect. Chuck Hagel, who was then Obama's secretary of defense, was appalled and believed that when the president ignored his own red line, it "debased the currency" and dealt Obama and the United States a "severe blow." In the days and months afterward, Hagel's counterparts around the world told him that "their confidence in Washington had been shaken over Obama's sudden about-face."[102]

While the confidence of friends may have been shaken, the confidence of Assad and US adversaries was given a huge boost. Assad could see that there were no circumstances in which the United States would use force. Barrel bombs, starvation sieges of cities, use of chlorine, you name it—he knew he could take all these actions with impunity. From within the administration, Samantha Power understood this, later writing, "Despite making the best of a terrible predicament, there was no getting around the fact that President Obama's own public statements prior to going to Congress reflected a firm conviction: what Assad had done merited using military force ... Assad paid some price—giving up chemical weapons—but he subsequently used the rest of his arsenal with even greater abandon. The costs to Syrians, the United States, and the world—would continue to grow."[103] And, as she added in the documentary *Corridors of Power*, America's "threat to use force meant less than it did before" the administration's failure to act on the red line.[104]

According to the French foreign minister at the time, Laurent Fabius, it was not just the effect on Assad but also on Putin that mattered. In an interview with Sam Dagher, Fabius said that Putin drew the conclusion that he could get away with a lot because the United States might talk tough—tell Assad he must leave power and draw red lines barring CW use—but ultimately, it was not prepared to take action to back its threats. And, for Fabius, this very much affected Putin's subsequent actions in Ukraine.[105]

Obama would certainly dispute Fabius's view, but deterrence and credibility reflect the psychology and perceptions of others. And, in this case, the perceptions of others in and around Syria created another set of consequences that ultimately created bigger problems for the United States—and led to America having to use force. The effect on the Syrian opposition and the majority of the Syrian public that opposed Assad was, according to John Kerry, devastating. As Kerry wrote, "Murderers should be punished, not just stripped of their killing arsenal," and the result of the administration's posture meant "to the members of the Syrian opposition, Assad was getting away with murder. If this horrifying attack did not justify intervention, nothing would."[106] But if that were the case, who do you turn to? You will turn to those forces that are the most ferocious in the fight against Assad: the Islamists, al-Nusra, and ISIS.

Nothing gave a bigger boost to ISIS and the group's regional and global recruitment than the CW attack on Ghouta—and the US and international response to it. Wa'el Alzayat, who was the State Department's Syria outreach coordinator, would, after leaving the department, decry the administration's non-response to Ghouta attack, explaining that it provided ISIS a seismic opportunity to expand its appeal as the defenders of the Sunnis.[107] Sam Dagher would go further, saying that, "No single event in the history of the Syrian conflict helped the Islamist extremists justify their terror and message of hate more than the CW attack and the way the international community handled its aftermath. It became a potent and resonant recruitment tool."[108]

Not surprisingly, not acting on the red line also affected the perceptions and behavior of America's regional allies and friends. There was shock and dismay, with Turkish president Abdullah Gul saying, "We expected more [of America]." The Saudis, who were not informed of the president's decision to pull back, felt it was a betrayal. At the time, Frank Gardner, the BBC's reporter in the Kingdom, called it a "seminal moment" and a turning point in fueling a more activist and militarist Saudi approach to the region.[109] King Abdullah and Prince Bandar—who had been assigned the role of working with the United States and the opposition in Syria—were furious and felt that the Kingdom must now provide arms to those in Syria most effective in the fight against Assad, irrespective of what the United States might want. That had always been the position of Turkey and Qatar, but they now felt even less of a need to be responsive to the United States.[110]

One other consequence of not acting militarily on the red line and in response to Ghouta was the impact it had on Syrians believing they must flee: at the time of the Ghouta sarin attack, the UN Refugee Agency (UNHCR) had 1.8 million registered refugees after roughly 2.5 years of the regime's war in Syria. One year later, that number was 2.9 million.[111]

Viewed through the narrow lens of getting most of the CW withdrawn from Syria, President Obama can take satisfaction in his decision on the red line. Derek Chollet can argue that the critics should be focusing on the result, not the process—and yet, when viewed against the larger objectives in Syria, the decision seemed to have helped Assad more than it hurt him and given a major boost to the very forces the United States would then have to act against militarily. Moreover, internationally, it is hard to conclude that it served America's broader interests. As was so often the case in the Obama administration, decisions were made based on an assessment of the costs of taking action; rarely were the costs of inaction given sufficient consideration and weight.

Even while Susan Rice can say, "The gap between our rhetorical policy and our actions constantly bedeviled US policymaking," there was also little thought given to the consequences of such a gap. To be fair, it was, as Hillary Clinton said, a "wicked problem." And one could argue that there were no good choices in Syria. But does that mean that the administration could not have done better, or that its statecraft and its marriage of objectives and means could not have produced a better result?

Could It Have Been Different?

Susan Rice would later write, "I believe that, as pained as we felt, as much as our values were offended, and as amoral the decision not to intervene directly in Syria's civil war seemed, it was the right choice for the totality of US interests."[112] She defined intervention in broad terms, including the provision of arms to the opposition, explaining that she questioned "the wisdom of arming and training the Syrian rebels since the level of our support was not sufficient to create more than a temporary stalemate, before Russian intervention tilted the conflict in Assad's favor."[113]

But the Russians did not intervene until the fall of 2015. True, I quoted earlier Putin's speech from July 9, 2012, about not letting another Libya transpire. Would Putin's calculus of the low risk of his intervention have been the same had the United States provided meaningful support to the opposition and used America's readiness to do so as a lever to organize both the opposition and its aid provisioners? That would have raised the stakes and potential cost to Putin, including the risks to his aircraft, if the United States had been willing to provide any air defense means to those fighting the regime. But the United States waited to provide any weapons until late 2013, and even once that decision had been made, the weapons were slow to arrive and were limited in their utility to deal with the threats facing the opposition. Moreover, Putin also knew, after the administration's non-response on the red line in 2013, that he ran few risks of America's intervention.[t]

Derek Chollet recounts the constant debates over what to do in response to Syria and even notes that the administration was "slow" to get in the game of providing arms at a time when so many were already flowing into Syria and going to "the wrong elements of the opposition."[114] He explains that part of the reason for the delay was "a lack of understanding about who the opposition was and worries that if we provided military assistance, it would end up in the wrong hands."[115]

In addition, he notes that in the White House, there were doubts about "effectiveness, accountability, and risk" of providing arms and what it would mean about sucking the United States into the conflict.[116] The subsequent problems with Timber Sycamore, including corruption, incompetence, and weapons falling into the wrong hands, seemed to justify the hesitancy to begin with. But here again, what if the administration had started this process earlier? What if it had conditioned US arms on greater organizational coherence on the part of the opposition, and on the Turks, the Qataris, and the Saudis providing arms only through the mechanism the United States would set up?

Even before I left the administration in the fall of 2011, I was pushing not just for lethal assistance, but to create a US-managed mechanism through which all weaponry would have to flow. I argued—as Clinton and Petraeus would in the summer 2012—that unless the administration provided arms, it would not be able to get others to respond to the United States. Already

---

[t] That he intervened in Crimea in 2014 with little green men suggests he still felt the need to test whether and how the United States might respond—and here again he saw how restrained America's response was.

in the fall of 2011, because of the brutality of the regime, the Qataris and the Turks were sending arms and money. Farouk Habib would tell me in January 2012 that the Muslim Brotherhood had money and arms; Mazen Darwish, a peace activist in Syria, would complain similarly that already in 2011, "when people like us were distributing slogans, [the Muslim Brotherhood] were giving money and food," they were determined to fight, and they had deep pockets. In Darwish's words, "The regime's barbarism and people's rage were channeled into a violent jihadist agenda." And the Islamists, those more extreme than the Muslim Brotherhood, had no trouble getting arms.[117]

This was "the mess" that Hillary Clinton referred to trying to fix. David Petraeus would later tell me that there would have been coordination if the United States had contributed real weapons and led. He added that had the president approved what they proposed in 2012, they would have gained control over the arms flowing into Syria—and it would have worked.[118] But one can ask, worked to what end? Would it have truly created structure and coherence of the opposition? It might well have permitted the moderates in the opposition to dominate, especially if the United States organized all those who were providing material and military assistance and ensured that one centralized mechanism would be used to channel all the support to one group. That would have required a serious investment on America's part and constant management to ensure the mechanism functioned as intended—with penalties for transgressions.

In other words, it would have required real American leadership and a continuous investment. The irony is that this would emerge only in 2014, when the Obama administration, with Secretary John Kerry and General John Allen leading the way, organized a broad international coalition to fight ISIS, with the US military in the lead and carrying out thousands of air strikes against Daesh. For Obama, the weight of Iraq and Afghanistan had been too heavy for him to play the same role against the Assad regime. Again, to be fair, we cannot know for sure that this kind of American leadership would have worked to truly force the opposition to function as an organized group. Yes, US leadership, readiness to provide arms, and the creation of one centralized mechanism could have prevented the Turks, the Qataris, and the Saudis from worsening the fissures within the Syrian opposition, but they would not have guaranteed success.

Interestingly enough, the administration would prove that it could work effectively with a local partner, the Syrian Democratic Forces (SDF), who would be the ones to root out ISIS and bear the brunt of the casualties in doing so. But the Syrian Democratic Forces, with its Kurdish leadership, was far more homogeneous than those who came to make up the diverse Syrian opposition forces. Even if we cannot know for sure, it is hard to escape the conclusion that had the United States embraced the moderates in the opposition early and provided them training, weapons, and money, the situation would have looked very different. If nothing else, it could have done a great deal to undercut the support that Assad had from the minorities in Syria.

Moreover, there was another option for affecting the nature of the conflict even if the administration chose not to provide weapons to the opposition through a centralized mechanism: the provision of a partial or total no-fly zone or zones within Syria. The US military said that the dense Syrian air defense made this impossible. As noted earlier, that vaunted, dense air defense network did not prevent the Israelis from carrying out countless air strikes—numbering well over 1,000. Hillary Clinton was trying to get a no-fly zone done in the summer of 2012, and the Turks were a very willing participant. Clinton also found that the French were willing to help enforce such a zone or zones. With Patriot missile batteries deployed to the Turkish–Syrian border, the US already had coverage of much of northern Syria; in any case, the United States could also have used Turkish bases to enforce a no-fly zone in northern Syria, much as it had been done for the no-fly zone in Iraq, which had been maintained for 12 years.

It is not hard to imagine what a no-fly zone just in the north of Syria, covering Aleppo and Idlib provinces, would have meant: it would have produced safe areas for refugees, and these areas could have been built up with assistance from the Saudis, the Qataris, and Turkey to accommodate them and to turn these areas into an economically viable region. The flow of refugees could have been dramatically reduced, and in so doing, the United States would have removed or at least limited one of the sources of instability growing out of the conflict in Syria. Such a no-fly zone would have also allowed the opposition to create governance in a space where they were not being subjected to barrel bombs and airstrikes. That could have allowed the opposition to demonstrate there was an alternative to Assad that was capable of functioning and governing, even as it alleviated a great deal of the suffering in Syria.

There may have been other benefits from establishing even a partial no-fly zone. For example, would Assad have used CW if the United States had already created a no-fly zone in at least a part of the country? Might he have judged America's likely responses differently had the administration already created a no-fly zone in the north? Might he have believed that the United States would do more in response?

Maybe Assad still would have acted, and maybe Putin still would have intervened in 2015, but both Assad and Putin would have to take into account what further action the United States might take. It is interesting to note that Putin has not been prone to test the United States where it has real capability and demonstrated the intent to use it, including even in Syria once we began to act militarily against ISIS.[u]

The point is that the administration had options and tools to do more in Syria. It would have had more options if it had provided arms and assumed greater leadership earlier in Syria; it had more options to limit Assad's use of barrel bombs and attacks on civilians at least in the northern Syria; it had more options to deal with the Syrian CW. Had it meaningfully acted on any of its options, the number of casualties, the number of refugees, the shape of Syria—and the perception of the United States in the region—might look very different today. The Assad regime's collapse tends to validate this point.

Conclusion

This is surely a case of statecraft done badly. The framing of the issue and the administration's goal—as Susan Rice has acknowledged—were mistakes. The assessments of the reality in Syria were poor and appear to have been influenced by the Intelligence Community's view that the administration wanted to do little. Their assessments were likely also influenced by having been burned in Iraq, and President Obama surely seemed, with some justification, to be leery of involvement because of the legacy of his inherited war, his own worldview, and his recognition of the domestic political realities he faced. He constrained America's means and ensured that they would bear little relationship to the administration's goals, and as a result, he reduced US leverage—the key to affecting the behavior of others.

At every juncture when something different might have been done to reduce the terrible costs of this conflict, President Obama's decision was not to act. He would later tell Jeffrey Goldberg that he might have been

---

[u] Note the US destruction of a Wagner Forces when, after several warnings, they refused to stop an advance toward a small American force on February 7, 2018, in Syria. At least 500 of the Wagner forces were killed, and the Russians did nothing about it—trying to keep the deaths hidden and not testing the US forces again in Syria. US forces have remained in Syria to prevent ISIS from rising again.

more willing to act in Syria if it had not been for Iraq. Again, this instinct is understandable, but the context of Iraq and that of Syria were very different. In Iraq, the United States had carried out regime change with no plan for what would come afterward. Syria, by contrast, was about a leader triggering a domestic uprising against his own regime. Yes, extremist outsiders came to help the opposition, but they did so in response to the regime's sheer brutality.

In making consistent decisions not to act, President Obama was constrained by his fear of the costs—not unreasonable for a leader. He constantly questioned those who argued for taking steps, asking them to, "tell me how this ends." But he never asked the corollary question, "tell me what happens if we do nothing." Those costs of inaction have proven to be very high, and had the statecraft in his administration been better, the costs almost certainly would have been dramatically lower. Good statecraft cannot guarantee success, but it certainly avoids the costs incurred by practicing poor statecraft. Here, the Obama administration did it poorly, with a range of terrible consequences, including the number of casualties, refugees, a backlash in Europe, the shape of Syria, and the perception of American judgment and reliability.

Chapter 10
Lessons of Statecraft for Today

German unification, Bosnia, the first Gulf War, Iraq, and Syria constitute very different cases of statecraft. In the case of Iraq, it is hard not to conclude that there were two totally different approaches to statecraft in the same administration, with one that was terrible and the other quite sound. From these case studies of good and bad examples of statecraft, it is possible to distill a number of lessons. Some are broad, and decision-makers need to be mindful of them in considering objectives and means. Let's start with the issue of timing.

The Importance of Timing

Earlier I said that timing is to statecraft what location is to real estate. Reading the timing and context well can be the difference between recognizing an opportunity and acting on it—or missing it and losing the possibility to transform the circumstances.

In Syria, there were a number of moments where an American intervention could have made a difference, but the American hesitancy meant that the Obama administration missed them. When an opportunity is missed, the means to achieve objectives become far more demanding. Maybe the most fundamental moment missed was not materially supporting moderate groups early, before the Islamists began getting money and arms principally from the Qataris and the Turks.

No doubt, Obama's worldview, and the legacy of Iraq as he saw it, help to explain why he chose not to act, and why this and other moments were then missed as a result. The point is that timing matters—sometimes it is missed or perhaps seized as a result of conscious decision-making. Other times, luck plays a role. Would German unification have worked as well if Saddam Hussein had decided to invade Kuwait on May 2 as opposed to August 2? The key questions on unification were resolved only in early June; even then, Gorbachev was facing enough opposition from the Politburo that he had

Statecraft 2.0. Second Edition. Dennis Ross, Oxford University Press. © Oxford University Press (2025).
DOI: 10.1093/oso/9780197698914.003.0010

Shevardnadze give a speech on June 22 in Berlin that walked back key concessions. Because enough momentum behind reaching an understanding on unification in NATO had already been achieved, it would probably still have been possible to do the deal. That said, I have no doubt that there would have been some new obstacles to overcome, especially since the issue and the amount of the financial assistance from Germany to the Soviets had not yet been finalized.

Finishing the deal on German unification would have been one thing, but Soviet readiness to partner with the United States on Iraq would probably have been quite another. If nothing else, resistance in the Soviet national security apparatus would have been greater, with some acquiescing in the final deal on Germany only with the proviso that the Soviets could not also essentially abandon their position in Iraq—their most important client state in the region.

In May or June, the absence of the unification deal would have meant that Gorbachev's trust and confidence in the United States would have been different, and there is a very real chance that the United States might not have had the USSR as the full partner it became in the run-up to the first Gulf War. So the Bush administration was surely good in practicing statecraft on both German unification and in mobilizing and sustaining the coalition before, during and after the first Gulf War, but it was also lucky that Saddam did not take Kuwait two or three months earlier.

Timing and knowing when to seize the moment were central to the outcome of American statecraft toward the Bosnian War and altering Serbian, especially Slobodan Milošević's, behavior. The non-response to the shelling of Dubrovnik in 1991 convinced Milošević that there would be no resistance to his effort to create a Greater Serbia. The decision after Srebrenica to use serious air power against Serb threats to the safe areas produced not just the Gorazde rules: it also produced a new diplomatic mission with Richard Holbrooke leading his small team with the aim of ending the conflict.

The Role of Leverage, Coercion, and the Danger of Over-Calibration

Holbrooke understood that he needed leverage and the ability to coerce Milošević to achieve the diplomatic goal. Holbrooke used the bombing of Serbian infrastructure by the United States to make the costs of the siege of Sarajevo very clear to Milošević. And Holbrooke resisted stopping the bombing when the Europeans, the Russians and even some in the Pentagon felt that the United States had run out of appropriate targets. Similarly, Holbrooke resisted calls to have the Croatians stop their military offensive that was taking back the land that the Serbs had sieged. Holbrooke knew that the Croatian offensive was changing the reality on the ground in a way that would help the diplomacy resolve the final boundaries as part of the settlement. In short, Holbrooke used the military tool to change the posture of the Serbs and make it possible to end the war.

Bosnia, thus, offers insight into the use of the military tool as a part of the application of smart statecraft. In fact, there are clear lessons to be learned from the way force was used in Bosnia, the Gulf Wars, and Syria. Early in the Bosnian War, the so-called pinprick attacks signaled how little the United States and others were willing to do in response to Serbian aggression. By showing that the United States was not just reluctant but in fact feared escalation, the administration conveyed to the Serbs that they had little to fear from threatening the UN Protection Forces and even taking them hostage. Instead of deterring the Serbs, the pinprick attacks made them more aggressive, not less—ultimately leading to their over-playing their hand and triggering a change so that the United States forged a consensus to attack Serbian forces and infrastructure in a far more serious and strategic fashion. Rather than becoming bogged down in a quagmire, the United States used meaningful air power to back diplomacy, and it worked.

The parallels are certainly not exact, but in the Biden administration, the fear of escalation in Syria and Iraq produced a very small number of highly limited, calibrated retaliatory strikes in response to Iranian proxy attacks on US forces. In the first 28 months of the Biden administration, American forces in Iraq and Syria were hit 83 times by Shia militias, who had been armed, trained, and financed by the Iranians.[1] The United States responded four times, declaring each time that the responses were proportional and precise.[2] The small number of responses—and their deliberately limited character—conveyed clearly that the United States feared escalation, just as the pinprick attacks did in Bosnia.

Given Iran's connection to these attacks, the United States needed the Iranians to fear escalation, not signal that the administration feared it. This is obviously not an exact science, but in a place where the United States has stakes high enough to justify a military presence, America also needs to produce deterrence, especially of attacks against US forces. Direct messaging in private, along with strikes that punctuate that message in a way that is understood the way it is intended, is essential. With the Serbs, the administration eventually got the mix of coercive diplomacy right. In this case, it worked because Holbrooke and his team understood who they were dealing with and implemented an intensive diplomatic game plan.

In general, that has not been the case with America's continuing small presence in Iraq and Syria. The US military are there to prevent the re-emergence of ISIS. But it is not part of a larger strategy for dealing with Iran and its proxies. In Chapter 12, I will suggest a statecraft approach for dealing with Iran. Here it suffices to say that America's responses to the proxy attacks generally look much like the pinprick attacks on the Serbs; while it may be too much to say that these limited attacks against the Iranian proxies have emboldened the Iranians, they certainly have done nothing to deter Tehran. In fact, the Iranians—as they increase their weapons supplies to Houthis and other proxies, and as they seize oil tankers and press ahead with their nuclear program—show little fear of the United States and clearly doubt that the United States will use force against them. That being said, when three American military personnel were killed on January 28, 2024, and the United States launched a one-time tougher response, with airstrikes on more than 85 IRGC-affiliated militia targets on February 2, strikes against American forces ceased until July, once again underscoring that the issue is not US capability, but credibility.

One critical lesson to be learned is that when attacked or facing local aggression, finely calibrated responses reassure America's regional adversaries rather than strike fear in their hearts. Not surprisingly, they also raise questions in the minds of America's regional friends who wonder what America's reluctance to do much in response to attacks against its *own* forces will mean for the willingness of the United States to come to their defense. This is a good reminder to think carefully, before deploying US forces, about what messages must be sent to those who might constitute a threat—and what military actions will be needed to reinforce those messages.

The Necessity of Credible Local Partners

The cases of the Gulf and Iraq wars and Syria highlight another lesson on America's use of force: if the United States considers military interventions (especially in the Middle East), it needs real local partners. General Abizaid's observation about foreign forces being rejected in the region, much like the body uses anti-bodies to react to a disease invading it, has merit. Much, however, depends on the size of those forces, how they are used, what their role and purposes are, and whether the United States has local partners. As noted in Chapter 2, America has learned the hard way that sending large numbers of ground forces to the region to topple regimes makes no sense. The administration of George W. Bush made that mistake. His father, by contrast, had Arab forces from Egypt, Syria, and Saudi Arabia join US forces, and the mission was to reverse the Iraqi aggression from Kuwait by expelling their forces. George H.W. Bush refused to change the mission and rejected the idea of marching to Baghdad. He also wanted a so-called Arab nationalist regime like Syria to be part of the coalition with the United States, believing that would give America's mission more credibility.

Notwithstanding all the hesitancy of the Obama administration in Syria, it deserves credit for working with a local partner that was willing to fight for itself against ISIS. Obama saw that the Syrian Democratic Forces coalition was fighting ISIS, was a natural partner as a result, and needed American assistance to be effective in the fight.

Earlier in Iraq, the Bush 43rd administration recognized that the Sons of Iraq were fighting al Qaeda. The surge helped this local partner, but it was not the reason the Sons of Iraq were fighting: these tribes felt that their existence was at stake. They were fighting al Qaeda to preserve themselves. They needed the material help, intelligence support, firepower assistance, and weaponry to do the job. At times, American advisors and troops embedded with them and helped them succeed. Much like the Syrian Democratic Forces, the Sons of Iraq were tied to the land and connected to their publics—and in many cases they were literally fighting for their homes. It was their willingness to fight and their organization that made them an effective fighting force and good partner.

If there is not a local credible partner willing to fight for itself and its people, the United States will not succeed in the Middle East; instead, it will run the risk of becoming bogged down in a quagmire. Almost certainly, America will make things worse and become even less able to use force when needed. Conversely, a local partner that is truly credible and ready to fight in circumstances where the United States has clear stakes can warrant an American intervention with limited forces.

Much depends on the assessment and understanding of the nature of the threat, of America's interests in the region, and of the character and capability of the putative local partner. Clearly, there is a need for the local partner to prove itself—something that the United States realized with both the Syrian Democratic Forces and the Sons of Iraq. Not surprisingly, we once again see how central good assessments are to conducting good statecraft.

The Role of Presidential Leadership

Another key lesson that emerges from the study of the cases analyzed in this book is that presidential leadership matters. In every one of the examples of good statecraft, presidential leadership and decisiveness were important factors. While its presence alone is clearly not sufficient—to wit, George W. Bush's decision to go to war in Iraq—the absence of strong presidential leadership tends to produce unclear objectives, general hesitancy in terms of means, and a propensity for opening up wide gaps between objectives and means. Bill Clinton in the first two years of Bosnia and Barack Obama on Syria were both willing to publicly declare ambitious objectives but were completely unwilling to apply means that fit those objectives. Both exuded hesitancy and avoided decisions that might have produced greater intervention.

It is noteworthy that Clinton would change on Bosnia by 1995, but Obama never changed on Assad. He would change on fighting ISIS, both in terms of carrying out air strikes in Syria, and in deploying American forces once again back to Iraq even without requiring the Iraqis to grant immunity to US forces based there. Obama's unwillingness to keep US forces in Iraq without such immunity led him to fulfill Bush's agreement to withdraw all US forces from Iraq by December 31, 2011. Without American forces on the ground, the perpetually suspicious Maliki reverted to his sectarian instincts and behaviors: he betrayed his promises to integrate the Sunni Sons of Iraq into the security establishment and pay them, even as he also hollowed out the Iraqi military by purging competent officers and replacing them with Shia loyalists.

In the instances when Clinton became decisive with the Serbs and Obama became more determined (at least on ISIS), they tended to match what George H. W. Bush did in German unification and the first Gulf War and what George W. Bush did with the surge. Presidential leadership and decisiveness are necessary conditions for better statecraft, but they are certainly not enough. Why might they be important?

Two factors stand out. First, the more decisive the president is, the more the administration's objective is likely to be clear, unambiguous, and coherent. In the cases of German unification and the first Gulf War, the objectives were shaped clearly and at the highest levels. The administration leaders believed the stakes were very high, and they accordingly mandated an intensive effort that they often led. Second, the more decisive the president, the more the national security bureaucracy—the State Department, the Defense Department, the Treasury Department, and the National Security Council—is likely to work in harmony toward that clear mandate. Good cases of statecraft reflect administrations working harmoniously and not without internal debate, but without extraneous internal competition. David Petraeus points out that what also made the surge effective was the whole-of-government effort that Bush produced by being not just decisive but hands-on.

We saw the opposite take place in the case of Bosnia during Clinton's first two years. President Clinton's indecisiveness resulted in no small part from the split in his administration between the Pentagon on the one side and the State Department and the National Security Council on the other—but it was also his hesitancy that deepened the divide, especially because he chose not to make a decision. His objectives may have been clear then in terms of wanting to end Serb aggression, stop ethnic cleansing, and bring the war to an end, but he was largely paralyzed by the Pentagon's opposition on the means to be used. When the circumstances changed on the ground with the massacre in Srebrenica (and with a new secretary of defense and chair of the Joint Chiefs of Staff), the president recognized the stakes. He had a line-up that was ready to act when he was—and that moment had arrived. At that point, the administration became unified on the objectives, and all parts of the administration worked together on implementing the means.

Once that point was reached, statecraft in Bosnia had much in common with the statecraft conducted on German unification and the first Gulf War. In these cases, the objective, stakes, and means were clearly in sync, and the national security apparatus was generally unified and fixated on achieving the objective. The diplomacy was intensive and continuous, and there was an ongoing and accurate assessment of the environment, openings, problems, sources of leverage, and role and effectiveness of potential partners. Finally, there was deep presidential interest and effective follow-through. (The latter was clearly also the case with the Iraqi surge in 2007–2008.)

In fact, in German unification, the first Gulf War, and Bosnia from August 1995, one sees policy not by slogan but by determined action. Nothing was left to chance or to hopeful assumptions. The case of Iraq in 2003, by contrast, reflects wishful thinking, as the confusion of objectives there led to confusion of means. The divisions within the administration were so poisonous that they made reality-based assessment impossible. Those who knew the most about the realities on the ground in Iraq were relegated to irrelevance because of their perceived opposition to the war and its purposes. The military's preferences for larger forces given the requirements— especially for creating law and order, controlling the borders, and subduing the area most likely to give rise to an insurgency—were rejected by the secretary of defense. Rumsfeld believed that the military's mindset on warfare was outdated in an era of mobility, precision weapons, and force-multiplying effects of intelligence and information technologies.

Planning for postwar reconstruction was not taken seriously by those given the responsibility for implementing it. Small wonder that with weak planning, there was weak follow-through. The surge stood in sharp contrast, as there was systematic planning and very determined follow-through, using political and military tools effectively. Not everyone agreed on the assumptions of the surge, but decisive leadership brought everyone along for the implementation. Presidential decisiveness can produce unity of action— something that is necessary for success—but it cannot overcome a poor understanding of the reality that US policy is designed to change.

Statecraft done well requires good planning and execution, employing all available tools. It requires administrations not at war with themselves. It requires effective assessments and accountability, with someone taking the lead and acting or ensuring that problems are anticipated and those that emerge are addressed quickly. In the cases of German unification, the first Gulf War, and Bosnia beginning in the summer of 1995, we saw all of those elements in action. There is one factor that separates Bosnia in 1995 from the other cases: the very apex of the Clinton administration was not consumed by Bosnia the way the apex of the Bush 41st administration was completely absorbed in dealing with German unification and the first Gulf War.

To be sure, Secretary Christopher played a pivotal role at certain strategic moments, especially in New York and at Dayton, where his interventions were decisive. But his involvement was episodic, not perpetual. The same is certainly true of President Clinton. Episodic involvement did not signal his lack of interest—far from it. Nor did it prevent him from making critical strategic decisions, one of which was to empower Richard Holbrooke and his team to do the job.

And that is the point. The continuous, intensive effort made in Bosnia was carried out by a level below the president and secretary of state. As such, Bosnia showcases a model of statecraft different from the cases of German unification and the first Gulf War insofar as with Bosnia, the administration employed a small interagency team that ran the policy in a way that certainly required presidential and secretarial involvement but did not demand nearly all of the president's and secretary's time and attention.

Empowering Sub-Cabinet Groups While Avoiding Groupthink

The Holbrooke group could work because Richard Holbrooke was empowered. He had access to the secretary of state whenever he wanted or needed it, and he had the secretary's backing for what he was doing. Of course, he had access to the national security advisor whenever necessary, but their relationship was complicated. Don Kerrick, a brigadier general serving on the National Security Council staff, was on Holbrooke's team and kept National Security Advisor Lake informed but also on board—getting him to back what the team was doing. The other members of the team played the same role with the other essential bureaucratic players. Wesley Clark, a three-star general, represented the Joint Chiefs of Staff and kept the chair apprised of what was going on and what the team needed to succeed—including keeping up the bombing when most of the allies (and the US military) were second-guessing it. James Pardew, who represented the secretary of defense, did the same, maintaining William Perry's support for what the team needed.

Without the team functioning in this way, the same bureaucratic divisions that hampered and at times paralyzed the policy from 1993 to 1995 might well have continued. Instead, the team, under Holbrooke's leadership, thrashed out what needed to be done on the road, and then got their home agencies to back them. The value of having checks and balances was preserved because the team itself debated every issue; they preserved a group dynamic but never fell victim to a dangerous groupthink—where alternative points of view are discredited and ignored—as was the case with the second Gulf War.

One additional factor helped to make this work: Holbrooke had the trust and active support of key people around Secretary Christopher, who also played an essential role in making the decision-making process work. Strobe Talbott, the deputy secretary, who was also close to the president and to Tony Lake, would often either make the case for Holbrooke or explain to him what he would need to do to overcome the opposition to the decisions he might be seeking. Tom Donilon, the secretary of state's chief of staff, with ties to the White House, also frequently acted to make sure the process did not fall apart.

Given this team concept and the active intervention of leading players in Washington to back the team, the president and the secretary of state played their roles and contributed to success. They did not have to be the central players in this process the way they were in German unification and the first Gulf War. In those cases, their internal discussions and high-level meetings, their travels and phone calls, left them little time for anything else. Would it have been better for the leaders of the administration and those immediately around them to be less consumed by German unification? Yes. They might have paid more attention to Saddam Hussein prior to his invasion of Kuwait. Similarly, if the run-up to the first Gulf War had not been so all consuming, the leaders of the administration might have had more energy and inclination to deal early with issues such as Yugoslavia falling apart or the need to secure Soviet weapons and scientists as the USSR collapsed.

The issue of fatigue—physical and emotional—in carrying out the duties of statecraft has received far too little attention. It is not just preoccupation and having little time for anything else that were certainly factors in German unification and the first Gulf War. But, especially in the case of the first Gulf War, the president and his senior advisors (the so-called group of eight) rode an emotional roller coaster from the time of the Iraqi invasion until the end of the war. Over an eight-month period, which followed immediately on the heels of the German unification effort, they were involved with an exhausting process of responding to the invasion, building an international coalition, and holding it together to see if pressure could force Saddam out of Kuwait or if war would be required to do so. Compounding the exhaustion was a gnawing uncertainty about the likely costs of war both politically and militarily. The burden that the president and his team bore was immense, particularly with the unknowns about the scope of American casualties and with the very real fears that they could be high.

It should come as no surprise that the success of the war produced exhil-
aration and relief—but also a letdown. It was not conscious, but it was
unmistakable. There was simply no energy, intellectually or emotionally, to
tackle new and different challenges. True, Secretary Baker was prepared to
launch an effort on Arab–Israeli peace, but that was seen as a continuation of
the effort, and in any case had been one of the promises made as the United
States built the coalition. And one deeply ingrained trait of both President
Bush and Secretary Baker was a profound commitment to living up to their
word. They had given it as part of the coalition development and had actively
planned an initiative after the war.

Given the timing, messiness, and the US military's reluctance even to
contemplate involvement, tackling something such as Yugoslavia was a non-
starter. One could argue that this might have been true even if the United
States had not just gone through an emotional binge at the top of the administration on Iraq. Perhaps, but there would have been more of a debate, more
of a discussion of America's stakes and the consequences of letting a conflict emerge in Europe with the potential for ethnic cleansing, large refugee
flows, and a widening of the war. There just was not the energy for such a
thrashing-out.

When the energy is not there, when there is such fatigue, assessments
and the will to act inevitably will be affected. And that, too, was seen at
the time in the Bush 41st administration, and not only in its dealing with
other potential conflicts. For example, there was little energy available to
persuade Congress that, with the collapse of the Soviet Union, the United
States would need to mobilize its own resources and those of others to secure
the Soviet weapons sites and Soviet scientists. Safeguarding the sites, con-
verting weapons materials to civilian purposes, and making sure nuclear
scientists were not becoming destitute (and therefore vulnerable to being
paid by the Iranians or the Libyans to hand over their nuclear know-how)
were all critical needs. To be fair, these needs were understood by the administration, and some effort was made to address each of these issues. But there
was simply no energy to mobilize the world, launch a major campaign, or
actively work Congress to finance what would be needed. In the end, the
initiative on these challenges came not from the administration but from
Senators Sam Nunn and Richard Lugar.[3]

The point here is not to criticize the Bush 41st administration for neglect-
ing what needed to be done or even to raise questions about the effectiveness

of its statecraft. The fact is that the George H. W. Bush administration's state-craft was conducted with extraordinary skill and effort. All the tools of the trade were understood and exploited. Rather, the point is to note that when the most senior leadership of an administration is consumed for extended times, there is bound to be a cost. And sometimes the cost is borne afterward. Certainly, there are times when there is no alternative to direct, consistent, and deep involvement by the leaders of the administration. If war is involved, it is not a choice but a requirement for the president and those closest to him to be deeply involved on an ongoing basis. The greater the stakes, and the more the administration wants to persuade political leaders of other countries to make hard choices and join the United States on tough issues, such as Iranian nuclear weapons, the more persuading the president and the secretary must do. Clearly, there are circumstances in which other political leaders need to hear directly from American political leaders about why certain choices are necessary, and leaving such communication to lower levels of the administration implicitly signals to others that the issue is not important enough to merit presidential or cabinet-level time and attention.

The question is not whether the president and secretary of state should be involved; they must involved and they also need to travel. The question is, rather, can their involvement be made more strategic, efficient, and deliberate and not so perpetual that they have little time for anything else? I would argue that it can.

Perhaps the Bosnia case with Holbrooke's approach provides the model for those situations where the stakes are high or where the administration has a keen interest in conflict resolution. The essence of the model is the creation of an interagency team that is senior and has access to the top leadership when it needs it; is capable of managing bureaucratic divisions and yet can call on all necessary bureaucratic resources for support; is seen as having authority not only domestically but with those it deals with internationally; and is able to bring in the president and secretary not just for decisions but also for persuasion of others at decisive moments.

I do not offer this assessment only as an observer of the Holbrooke team. I led a team in managing America's approach to Middle East peacemaking for nearly all of the Clinton administration. My team was not as high-level as Holbrooke's, but it did involve the senior experts from the National Security Council staff and the State Department; when I needed support from the Defense Department, I had it—even taking lieutenant generals with me on trips to Syria when I felt it was required. When not on the road, I had daily meetings in my office at 10:00 a.m. to plan what we were doing and to make sure that nothing was going on in the administration that might be inconsistent with what our diplomacy required. I had authority across the administration and access to the secretary at all times and to the president when necessary. Bureaucratic impediments were managed in this fashion, and support across the administration, including from the Intelligence Community and the Agency for International Development (USAID), was something I could always call and count on. If nothing else, this shows that a Holbrooke-type model with lower-level officials is sustainable over time and not only for short, intense bursts of activity. It is a model, at least mechanically, for how to make statecraft effective.

Clearly, statecraft is not just about defining objectives, assessing how to relate means to those objectives, and then acting on them. Statecraft must necessarily also involve organizing bureaucratic agencies so they work together and can be managed effectively to maximize available tools. Presidential leadership is needed to mandate such harmony, and cabinet officials should be selected with that in mind. When there is bureaucratic disagreement, presidents must be prepared to make decisions, or at least authorize a Holbrooke-type model that can contend with the problem.

President George H. W. Bush hated the bureaucratic warfare in the Reagan administration, and he conveyed very clearly to his entire national security team that he would not tolerate such bureaucratic dissonance in his administration. President Clinton initially did not resolve the bureaucratic disharmony in his administration, but eventually he chose Holbrooke-type envoys and teams to lead American efforts on the Middle East, Russia, and North Korea as a way of overcoming bureaucratic prerogatives and priorities that produced stalemate. President George W. Bush's first term was characterized by bureaucratic stalemate until 9/11. After 9/11, he effectively delegated enormous responsibility to Secretary of Defense Rumsfeld, relegating Secretary of State Colin Powell to a decidedly secondary position. Even when Bush decided to send Powell to the Middle East to deal with the burgeoning Palestinian second intifada—at the point after the Israeli military had been sent back into the West Bank cities with the aim of quelling the acts of terror in Israel coming from the Palestinian territories—he rejected Powell's proposal to convene an international conference. Why? Because Rumsfeld and Cheney opposed the proposal, saying that it rewarded terrorism and that the United States should give the Israelis a free hand to defeat it. Bush thought little about the consequence of undercutting his secretary of state while Powell was still in the Middle East and had broached this proposal with those in and outside the region.[4,a]

Because George W. Bush elevated Rumsfeld and Cheney in the first term—and largely deferred to them—he guaranteed that much of the foreign policy apparatus was excluded from the decision-making process. It was as if he felt little need to rely on anyone else. In the second term, he made a big switch in personnel: forcing out Powell and replacing him with Condoleezza Rice, and elevating her deputy at the National Security Council, Stephen Hadley, to national security advisor. Where there had been little meaningful interagency process in the first term, it very much defined what guided the administration in the second term—even though Rumsfeld still resisted intrusion into what he saw as his domain. When Rumsfeld resigned after the midterm elections in 2006, the bureaucratic exclusion and division that had characterized the first term was replaced by a process that looked much like what one saw in the Bush 41st administration.

With the surge, George W. Bush brought the military chiefs along, had his national security advisor shape a process that included everyone bureaucratically, and no longer delegated to others. Bush ultimately made a decision on an option that he had preferred for some time and that Stephen Hadley made sure was part of the mix—but it was an option that had been thoroughly analyzed and discussed. Bush then created a model that was a hybrid, depending heavily on two people—General David Petraeus and Ambassador Ryan Crocker—who were in Baghdad and managing the military and political strategy in Iraq. The president would do a secure video call with them daily—something that allowed them to explain what they needed from Washington, and the president's instructions afterward ensured responsiveness from agencies that might have resisted or slow-rolled some of their requests otherwise. Petraeus and Crocker—and their staffs—worked as a team and much like the Holbrooke approach thrashed everything out. Such a model fit the circumstance and might not work all the time, but it was effective and was very much tied to the realities on the ground—something that marked a very clear difference from George W. Bush's first term.

It seems that George W. Bush did learn from some of the mistakes of his first term, and not only on Iraq. On Iran, the administration spent its first term without a policy toward Tehran largely because the Pentagon and

---

[a] Powell would conclude that he was being set up to fail, and he would become far more reluctant about taking initiatives as a result.

Vice President's Office advocated isolation and regime change while the State Department preferred engagement. Unwilling or unable to resolve this internal conflict, President Bush and his National Security Council deferred the issue and wasted valuable time as Iran continued to progress in its quest to acquire nuclear weapons. During the second term, the president backed the secretary of state's support of European engagement with Iran, her successful efforts to organize UN Security Council sanctions against Iran, and direct US participation in the 5+1 talks with the Iranians.

When it comes to exercising statecraft, the starting point, at least organizationally, is to prevent bureaucratic dysfunction or paralysis. To ensure that the executive branch functions well and maximizes the full potential of America's assets, it is essential to be able to integrate all bureaucratic tools and have someone responsible for spearheading them in a way that responds to the administration's strategic aims. George W. Bush did that himself on the issue of the surge. But a president clearly cannot always do that, and it is not necessarily a simple thing to ensure. As Joseph Nye points out, the task is made infinitely more difficult by the fact that "official instruments of soft power—public diplomacy, broadcasting, exchange programs, developmental assistance, disaster relief, military-to-military contacts—are scattered throughout the government, and there is no overarching strategy or budget that ever tries to integrate them with hard power into an overarching national security strategy."[5]

This remains a challenge for all presidential administrations. At a minimum, statecraft done well demands having a keen eye for organizations and knowing how to gain control over all the relevant means the administration has in order to employ them synergistically. The president must designate someone—presumably the national security advisor or the White House chief of staff—to make sure that all bureaucratic assets are being used in a complementary or reinforcing fashion to help achieve policy objectives. (George W. Bush used his daily video calls to Baghdad to give his national security advisor marching orders to the different departments—but that also meant that he, much like his father during the first Gulf War, was fixated on Iraq from the time the surge was launched. Understandably, wars create huge stakes and have a way of concentrating any president's mind.)

Of course, statecraft is not just about the orchestration of the means or the tools of the trade. Ultimately, to be effective, statecraft is about identifying and acting on the right objectives. And, as I outlined in Chapter 2, there are a number of reasons for why that might not be done.

One can certainly argue—and I have publicly—that given who Yasser Arafat was and his inability to make peace, the administration pursued the wrong objective; rather than working on a conflict-ending agreement, the United States should have focused on increasing the scope of Palestinian independence from Israeli control and on broader cooperation between the two societies until after Arafat passed from the scene. That could have created the conditions for peacemaking in the post-Arafat period.

Here we are reminded that if the objectives are wrong, one can employ tools and leverage effectively and still produce bad outcomes. Sometimes one might identify the right objectives in the near term, but not necessarily adjust to recognize the right objectives as they evolve over time. Margaret Thatcher was convinced that German unification in NATO was the wrong objective because it would cost us Mikhail Gorbachev; perhaps the United States would win the new "battle" for Europe but lose the war by undermining a reformer in Moscow who would serve America's longer-term aims of genuine partnership with the Soviet Union. The Bush administration made the judgment that shaping a new architecture in Europe, with Germany embedded in Western institutions, was a surer way to safeguard America's long-term interests than letting Gorbachev's needs be the arbiter of what was possible in Europe.

This is not to say that the Bush administration was indifferent to Gorbachev's needs—far from it. But the president and his advisors, while wanting Gorbachev to succeed, made an assessment that his success over time was ultimately beyond their control to affect. They thought that they might do all they could to help him, and still he might not succeed. If the United States had mortgaged the future of Europe by accepting a neutral Germany as the price of helping Gorbachev, America might have ended up losing on both counts—and with disastrous consequences as a result.

In other words, the Bush administration made a judgment. It focused on the most important objective even as it sought to minimize the costs to Gorbachev, and worked with him to do so. The administration also made a judgment call on how to end the first Gulf War. Would it have been better to alter the objective either to regime change or even to the destruction of the Republican Guard, the main forces that protected the regime? Would doing so have prevented the war in 2003?

Looking at the enormous difficulty and costs of the American involvement in Iraq, the veterans of the George H. W. Bush administration would answer that their judgment of ending the war the way they did has been vindicated.

Others might argue that altering the objective at least to destroying the key military forces underpinning Saddam's rule would have been the wiser course when thinking about the future.

Is the answer in such a debate obvious? I think not. And that is also going to be true for every administration as it conducts statecraft. Defining the right objectives is enormously important, but also enormously difficult if one is trying to find a balance between near and long-term objectives. Choices have to be made. Oftentimes there will be tensions between objectives, and leaders and their advisors have to choose based on the best assessments they can make. The point is to make assessments so that at least the choices are conscious and deliberate, not inadvertent or habitual. Decision-makers must at least consider which objectives are ultimately the most appropriate for now and for later.

This consideration calls for assessments that take all factors into account, and faith-based or ideologically driven assessments obscure what needs to be considered. The Bush administration in 2002–2003 proved the folly of such an approach.

So what does all this mean for how to think about statecraft? To be effective, statecraft starts with being able to define clear, understandable, and meaningful objectives. Hardheaded assessments are essential for refining the objectives to fit reality, relevant ambitions, and means, including the means the United States can marshal with others. It is also critical to be able to frame what is at stake in a way that not only can mobilize and sustain domestic support but also does so in a way that makes America's objectives legitimate internationally and raises the costs to those who would oppose them. Active diplomacy is an essential element for anticipating problems and managing or overcoming them. Back channels are a crucial part of active diplomacy, crucial because they permit brainstorming, discussion of politically sensitive issues without fear of exposure, and ability to explain political needs and limitations; they are also trust-building by nature. Back channels tend to be a key lubricant in making active diplomacy successful. In the end, good statecraft is all about achieving leverage—and knowing how and when to orchestrate inducements and penalties, including threats and coercion, in order to achieve defined objectives.

To this point, I have defined statecraft, explained in general terms why it is necessary, showed how it has worked effectively in some cases and not in others, and drawn some general lessons. Now I would like to turn to applying it to several current policy challenges.

Chapter 11
Practicing Statecraft: How to Deal with China

Much like the Trump administration before it, the Biden administration saw China as posing the greatest threat to American interests and the most significant challenge America faces on the world stage. In its National Security Strategy, the Biden administration explained that while Russia "poses an immediate threat to the free and open international system ... [with] its brutal war of aggression in Ukraine," China is the much bigger threat. It is "the only competitor with both the intent to reshape the international order and, increasingly, the economic, diplomatic, military, and technological power to do it." Moreover, it has "ambitions to create an enhanced sphere of influence in the Indo-Pacific and become the world's leading power."[1] Because of China's ambition and the multifaceted threat it poses—a threat that includes a dramatic buildup of nearly every aspect of its military—the Pentagon, in its National Defense Strategy, declared that the Chinese military, also known as the People's Liberation Army (PLA), is the "pacing challenge" it must plan against.[2]

Nonetheless, even as President Biden made clear in an address to the UN General Assembly that the United States would "push back on aggression and intimidation" by China, he denied that the United States was trying to "contain" China. To emphasize this, he said, "We seek to responsibly manage the competition between our two countries so it does not end up in conflict."[3] That makes perfect sense but, of course, it will not simply happen on its own, especially at a time when, as some argue, the United States is already in a cold war with China.[4]

For those who suggest that the Cold War is the best way to think about the US–China relationship, it is important to understand the limits of that analogy. China is a very different challenge than that posed by the former Soviet Union. The Soviets were a military threat but never an economic competitor. Their economy was minuscule by comparison; other than farmers selling wheat to the USSR, no other US constituency, for most of the

Statecraft 2.0. Second Edition. Dennis Ross, Oxford University Press. © Oxford University Press (2025).
DOI: 10.1093/oso/9780197698914.003.0011

Cold War era, had any economic interest in trade with the Soviets. China, in an era of globalization, is a completely different story. American and Chinese economies are intertwined. US corporations, seeing a huge market, have invested heavily in China, and the Peoples Republic, by holding over $1 trillion in American bonds, helps to finance American debt. Transnational dangers—whether climate or health driven—do not respect borders or national sovereignty and cannot be solved without American and Chinese cooperation.

From this standpoint, a cold war that makes cooperation difficult will threaten both sides involved. And yet, the competition and conflicting interests may yield that result. Moreover, without skillful management, cold wars can turn into hot wars. Put simply, there are few challenges that more clearly require the effective use of statecraft than those the United States faces with China.

The starting point for effective statecraft is having clear and achievable objectives—meaning that the United States must be able to marry its objectives and means. That, as we have seen, is often easier said than done. While high stakes help define—even dictate—objectives, they do not guarantee their achievement. US policymakers must understand the nature of challenges or threats America faces and find the best means for countering or altering those threats. And that must begin with a clear assessment of what drives China's leaders, how that may be evolving, their hopes and fears, their capacity for change, and their perceptions of the United States and how America's actions affect them. US policymakers must be clear-eyed about China's strengths but also its weaknesses. The latter are a reminder that it is essential to keep the nature of the Chinese threat in perspective even as one thinks carefully about how best to use America's leverage to affect China's behavior.

Assessing China

Even before Xi Jinping, China's leaders were heavily influenced by what they refer to as the "century of humiliation," the period from 1839 to 1949 which ended with the establishment of the People's Republic of China at the conclusion of the civil war.

The century of humiliation began with the Opium Wars, which took place between 1839 and 1842. Following these wars and throughout the remainder of the nineteenth century, China faced foreign diktats that included unequal treaties on trade, the ceding of Hong Kong to the British, the German establishment of a colony at Qingdao on the Chinese mainland, and the loss of other territories, including Outer Mongolia to Russia and Macau to Portugal. From 1894–1895, China was defeated in the first Sino-Japanese war. As a result of that loss, China was forced to recognize Korean independence, surrender Taiwan and parts of Manchuria to Japan, and was unable to prevent Japan from annexing what the Chinese refer to as Diaoyu Dao and the Japanese call the Senkaku Islands in the East China Sea.

Earlier, a bloody civil war from 1850–1864 had taken its toll, leaving China even more susceptible to foreign exploitation and interventions, which at the turn of the 20th century would lead to multinational forces, under the command of a British general, putting down the Boxer Rebellion of 1899–1901. The Boxer Rebellion was especially noteworthy because it was largely a rebellion against the foreign presence in China. It was defeated by forces that included contingents of British, American, French, German, Russian, and Japanese troops. Once again, China had to make trade concessions, with John Hay's Open Door policy designed to ensure that the United States received the same privileges and access that others had in China.

China remained largely at the mercy of others in the first several decades of the twentieth century. The end of the imperial system—and its replacement with a weak republican government in 1912—did little to change China's vulnerability to outside forces. At the outset of World War I, China's new president, Yuan Shikai, would declare his country's neutrality, but in time, he would offer to provide 50,000 troops to the British to retake Oingdao from the Germans. The British did not take Shikai up on his offer, preferring the help of the Japanese, who were part of the Entente. Still, Shikai would formally end China's neutrality in the war when he declared China's support for the Entente in 1916.[5]

While China would provide no troops to the allies, it would send laborers, with Chinese peasants digging the trenches in Europe—trenches that came to characterize the very nature of World War I. The expectation was that, given the very practical support that China had provided, and President Wilson's 14 principles and support for the Chinese cause, China would not only have a seat at the table at the peace conference at Versailles but that all the unequal treaties imposed on Beijing would be undone. That assumed recompense never materialized, as Wilson prioritized Japan's support for and participation in the League of Nations at Versailles. As a result, he supported

Shantung being awarded to Japan—meaning that the United States joined in recognizing Japan's expansionist aims in China, even beyond those areas taken from the Germans.

Wilson's principles meant little when it came to China, and Mao Zedong would later refer to the Europeans, the Japanese, and the Americans as a "bunch of robbers."[6] America was again to disappoint the Chinese when it adopted a hands-off posture in response to Japan's invasion of Manchuria in 1931. Herbert Hoover would say that "Japan in Manchuria did not challenge the deep interests or values of the United States."[7] The American telling of the relationship between the United States and China paints Washington as a supporter of China, at least prior to the takeover of the Communist Party. Indeed, American historical memory emphasizes the missionaries who built schools and hospitals, the fact that the United States claimed no territories, Wilson's rhetorical support, practical assistance during World War II, and Franklin Delano Roosevelt's insistence that China be one of the five permanent members of what became the UN Security Council. The Chinese perception of America, and the telling of its own story, are quite different.

In the broader Chinese narrative, internal division, weakness, and the absence of strong centralized leadership produced the century of humiliation. According to the Chinese narrative, China had a grand destiny that had been derailed, and the Chinese Communist Party (CCP) restored China's stability, ended the exploitation by others, and built the country and the respect it garners on the world stage. Michael Beckley suggests that the CCP's prime role has been to ensure that China is never bullied or divided again, and its leaders believe that this task requires "relentlessly amassing wealth and power, expanding territorial control, and ruling with an iron fist."[8]

Mao, having been a founding member of the CCP and the Red Army, and the leader who ultimately led the CCP to victory in the civil war, would rule China from 1949 until his death in 1976. He guided everything with his ideological maxims and his version of Marxism–Leninism. He concentrated power in the party under his aegis. While the country did develop during his rule, it was often at a terrible price. Arbitrary rule was the norm, but if the circumstances required pragmatism, Mao would exhibit it—as evidenced by his acceptance of the opening to the United States in 1972, a step taken largely because of the worsening conflict with the Soviet Union. Still, during the course of his reign, Mao subjected the state and the party to mass campaigns like the Great Leap Forward and the Cultural Revolution which produced disruption and upheaval, resulting in economic collapse and tens of millions of deaths. The Cultural Revolution was Mao's last campaign, designed in theory to purify the CCP, but it died with the Chairman in 1976.

Deng Xiaoping succeeded Mao, and his main task was to end the campaign and clean up the wreckage that the Cultural Revolution had wrought. Deng understood that China needed to recover before it could advance— and no real progress could be made unless he opened China economically to the outside world. He launched an era of reform in which he embraced market forces, provided incentives to help the private sector emerge and grow rich, and put a premium on creating openings for trade with the West and foreign investment in China.

The opening to the outside world, in particular to the United States, included encouraging study abroad, with thousands of Chinese students enrolling in advanced degree programs at American universities. The surveillance state of today's China did not exist during Deng's rule, and the relative openness of that time even extended to tolerance for religious practices that are banned in China today.

Deng was mindful that outreach to the West and investment in China could be undermined if the People's Republic looked threatening or aggressive toward the outside world. As such, his guide to action internationally was simple and direct: "Hide your strength; bide your time; never take the lead."[9]

Humility was the watchword, but openness did not mean that economic liberalization would equal political liberalization or tolerance for dissent. For example, in 1979, when thousands of people put up posters protesting political and social issues on what became known as the Democracy Wall in Beijing, Deng suppressed the effort when it seemed poised to become a movement. Similarly, he was not prepared to accept the demands of the students who occupied Tiananmen Square and ordered what became known as the Tiananmen Square massacre.

Moreover, Deng was also clear that his reforms were not designed to weaken the CCP's role as the overseer of the government or society. In his words, he was "opening the window to breathe fresh air," but the party's responsibility was to "swat away the flies and insects that come in."[10]

Jiang Zemin would succeed Deng in 1989, and he continued and expanded upon the economic policies that Deng had launched. He provided even more support for the private sector, pushing for Chinese access to the World Trade Organization (WTO). That feat was achieved in 2001, and it gave a huge boost to Chinese manufacturing and exports, as it not only opened international markets to China's enterprises or businesses (state and private) for their products but also gave them much needed capital to expand.

Cai Xia, a former professor at the Central Party School of the CCP, has written that Jiang continued to emphasize the central role of the Party even as he pronounced that it had three key responsibilities: to develop the requirements of advanced productive forces, ensure cultural progress, and address the interests of the majority. For Cai, the first of Jiang's responsibilities meant abandoning the Marxist idea that capitalists were an exploitative group—and as a result, Jiang opened the CCP "to their ranks."[11,a]

Jiang was as determined as his predecessor to ensure that there was neither a challenge to the party nor a repetition of the Tiananmen protests, especially as more Chinese went to the United States and Europe for education and were exposed to Western political culture. To that end, he promoted a patriotic education campaign in the early 1990s to both reinforce political orthodoxy and alert Chinese professionals who would be educated in the United States to the dangers posed by Western values. The campaign played on nationalism as well, calling on those studying abroad never to forget China's "national humiliation" by Japan and the West.

As Kevin Rudd points out, Jiang was also mindful of the need for the CCP to present contemporary Chinese history in a way that would not have China fall victim to "the peaceful evolution plot of international hostile powers."[12] Jiang, like Deng before him, understood the need both for Chinese corporations' access to the United States and also access for US corporations to China. It is noteworthy that this access, which he believed was necessary for Chinese economic growth, did not alter his view that the United States constituted a threat to China's interests, and he wanted those going to America to understand this. America was, in his words, a hostile power, and its strategy was to have China evolve in a way that would change who and what it was.

---

[a] Cai Xia was educated at the Central Party School of the CCP, received her doctorate there and became an instructor. In that role, she taught many students who later became high-ranking members of the CCP. She favored political liberalization and a reduction in the role of state enterprises in the economy, believing initially that Xi Jinping would be a reformer. When instead of reform he reversed economic policy and limited discussion within the party, she became critical and was warned about the consequences of her views. Mindful of the warnings, she chose not to return to China when abroad and now lives in the United States.

The belief in both the Clinton and Bush administrations was that since China had to play by the rules of the WTO, China's economic transformation would, in time, lead to a political transformation as well. The path that Deng had set, and that Jiang had developed further, at least seemed to suggest that market forces were increasingly shaping the Chinese approach to the economy. Wouldn't political liberalization necessarily have to follow? The answer in China was "no" at a political level; however, it *was* allowing the private sector to increasingly drive the economy and for a middle class to emerge—and both had expectations and interests in expanding what they could do both domestically and abroad. Under Hu Jintao, Jiang's successor, these realities and trends became more pronounced, and the result was increasing freedom of travel for China's middle class and more foreign contacts for those who traveled and did business outside China. More differing opinions began to be published, and NGOs were even permitted.

But there were stresses as well. Hu would offer his "Scientific Outlook on Development"—a doctrinal effort to justify the mixed model of development that was driven both by the state and private sector. In Cai Xia's words, Hu's explanatory effort failed to deal with the big questions facing China: its breakneck development was producing social conflict as farmers' land was seized for development, and factories squeezed workers for profits. The number of petitioners seeking redress from the government increased dramatically—and nationwide demonstrations exceeded 100,000 per year. Cai said: "To me, the discontent showed it was becoming harder for China to develop without liberalizing its politics."[13]

This was precisely what the Clinton, Bush, and then the Obama administrations expected: China's growth necessarily would produce a political evolution toward the United States. In the Obama administration, this expectation led some to believe that these two countries, now with the world's two largest economies, could form a G-2 to lead the G-20 countries.

Hu might have liked the recognition; after all, it signified an acceptance that China had a leading role to play on the world stage. But this would still be an American-dominated global stage, and he was not prepared to play by the US rules that this would have meant. By definition, these rules would limit China and would have required Hu and the Chinese to give up their preferred posture of favoring multipolarity internationally—a reality that would produce constraints or limitations on the United States, not China. As China's leaders have been wont to do, Hu offered a vague formula calling for a "new type of great power relations." Who could complain about a new type of relations in a new era of growing economic ties? Here was Hu acting very much in concert with Deng's maxim of hiding one's strength and biding time. China could continue to develop, and rivalry with the United States could be deferred until China was "fully equipped to deal with [the US], and, if necessary, prevail."[14]

This is the posture that Xi Jinping would inherit in 2012 when he succeeded Hu. Xi also inherited a country that was growing and, in the words of *The Economist*, was "changing fast. The middle class was growing, private firms were booming, and citizens were connecting to social media. A different leader might have seen this as an opportunity. Mr. Xi saw only threats."[15]

Xi would act to reverse course across the board, perhaps not immediately, but certainly unmistakably. No longer would China adhere to Deng's maxim of hiding its strength and biding its time. China would become increasingly aggressive with "wolf warrior" diplomacy in pressing its interests abroad. At the 2023 National People's Congress, Xi unveiled a formula vastly different from Deng's: "dare to fight."[16] His policies had long since turned to asserting China's role and prerogatives internationally, and while Xi's predecessors also saw the United States as a threat to China's long-term interests, their approach was not to provoke the United States to respond. But Xi has been different. He began to act on Chinese claims in the South and East China Seas, including by unilaterally declaring, as early as November 2013, an Air Defense Identification Zone (ADIZ) over the entirety of the East China Sea—a zone that conflicted with the ADIZs of Japan, South Korea, and Taiwan.

Internationally, Xi has been far more convinced that China's time had come. In 2021, he told party leaders that "time and momentum are on our side."[17] From early in his rule, he engineered a major military buildup and modernization plan to underpin China's global reach. All this was part of what Xi saw as a plan for national rejuvenation which would lead to the reunification with Taiwan, secure China's other long-standing territorial claims, and add to the appeal of its model internationally. His "no limits" partnership with Russia would counter the United States and prevent it from sustaining its rules internationally. It is precisely for this reason that Xi has called Beijing's relationship with Moscow "the world's most important bilateral relationship."[18]

Xi's assertiveness, however, including in the form of cyber hacks, soon began to produce American responses. During the Obama administration, the decision to "pivot to Asia" was seen as rebalancing America's policies—shifting greater priority to the dynamism and growth in Asia but also to the competition with China. The United States increased its military presence in the Indo-Pacific, with an ongoing contingent in Australia, and negotiated the world's largest free trade deal, the Trans-Pacific Partnership (TPP). The TPP excluded China and included 12 Pacific Rim countries which collectively constituted 40 percent of the global economy. It was an effort to rebalance trade and reduce China's economic leverage on those in the Indo-Pacific and beyond. The Obama administration believed the TPP would yield economic and geopolitical benefits, promoting American leadership in Asia and bolstering its alliances in the region. Moreover, as President Obama explained, the TPP would help ensure that "the United States—and not countries like China—is the one writing this century's rules for the world's economy."[19]

While Obama saw the TPP reversing trends in Asia and on trade that favored China—and not playing by the rules—the TPP would fall victim to the populist protectionist politics in America in 2016. Trump's argument that the TPP and previous trade agreements like NAFTA had sent US jobs overseas and were unfair to American workers had great political resonance with the American electorate. During the campaign, he declared that he would withdraw from the TPP, and upon assuming the presidency, he did just that.

That did not mean that Trump did not see China as a threat. On the contrary, his administration would make the pushback on China even more pronounced, with Trump proclaiming that trade wars were easy to win. While he would, in time, reach a trade agreement that would be only partially implemented given the onset of COVID, his tariffs and national-security-imposed limits on trade of certain high-tech items, like advanced semiconductors, would not only be mostly embraced by the Biden administration but actually enhanced. Biden, too, would continue the military buildup and also form new bilateral and multilateral partnerships in the Indo-Pacific region.

Without any sense that China's policies may have contributed to the American posture, Xi would declare that the United States was engaged in a policy of "all-around containment, encirclement, and suppression of China," adding that American sanctions and diplomatic pressure was bringing "unprecedented severe challenges" to China.[20]

One might think that increasing perception of an external threat to China would feed an instinct for greater domestic political control and the promotion of stronger expressions of nationalisms. That certainly has been the case with Xi's policies, but the reality is that Xi moved to strengthen the CCP's control and press national assertiveness well before the United States began to push back. Soon after assuming power, Xi launched an anticorruption campaign designed to remove opponents and purify party and state institutions at both the provincial and central levels.

Cai Xia has described how, when Xi released his so-called comprehensive reform plan in 2013, it became apparent that Xi was not a reformer—just the opposite: he was turning the clock back economically and on political openness. Indeed, rather than freeing up the private sector from political controls, he reinforced those restrictions. Cai also believes that even Xi's emphasis on anti-corruption was a sham, arguing that "China's long standing problem of corruption, public debt and unprofitable state enterprises was rooted in party officials' power to meddle in economic decisions without political supervision."[21] In addition, she described Xi's plan as one that was all about solidifying centralized control under the rubric of "governance, management, service and law." She added that the package of legal reforms that Xi unveiled in 2014 further exposed that he was using the law to maintain total control and to impose repression, something that became apparent when, starting in 2015, the CCP rounded up hundreds of defense lawyers. His move to prevent any criticism of the party became more pronounced in 2016, when he attacked and subsequently jailed real-estate tycoon Ren Zhiqiang for criticizing growing censorship of diverse views in the Chinese media.[22] This would presage other moves against some of the biggest moguls like Alibaba Group's co-founder Jack Ma.

New themes of "common prosperity" were populist in character but designed to send a message that Xi would deal with economic disparities and inequalities in wealth. He would not explicitly proclaim this theme until 2021, but foreshadowed it in 2017 when he declared that after decades of very rapid economic growth, the "principal contradiction" was "between unbalanced and inadequate development and the people's ever growing needs for a better life."[23]

In theory, Xi was addressing a contradiction in a country supposedly based on Marxist ideology; he would correct the great disparities in wealth, an effort that, much like his anti-corruption campaigns, had great public appeal. While ideologically satisfying, it also allowed him to go after the growing private sector and a burgeoning entrepreneurial class that seemed beyond party control and was clearly eclipsing the party apparatchiks.

And this is the essence of Xi: the centralization of power, the dominant role of the party, the use of anti-corruption campaigns to purge anyone not loyal, the preoccupation with internal security, grand domestic ambitions (raising China on a per capita basis to a middle-income country, at a time when 600 million people still have an income of less than $140 a month), and, internationally, eclipse the United States as global leader. With his "made in China campaign," he set his sights on surpassing America in technologies like AI and quantum computing by 2025. That goal is no longer in the cards, but Xi continues to believe that China can win the competition with the United States by mobilizing its means of producing electronic vehicles, semiconductors, and other advanced technologies.[24]

As we will see, Xi's problem is that his commitment to control and party dominance undercuts his goal of economic growth—growth which has been the key to the basic social contract with the Chinese public: we provide you a better life, and in return, you grant the CCP total political control. That contract may be increasingly difficult to sustain unless Xi can adapt his instinctive approaches domestically and internationally. Still, China as a competitor must not be underestimated; from the statecraft perspective, it is important to understand both its strengths and weaknesses. That understanding can better guide the United States on how to think about both its objectives and the means it will need to employ to achieve them.

China's Strengths and Weaknesses

China has many strengths. It is the world's biggest manufacturer; its infrastructure in terms of ports, fast trains, airports, highways, and telecommunications is highly advanced—and in many areas much superior to that of the United States. Its information and communications technology company Huawei has been the largest supplier of equipment needed to operate the global internet—despite American sanctions. China is the largest trading partner with over 120 countries (including close American allies like Germany), and that number may be as high as 140—a reality that gives to China economic leverage with many who cannot afford to antagonize the country that has proven it will impose penalties on its critics.[25]

China's stimulus package in 2008–2009 helped the world to recover from the global financial crisis. China continues to be, in the words of its ambassador to the United States, Xie Feng, "the most important driver of global growth." In fact, Xie Feng also notes that China has been responsible for 40 percent of the global economic growth over the last decade, compared to 22 percent for the United States.[26]

China also has a major advantage in the area of renewables. It dominates many of the renewable supply chains and is by far the biggest producer of batteries, electric vehicles, solar panels, power control systems, and wind turbines. It already controls as much as 60 percent of the solar market—and Dale Aluf points out that in the last decade alone, China accounted for 36 percent of the world's total renewable generation capacity.[27]

What may be even more significant is China's control over the mining and production of the rare earth metals (also known as rare earth metallic elements) essential to many high-tech devices. Whereas in 1993, China accounted for 38 percent of the world's production of rare earth elements and the United States for 33 percent, by 2011, China accounted for 97 percent. The rare earth elements are necessary components "of more than 200 products across a wide range of applications, especially high-tech consumer products, such as cellular telephones, computer hard drives, electric and hybrid vehicles, and flat screen monitors and televisions. Significant defense applications include electronic displays, guidance systems, lasers, and radar and sonar systems."[28]

Ursula von der Leyen, the European Commission President, has called attention to concerns about dependence on China for rare earth materials, saying that this "is an area where we rely on one single supplier—China— for 98% of our rare earth supply, 93% of our magnesium, and 97% of our lithium, just to name a few." In light of such concerns, the EU proposed the Critical Raw Materials Act in May 2023 to diversify and secure supplies.[29]

The concerns in this area have become especially pronounced because of the role that some of the rare earth elements play not only in clean energy technologies but also in defense applications. One example is that China has a near monopoly over raw Gallium, producing 98 percent of the world's supply. This metal is used to produce some of America's most advanced military technologies and is particularly critical for radar systems used in a variety of platforms, including the F-35 stealth aircraft as well as THAAD and Patriot missile defense systems.[30]

As a sign of its leverage, in July 2023, China imposed new export restrictions on Gallium and key Gallium compounds in retaliation for American, Dutch, and Japanese export controls on advanced chips and chip-making equipment. With Gallium chips beginning to replace silicon chips as a means of increasing computing power, China's near monopoly on Gallium poses a real threat across the board, but especially in the military-security arena, in which there can be little doubt that China is determined to compete.

The development of China's military power, giving it not just regional dominance but global reach, has been a hallmark of Xi's rule, but the buildup of the Chinese military preceded Xi Jinping coming to power. If there was a turning point in the development of China's modern military, it was probably hastened by the Kosovo war. One factor that almost certainly contributed to the new emphasis on modernizing the Chinese military was the accidental American bombing of the Chinese embassy in Belgrade on May 7, 1999. China did not accept the Clinton administration's explanations that the strike was a mistake, and the bombing provoked bitter demonstrations with thousands of students rallying outside the US embassy in Beijing. Ten years after Tiananmen Square, there is no way the regime was interested in spontaneous demonstrations by students—meaning it clearly orchestrated the demonstrations and the nationalist response.

That the bombing remained etched in the minds of Chinese military leaders was indicated by the comments of former Chinese defense minister, Wei Fenghe. In visiting Belgrade and meeting the Serbian president on April 1, 2021, nearly 22 years after the bombing, Wei referred to the bombing, saying, "The Chinese people will never forget this period of history. And, the Chinese People's Liberation Army will never allow such history to repeat itself." He would add that "China is fully capable and determined to defend national sovereignty, security, and development interests."[31]

Judging from Wei's words all those years later, it is not unreasonable to assume that the bombing provided a spur to developing the military, especially because they saw the United States striking a symbol of Chinese national sovereignty with impunity. But M. Taylor Flavel and John Ikenberry argue that America's decision to fight the Kosovo war without a mandate from the UN Security Council was even more significant from another standpoint—it convinced the Chinese leadership that they could be facing something much more serious from the United States: a readiness to intervene over Taiwan. Moreover, the way the Americans fought the Kosovo war, succeeding without using ground forces, also signaled that the United States was far ahead in the modern technology of war-fighting; China, which had not fought a war since 1979, needed to catch up.[32]

In March 2000, the Chinese military's National Defense University provided a detailed assessment of the war in the former Yugoslavia. Among its critical conclusions, the report stated: "In modern wars, information superiority is the basic superiority. Whoever has information superiority ... will be able to gain the initiative in war."[33] Additionally, in the report's conclusions, there was a heavy focus on the lethality of air strikes in modern warfare and the need for China to develop countermeasures—along with the importance of using "short-range and long-range air strikes, precision strikes and stealth aircraft."[34]

To show how seriously the Chinese leadership took the need to upgrade the Chinese military and transform it to take account of the changed nature of warfare, President Jiang Zemin gave a speech in December 2000, in which he said:

> High technology local wars since the Gulf War demonstrate that information technology plays an extremely important role in modern warfare ... The new military transformation is essentially a revolution in military informatization. Informatization is becoming a multiplier of the combat effectiveness of the armed forces.[35]

The military was reorganized both to reflect the role of information dominance but also to take account of joint operations. By 2014, with Xi now in power, there was a new strategic guideline: "Winning Informatized Local Wars."[36] By 2015, information went from being an "important condition" for success in warfare, to being described as playing a "leading role."[37]

The military's role and responsibility was also further spelled out in terms of safeguarding China's needs and interests: the strategy formulated in 2014 balanced "defense of China's rights and interests with the maintenance of stability, firmly safeguarding national territorial sovereignty, unification and security, [and] supporting China's development."[38]

While this guideline, with its reference to unification, was indicating that Taiwan was a major part of the military's mission, it was also signaling that widespread organizational reforms would be necessary to fulfill broader responsibilities. At this time, China also shifted the focus of its military doctrine from territorial defense to extended power projection. Apropos of this shift, China's May 2015 Defense White Paper stated that the Chinese navy's strategic concept "will gradually shift from near-seas defense to the combination of near-seas and far-seas protection."[39]

The new doctrine also drove far-reaching structural reforms as President Xi increasingly put his imprint on the military. Seven military regions were transformed into five theater commands; a separate ground-forces command was created even as 300,000 forces were cut from the armed services, reflecting the reduced focus on territorial defense; Second Artillery, featuring longer-range fire support was elevated from a branch into a service; and the Strategic Support Force was established with a focus on the cyber and space domains—something that also reflected the new emphasis on information dominance.[40]

Since then, there has been an extensive buildup in the quantity and quality of China's air, sea, and missile forces. Attack drones have been part of this buildup along with stealth aircraft; hypersonic weapons have been developed; the Chinese navy (known as PLAN) has deployed its third aircraft carrier; and the PLAN ships now outnumber those of the US Navy.[41] Not surprisingly, China has in the last few years also been pressing the development of AI for its military and space applications.

The buildup has meant increasingly larger defense budgets and greater spending. From 2013 to 2023, the published Chinese defense budget approximately doubled to $224 billion, and the budget was announced to increase 7.2 percent further for 2024. Those announced budget figures, however, appear to dramatically understate the actual defense spending, as the costs associated with many military functions are accounted for in separate budgets. To give but two revealing omissions from the defense budget, neither the Chinese Coast Guard nor the People's Armed Forces Maritime Militia appear as line items—both entities are funded separately from the rest of the Chinese military. One observer argues that the actual spending on defense is over $700 billion—making Chinese spending on defense far closer to the size of America's budget for the Pentagon and the US military than had been assumed.[42]

The military's development and reach is a significant strength, reminding everyone that China is a superpower both economically and militarily. At the same time, China has been increasingly active diplomatically, determinedly building new regional institutions and insinuating itself in UN bodies. Yes, it wants to give new expression to the multipolar nature of the world and the institutions that reflect it. But this is also a sign that China believes it can outcompete the United States in multinational institutions, gaining favor and setting the agenda in these organizations and, in effect, coming to dominate rule-making in these international bodies. It is not that the Chinese are against rules or norms internationally; on the contrary, provided China is setting the terms, they welcome the stability and predictability that rules and norms bring. Hence, one sees China's active pursuit of leading roles in a variety of the UN agencies: UN Food and Agricultural Organization, UN Department of Economic and Social Affairs, UN Industry and Development Organization, International Civil Aviation Organization, International Telecommunications Union, Interpol, etc.

These efforts allow China to present itself as a good global citizen and, increasingly, steward—something it used to contrast itself with the Trump administration's lack of interest in international institutions and the views of global audiences. But it also has meant that China has been building its ability to influence the work of these functional agencies and how they approach their responsibilities. One might say that this is a subtle way to promote China's soft power, inserting Beijing's values and its developmental model into agencies that play a role in the developing countries of the Global South. With Chinese appointees in leading positions, these agencies gradually come to take account of Chinese interests more and more and are unlikely to ever adopt positions not shared by the Chinese government.

While the Chinese extol the virtues of multipolarity and international institutions, President Xi, as noted in Chapter 1, had no problem ignoring the Permanent Arbitration Tribunal, appointed under the terms of the UN Convention on the Law of the Sea, when it found against China on the nine-dash line in 2016. Hence, we can observe the interesting Chinese duality of promoting these international institutions: knowing that these institutions have an appeal to Global South countries as forums to express their views and get potential redress but simultaneously feeling free to ignore any finding that does not suit China. (The Permanent Arbitration Tribunal even producing such a finding now seems far less likely given China's expanding role in these UN institutions and agencies.)

From building alternative financial institutions, like the Asian Infrastructure Investment Bank and the New Development Bank, to promoting new regional groupings, like the Shanghai Cooperation Organization (which has a security focus and keeps expanding its membership, with India and Iran now as full members, and Saudi Arabia and the United Arab Emirates as observers), China is showing that it may not have alliances like the United States, but it has partnerships in regions ranging from Asia to Africa to Latin America. Though most of these groupings began with an economic orientation, the focus is not just on economics. If nothing else, these institutions and groupings, to include the BRICS countries, mean that China's concerns can rarely be ignored.

Perhaps the most spectacular of China's efforts to spread and cement its economic ties has been the Belt and Road Initiative (BRI). By financing and constructing extensive infrastructure internationally, China has also been extending its reach, deepening commercial relationships, and reducing the vulnerability of its trade through land and sea networks of rail-lines and ports. It has promoted partnerships and built dependencies in the process, even as it has demonstrated enormous financial clout. Xi articulated the logic of the BRI in Kazakhstan in 2013, inaugurating what he described as a new era of trade and friendship between China and the rest of Central Asia and declaring that "a near neighbor is better than a distant neighbor."[43] China would expand the BRI eastward toward Indonesia, southward to Pakistan, and to the Middle East, Africa, and even Latin America. To date, 147 countries, making up roughly 40 percent of the global GDP, have signed BRI projects or expressed interest in them.[44]

As of 2021, BRI had funded 2,600 projects in 100 countries, totally roughly $3.7 trillion.[45] Many of these projects—especially those in and around the Indian Ocean, which included the development of ports collectively referred to as the "string of pearls"—probably have greater military than economic value, especially as they practically support China's ability to deploy its blue water navy and project power. But focusing principally on the military aspect of the BRI would be a mistake and miss the impact of the initiative, especially in the Global South. Indeed, for many of these developing countries, the BRI was the only source of funding available to them to build critical infrastructure essential for those nations' economic development. As such, the BRI has been a remarkable manifestation of Chinese strength and has certainly built its soft power—as well as dependencies of other countries on China. But dependencies often also breed resentments.

And, that reminds us that there is another side to the BRI: it is not all good news for China or for those who have become dependent on its infrastructure projects. To begin with, not all of the projects have been well constructed, but nearly all have become debt traps. The Chinese finance the projects with loans, but those loans are burdensome for developing economies and have led to a large number of defaults, adding to China's burgeoning debt burden. China's answer has often been to seize assets or coerce essentially long-term, low-cost leases, as in the case of Sri Lanka. Overwhelmed by its debt to China for its infrastructure development, the island nation granted China a 99-year lease to its deep water port in Hambantota. That and related deals involving a Chinese company acquiring a 70 percent stake in a joint venture with the state-run Sri Lanka Ports Authority, produced protests and opposition within the country. Namal Rajapaksa, a member of the Sri Lankan Parliament and son of the former president, tweeted at the time: "Government is playing geopolitics with national assets? #stopsellingSL."[46]

With more countries facing debts to China that they cannot service— and China's reluctance to reschedule these debts—the BRI, which once enhanced Chinese soft power, is now a public image liability. China is under increasing pressure internationally to reschedule debts and ease the pressure it is putting on Global South countries.

Moreover, the actual commercial benefits or even viability of many of these projects are increasingly dubious. Big projects like Indonesia's bullet train—being built and financed by China—show little prospect of returning a profit any time soon or at all. The Indonesians are now pressing China Railway "to transfer its technology to Indonesia so it can produce the trains domestically."[47] The initiative that once seemed to exemplify Chinese ascendency on the world stage has become a critical weakness for Beijing. It serves as a reminder that for all of China's strengths, there are corresponding weaknesses that are often outgrowths of apparent advantages.

An example of a strength that often turns into a weakness is China's ability to make a decision and efficiently mobilize great resources to implement it. So much of Chinese infrastructure development emerged from the single-minded decision and implementation process. Big decisions can be made and implemented—something that Xi often uses to contrast the Chinese model with what he describes as American dysfunction. There surely is dysfunction in US policymaking and implementation. (Look no further than the inability of administrations to pass new budgets as opposed to continuing budget resolutions or the efforts that have proven consistently needed to avoid government shutdowns.)

The problem for China, however, is that some of those big decisions that its leaders impose and implement can prove to be disastrously wrong. One recent example is "zero-COVID" policy, which shut down whole cities due to a single case or very few cases of COVID—stopping economic activity, imposing terrible hardships in these cities, and preventing the emergence of immunities in the general public. At one point in 2022, 373 million people in 45 cities were under partial or complete lockdown.[48] The economic price was immense, but so was the social price. It ultimately led to a political backlash, with spontaneous public protests over the continuing shutdowns of cities finally erupting. Then, suddenly, as if the protests were getting out of control, Xi made the decision to instantly end the zero-COVID/shutdown strategy. However, there was no preparation for the dramatic surge of COVID cases that ensued, no putting hospitals in a position where they could absorb the sick, and little or no practical support to help local areas be able to handle and dispose of the dead.

Consider another transformative decision during Deng's time: the one-child policy, implemented in 1980. At the time, the idea was to stem population growth given the limits on capital, natural resources, and consumer goods. But that decision has now produced huge demographic problems—with far-reaching economic implications—so severe that Xi ended the policy in full in 2016.[49]

The zero-COVID and one-child policy decisions are both vivid examples of big decisions from a highly centralized leadership that have yielded disastrous consequences and help to contribute to what some observers are now describing as "peak China." These observers see slowing economic growth as an indication that China's economy will not surpass America's, at least for the foreseeable future. The expectation that China would overtake the United States and become the world's leading economy, first raised seriously by Goldman Sachs in a 2003 forecast, is now being replaced by the assessment that, at a minimum, China is decades away from being able to overtake the United States economically.[50] Moreover, there are those who believe that China has already hit its high point and will decline.[51]

Making big decisions that prove to be very wrong is one factor that contributes to greater pessimism about China's future. That President Xi is so determined to centralize power and increase the CCP's control in all sectors, especially in the economy, only adds to the view that he will compound bad decisions even as he makes more of them. Indeed, his propensity to make big decisions seems to be very much a part of his mindset, and yet these decisions frequently undercut his own objectives on economic growth. Arbitrary decisions like imposing zero-COVID, and then simply lifting it, undermines the confidence of the private sector, reluctant to make investment decisions that could be completely undermined by a change in governmental policy or imposition of new rules—like the new national security regulations that have scared off foreign investors. As Adam Posen points out, it is not just the private sector that becomes dramatically more conscious about investment decisions, but the public does as well. Both become wary and save rather than invest or consume. In Posen's words, "Once an autocratic regime has lost the confidence of the average household and business, it is difficult to win it back."[52] Not only are the effects of disastrous decisions debilitating in their own right, but the centrality of the party, and indeed of Xi himself, in these decisions ensure that leadership has very little plausible deniability or ability to effectively scapegoat.

At a time when China's initial and successful growth model must change from huge investments in infrastructure-, property-, and export-driven policies to services and consumer spending, the arbitrary decisions that are so much a part of Xi's centralization of power vitiates the prospects for China's continual growth—and among other things, that also threatens the basic social contract noted earlier: if the public does not get a continuing improvement in the quality of life and economic betterment, then the CCP's monopoly on political power will not go unquestioned.

But what happens if the government begins to be questioned because it can no longer deliver on its part of the bargain/contract? Will stability that is so highly valued in China be put at risk? It is at least a question worth asking because China does have a number of structural weaknesses that will not be easy to overcome—especially, if President Xi's way of governing does not change.

To begin with, expectations were high that Chinese economic growth would rapidly recover after COVID—and that has not happened. There are multiple reasons for that, including that the drivers of the economy in the past—like housing, real estate, and infrastructure development—are all facing monumental problems. Housing and real estate are in crisis, with the bankruptcies of the two largest developers in the country: Evergrande and Country Garden. The fallout from their bankruptcies is hard to exaggerate, ranging from the impact on private household wealth to the funding of local and provincial governments. To put this in perspective, housing represents 30 percent of the Chinese economy and 80 percent of the household wealth.[53] In 2021, the year Evergrande failed, land sales plunged 90 percent in the country.[54,b] Since the 1990s, real estate has also provided over

---

[b] Country Garden's bankruptcy came only in 2023.

40 percent of the revenues of local governments, with roughly 1/3 coming from land sales and up to an additional 15 percent from taxes on development.[55] With the bankruptcies of the largest developers—and many smaller ones—there was a big decline both in the sale and development of property, and that meant that local governments were losing the means to fund health care, pensions, education, environmental cleanup, and basic services. As one municipal official put it, "Beijing says that we need to keep the government up and running. But if land sales continue to weaken, we will have real trouble making ends meet."[56]

Moreover, with so much of the household wealth tied up in property, it was not just local governments being affected but also private consumption. Gary Na, an economist at a Hong Kong firm, said that "because a large part of Chinese households' assets are attached to real estate, when home prices aren't growing, or if they expect a weakening outlook on property, people naturally feel they do not have much money in their pockets."[57] The problem in 2023 was that the price of houses was not just weakening, it was declining—note, for example, that the existing value of houses declined 1.4 percent in June from the prices in May, accelerating a decline from the preceding months.[58]

There was no secret for why the price of houses was declining: China may have as many as 130 million empty apartments.[59] Visitors to China describe the existence of "ghost cities," with Mark Mobius describing how the outskirts of many cities are dotted with vacant high-rises, "many constructed by the troubled property giants Evergrande and Country Garden."[60] It is fine to talk of a new growth model for China in which consumption increases, but the real-estate collapse has undermined that prospect for some time to come.

Xi has not been prepared either to rescue the failing real-estate developers or to provide a major stimulus package, the traditional way the CCP has promoted growth when there was a slowdown. His ideological predispositions, and his commitment to overcoming income inequality, have contributed to his being unwilling to bail out the big developers who had amassed such wealth but whose companies had acquired huge debts as they continued to build. Xi, in letting them fail, made another big decision either without fully considering the far-reaching consequences or simply dismissing them.

Einwar Prasad, formerly the head of the China division of the International Monetary Fund, described these consequences: "Beijing is discovering the huge costs of rectifying imbalances in a sector that it had long been relied on to prop up growth, boost local government revenues, and contribute to household wealth accumulation. The sector's influence over practically every aspect of the economy, financial markets, and society, make it a thorny issue to fix."[61] Xi clearly has not fixed it and at this point is not permitting polices that might do so. To be fair, it is not only real estate that has been terribly overbuilt; it is also infrastructure. Ghost cities are complemented by massive highways with no cars, huge modern airports in provincial cities with little or no air traffic, and local governments who may be strapped for revenues but are still borrowing to finance big infrastructure projects; all of that is feeding an ever-spiraling assumption of debt.

Xi has a strong incentive not to add to the growing debt, but he has yet to change the development model that remains embedded in the psyche of CCP's central and provincial planners. Edward Luttwak says that it is not just the psyche and habits of the CCP and state functionaries but also the inherently corrupt nature of the system, and what is necessary to enjoy its fruits or avoid its penalties. In Luttwak's words, semi-private joint ventures are financed by "loans of local branches of state banks, whose managers could not just say no to local party bosses, who could choose to invite them to sumptuous dinners in pretty company or lock them up for a corruption investigation if they saw fit."[62]

Luttwak's observations may be overly cynical about what is driving so much of the debt and the overbuilding of housing and infrastructure, but there is no denying that the provincial officials continue to borrow and build even when there is no need. They are driven by central plans and economic targets that they must meet; these plans and targets are often divorced from reality. Take the example of Yunnan Province: in the summer of 2023, its local officials said the local government would spend millions of dollars to build a new COVID-19 quarantine facility, "nearly the size of three football fields, despite China having ended its 'zero-Covid' policy months ago, and long after the world moved on from the pandemic."[63]

Yunnan is not unique. Like Yunnan, other localities keep borrowing, and the debt has ballooned dramatically, so much so that China's debt is now greater than that of the United States. As recently as 2020, the US debt-to-GDP ratio exceeded China's. That is no longer the case. Milton Ezrati points out that China's combined public and private debt in all sectors amounted "to the equivalent of $51 trillion, almost three times the size of China's economy as measured in the country's GDP." According to Ezrati, China's relative debt burden as of mid-2022 stood 40 percent higher than America's.[64] The

International Monetary Fund reports that Chinese cities alone accumulated a debt of more than $9 trillion.[65]

The scale of China's debt and the resources needed to service it will make it difficult to invest in Xi's priorities—producing technological self-sufficiency, doubling the size of the economy by 2035, and addressing the economic expectations of the Chinese public. If the debt was not a big enough problem, the demographic trends are certain to make the situation worse. China's population is already declining. For the first time since 1961, when there was widespread famine and death caused by Mao's Great Leap Forward, the population of the country actually declined in 2022, with 9.56 million births and 10.41 million deaths.[66]

For the last five years, the birthrate has been declining. Professor Wang Feng has predicted, "The year 2021 will go down in Chinese history as the year that China last saw population growth."[67] This was not expected until at least 2029, and the UN now projects that by the end of the century, China's population of 1.4 billion will be 800 million.[68] Historically, only calamities produced such a dramatic decline; today, the trajectory comes as a result of calamitous policy missteps made in the name of efficiency. In the words of Professor Yi Fuxian, "China is facing a demographic crisis that is beyond the imagination of the Chinese authorities and the international community."[69]

By definition, China's population is graying; its working age cohort is already withering and is projected to be the same size in 2050 as it was in 1990. Those over 60 are projected to total roughly 36 percent of the population by the mid-twenty-first century. These numbers have profound implications not only for economic growth, with fewer workers meaning less productivity, but also for the China's labor market—where the ratio of workers to pensioners will continue to fall in the coming years. An already weak welfare system will be stressed further as tax revenues decline.[70]

Several factors could change this for the better. China could require people to retire at an older age—though that may be seen as a reversal of the social contract. It could greatly improve labor productivity—though the trend in China is actually moving in the opposite direction. And, of course, it could encourage higher birth rates—something the leadership has been promoting since 2016, with the reversal of the one-child policy and the initial permission to have two children per couple being raised to three children in 2021. But social engineering of that sort is not easy to produce, and younger

Chinese generations are thus far not demonstrating a willingness to shape their personal lives to correct for mistakes of the state.

Women want careers and are either getting married later or not at all. Indeed, some women are refusing to get married because they believe they will be pressured to have children, and that will reduce their options. However, many of those who do get married are choosing with their spouses not to have children given the high cost of living—and the couples that *do* decide to have kids are deciding to have only one in order to preserve their quality of life. Even many of those who might have considered having more than one child have decided against it, believing that the key to success is a good education. Competition to assure academic success led to a thriving tutorial sector, which was very expensive and led few to believe they could afford to pay for more than one child.[71]

There was, of course, another factor affecting the low birth rate: the legacy of the Deng policy of having only one child, which ended only in 2016. Fewer girls were born during this period, and this has affected the number of women of child-bearing age today and for some time to come.

The government clearly recognized the problem, and that is why the one-child policy was reversed. Its efforts to stimulate the birthrate have included tax incentives for having children, new laws penalizing discrimination against working mothers, and even banning private tutoring to reduce the costs of education to "rein in the competitiveness among young parents."[72]

However, nothing has worked to change the birthrate. The demographics problem and debt are not going away and will create real structural barriers to growth. The engine of growth has been the private sector, accounting now for more than 60 percent of national output, 70 percent of national wealth, and 80 percent of urban employment.[73] In theory, the more successful the private sector is, the more the Chinese might be able to mitigate the effects of demographics and debt.

Here again, however, we see Xi's ideological predispositions undercutting the best generator of economic growth and productivity. It is not as if the government, and Xi's chief lieutenants, did not know the importance of the private sector for driving the economy. Former Vice Premier Liu He, speaking to a gathering of entrepreneurs in 2018, said that the "private sector was responsible for 90% of new employment growth, 80% of urban development, 70% of technology innovations, and 50% of the country's taxation."[74] These figures demonstrate the significance of the private sector. And yet, Liu's acknowledgment of the importance of the private sector has not prevented a crackdown on it.

Indeed, this crackdown has had several elements. It has included silencing leading figures of the private sector—like Jack Ma, one of the founders of the e-commerce giant Alibaba and one of China's wealthiest men, who criticized financial regulators for constraining the financial technology sector with their "pawnshop mentality." Not only was Ma silenced and disappeared for three months, but the planned IPO of his company Ant Financial Group was stopped. Companies including Alibaba and TMall (an online market vehicle) were fined huge amounts, the ride-hailing group Didi was forced to delist, Ant was restructured, and its consumer finance branch faced new regulation. The micro-blogging platform Weibo was fined 44 times in 2021 alone and, along with the short video app Byte Dance, was forced to give the government 1 percent ownership and board seats. The education-tutorial groups were put out of business entirely.[75] All of these different high-tech and gaming companies generated lots of jobs, especially among younger people; the straight-jacket these companies have been forced to operate in has produced serious losses—and those losses help to account now for high youth unemployment, which was last measured at 21.4 percent. That figure probably understates the real numbers, which are running so high that China has stopped releasing statistics.[76]

Beyond regulation and fines, social media and entertainment platforms began to face increasing censorship of content. Gong Yu, the CEO of one of these platforms said, "The biggest problem for our industry is severe shortage of content supply." Facebook and Twitter were banned in China after riots in Xinjiang province in 2009, and Instagram was banned five years later during pro-democracy protests in Hong Kong.[77]

The regulations, the fines, the censorship, and the deliberate targeting of the country's biggest private enterprises is not only limiting the private sector, but demoralizing it. Fearing they too could be targeted, and with little recourse, many entrepreneurs are taking their businesses and wealth and leaving China. Singapore is one of the preferred destinations, and now four of the wealthiest Singaporeans are Chinese immigrants.[78] Li Yuan interviewed a number of entrepreneurs who had left China, and they said that they had decided not to put themselves or their businesses "under the thumb of the Chinese Communist Party again" as they want to live free of fear.[79]

Xi's emphasis on party control as well as his ideology drove the crackdowns. According to one report, Xi is of the opinion that "the private sector had become detached from national interests and drove up systemic risks in the financial sector, an issue that could only be addressed with more control."[80] For Xi, the party must dominate and demand obedience from those companies and individuals that can contribute to national construction.

Xi offered a so-called New Development Concept (NDC) that very much justified party control while putting an emphasis on common prosperity. Kevin Rudd describes Xi's NDC as prioritizing political stability, equality over rapid individual wealth accumulation, social cohesion over economic efficiency, and national self-sufficiency over the benefits of open international exchange.[81] Xi might talk about the private sector and the market, but he has steadfastly favored state enterprises over private companies, shaping China's economic landscape according to the needs of the party, rather than the market.

Of course, he wanted and needed economic growth, but his ideologically driven decisions ran counter to that need. The crackdowns on the private sector, the new national security regulations, the tension with the United States, and the trade wars—all contributed to a serious decline in foreign direct investment. Understanding and trying to correct that, China organized a lavish dinner with American business leaders in San Francisco on the margins of the Asian-Pacific Economic Cooperation Forum in November 2023. Xi addressed the dinner in an attempt to assuage guests' skepticism: "No matter how the international situation evolves, China's resolve to foster a market-oriented, law-based and world class business environment will not change."[82]

His policies, however, belie that statement. He can appeal to businesses, as he did in San Francisco, by speaking of China's "super-large economy and a super-large market," and pledge to make the "cooperation list longer," but the US private sector has seen what has happened to their Chinese counterparts. Moreover, they have seen the new Chinese counter-espionage laws produce raids on foreign firms, and that has created fear among businesspeople about doing business in China—a fear that extends to their physical well-being while there.[83]

Once again, Xi's need to centralize control and put a premium on internal security is undermining his stated goal of advancing China's economy and making it a middle-income country based on per capita income. Xi may want to shape a new model based on growth in consumption, services, and high-tech self-sufficiency, but China has a long ways to go. Household consumption is only 38 percent of GDP—a far cry from the roughly 68 percent in the United States—and that gap has not changed over the last few years.

China also lags behind in advanced semiconductors and their advanced chips—probably on the order of five to seven years.[84]

Having said all this, one should not underestimate China's ability to mobilize great resources—including human scientific ones—to tackle specific tasks. While there is great risk in allocating resources to decisions that might be more aptly characterized as whims, there can also be great reward if those decisions are not strategic failures like zero-COVID or the one-child policy. Moreover, China has proven having the ability to adapt. One example is Huawei surviving US sanctions and showing a profit based on actually being able to produce the Mate 60 series, a smartphone that is powered entirely by domestically produced chips. Even if these chips were not as advanced as those in the Apple smartphones, they were functional, and were produced more quickly than had been anticipated following America's imposition of sanctions on Huawei and on semiconductor technology.[85]

So, America faces a determined competitor. Its economic, political, and military strengths are considerable. Nationalism has become an increasingly important tool that Xi uses to build legitimacy; and, as generating economic growth becomes harder to deliver, will he rely more on nationalist fervor and become more threatening and adventurous on the outside? The Council on Foreign Relations' Task Force on Taiwan contends that this is real possibility:

> As China's economic growth has slowed under Xi, he has increasingly turned to nationalism to justify the CCP's monopoly on power. With a further downturn, he could turn to the Taiwan issue to rally support for the CCP and his personal rule.[86]

If nothing else, this risk certainly argues for the United States to ensure that it has a real deterrent capability in the Indo-Pacific region. Deterrence is about preventing not just Chinese aggression but also its coercion and intimidation of its neighbors and US partners. American policy undeniably needs to take both China's strengths and its weaknesses into account. Both will call for the US to work with others, but cooperation is a means, not the ultimate objective. We have seen cases where the means defined the objective rather than the other way around. Here, having offered an assessment of the challenge that the United States is facing with China, and Beijing's strengths and weaknesses, let us turn to a discussion of what America's objectives should be in this competition, and then we can turn to the means that the United States can use to achieve them.

Objectives

At the outset of the chapter, I quoted President Biden saying that the United States seeks to manage its competition with China while avoiding a conflict. That could be a reasonable objective, but it is mostly preventing a negative. Secretary of State Blinken encapsulated the objective somewhat more positively, saying that "our relationship with China will be competitive when it should be, collaborative when it can be, and adversarial when it must be."[87] In other words, Blinken offered what might be described as a mixed-model approach designed to keep the competition within bounds while making cooperation possible. Both statements imply that an essential objective is preventing a war—and, with a fundamentally competitive relationship, it is easy to understand why that should be America's objective with China.

But precisely because China poses not just a military but also an economic challenge, there is an additional need to find ways to cooperate because, like it or not, economies of the United States and China are in many ways structurally interdependent. A downturn for one means economic suffering for the other. These countries also share vulnerabilities to transnational threats such as pandemics, climate change, nuclear proliferation, and terror—challenges that can be neither resolved nor effectively managed by either of the two countries independently. Kevin Rudd takes account of the duality of Chinese and American interests, describing how each country has a stake in creating "guardrails" in their relationship, even as they offer two competing models to the world. He calls for creating a joint strategic framework to avoid conflict and permit both competition and cooperation. To that end, he outlines three tasks that this joint framework must address:

- agree on principles and procedures for navigating each other's redlines;
- identify areas of non-lethal competition across the spectrum of national security as well as foreign, economic, and technological development policy;
- define areas where cooperation, not competition, is recognized and promoted.[88]

Rudd's joint strategic framework is driven by his concern about the real possibility of war given what he sees as fundamentally clashing American and Chinese interests, including in those areas that can easily become flashpoints for conflict like Taiwan or the South China Sea. If one believes that war is likely or certainly possible, it is understandable that the main objective should be preventing it. Rudd argues that if a joint framework was possible to reduce the risk of conflict between the United States and the Soviet Union and was agreed at their summit in 1972, then surely such a framework should also be possible between the United States and China. He believes that these two countries should aim for a framework and an international order where territorial integrity, political sovereignty, and a pathway to national prosperity are assured for large and small states alike.[89]

In effect, Rudd's objective is to preserve something very much akin to the existing international order that Biden has wanted to safeguard—and his joint framework is part of the means for achieving that objective. Other China watchers take a similar approach. For example, Roger Fontaine argues that America's objective should not be regime change or even getting along with the Chinese; instead, America's focus should be on what the United States needs to do with China to maintain the current international order—one in which rules, not brute force, govern the order; where disputes are handled peacefully and borders are respected; and where democracies are able to flourish with markets generally open and human rights respected. In his words, "The aim of the United States should be to ensure that China is either unwilling or unable to overturn the regional and global order."[90] That might be achieved, he argues, if China's leaders understand that trying to overturn the elements of the liberal order is futile given the strength of the countries committed to preserving these elements and "the vigor with which they will oppose China's efforts to disrupt them."[91]

Here again, we begin to see the very general means that Fontaine wants to use to achieve his objective of preserving the order. He contends that should China believe that it cannot undermine the order or alter it to serve its interests, China's leaders might one day come to the conclusion that their nation's interests will be best served by preserving the liberal order.[92] Ryan Haas shares this view, and he believes that this objective is achievable. He suggests that the United States can "entangle" China, making the case that "Washington should aim to preserve a functioning international system that supports US security and prosperity," and includes China rather than isolating it.[93]

Robert Zoellick believes that such an objective is achievable but only after Xi. He makes the case that Xi will not last forever and that there are many Chinese in the system who are practical and understand that cooperation with the United States can serve the mutual interests of the two countries.

They do not necessarily see the relationship is zero-sum terms.[94] For the remainder of Xi's time in power, Zoellick believes that America's goal must be to prevent China from achieving political, security, and economic dominance in the Indo-Pacific region. No doubt, in the eyes of Fontaine and Haas, such regional gains for China would convince the leadership in Beijing that they need not adjust their positions. On the contrary, geopolitical gains in the Indo-Pacific would likely strengthen the hands of those in the Chinese elite who see cooperation driven by weakness and not strength—and thus would reduce their interest in compromise and acceptance of the US rules-based system.

Generally, the debate among China watchers and policy practitioners is less about objectives, where there is broad agreement, and more about the strategies and means needed to achieve those objectives. Those who favor "engagement" as the means believe that dialogue with the Chinese will bring them around both practically and more safely—they also think an engagement strategy is in keeping with America's own values of greater openness. Others take a tougher approach, believing that actively countering the Chinese is necessary to convince them to alter their behavior, which in time, they argue, will reduce the risk of conflict. They favor containment.

While commentators who favor engagement (let's call them "engagers") very much prefer outreach and dialogue, those calling for containment ("containers") focus far more on creating deterrence and countering all areas where the Chinese adopt aggressive postures. Engagers, however, worry that tough postures will feed the worst Chinese instincts and responses. Susan Shirk, both as an academic and a practitioner, suggests that the "the most urgent priority for both sides ... [is] a return to traditional diplomacy and confidence-building, to reduce hostility."[95] She acknowledges the value of those calling for guardrails but emphasizes that "another crucial objective is to dispel hostility and restore motivation for compromise."[96] She sees statements by officials accusing Beijing of genocide against Uyghur Muslims in Xinjiang and identifying China as a bigger threat than Russia as damaging because they communicate "an unequivocally adversarial stand against China."[97]

For Shirk, such a posture inevitably triggers Chinese perceptions that they must counter the efforts of an America determined to keep China down. Rather than making China think that the United States is hostile and unrelenting in trying to preserve its dominance, Shirk feels there is a need to reassure the Chinese. Indeed, in her words,

The US aim should be not to hold on to the top slot in a global pecking order. Instead, its overriding goal should be preventing a war by motivating China to behave constructively and not aggressively toward other countries, even if in some dimensions it outdoes the United States.[98]

Shirk is very mindful of not feeding stronger nationalist instincts in China, noting that anti-Americanism had not been a major factor in China until Trump—and she believes that such sentiments place limits on any impulse to compromise. As a result, Shirk urges US policymakers to weigh how their actions will affect public views in China toward the United States.[99] Antagonizing the Chinese public and stoking vitriol toward the United States could make a successor of Xi more constrained in attempts to pursue a more constructive, cooperative relationship with Washington.

There are certainly Chinese commentators who seem to validate Shirk's view. For example, Wu Xinbo, a leading Chinese academic, in speaking about the factors driving China, said, "China wants to feel that we are a force in international affairs on par with our growing national power. But another factor is the US's attempts at containing China. They want to isolate us, suppress us, demonize us, and so we need to acquire the ability to resist those efforts."[100]

All this leads Shirk to call for "communication at all levels, including the leader level." Each side should "identify a short list of issues that they think are very, very important and [that are] amenable to possible give-and-take and resolution through diplomacy."[101] Indeed, Shirk proposes that it is essential to restore the diplomatic track.

Along with engagers' belief in reassurance, communication and diplomacy are the hallmarks of this approach. Understandings can be hammered out—provided, as Adam Tooze asserts, that there is "accommodation of China's historic rise."[102] Containers see it differently. China has not played by the rules: it has ignored its obligations under the WTO, provided state subsidies for unfair competitive advantages, consistently stolen intellectual property, and coerced American companies to provide China's companies their advanced technology. As if that were not enough, they argue, it has threatened and coerced its neighbors. For containers, none of this is a surprise because China is bent on surpassing the United States and rewriting the global rules to fit Chinese interests at the expense of those of the United States. As Michael Beckley observes, the vital interests of the United States and China are in conflict. He argues that the United States and its allies must deter Chinese aggression in the near term and avoid concessions that would give Beijing an advantage in the longer term.

For Beckley, merely talking more will neither make our differences disappear nor alter our great power rivalry, and, by definition, our rivalry requires strong deterrence and a stable balance of power. Blunting Chinese aggression can eventually play on its internal contradictions—contradictions that Xi exacerbates with the centralization of party control, shackling of the private sector, vast overbuilding of housing and infrastructure, and structural weaknesses ranging from debt to demography. As if that were not enough, China's threatening posture has produced a backlash from many of its neighbors. Echoing the logic of George Kennan's original concept of containment of the Soviet Union, those who advocate containing China today believe that in time, either China's leaders will come to see that eclipsing American dominance is not achievable and alter their course. Or, as Hal Brands suggests, effective containment, including denying China's access to key technologies, can lead to a loss of Chinese power or the way it is governed. Effectively, Brands believes in regime change but acknowledges that if this is the explicit objective, it will be hard to mobilize the necessary counter-coalitions to ensure the success of containment.[103]

Joseph Nye, another academic and practitioner, is not necessarily in either the engagement or containment camp. He acknowledges that he was once an advocate for engagement but he came to believe that it was certain to fail once Chinese elites concluded that America was in decline and China would surpass it—a view that was triggered by the global financial crisis of 2008. Yes, Nye believes that Donald Trump and Xi Jinping "played important roles in ending Sino-American engagement," but for Nye the fundamental problem was that engagement could not transform the Chinese system, and sooner or later its failings would produce a different path for the relationship. He notes that "managed competition" or "competitive co-existence" has replaced engagement, and that the latter should "RIP."[104]

Those who favor managed competition or competitive co-existence may not be engagers, but they are also not containers. Like the containers, they believe in the importance of strong deterrence of China. Unlike the containers, who already believe that the United States is in a cold war with China and should not make life easier for Beijing, the "competitive co-existers" believe that cooperation is possible and can be in the mutual interests of the two countries. They also see a risk of the containers (or new cold warriors) making conflict a self-fulfilling prophecy. Competitive

co-existers like Jessica Chen Weiss seek a balanced approach that both recognizes the need to counter the Chinese but also accepts that it is in America's
interests to build a positive relationship with them. Note Weiss's words:

> There is no doubt that China—whatever its trajectory—poses a huge and
> complex policy challenge for America. But exaggerating fears of an "exis-
> tential struggle" increases the likelihood of conflict, crowds out efforts
> to tackle shared challenges like climate change and creates a with-us-or-
> against-us framing that could alienate the United States from allies and
> much of the world.[105]

Weiss does not presume that China's leaders necessarily have benign intentions toward America, but she also believes that fostering cooperation is both
possible and very much in America's interests. She wants policymakers "to
pair deterrent threats with more robust efforts to seek a constructive relationship with China, while also protecting the core values and interests of
an inclusive international order and calling on Beijing to offer more credible
reassurances of its intentions."[106]

Like the engagers, Weiss is mindful of how the Chinese read US actions as
attempts to preserve American dominance at China's expense. She believes
that this needs to change, and US policymakers should have a "positive-sum
vision of a reformed international system that includes China and meets the
existential need to tackle shared challenges."[107] Moreover, she worries that as
US policymakers continue to respond to Beijing's actions with sanctions and
tariffs on commercial and scientific exchanges, the United States is moving
away from its principles of openness and nondiscrimination that have long
been a comparative advantage of the United States.[108] Others, like former
secretary of the treasury Henry Paulson, share that view. He says that the
"test for US policy-makers will be whether we lose confidence in our system
by continuing to attempt to beat China at its own game—or whether we trust
in our economic principles that have made our economy and our companies
leaders in the world."[109]

No one fits perfectly in any of these categories of engagement, containment, and competitive co-existence. The right approach probably combines
elements of all three. Striking the right balance is difficult because, as Weiss
observed, China poses a complex set of challenges—and it certainly prefers
a world where democracy and individual rights are eclipsed. But given
China's history—and the deep-seated Chinese perception that the United

States seeks to limit it, keep it vulnerable, and, therefore, in Xi's eyes, even force regime change—it is difficult to take steps that are not misread by the Chinese leadership.

Steps the United States takes to compete with the Chinese are interpreted as a threat or an effort to hold China down. Steps taken to deter the Chinese from further militarizing the South China Sea, potentially invading Taiwan, or continuing unfair trade practices are seen as simply the latest example of American stifling of Chinese potential. And the calls for respecting the norms of a rules-based liberal international order are taken skeptically, as a means to make China conform to America's rules, or are seen as hypocritical because when America's interests diverged from the order it constructed, whether in Iraq or related to keeping markets and trade truly free, the United States flouted its own rules.

This is not to defend the Chinese; instead, it is a reminder that almost regardless of how the United States chooses to compete with China, its leaders will tend to read America's actions negatively. If that is true, then why not do the maximum, as the containers suggest, to deter Beijing and deny them the technologies that would allow them to gain greater leverage over the United States? The simple answer is that such a path may well produce a conflict not by design but by miscalculation. That said, if the Chinese are prone to misreading America's actions, it is hard to believe that the United States will be able to reassure them the way the engagers want. And here the containers are probably right that simply engaging in more diplomacy will not make the interests of China and the United States, which are at best simply different and at worst irreconcilable, magically disappear. So, are the competitive co-existers right?

Probably. The balanced approach of the competitive co-existers makes the most sense but with an emphasis on the areas where common interests require cooperation. Publicly, the United States cannot appear to be acquiescing, but it is possible to emphasize that American interests on climate, pandemics, cyber dangers, terror, nuclear proliferation, and even macroeconomics require working with, not against, the Chinese. It is not a favor that the United States would do for China; it is how the US government protects Americans and their well-being now and in the future.

Privately, it would make sense to say to China, "Where we disagree, so be it, but let's address what we both need." Kevin Rudd, who can be described as a competitive co-exister, essentially argues that China and the United States will inevitably compete because they have different worldviews and different models of development. Each one thinks that theirs is better: let them play out. That is the right diplomatic approach, and, in time, there is the possibility that Chinese leaders could see America's determination to compete as one that is taking place within a framework of emphasizing areas of mutual interest and need.

Again, Kevin Rudd's three tasks of his joint framework provide a useful guide for how to act on the objective of managing a competitive relationship that must be made not just safe but also capable of producing cooperation and coordination in areas of mutual needs. This has implications for how US politicians should structure meetings with senior Chinese officials. For example, it is crucial to make the first item on agendas for meetings the discussion of issues on which China and the United States have common needs and mutual interests. Making the areas of common interests the first part of discussions with senior Chinese officials can begin to create a pattern for such interactions. As the Chinese at the highest levels come to understand that the American agenda for discussion will always start with the areas of common interests, they too will begin to prepare for talks on those issues and will gradually begin to come to the table with their own points about those issues.

This is not to suggest that just as one can make conflict a self-fulfilling prophecy by always emphasizing it, that the opposite can be done just with an emphasis on mutual need. Indeed, it will take time for attitudes and habits of thinking to change. But it is possible to start a process of reorienting thinking, and the United States should make the effort to do so.

Means and Tools for Achieving the Objectives

To be sure, much depends on the context and issues and on possible crises, and, of course, also on how the United States uses all the tools/means at its disposal. It is essential to realize that the United States has structural advantages in that it is not surrounded by hostile countries while China has disputes with nearly all of its neighbors. The United States has a strong global alliance system built as much on shared values as shared interests, while China's relationships are far more transactional. That suggests that the United States has a built-in ability to organize coalitions of allies and partners that can limit China's choices and enhance America's leverage. Even before the Biden administration, there was a recognition that India might not be one of US allies but could become an increasingly important partner, especially given China's aggressive posture toward its border dispute with India and its support for India's historic rival, Pakistan.

But American allies and potential partners find it easier to join with the United States if it does not appear to be trying to corner China or act with excessive hostility toward Beijing. Collectively, many of US allies and partners have economic interests in China and certainly do not see it as an existential threat. How US policymakers frame their objectives (and related policies) is critical. In fact, public framing of objectives (an important means) is a crucial factor in positioning oneself not just with allies but more generally on the world stage. Proper framing of objectives—as we saw in cases like German unification in NATO and the first Gulf War—leads others to respond to situations based on America's definitions of the issues and on America's calculations of what is at stake. Framing policy as one in which there are global problems that require common approaches by the United States and China (i.e., climate) is likely to put China in a position where it either needs to be responsive or it will be put on the defensive. Since the United States and China are the two biggest emitters of carbon dioxide, it is essential for the United States to consistently and publicly call for joint actions with the Chinese, and for the two countries to take the lead in producing zero-based emissions.

Effective framing of issues helps align other states' thinking with that of the United States and leads them to support Washington's responses. It is an underappreciated tool or means of statecraft. When done well, it makes coalition-building much easier and deepens another one of America's tools: soft power. China has been mindful of the importance of soft power, and it sees its potential advantages, especially with the Global South. China seeks to exploit the resentment of the United States and its supposed double-standards when it comes to conflicts like Russia and Ukraine. Countries in the Global South like South Africa ask, "Why does the US single out Russia for its invasion when the US invaded Iraq and has done so little to stop Israel in its war in Gaza?"

The differences may seem obvious to US policymakers, but they are a reminder that America's framing of what is at stake is also more compelling when soft power—meaning the power of attraction—is stronger. The United States does have a problem with the Global South that requires more outreach, more sensitivity to the source of resentment, and more recognition of the role that these countries can play in America's competitive-cooperative relationship with China. China's own relative strength in the Global South is bedeviled by the growing debt burden these countries are carrying because of China. Moreover, while China's readiness to share its COVID vaccine with developing countries earned it points early on, its image was later damaged, even with some countries in the Global South, when its vaccine proved much less effective than the mRNA vaccines, and when its zero-COVID lockdown policies backfired.[110]

China's support for Russia in Ukraine may not have greatly damaged its soft power in the Global South, but it surely did so in Europe. Early on, there were voices in China that argued that support for Putin's invasion of Ukraine would impose real costs on China's image and its soft power. Hu Wei, writing two weeks after the invasion, said that "this military action constitutes an irreversible mistake." He pointed out that Putin's invasion meant that "China was on the wrong side of the world," and contradicted China's principle of respecting national sovereignty and territorial integrity of states.[111,c]

But Wei and others making this case in China were soon silenced as President Xi made his decision that alignment with Putin was more important than the loss of soft power. That said, Xi would announce new formulations to show that China was trying to lead in promoting stability internationally. His Global Security Initiative—which pushed slogans such as comprehensive security, common security, indivisible security, sovereignty, territorial integrity, and non-interference in other countries' internal affairs—seemed very much like an effort to showcase China working for the common good in order to restore China's image that support for Putin was eroding. However, the so-called principles of the Global Security Initiative rang as hollow as Xi's remarks to American business leaders in San Francisco: enticing on paper, but hardly reconcilable with Xi's actions.[112]

Of course, in building leverage, the United States has additional tools beyond how it frames issues and its soft power. And the Biden administration has been quite effective in terms of organizing political, economic, and security coalitions or groupings of states—all of which were designed to ensure that these countries could resist China on issues, whether it was on economic coercion, military aggression, illiberal technologies, and/or human rights abuses.[113] In fact, the groupings that the Biden administration either upgraded or put together are quite impressive: it raised the

---

[c] It would be taken down from the site shortly after the translation appeared. Hu Wei at the time of this writing was the vice-chairman of the Public Policy Research Center of the Counselor's Office of the State Council, chairman of the Shanghai Public Policy Research Association.

Quad—the United States, India, Japan, and Australia—to the level of leaders with an early virtual summit. India, Japan, and Australia have all been the targets/victims of aggressive Chinese efforts at coercion, and while the Quad does not necessarily have a military focus, it is interesting that Subrahmanyam Jaishankar, the Indian Minister of External Affairs, observed that from India's standpoint, the Quad had a much "larger resonance" following the border clashes with China. It certainly fostered greater "comfort levels" in the United States and India, he said, on the need "to engage much more intensively on matters of national security."[114]

The formation of AUKUS—Australia, the United Kingdom, and the United States—on the other hand, is very consciously designed to enhance security by doing a great deal to extend the collective naval-military reach of these three countries in the Indo-Pacific. Tom Donilon, Obama's national security advisor, sees (much like Robert Zoellick) the immediate imperative to be preventing China's dominance in this region; in his eyes, AUKUS is an important mechanism for helping to do that.[115] The partnership creates a new level of trilateral security cooperation, with the United States and the United Kingdom assisting Australia in acquiring the most advanced nuclear submarines capable of patrolling in much more distant waters. Beyond the submarines, the British, the Americans, and the Australians will collaborate on cyber defense, electronic warfare, artificial intelligence, and hypersonic/counter-hypersonic weapons—meaning that this trilateral arrangement is designed to bolster their collective military capabilities as they face China's increasing military prowess in the Western Pacific.

The Biden administration has acted in other ways to increase its own power projection and maintenance capabilities in the region. It has been able to reacquire access to naval bases in the Philippines and has sent a carrier and two guided missile cruisers in a port call to Da Nang in Vietnam. The latter is part of an effort not just to expand cooperation in security and economic relations with Vietnam but to collaborate with those countries like Vietnam and the Philippines that are resisting Chinese claims in the South China Sea.

Even more broadly, the United States, overcoming years of strained relations between Japan and South Korea, brokered a number of trilateral defense initiatives, joining Tokyo and Seoul in three-way multi-domain air, sea, land, and cyber exercises, ballistic missile defense cooperation, and coordination on building greater security of defense supply chains. In announcing the breakthrough at the trilateral summit at Camp David in

August 2023, President Biden said: "We're elevating our trilateral defense collaboration to deliver in the Indo-Pacific region. This is not about a day, a week, or a month. This is about decades and decades of relationships that we're building." The scope of the understandings was quite broad, extending beyond defense and encompassing how the three can work together to reduce dependencies on critical materials (like cobalt, gallium, and lithium) largely dominated by the Chinese.

This was smart statecraft in practice. The Biden administration understood that to build America's leverage toward China, the United States needed its means to be joined with the means of others—and it was very clear that America's means would be dramatically enhanced if combined with those of Japan and South Korea. All previous efforts at forging real three-way collaboration had foundered on the enduring tensions between Japan and South Korea. Indeed, notwithstanding their common threat perceptions of China and North Korea, historical issues—related to apologies, comfort women, and compensation—held such weighty political baggage that the desired cooperation was never achieved. These historical barriers, however, were surmounted by the Biden administration, when the senior policy official on Asia at the White House, Kurt Campbell, made it a mission to overcome the differences and forge an understanding.

The Biden administration sought similar multilateral understandings in non-military areas. Both to show an alternative to China's Belt and Road Initiative and to forge new port, rail, and energy infrastructure designed to foster trade and development linking India to the Middle East and to Europe, President Biden announced the India–Middle East–Europe Economic Corridor on the sidelines of the G-20 meeting in India in September 2023. The corridor, in Prime Minister Narendra Modi's words, was a "big connectivity initiative," that could bind all the countries in it closer together and would use public and private moneys to build the infrastructure.

In the context of means, the Biden administration used its mobilizing and convening power (which is a tool)—as well as the interests of all these parties to draw closer to the United States and each other—to forge an understanding that showed very clear alternatives to China when it comes to infrastructure development.

In short, Biden's America was effectively using its means to compete. Just as his administration made a decision to generate legislation that would subsidize the US semiconductor and chip industry to ensure that America would stay ahead of China, the United States was showing that it had both the means to compete and the will to use them. The question remains, what is the aim of the competition? The competitive co-existers would say that the United States needs to compete, not to isolate China or to make it defensive, but to give it incentives to join with America. The containers would say that China must see that it will lose if it persists in trying to surpass America or reshape the order against the United States. The co-existers would say that providing both positive and negative incentives can bring the Chinese to adjust their behavior. For them, promoting cooperation, even as the United States enhances deterrence by being strong militarily, can produce that.

But one still needs to explain policies, and not just in public. It is easy to misread policies, assuming the worst intentions. The Chinese, given their innate suspicion about American intentions to limit them, contain them, and subordinate them, are prone toward such interpretations. But so are the Americans.

Moreover, there are real potential flashpoints of conflict, with Taiwan being the most prominent. That especially requires clear discussions in which the United States reaffirms its acknowledgment of the One China policy, acceptance of unification provided it is done peacefully, and commitment to avoiding provocative symbolic moves, like House Speakers Pelosi's and McCarthy's visits to Taiwan that do nothing for the island's security or deterrence but *do* unnecessarily provoke China. Provided that posture is clear and consistently communicated, the United States can make deterrence stronger by helping to build Taiwan's self-defense capabilities without provoking China. In the end, Xi and others must see the high costs of trying to impose unification by force.

Clearly, however, the sensitivity of the issue in China—and the potential that nationalist impulses will become stronger as economic growth declines—call for unfiltered channels of communication between the United States and Beijing. Kevin Rudd and Robert Blackwill independently make the case for a high-level political channel of individuals close to the two presidents. Rudd, arguing, as noted earlier, for a joint strategic framework, writes:

> The framework would need to be negotiated between a designated and trusted high-level representative of Biden and a Chinese counterpart close to Xi. Only a direct, high-level channel of that sort could lead to confidential

understandings that could be respected by both sides. These two people would become the points of contact when violations occurred ... and the ones to direct enforcement of consequences for any such breaches.[116]

Blackwill suggests something similar, arguing that "both sides should agree to launch an intense bilateral dialogue led by their national security advisors to discuss their respective vital national interests and redlines for the other's behavior, as Dr. Kissinger has proposed."[117]

Their suggestions for the formal communication channel make sense; such a channel is an important, even necessary, means. But there is a different kind of channel that is also needed—a true back channel. When the national security advisors meet, by definition it is formal, and each side sees it as committing. Brainstorming is not the province of such senior officials, and trying out ideas is rarely done in such environments for fear that one will be held to them. This is not an argument against regularizing such meetings—a recommendation that both Rudd and Blackwill make—but back channels can prepare the ground for such meetings to be more productive.

In the cases of both German unification and the first Gulf War, the back channels worked very effectively. I developed a relationship of trust with Sergei Tarasenko, who was Soviet Foreign Minister Eduard Shevardnadze's closest assistant/advisor. On the issues related to the Soviets, I had a similar relationship with Secretary of State James Baker. The more Sergei and I met, the more we worked together to prepare the meetings of our two ministers, the more we would anticipate problems or identify opportunities, and the more we could do together.[d]

Unlike meetings of the national security advisors—or of secretaries of state and foreign ministers—the meetings of their aides can be secret. No public explanations are required, and there is no need to posture. Back channels need to be essentially one-on-one; it is far easier to build trust this way, there is no playing to an audience, and ground rules for the discussions can be established from the beginning. The best way to establish these kind of channels is for the president or the secretary of state to tell his counterpart

---

[d] One example of the depth of the trust was, as noted earlier, when Sergei sent through a secure channel a highly sensitive message about Yevgeny Primakov's mission to Washington—a mission designed to undercut Shevardnadze and thwart cooperation. Robert Zoellick had a similar channel with Frank Elba, the German foreign minister's closest aide, and Robert Blackwill had a similar one with Horst Teltschik, the national security advisor to the German chancellor.

that he would like a discreet, trusted way to communicate, with several aims in mind:

- to explain America's thinking, what it is trying to do, and how it perceives its counterparts' thinking and behavior—and to permit them to do likewise;
- to manage or even anticipate potential problems;
- to provide early warning on steps that might have to be taken for political reasons and address what might be done to mitigate any damage or compensate for the step being taken;
- to identify steps that could build mutual confidence and make cooperation more likely, including by establishing parallel or reciprocal moves;
- to reach informal understandings that can then be given to the formal channels to finalize;
- to explore possible opportunities for breakthroughs on issues that matter.

It is hard to exaggerate the value of such channels, especially because they create a much stronger basis for fostering understanding even on issues where agreements are not possible—meaning they can be critical to managing differences.

Some may think that intelligence channels can be used this way—and they can, to a certain extent. However, they often have an inherent limitation in that they are better for sending sensitive messages than for actually producing serious discussion on new or different policy approaches.

There can also be different kinds of back channels—some that involve officials, and others that only involve former officials or people known to be close to decision-makers. When those no longer serving in government are involved, the back channel by definition is more deniable, and those involved are likely to feel freer to brainstorm and think outside the box. As an example, someone like Tom Donilon, who has known President Biden for a long time and has had a long-standing relationship with the Chinese and dealt with Xi, would have been perfect to play a role in such a channel during the Biden administration. Maybe the Chinese would have hesitated, but the effort to establish such an "unofficial" channel was never made. And, had Donilon been meeting with someone whom Xi designated, that channel could have produced a deniable problem-solving and problem-avoidance set of discussions. I know from experience that the work of such back channels can be given over to front or formal channels, setting the stage for actual agreements.[e]

Conclusion

No set of tools or means is a panacea for dealing with a relationship as complex and inherently competitive as that between the United States and China in the twenty-first century. The United States will need to use all of its means and seek to show its readiness to emphasize mutual interests on those issues that bedevil both countries, even as they compete. Intrinsic suspicion will not magically disappear, and the reality is that both Robert Zoellick and Ryan Haas may be right: with Xi, the combination of aspirations and suspicions may fundamentally limit what is possible. Maybe that will require more focus on management than accomplishment. But even with Xi, the aim must be to adopt policies and tools that do not preclude a better future.

Robert Zoellick suggests that sooner or later, Chinese leaders are likely to see the internal contradictions and the failure of their growth model. When they do, he asks, shouldn't the United States be the champion of open markets, rule of law, and what have been the hallmarks of the liberal international order and welcome the Chinese into it?[118]

Ryan Haas sees a similar evolution on the Chinese side, saying that if history is a guide, there is a strong possibility that the pendulum will swing when Xi leaves the scene: "When that day comes, China's leaders will need to decide whether they can better reach their goals by integrating into the global economy or by turning to more self-reliance and limited partnerships with the developing world."[119] Like Zoellick, Haas wants to be sure that America's policies have not only left China's leaders that choice but that the United States is also embracing it.

If the United States is able to put itself and China in that position, it will be fair to say that America has practiced statecraft well toward the People's Republic of China.

---

[e] As we will see in Chapter 13, I had very fruitful discussions in a back channel on the Israeli–Palestinian conflict that would have been far better exploited by the front channel if Hillary Clinton and Tom Donilon had remained in their positions.

Chapter 12

Iran: What Is Necessary to Conduct More Effective Statecraft Vis-à-Vis the Islamic Republic

No country presents a more complex set of international challenges to the United States than China. As we saw in Chapter 11, the relationship with China needs to take account of threats and mutual needs—and it is possible to address both with the right mix of tools, leverage, and channels. Iran, on the other hand, may not be a global challenge, but it is a terribly difficult regional one. It poses threats across a variety of dimensions: nuclear and missile proliferation, terrorism, exploitation of existing conflicts, use of proxies, destabilization, and determination to upset the regional order. (The fact that it abuses the basic human rights of its citizens, especially women and minorities, clearly also challenges American values.)

Henry Kissinger often said that Iran had to decide whether it was a "cause or a country." If it is the former, the challenge has one set of implications for America's objectives and the means the United States uses to achieve them—and US leaders will inevitably be driven to do more to defeat the ideology and demonstrate its failures. If it is the latter, US policymakers should theoretically be able to more easily shape an approach that presents Iran's leadership with choices that affect its calculus and the country's well-being.

Of course, like most countries—certainly including the United States—Iran is a mix of both ideology and nationhood. Regardless of which characterization *more* correctly describes the Islamic Republic, one thing is clear: it continues to be a problem, posing real threats to American interests and values and to broader regional and indeed global stability and security.

The most profound of those threats is presented by the Iranian nuclear program. Today, Iran has become a threshold nuclear state. It enriches uranium to near weapons-grade levels. Rafael Grossi—the director of the International Atomic Energy Agency (IAEA), the UN's nuclear watchdog—has said that the Iranian nuclear program is "galloping ahead" and that there

Statecraft 2.0. Second Edition. Dennis Ross, Oxford University Press. © Oxford University Press (2025).
DOI: 10.1093/oso/9780197698914.003.0012

is no justifiable civilian purpose for enriching uranium to 60 percent—and yet, Iran is now producing nine kilograms of uranium enriched to that level per month.[1] Turning this uranium into weapons-grade fissionable material would take very little time, and Iran—whether by a mistake or design—re-piped some of its centrifuges and produced uranium enriched to 83.7 percent. For comparison's sake, the first atomic bomb that the United States dropped on Hiroshima was enriched to 80 percent.

So, producing weapons-grade uranium is something that Iran can already do—and do quickly. And, Iran is now accumulating or stockpiling enough weapons-grade material for several bombs. Should enrichment of nine kilograms of uranium per month continue without interruption, it is very possible that at some point during 2025, Iran could have 10 bombs' worth of highly enriched uranium (HEU). The more it accumulates, the easier it will be for Iran to divert that material to secret sites that the United States may not know about.

To be sure, having weapons-grade fissionable material is not the same as producing bombs, but it is the most difficult technological and engineering obstacle that must be overcome to be able to create nuclear weapons. Moreover, with Iran no longer allowing the IAEA to have 24/7 coverage with all its cameras, or even access to the data from operating cameras, it is not surprising that Grossi in an interview said, "We don't know what's happening with the Iran's nuclear program."[2] The lack of transparency means that Iran has the potential to divert HEU without the knowledge of IAEA inspectors—who at least still have weekly, but no longer daily, access to known enrichment facilities. Unfortunately, since President Trump walked away from the Joint Comprehensive Plan of Action (the JCPOA, also known as the Iran nuclear deal), the IAEA no longer has any coverage of centrifuge assembly sites, meaning that there is now also the risk that covert assembly of centrifuges as well as enrichment could be taking place.

What compounds the problem is that weapons or bomb development is more difficult to track and monitor than enrichment. It is true that the Iranians do not know what the Americans know, and that could make them cautious in pursuing an actual covert weapons program lest the United States discovers it and acts militarily against it. In fact, Israel's ability to assassinate the leader of Iran's nuclear program, Mohsen Fakhrizadeh, and also steal 55,000 documents of Iran's nuclear archive from downtown Tehran, demonstrates that the Israelis have Iran deeply penetrated, adding to Iran's caution on this issue.[a]

---

[a] The Iranians no doubt assume that anything the Israelis know, the United States knows as well.

Still, even without a covert program, if the Iranians decided that they were not going to test a bomb but simply wanted to produce a crude nuclear device—one not fitted for ballistic missiles—they could do so in several months. This is why former chairman of the Joint Chiefs of Staff, General Mark Milley, warned that Iran could have a nuclear bomb within months, not years.[3] Given Israel's view that a nuclear Iran poses an existential threat, it is a fair question to ask whether Israel will continue to wait to strike Iran's nuclear infrastructure if it thinks that Iran is on the brink of creating a nuclear a weapon.

Maybe Israel will not act if it thinks that Iran will stop short of crossing the threshold to a weapon—but even that posture is only likely if the Israelis are confident that they know where the Iranians are in terms of developing a weapon, the location of the effort, and whether they believe they will have sufficient early warning to be able to take it out. The danger, of course, is that the more the Iranians accumulate, Israel (and the United States) may not know where all the material for bomb-making and producing is located. In other words, the longer Iran accumulates close to weapons-grade fissionable material, the more difficult it will be for anyone to destroy their ability to make nuclear weapons. To make sure that is true, Iran is now developing an enrichment site close to its existing facility at Natanz; the new facility is being dug so far underground—80–100 meters—that it is too deep even for the US Massive Ordinance Penetrator (MOP) to be able to destroy it—meaning that Iran is preparing an enrichment facility that is largely invulnerable.[4]

That may be just what Ali Khamenei, the Supreme Leader, is seeking—to leave his successors the option to have a bomb should they decide to take that step. But even that threshold status, especially given ongoing accumulation of HEU, may create incentives for other regional states to, at a minimum, be able to match what the Iranians are doing. Saudi Arabia has already declared its intent to create a large nuclear industry and wants to enrich on its soil—ostensibly to become a supplier of nuclear fuel. Yes, they are prepared to provide all sorts of safeguards to ensure that their program is solely for civilian purposes, but Crown Prince Muhammad bin Salman, the de facto leader of the Kingdom, has repeatedly said if Iran gets a nuclear weapon, the Saudis will get one too. It is a safe bet that others in or near the region (e.g., Egypt and Turkey) will follow suit.

A nuclear-armed Middle East significantly increases the risk of the use of nuclear weapons, particularly given the reality and danger of conflicts in the region. Moreover, one should not necessarily assume that the logic of the balance of terror or mutually assured destruction will apply in the Middle East. There is a near certainty that for some period of time, Middle Eastern states that acquire nuclear arms will lack an assured second strike capability, meaning that the temptation to strike first in a crisis and avoid a "use or lose" posture would be very strong—and very dangerous. In a tinderbox like the Middle East, America's aim needs to be to enhance crisis stability, not see it undermined, which would likely be the effect of Iran crossing the nuclear arms threshold and triggering others to do so as well. What is more, if countries in the Middle East decide to go nuclear, it is fair to ask whether countries in other regions will continue to adhere to the nuclear non-proliferation treaty. That is certainly an open question. The last thing we all should want to see is one of the most effective and enduring international treaties limiting the number of nuclear weapon states collapse.

If nothing else, this shows that Iran's nuclear program poses a very significant danger, and the United States has a large stake in preventing Iran from becoming a nuclear-armed state. But, of course, the development and direction of Iran's nuclear program is not the only threat that the Islamic Republic poses. The Iranians have cultivated, armed, trained, financed, and guided Shia militia forces—and they have become an instrument for coercion, leverage, and threats throughout the Middle East. Iran and its proxies may not be the source of all conflicts or instability, but they are quick to exploit them. Iran may not have known in advance about the plan of Hamas, the Sunni militia Iran supports, to perpetrate the onslaught against Israeli citizens on October 7, 2023. But Iran was quick to celebrate this attack, and all of its proxies from Gaza (Islamic Jihad) to Lebanon (Hezbollah) to the Red Sea (Houthis) to Iraq (Kata'ib Hezbollah and others) joined in attacks against Israel and American interests—including US bases in Iraq and Syria and freedom of shipping in the Red Sea and the Gulf of Aden.

Iran saw an opportunity to use its proxies to support the Palestinians in a war in which Israel was inflicting a very high toll on civilians—the byproduct of Hamas having embedded itself under the Gazan population. For the Islamic Republic, here was an opportunity to put Arab regimes on the defensive and to promote Iranian support for the Palestinians and their cause—one that resonates throughout the region. For Iran's leaders, it was also a reminder of its coercive power and its ability to unleash its proxies on Arab states as well. While true, it also showed Iran's capacity for miscalculation. Had it known that Israel would be able to devastate militarily not just Hamas but also Hezbollah—and that would trigger events that would lead to the collapse of the Assad regime—Iran's leaders would not have had Hezbollah open its front against Israel. Assad's demise dramatically weakens

Iran's "axis of resistance" and represents a strategic defeat for Iran and its proxies—even if it is too soon to grasp the full implications of their losses.

Whether with its nuclear program or its use of proxies, Iran has the power to provoke and promote instability in the region. But Iran's trouble-making is not limited to the Middle East. It has been responsible for killing dissidents in Europe, targeting US officials and expatriate

Iranians in America, acts of terror elsewhere internationally, and now is providing the Russians with drones and missiles to carry out their aggression against Ukraine.

Iran has consistently opposed the United States' interests, friends, and military presence in the Middle East, and this is far from a new stance. In fact, Iran has been threatening US interests for a long time and damaging American presidents for nearly the entirety of the Islamic Republic's existence. Its taking of American hostages in 1979 contributed a great deal to Jimmy Carter's defeat by Ronald Reagan in 1980.

The point worth noting is that the Islamic Republic has been hostile to the United States since its creation, and it remains so today. As Suzanne Maloney points out, every president since Jimmy Carter has basically tried the same approach to Iran—penalize and try to negotiate—and none has succeeded in fundamentally altering Iran's behavior.[5] She argues for an end to illusions in dealing with Iran. While I generally agree, I see some distinctions among approaches of different administrations and believe that some lessons can be drawn from them in applying more effective statecraft toward Iran. With that in mind, what follows is an overview of each administration's approach to Iran from Carter onward. Having been a part of several of these administrations, I will offer greater detail of those administrations, with an eye toward distilling key lessons.

The Policies of US Administrations toward Iran: From Carter to Biden

Jimmy Carter hoped that after the revolution in Iran, the United States would be able to work with the new regime. At one point, his national security advisor, Zbigniew Brzezinski—who had taken a hard line in trying to save the Shah and even favored a military coup after his fall—met in Algiers with the head of the Iranian Provisional Government, Mehdi Bazargan.[6] The aim of the meeting was to forge understandings and develop relations with the new Iranian leadership. But at a time when there was a division between the new provisional government, seeking to establish the means to govern, and

Ayatollah Khomeini with his concept of a revolutionary regime, the meeting was interpreted as a threat by those around the Ayatollah. Their suspicion of the United States had deepened, especially in the aftermath of the Shah arriving in the United States for medical treatment. They saw Washington as a threat to the revolution, with the United States plotting to restore the Shah to power.

That was the context in which the Brzezinski–Bazargan meeting took place on November 3, 1979. The following day, several hundred students loyal to Ayatollah Khomeini took over the American embassy in Tehran and seized American hostages—who were then held until the end of the Carter presidency.

Carter, whose commitment to human rights made him ambivalent about the Shah, was inclined to believe that the change in Iran might be a good thing. For the first several months after the fall of the Shah, Carter was convinced that it was possible to work with the new regime—and Brzezinski's meeting with Bazargan was a reflection of that optimism. The seizure of the hostages changed expectations, but did not end the administration's efforts at negotiating with the regime—the problem was the challenge of determining who represented the regime and could make authoritative decisions and act on them.

While the administration was frustrated in trying to discern that, it would try multiple approaches to affect the Iranian leadership and free the hostages. Carter imposed unilateral penalties (freezing assets), sought to isolate Iran politically by mobilizing international condemnation and punishing it with multinational sanctions, and made a failed effort to rescue the hostages—even as the administration sought to negotiate their release. At times, Carter believed that the United States was close to a deal with Iranian president Bani Sadr, only to realize that Sadr could not deliver. Eventually, the Algiers Accords, mediated by Algeria, were concluded the day before the end of the Carter administration. They produced the release of the hostages and created a special tribunal to unfreeze Iranian assets and resolve commercial disputes. The tribunal still exists, but the accords did not end Khomeini's instinct to humiliate Carter—the Iranians would only release the hostages after Ronald Reagan was sworn in as president on January 20, 1981.

To be sure, the United States did not lift all sanctions, as President Reagan came in with a decidedly tough posture toward the Islamic Republic—not a surprise given the legacy of the hostage crisis. Not only did his administration not lift all sanctions as called for in the Algiers Accords, but it would decisively tilt toward the Iraqis in the war that Saddam Hussein had launched by invading Iran in September 1980. The United States removed Iraq from the state sponsors of terrorism list; provided Iraq $500 million in credits to buy American agricultural products; sold the Iraqis TPQ radars, which provided a major force-multiplier effect on the battlefield; and eventually reflagged oil tankers to protect them from Iranian attacks and permit Iraq to overcome the Iranian effort to block the Iraqi oil trade. Iran was seen as a threat, and the United States was prepared to counter it and show that Tehran would pay a price for its aggressive posture toward America and its regional friends.

But was Iraq really a friend? Only to the extent that it was fighting the Iranians and imposing a very high price on them. Reagan's posture exacerbated the Iranian perception that America was determined to overthrow the Islamic Republic and the revolution. Of course, Khomeini's hostility toward America predated the Reagan administration and was fed by a narrative in which the United States wanted to preserve its dominance in Iran, having blocked the will of the Iranian people with the overthrow of nationalist Prime Minister Mohammad Mosaddegh in 1953.

Nonetheless, while tilting toward Iraq in its war with Iran, Reagan harbored hopes about a relationship with Iran—a factor that was one of the drivers in the Iran–Contra affair. The main factor, of course, was Reagan's desire to get American hostages whom Hezbollah was holding in Lebanon released. When Robert C. "Bud" McFarlane, Reagan's national security advisor from November 1983-December 1985, was approached by Israel with the possibility of creating a connection with moderates in Iran, saying that those moderates were willing to act to get US hostages released, the temptation was too great for Reagan. For him, the best indicator that these were moderates was that they were willing to work with the United States to get the hostages released. That unfortunately blinded him to the reality of what they were peddling: their help for getting the hostages released in return for the United States providing weapons to Iran. Reagan never saw this as an arms-for-hostages deal, only belatedly acknowledging that others came to perceive it that way.

Later in writing his memoirs, Reagan would emphasize that he had much broader strategic aims in mind. He wrote that he had seen a strategic opening with Iran because he believed that the Iranians whom the administration was dealing with—and whom Bud McFarlane would meet in Iran—were of the Iranian elite. Reagan was sure they wanted to reach out to the United

States because, in his words, they wanted to end "the tyrannical theocracy imposed on them by Khomeini," to stop the war with Iraq, and to create a new day in Iran and in the Persian Gulf. He would add, "Here was a bona fide opportunity to shape the future in the Middle East."[7]

But in reality, there was no such an opportunity, and the so-called moderates were, in fact, arms dealers whom the Iranian regime used effectively to try to entice the Reagan administration into providing them arms and possibly ending the American tilt toward Iraq. By 1987, when the United States was reflagging tankers to preserve the oil trade generally, while helping the Iraqis in the process, America would end up sinking Iranian fast boats and naval vessels and destroying Iranian oil platforms. When the United States mistakenly shot down an Iranian civilian airliner—and the Iranians saw the danger of a war with the United States—Khomeini would accept a cease-fire to end the war with Iraq. The Reagan administration had used both hard power and outreach—albeit through dubious Iranian middlemen—both to try to alter Iranian policy and see if a new day was possible with Iran.

Reagan's approach to Iran was unquestionably shaped by the legacy and reality of Iran and its proxy in Lebanon, Hezbollah, holding US hostages. For George H. W. Bush, it was Iran–Contra that shaped the environment and limited options toward Iran. The scandal triggered criminal proceedings because the sale of the arms to the Iranians were off the books, and the proceeds were then given to the Contras in Nicaragua—something that expressly violated laws adopted by Congress. Bush as a result saw the Iranian issue as politically toxic, and the administration did very little toward Iran. At this point, the Iranians were in need of a respite given the high costs of their eight-year war with Iraq.

The Bush administration made no effort at outreach to Iran; its priorities in national security were focused on East–West issues: pursuing German unification in NATO and, after that, reversing Saddam Hussein's invasion and occupation of Kuwait. As the administration built up American forces against Saddam, Iran sent signals that it would stay out of this conflict. That should hardly have come as a surprise, as Saddam Hussein had adopted a posture that the Iranians saw as leading to a conflict with the United States— meaning that Iraq, with whom Iran had just fought an eight-year-long war, would emerge weaker. This was a good thing from the perspective of Iran's leadership, provided, of course, that the United States did not become too strong on its border.

The Clinton administration adopted early on a posture it called "dual containment." It labeled both Iraq and Iran as threats to the region, and, as such, America's policy was to contain them both. But the focus, at least initially, was more on Iraq, beginning with Saddam's assassination plot against George H. W. Bush when he visited Kuwait in 1993. In response, Clinton authorized a strike against Iraq's intelligence headquarters in Baghdad. For much of Clinton's first term, the administration was contending with Saddam's constant game of "cheat and retreat" with inspectors sent into Iraq to implement UN Security Council resolutions requiring the identification and dismantling of all Iraqi capabilities for creating weapons of mass destruction. The administration became preoccupied with what it saw as two imperatives in Iraq: pressing to get access for inspectors and sustaining sanctions so that Saddam would be kept in a box.[b]

Even if Iraq commanded more attention than Iran, dual containment was the policy because Clinton was determined to prevent the trouble-making of both countries in order to create the space for his real priority in the Middle East: peacemaking. The president saw the opportunity to make peace between Israel and Syria and between Israelis and Palestinians. It was the latter conflict in which Iran emerged as a major threat. Increasingly, terror threatened the peace processes—and it was Iran pushing Hamas and Islamic Jihad to carry out those acts of terror.

As the US envoy on Arab–Israeli peace, I was constantly presented with intelligence that showed Iran pressing for new bombings, even at one point offering to provide greater financial rewards if more Israelis could be killed by the "resistance." The attacks were never on military targets.

The Iranian actor driving the terror was the Iranian Ministry of Intelligence and Security. The ministry paid and recruited terror bombers, believing this violence could successfully derail the peace process. Three months after a fanatical right-wing Israeli assassinated Yitzhak Rabin, four Hamas and Islamic Jihad bombs in nine days threatened to undermine the government of Rabin's successor, Shimon Peres. The United States would make strenuous efforts to shore up the Peres government, putting together a summit of peacemakers in Sharm al Sheikh to show the region coming together

---

[b] Both proved problematic, as sanctions did little to actually hurt Saddam, but it impoverished his public, and his blocking of inspectors eventually culminated in 1998 with four days of intensive bombing of sites associated with weapons of mass destruction and command-control. Saddam would allow no inspectors in after that.

to fight terror. In advance of the Israeli elections in late spring 1996, President Clinton and I knew it was essential that there be no more acts of terror in Israel if Peres were to have any chance to win. The administration used multiple channels to the Iranians to convey that America would impose a steep price on them if the terror did not stop. Secretary of State Warren Christopher would also press the Germans to use their influence in Tehran to stop the acts of terror in Israel.

Once again, the logic of penalties and outreach was being applied to the Iranians. (There were no bombings in Israel before the election, but Bibi Netanyahu wound up defeating Peres by a narrow margin, campaigning that the earlier terror had proven there was no peace, and only he could provide security.)

Washington's view of Iran began to change in May 1997, with the surprise election of Mohammad Khatami as president. Here was an avowed reformer who had been overwhelmingly elected in an election in which there was an 80 percent turnout. The potential for change in Iran seemed real, and the administration again began to pursue a quiet approach to outreach. In 1998, the effort at outreach was more public with Secretary of State Madeleine Albright giving a speech in which she said that the United States could "develop with the Islamic Republic, when it is ready, a roadmap leading to normal relations." For America's part, it was ready to explore "further ways to build mutual confidence and avoid misunderstandings."[8] The administration would lift some sanctions, permitting the import of Iranian carpets and almonds as a sign of America's interest in improving relations.

But the Clinton administration's interest in outreach was not something that Khatami was permitted to engage on. While he might call for a dialogue of civilizations and cultures, he was not permitted by Khamenei to engage in a direct dialogue with the United States. The US remained hopeful thanks to Khatami's public posture, which included, at one point, condemning acts of terror against Israelis and saying that it was up to the Palestinians to decide for themselves how to resolve the conflict. But there was a duality of Iran's actual policy, as the administration continued to see the Iranian Ministry of Intelligence and Security trying to unleash acts of terror. In addition, the United States also began to pick up increasing signs that Iran was covertly developing its nuclear program—a reality that led the Israelis to flag their concerns in their discussions with the administration.

Just as the Carter administration found that Barzargan and later Bani Sadr were potentially open to doing deals with the United States but were unable to deliver, so too would the Clinton administration find that Khatami could not act on public and private signals he sent to the United States—and US outreach led to no responsiveness.

With George W. Bush, circumstances changed after 9/11. Negotiators for the Bush 43rd administration worked with the Iranians on Afghanistan after the US invasion and set up a conference, which the Iranians participated in, to establish the new Afghan government. However, by 2002, the president was calling out the Iranians and identifying them as part of the "axis of evil". Regime change was the leitmotif of the Bush administration, especially in its first term. States that were sponsors of terror were not going to be tolerated, and the administration was prepared to apply great pressure on them.

After it took the US military three weeks to defeat Saddam Hussein's army—the military force that Iran could not overpower in eight years—Iran was looking to propitiate the Americans. It even made a proposal through the Swiss that would have suspended uranium enrichment and ended Iran's military support for Hezbollah and Hamas, in return for understandings with the United States on normalizing relations with the regime, an end to economic boycotts/sanctions of Iran, and acceptance of Iran having civil nuclear power.[c]

I will have more to say about this proposal later and what it reveals about the Iranian calculus, but the key point here is that the Bush administration did not pick up on the significance of the Iranian proposal. The first term of George W. Bush was dominated by the neo-conservatives in the aftermath of 9/11, who interpreted the proposal as a sign of the desperation and paranoia of the Iranian regime after the United States had removed Saddam. If the regime was, in fact, desperate, why should the administration rescue it? Those closest to President Bush saw negotiations and a possible deal as giving the Islamic Republic a lifeline, and the United States was in the business of changing such regimes, not helping them survive.

Unfortunately for the Bush administration, America's position weakened toward Iran as the United States got bogged down in a terrible sectarian war in Iraq. Grand bargains of the sort that Iran seemed to be suggesting in the fax in 2003 were off the table as America's position weakened. The administration remained loath to engage with Iran, but in Bush's second term, it began to back European diplomacy with the Iranians.

---

[c] The proposal was conveyed in fax from the Swiss ambassador in Iran, Tim Guldimann. A copy of the fax can be found at http://media.washingtonpost.com/wp-srv/world/documents/us_iran_roadmap.pdf.

Shortly after the US presidential election in November 2004, the British, the French, and the Germans—the so-called "EU three"—succeeded in convincing the Iranians to announce a "voluntary suspension" of uranium enrichment. The Iranians declared that they would review their voluntary suspension in three months. For its part, the EU three sought to make the suspension permanent in return for providing both economic and political incentives.

President Bush, following his February trip to Europe at the outset of his second term (with a new secretary of state, Condoleezza Rice, and a new emphasis on diplomacy), authorized not only coordination with the EU three on Iran policy but also permission for them to offer limited incentives to the Iranians on America's behalf. The essence of Bush's new approach was to let the Europeans talk to the Iranians, warn Tehran of the consequences, including sanctions to be imposed if they persisted in their nuclear efforts, and offer limited inducements to the Iranians to cease their program.

Even when the Iranians resumed their conversion of uranium ore to uranium gas (hexafluoride)—a precursor to resuming enrichment—the Bush administration continued its coordination with the Europeans. This showed how much Bush's approach had changed from the first term. Consider that the EU three had warned the Iranians in the summer of 2005 that if they resumed such conversion, it was a red line, and they would stop negotiations. While the Europeans would keep that position for nearly six months, they would subsequently relent and resume talks—and the Bush administration accepted their posture and continued to coordinate with them.

But the administration, with its renewed emphasis on diplomacy, also widened its approach, seeking to build an international consensus on the need to stop Iran's nuclear development and to ensure that Iran would be isolated if it did not cease advancing the program. To that end, Secretary Rice established a regular coordinating forum of six, with the British, French, Germans, Russians, and Chinese taking part. Agreement within that forum helped to produce a decision in the IAEA Board of Governors to refer Iran's non-responsiveness on its nuclear program to the UN Security Council in early 2006 for a discussion on sanctions. To preserve a united front against the Iranians on the issue of punitive sanctions, the administration took a number of steps: first, it did not press immediately for a sanctions resolution; second, when others were ready to support at least limited sanctions, the administration scaled back what it decided to press for to make a UN Security Council resolution possible; third, Secretary Rice announced that the United States would deal directly with the Iranians if they would suspend enrichment activities; and fourth, the administration agreed to support the EU three's incentive package for the Iranians, which included light water reactors for the Iranians in return for a halt to enrichment.

When the Iranians rejected the European offer, claiming it was their right to enrich and they could not be pressured to surrender that right, there was an agreement to move to adopt sanctions. That sanctions resolution—UN Security Council Resolution 1737—was adopted in December 2006. The resolution fell far short of what the Bush administration originally had in mind—i.e., a sanctions resolution that would make doing any business with Iran very difficult. Still, rather than losing the chance to adopt a Chapter VII sanctions resolution, the administration (and the Europeans) agreed to go along with what the Russians and the Chinese were willing to accept. As a result, the resolution's sanctions focused narrowly on individuals and the nuclear- and missile-related industries that could contribute to Iran's enrichment and missile producing capabilities. While narrow, the resolution did establish a precedent of imposing penalties on Iran for refusing to cease its nuclear program. It would be followed by UN Security Council Resolution 1747 in March 2007, which expanded the number of Iranian entities and individuals whose assets would be frozen, and also outlined restrictions on Iran's sale or procurement of conventional arms.

The shift toward emphasizing diplomacy with Iran continued into 2008. Already in 2006, Secretary Rice had crossed a threshold—especially given where the Bush administration had been in its first term—when she offered to engage directly with the Islamic Republic if it ceased enrichment. In 2008, with Iran enriching and being sanctioned, the administration announced in the summer that William Burns, the under secretary of state for political affairs, would join the 5+1 talks with the Iranians.[d] Not only did Burns join the others in the talks, meeting directly with the Iranians on the sidelines, but the administration joined a new proposal that was made to the Iranians—one that repeated the offer of incentives if Iran would stop enrichment and introduced the element of a "freeze for a freeze" in which, if the Iranians would halt any additional enrichment, the United States would freeze sanctions where they were and not add new ones.

Once again, the Iranians would reject any halt to enrichment, even for inducements. By the end of the Bush administration, its approach to Iran

---

[d] These were the five permanent members of the UN Security Council plus Germany.

had run the gamut: direct dealings with the Islamic Republic on Afghanistan after 9/11, to rejection of any negotiations with Iran and a preference for regime change, to coordination with others dealing with Iran but no direct talks, to joining others meeting Iran but no strictly bilateral settings for talks. The duality of pressure and engagement may have tilted much more toward pressure in Bush's approach, but it followed the earlier logic of penalties and outreach or engagement. In the end, for Bush, it proved no more promising than earlier efforts at outreach and engagement.

During his campaign for the presidency, Barack Obama spoke of engagement with even rogue regimes. He criticized the Bush administration for not being willing to talk and made clear that there would be outreach in his presidency. Unlike Bush, who saw engagement as a possible reward, or tied to rewards, Obama saw engagement as a way to reassure those who might be highly suspicious of US motives regarding regime change as the objective.

Upon becoming president, engagement was a lodestar for the Obama administration. I began in the administration in the State Department with a responsibility for developing policy toward Iran, co-chairing an interagency group given that responsibility.

I saw engagement as a useful tool for building pressure on Iran from two different standpoints. First, it would allow the Obama administration to correct an impression that internationally had taken hold—i.e., that it was the Bush administration's reluctance to engage the Iranians directly that was the source of the problem, not Iran's behavior. It mattered little that in reality Bush had evolved in the second term because that was not perceived to be the case around much of the globe. By broadcasting America's readiness to engage with the Iranians, the Obama administration shifted the onus for no negotiations to them. Second, I knew that dealing directly with the United States would roil elite politics in Iran, especially given the split within the Iranian elite between those hardliners who always opposed talking to the United States and the more pragmatic elements who saw understandings with the United States as crucial for relaxing conditions internationally and domestically. Since the Supreme Leader, Ali Khamenei, was always skeptical of dealing with America, the administration knew that its offer to talk would create pressures and splits within the regime.

In other words, America's outreach to produce direct talks was both genuine and instrumental. Obama genuinely believed that direct diplomacy was necessary to stop, or at least slow, the Iranian nuclear program. He also understood that diplomacy gave leverage to the United States, particularly because America gained both greater international support and enlisted others to pressure Iran to talk to the administration. The net effect of the approach was to put the Iranians on the defensive for resisting direct talks with the United States.

To signal to the Iranians that the United States was not pursuing regime change, the administration consciously decided to refer to Iran as the Islamic Republic in the 2009 Nowruz (New Year) message—implying America's acceptance of it. President Obama presented the message in a videotape, and the essence of the message was about outreach. While observing that the United States and Iran had long-standing differences, the president addressed Iran's leaders, saying that "in this season of new beginnings," his administration was "committed to diplomacy that addresses the full range of issues before us, and to pursuing constructive ties among Iran, the United States and the international community. This process will not be advanced by threats. We seek instead engagement that is honest and grounded in mutual respect."[9]

The message was followed up by William Burns—who remained as the under secretary of policy in the State Department—being sent again to take part in the 5+1 talks on Iran's nuclear program, but this time, unlike previously, with an explicit mandate to hold bilateral side-discussions with his counterpart. But these were not the kind of bilateral meetings Obama had in mind. He wanted an authoritative channel tied directly to the Supreme Leader. Following several internal discussions over which Obama presided, he made the decision to send a secret letter to Ali Khamenei, the Supreme Leader, in which he proposed setting up a private channel for serious discussions.[e]

The Obama letter would go through multiple drafts before being finalized. While acknowledging the differences between the two countries and expressing America's desire to overcome them, the letter proposed establishing a private channel for discussions between representatives of the president and the Supreme Leader. The administration sought a private channel to allow for frank discussion without a need for public posturing.

---

[e] Because of Iran–Contra, there has been a suspicion in different US administrations about whether secret approaches that would be received from Iranians were really authoritative. In the first several months of the Obama administration, I would receive multiple messages, ostensibly from those representing the Iranian regime, wanting to open a channel. Always, they would suggest that much wider understandings would be possible with Iran if a channel was created. All these approaches would be shared with the White House, and they actually contributed to the decision to do the presidential letter.

The full range of issues would be on the table, but the most immediate one was the Iranian nuclear program. Susan Rice, US ambassador to the UN, gave the letter to her Iranian counterpart, who conveyed it to the Supreme Leader.

We would hear nothing for over a month, and when we finally got a response, it was a long, meandering letter—offering a litany of historical grievances about what the United States had done to Iran. However, toward the end of the letter, the Supreme Leader expressed a willingness to consider such a channel. The language was qualified and couched in skepticism, but he seemed to be agreeing to establish such a channel.

We would have several small meetings at the White House to discuss the response to the letter, how to operationalize the channel, and who would represent President Obama. We sent a response to the Supreme Leader's letter shortly before the Iranian election in June. A response from Ali Khamenei never arrived. Instead, as the demonstrations in Iran against what the public perceived to be a stolen election brought several million people to the streets of Tehran and other cities, the Supreme Leader in a Friday sermon publicly revealed that he had received a letter from the president. However, he talked about it in the context of charging the United States with perfidy, as he accused the US of offering to talk to Iran's leadership even as he claimed it was behind the protests.

The United States was not behind the protests; in fact, the cautious US response to the demonstrations in Iran triggered criticism that the American interest in engagement was the reason the Obama administration was so tepid in reaction to the Iranian protests and the regime's crackdown that ensued. While it is true that there was a strong desire to engage the Iranians—especially because President Obama was convinced that if the United States could not alter the path of Iran's nuclear program, Israel would act militarily against it—Obama feared that it would trigger a regional war into which the United States would inevitably be drawn. But that was not the reason for the low-key response. In fact, I was called into the Oval Office for a meeting on the Saturday morning following the election. The president wanted to discuss how we should respond. He wanted to show support for the demonstrators and for the principle of peaceful protest, but he also wanted to be sure that what we were doing would be helpful, not unintentionally hurtful, to them.

At this time, we were hearing from those associated with the Green Movement—the protest movement—in and outside of Iran. Those within

Iran were conveying to us that the regime was trying to paint them as being tools of the Americans, and our public posture needed not to play into their hands. Those outside of Iran wanted a forceful American reaction, including with threats against the regime. The views of those on the inside affected my advice which was, "Let's emphasize that the world is watching; that Iranians are expressing themselves and must have the right of peaceful protest; and that a violent response by Iran's leaders can only discredit them." Obama took my advice.

In other words, the US posture was not shaped by the administration's desire for engagement or the fact that we had not yet heard a response from the Khamenei to our second letter. On the contrary, I argued in this meeting that the fact that Khamenei had publicized the president's first letter, and was suggesting this was another example of America's duplicity, was a clear signal that he had no intention of going ahead with a channel any time soon—and President Obama agreed.[f]

In the context of the crackdown in Iran, particularly after the killing of 21-year-old Neda Agha-Soltan on June 20, 2009, eight days after the election, the administration did begin to ratchet up its rhetoric. Talk of sanctions did not begin immediately. But it is worth noting that prior to the Iranian election, Obama told newly elected Prime Minister Benjamin Netanyahu during his visit to Washington in May, that if the engagement approach did not bear fruit by the end of the year, the United States would switch to a sanctions approach and impose penalties on Iran for its nuclear program.

In fact, because of the ongoing protests in Iran and the crackdown, the administration could have begun to promote sanctions much earlier, even during the summer. But Mohammad ElBaradei, then the head of the IAEA, came to the administration in July and explained that the fuel plates for the Tehran Research Reactor—a reactor that the United States had built during the Eisenhower administration and that produced medical isotopes—needed replacing. The United States had stopped providing the plates, and Argentina had begun to do so but could no longer. The Iranians had now gone to the IAEA to explain that the supply of these plates was nearly exhausted; the implication was that if the IAEA could not provide an alternative supply, Iran would start enriching to 20 percent in order

---

[f] In retrospect, I think my advice was wrong—we should have been much tougher and made the regime fear the consequences of a crackdown. We needed to raise the cost of what it was doing, especially because the regime was going to charge the protesters with being our tools regardless of what we did.

to produce these plates.[g] ElBaradei informed the Obama administration of this, and Bob Einhorn and Gary Samore came up with the idea of offering the Iranians an alternative supply of the fuel plates in return for using what amounted to 80 percent of their existing stockpile of 5-percent-enriched uranium to provide the feeder material for the plates.[h]

The Einhorn–Samore proposal was simple and would mean that Iran would deplete most of its accumulated enriched uranium for a genuine civilian purpose, meaning that it would not have sufficient material even for one bomb. The administration got Russian support for this approach, and ElBaradei agreed to propose it to the Iranians. Perhaps, because it was the IAEA presenting it, with Russian support, Iran's president Ahmadinejad agreed in principle to the proposal with ElBaradei. In follow-on negotiations between the 5+1 and the Iranians, Ahmadinejad faced resistance in Iran, could not deliver, and the deal fell apart in November 2009. It was in the aftermath of the collapse of the deal that President Obama decided that, having made a real effort at engagement and even having offered a creative solution that did not require an Iranian concession, it was time for a more punitive approach, especially given the ongoing advance of the Iranian nuclear program. As a result, the administration shifted to producing a new UN Security Council resolution that would impose much greater penalties on the Iranian economy than Resolutions 1737 and 1747.

Diplomatically, that meant a full-court press to gain support from the Russians and the Chinese not only to ensure that there was no veto in the UN Security Council, but also to demonstrate that the Iranians were truly isolated. While the Russians and the Chinese were not prepared to go as far as the United States on imposing a price, they too had supported the Tehran Research Reactor deal and were frustrated by the Iranian acceptance and then rejection of it. They too were surprised and were not prepared to defend the Iranians when the United States shared its discovery of a new covert enrichment site at Fordow—a violation of the nuclear non-proliferation treaty's reporting requirement of the development of a nuclear site. And the Chinese in particular were concerned that Iran's continuing march toward

---

[g] Twenty percent enrichment is the dividing line between low and highly enriched uranium, so such enrichment would move Iran much closer to producing weapons-grade fissionable material.

[h] Einorn and Samore had the lead on proliferation issues in the Obama Administration, with Einhorn at the State Department and Samore at the National Security Council and the White House. Since the Iranians were saying they were enriching only for civilian purposes, the logic was "Okay, you provide the low enriched material as the source and an outside supplier will fabricate the fuel plates out of that."

a nuclear weapon could trigger Israeli military strikes against the Iranian nuclear infrastructure—a concern that the United States shared and played on with China. While it would take until June 2010 to adopt UN Security Council Resolution 1929, the Obama administration succeeded in imposing real restrictions on Iranian banking, financial, and insurance transactions—limiting Iran's ability to do business internationally. It did not specifically prevent the sale of Iran's oil, but it laid the predicate for doing so by raising the connection between oil sales and the advance of Iran's nuclear program. At the very end of the year, Europe made the decision to boycott Iranian oil. Since Europeans, unlike the United States, were big buyers of Iranian oil, this made the sanctions in Resolution 1929 far more impactful.

Throughout 2010 and into 2011, the administration was dealing with another issue, involving three young Americans from Berkeley who decided to hike along the Iraq–Iran border, crossed an unclearly marked area into Iran, and were imprisoned. I would spend a great deal of time with the families of Sarah Shourd, Shane Bauer, and Joshua Fattal as we worked to free them. There were many who offered help internationally, but only the Omanis—and specifically Salem Ismaili and his boss the Sultan Qaboos—delivered. Salem had visited me in 2009, laying out an agenda he said the Iranians had agreed to for talks. While the agenda seemed promising, it was like several others that were all conveyed indirectly, and we had no reason to believe that any were authoritative. Indeed, it was these competing probes that contributed to the decision to send the first presidential letter to the Supreme Leader. After the Omanis were able to get the three hikers released, we accepted that Sultan Qaboos was an effective channel to the Supreme Leader.

Given that, the president decided that we should send a message through Qaboos to Ali Khamenei, and I was sent, along with Puneet Talwar, secretly to Oman to deliver the message.[i] I told Qaboos that we had come because President Obama wanted to establish a quiet, authoritative channel of discussions with the representatives of the Supreme Leader; that President Obama did not know if an agreement on the nuclear issue was possible but he wanted to determine whether it was; that to that end, he was prepared to engage in good faith talks with the Iranians, provided the talks were with authorized representatives of the Supreme Leader; and that we were prepared to accept an Iranian civil nuclear program so long as it could not

---

[i] Puneet accompanied me, but it was largely left to me to craft the message.

be converted into a military one. I concluded by saying that the president was serious about finding a diplomatic outcome if that was possible, but we needed to make sure that his willingness to talk was not misread by the Iranians: if the Iranians were not prepared to accept only a civil nuclear program, the United States would take whatever actions necessary, including military, to prevent Iran from acquiring nuclear weapons.

Qaboos said that he understood us, that he believed this was a good approach and that a deal would be possible. He understood the consequences of not reaching an agreement and would make sure that the Supreme Leader received the message as I had conveyed it. I told him that once we had a response, President Obama would want to do a secure call with him.

There would, in fact, be two secure calls between the president and Qaboos before a genuine back channel would be set up and take place in Oman. Discussions began in 2012, but the talks did not get serious until after Hassan Rouhani was elected in 2013 and the Iranians showed much more interest in reaching an understanding.[j]

The back channel would produce, by the end of 2013, an interim agreement—the Joint Plan of Action (the JPOA) —which would freeze the Iranian nuclear program and have the Iranians dilute their enriched material to 20 percent, thus reducing it below HEU. For America's part, it would freeze any additional sanctions and also relieve some existing sanctions, providing the Iranians about $4 billion over the life of the JPOA. Why an interim deal rather than what came to be known as the JCPOA, which was achieved about 18 months later? The Iranians argued that they needed to show that something could be achieved first to make it possible to achieve a longer-term understanding on their nuclear program. Obama saw merit in the deal because it was both freezing the nuclear program and actually reversing the enrichment to 20 percent—something that Israeli Prime Minister Netanyahu had declared was a red line for Israel.

There was a significant concession that the administration would make in the JPOA—as it acknowledged that the negotiations on the follow-on agreement would be about the scope of Iran's enrichment capability. While technically not acknowledging an Iranian right to enrich, the administration had agreed that the next negotiations would be about how much enrichment would be acceptable.

---

[j] I left the administration in December of 2011, and Rouhani had run saying he would engage in diplomacy to end the sanctions that were costing the Iranians so much.

In the first term of the Obama administration, our internal discussions had always assumed that as our very last concession in such talks, we would accept a small, symbolic enrichment facility in return for a dramatic scaling back of the size of the Iranian nuclear infrastructure. The trade-off would be acceptable because Iran would be demonstrably giving up the capability that could give it an option for going for a weapon. The shift embodied in the JPOA reflected the judgment of the negotiators that a deal was possible to constrain the Iranian nuclear program but only if the United States conceded on enrichment in return for very intrusive verification means. Effectively, the size of enrichment for verification trade-off assumed that the combination of a partially scaled back Iranian program with intrusive monitoring would provide the United States plenty of early warning if the Iranians decided to cheat and go for a weapon.

The JCPOA embodied this trade-off. It constrained the program for 15 years and gave to the IAEA access to monitor the assembly of centrifuges and to every step of the fuel cycle process—from uranium mining to conversion of uranium ore, to yellowcake, and to the enrichment itself. Plus, it reduced the stockpile of enriched uranium from nearly 12,000 kilograms to 300, or less than one bomb's worth—and all of the excess had to be shipped out of the country. Combined with the shrinking of the number of active centrifuges from nearly 20,000 to roughly 5,000, the Obama administration felt confident that it would have close to a one year warning time if the Iranians sought to break out to producing weapons-grade fissionable material. While true, critics made many arguments: after 10 years, limited production of advanced centrifuges could begin; snapback sanctions would also lapse after 10 years; all the quantitative and qualitative limits on the program (though not verification protocols) ended in 2030—meaning at that point the combination of being able to enrich to any level, including weapons grade, and the sheer size of the infrastructure would mean that Iran was deferring but not giving up the option of a nuclear weapon. What the critics ignored, however, is that the JCPOA was buying up to 15 years, and what mattered was how the United States and others would use this period to enhance deterrence of the Iranians.

But we would never find out because Donald Trump, having declared the JCPOA the worst agreement ever made, was bound and determined to walk away from it. His initial secretaries of state and defense, Rex Tillerson and General James Mattis, were both against leaving the JCPOA, particularly if the Iranians were living up to their obligations and the Intelligence Community said they were doing so. For one year, they persuaded Trump not to leave the agreement, but his threats to do so produced negotiations with British, French, and German allies of the United States—all of whom acknowledged that there did need to be a follow-on agreement that would continue to constrain the Iranian nuclear program. For several months, their representatives negotiated with Brian Hook, who had the Iranian portfolio at the State Department, and from my discussions with Hook and with all the representatives of the EU three, it was clear that they made considerable progress. In spite of that progress, however, Trump made the decision to walk away from the JCPOA in May 2018.

His declared policy was one of "maximum pressure"—which he argued would compel the Iranians to give up more than they had in the JCPOA. While Trump spoke of maximum pressure, he actually did not apply it at the time of his withdrawal from the deal. At the time of the president's withdrawal in May 2018, he granted waivers to eight countries buying Iranian oil—permitting Iran to maintain its oil exports and preserve those revenues. During this year, the Iranians announced that they would no longer respect the limits imposed on them in the JCPOA, but the European countries maintained their commitment to stand by the deal—and while Iran over the course of the year began to transgress some of the limits on the level of enrichment and research and development on advanced centrifuges, these moves were incremental and limited.

This would change in May 2019, when Trump announced that he was revoking the waivers to those countries buying Iranian oil, making them subject to US sanctions should they continue to do so. Ending the waivers dramatically affected Iranian oil sales, cutting back to as little as 100,000 barrels a day.[10] And the Trump administration would take credit for squeezing the Iranians so much so that it meant that Iran was forced to reduce its payments even to its most important proxy, Hezbollah. Brian Hook would tout that Hezbollah had been forced to do its own tin-cup exercise to try to cover its financial needs.[11]

While Iran was being squeezed, it not only did not alter its behavior on its nuclear program, but it also produced an Iranian version of applying maximum pressure against US interests and friends in the region: attaching limpet mines to tankers, increasing harassment of and threats to shipping in the Gulf; unleashing Houthi missile attacks into Saudi Arabia; launching, from their own territory, cruise missiles and drones against Abqaiq, the most important Saudi oil processing facility in the Kingdom; and the shoot-down of an American drone.

Trump's response to these attacks was minimal. He said that the attack on Abqaiq was an attack on Saudi Arabia, not the United States. Similarly, on the threats to shipping in the Gulf, Trump said that the Europeans and others got the oil from there, while the United States did not, so "let them deal with it."[12] As for the destruction of the US drone, he contemplated a retaliation for its downing but ultimately decided against it on the grounds that no American had been killed. If he had a red line on Iran, it was the killing of Americans. It was this that he later used to justify the targeted killing of Qassem Soleimani, the head of the Qods Forces (the action arm of the Revolutionary Guard in the region). For sure, this was a blow to Iran's operations in the region and to Ali Khamenei personally given his ties to Soleimani, but the Iranian nuclear program would continue to gradually advance, unaffected by Trump's pressure.

When Trump sought a meeting with Iranian president Rouhani, he was rebuffed. Trump's claim that with maximum pressure, he would change Iran's nuclear trajectory proved hollow. To be fair, although the Iranians stopped respecting the limits in the JCPOA during Trump's term, they would only begin to scale up dramatically their violations of the agreement once Biden was elected. Only then did their transgressions become much more pronounced in terms of rebuilding their stockpile of enriched uranium, enriching to HEU, including to near weapons-grade at 60 percent, and to deploying many more cascades of advanced centrifuges that are vastly more efficient and capable of enriching HEU much more quickly. (They would do this even in Fordow, where the JCPOA mandated there should be no enrichment.) Moreover, Iran also began to use its proxies more actively and aggressively than before. Yes, this became much more pronounced after the Hamas onslaught against Israel on October 7, 2023, and the subsequent war—but there were signs of this before, especially in places like Iraq.

Trump may have ended the JCPOA without a serious strategy for what could replace it or a game-plan in case the Iranians responded to his maximum pressure policy with counter-pressure of their own, but Biden's approach also proved to be unsuccessful. Iran was more aggressive in the region, and its nuclear program greatly accelerated.

What was Biden's approach? He made clear during his 2020 campaign that he wanted to restore the JCPOA—after all, he argued that it had rolled back the Iranian nuclear program and had been succeeding in preventing an advance. But the administration confronted an early problem: the Iranians were not willing to speak directly to the United States, only to the other members of the 5+1 who had been parties to the JCPOA; what is more, Iran insisted on receiving compensation for the billions it had lost because of the re-imposition of US sanctions under Trump. For its part, Biden did not want to be making concessions to the Iranians while they were violating the terms of the JCPOA.

The Biden administration chose not to make an issue of the Iranians being unwilling to meet directly and agreeing to talk to the United States only indirectly in what amounted to proximity talks. Why not insist that the administration would only deal directly with the Iranians, decrying their unwillingness to meet as an indication of their lack of seriousness? No doubt, because there was a view among some of US partners that the United States had walked away from the JCPOA and that justified some conditions by the Iranians. But that is not the whole story. Within the administration, there was a concern that if the United States could not reach an agreement before the Iranian election in May 2021—while Rouhani was still president and Javad Zarif was still foreign minister—their replacements (who would likely be hardline) might make any deal impossible.[k]

As a result, through the first few months of the Biden administration, there were many meetings in Geneva, and the outlines of a roadmap began to take shape: one in which the United States would take a limited first move to relax some sanctions and the Iranians would then respond by moving step by step back into compliance, in parallel with US moves on lifting sanctions. What seemed to work for both sides did not work for the Supreme Leader; he rejected any such agreement and clearly sent the signal that he wanted to wait for the outcome of the election and then the inauguration of President Ebrahim Raisi.

Raisi, too, was in no rush, and his appointment for foreign minister, Hossein Amirabdollahian, was also in no hurry. His newly appointed negotiator, Ali Bagheri Kani, took his time, and when the indirect meetings resumed in November 2021, Kani signaled that the new conservative Iranian government and its representatives were going to put their own stamp on the talks and their content. They did not embrace the roadmap that had been developed, again emphasizing that compensation from the United States was necessary before talks could move forward. Moreover, they also insisted that the Biden administration must guarantee that its successor would be bound by an agreement should one be reached.

---

[k] A hardline victory for the presidency and in the Parliament was assured when the Guidance Council disqualified nearly all those representing not just reformers but even traditional conservatives—like Larijani, the speaker of the Parliament.

If the United States still hoped to negotiate a trade-off on Iran coming back into compliance with the JCPOA in return for relief on sanctions, Russia's invasion of Ukraine on February 24, 2022, suddenly seemed to dash those hopes. Russia had generally been helpful in the negotiations until this point. This support would stop, as Russia itself became the target of sanctions and was making common cause with Iran—in part to see how to evade sanctions. For the Iranians, it was also a sign that Iran would not only face less of a united front from the 5+1 negotiators, but that Iran need not fear being politically isolated given Russian support and the Chinese tendency to side with Russia.

Still, Iran was under sanctions, its economy was being devalued, and inflation was running over 40 percent a year, which was feeding alienation in Iran—an alienation deepened by a conservative government that seemed to have little clue about what needed to be done to deal with Iran's domestic challenges.

And yet, Iran acted as if it had all the time in the world—perhaps because it was increasing pressure on the administration and the Europeans by enriching to 60 percent, even as Rafael Grossi of the IAEA declared that enrichment to that level had "no justifiable civilian purpose." For their part, the Iranians implied that the enrichment to 60 percent was a response to an alleged Israeli attack against its Natanz facility that damaged a hall where centrifuges were enriching.[13,1]

Other than strong words of criticism, the Biden administration and the Europeans had no meaningful reaction to Iran's enriching to near weapons-grade. But with concern rising about the accumulating amount of Iran's 60-percent-enriched stockpile, Josep Borrell, the foreign policy chief of the EU, would present a new proposal in the summer of 2022. Expectations rose in August that there would be a deal when Borrell presented his proposal, one he described as the last chance, and one that produced an Iranian response that he characterized as "reasonable."[14]

But with Iran, answers are often never final, and the Iranians would subsequently add qualifiers to their response that neither Borrell nor the administration were prepared to accept. Might there have been an agreement if it had not been for the arrest and killing in custody of Mahsa Amini, a 21-year-old Kurdish woman, for not wearing her hijab appropriately—and the subsequent explosion of protests throughout the country under the

---

[1] Iranian State television called the announcement on enrichment "a show of power against terrorist rascality."

slogan of "women, life, freedom?" My guess is that there might still have been an agreement. The Supreme Leader might well have approved a deal which could certainly have eased some of the currency and inflation problems plaguing the country and in a way that might have made Raisi and the hardliners get credit for the improvement. But there was no way that was possible once the country was convulsed by widespread demonstrations with the regime responding brutally, including killings, executions, and mass arrests.

As if that had not been enough, the Iranians then began selling drones to Russia. Under such circumstances, a deal with the Iranians was politically unthinkable for the United States. The reality of Iran continuing to enrich to 60 percent was ongoing and dangerously close to weapons grade. To make matters worse, the Iranians had paid no price for doing it, and given that, there was reason to worry that the Iranians might decide to go ahead and enrich to 90 percent: weapons-grade.

At this time, I was told by senior Israeli security officials that before the Iranians decided to enrich to 60 percent, there had been an internal debate with some in the Iranian elite arguing that enriching to that level risked a dangerous reaction from the United States. When nothing happened, those who had warned of the risks of pressing ahead with the nuclear program were undercut, and their counterparts were strengthened. Again according to these Israeli officials, the Biden administration was well aware of this information about the debate.

I was subsequently told by two senior officials in the Biden administration that at this point, the administration did warn the Iranians both directly and through others that the United States would interpret the Iranian decision to enrich to 90 percent as proof that the Iranians intended to go for a weapon—and Tehran knew (or should have known) that the United States would act to prevent that.

The United States would also warn the Iranians over the increasing aggressiveness of Shia militias in Iraq against the US presence; it had to stop, or there would be consequences. It was in this context that the American approach began to shift to producing understandings without a formal agreement.

In the summer of 2023, Brett McGurk, the Middle East coordinator on the National Security Council staff at the White House, engaged in quiet proximity discussions in Oman and worked out two understandings with the Iranians. According to the first one, the United States would gain the release of five US citizens who had been seized and imprisoned in Iran, and in return, several Iranians in US jails would be released, and $6 billion of Iranian money frozen in South Korean banks would be transferred to an account in Qatar that Iran could use on an item-by-item basis to buy humanitarian goods. According to the second understanding, attacks against US forces in Iraq and Syria would cease, Iran would reduce the amount of 60-percent-enriched uranium in its stockpile (by diluting it) and the Iranians would not enrich to 90 percent. In return, the United States would not enforce sanctions that had precluded China from buying Iranian oil, and US sanctions that prevented Iraq from paying the Iranians for up to $11 billion for the provision of electricity would be suspended to enable payment in installments. Once the second informal understanding was fully implemented, there would then be talks on a possible longer-term arrangement.[15,m]

It was the desire to produce calm by being able to stop and even reduce the buildup of Iran's 60-percent stockpile of enriched uranium—and also stop the attacks on US forces in Iraq—that led the Biden administration to seek these informal understandings. The politics did not permit formal agreements, but the need to change the trajectory of Iranian actions required informal ones. The interesting point is that the Iranians clearly also had an interest in reaching these understandings, and both they and the Biden administration began to fulfill them. Indeed, the IAEA reported that Iran did reduce its 60-percent stockpile; parallel to this, the proxy attacks on US forces in Iraq did, in fact, stop. According to Ali Vaez, talks to build on these understandings were to commence on October 18, 2023—but the Hamas onslaught of October 7th and Iran's unleashing its proxies a week later precluded any possibility of those talks taking place.[16]

Interestingly, after October 7 and Iran's unleashing of its proxies, there were talks again in Oman in January 2024, with the United States seeking to get the Iranians to get the Houthis to stop attacking shipping in the Red Sea and the Gulf of Oman. That clearly did not materialize. Something else did not materialize for the Iranians. They were seeking to be able to draw on the account in Qatar, and that also did not happen, at least at this time. While the United States did not freeze the funds, the process of identifying companies that were cleared to sell humanitarian goods simply did not

---

[m] My discussions with senior officials revealed this.

move—meaning, at that time, that the Iranians were still not able to draw down the money.[17]

Apart from the indirect talks, the Biden administration did signal to the Iranians with the use of force. On January 28, 2024, three American soldiers were killed at Tower 22 in northern Jordan by a Kata'ib Hezbollah drone attack; the US retaliated on a scale not seen before, hitting 85 targets on February 2. True, the administration waited five days before carrying out the attacks, but it hit those it believed were behind the strike on Tower 22, and days later in a targeted hit in Baghdad, the US military also killed senior leader in Kata'ib Hezbollah, Abu Baqir al-Saadi—the person who was believed to be responsible for the attack. The head of the Qods Forces, Esmail Qaani, after the Tower 22 attack, visited Baghdad and told the leaders of the Shia militias "to manage their behavior in a way that will not allow America to engage Iran."[18] On January 30, the head of Kata'ib Hezbollah, Ahmad al-Hamidawi, announced a suspension of attacks following Qaani's visit—and even the US killing of his deputy commander afterward did not produce a response.

Lessons from the Past

Suzanne Maloney is right that nearly all administrations since Carter's tried variations of the penalize-and-engage approach with the Iranians—not necessarily in the same sequence, but using both means to try to affect Iran's policies. No administration succeeded in altering the basic approach of the Islamic Republic toward the United States, but clearly some administrations had more luck than others in getting the Iranians to make at least tactical adjustments in their behavior. Who failed to achieve even tactical adjustments? Carter was probably the most spectacular failure—not only with hostages taken but with their release coming minutes after Carter was out of office. True, the Iranians agreed to mediation through the Algerians and a settlement was reached leading to the release of the hostages, and, as part of the Algiers Accords, the United States lifted the freeze on nearly $8 billion in Iranian assets and committed to ending litigation against Iran.[n]

---

[n] There were five main provisions to the accords: (1) the US would not intervene politically or militarily in Iranian internal affairs; (2) the United States would remove the freeze on Iranian assets and trade sanctions on Iran; (3) both countries would end litigation between their respective governments and citizens, referring them to international arbitration in the Claims Tribunal for

Reagan might get the benefit of the hostages being released after he had become president, but he would breach the Algiers Accords by not acting to terminate all litigation. His administration had a mixed record: he lost 241 US soldiers in Beirut with Hezbollah's bombing of the marine compound at the airport—and Hezbollah was Iran's creation. Moreover, Iran–Contra reflected the Iranians playing on his desire to get the US hostages in Lebanon released, and using the secret talks to get something for Iran—namely, arms. But his tilting toward Iraq in the war and then reflagging oil tankers, sinking Iranian ships, and destroying Iranian oil platforms, ultimately led the Iranians to decide to end the war with Iraq. Clearly, his administration forced the Iranians to, as Khomeini was to say, drink "poison from a chalice" and bring the Iraq–Iran war to an end.

As noted above, George H. W. Bush did not focus on Iran, but he did use different channels to the Iranians to make clear that if the United States used force to expel Iraq from Kuwait, the US military would not engage the Iranians, and they should stay out of any conflict. Tehran sent messages back that they were not a part of this conflict and would do nothing unless attacked. Iran was not invited to the 1991 Madrid Conference, nor were they included in the multilateral working groups that were set up as part of the process it had launched. Though there were some countries in the region who felt that Iran should be included, the Bush administration had little interest in that— and was probably the one administration that did not have an engagement strategy toward Iran. Deterrence yes, engagement no.

With Bill Clinton, the policy of dual containment was followed by a genuine effort at engagement, but there was no Iranian responsiveness. Like Carter who discovered that divisions in the Iranian elite undermined any possibility of agreements, Clinton too found that the hardliners would prevent any Iranian responsiveness to America outreach. George W. Bush avoided engagement in his first term—not even testing the proposal that was transmitted by the Swiss. Fear that the Iranians might be next after the US military removed Saddam produced an Iranian proposal designed to address US concerns and prevent American adoption of regime change in Iran as an objective. The drafter of the Iranian proposal was Sadegh Kharrazi, at the time the Iranian ambassador to France and the son of the Iran's

---

Iran–United States that the accords established; (4) the United States would ensure that US court decisions regarding the transfer of any property of the former Shah would be independent from "sovereign immunity principles" and would be enforced; and (5) Iranian debts to US institutions would be paid.

foreign minister, Kamal Kharrazi. He would describe the thinking behind the faxed letter in a speech he gave in 2007:

> [I]n 2003, there was a wall of mistrust between Iran and America and in any second there was the possibility for an American attack! For that reason with my suggestion the 8th government [Khatami's] wrote a letter to America and announced our agreements with some of America's policies in the Middle East such as peace in Palestine and the need for transformation of Hezbollah of Lebanon to a political party and also making nuclear activities of Iran more transparent."[19]

Ali Bagheri Kani, who became the Iranian nuclear negotiator in Raisi's administration and who has traditionally been a hardliner close to Ali Khamenei, confirmed the reality of this letter and its content in a critique of it in an Ofoq television interview that aired on May 3-4 2020. Much to Bagheri's disdain, he said that Khatami, less than two months after the United States invaded Iraq and overthrew Saddam, offered to force Lebanese Hezbollah to end its anti-American posture and armed resistance against Israel, and transform into a political party.[20] Bagheri made clear that he believed it was fortunate that the Bush administration rejected this effort to reach out to it and address America's concerns.

The Iranians lost their fear of what the United States might do by Bush's second term, and the administration's efforts at sanctions and engagement failed to produce any change in Iran's nuclear or regional posture.° In short, the Bush administration failed to achieve any real objectives it had toward the Iranians, and the same is true of the first Trump administration.

Perhaps one could argue that in both the Bush and the Trump administrations—where pressure more than engagement was the priority—Iran's behavior could have been worse. In Trump's case, the killing of Qassem Soleimani did not set the region on fire as many critics of the administration predicted. Instead, the Iranians hit the al Asad base in Iraq as retaliation—and apparently gave the United States early warning of what they were going

---

° There were meetings between Ambassador Ryan Crocker and General Petraeus with the Iranian ambassador to Iraq who was tied to the IRGC. At one point, American forces also seized five IRGC officers in a raid; their release was worked out by the Iraqi government, and there was some defusing of tensions afterward with the Iranians, but proxy attacks never stopped. American retaliations were limited to going after the Shia militias in Iraq. The Obama administration would use the channel in Iraq to pass tough messages to the Iranians on attacks against US forces in Iraq.

to do via the Iraqis.[21,p] Trump did not respond further, and once again we saw evidence that the Iranians are risk averse when possible—keen to avoid direct conflict with the United States.

Preventing negative actions is important, but it is certainly not the same as getting the Iranians to adjust their behavior or policy in a more favorable direction. One could argue that both Obama and Biden at different points produced some adjustment in Iran's behavior. In Obama's case, the JCPOA produced a scaling back of the Iranian nuclear program and the buying of 15 years; true, the Iranians received what they saw as legitimization of having a large nuclear industry and infrastructure that preserved for them the option of having a nuclear weapon later. And it is also a fact that Iran became even more active and aggressive in the region, especially in Syria, after doing the deal. Similarly, in Biden's case, the nuclear program advanced, but the Iranians were prepared to scale back its 60-percent enrichment and even lean on their proxies in Iraq to stop attacking US positions in Iraq and Syria.

What Obama and Biden had in common was pressure and engagement. Obama helped to produce economic and political isolation as embodied in UN Security Council Resolution 1929 and then in the EU's decision to boycott Iranian oil. Afterward, the United States negotiated and produced the JCPOA. What is interesting is that the Iranians had declared, before the administration pushed to get UN Security Council Resolution 1929 adopted, that they would never negotiate on their nuclear program so long as they were under sanctions. And after the United States literally tripled down on them and the EU boycotted their oil, they negotiated the JPOA and then the JCPOA.

In Biden's case, tough messages in private, especially on enriching to 90 percent and attacks against US forces, led to some tactical adjustments on the Iranian side. To be sure, Iran's leaders saw real gains—effectively, they created a new baseline in enrichment at 60 percent. Even agreeing to dilute and reduce some amount of it still left it as a new baseline. That tends to fit with what Michael Singh has described as the Iranian "feint and advance strategy, by which it agrees to limited deals to stave off pressure" from the United States, the IAEA Board of Governors or the UN Security Council. In Singh's

---

[p] The Iraqi Prime Minister Adel Abdul Mahdi, issued a statement explaining he was warned in advance by the Iranians.

words, these limited deals have the added benefit of "shifting the diplomatic goalposts and cementing the advances Iran has made in contravention of its previous commitments. Tehran then proceeds to ignore even these diluted commitments and move the goalposts further."[22]

So was that what the Iranians were doing with Obama and Biden? The JCPOA was clearly more than feint-and-advance because the Iranians were agreeing to real limits for an extended period of time. The quiet understanding with Biden might more closely fit the feint-and-advance approach, but the understandings did extend beyond their nuclear program to attacks against US forces stopping for several months until after October 7. Put simply, the Iranians did adjust their behavior, but in different ways with the Reagan, Obama, and Biden administrations.

That the Iranians will enter agreements that they think serve their interests makes them no different from anyone else. Indeed, just like anyone else, they will make these agreements for both offensive and defensive reasons, meaning to make gains or prevent losses. And here there is a pattern of Iran making adjustments when the pressure imposes a cost on Iran. With increasing military conflict with the United States near the end of 1987, Khomeini ended the war with Iraq the following year. In the 1990s, when the Europeans threatened sanctions over the killing of dissidents in Europe, the Iranians stopped the assassinations. In 2001, after 9/11, the US invasion of Afghanistan, and the toppling of the Taliban, the Iranians were quick to cooperate with the United States. In 2003, when they thought they were America's next target after Saddam, the Iranians drafted their proposal to address American concerns. In 2013, they negotiated and reached agreements on their nuclear program after saying they would not do so unless sanctions were lifted—and given the economic pressure. The Iranian reaction to both killing of Soleimani and the United States hitting 85 targets after the proxy attack on Tower 22 suggest that the Iranians back off when they think they could face direct conflict and escalation with the United States.

Put simply, the Iranians make rational choices given who they are and what they value. Protecting the regime is by far the first priority. Before turning to what America's objectives should be and the means needed to achieve them, it makes sense to take a closer look at what matters to the Iranian regime and some of the problems it must contend with.

Assessing Iran

There is certainly an Iranian regime with different institutions and factions. In his book *Hidden Iran*, published in 2006, Ray Takeyh focused heavily on the interplay of the factions, which he concluded was the dominant factor in determining Iran's policies.[23] Takeyh no longer believes the conclusion he drew in 2006. Today, he believes that factional interplay is no longer an important factor in shaping Iranian policy because the Supreme Leader, Ali Khamenei has tilted so heavily in favor of hardline groups and forces like the Revolutionary Guard over pragmatic reformers. In fact, until the presidential election to replace Ebrahim Raisi, who had been killed in a helicopter crash, Khamenei had acted to ensure that hardliners would control all the key institutions: the presidency, the Parliament, the judiciary, the Guidance Council, the Assembly of Experts, Expediency Council, etc.[24] Having dominated the political landscape for so long, Khamenei seemed determined to have his worldview and ideology shape the acceptable political boundaries for the future. As Alex Vatanka—a longtime Iran watcher—said, Khamenei "is focused on consolidating control in the hands of very few hardline loyalists that he wants in positions when he eventually dies."[25] And yet, he permitted Masoud Pezeshkian to win in an election in which Pezeshkian was pitted against hardliner Saeed Jalili. During the brief campaign, Khamenei signaled his support for Jalili's views and raised his concern about "America lovers"—a not-so-subtle dig at Pezeshkian, who made clear his desire to end sanctions and his readiness to engage the West.[26]

Why after acting to make sure that hardliners would dominate each institution, would Khamenei allow a "reformer" to run and win the presidential election in July 2024? There are several reasons. First, as I will explain more fully, the decreasing participation in elections undercut an argument that Khamenei has always used to showcase internationally the legitimacy of the Islamic Republic what that lesson is. It's implied, but would benefit from explicitly laying it out. Second, he understood that if the election were stolen, there was a clear risk that anger among the public would erupt again—only now in a context where the public's alienation since the Women, Life, Freedom movement is much deeper and more widespread. Third, Jalili was so extreme that conservatives, who generally share the Supreme Leader's views, felt his governance would be terrible and would inevitably foster greater anger and upheaval within the country. (Many of the supporters of conservative Mohammad Qalibaf—the former Islamic Revolutionary Guard Corps Air Force Commander and speaker of the Parliament—supported Pezeshkian after Qalibaf finished third in the first round of voting and did not make the run-off.) Fourth, Khamenei knew that with conservative hardliners in all the institutions, especially the Parliament, they would oppose any meaningful liberalization that Pezeshkian might pursue—and in any event, he was the ultimate decision-maker.[27,q]

To put this last point in perspective, Ali Khamenei has been the Supreme Leader since his election by the Assembly of Experts on June 4, 1989. For his first few decades in power, Khamenei seemed to favor the role of being an arbiter among the different competing forces in the elite, never letting anyone become too powerful. But over the last several years, he stopped favoring balance; instead, he tilted toward hardline forces, favoring the Revolutionary Guard on the outside and ultra-conservatives on the inside. According to the former Iranian foreign minister Javad Zarif, Khamenei permitted the Revolutionary Guard Corps to call the shots, saying, "In the Islamic Republic, the military field rules," and he had to sacrifice "diplomacy for the military field rather than the field servicing diplomacy."[28,r]

Domestically, it was no different. Khamenei acted to weaken reformers and pragmatists in favor of ensuring the dominance of hardline views and groups—even disqualifying Hassan Rouhani as a candidate to remain in the Assembly of Experts and vetoing Ali Larijani's candidacy for the presidency twice. Because Khamenei had criticized Rouhani during his presidency for his government's "trust" of the United States and Western countries and for his reformist agenda, it was no surprise that he denied him the right to be elected to stay in the Assembly of Experts. But Larijani was a different story; he was always seen as a conservative, especially when compared to the reformers, but he was also a pragmatist. That someone like Larijani, who came out of the Islamic Revolutionary Guard Corps and was speaker of the Parliament for a decade, proved not to be hardline enough, says a lot about what Khamenei wants the future leadership to be. That said, letting Masoud Pezeshkian win is a reminder that Khamenei is prepared to adjust when he thinks the circumstances require it.

q Karim Sadjadpour also argues that Pezeshkian is not actually a real reformer. As Sadjadpour conveyed to me, Pezeshkian "self identifies as a 'principalist'—someone committed to the ideological principles of the revolution—and has been clear about his devotion to the Revolutionary Guards and Ayatollah Khamenei ... None of his words or conduct the last four decades suggests he is a liberal reformer."

r In a leaked videotape, Zarif referred to how Qassem Soleimani, the head of the Qods Force, undermined the nuclear deal and adopted policies toward Syria's war that damaged Iran's interests.

Having served so long as the Supreme Leader and having spoken and written a great deal, Khamenei's worldview matters—and he clearly wants it to inform present and future Iranian policies.[s] One thing is clear: he has been remarkably consistent in his views over the years.

Indeed, his views of the United States show no sign of change or moderation. He is convinced that America's leaders are determined to dominate Iran and the region. More than 20 years ago, he said, "The United States government has not lost its insatiable greed for domination of our country."[29] It is the greed, the quest for domination that defines the United States in Khamenei's eyes and is why he refers to America as "the arrogant power." In 2022, he explained that America has a problem with the Islamic Republic because the US can no longer do what it thought it could—namely, "use the abundant resources available here without fear or worry."[30] Moreover, its real problem with Iran, according to Khamenei, is that the Islamic Republic leads the forces of resistance, not submission, in the region—and he declared that, "Resistance means refusing to submit to US coercion, greed, and interference."[31]

Earlier in 2015, to show that he was not walking away from his view of America or his ideology by accepting the JCPOA, Khamenei said after its achievement, "if we want to give an example of who [the] enemy is in the outside world, we should refer to the regime of the United States of America." He explained that "by 'enemy' we mean global arrogance ... whose existence depends on dominating others, interfering in their affairs and possessing their financial and vital resources."[32]

So why did he accept the JCPOA? He answered this question saying, "The reason we entered into negotiations and made some concessions was to lift sanctions."[33] Khamenei may have accepted the JCPOA to get sanctions lifted, but there would be no détente with the United States. That would mean opening Iran to US cultural influences—something that led Patrick Clawson to observe that the Supreme Leader worries more about a cultural invasion than a military invasion, meaning that "he fears Hollywood more than he fears Washington."[34] While that may be an exaggeration, Karim Sadjadpour has also written about Khamenei's fear of a Western political and cultural intrusion and its impact on Iranian society—ranging from playing on differences within the Iranian elite to undermining traditional society to fostering "ethnic and sectarian unrest."[35]

---

[s] While he is 85 (as of 2024) and from time to time has apparently had health problems, his public events now are much more frequent, and no one knows how much longer he will be the Supreme Leader—but assuming it will only be for a short while is probably not wise.

In other words, Khamenei wants to safeguard Iran from US influence. He may countenance negotiations as necessary at times but feels the need to warn against the consequence of making concessions to the United States, and of the danger of surrendering Iran's revolutionary principles. Doing so will, he believes, feed the appetite of the United States to demand more and more. Note his words: "If the officials of a country get daunted by the bullying of the arrogant powers, and make concessions to those powers, these concessions will never come to an end!" He added, "They will never stop obtaining concessions from you through pressure and intimidation, and you will be forced to retreat from your values and principles step by step! Indeed, the end to US pressure and intimidation will only come when Iranian officials announce they are ready to compromise Islam and their popular government of the Islamic Republic, and the United States may bring to power in the country whoever it wants." Khamenei made this statement after the Bush administration had rejected the proposed concessions in the fax presented by the Swiss.

This was his answer to those who wanted to address US interests in the region. Having signed off on the fax proposal–no doubt grudgingly– Khamenei here was essentially saying to those that had argued for this proposal to the Americans that "I told you so" and it was a mistake.

Circumstances could lead Khamenei to make tactical adjustments, but never to deviate from his revolutionary principles. In one speech in 2022, he said, "Of course, dear brothers, dear sisters an important point is to remain revolutionary," explaining that, "Revolutionary slogans are to the advantage of the country ... Contrary to what some people say—that revolutionary slogans and revolutionary ideals are a source of trouble for the country— ... [they] are a cure for the problems."[36] Undoubtedly, the "some people" were those who were more pragmatic, who wanted to deal with domestic problems like the economy and the alienation of the public—for example, Rouhani and Zarif, who saw agreements with the United States helping to ease Iran's problems by ending sanctions and limiting confrontation with the United States and the West. For Khamenei, they were the problem—for they would let revolutionary zeal die, and that would threaten the Islamic Republic.

Here is the explanation for Khamenei's tilt to the hardliners. The pragmatists were a danger because they would threaten the survival of the revolution, they would concede to the United States and the West, grant them access to Iranian society, and fail to build a "resistance economy"—and there was no need to accommodate the Americans and the West because they were losing power. In Khamenei's words, "The US as an arrogant power has become weak and is continuously becoming weaker." He added that the "Western Arrogant Powers are becoming weak. This is not a slogan. It is a reality. It is something they are saying that the indicators showing the authority of the US is declining."[37]

For Khamenei, Afghanistan was an indicator that the United States could no longer dictate change in other countries as it once had. And there was the emergence of other powers—China and Russia—that seemed to show that Iran had options.[38]

None of this meant that Khamenei was unaware of economic problems or the loss of belief in the system and its ideology; in his speeches, he is constantly imploring the need for greater development and self-sufficiency, dealing with inflation ("expenses are high, especially regarding some food items and high housing prices" and "people see these things"), and the need to infuse the youth with the proper education.[39,t]

But it is to suggest that he is incapable of dealing with the problems if it means altering his basic principles. He may make foreign and domestic policy adjustments as when he thinks the circumstances require it. Allowing Rouhani to win the election in 2013 and Pezeshkian in 2024 no doubt reflected Khamenei's awareness that getting sanctions relief and offering a hint of liberalization could ease the mood domestically. But he will not yield on anything he considers to be fundamental. For example, giving in on the hijab after the killing of Mahsa Amini by the morality police was a bridge too far. As Karim Sadjadpour wrote two months after Amini's death,

> Mr. Khamenei's ruling philosophy has been shaped and reinforced by three notable authoritarian collapses: The 1979 fall of Iran's monarchy, the 1991 dissolution of the Soviet Union and the Arab uprisings of 2011. His takeaway from each of these events has been never compromise under pressure and never compromise on principle. Whenever Mr. Khamenei has faced a fork in the road between reform and repression, he has always doubled down on repression.[40]

In essence, Ali Khamenei is not indifferent to domestic challenges but will not make fundamental concessions on them; he may concede tactically

---

t This is almost a year after the killing of Mahsa Amini and these are his answers.

on the outside if he thinks it either can avoid military confrontation that could threaten the Islamic Republic's survival or if he thinks it can offer economic benefits that eases public alienation because life becomes easier. Buying off the public with economic improvement is acceptable; making any concessions on political liberalization is not.

If nothing else, this suggests that Iran's economic vulnerabilities or other domestic or structural problems that affect the quality of life can be sources of leverage used to alter Iran's behavior at least tactically. The vulnerabilities are real. To begin with, there is deep public alienation, and it has been manifested even before the Women, Life, Freedom protests.

Since 2017, nearly every year has been marked by widespread protests in Iran, typically triggered by economic concerns or grievances. In late 2017, protests erupted in the traditionally conservative city of Mashhad over high prices of basic goods—police used water cannons and arrests to break up the demonstrations there, but the protests then spread to 21 other cities with chants against corruption and the leadership. The protests lasted for several weeks. Abbas Milani, a specialist on Iran at Stanford University, explained that deep frustration triggered these protests: the "gradual grind of double-digit unemployment, no prospects of economic improvement, the remarkable cronyism, recent publication of budget figures that show millions of dollars have been given to religious endowments that have done virtually nothing to contribute, all of that created a tipping point."[41] What seemed to make these protests different is that they took place in conservative cities and rural areas—traditionally known for their support for the regime. It took the Islamic Revolutionary Guard Corps deploying to three provinces to quell the riots.

In 2019–2020, riots that became known as Bloody November were triggered by increases ranging from 50 to 200 percent in fuel prices. These protests also began peacefully but quickly spread around the country, involving up to 104 cities, and were put down brutally, with reports that more than 300 protesters were killed. In 2021, riots were triggered initially by protests against water shortages and later by President Ebrahim Raisi's reduction of food and fuel subsidies—once again, the internet was shut down, arrests were made, and many protesters were killed, although not as many as in 2019–2020. All of this was a prelude to what happened in the aftermath of the killing of Mahsa Amini while in custody. The protests covered the country, were active for months, were not centrally organized—both a strength and a weakness of the movement—and were led largely by young people and women of all ages.

The nature of the crackdown and the brutalization of women seemed to provoke greater anger toward the regime and sustain the protests across wide swaths of Iranian society. According to the March 2024 UN Fact-Finding Mission Report on the Iranian crackdown, the regime would kill more than 550 people when putting down riots, execute dozens more, and arrest more than 20,000—with the average age of those arrested being 15. The UN report spoke of torture and widespread sexual abuse, with rapes of young women and men.[42,u]

The level of alienation is deep and is reflected in how the song "Baraye" ("because of" in Farsi) became the anthem of the protest movement, is sung by schoolgirls, and has become part of chants at major sporting events in Iran—along with chants of death to the dictator. While the regime did release over 20,000 from the jails, there has been no relaxation on the requirement to wear the hijab, with women being fined or losing jobs, or restaurants or shops forced to pay a fine if they serve women who are not wearing one.

Alienation is also reflected in the declining level of voter participation in Iranian elections. Partly, that results from the elimination of any candidate who is not a hardliner. Turnout during the March 2024 elections for the Parliament and the Assembly of Experts was the lowest ever, with the state reporting 41 percent turnout—and critics all saying that even this low figure was inflated. The low turnout came despite Khamenei's repeated calls for people to vote, saying at one point, "If the elections are weak, everyone will be hurt. I am not accusing anyone, but I remind everyone that we should look at the elections from the perspective of our national interests."[43]

He has always used Iran's elections to showcase the Islamic Republic's legitimacy; not surprisingly, he and the regime always accompany the elections with a campaign exhorting people to vote. But the boycott in this election reflected the disqualification of all reformist candidates—so much so that former president Khatami chose not to vote. He referred to the elimination of any candidates besides those who were chosen, saying that such selection "undermines the nation's confidence in the system."[44] The contrast with when Khatami ran, when 80 percent turned out to vote, is revealing. At that time, Iranians had hope. Now frustration has replaced hope, and Khamenei's decision to allow Pezeshkian to run and win indicates that the Supreme Leader understands that.

---

u In the report, human rights groups are cited saying those arrested actually numbered around 60,000.

This reality helps to contribute to a climate in which missteps by the regime can easily provoke new waves of protests and demonstrations. True, the regime seems to believe it can handle them, but in reality, it never knows when the next outbreak can happen. Its pre-emptive arrests and warnings in September 2023 prior to the anniversary of Mahsa Amini's death reflected its expectations that it would face new rounds of protests—and it was right, but its pre-emptory actions did not prevent protests around the country.

Aside from poor governance, favoritism of the hardliners, and corruption, economic problems will also continue to perpetuate popular unhappiness. Even though there is leakage in the sanctions regime, with the Biden administration choosing to turn a blind eye to Iranian oil exports going to China (which at the time of this writing accounts for 91 percent of Iranian oil exports), the economy remains bedeviled by structural problems.[45] In fact, while the unemployment rate has dropped from double-digit to single-digit figures, inflation remains roughly 40 percent, the currency keeps being devalued and is riddled with multiple exchange rates, contributing to capital flight, and per capita incomes are declining.[46] Bijan Khajehpour points out that there has been an accelerating loss of purchasing power, with GDP per capita from March 2023 - March 2024 being 28 percent lower than the year prior.[47,v] Relieving sanctions would improve economic performance, in part because investment is desperately needed to generate growth and sanctions continue to preclude most foreign investment, and in part also because access to consumer goods would be more plentiful and far cheaper.

But sanctions relief is not going to happen if there is no deal on Iran's nuclear program, and this program is headed in the wrong direction. And even if there was sanctions relief, it is not a panacea. For one thing, the international banking system would still be reluctant to work with Iran's banks given their need for reform that adopts and then acts on anti-laundering and anti-terror provisions. So long as Iranian banks directly and indirectly finance terror groups, little will be possible, especially because financial institutions internationally will fear doing business with them.[w]

Put simply, sanctions relief would help, but it would not solve distortions, mismanagement, and misplaced priorities in the Iranian economy. In the

---

[v] The fiscal year for Iran is tied to their new year.

[w] The Financial Action Task Force, an international body for countering terror, engaged Iran for several years but eventually gave up, as Iran's definition of resistance meant it would keep using its banks to finance groups that many in the international community regard as terrorist. This was an issue that Pezeshkian raised in the campaign and argued must be addressed. Will he actually be able to do so if it requires giving up the financing of Hamas and Hezbollah? Probably not.

words of Iranian economist Hossein Assadi Nia, "Our problem is internal and caused by the structure of our economy. Unfortunately, there are no signs of improvement."[48]

As problematic as the economy is for Iran's public, Iran's water shortages might be even worse, and there is no sign of the leadership or government's capacity to deal with this situation, which could be catastrophic for the country. The problem is so profound that Iran's former minister of environment warned that the continuing mismanagement of water resources could mean that 50 million Iranians—70 percent of the Iran's population—"will have no choice but to leave the country."[49]

In other words, water shortages will render the country incapable of sustaining its own population. Iranian water specialists point out that climate change compounds the problem, but Iran is doing next to nothing to stop the reality that 70–80 percent of rainwater in the country is lost through evaporation. The combination of mismanagement, political decisions on water allocation, destructive land use, poor water pricing leading to waste, and the inability of farmers to optimize irrigation systems all contribute to the increasing water shortages.[50] There are policy decisions that can ease the crisis, but they require multiple steps: stop over-withdrawal of ground water in the main plain of the country, use water recycling, avoid construction of hydraulic structures without environmental and social considerations, employ de-salination, reduce consumption in agriculture and industry, upgrade irrigation techniques generally and, in particular, use underground irrigation to limit evaporation, prevent water contamination, etc. All of these necessary steps are possible but are currently not being taken in Iran.

Water is so basic that Iran will need help, and it can be a basis on which to deal with the Iranians—especially as an inducement but also as a lever by publicizing America's willingness to help.

Objectives and Means

At a minimum, the objectives toward the Islamic Republic should be straightforward: prevent Iran from threatening its neighbors or using its proxies to intimidate and spread instability in the region, and stop, if not reverse, its nuclear program. These objectives are essentially negative. They are not necessarily equal in importance or urgency; with Iran already having achieved threshold status for nuclear weapons, it is important first and foremost to ensure that it does not cross that threshold. Of course, even at threshold status, others may seek to achieve the same level, but making sure that Iran does not go for a weapon and trigger others to do the same is essential and, I would argue, urgent; otherwise, we might soon see a nuclear-armed Middle East with all its potential dangers.

Could there be positive objectives? Could the United States set its sights higher and change the character of the Islamic Republic, so it is not a rogue actor in the region determined to threaten US interests—and so it is even willing to cooperate with America? If there is one overriding lesson from the past, it is that nobody is going to be able to change the character of the Islamic Republic from the outside—and there is no combination of inducements or penalties that will alter Iran's strategic orientation. Iran is and has been fundamentally hostile to America and its purposes, and Khamenei is acting to ensure that he will be succeeded by like-minded leaders.

That is why some Iranian watchers, like Reuel Gerecht and Elliot Cohen, are convinced that the only answer must be regime change. With this objective, the means become much more total and unrelenting: squeeze the regime economically with sanctions fully implemented; play on ethnic and sectarian fissures from the outside; help those on the inside with virtual private networks to get information and communicate; actively target Iranian intelligence operatives in the region as a way of raising the costs to them and anyone who might succeed them; use "active measures to weaken the regime's control of its population, which means in every possible way undermining and attacking its secret police," and respond to attacks by proxies on the United States and its allies with "massive, disproportionate, and above all lethal attacks against Iran's Quds Force and IRGC units and command structures."[51]

Such means are obviously designed to play on the vulnerabilities of the regime—with a public that is increasingly difficult to control—and, in Elliot Cohen's words, demonstrate that America's leaders are "just as implacable toward Iran as its leaders are toward the United States." Would that inspire the Iranian public and possibly also cause greater fissures in Iran? It might. But this strategy might also convince the regime that it has nothing to lose, which could prompt it quickly and covertly to develop and then announce it has a crude nuclear device. Would that trigger a US readiness to act militarily against Iran, or would it make even Trump more cautious? If Khamenei et al.

felt that they were in the corner and regime survival was already at stake, they might roll the dice.

If we accept that Iran is going to remain implacable during the rest of Ali Khamenei's time in power and at least for some time after he passes from the scene, what should the objective be? Simply containment and deterrence? Some might define containment as meaning containment of an Iran nuclear weapon after its achievement. In June 2023, I wrote a piece in *The Washington Post* in which I pushed back against that view, arguing that the Biden administration must stick to a policy of prevention of Iran having a nuclear weapon. I feared that accepting Iran's enrichment to 60 percent indicated that the United States was accepting there was little it could do to stop the Iranians from possessing nuclear weapons, at least at an acceptable price. In essence, the administration's posture, which was putting little or no pressure on the Iranians—even with the informal understandings—seemed to suggest that the Biden administration was prepared to live with containing a nuclear Iran, rather than exert the pressure necessary to prevent it.

We need not live with that. As has been established, Iran remains risk-averse when it comes to possible direct conflict with the United States. The Trump administration's objective needs to be prevention of Iran's nukes by making clear that the United States will use or support the use of force to stop it. That may be far more convincing in the aftermath of Israel having destroyed most of Iran's strategic air and missile defenses in its military strikes on October 25, 2024. With Donald Trump's election, and the likelihood that he might give the Israelis the green light and the means to attack the Iranian nuclear infrastructure, Iran's leadership is likely to take those threats far more seriously–especially if Khamenei et al. fear the US would inevitably be drawn into the conflict.

As for the region, the administration's posture should be one of deterrence of Iran's aggressive behaviors in the area. Is that containment? Containment is purely defensive, and while that might be good enough for curtailing Iran's threats against US partners in the region, it is not sufficient to prevent them altogether. Once again, it is possible to raise the costs to the Iranians of what they are doing with proxies so that the Iranians choose not to run certain risks. That does not mean all threats will disappear, but they can be mitigated. And, after what Israel has done to dramatically weaken Hezbollah and Hamas, Iran is likely to want its proxies to be able to reconstitute themselves; that likely argues for adopting less threatening postures and actions, as least for some time to come.

Suzanne Maloney has no illusions about the Iranians and is dubious about what engagement can produce. She does not argue against engagement, but she contends that it is unlikely to produce much. She does not favor regime change as an American objective—even though she has come to believe that the regime will not survive over time. That said, Maloney wants the United States to support the aims of Iran's protesters—who she believes are "far less interested in acquiring nuclear weapons or promoting insurgencies."[52] But she also observes that the "United States has the most tangential reach into the halls of power in Iran and holds little sway on the streets." The US is not going to determine the future of the country, "Iranians will."[53] She wants the United States to shine a spotlight on the heroic efforts of Iranian protesters, to expose the regime's repression, and to try to hold the regime accountable.[54]

Maloney's approach might be described as deterrence and minimizing bad behavior by raising costs and finding ways to support the Iranian people. My objective would be similar, but I see the regime's risk aversion as meaning not only that deterrence can work, but also that there are times when the desire to buy off the Iranian public can make tactical adjustments in Iran's behavior possible. And tactical adjustments can have strategic consequences.

The desire not to make life easier for the regime can be an argument against the tactical adjustments, but if the regime is not about to be overthrown, is it not of value to improve life for Iranians? Yes, there certainly could be a cost to relaxing sanctions. Henry Rome has shown the data that demonstrate that every time sanctions have been relaxed, Iranian defense spending went up—and when imposed, it has gone down. Certainly, for Khamenei's time, the Islamic Revolutionary Guard Corps maintained the privileged place in defense spending.[55]

Before concluding, let me encapsulate the means that could be used to achieve the deterrence and tactical adjustment objectives. Regardless of whether we are focused on Iran's nuclear or regional behavior, it is important to think in terms of military, economic, political, diplomatic, and declaratory tools. On deterring Iran from crossing the nuclear-weapon threshold, the administration needs to be clear in private and in public that the United States, regardless of what Israel does, will use force to destroy Iran's entire nuclear infrastructure if: its moves toward weaponization become obvious, Iran goes to 90-percent enrichment, or Tehran walks away from the nuclear non-proliferation treaty. An Iranian leadership whose priority is regime survival must have no doubt about what the United States would do in any of these cases. Why put a walk-away from the nuclear non-proliferation treaty in this category? Because the cascading effects of such a rebuke would be far-reaching, making the world far less stable, and the Iranian leadership must know the consequences of taking this step.

A number of steps would reinforce the threats articulated by the United States:

- conduct US military exercises in the region that simulate both attacks against remaining air defenses and air-to-ground attacks on hardened targets;
- provide Israel the heavier bunker buster bombs that it has denied until now;
- conduct joint exercises with the Israelis focused on air-to-air refueling and ground attacks;
- accelerate delivery to Israel of the next generation aerial refueling aircraft, something that is essential to increase Israeli aircraft time on target for attacks;
- work to more fully integrate air and missile defenses with the Saudis, Emiratis, and Bahrainis, and run exercises to show that U.S. Central Command can blunt Iranian missile and drone attacks against America's regional partners;
- develop a successor to the massive ordinance penetrator (MOP) if Iran's new underground facility next to Natanz is too deep to reach it.

The focus on Israel is important for deterrence because even after its wars with Hamas and Hezbollah, and maybe even because of them, the Israelis will be even more sensitive to not acquiescing in what they believe could be existential threats. Iran's leaders may continue to believe that Israel is even more willing to act than the United States—and in any case, US cooperation with Israel will signal not only that the United States will not hold the Israelis back, but also that America will support Israel and perhaps even join with it.

US military presence and exercises in the region are likely to be useful for deterring Iran's use of its proxies in the region, especially if the United States increases efforts to interdict Iranian military supplies to proxies like the Houthis. One key to deterring Iran's use of regional proxies, especially when used against the United States, is to hit back hard whenever US forces are attacked—and not only if US soldiers are killed. Hitting Iranian training camps in Iran, without acknowledging it, would signal that America's toler-ance level is low, and yet would not require the Iranians to retaliate or lose face. It would show that the United States is prepared to attack Iran directly, but in a way that preserves some degree of deniability for both countries.

The point is to raise the costs and risks for the Iranians and show that the United States is not self-deterring because of the fear of escalation. If deter-rence is going to work, Iran, not the United States, needs to fear escalation. Of course, the United States should not be using only military tools. Iran's domestic needs create leverage and the possibility of producing some tacti-cal adjustments. The United States can move to tighten the economic noose but also demonstrate a willingness to loosen it should certain benchmarks be met. The administration can make clear that it will do snapback sanc-tions and keep them as part of the nuclear file rather than let them lapse. Similarly, the administration can do more to make sanctions evasion diffi-cult, especially working with Azerbaijan, Kazakhstan, and Turkmenistan to "expose Iranian–Russian links"[56]

In addition, it is essential to think about China and its potential to affect Iran's behavior. Yes, China competes with the United States, but it has no interest in conflict in the region. Unlike Russia or Iran, China values stable oil markets and lower prices. With the Chinese, the United States should be focused both on the Iranian nuclear program and its use of proxies. On the former, getting China to reinforce America's red lines with the Irani-ans may well be possible if the alternative is the use of force. On the latter, much will depend on whether the actions of the proxies impinge on Chi-nese interests—the Houthis attacks on international shipping were not a positive development from the Chinese standpoint, and they apparently let the Iranians know it.[57] Without exaggerating the potential Chinese role, the administration has an interest in seeing where the Chinese may be able to have an effect.

That is still likely to be more impactful in terms of limiting Iranian bad behaviors, but the United States certainly has the potential to move the Irani-ans more positively, if still only tactically. Khamenei moved tactically before, when he felt it was useful to ease domestic conditions and public anger—at least as directed toward the economic circumstances. Earlier I mentioned Iran's water crisis. What if the United States (alone or together with Europe) offered a package of water and economic assistance in return for a scaling back of the Iranian amount of HEU and a concrete reduction in material sup-port to different proxies? As the water problem becomes more acute, such an offer could put much more pressure on the regime. And Iran's leaders might even feel compelled to be responsive.

The point is that it is important to be mindful of when Iranian needs might create openings for tactical changes. One such opening may come when Khamenei dies. Succession periods always stress authoritative systems as the potential for leadership contests create competition, uncertainty, and friction. Such systems often seek to send a message of relaxation and easing of conditions to their publics. That might be the moment to see what is possible in terms of openings.

Conclusion

Iran has bedeviled US policy for decades. As always with statecraft, the key challenge is understanding and acting on the right objective. With the Iranians, it is essential to understand what is and is not possible. It will probably not be possible to transform Iran from the outside. Only Iranians will be able to create change; but so long as there is, in the words of Karim Sadjadpour, a regime that is ready to kill and a population that is not willing to die, we are unlikely to see an internal transformation. Yes, we have seen more Iranians express their opposition to the regime, and that, by itself, may well create greater fissures in the regime.

Ali Khamenei knows only one way to respond to those who seek domestic change: repression. But many in the elite may not be so willing to separate themselves from the public, including their own children, and Khamenei's favoritism of the hardline figures who have no capacity to deal with Iran's structural challenges could provoke change after he is gone. In any case, the task of American statecraft vis-à-vis Iran is to deter its most dangerous behaviors and take advantage of possible openings for limited changes—the kind of changes that could foster more strategic consequences over time.

Chapter 13
The Israeli–Palestinian Conflict: Can Statecraft Work?

As with all questions of applying statecraft, the issue is not whether statecraft can work but to what end. If one sets an objective that is not achievable, then the statecraft, by definition, will be poorly applied. Statecraft involves applying the tools, the leverage, and the wherewithal that a country can marshal in the pursuit of an objective. Declaring that the aim of the United States is to end the Israeli–Palestinian conflict need not be beyond the application of smart and effective statecraft if it is understood that achieving that outcome cannot be realized any time soon. Instead, the aim of statecraft now with this conflict should be to change the circumstances and conditions to the point that what is not possible today can become possible over time.

In that connection, an essential element for effective statecraft is having a good understanding of the reality that has to be addressed. What I call making a sound assessment is a starting point for knowing what needs to be done and how to do it. Understanding what is feasible is certainly one essential factor in defining objectives—certainly near-term objectives. Having spent nearly four decades working on the Arab–Israeli and Israeli–Palestinian conflicts, I will draw on those experiences (and contacts) in outlining how to employ statecraft to try to ameliorate and transform what is a terrible reality at the time of this writing.

Assessing What Is Possible

Prior to October 7, 2023, and the onslaught by Hamas into Israel—and the Israeli war against Gaza it had provoked—the region and the possibilities looked very different from how they appear now. There is value in understanding where things stood prior to the invasion of Israel by Hamas, not because there is not dramatic change after it, but because some of the contextual realities remain the same. For example, the countries that signed

Statecraft 2.0. Second Edition. Dennis Ross, Oxford University Press. © Oxford University Press (2025). DOI: 10.1093/oso/9780197698914.003.0013

Abraham Accords have not walked away from their agreements with Israel, even if they are going slower in developing relations. And this is noteworthy because it is a reminder that what drove these countries—and especially the United Arab Emirates, which was the initiator of the accords—was their self-interest.

Something clearly changed in the region that prompted the Abraham Accords. When I was asked how the accords were changing the Middle East, I would respond by saying that was an important question but not the right one. The right one was to ask what had changed in the region that made the Abraham Accords possible. For one thing, the Arab view—or at least the Gulf State views—of Israel and the Palestinians changed following the second intifada.

By 2007, when I would travel to Gulf, I began to hear more and more frustration with the Palestinians and their leadership. The division between the West Bank and Gaza after the Hamas coup in 2007 convinced those I would meet, especially in Saudi Arabia and the Emirates, that Palestinians, given their leadership, would never be able to help themselves. In the Saudi case, their frustration grew out of their having brokered, after the coup, what they believed was a reconciliation agreement between Hamas and Fatah (or Hamas and the Palestinian Authority) with both having then walked away from the agreement.[a] So long as Abdullah bin Abdulaziz was the King of Saudi Arabia, the Palestinian issue remained a source of deep concern to him—and his instincts toward Israel were largely negative. Abdullah bin Abdulaziz would tell President Obama in June 2009 that he would be the last one to make peace with Israel in response to the president asking him to make a public gesture toward the Israelis. While King Abdullah was not prepared for any public outreach, he inherited a secret channel between Mossad and Saudi intelligence that he permitted to operate and develop.[b]

In fact, it was in the security area where covert cooperation developed between Israelis and many Gulf States as well as states like Morocco. The more Iran became the preoccupation of the Saudis, the Emiratis, and others in the region, the more the security/intelligence cooperation began to grow between the Israelis and the United States. As early as 2007, when Secretary

---

[a] This was hardly an exception, with at least 11 reconciliation agreements reached since that time and none held or implemented.

[b] I was not involved with this covert intelligence channel, but during the Clinton administration I did set up and take part in three-way meetings between senior Israeli and Saudi officials. It was after Obama's trip to Riyadh in June 2009, in which he felt his meeting with King Abdullah had not been properly prepared, that he asked me to leave the State Department and move to the White House to assume a broad role in the Middle East.

of State Condoleezza Rice met all the foreign ministers of the Gulf Cooperation Council to tell them she was going to launch an initiative to resolve the Israeli–Palestinian conflict, she discovered that Iran was their main preoccupation, not the Palestinians. In her words, "This is pretty interesting, I thought. The Israeli–Palestinian issue has fallen down the list of priorities. Iran is number one, two, three, and four."[1]

Early in the Obama administration, I would see how much convergence was being developed between the United Arab Emirates and Israel. In February 2009, Yousef al-Otaiba, the Emirati ambassador to the United States, asked if he could have a discussion on Iran not at the State Department or in his office but in his suite at the Ritz Carlton in downtown Washington. When I arrived and he opened the door, Sallai Meridor, the Israeli ambassador to the United States, greeted me along with Otaiba. It became clear in our discussion that the two were not just aligned on Iran but were cooperating and coordinating their approaches—and wanted the US policy to be aligned with theirs on Iran.

What drove the quiet relationships Israel was developing with a number of Arab states beyond Egypt and Jordan, with whom it had peace agreements, was the convergence of strategic threat perceptions. With that as a baseline which created increasing trust, there was a further development in ties after the Arab Spring in 2011. The Emirati, Saudi, and Bahraini leaderships, in particular, became increasingly dubious about President Obama's commitment to them given their perception that in the face of the protests in Tahrir Square, he had quickly walked away from Egyptian president Hosni Mubarak and "thrown him under the bus." Muhammad bin Zayed, the Crown Prince and at the time de facto leader of the Emirates, called me and asked, "If we have a demonstration in our main square, will America walk away from us too?" I sought to reassure him, but his doubts remained.[c]

His doubts were mirrored by others in the region, with the Israelis literally using the same terminology of "throwing Mubarak under the bus." The UAE and other Arab states would draw even closer to the Israelis as a result of the Iran nuclear deal (the JCPOA) in 2015, becoming convinced that the Obama

---

[c] I said that the United States would not walk away from the United Arab Emirates. But I then explained that it was not just the demonstrations, but that Mubarak showed no sign of recognizing what was going on in Egypt, had no plan to deal with it, and was dismissing that he had a problem. The administration wanted him to take steps and create a transition to the future and not leave precipitously, but he lost the support of the military—and that dictated his departure, not the United States. I said, "In the United Arab Emirates, you focus on producing good governance, not tolerating corruption, and promoting education to enable the country to transform its economy and produce a resilient society. If that were the case in Egypt, we would not be having this conversation."

administration had ignored their concerns in reaching the agreement and turned a blind eye to what Iran was doing in the region—something they argued would get worse when Iran was no longer under sanctions.[d] Prime Minister Benjamin "Bibi" Netanyahu's May 3, 2015 appearance before a joint session of the U.S. Congress to challenge the prospective Iran deal before it was finalized made the Arab states value the Israelis more. Some leading Arab officials told me they admired Netanyahu's readiness to stand up to the United States and its president who, as they increasingly doubted, could be counted on to live up to any security commitments he might make to them.

The combination of Obama's approach to Mubarak, his policy toward Syria (including his failure on the red line), his deal with the Iranians, and the "tilt to Asia"—all combined to raise basic questions about the United States. In fact, the tilt toward Asia, or what the administration referred to as "rebalancing," was interpreted as the United States leaving the Middle East— and, perhaps not surprisingly, I began to hear from Gulf State officials that "at least we know that Israel can't leave the region." While Israel could not substitute for the United States, its opposition to Iran was clear and its policy of increasingly bombing Iranian efforts to transfer weapons into Syria and to Hezbollah in Lebanon meant that it was the one country that was actively countering Iran and its expansionist, aggressive policies.

As a result, cooperation (largely below the radar screen) developed further—and it began to involve Israel's private sector as well. By 2019, I was told by Israeli officials that 500 Israeli companies were active in the Gulf States. True, the Israelis doing business were holders of two passports and were going to the Gulf States on their foreign passports. But everyone knew they were Israelis—and that was part of the attraction. The image of Israel as the "startup nation" with cutting-edge technologies was creating its own form of attraction, especially in the Gulf States, that drew lessons from the Arab Spring about the need for effective governance to prevent frustrated publics from erupting in anger. Digital and information-based economies were needed to modernize and compete; water security, food security, health security, and cyber security all became important for effective governance—and Israel was seen as being a valuable partner. What began as quiet but meaningful security partnerships increasingly included Israeli high-tech firms coming and doing business in the Gulf States.

---

[d] Their main argument was, "If Iran could cause this much trouble when it was under sanctions, imagine how much more it could do with its proxies when it had many more resources because sanctions had been lifted."

In the United Arab Emirates, starting as early as 2015, there was a readiness to permit an increasingly open Israeli presence. For example, Israel was permitted in 2015 to establish a diplomatic office in Abu Dhabi in the International Renewal Energy Agency. This would be followed by Israeli wrestling and judo teams being allowed to compete in tournaments in the Emirates, Israeli cultural and sports ministers allowed to visit the country, and Israel being invited to set up a pavilion in Expo 2020 in Dubai. All this took place before the announcement that the UAE would normalize its relations with Israel in August 2020 and the formal signing of the Abraham Accords one month later.

It is worth noting that earlier, well before the accords, the Trump administration had been seeking a statement of non-belligerency between four Arab states and Israel. But once the Trump Peace Plan was unveiled in agreement with Israel on January 28, 2020, and Prime Minister Netanyahu announced that evening that he would annex the territory allotted to Israel in the West Bank, there were no takers on the Arab side. In June 2020, Yousef al-Otaiba would publish an article in the Israeli newspaper *Yediot Aharonot*, saying that Israel could have normalization or annexation but not both. The Emiratis, seeing great benefit in the relationship with Israel and wanting to develop it much further, believed that Israeli annexation would produce such a public backlash in the region that it would jeopardize their plans. Otaiba and his boss Mohammad bin Zayed had hoped that the article would trigger a change in Israel or get the Trump administration to see that normalization was possible provided there was no annexation. When that change did not happen, Otaiba was authorized to go to Jared Kushner and offer a normalization deal provided there was no annexation, and the United Arab Emirates was permitted to buy F-35s and Reaper attack drones—both weapons systems that the Emiratis had been denied until that time on the grounds of preserving Israel's qualitative military edge.

Jared understood the import of the offer and persuaded his father-in-law to embrace it. Jared would then put pressure on Bahrain to join the Abraham Accords, offered recognition of Western Sahara to get Morocco to join, and took Sudan off the terrorism list to get it to become part of the agreement.

The Saudis did not join the Abraham Accords but raised no objections to their being signed in September 2020, and this was especially significant for Bahrain. With Bahrain dependent on Saudi Arabia for about 2/3 of the government's revenue—the result of sharing the Fasht Abu Safa offshore oil field run by the Saudi oil company, Aramco—the Bahrainis could not have proceeded over Saudi objections. But the Saudis did more than acquiesce in Bahrain and the Emirates normalizing with Israel. The Saudis would also allow Emirati airlines to overfly the Kingdom to and from Israel in the aftermath of the Abraham Accords.

Additionally, the Kingdom signaled its support by allowing Bandar bin Sultan, the former longtime Saudi ambassador to the United States and subsequently the Saudi national security advisor, to appear in a documentary which ran initially for three nights in August 2020, after the normalization deal between the United Arab Emirates and Israel was announced but before the formal signing of the Abraham Accords.[2] The documentary was a high-production film in which Bandar described the history of the conflict and how Palestinian leaders had multiple chances to achieve a state and peace with Israel but never took advantage of the opportunities. The core of Bandar's message was, the Saudis were right to support the Palestinian people but could no longer afford to forgo their own interests on behalf of Palestinian leaders who were incapable of ending the conflict.[3,e]

Bandar's public message was essentially what the United Arab Emirates, Bahrain, and Morocco were signaling: these countries had their own needs, and they could no longer permit the Palestinians, whose leaders they perceived to be incapable of ending the conflict, to force them to forgo and deny what was in their countries' interest.

They were collectively reversing the concept of linkage that had traditionally guided the Arab approach to Israel. Linkage meant that there could be no normalization with Israel until Israel had ended its occupation of Palestinians. In other words, Israel could not reap the reward of being accepted in the region so long as its occupation of the Palestinians continued. For Palestinians, this was an article of faith, and they accused the Emirates and the others of a "betrayal" and a "stab in the back," assuming, or at least hoping, that this might trigger a mobilization in the region against them—but it did not. Mahmoud Abbas, and those around him, failed to see how the region was changing, and how threats from the Iranians, the Islamists, and restive publics could create dangers that required security partners on the outside and partnerships that could help with governance needs on the inside.

---

[e] I would preview the Clinton parameters in December 2000 with Bandar before President Clinton presented them to the Israelis and Palestinians. As I explained to Bandar at the time, the parameters came as a response to the Israelis and Palestinians requesting the United States to bridge their differences; upon hearing what they would be, Bandar said to me, "if Arafat rejects them, it won't be a mistake, it will be a crime."

Still, while the Saudis may have supported the others normalizing with Israel, they did not join the agreement themselves. The Trump administration spoke of expanding the Abraham Accords, and might have succeeded in doing so with the Saudis had there been a second Trump term. While Joe Biden in the campaign supported the accords, the Middle East was not a priority when he became president. Moreover, because of the October 2018 murder of Jamil Khashoggi, the Saudi journalist killed by a Saudi hit squad in Turkey, Biden had referred to the Kingdom (and Mohammad bin Salman, its Crown Prince) as a pariah, and was unwilling to have direct contact with its de facto leader. This would change after Russia's invasion of Ukraine.

The need to limit Russian revenues and therefore limit its sale of oil suddenly gave the Biden administration an interest in the Saudis and their oil production. Moreover, with China essentially supporting Putin, Biden understood that the Saudis were important in the larger strategic contest between his desire to shape and preserve a rules-based order and the joint Russian–Chinese intention to upset it. He would take a trip to Saudi Arabia in the summer of 2022, and his administration would broker a deal in which Israel would acquiesce in Egypt's transfer to the Saudis of two small islands (in the Straits of Tiran), which the Saudis wanted to develop for broader tourism plans in the Red Sea; in turn, the Saudis would agree to allow Israel's national airline, EL AL, to overfly the Kingdom—saving millions in fuel costs and time for its flights to India and Asia.[f]

In the aftermath of this agreement, Prime Minister Mohammed bin Salman Al Saud of Saudi Arabia (popularly known as MbS) began to speak to visiting American groups in the fall of 2022 about his readiness to normalize with Israel.[g] Since this would pose some risk, and his public needed to see why taking this step served Saudi interests, he said he needed three things from America before doing so: a formal defense treaty with the United States, a nuclear partnership with America much like the one that allowed the Saudis to develop their oil industry, and a free trade deal or something akin to it. These were not small asks—there has not been a new bilateral defense treaty concluded by the United States for 60 years, and such a defense treaty would require a two thirds senate majority to be adopted. And yet, in

---

[f] The islands were covered by the Egyptian–Israeli peace treaty, and the terms needed to be respected by the Saudis.

[g] One such group was from the Washington Institute for Near East Policy—which is my base as of this writing.

2023, the Biden administration became convinced not just of the importance of producing Saudi–Israeli normalization but also that it could be achieved.

Initially, MbS told his US visitors that if these three conditions were met, he did not need anything else. However, after the emergence of the new Netanyahu government at the end of 2022, with its far-right ministers and their aggressive settlement policies in the West Bank and growing Palestinian violence, MbS began to say that he would need something on the Palestinian issue. Still, in my conversations with senior Biden administration officials, there was increasing confidence that they would reach a normalization deal before the end of 2023—and that confidence was matched in my discussions in the Kingdom. In the Kingdom, I would learn that there was also confidence that once the agreement was reached, others in the region and large Muslim-majority countries like Indonesia and Malaysia would follow suit and normalize with Israel. The Saudis, the Israelis, and those in the Biden administration correctly saw normalization as a transformative development in the Middle East and beyond it—and these expectations were emerging in public.

This was the context before October 7, 2023. Surprisingly, there was little consideration given to what spoilers might try to do to frustrate such a transformative agreement. To the extent that the Israeli security establishment thought about Iran and its proxies as possible spoilers, Israeli leaders were focused on their northern border with Lebanon and the West Bank. In the north, Hezbollah was becoming increasingly provocative, sending a terrorist into Israel, deploying military outposts right along the border, and even setting up two tents on the Israeli side of the Blue Line. In response, Israel greatly increased the presence of Israel Defense Forces in the north. In the West Bank, the Iranians were providing money and actively trying to smuggle in arms from Lebanon and Jordan to those groups who were largely unaffiliated but becoming more violent—and here as well, the Israelis greatly increased their military presence and tempo of operations to make pre-emptive arrests and blunt terror attacks.

Only in southern Israel along the border areas next to Gaza was there no particular concern. As I was told in June 2023 by senior Israeli security and intelligence officials, the Hamas leader in Gaza, Yahya Sinwar, had a "prisoner's mentality." He would raise pressures from time-to-time to gain Israeli concessions—like more permits for workers to come into Israel, more extensive fishing areas for Gazan fishermen, and greater access for Gazan businesspeople. My contacts added that Yahya Sinwar would also periodically raise tensions because he knew that the Qataris would provide monies to keep things calm between Hamas and Israel.

As in any case of strategic surprise, Israel had all the early-warning indicators that something major was being planned—acquisition of arms, training exercises that looked surprisingly like rehearsals, increasing demonstrations along the barrier with Israel—but the basic assumptions forged a prism through which all the information was seen and interpreted.[4,h]

In retrospect, it is, of course, all clear and self-evident —including the stake of Hamas in acting, especially given the risk that Saudi normalization with Israel would pose to the position and goals of Hamas. For me, their actions are completely consistent with what Hamas did throughout the 1990s. Then, quite literally whenever we were making progress toward peace, we got Hamas bombs. Three months after the assassination of Rabin, when the right wing in Israel had been discredited, when the Israeli public was moved by the Palestinian mourning of Rabin's murder, and when leaders of Likud were telling me that Shimon Peres, Rabin's successor, could achieve with the Palestinians what Rabin in life could never have achieved, Hamas struck with four suicide bombing attacks in nine days. The bombings altered basic attitudes in Israel, raising questions about whether this was the peace that Peres promised—one where Israelis could not get on buses for fear of suicide bombings? Peres would narrowly lose the election three months later to Bibi Netanyahu.

Preventing peace with Israelis has always been one of the guiding principles of Hamas—an Arabic acronym for the Islamic Resistance Movement. October 7 may not have produced what Yahya Sinwar envisioned—a region-wide war with Hezbollah going all-out from the north, the West Bank exploding, and the Israeli Arabs rising up—but his most immediate aim was at least to prevent the normalization of Saudi Arabia and Israel. While he may not have killed it, his actions definitely put it on hold.

How October 7 Changed the Context for Peacemaking

It is commonplace to hear Israelis say that Israel is not the same country after October 7, 2023. Israelis have lost the sense of security that they previously had. The shock is hard to exaggerate. It was not just the scale of the

---

[h] An intelligence unit made up of women conveyed repeated warnings of preparation for an attack along the lines of what took place on October 7, and their warnings were considered fanciful and not reported up the chain.

surprise or even the inability of the Israel Defense Forces to respond quickly and to blunt an attack that took the lives of 1,200 people. It was the brutality and the atrocities—with children killed in front of parents and parents in front of their kids. The rapes, the mutilations, and the sheer joy reflected in the videos that Hamas marauders were taking, along with the kidnappings of those as young as nine months and as old as 85 (and in a wheelchair), seemed to suggest no limits, no humanity, and no decency. Israelis consciously understood terror bombings or shootings; they did not accept them, but they were familiar. This was nothing anybody could have imagined. This was dehumanization at the most dramatic level—and pictures from Gaza of crowds cheering some of the kidnapped being paraded around added to the sense that in Gaza there was no distinction between Hamas and the Palestinians who lived there.

As one Israeli friend of mine, Avinoam Bar-Yosef, who lives in a suburb within pre-1967 Israel—just like the areas invaded on October 7 in the south, plaintively asked me, "Is this what the Palestinians who live just across from us in the West Bank would do if they had the chance?" It will take time for the Israelis to overcome the trauma, and their views of the Palestinians will not change overnight. Already, the Israeli reaction to the idea of a Palestinian state has changed dramatically for the negative. In an Israel Democracy Institute poll in February 2024, 71.5 percent of Jewish Israelis opposed a de-militarized Palestinian state.[5] Maybe any poll taken during the war was going to reflect deeply negative views of a Palestinian state, especially because any Palestinian state was seen as likely to be run by Hamas. Once beyond the war, particularly if the Israelis have succeeded in dismantling Hamas military forces and infrastructure, the attitudes in Israel could change. But the starting point for that is seeing that Palestinians will demonstrate their rejection of Hamas.

Given the collective hurt and sense of trauma on the Palestinian side, one should not expect that Palestinians will reject Hamas any time soon. Certainly, that is what polls of Palestinians show, with 59 percent believing that Hamas should control Gaza after the war, 71 percent feeling that it was right to carry out the attack on October 7, and 97 percent believing that Hamas committed no atrocities.[6] Much like with Israelis, the trauma that Palestinians feel because of the death and destruction in Gaza makes them incapable of feeling anything except their own pain. Just as Israelis at this stage do not see the images of suffering in Gaza, almost as if it was not possible to be aware of anyone's pain but their own, the Palestinian denial that Hamas committed atrocities reflects a similar inability to acknowledge that the other side has suffered or had victims.

Maybe the attitudes on both sides can change when the war ends and the Israelis withdraw from Gaza, but there should be no illusions: Israelis and Palestinians are not going to believe in possibilities of peacemaking any time soon. It will take time to restore any sense of possibility, much less hope in the future. Basic lack of trust in the other is likely to endure for some time to come. Israeli perceptions that Palestinians will remain fundamentally hostile to a Jewish state, as well as Palestinian beliefs that Israel will never accept an independent Palestinian state, are not going to magically disappear.

And that certainly has implications for what the American objective should be with regard to this conflict. America's stakes in a stable Middle East—one that is not constantly being a source of disruption, conflict, nuclear proliferation, escalation, and terror—remain high. The region connects continents and international-trade routes, with 20 percent of the world's oil passing through the Straits of Hormuz and 12 percent transiting the Bab el Mandeb and the Red Sea. On top of that, 30 percent of the world's container traffic goes through the Suez Canal and the Red Sea.[7] With Houthis declaring that they are targeting ships serving Israel in response to the war in Gaza, but in fact attacking vessels far more indiscriminately, the supply lines are once again being affected and the costs of trade are going up.

Leaders of Hamas are not wrong to claim that they have put the Palestinian issue back on the world's agenda. But that agenda is not the same as the agenda of Hamas—for they reject a two-state outcome and that is what the United States and Arab states want to focus on. That might be the right endgame—in fact, I believe it is because a one-state outcome is a prescription for endless conflict. There are two national movements with distinct national identities very much tied to the same land. Neither will submerge itself in one state and neither will disappear. And yet, achieving two states any time soon is psychologically and practically impossible.

I say this not just because neither population will be able to contemplate concessions to the other for some time to come. I say it because the Israelis must go through a political reckoning for the responsibility for the strategic failure of October 7th. That will come; in fact, an election is likely before the formal work of the inevitable State Inquiry Commission has been completed. (In fact, Prime Minister Netanyahu continues to oppose one before the war ends.) What is certain is that at some point, there will be political changes in Israel and, in time, the basic assumptions that guided the pre–October 7 policy toward the Palestinians will also be debated. The reality of the Israeli democracy, the certainty of elections, and the tradition of no-holds-barred State Inquiry Commissions will guarantee both political change and a debate. But, realistically, as I write this in the fall of 2024, we can expect it will take at least at least year or even two for all this to play out.

Soul-searching on the Palestinian side is also needed but, frankly, has never taken place. The Palestinians have neither the institutions nor the history of deep questioning of the posture of their leaders or groups, much less debates about the lessons to be learned from policies that have imposed such high costs on them. Will such a hard questioning or systemic debate come any time soon? It is hard to imagine that being possible before real reform and the emergence of a leadership that seeks to resolve the fundamental question of the identity of the Palestinian movement takes place. To wit, what separates Hamas on one side and the Palestinian Authority and Fatah on the other is a fundamentally different view about who and what the Palestinians are to be. Hamas are Islamists who are guided by their belief in armed resistance and dual rejection of peace with Israel and the idea of a secular state of Palestine. For Hamas, a Palestinian state must be run exclusively on the basis of their interpretation of Sharia or Islamic law. For Fatah (which was founded by Yasser Arafat) and the Palestinian Authority, the Palestinian movement is a national and secular one—the Palestinian state should not be a religious one. While accepting that resistance is legitimate, they do not believe it must be violent or armed and they favor negotiations as a means for settling the conflict.

Resolving this identity question must be part of an intra-Palestinian dialogue—and must precede any possibility of generating a process designed to result in a two-state outcome. With Hamas largely destroyed as a military force, it is possible that it can be weakened as political one as well. But for the Palestinian Authority to take advantage of the aftermath of the war in Gaza, it must credibly reform and open up its ranks to younger and well-educated Palestinians.

This is unlikely to happen without the insistence from the United States and other donor states. Collectively, they have leverage that stems from continuing material assistance to the Palestinian Authority—and they need to use it. Arab states, like Saudi Arabia and the United Arab Emirates, can be especially effective not only because they have the means to contribute significant assistance, but also because they, themselves, are focused on delivering decent, efficient governance, genuine modernization, and the development of digitally driven economies. They can focus on bringing these kind of changes to the Palestinian Authority, provided that Palestinian leaders clean up their governance and end their corrupt practices. With a genuine makeover of the Palestinian Authority, the Emirates and the Saudis could commit to invest in the Gaza and the West Bank. From my talks with Emirati and Saudi leaders, it is clear that they are prepared to invest in reconstructing Gaza and modernizing the West Bank infrastructure, including in broadband, but they will do so only if the Palestinian Authority stops the corruption and takes demonstrative steps to prove their commitment to reform. As one senior Saudi official told me, providing direct assistance to the Palestinian Authority at this point made no sense; in fact, he said, "we would be smarter just to ask the Palestinian officials for their Swiss bank accounts numbers." The Emiratis are no less cynical about the corruption in the Palestinian Authority, and are ready to do a great deal on the ground if they see a serious approach to reform—indeed, one that reflects what the United States insisted on back in 2007.

Back then, the Bush 43rd administration organized all the donors to the Palestinian Authority—Western allies, Japan, and the Gulf States—and told Mahmoud Abbas, the president of the Palestinian Authority, that no more assistance would be provided unless he appointed an empowered prime minister. At that time, Bush insisted that Salam Fayyad be appointed in that role, with support from Abbas but no interference. Fayyad had come out of the International Monetary Fund/World Bank system, where he had worked for 20 years before becoming the finance minister of the Palestinian Authority. Abbas acquiesced in making Fayyad the prime minister and did empower him.

It is important to recall the circumstances: the Palestinian Authority had lost Gaza in the Hamas coup damaging its legitimacy, there was complete lawlessness in the West Bank, with gangs operating in every city, and corruption and diversion of assistance was widespread. Fayyad tackled security first, saying that there would be no economy without security, and succeeded in overhauling the security services, professionalizing them and restoring law and order throughout the West Bank.

Fayyad served as prime minister for close to five years, launching over 1,000 projects on the ground. Additionally, he succeeded in collecting taxes and producing a system where payment was actually achieved for consumption of water and electricity. Yes, his actions generated resentment from within Fatah and increasing jealousy from Abbas for all the credit that Western countries gave him. Fayyad achieved a great deal but could have achieved much more if Arab states had been willing to invest more in his efforts and if the Israelis had permitted the sale of Palestinian goods in Israel, reduced impediments to doing business, obstacles to movement, and restrictions on building in area C (60 percent of the West Bank).

Neither the Israelis nor the Arabs acted in a way that could have enhanced Fayyad's delivery of real goods, and could have built his authority by showing that his way was working. It was not only the Arab states and Israel that failed to help a reforming Palestinian prime minister to succeed; the Obama administration was also missing in action, neither insisting on reform nor telling Abbas that he would lose support from the United States and other donors if he fired Fayyad. The administration was largely passive on the reform and then on Abbas's firing Fayyad; unfortunately, the administration's emphasis was far too much on the political negotiations and far too little on the delivery of goods by the Palestinian Authority to its public.

Still, Fayyad demonstrated that real reform was possible; he showed that the starting point for shaping a Palestinian future after the Gaza war involves not just reconstruction in Gaza but also real reform in the West Bank.

Where Do We Go from Here?

The sad reality is that peacemaking is simply not possible now. But the ground can and must be prepared for it. The US objective between Israelis and Palestinians needs to be focused on bottom-up efforts to show that life can get better, that functional cooperation is possible, that mutual security is necessary, that rejectionists will be countered, and that a coalition of those who seek a better future for the region can be built and sustained. There is an Arab role in peacemaking that for the most part has always been lacking, but may be possible now given the stakes of Arab states.

They have learned that if they want stability in the region, the Palestinian issue cannot be ignored. They see how it can be exploited by the Iranians. The United States also sees this. But there is a tendency for the Arabs and the United States to want to achieve an outcome quickly, and that is not possible in this case.

An essential starting point, as we often see with effective statecraft, is framing the issue and the objective the right way. While the two-state solution is not possible soon, it is essential to explain why one state is a prescription for a never-ending conflict, emphasizing that neither national identity can be fulfilled in a binational state. In the Middle East, the post-nationalism phase has not yet begun. Wherever there is more than one identity—national, tribal, or sectarian—that state is either failed, failing, paralyzed or at war with itself. Look no further than Lebanon, Syria, Libya, Yemen, and Iraq—and that should not be the future sought for Israelis and Palestinians.

In other words, it is essential to explain on a consistent basis why one state is a prescription for enduring conflict, not peace. Those who speak of a one-state reality may not be wrong to say that it is emerging, but they are wrong to think that a binational state will end the conflict. By continually explaining that one state guarantees endless conflict, the two-states-for-two-peoples outcome can be seen for what it is: the only possible way to settle this historic conflict.

With both Israelis and Palestinians seeing it as an impossibility now, both must also be reminded why there is no alternative to it and why one state is a danger for both. The framing should also emphasize that separation and divorce of Israelis and Palestinians may be more realistic than images of peace and reconciliation. While desirable, Israelis and Palestinians cannot envision it now, and emphasizing that as the goal tends to add to their disbelief.

However, separation need not mean no practical or functional cooperation. On health, environmental, and water issues, there is a need for functional cooperation, especially because these issues respect no borders—and have existed for very practical reasons before. Moreover, in the near-term, there remains a Palestinian dependency on Israel for transfer of collected taxes and for much of the movement of goods and trade.

Before October 7, the earnings of Palestinian workers in Israel contributed about 1/3 of the GDP of the Palestinian economy in the West Bank. After October 7, the body politic in Israel sees Palestinian workers as a threat—and it will not be easy to allow workers to come back.

And serious investment in both Gaza and the West Bank will be needed to begin to create an economy that is far less dependent on Israel. Gaza will need enormous reconstruction, and the West Bank economy having shrunk 30 percent in the aftermath of October 7, with workers no longer able to go to Israel, will need a great deal of investment as well. Investment in infrastructure, housing, and industrial zones could all provide employment. Backing up the banking system and buying up its debt will be essential for preventing its collapse, understanding that because the Palestinian Authority is not a state, its banks cannot get help from the International Monetary Fund or the World Bank. The Gulf States in particular could and should play a major role in providing support.

So what are the building blocks that need to be put in place to restore peacemaking? And what are the key objectives that US statecraft should now be pursuing? Reconstruction of Gaza and an alternative to Hamas rule are essential. Two states will never be possible so long as Hamas is in control in Gaza. Hamas has demonstrated over time that its priority is building military capability to keep attacking Israel. After the conflicts in 2009, 2012, 2014, and 2021, Hamas did not make an effort to rebuild Gaza or seriously improve its economy; instead, Hamas created over 300 miles of tunnels and a military-industrial base underground. Thirty thousand tons of cement, probably close to 8,000 tons of metal, huge amounts of wiring, piping, tiles, and even wood—all could have been of enormous use above ground for building Gaza. But advancing the well-being of Gazans is not, and has never been, the aim of Hamas.

Israel, having largely demilitarized Gaza, needs to be assured that it cannot be remilitarized, and that suggests a basic formula for Gaza: reconstruction for assured demilitarization. The United States needs to mobilize support for a "demilitarization for reconstruction" formula. Reconstruction must also be conditioned on Hamas not being in control of Gaza politically—no one will invest in reconstruction if Hamas retains control because it is a given that at some point it will try to attack Israel again. As noted earlier, the United Arab Emirates is prepared to play an unprecedented role on the ground, including by providing forces to create security. But it will require assurance that there is a Palestinian alternative to Hamas for governing Gaza so that its presence is a bridge to a Palestinian future and not a replacement for it. That is only possible if the Palestinian Authority is transformed as it was earlier under Salam Fayyad.

However, bringing a reformed Palestinian Authority back to Gaza is necessary not just to ensure that the United Arab Emirates, and probably the Egyptians, are not going to be responsible for it forever—a prospect that would preclude their being willing to play this transitional role at all; it is also essential if there is ever to be a hope for a two-state outcome. If the West Bank and Gaza are not reunified politically, two states are not even possible. From the standpoint of the two-state solution, reconstruction for demilitarization and a reformed Palestinian Authority are essential for transforming the environment and setting the stage for future progress.

Israelis must see that a different Palestinian entity, with very different governance and priorities, is taking shape. Under such circumstances, low-level, functional cooperation from security to economic and health issues should be promoted. For two states, the Palestinians must demonstrate with actions that it will meet a number of standards or benchmarks that indicate what kind of a state it will be. In other words, Palestinians must show that they are prepared to accept responsibilities that must go with statehood, including the following conditions:

- neither Hamas nor extremist groups can lead the Palestinian state;
- the state cannot form alliances with those who reject Israel's right to exist, and will not be a member of the Iranian axis of resistance;
- the state will commit to co-existence with Israel and to resolving all differences through nonviolence and negotiations;
- leaders of the Palestinian state must acknowledge the historic Jewish connection to the land, something that is essential to accept Israel's legitimacy and not just its de facto existence;
- the Palestinian state will educate its citizens for peace, perhaps working with the United Arab Emirates on developing a new curriculum and centers of excellence that can foster the skills necessary for its people to be competitive in a modernized, digital economy;
- the Palestinian state will develop institutions and the rule of law to ensure that it does not become a failed state.

Israel, too, must assume a set of obligations. It cannot be that only the Palestinians have obligations. Even if it will take time to create the conditions for two states, Israel must not, in the meantime, take steps that make a Palestinian state impossible. It must, therefore, not expand the settlements or take more land for settlements that exist outside the bloc areas. Eighty-five percent of the Israeli settlers live in the 8 percent of the territory closest to the Green Line (the 1967-borders).[8] Building in those areas where the vast majority of Israeli settlers reside is consistent with a two-state outcome. Building outside those bloc areas or to the east of the security barrier is not.[9,i] Acting against extremist settlers that threaten Palestinians must be done unequivocally, and based on the premise that Israel is a country of laws and will prevent lawlessness and vigilantism.

---

[i] There are 130 settlements: 55 to the west of the security barrier, which runs along 8 percent of the West Bank, and 75 to the east of it. Those 75 is where 15 percent of all the people who live to the east of the Green Line reside.

Additionally, Israel must also:

- recognize that Palestinians are a people and have a right to self-determination and a state, provided they fulfill their responsibilities;
- permit Palestinian access to area C for housing, economic activity, tourist development in the Dead Sea, and the development and even ownership of rock quarries given the importance of stone masonry in the West Bank;[10,j]
- make life easier, not harder, for a reforming Palestinian Authority—meaning, ease movement, lift bureaucratic restrictions on banking and excessive red tape on foreign investments in the West Bank and Gaza;
- open the Israeli market to a wide range of Palestinian agricultural produce and products, including pharmaceuticals if they meet Israeli standards;[k]
- make clear that the more Palestinians do on security, the less the Israelis will do (this is a formula that worked in the past; a truly reforming Palestinian Authority that gets serious and is capable of producing law and order may seek this approach again, and the Israelis should be open to it).

There are several points worth noting about these mutual obligations.

First, there is a parallelism here in terms of the two sides for the first time accepting the legitimacy of the other. Israel recognized the Palestinian Liberation Organization but never acknowledged the legitimacy of Palestinian statehood aspirations. Similarly, Palestinians never accepted that the Jews and their nationalist movement, Zionism, was legitimate with long-standing attachment to the land. Precisely because the onslaught on October 7 and the Israeli response to it revealed the existential nature of the conflict—essentially bringing us back to 1948 and the denial and rejection of each other—it is necessary not to repeat the mistakes made in the Oslo process. Back then, each side recognized the fact of each other, but not the legitimacy of each other's national identity and aspirations. As a result, every time there is a new flare-up or re-emergence of the conflict, the same fundamental

---

[j] Ten years ago, the World Bank estimated that the economy of the Palestinian Authority would improve by as much as 35 percent if it had access for this kind of activity in the West Bank. This estimate is still valid.

[k] Palestinian pharmaceuticals are sold to Europe but are not allowed in the Israeli market.

issues re-emerge. It will not be possible to get to a two-state outcome without resolving these issues once and for all.

Second, these mutual obligations remind both sides that they have rights and responsibilities. Each side has been very good at focusing on the other side's obligations without much acknowledgment of their own. To be fair, because the Palestinians have not had a state and have made being a victim their strategy, they act as if they have no responsibilities and as if statehood must be simply granted to them and not earned. That view must change, but the Israelis also need to understand that they have an obligation to facilitate Palestinian development if the Palestinians are doing their part and actually fulfilling their responsibilities.

Third, others can help create the conditions that will make two states possible over time. The United States already trains Palestinian security forces, and it is possible for the United States to do more in this regard, especially if there is a reforming Palestinian Authority that is restoring its legitimacy in the eyes of its public. Likewise, Arab states can provide the investments that can help allow the Palestinian Authority to develop an economy that is not perpetually dependent on donors but becomes increasingly self-sustaining. They should not provide the investments unless the Palestinian Authority is transformed in a way that makes it possible for them to showcase that the West Bank and Gaza will produce decent governance, transparency, and a basis for a return on investments. The scope of reconstruction needs in Gaza will be immense but that can also mean that Palestinian employment needs can be addressed.

The role of the Arabs will be important not only in terms of assisting economically but also in terms of security. I am referring to the role that Egypt can play in Gaza, and Jordan can play in the West Bank. When my colleagues and I were at Camp David in the summer of 2000, we envisioned a security role that brought the Egyptians, the Palestinians, and the Israelis together on Gaza, and the Jordanians, the Palestinians, and the Israelis together on security. The scope of Egyptian and Jordanian security cooperation with Israel is far beyond what anyone acknowledges in public—and creating three-way cooperation could, ironically, reassure the Israelis and the Palestinians. The Israelis have confidence in the security establishments and their relationships with Egypt and Jordan—and the Palestinians could see their two Arab neighbors playing a supportive role for them. Ahmed Korei, better known as Abu Ala, was for some time the leading Palestinian negotiator and he once said to me, "Dennis, you know that Israelis will never feel fully confident in their security if the West Bank is not anchored with the Jordanians. I can't raise that but you can, and I can work to get it accepted on our side." Abu Ala is now gone, but it is time to follow the wisdom of his suggestion.

Fourth, security cannot be viewed only locally, especially with Iran and its proxies being a threat to the Israelis and all their Palestinian and Arab partners. The possibility of normalization between the Saudi Arabia and Israel creates a more overt potential for a regional coalition against Iran and its proxies. In the US Central Command there is already a great deal of practical security coordination and cooperation between the US military, the Arab military, and the Israeli Defense Force. Early-warning coordination already exists, with radars that are connected and identify a missile launch anywhere. An integrated air and missile defense is very much within reach, and on the night of April 13–14, 2024, it was demonstrated in fact, not in theory. The United States, with the British, the French, the Jordanians—and important intelligence assistance from the United Arab Emirates and Saudi Arabia—intercepted nearly 100 of the Iranian cruise missiles and drones that Iran launched against Israel. While Israel's defense was nearly flawless and was responsible for intercepting the ballistic missiles and downing 2/3 of the cruise missiles and drones, its defense would have been far more stretched and stressed without the active intervention of the US Central Command and its regional partners—an intervention that was unprecedented and would have been unthinkable in the past. This intervention showed that the traditional Israeli ethos of defending itself by itself might no longer be practical or even desirable.

In short, the US Central Command has already forged an essential foundation for a regional security coalition. More can be done collectively on countering the Iranian proxies, on sharing intelligence, interdicting weapons deliveries, and even developing common strategies based on the comparative advantages of the different militaries.

And here we see the means that the United States is already using and is able to develop further. Training of the militaries, creating common counter-terror facilities, developing counter-drone capabilities, fostering greater cyber-force collaboration, and expanding the naval-task forces that the United States has deployed with Middle Eastern countries, including Israel—will all become even more doable with Saudi normalization with the Israelis—especially because others are likely to follow.

American diplomacy can and should drive this process. The United States should also mobilize its European allies to play a role that can develop coalitions in and beyond the Middle East even further. In addition, the United States can broker the Saudi–Israeli normalization deal that will be driven by the US offer of a defense treaty with the Kingdom. But as part of that deal, the Saudis will require that they must achieve something meaningful for the Palestinians as part of the package.

Here we come full circle. The Saudis want to show that there is, in Secretary of State Tony Blinken's words, "credible pathway to a Palestinian state." As one Saudi senior official said to me, "We will normalize with Israel—it is only a matter of time. But when we do normalize, we have to show that we got something more for the Palestinians than they had received before." In response, I said that a Palestinian state without benchmarks demonstrating performance is a state that will not contribute to stability and could easily be a failed state. I asked him whether that was what he was seeking—and, of course, his answer was "no." He added, "It is up to the United States to figure out how to move us toward a Palestinian state that will be good for stability in the region and not bad."

In this chapter, I have tried to show that essential building blocks in Gaza, with a reformed Palestinian Authority in the West Bank, and the socialization of mutual obligations on the part of Israelis and Palestinians are all necessary to change the environment so a Palestinian state can become possible. The means will involve the right framing of the objective, and then the United States mobilizing security, diplomatic, economic, material assistance, and intelligence tools in putting all the pieces in place.

It is not simple; it requires careful orchestration of key steps and their timing; it will require American assurances to the Israelis and others about security and a role for Arab states in peacemaking that they have traditionally avoided. But they may now see that the price of doing little on the Palestinian issue has become too high and their stakes dictate a more direct role. As if all that were not enough, new Israeli and Palestinian leaderships will be a sine qua non for making the decisions and for taking the steps that can make it possible for a Palestinian state to emerge in time.

Right now, this may all seem too difficult. Having collectively seen the consequences and costs of inaction, there is a potential for smart American statecraft to begin to put the right building blocks in place. No one else has the potential either to influence the Israelis or to mobilize the Arabs and US allies to take the steps that will be necessary to succeed.

Chapter 14

Conclusion: Statecraft and New National Security Challenges

One conclusion that emerges from this book is that to practice statecraft effectively it is necessary to ask basic questions. Notwithstanding that, I have often told my students that statecraft cannot be practiced mechanically—I now think I was wrong about that. Indeed, the longer I served in senior government positions and the more I have reviewed past cases, the more I have come to realize that policy and statecraft requires going through a checklist of questions—and being very explicit in doing so.

One basic reason for doing so is that objectives are so often poorly thought through. As I explained in Chapter 2, many factors play a role, including political considerations for adopting an objective. Of course, one cannot wish away political factors and pressures, but being required to be explicit about the assumptions guiding the objective can make policymakers more aware of what they are choosing and why. Similarly, even if one is more explicit about the objective, poor assessments can still bedevil statecraft and the employment of the appropriate tools. But here again, the more policymakers are forced to think through what means they have to achieve the objective, the more they are likely to want to know more about what they are getting into. Certainly, the more questions will be asked about how the means we have—or can mobilize from others—match up with the objective we have adopted, the better chances for developing successful policies.

The problem so often with policymaking is not just that the assumptions are rarely explicit or questioned but that policies often also take on a life of their own, with drift and habit guiding them more often than deliberate thought. This is not unique to the United States. Israel's response to the onslaught of October 7, 2023, has been, not surprisingly, shaped by an objective of the need in Benjamin Netanyahu's words for "total victory." This objective is understandable, given the shock and sheer brutality of the attack, but what does "total victory" mean, exactly? Does it mean that Hamas should

Statecraft 2.0. Second Edition. Dennis Ross, Oxford University Press. © Oxford University Press (2025).
DOI: 10.1093/oso/9780197698914.003.0014

be eradicated? Does it mean that every Hamas fighter must be found and disarmed? Neither of these are real possibilities. Hamas is not just a military; it is also an ideology, and Israel cannot just not eradicate it. Similarly, the Israeli military would not be able not find every Hamas fighter embedded in over 300 miles of tunnels; nor would it be possible to identify those who are able to blend into the population when not literally underground. However, there have been achievable objectives—like the demilitarization of Gaza, the defeat of Hamas militarily, and the destruction of the bulk of its military infrastructure. But to prevent the reconstitution of Hamas, its rearming, or its ability to return to power and control in Gaza, Israel also needs to recognize that it cannot leave a power vacuum. It needs others in the region to step in and provide a bridge to a Palestinian alternative to Hamas—Israel cannot create such an alternative if it is to be accepted and have any legitimacy. In a similar vein, Israel needs to preserve enough international and regional support for others to be willing to commit to a formula of reconstruction for assured demilitarization—meaning a credible mechanism has to be established that could ensure that all materials coming into Gaza were monitored from entry to end-use to ensure no diversion to purposes other than reconstruction.

In other words, Israel's objectives in Gaza need to employ means that would retain international and regional support. Had Israel's leaders asked the right questions up front–how much of the Hamas leadership, command-control, military, its underground infrastructure, and its ability to smuggle do we need to be able to destroy to make it hard for Hamas ever to reconstitute itself? What regional or international role will be necessary to ensure the IDF does not have to remain in Gaza or face a dangerous vacuum there? Had Israel's approach been guided by a statecraft checklist or mindset, its challenge still would be daunting—after all, Hamas has constructed hundreds of miles of interconnecting tunnels and embedded itself under a population that it has been willing to sacrifice. Indeed, Hamas has treated its population as if they are willing to be martyrs without giving them a choice. For sure, Israel has faced a cruel dilemma: it cannot root out Hamas militarily without there being large numbers of civilian casualties; but if Israel is not willing to destroy Hamas as a military, the strategy of Hamas will win, its ideology will be validated, and it will surely threaten Israel again.

In their immediate response to October 7, it was essential for Israelis to do all they could to address the humanitarian needs of Gazans—precisely because Israel would inevitably inflict civilian casualties. Only such a posture could have made it possible for Israel's military strategy to succeed and shape a political outcome in Gaza without doing terrible damage to Israel's image internationally.

Regrettably for Israel, Prime Minister Netanyahu shaped his objectives based on the genuine outrage of the Israeli public and the political pressures coming from the extreme right of his coalition. The former made it difficult to provide or permit humanitarian assistance so long as Hamas held hostages and denied any humanitarian access to them; the latter made it difficult to allow even a reformed Palestinian Authority to return to Gaza. The politics were difficult and made it natural to drift and pursue a policy guided by an unachievable objective–so-called "total victory."

Leadership requires a clear-eyed approach, with a strategic understanding of what could be achieved and the means necessary to employ to achieve it. Unfortunately, Netanyahu's repeated calls for total victory were a slogan, not a real objective. And the means used to achieve that slogan too often appeared to show too little regard for the costs in Palestinian lives—a perception that gained far more currency given the restrictions imposed on humanitarian assistance.

The absence of strategic considerations taking precedence over political ones has cost Israel on the international and regional stage and limited the effect of its real military successes. Could Prime Minister Netanyahu have done a better job of leading and explaining to his public why permitting humanitarian assistance to get into Gaza at the necessary levels was not only moral but also a practical necessity—indeed, that it was not a favor Israel was doing for Palestinians, but a strategic imperative to give Israel the time and space it needed to defeat Hamas and dismantle its military? Yes, but he did not offer that explanation.

For him, the domestic political realities predominated. They, of course, will always be present, and good statecraft does not ignore such pressures; instead, it focuses on explanations and framing of issues and stakes to either overcome the obstacles or at least lessen their impact. Having political considerations dominate is not unique to Israel, or to Netanyahu as a leader. Leaders make judgment calls about stakes to themselves and to the country. They make choices. Barack Obama decided to stop pursuing peace efforts between Israel and the Palestinian Authority in 2011, when there was a potential for success—because he did not think the prospects were great, but also because he saw it requiring him to take steps that would be costly as he looked ahead to his re-election campaign in 2012. And that was not a political price he was willing to pay.

The point is that good statecraft takes account of political realities and seeks to shape them in a way that makes it possible to pursue the right objectives and sustain that effort. That, too, can come from asking the right questions from the outset and thinking through how the objective and the issues it raises can be framed to gain support both domestically and internationally.

Objectives should be shaped by stakes and feasibility. Stakes, by definition, tell us how much we stand to lose (or potentially gain). George H. W. Bush felt that Saddam Hussein's invasion and seizure of Kuwait could not stand because it would mean big states could engage in aggression and seize their smaller neighbors. Joe Biden saw Putin's invasion of Ukraine in much the same way. Both felt that basic norms in the international system were at stake if the United States did not reverse the Iraqi aggression (in Bush's case) or make Putin pay such a high price that he would look for a way out (in Biden's case). Each saw the world becoming much less stable if such behaviors were normalized—and that meant the stakes were high. They both also believed that the objectives were feasible and, therefore, achievable.

Feasibility is a judgment call. The higher the stakes, the more policymakers will decide that they will run risks necessary to make sure the objective is achieved. Still, they will want to understand what they are facing and the means they must employ to be able to be successful. In other words, they will need sound assessments so they understand the reality, the challenges, the possibilities, the dangers, and who else can play a role. There is a continuum of stakes and feasibility: the lower the stakes, the more the feasibility will matter. In any case, assessments are important in determining objectives, but are more likely to shape objectives in those cases where the stakes are perceived to be lower.

In the German unification case, the objective was shaped by the president and the secretary of state, both of whom saw the stakes as very high. Notably, officials in the State Department and the Intelligence Community below the most senior political levels actually opposed the idea of German unification in NATO, believing that it was not achievable given Soviet, British, and French opposition. They did not read the stakes the same way. In the Yugoslav case during Bush's presidency and in the Syrian case during the Obama administration, the bureaucratic, non-political level officials, believed that the stakes warranted much greater US intervention—or at least a greater role. But Presidents Bush and Obama both doubted the feasibility and adopted the objective of avoidance. For both Bush and Obama, the stakes were not seen as so high, and their fears of a quagmire were decisive.

Their fears, their assessments, were probably too strong to get them to change their predispositions even if there had been more systematic questioning about the consequences of avoidance as an aim. Nonetheless, as a rule, asking more questions makes sense both on objectives and on means, and especially on how the means fit the objective. When in the Situation Room meeting on Libya, I pointed out that either the group had to persuade President Obama to change his publicly stated objective of preventing a massacre in Benghazi, or those in the room had to change the means they were prepared to use in Libya, because there was a huge gap between the two positions. No one in the room acted as if there was a relationship between objectives and means, and that is why I raised it. It had occurred to no one in the Situation Room—and even after I raised this, I was asked if I was pushing for a military intervention. The question indicated that the very idea of challenging the group to think about the gap between objectives and means was not taken as a natural way of deciding on the right course, but rather as a signal that I had a problem with the emerging consensus.

And yet, the starting point for good statecraft must be treating objectives and means as organically linked. It has to be part of the discussion of thinking through the objective and how it can be achieved. It is the first-order question regardless of the stakes—indeed, the higher the stakes, the greater the need to think through all the tools for achieving what is necessary. The lower the stakes, the more thinking through the tools, or the partners who have means, will be important for shaping what the objective should be.

One set of means that needs to be employed early is framing the issue. Seizing the initiative in shaping how the issue—which really means the objective—is thought of is essential. With the Berlin Wall having come down and German unification becoming a certainty, Baker's four principles had the rest of the world reacting to the US framing of the issue—Germans had to decide their future, unification would need to take place in the context of the continued German commitment to NATO, but with due regard for the legal role and responsibilities of the four powers; it had to take place gradually, and with full respect for the inviolability of existing borders. The principles meant that the outcome would be unification in NATO, but in a way that was not rushed and took account of the concerns of the British, the French, and the Soviets (three of the four powers).

Seizing the initiative is important while always thinking of leverage. Leverage is all about getting others to do what we want regardless of what they may want. It is important with allies, partners, neutrals, and adversaries. It may not always be easy to apply leverage, but it is always necessary, and doing it well and in a timely fashion is essential. Did the Biden administration apply leverage effectively with Israel or with Qatar in Gaza? If humanitarian assistance was so critical to the American support, the pressure that the president needed to apply to Prime Minister Netanyahu on this issue needed to be very real, very early on. After Israel's mistaken killing of the seven aid workers of the World Central Kitchen, President Biden told Netanyahu that the administration would reassess its posture on Gaza and support for Israel if immediate concrete steps were not taken to allow much more humanitarian assistance into the Gaza Strip. For six months, Netanyahu had rejected opening the northern crossing point from Israel and permitting the number of trucks to reach into the hundreds. After Biden's warning, Israel's posture changed, and what had not been acceptable for six months was finally done. Yes, the context had changed and the threat was more believable to Netanyahu, but it needed to happen earlier.

Similarly, the Biden administration should have put real pressure on Qatar to use its leverage on Hamas–leverage that was the product of both Hamas dependency on Qatar for money and the fact that its political leaders resided in Doha. In fact, having given the Qataris the status of being a "major non-NATO ally" in March of 2022, the administration should have made it clear from the outset that Doha needed to use its relationship with Hamas to get the American hostages—at a minimum—released immediately or the United States would not be able to rationalize why Qatar should be accorded such a status. The Qatari argument that its relationship allowed them to reach out to Hamas and moderate its positions seemed to be taken at face value by the Biden administration—largely, perhaps, because the administration was desperate to have a channel to Hamas. In truth, there was little to indicate that Qatar affected Hamas's calculus, while there is much to indicate that Hamas used the relationship with Qatar to benefit the organization's goals. There was very little sign that Qatar pressured Hamas in a meaningfully way. In fact, for months after October 7, the Qataris acted as a mediator, passing messages but not exerting any of its presumed leverage. As one of the senior Israelis responsible for negotiating with Qatar on getting the hostages out told me, "from everything we see, Qatar could apply pressure but largely refrains from it." The United States itself should not have refrained from applying pressure on Qatar, yet at least until just before Ramadan in March 2024, it was apparently applying very little.[a]

To be fair, maybe Qatar's leverage on Hamas was not that great, especially on the military wing of Hamas and its leader, Yahya Sinwar, who was the keeper of the hostages. But if so, shouldn't the administration have conveyed to the Qatari leadership that they needed to let Hamas know that the Qataris would end its material support for Hamas and its political leaders? Shouldn't the political leaders of Hamas like Ismail Haniyeh, Khaled Mashal, and Abu Marzouk know that they would not be allowed to remain in Qatar any longer or use Al Jazeera as a platform?

Knowing how to apply leverage—and when—is another foundational element for effective statecraft. Richard Holbrooke instinctively understood it in Bosnia and persevered when others thought that the United States needed to stop the bombing of Serbia or the Croatia offensive that was changing the realities on the ground. He was unwilling to do either. He understood that the bombing and the Croat offensive were moving Milošević. But he also understood that the United States could not apply only coercion and negative pressure if the objective was to finalize an agreement. Incentives had to be provided as well—and it was Holbrooke who pushed for easing sanctions on Serbia on the eve of going to Dayton to show Milošević what could be gained. In trying to resolve historic conflicts, both pressure and possible gain must be present. One of the most unfortunate terms used in the Biden administration was "relentless diplomacy"—as if talking more would resolve conflicts. Like Obama after Bush, Biden wanted to show the contrast with Trump and his disdain for alliances and traditional diplomacy. But diplomacy without applying leverage is doomed to fail; it represents a failure to understand the roots of good statecraft.

Statecraft means using all our tools; hence, in most high-stake conflicts or competition, back channels need to be employed. Back channels permit the introduction of ideas or testing of possibilities in a way that formal talks simply preclude. But back channels have to be cultivated and nurtured; they take time to develop and typically are a function of building relationships—often meaning that they may need to employ those who are not part of the existing administration but who have long-standing ties with those with whom the

---

[a] After that, I was told that Bill Burns, the CIA Director during the Biden administration, did warn the Qataris that there would be consequences for the bilateral relationship between the United States and Quatar if the administration did not see progress made on the hostage releases. But why wait for months?

administration seeks at least some understandings. Henry Kissinger had ties and credibility with the Chinese. Robert Zoellick (former deputy secretary of state and head of the World Bank) and Tom Donilon (former national security advisor) could be his likely successors with China. Officials within administrations can develop these relationships—like the ones I developed with Sergei Tarasenko (the Soviets), Sallai Meridor and Yitzhik Molho (the Israelis), or Abu Ala (the Palestinians). But there has to be a recognition within the administration that building these relationships takes time, the ability to show understanding of the other side's concerns, proof of credibility, and the ability to deliver—and that the most sensitive discussions will never be exposed.

Back channels clearly require a mindset and the use of those who are very close to the president or secretary of state and are seen as authoritative. Presidents and secretaries of state need to appreciate the value of back channels and, in circumstances where those might be difficult to establish, use people on the outside (like Henry Kissinger in the past) to initiate them.

In terms of a checklist to go through to employ statecraft effectively, decision-makers need to satisfy themselves that they have defined clear, understandable, and meaningful objectives. Hardheaded assessments are essential for refining the objectives so they fit reality, relevant ambitions, and means, including the means that can be marshaled from others. Decision-makers must focus on how to frame the issues and what is at stake in a way that not only can mobilize but sustain domestic support—and at the same time legitimize objectives internationally while raising the costs to those who would oppose them. The more soft power is available, the easier it will be to attract others to the established objectives, but smart and early framing of issues and stakes can help promote soft power while conditioning attitudes and expectations more generally. Active diplomacy (including back channels) and the careful orchestration of inducements and penalties—to include threats and coercion—is an essential means for achieving the objectives. To that end, decision-makers must ask what steps will be taken, which other players can help, what will it take (in terms of assistance or assurances or pressure) to get them to play the necessary role, and what fallbacks need to be adopted if the stated objectives cannot be achieved at this juncture.

One might ask how would such a checklist of questions and considerations work with a president like Donald Trump who is known to make decisions more on impulse than deep consideration? The short answer is that those working for him have an obligation to think everything through along the lines of what I just outlined. He instinctively understands leverage, so that is not the issue. What is critical is that he be able to adopt the right objectives–and here the task may not be so difficult: he defines everything in terms of "wins" and "losses"–and those around him must be able to show how, with the objective they propose, America (and he personally) wins and with the alternative objectives, America (and he personally) loses. To be fair, most political leaders personalize the meaning of their decisions and rationalize that it serves the larger good. Trump is just more open about it.

Put simply, those around him must be sure to embrace the checklist or set of questions I outlined that help to govern good statecraft. That checklist applies not only to traditional national security challenges; it also can and should be applied to the new ones of today: climate change, pandemics, and cyber threats. All three respect no borders, and none of them can be handled on a unilateral basis. Each challenge poses its own threats to national security. Consider climate change: droughts drive migration and, in cases like Syria, might provoke terrible internal wars. They may increasingly produce wars over water unless water availability can be expanded. In fact, as John Kerry pointed out in a speech in 2021, climate change has been provoking wide-ranging dangers internationally: "Climate change is a threat multiplier that will create untold number of refugees and migrants, disrupt food supplies, put military installations at risk, and create increasingly fragile states and societies where extremists and terrorists can flourish."[1] How should one encapsulate objectives, means, and leverage with climate change, pandemics, and cyber threats?

Climate Change

The irony of climate change is that in 2015, at the UN climate conference, a consensus was forged on making sure that the increase in global temperatures did not rise by two degrees Celsius above pre-industrial levels. The next year in the Paris climate agreement, nearly 200 nations not only agreed to this objective but went further and pledged efforts to keep the growth below 1.5 degrees Celsius. Scientists have warned that if temperatures rise by more than 1.5 degrees, coral reefs will not survive and the Arctic sea ice will melt—raising the ocean levels and threatening islands and coastlines, not to mention the more severe weather it will produce.

In 2023–2024, for the first time, the global temperatures rose by 1.5 degrees Celsius from pre-industrial levels. Perhaps that is why we are already experiencing severe weather, meaning more intense hurricanes and tornadoes, extreme droughts, greater heat waves, and huge winter snow and ice storms—and related developments like terrible flooding and more extensive fires that take place year round and not only in what used to be called fire seasons. The objective stated in the Paris climate accord is clear, and countries did pledge to reduce carbon emissions. However, those pledges were voluntary, and while investment in green technologies and carbon capture are increasing, economic growth still depends on using cheaper fossil fuels and, in nearly every country, there are those who resist making decisions on climate that will inevitably involve some economic sacrifice in the near term. Moreover, countries in the Global South say that since they did not contribute to the global warming problem, they should not be denied their ability to develop and modernize—and, at a minimum, there must be contributions from the developed countries to help them cope with the consequences of climate change and also adjust their economies. To that end, there have been pledges to create a fund of $100 billion for developing countries, but that is far short of what is needed—and even these pledges have not been fulfilled. Moreover, as Lawrence Summers and N. K. Singh point out, instead of providing the developing countries with the moneys and capital they need, more money is flowing out of these countries than in, as they are forced to pay more to private creditors than they are receiving.[2]

So the objective may be clear, but even in the United States, there is no consensus on the needed steps. Many Republicans still question the science related to global warming, declaring that it is not human-made and simply part of a historic cycle. Indeed, President Trump once referred to global warming as a hoax. But it is interesting that in a politically "red" state like Florida, there is increasing concern about the danger of the sea rising and threatening cities and infrastructure along the coast. The point is that it is possible to create pressures domestically to emphasize the need to address the increasingly perilous consequences of climate change.

But what about acting internationally? What are the means the United States can use to move toward the necessary goal of reducing heat-trapping carbon emissions to the point where warming is controllable and maybe reversible to at least some extent? There already is an international mechanism, the Conference of the Parties (COP), that meets annually to assess the efforts to fulfill the Paris Agreement; the COP asks countries to showcase what they are doing to meet the targets they have committed to reaching on reducing emissions and working toward becoming carbon-neutral. This questioning can implicitly create pressure on those who are not doing so; indeed, one aim in COP meetings must increasingly become focusing on those countries that are failing to meet their targets and generating pressures and inducements for them to change the trajectory of their efforts.

In addition, as we think about means for reaching the objective, each COP meeting creates an opportunity (actually, an imperative) to prepare for the event by working with US allies, especially European and Japanese, to see what the countries can do collectively and with the international financial institutions to address the needs of the Global South. Since both the Saudis and the Emiratis have an interest in showing their commitment to becoming good global citizens and leaders in renewables, it is important to actively seek to bring them more into these new financing efforts.[b]

In this connection, much remains to be done to ensure that the World Bank, the developmental banks, and the International Monetary Fund become instruments for helping developing countries cope with the climate crisis and adapt their economies to be more sustainable and more carbon-neutral. Summers and Singh argue that the Multilateral Development Banks (MDBs) need to become "big, risk-taking, climate focused banks." They are not lending with this as the priority now and will only do so if the wealthy countries that are the biggest stakeholders in the multilateral system "provide the political support for that risk-taking."[3]

The MDBs are one of the tools that need to be employed, but they will only play the role if the United States mobilizes its allies to enable them to do so. In theory, especially with its global pretensions, China's role here could be helpful as well. It did help to strengthen the International Monetary Fund's financial capacity through contributions to its concessional lending instrument for low-income countries, but it continues to press for greater voting power to reflect its economic clout without increasing its overall contributions to the Fund.[4,c]

US public diplomacy—and the framing of America's response to the climate crisis—should emphasize the responsibility that the wealthier states

---

[b] The Emirates did make a financial contribution when they hosted COP 26.

[c] The United States has been proposing an "equiproportional" increase in International Monetary Fund quotas—with quotas being the money that member states contribute to the fund—being the step first before altering voting shares.

have to help countries in the Global South cope with the climate crisis; in that context, the United States should be calling publicly on China to do more to help others in need. This is a vulnerability of China as it claims to represent the needs and interests of the Global South while its help usually ends up creating greater indebtedness to the Chinese.

Once again, we are reminded of the importance of framing in general, and particularly how important it can be for dealing with the challenge of climate change. To mobilize others on climate, it is important to be consistently framing the issue in way that highlights the dangers and the risks of not acting—as well as the steps we are taking to combat it. John Podesta, who replaced John Kerry as the climate czar in the Biden administration, made an effort to do both in his speeches. In a speech in April 2024, Podesta highlighted that 2023 was the hottest year on record and that the months from the summer of 2023 to March 2024 were the hottest ever recorded. He spoke of the deaths caused by the heat and said that in Iran, the heat index at one point hit 152 degrees Fahrenheit, "nearing the limit for human survival." But he also spoke about the steps the United States is taking, to include "mobilizing a whole-of-government approach to cutting carbon pollution across every sector: power, transportation, building, industry, agriculture, forestry ... And by passing the Inflation Reduction Act—the largest investment in climate and clean energy in history."[5]

Framing and leading by example should be taken as a given. Working in subgroups with allies, especially those like the British and the Germans who are meeting targets they have set for themselves in becoming carbon-neutral, is another way to demonstrate how the United States and others are making progress. The United States can be calling on others to match its efforts—asking them to demonstrate their own commitment the way Americans are demonstrating theirs is another way to exert leverage on China and give it a reason to do more. The Chinese do show sensitivity to anything that exposes their role as the world's biggest emitter of carbon gases. In general, one should not be hesitant to think about the tool of naming and shaming those who are contributing to the climate crisis—sometimes recognizing that the private threat of going public may be sufficient to get responsiveness to the behaviors that the United States seeks to change. That may be especially true with the Chinese.

Beyond framing and both publicly and privately using threats to name and shame as a tool, the United States needs to think about how to develop and exploit public–private partnerships on the climate challenges. Major energy companies have the means and incentives to invest in renewables, particularly as they seek to become the leading suppliers of new alternative and cleaner forms of energy. Moreover, they also have an interest in showing that they are responsible social actors—meaning, they are likely to have a big stake in investing in the new technologies that have the potential to mitigate warming. These technologies are grouped in a category that is called geo-engineering, and they range from literally sucking carbon out of the atmosphere and injecting it into rocks—where much carbon has already become minerals—to deflecting the sun's rays so as to reduce heat. In the past, these technologies might have appeared to be science fiction rather than fact, but they are no longer simply the figment of fertile imaginations.

The multinational energy companies are pursuing green technologies, including the development of both blue and green hydrogen.[d] A great deal of investment is needed to create blue or green hydrogen on scale, and companies and countries are already working collaboratively on this, though more of such collaboration is surely possible. Already in August 2021, John Kerry spoke about developing hydrogen, "From Saudi Arabia to India to Germany to Japan we're setting up hydrogen partnerships around the world to advance this critical technology that every country understands has the opportunity to play a vital role in the clean energy transition."[6] Critics of the focus on hydrogen say it is too expensive and not as clean ultimately as wind and solar—where they would like to see greater investment and collaboration take place.

The larger point is that the private sector is investing in the green technologies because it sees the need, the market, and potentially the governmental interest. That interest existed in the Biden administration. Will it exist in the Trump administration? Precisely because the private sector is being drawn to investing in the green technologies, the Trump Administration is likely to have an interest as well and see the virtue of forging public-private partnerships.

One can also see President Trump being drawn to the exotic technologies that can actually cool the planet on a temporary basis.[e] Because the exotic, but increasingly applicable, technologies involve re-engineering the

---

[d] The main difference between the two is that blue hydrogen is made from a chemical process using natural gas, which does release carbon in the process, but the effort is made to capture carbon so it is not released into the atmosphere; while green hydrogen is made from renewable sources of power (e.g., wind, solar, or water.

[e] One technology involves testing a system to disperse a cloud of tiny reflective particles about 60,000 feet in the altitude, reflecting sunlight away from the Earth to cool the atmosphere. An Israeli

weather, they require careful consideration and a very clear statecraft mind-set and approach. After all, they raise basic questions about re-engineering the weather with the very real possibility that changing the weather over one country can affect it potentially negatively over another.

In this regard, an editorial in *The Washington Post* smartly calls for "a concerted diplomacy" to "establish agreed upon guardrails around a tech-nology that remains little understood but whose deployment would have widespread and yet unequal effects for different countries around the world." For example, as the editorial asks, could a major effort to cool Saudi Arabia or Gulf States alter the monsoon season in India and with what effects?[7]

The new technologies offer a pathway to compensate for the reality that countries are not meeting their own declared targets on greenhouse emis-sions; the danger is waiting too long to take the necessary steps and hoping for a technological fix—each of which might produce uncertain conse-quences. But this is a challenge for using the tools of statecraft, and the private sector is likely to provide a means to help achieve the climate change objectives. The Trump administration needs to see there is a tool here. It would also need to see the additive value of working with allies and part-ners in part because of the sheer size of the investments required and also to maximize collectively what the private sector and new technologies can do—even as everyone works together to manage and minimize some of the negative consequences.

There is irony here as well. An administration like Biden's can show it is not only about regulating the private sector or managing it, but can work in partnership. And an administration like Trump's might discover that it can make a lot of money for the private sector while producing a winning hand.

Pandemics

There is an obvious connection between climate change and health. Already over 700 million people a year get mosquito-borne diseases, with one million dying as a result. Diseases such as the Zika virus, Dengue fever, and malaria are spread by mosquitos. Higher temperatures are going to make these dis-eases worse and expand globally those areas where people are going to suffer from them. The diseases will become worse because higher temperatures

company called Stardust Solutions is developing this technology, which can produce what is called "solar radiation management."

make mosquitos hungrier, and within them, shorten the incubation period of the virus before they become infectious.[8] In addition, hotter temperatures also expand the habitats for mosquitos and introduce these diseases to areas where they had previously not occurred.[9]

Similarly, hotter temperatures will threaten health in another way: there is a distinct possibility that novel antibiotic-resistant bacteria and viruses that have been trapped, literally frozen in the permafrost, will be released as it melts.[10] And, as we saw with COVID, new viruses can cause pandemics when populations have little or no immunities. Pandemics can overwhelm healthcare systems, wreck economies, devastate militaries, and produce death on an enormous scale. The so-called Spanish flu pandemic of 1918 infected an estimated 500 million people, 1/3 of the world's population at the time, and killed roughly 50 million. The United States lost more people to the Spanish flu than all of the American fatalities in two world wars combined with the Korean and Vietnam wars.

The numbers of deaths from COVID, which still numbered in the millions, might have been dramatically worse had it not been for the rapidity in which the mRNA vaccines were developed. They proved to be very effective not necessarily in terms of prevention of the illness but in terms of its mitigation and prevention of death. In addition to huge resources that were immediately committed to dealing with COVID, two factors help to explain why the vaccines were developed so quickly. First, the genetic code of the virus was submitted to a National Institute of Health database known as GenBank.[11,f] Once it was published in GenBank, scientists in different labs internationally investigated the sequence and quickly came to recognize the similarity to the SARS virus, which had been discovered in Asia in February 2003. Second, when SARS was discovered, funding was provided for research into it. That funding also led to the development of possible vaccines, to include mRNA vaccines to deal with it. That prior work proved pivotal when dealing with COVID.

There is a lesson here for dealing with pandemics: the most important objective is preparedness. The means flow from that. So what is the starting point? According to Dr. Daniel Douek, a senior researcher at NIH who also is charged with doing preparedness for pandemics, there are two essential means that are necessary to achieve this objective: first, create a repository

---

[f] It actually could have been published in the database earlier had the Chinese been more transparent and forthcoming.

of vaccines effective against a range of virus strains that could emerge; and second, create excess manufacturing capacity for producing the potential vaccines that will be necessary. Both, of course, require money, but both permit early identification of a vaccine that can work, and the production capability to make huge quantities of it.[12]

One of the failings of the United States and the international response to COVID was the slow response to providing vaccines to Africa and Latin America. Because there was no way to hermetically seal any country from the infection—though clearly some countries tried with varying degrees of success—it was always in the American interest to create wide distribution of the vaccines. Like other countries, the United States wanted to conserve and use its vaccines for its citizens first; this was a natural response, and it is likely to be the case again not just for America but for the Europeans, the Chinese, the Japanese, the South Koreans, etc.

The problem is that pandemic viruses respect no physical border and will spread wherever there are those who have no immunities. The aphorism that scientists use when talking about pandemics is, "An outbreak anywhere is an outbreak everywhere." When the United States is arranging for vaccines to be provided to others, it is not only the morally right thing to do, but also profoundly in America's national self-interest.

That should remind US administrations that they have an education and framing job to do as part of shaping responses to a new pandemic—and that too needs to be part of administrations' toolkit as they meet the objective of preparedness. Perhaps, America's poor and inconsistent initial messaging on COVID—lockdowns vs. no lockdowns, masks vs. no masks, travel vs. no travel, and open borders vs. closed borders—was the result of not knowing enough about the virus and how it spread. But learning the lessons of COVID should put current and future administrations in a better place to explain what they can do to reduce the risk and consequence of the next infection, whenever it might happen.

From the beginning, it will be important to remind everyone what we all have learned in dealing with the COVID pandemic. If the next pandemic is as dangerous as COVID, then the starting point will be minimizing exposure and infection until a vaccine has been developed. The good news is that scientists have demonstrated that they can collaborate internationally, as labs very far removed from each other shared discoveries and insights about the genetic code of the virus and the best ways to counteract it. Even if leaderships of some countries were initially not so prone to cooperating, scientists and researchers ignored political constraints and generally worked together.[13]

The less dangerous the virus, the less the cost of letting people get it and develop immunities—indeed, to develop a herd immunity to it. In other words, lockdowns do not make sense if the population at large is generally not in danger from the virus—and steps can be taken to protect vulnerable groups prior to the development and distribution of vaccines. The converse is true: lockdowns become essential if the virus is virulent, easily spread and life-threatening. Understanding this difference is essential. Similarly, understanding the importance of making sure that vaccines are produced and distributed to all the countries is an essential self-interest of the global community if it wants to control the virus and limit its impact.

Here we see the importance of investing in greater production capabilities for being able to surge what can be produced in a crisis. This preparedness must not be limited only to the United States. Part of being prepared for such a dangerous pandemic must be generating manufacturing capability in Africa and Latin America so the production can be done regionally and locally. Clearly, someone must drive the process to develop these factories. Too often, if the United States does not mobilize the international community, it simply does not get mobilized and organized. The best tool for generating the money and investment in developing the production capabilities in Africa and Latin America is probably some combination of the G-20 countries working with the World Bank, the Regional Development Banks, the International Monetary Fund, and also with big pharmaceutical companies. Developing the manufacturing capability not only would provide for a surge capacity to produce vaccines when critically necessary but, once these factories exist, they can be used for production of other medicines during non-pandemic times.

Once again, we see the importance of preparedness and the steps that can create the necessary infrastructure in advance. One step that the United States should be organizing and creating in advance are mechanisms that can produce systematic and collective, collaborative and non-competitive responses to a pandemic. This includes health responses, but it also multilateral actions designed to deal with managing trade, travel, and economic needs and assistance internationally. This should not be an exclusionary approach as pandemics do not respect political or ideological differences.

To be fair, there are structures and mechanisms internationally that are inclusive and are designed to enhance preparedness—and they do involve experts. For example, the World Health Organization (WHO) is certainly charged with dealing with pandemics. And the director-general of the WHO as of this writing, Tedros Adhanom Ghebreyesus, clearly understands the need to do more. In a speech in September 2023, he said that the WHO recognizes "the need for a stronger architecture for health emergency preparedness and response." To that end, he explained that the WHO was already involved in negotiating a legally binding accord on pandemic preparedness and response; in addition, the WHO was piloting a Universal Health and Preparedness Review. He added that the WHO was also developing a concept note for an "interim mechanism to coordinate timely and equitable access to medical countermeasures for pandemic and epidemic threats."[14]

These are laudable efforts, but they fall far short of what is necessary. Only five countries have signed onto the legally binding document he described—and they are all small countries. While there have been international pledges to create a $1.7 billion fund to deal with pandemics, that amount is far below what is needed, and even this figure has not been met, only pledged.

The basic problem is that preparedness is being handled at an expert, functional level, not at the level of political leadership. Unless the level is raised, preparation will drift along producing incremental improvements at best. Like with climate change, political leaders must seize the issue, and one way to do so is to create a standing committee of the G-20 charged with preparedness. Yes, the G-20 did create a Finance-Health Task Force, but what is needed is a high-level standing committee that is charged with identifying key targets and benchmarks for preparedness and reporting on the progress or lack of it to each annual meeting. Indeed, preparedness needs to be on the agenda of the G-20 each year. Just as the COP provides an annual basis on which to showcase both the good and the bad of climate change, the G-20 needs to be similarly committed to creating pandemic preparedness from every standpoint—e.g., sharing information on an outbreak quickly, preparing a stockpile of vaccines for a range of potential viruses, expanding production capabilities, increasing the availability of critical health materials (masks, hypodermic needles, ventilators), anticipating how to manage trade and travel in the event of a pandemic outbreak, etc.

Such a standing committee should have a secretariat that runs its work throughout the year—organizing meetings, creating agendas for these meeting, and flagging potential problems. Creating this approach within the G-20 will mean more if leaders are truly committed to the issue; in this connection, preparedness needs to be put on the agenda of bilateral summit meetings. If US presidents are raising this with their counterparts in summits (and those like Xi, Macron, Starmer, and Scholz know that this topic is going to be discussed), the sense of commitment and urgency will grow and the results will be far different from leaving this to the WHO, or even to the standing committee of G-20 that I propose.

Those who think it will be difficult to raise preparedness to a political level may prove to be correct. But the more public exposure there is of possible new pandemics, the more political leaders will not want to look like they are not addressing it. And as one listens to scientists like Daniel Douek speak of the increasing risks of a new pandemic—with all what it might mean to economy, security, physical and societal health—the more important it will be raise the political urgency of preparedness as an objective and the value of adopting a statecraft approach in which the United States uses all of its tools, soft power, and leverage to address it.

Cyber Threats

We live in a digital world where information and misinformation can travel fast—and where dangerous disinformation can go viral very quickly. With so many younger people getting their news almost exclusively from Tik Tok and other social media in a skewed and often misleading form, it is no simple task to keep publics informed and help them understand what is really going on in the world. Those who threaten America's interests and values use these platforms to present reality differently and to sow doubts about what America is and what it is doing. Indeed, in the information space today, whether dealing with how AI can be misused to distort reality or how social media can be exploited to tell a story that seems to legitimize the indefensible, the challenge to frame issues is far more difficult than ever before. On the one hand, it will almost certainly take new techniques to capture attention and frame discussions in ways that explain policies and gain support for them. On the other hand, the need to move with great speed to discredit misleading or dangerous posts or videos that can shape the way millions may think about an event puts a premium on moving fast. Unfortunately, that can mean moving without necessarily being in a position to be certain of all the facts—and yet if one waits too long the image is set and is hard to reverse.

Take the October 2023 example of an Islamic Jihad missile hitting the parking lot of the al Shifa hospital in Gaza city, causing a fireball and killing dozens. Hamas immediately claimed that this was an Israeli bomb, and the videos of the fireball and the deaths were immediately compelling. The Israeli Defense Force did the responsible thing, declaring that they were checking on what happened. Internationally, social and traditional media immediately went with the charge made by Hamas, and the impression was created that Israel did it, fortifying the view that Israel was indiscriminately bombing Palestinians and hitting targets that should have been off limits. Subsequently, Israel would release radar data that showed the launch of a barrage of Islamic Jihad rockets from next to the hospital, one of which misfired and crashed and its fuel ignited, creating the fireball. Israel also released an intercepted conversation between commanders of Islamic Jihad and Hamas, with the Islamic Jihad officer explaining that one of its rockets misfired and the Hamas official saying that they would blame it on the Israelis—and that is the image that prevailed.

As I have repeatedly pointed out, effectively framing issues is an essential form of statecraft. While social media makes it more of a challenge to seize the initiative and frame issues successfully, it certainly also creates more opportunity to do so. If there was a time when the United States Information Agency (USIA) was the vehicle that different administrations used as the American tool for public diplomacy—and ad agency executives were often selected to run it—today when the USIA no longer exists, social media wizards may be needed to play a leading role in public engagement internationally. Combining expertise on the substance of the issues with those who can package it in a compelling and alluring way will be one of the means the United States will need to be able to employ to affect the public information space.[g] (Maybe another is to invest in media literacy education as the US Department of State is doing.)

The cyber domain clearly affects the atmosphere in which the United States conducts foreign policy. Cyber tools necessarily must be wielded effectively by US administrations, especially as cyber-attacks pose increasing threats to American security and well-being. A cyber-attack, using malicious computer code, can target "an enterprise's use of cyberspace for the purpose of disrupting, disabling, destroying, or maliciously controlling a

---

[g] The State Department has an office of public engagement as an adjunct to its spokesperson operation. It uses all social media platforms. This function probably needs to be more centralized, taken seriously as a tool of policy, and needs to become more agile. While instant reactions are important, getting things wrong will discredit what we say more generally so it is a hard balance to strike.

computing environment/infrastructure; or destroying the integrity of the data or stealing controlled information."[15]

These attacks or threats come in many forms. Some are obvious: cyber-attacks against critical infrastructure can shut down systems ranging from electrical grids to water; cyber-attacks against the banking system or ability to conduct commercial or stock transactions could paralyze the economy; cyber-attacks against health or transportations systems—or transmissions of energy and fuel—can be both disruptive and dangerous. Moreover, cyber threats can come from state actors and non-state actors, including criminal actors that states can employ.

In this connection, nearly all sectors of the US economy have been subjected to ransomware. Hospitals have been locked out of their own data banks and medical files—and unable to access them unless they pay off the group that penetrated their systems. Fuel transmission systems have been the target of ransomware. Darkside, a criminal gang operating out of Russia, shut down Colonial Pipeline, which disrupted gasoline supplies in the southeastern United States and forced a dramatic increase in prices. Was Darkside operating with the Russian government's permission, doing its bidding? This is unclear. One thing is for sure: Russia was doing little to stop it or put it out of business, at least until the shutdown of Colonial Pipeline raised the profile of Darkside and created pressures on the Biden administration to impose a price on Russia.

No doubt those pressures were higher because of Russia's use of cyber tools to interfere in the US election in 2016. China has actively employed cyber tools for intelligence aims, for industrial espionage purposes, and even for penetrating the personnel records of the Office of Personnel and Management of the US government—a hack that exposed the private personal information of everyone who had worked for the federal government at that time.

The expectation that cyber could play a pivotal, disarming role in wartime has proven to date to be overblown, with the Russians able to do little against the Ukrainians in this domain. That does not mean that there are no cyber threats to be concerned about in the military realm or during conflicts, but, as Jacquelyn Schneider points out, the biggest concern is the ability of US adversaries to use cyber tools to sow mistrust in political, economic, and defense systems of the United States.[16]

Given the wide array of cyber threats, the most important objective is to be able to counter or blunt them. At a fundamental level, it is essential to make sure that cyber tools cannot be used to pose threats to America's national well-being and faith in US institutions. To that end, the Biden administration adopted a National Cyber Security Strategy in 2023 which was based on five pillars: (1) defend critical infrastructure, (2) disrupt and dismantle threat actors, (3) shape market forces to drive security and resilience, (4) invest in a resilient future, and (5) forge international partnerships to pursue shared goals.[17]

These pillars addressed areas of vulnerability, were designed to plug the holes in US data systems, and reflected an understanding that an approach emphasizing digital solidarity among domestic and international partners was necessary. There are few challenges that require effective statecraft more than cyber threats. Indeed, it requires a whole-of-government approach, calling on intelligence—technological and scientific—as well as on diplomatic, economic, financial, military, and informational means. It is essential to forge and build partnerships domestically and internationally with all those partners who can play a role.

In fact, fostering digital solidarity will be essential for blunting threats. In producing digital solidarity, Secretary of State Blinken stated that the effort required "working together to offer mutual assistance to the victims of malicious cyber activity and other digital harms; assist partners—especially in emerging economies—in deploying safe, secure, resilient, and inclusive innovation economies that can shape our economic and technological future." To that end, he said that the Biden administration is "rallying coalitions of governments, businesses, and civil society to shape the digital revolution at every level of the technology 'stack'—from building subsea cables and telecommunication networks, to deploying cloud services and trustworthy artificial intelligence, to promoting rights-respecting data governance and norms of state behavior."[18]

Public–private partnerships are essential. The private sector needs to work hand in glove with the government to identify breaches or gaps in the networks, and to fix them. Microsoft, Meta, Google, X, and other high-tech companies need to be in active partnership with the government to provide active cyber defense, with the ability to patch vulnerabilities as they emerge. Collectively, they need to provide best practices to minimize vulnerabilities and to protect data and systems.

Within the government, there needs to be a central address to coordinate all governmental agencies and manage threats. As Sue Gordon and Eric Rosenbach point out, the Cybersecurity and Infrastructure Agency in the Department of Homeland Security needs to be the authority of all domestic cybersecurity operations over intelligence agencies, law enforcement agencies, and the military.[19] Gordon and Rosenbach also argue that US Cyber Command needs to function like the Joint Special Operations Command to be able to respond quickly and flexibly to any attack.[20]

In other words, defense cannot be passive. Deterrence is clearly essential but it cannot be only the deterrence of the nuclear era which was essentially deterrence through punishment. Indeed, deterrence cannot be limited to the threat of inflicting a high price—although assured destruction of critical infrastructure is bound to be effective against countries like China and Russia. Both probably assume that the United States has planted malware in critical infrastructure, allowing it to be activated if America's leaders believe that either the Chinese or the Russians were going to cross certain thresholds in cyber-attacks against the United States. (If they do not assume it, the administration should be privately conveying to their leaders not only what the United States is capable of doing—in terms of shutting down their countries—but also what it will do if they carry out certain kinds of cyber-attacks.)

In addition to the threat of punishment, deterrence must also be based on denial. Deterrence through denial has meant active defense, it has meant defeating the attempts to use force against the United States. In the cyber realm, the United States needs to be able to blunt attacks and defeat them—not only inflict a cost. If those trying to use cyber tools know that their attacks will not work and the United States will then impose a high price on them for trying, deterrence is much more likely to work. In fact, on this basis, certain broad understandings might prove possible.

The Obama administration did make threats to impose sanctions. Obama may not have been actively threatening to do to China what its hackers were doing to the United States, but he was making clear that the United States would impose sanctions and publicly reveal what the Chinese were doing. For President Obama to reach an understanding with President Xi on limiting cyber theft of intellectual property for commercial gain was sufficient in 2015. This understanding was subsequently embodied two months later in a G-20 communiqué which affirmed that "no country should conduct or support ICT-enable theft of intellectual property, including trade secrets or confidential business information, with the intent of providing competitive advantages to companies or commercial sectors."[21]

While a good start, the understanding between Obama and Xi was limited to imposing prohibitions only on cyber espionage for commercial purposes and not for national security purposes. That certainly seemed to contribute to the Chinese not living up to the understanding for very long. Why? With many emerging technologies being dual-use (having both civilian and military applications), either the Chinese have rationalized that dual-use technology was fair game for hacking because it had a national security purpose or they had always intended to violate the understanding. Regardless of the reason, the Chinese are now hacking as much if not more than ever before. One observer reported that Beijing targets "valuable actors and specific industries with laser-like precision, including defense contractors, telecommunications firms, government agencies and technology companies."[22] Moreover, John Hultquist, head of Mandiant Threat Intelligence at Google Cloud, says that "Chinese hackers have also become far more adept at hiding and diversifying the infrastructure they use to carry out attacks."[23]

How can the United States affect the Chinese calculus so more meaningful understandings can be forged to limit their hacking? First, it is important to decide where China's hacking fits in the overall relationship between China and the United States, and determine the most important behaviors that the United States seeks to alter. Second, even as the United States weighs what it is trying to affect, it will make sense to employ both private and public approaches to China. The more the administration regards China's cyber behavior as a priority, the more the message that the administration is sending to China in private should be a tough one. The administration should convey that unless China is prepared to agree to and respect certain boundaries of acceptable cyber behavior, the United States will have little choice but to start carrying out its own attacks on Chinese systems. In addition, absent such understandings on permissible cyber use, the administration will be prepared to publicly expose what the Chinese are doing not just to the United States with their hacking and cyber assaults but what they are doing to others. Necessarily, such exposures would likely embarrass the Chinese and impose a cost in their relationships with others. Obviously, some of what the United States could expose could be more embarrassing also before their own public in terms of the wealth of Chinese leaders. That is also an approach that could be used with Russia and Putin.

The point is that the administration does not have to be focused only on defense—there are possible offensive uses of cyber tools that can alter the calculus of America's adversaries. Obviously, there are also offensive uses of cyber that can be used to affect threatening programs as well. Much has been written about the Stuxnet worm and how it was used to alter the rotor speeds of the Iranian IR-1 centrifuges—centrifuges that were joined to the Siemens S7-315 and S7-417 industrial controllers. While successful in destroying large numbers of Iranian centrifuges and setting the Iranian nuclear program back about a year, those who implanted the worm were not able to keep it in the machines at Natanz. As Lucas Kello points out, those who inserted the malware into the Iranian Centrifuge Drive System at Natanz wanted it to stay within the facility, but it escaped the air gap that "enveloped the facility" and "traveled speedily beyond its designate logical habitat, infecting tens of thousands of other machines in more than 100 countries in less than one year."[24]

Clearly there are offensive uses of cyber tools for reasons of deterrence and leverage and for disrupting threatening programs like the Iranian nuclear program. But there are also inevitable risks with such use that can also have unintended consequences. With the interconnectedness of computers and networks, offensive uses of cyber tools can bounce back and create real problems for those who employ the malware. The United States chose not to take down servers in the Iraqi financial and banking sector at the outset of the Iraqi invasion in 2003 out of fear that it might also disrupt cash dispensers in Europe.[25] Yes, the United States may be better able to target malware since that time, but the interconnectedness of systems and networks may still create problems that cannot be fully anticipated. Joseph Nye speaks of what he calls "entanglement" and mutual economic dependencies with China that ironically can make cyber tools both more effective as a deterrent but also problematic if their offensive use can create unintended blowback.[26]

Deterrence, defense, and offensive use of cyber tools can create incentives for understandings or creating boundaries of tolerable uses of cyber. Diplomacy should be used deftly to see what is possible. As in all statecraft, leverage is crucial for using diplomacy to alter behaviors with foes and even with friends. With so much of effective statecraft on the cyber domain depending on how the United States forges the digital solidarity that Secretary Blinken spoke of, it is worth noting that there are some collective understandings that can make America more secure. For example, it is possible to develop a "white list" that permits everybody to recognize and distinguish malicious from legitimate code. Such a list would create a case-by-case verification mechanism in which "all installed software ... is digitally signed and any unauthorized modifications can be recognized ... [and] Common integrity breaches caused by CIS [cyberweapons] can be identified and countered in real time."[27]

In the end, like all threats, the cyber threat is evolving. Technological advances are rapid—and both offensive and defensive means are progressing. The partnership with high-tech companies and cyber-security specialists will remain essential—and so will creating close collaboration with US allies and their security and tech specialists. Testing the systems, overseeing how private companies use best practices and protect data, and constantly providing intelligence on threats and how they are evolving must be part of an approach that employs all the available tools.

Good statecraft effectively and efficiently employs the tools the United States has or can mobilize from others. When thinking about these non-traditional threats to America's security—whether climate change, pandemics, and cyber threats—several conclusions are very clear: the United States has to be more agile in using its tools; the United States has to be smarter in terms of how it works with others and mobilizes their means and its own; and the United States has to be clear about identifying, on its own and with others, priorities for dealing with each of these threats. None of this may be easy, but smart practitioners of statecraft will understand the limits of what the United States can do on its own, and how others can help America meet the fundamental task of good statecraft: understanding the threats and opportunities and then being able to marry objectives and means to deal with them.

Endnotes

Preface

1. Gordon Craig and Alexander George, *Force and Statecraft: Diplomatic Problems of Our Time*, 3rd ed. (Oxford, UK: Oxford University Press, 1995), p. xi.

Chapter 1

1. Julian E. Barnes and Helene Cooper, "Trump Discussed Pulling U.S. from NATO, Aides Say amid New Concerns over Russia," *The New York Times*, January 14, 2019.
2. Joe Biden, "Remarks by President Biden on America's Place in the World," Washington, DC, February 4, 2021.
3. Joe Biden, "Remarks by President Biden before the 76th Session of the United Nations General Assembly," New York, NY, September 21, 2021.
4. John Hudson and Missy Ryan, "Withdrawal from Afghanistan forces allies and adversaries to reconsider America's global role," *The Washington Post*, August 17, 2021.
5. Yaroslav Trofimov, Nancy A. Youssef, and Sune Engel Rasmussen, "Kabul Airport Attack Kills 13 U.S. Service Members, at Least 90 Afghans," *The Wall Street Journal*, August 27, 2021.
6. Ivo H. Daalder and James M. Lindsay, "Why Putin Underestimated the West," *Foreign Affairs*, April 7, 2022.
7. Andreas Kluth, "The West's Biggest Enemy, And Putin's Greatest Ally, Is Disunity," *The Washington Post*, January 21, 2022.
8. Joe Biden, "Remarks by President Biden in Press Conference," Madrid, Spain, June 30, 2022.
9. Joe Biden, "Remarks by President Biden on the United Efforts of the Free World to Support the People of Ukraine," Warsaw, Poland, March 26, 2022.
10. Antony Blinken, "Secretary Antony J. Blinken at a Press Availability" Bali, Indonesia, July 9, 2022.
11. Ibid.
12. Antony Blinken, "Secretary Antony J. Blinken With Kiratikorn Naksompop Blauw of Thai PBS," Bangkok, Thailand, July 11, 2022.
13. Ibid.
14. Homi Kharas and Meagan Dooley, "The Evolution of Global Poverty, 1990-2030," Brookings Center for Sustainable Development, February 2, 2022; World Inequality Database, "World Inequality Report 2022," December 7, 2021.
15. Vladimir Putin, "Speech and the Following Discussion at the Munich Conference on Security Policy," Munich, Germany, February 10, 2007.
16. Francis Fukuyama, *The End of History and the Last Man* (Harlow, England: Penguin Books, 1992).
17. Vladimir Putin, "Speech and the Following Discussion at the Munich Conference on Security Policy," Munich, Germany, February 10, 2007.
18. Ibid.
19. CSIS China Power Team, "How Much Trade Transits the South China Sea?" August 2, 2017. Updated January 25, 2021.
20. Tom Phillips, Oliver Holmes, and Owen Bowcott, "Beijing rejects tribunal's ruling in South China Sea case," *The Guardian*, July 12, 2016.
21. Ibid.
22. "MH17 Ukraine plane crash: What we know," BBC, February 26, 2020, at: https://www.bbc.com/news/world-europe-28357880
23. Peter Juul, "A Whole New World," *Liberal Patriot Blog*, February 17, 2022.
24. Antony Blinken, Robert Kagan, "'America First' is only making the world worse. Here's a better approach." *The Washington Post*, January 1, 2019.
25. Vladimir Putin, *First Person* (New York, NY: Public Affairs, 2000).

26. Vladimir Putin, "Address by the President of the Russian Federation," Moscow, Russia, February 24, 2022.
27. Richard Haas, *The Opportunity* (New York, NY: Public Affairs, 2006).
28. International Monetary Fund, World Economic Outlook (April 2022).
29. Benn Steil and Benjamin Della Rocca, "Belt and Road Tracker" *Council on Foreign Relations*, Updated June 1, 2022.
30. Mohammed bin Salman, "Saudi crown prince: If Iran develops nuclear bomb, so will we" *CBS News*, March 15, 2018.

Chapter 2

1. David A. Baldwin, *Economic Statecraft* (Princeton, NJ: Princeton University Press, 1985), p. 8.
2. K. J. Holsti, quoted in Baldwin, pp. 8–9.
3. Chester A. Crocker, "A Dubious Template for American Foreign Policy," *Survival*, vol. 47, no. 1 (2005): 58–59.
4. Joseph S. Nye Jr., "Whatever Happened to Soft Power?" *Project Syndicate*, January 11, 2022.
5. Ibid.
6. Xi Jinping, "Keynote Speech by Xi Jinping at the World Economic Forum," Davos, Switzerland, January 17, 2017.
7. Alexandra Stevenson and Zixu Wang "China Locks Down Major Southern City of Chengdu," *The Washington Post*, September 1, 2022.
8. "China Locks Down 65 million, Discourages Holiday Travel," *Associated Press*, September 5, 2022; Eva Dou, "Deadly Bus Crash in China Stirs Fury, Grief over Strict 'Zero Covid' Policy," *The Washington Post*, September 20, 2022;Vivian Wang and Joy Dong, "Crash of Bus Headed to Quarantine Stirs Outrage in China Over 'Zero Covid,'" *The New York Times*, September 20, 2022.
9. Timothy Andrews Sayle, Jeffrey A. Engel, Hal Brands, and William Inboden, *The Last Card: Inside George W. Bush's Decision to Surge in Iraq* (Ithaca, NY: Cornell University Press, 2019), pp. 207–238.
10. Berry Gewen, *The Inevitability of Tragedy* (New York, NY: W.W. Norton & Company Inc., 2020), p. 224; Hans Morgenthau, *A New Foreign Policy for the United States* (New York, NY: Frederick A. Praeger Publishers), p. 84.
11. William J. Fulbright, *The Arrogance of Power* (Baltimore, MD: Johns Hopkins University, 1966).
12. Jeffrey Goldberg, "The Obama Doctrine," *The Atlantic*, April 15, 2016, p. 89.
13. Robert Gates, "The Over-Militarization of American Foreign Policy," *Foreign Affairs*, June 3, 2020.
14. Robert Gates, *Exercise of Power: American Failures, Successes, and a New Path Forward in the Post-Cold War World* (New York, NY: Knopf, 2020), pp. 297–302.
15. Barack Obama, "Remarks by the President in Address to the Nation on Libya," Washington, DC, March 28, 2011.
16. "U.S. Assistance to Egypt, Tunisia and Libya" *Wilson Center*, September 10, 2012.
17. Reuters Staff, "Trump Tweets: 'Trade Wars Are Good, and Easy to Win,'" *Reuters*, March 2, 2018.
18. Frederick W. Kagan, Jasan Zhou, Kyra Rauschenbach, Nicholas Heras, "Iranian Escalation Timeline," *Institute for the Study of War and the Critical Threats Project at the American Enterprise Institute*, January 10, 2020.
19. Brian Bennett, Vera Bergengruen, Massimo Calabresi, Edward Felsenthal, and W. J. Hennigan, "Exclusive: President Trump Calls Alleged Iranian Attack on Oil Tankers 'Very Minor,'" *TIME*, July 17, 2019.
20. Michael R. Pompeo, "After the Deal: A New Iran Strategy," Washington, DC, May 21, 2018.
21. Dennis Ross and Dana Stroul, "The Flaw in Trump's Maximum Pressure Campaign toward Iran," *The Washington Post*, August 29, 2019.
22. Dan Lamothe and Shane Harris, "Afghan Government Could Fall within Six Months of U.S. Military Withdrawal, New Intelligence Assessment Says," *The Washington Post*, June 24, 2021.
23. Barack Obama, "Remarks by the President to the White House Press Corps," Washington, DC, August 20, 2012.

Chapter 3

1. Berry Gewen, *The Inevitability of Tragedy* (New York, NY: W. W. Norton & Company Inc., 2020), p. 326.
2. Walter McDougall, *Promised Land, Crusader State: The American Encounter with the World Since 1776* (New York, NY, HarperCollins Publishers, 1998), p. 17.
3. Ronald Reagan, "Farewell Address to the Nation," Washington, DC, January 11, 1989.
4. Quoted in McDougall, op. cit., p. 18.
5. Robert Dallek, *The American Style of Foreign Policy: Cultural Style and Foreign Affairs* (New York, NY: Knopf, 1983), p. 64–65.
6. Barack Obama, "Remarks by the President at the United States Military Academy Commencement Ceremony," West Point, NY, May 28, 2014.
7. McDougall, op. cit., p. 37.
8. McDougall, op. cit., p. 36.
9. Robert Zoellick, *America in the World* (New York, NY: Grand Central Publishing, 2021), p. 447.
10. Douglas Irvin, *Clashing over Commerce: A History of US Trade Policy* (Chicago, IL: University of Chicago Press, 2017), p. 617.
11. Ibid., pp. 68–69.
12. Quoted in McDougall, op. cit., p. 31.
13. Quoted in McDougall, p. 46.
14. Quoted in ibid., p. 50.
15. Walter Russel Mead, *Special Providence: American Foreign Policy and How It Changed the World* (New York, NY: Random House Publishing, 2021).
16. Henry Cabot Lodge, "Senate Speech Opposing the League of Nations," Washington, DC, February 28, 1919.
17. Zoellick, p. 170.
18. Quoted in ibid., p. 172.
19. Ibid., p. 191.
20. Ben Samuels, "Two Years after Abraham Accords, Why the UAE F-35 Deal Remains Grounded," *Haaretz*, September 13, 2022.
21. Mike Lanchim "SS St Louis: The Ship of Jewish Refugees Nobody Wanted," *BBC World Service*, May 13, 2014.
22. Franklin Delano Roosevelt, "Campaign Address by the President," Boston, MA, October 30, 1940.
23. Henry Kissinger, *Diplomacy* (New York, NY: Simon and Shuster, 1994), p. 412.
24. Kissinger, op. cit., p. 413.
25. Quoted in Robert Dallek, *Franklin D. Roosevelt: A Political Life* (New York City, NY: Viking Publishing, 2017), p. 520.
26. Quoted in Zoellick, op. cit., p. 220.
27. Quoted in Zoellick, op. cit., p. 241.
28. Melvyn Leffler, *A Preponderance of Power: National Security, The Truman Administration, and the Cold War* (Stanford, CA: Stanford University Press, 1992), p. 63.
29. Winston Churchill, "Iron Curtain Speech," Westminster College, New Wilmington, PA, March 5, 1946.
30. Martin Gilbert, *Winston S. Churchill, vol. 8, Never Despair, 1945–65* (Hillsdale, MI: Hillsdale College Press, 2013), p. 194.
31. *Foreign Relations of the United States, 1947, vol. V, part 1, The Near East and Africa* (Washington, DC: Government Printing Office, 1971), Document 24.
32. Dean Acheson, *Present at the Creation* (New York, NY: W. W. Norton, 1969), p. 219.
33. Harold Truman, "Address of the President of the United States," Washington, DC, March 12, 1947.
34. Quoted in Zoellick, op. cit., p. 219.

Chapter 4

1. Abby Phillip, "O'Reilly Told Trump That Putin Is a Killer. Trump's Reply: 'You Think Our Country Is So Innocent?'" *The Washington Post*, February 4, 2017.
2. McDougall, op. cit.
3. McDougall, ibid.

4. Mead, op. cit.
5. Stephen Wertheim, "The Crisis in Progressive Foreign Policy: How the Left Can Adapt to an Age of Great Power Rivalry," *Foreign Affairs*, August 24, 2022.
6. Donald Trump, "Inaugural Address of President Donald Trump," Washington, DC, January 20, 2017.
7. Donald Trump, "Remarks by President Trump to the 73rd Session of the UNGA," New York, NY, September 25, 2018.
8. Donald Trump, "Remarks by President Trump to the 74th Session of the UNGA," New York, NY, September 25, 2019.
9. Ibid.
10. Michael Anton, "The Trump Doctrine," *Foreign Policy*, April 20, 2019.
11. Ibid.
12. Yoram Hazony, *The Virtue of Nationalism* (New York, NY: Basic Books, 2018).
13. Donald Trump, "Remarks by President Trump to the 75th Session of the UNGA," New York, NY, September 25, 2019.
14. Hazony, p. 3.
15. Ibid.
16. Trump, UNGA Session 73, op. cit.
17. Anton, op. cit.
18. Ibid.
19. Michael Anton, "America and the Liberal International Order," *American Affairs*, vol. 1, no. 1 (Spring 2017): 113–125.
20. Lily Kuo, "China Again Holds Firm on 'Zero Covid,' Despite the Worsening Toll," *The Washington Post*, November 7, 2022.
21. Richard Wike, Jacob Poushter, Laura Silver, Janell Fetterolf, and Mara Mordecai, "U.S. Image Suffers as Publics around World Question Trump's Leadership," *Pew Research Center*, June 26, 2017.
22. Rand Paul, "Restraint and Support for Freedom Abroad," *The American Conservative*, March 14, 2022.
23. "About Responsible Statecraft," *Quincy Institute for Responsible Statecraft*.
24. Andrew Bacevich, "Why Washington Can't Learn," *Quincy Institute for Responsible Statecraft*, January 23, 2022.
25. Ibid.
26. Stephen Wertheim, "The Only Way to End 'Endless Wars,'" *The New York Times*, September 14, 2019.
27. Ibid.
28. Ibid.
29. Ann Wright, "The US and NATO Escalate Tensions in Asia-Pacific War Games," *Quincy Institute for Responsible Statecraft*, July 9, 2022.
30. Rand Paul Defends Troop Withdrawal in Syria, Afghanistan: "Can the People Who Live There Not Do Anything?" *CBS News*, December 23, 2018.
31. Wertheim, op. cit., *The New York Times*.
32. Stephen Walt, "A Manifesto for Restrainers," *Quincy Institute for Responsible Statecraft*, December 4, 2019.
33. Jeffrey Sachs, "Ukraine Is the Latest Neo-Con Disaster," *OtherNews*, June 27, 2022.
34. John Mearsheimer, "John Mearsheimer on Why the West Is Principally Responsible for the Ukrainian Crisis," *The Economist*, March 19, 2022.
35. Quoted in Nahal Toosi, Alexander Ward, and Quint Forgey, "National Security Daily," Politico, July 7, 2022, at: https://www.politico.com/newsletters/national-security-daily/2022/07/07/that-conversation-is-over-jason-greenblatt-talks-on-khashoggi-israel-and-saudi-arabia-00044313
36. "NatSec Expert Resigns from Quincy Institute over Ukraine," *Think Tank Watch*, July 7, 2022; "America's Top Anti-War Think Tank Is Fracturing Over Ukraine," *Mother Jones*, July 8, 2022.
37. Andrew Bacevich, Trita Parsi, Paul Pillar, and Annelie Shelin, "A New Paradigm for the Middle East: Ending America's Misguided Policy of Domination," *Quincy Institute for Responsible Statecraft*, July 2020.
38. Wertheim, op. cit., *Foreign Affairs*.
39. Ibid.

40. Graham Allison, "The Myth of the Liberal Order: From Historical Accident to Conventional Wisdom," *Foreign Affairs*, July/August 2018.
41. Graham Allison, "The New Spheres of Influence: Sharing the Globe with Other Great Powers," *Foreign Affairs*, March/April 2020.
42. Peter Beinart, "America Needs an Entirely New Foreign Policy in the Trump Age," *The Atlantic*, September 16, 2018.
43. Beinart, op. cit.
44. Allison, op. cit., *Foreign Affairs*, March/April 2020.
45. Allison, op. cit., March/April 2020.
46. Reuters Staff, "Hailing Peter the Great, Putin Draws Parallel with Mission to 'Return' Russian Lands," *Reuters*, June 9, 2022.
47. Kevin Rudd, "The World According to Xi Jinping," *Foreign Affairs*, November/December 2022.
48. Beinart, op. cit.
49. Walt, op. cit.
50. John Mearsheimer, "John Mearsheimer on Why the West Is Principally Responsible for the Ukrainian Crisis," *The Economist*, March 19, 2022.
51. Stephen Walt and John J. Mearsheimer. "The Israel Lobby and U.S. Foreign Policy." *KSG Faculty Research Working Paper Series* RWP06-011, March 2006.
52. Henry Kissinger, *Years of Renewal* (New York, NY: Simon and Shuster, 2000) p. 1071.
53. Hans Morgenthau, "The Tragedy of the German Jewish Intellectual," in Bernard Rosenberg and Ernest Goldstein, *Reminiscences of Jewish Intellectuals of New York* (New York, NY: Columbia University Press, 1982) pp. 79–80.
54. David Tal, "Kissinger's wrath: the reassessment of the US-Israel relationship (March 1975)," Middle Eastern Studies, 60(5), 777–794. https://doi.org/10.1080/00263206.2023.2270430
55. Dennis Ross, *Doomed to Succeed* (New York, NY: Farrar, Straus and Giroux, 2015) pp. 138–140.
56. Grant Rumley, "China's Security Presence in the Middle East: Redlines and Guidelines for the United States," *The Washington Institute for Near East Policy*, October 18, 2022.
57. Hans Morgenthau, *Politics Among the Nations: The Struggle for Power and Peace*, 4th ed. (New York, NY: Alfred A Knopf, 1967) p. 25.
58. Quoted in Barry Gewen, *The Inevitability of Tragedy* (New York, NY: W. W. Norton & Company Inc., 2020) pp. 198–199.
59. Quoted in Gewen, op. cit. p. 205.
60. Hans Morgenthau, *The Decline of Democratic Politics* (Chicago, IL: University of Chicago Press, 1964) p. 330.
61. Ibid.
62. Gewen, op. cit. pp. 220–223.
63. Hans Morgenthau, *Vietnam and the United States* (Washington, DC: Public Affairs, 1965) p. 5.
64. Henry Kissinger, *American Foreign Policy: Three Essays* (New York, NY: W. W. Norton & Company) p. 92.
65. Melvyn P. Leffler, "9/11 and American Foreign Policy, Diplomatic History Roundtable: The Bush Administration's Foreign Policy in Historical Perspective," *Oxford University Press*, vol. 29, no. 3 (June 2005): 395–413.
66. Quoted in Gewen, op. cit. p. 376.
67. Among other works, see Ash Jain and Matthew Kroenig, "Present at the Recreation: A Global Strategy for Revitalizing, Adapting and Defending a Rules Based International System," *Atlantic Council*, October 30, 2019.
68. Robert Kagan, "The World America Made—and that Trump Wants to Unmake," *The Atlantic*, September 28, 2018.
69. Jon Ikenberry, "Why American Power Endures," *Foreign Affairs*, November/December 2022, p. 62.
70. Ibid.
71. Kagan, op. cit.
72. Ikenberry, op. cit. p. 63.
73. Ikenberry, op. cit. p. 67.
74. Ibid.
75. Ibid.

76. Dina Smeltz, Ivo H. Daalder, Karl Freidhoff, Craig Kafura, and Emily Sullivan, "2022 Survey of Public Opinion on US Foreign Policy," *The Chicago Council on Global Affairs*, October 20, 2022.

Chapter 5

1. Barthalomew Sparrow, *The Strategist: Brent Scowcroft and the Call of National Security* (New York, NY: PublicAffairs, 2015).
2. Philip Zelikow and Condoleezza Rice, *Germany Unified and Europe Transformed: A Study in Statecraft* (Cambridge, MA: Harvard University Press, 1995), p. 51.
3. Ibid., p. 51.
4. Ibid., p. 58.
5. Ibid., p. 62.
6. Quoted in Zelikow and Rice, p. 99.
7. Quoted in ibid., p. 93.
8. Quoted in ibid., p, 98.
9. Quoted in ibid., p. 26, and recounted to the author by Robert Zoellick.
10. Zelikow and Rice, p. 28.
11. Robert Zoellick, "Two Plus Four," *The National Interest* (Fall 2000): p. 19.
12. Zoellick, p. 19.
13. Philip Zelikow and Condoleezza Rice, *To Build a Better World: Choices to End the Cold War and Create a Global Commonwealth* (New York, NY: Twelve, 2019).
14. Quoted in James A. Baker III, *The Politics of Diplomacy: Revolution, War and Peace 1989–1992* (New York, NY: G. O. Putnam's Sons, 1995), p. 234.
15. Quoted in Zelikow and Rice, p. 137.
16. Quoted in Baker, p. 235.
17. Quoted in Zelikow and Rice, p. 266.
18. Quoted in ibid., p. 96.
19. Quoted in ibid., p. 98.
20. Quoted in ibid., p. 207.
21. Quoted in Baker, p. 167.
22. Zelikow and Rice, p. 152.
23. Quoted in ibid., p. 204.
24. Quoted in ibid., p. 215.
25. Quoted in ibid., p. 217.
26. Quoted in ibid., p. 127.
27. Baker, pp. 258–259.
28. Quoted in ibid.
29. Vladimir Putin, "Speech and the Following Discussion at the Munich Conference on Security Policy," Munich, Germany, February 10, 2007.
30. Peter Baker, "In Ukraine Conflict, Putin Relies on a Promise That Ultimately Wasn't," *The New York Times*, January 9, 2022.

Chapter 6

1. David Halberstam, *War in a Time of Peace: Bush, Clinton, and the Generals* (New York, NY: Scribner, 2001), p. 29.
2. Baker, p. 636.
3. Ibid.
4. Ibid.
5. Quoted in Jutta Paczulla, "The Long, Difficult Road to Dayton: Peace Efforts in Bosnia-Herzegovina," *International Journal*, vol. 60, no. 1 (Winter 2004/2005): 258.
6. Quoted in Halberstam, p. 86.
7. Halberstam, p. 38.
8. Colin L. Powell, "Why Generals Get Nervous," *The New York Times*, October 8, 1992, p. A35.
9. Halberstam, p. 126.
10. Quoted in ibid., p. 155.
11. David Owen, *Balkan Odyssey* (New York, NY: Harcourt Brace, 1995), p. 107.

12. Quoted in Derek Chollet, *The Road to the Dayton Accords: A Study of American Statecraft* (New York, NY: Palgrave Macmillan, 2005), p. 6.
13. Quoted in Chollet, p. 28.
14. Chollet, pp. 28–29.
15. Ibid., p. 36.
16. Madeleine Albright, *Madame Secretary* (New York, NY: Miramax Books, 2003), p. 190, and quoted in Chollet, p. 40.
17. Quoted in Chollet, p. 60.
18. Richard Holbrooke, *To End a War* (New York, NY: Random House, 1998), p. 191.
19. Quoted in Paczulla, op. cit., p. 263.
20. Quoted in Holbrooke, p. 195.
21. Derek Chollet and Samantha Power, *Unquiet American: Richard Holbrooke in the World* (New York, NY: PublicAffairs, 2012) p. 206.
22. Carol Schaeffer, "How the West Failed Bosnia," *The Nation*, December 27, 2022.
23. "Bosnia: 25 Years After the Dayton Accords Conference Panel 1—Reflections on Bosnia Since 1995," *Yale University Genocide Studies Program*, December 21, 2020.
24. Carl Bildt, "Dayton Revisited: Bosnia's Peace Deal 20 Years On," *European Council on Foreign Relations*, November 1, 2015, p. 4.
25. Ibid.
26. Edward Morgan-Jones, Neophytos Loizides, and Djordje Stefanovic, "20 Years Later, This Is What Bosnians Think about the Dayton Accords," *The Washington Post*, December 14, 2015.

Chapter 7

1. Quoted in "THE WORLD: Excerpts; Fighting The War of Words Over Kuwait" New York Times, August 12, 1990, at: https://www.nytimes.com/1990/08/12/weekinreview/the-world-excerpts-fighting-the-war-of-words-over-kuwait.html.
2. Quoted in ibid., p. 260.
3. "Interview with Robert M. Gates, July 23–24, 2000," George H. W. Bush Oral History Project, Miller Center of Public Affairs, p. 88, https://s3.amazonaws.com/web.poh.transcripts/Gates_Robert.ARCHIVE.pdf.
4. Baker, p. 276.
5. George Bush and Brent Scowcroft, *A World Transformed* (New York, NY: Knopf, 1998), p. 303.
6. Ibid.
7. Baker, p. 278.
8. Bush and Scowcroft, p. 330.
9. "Interview with Richard Cheney, May 16–17, 2000," George H. W. Bush Oral History Project, The Miller Center of Public Affairs, p. 88, http://web1.millercenter.org/poh/transcripts/ohp_2000_0316_cheney.pdf.
10. Baker, pp. 277–278.
11. Ibid., p. 279.
12. Baker–Aziz meeting in Geneva (January 9, 1991), in which I was a participant.
13. Bush meeting with outside experts, which I attended.
14. Quoted in Michael Watkins and Susan Rosegrant, *Breakthrough International Negotiation: How Great Negotiators Transformed the World's Toughest Post–Cold War Conflicts* (San Francisco, CA: Jossey-Bass, 2001), p. 199.
15. Bush and Scowcroft, p. 304.
16. To create a less formal atmosphere for ministerial meetings, Baker held them with Shevardnadze in Jackson Hole, Wyoming, and Shevardnadze reciprocated by hosting us at a retreat on Lake Baikal, in the Soviet hinterland.
17. Quoted in Baker, p. 2.
18. Quoted in ibid., p. 286.
19. Bush and Scowcroft, p. 378.
20. Baker, p. 304 [emphasis added].
21. Ibid., p. 305.
22. Watkins and Rosegrant, p. 194.
23. Watkins and Rosegrant, p. 189.
24. Quoted in ibid., p. 195.

25. Bush and Scowcroft, p. 452–453.
26. Quoted in Bush and Scowcroft, p. 389.
27. Ibid., p. 399.
28. Baker, p. 336.

Chapter 8

1. Timothy Andrews Sayle, Jeffrey A. Engel, Hal Brands, and William Inboden, ed., *The Last Card: Inside George Bush's Decision to Surge in Iraq* (Ithaca, NY: Cornell University Press, 2019), p. 20.
2. David Satterfield, interview with the author, May 17, 2023.
3. Quoted in George Packer, *The Assassins' Gate* (New York, NY: Farrar, Straus and Giroux, 2004), p. 23.
4. Ibid.
5. Michael R. Gordon and Bernard E. Trainor, *Cobra II: The Inside Story of the Invasion and Occupation of Iraq* (New York, NY: Pantheon, 2006), pp. 13–14. According to Gordon and Trainor, Clinton suggested a different set of priorities, starting with Al Qaeda, Middle East diplomacy, North Korea, the nuclear competition in South Asia, and only then Iraq. Bush did not respond.
6. Packer, p. 36.
7. Richard A. Clarke, *Against All Enemies: Inside America's War on Terror* (New York, NY: Free Press, 2004), p. 32.
8. Gordon and Trainor, p. 17.
9. Quoted in Packer, p. 41.
10. Bob Woodward, *Plan of Attack* (New York, NY: Simon and Schuster, 2004), p. 2.
11. Gordon and Trainor, pp. 30–31; and Packer, p. 45.
12. Quoted in Packer, p. 45.
13. Quoted in Elisabeth Bumiller, "A Partner in Shaping an Assertive Foreign Policy," *The New York Times*, January 7, 2004, https://www.nytimes.com/2004/01/07/world/a-partner-in-shaping-an-assertive-foreign-policy.html.
14. Brent Scowcroft, "Don't Attack Saddam," *The Wall Street Journal*, August 15, 2002, https://www.wsj.com/articles/SB1029371773228069195.
15. The Scowcroft article fed other stories that in some cases were misleading or actually wrong. Todd Purdum and Patrick Tyler reported in *The New York Times* that Henry Kissinger and other Republicans shared Scowcroft's position and opposed the administration's course on Iraq. Yet Kissinger wrote an article that, while somewhat more nuanced, basically supported the administration's posture. Baker, too, authored a piece that emphasized the value of going to the UN as the next step in dealing with Iraq and creating more of a legitimate basis for using force against Iraq if that proved necessary to get Iraq to disarm.
16. Woodward, *Plan of Attack*, pp. 160–161.
17. See ibid., p. 160.
18. Quoted in ibid., p. 161.
19. "Remarks by the Vice President to the Veterans of Foreign Wars 103rd National Convention," Nashville, TN, August 26, 2002, https://georgewbush-whitehouse.archives.gov/news/releases/2002/08/20020826.html.
20. Elisabeth Bumiller, "Traces of Terror: the Strategy; Bush Aides Set Strategy to Sell Policy on Iraq," *The New York Times*, September 7, 2002, https://www.nytimes.com/2002/09/07/us/traces-of-terror-the-strategy-bush-aides-set-strategy-to-sell-policy-on-iraq.html.
21. "Threats and Responses; The Rationale for the UN Resolution on Iraq, in the Diplomats' Own Words," *The New York Times*, November 9, 2002, https://www.nytimes.com/2002/11/09/world/threats-responses-rationale-for-un-resolution-iraq-diplomats-own-words.html.
22. The additional concession at the end of the negotiations to secure the votes and the agreement of France made it harder, not easier, to find Iraq in material breach. According to the language of the resolution, Iraq had to be guilty of false statement or omission in its declaration *and* failure to comply with inspections. While this concession enabled the passage of the resolution, it foreshadowed the differing standards the United States and France would have to find Iraq in material breach. In other words, the Iraqi declaration could be agreed to be incomplete, but if the French interpreted Iraq as allowing further inspections, they would not view Iraq as in material breach—which was precisely the dispute that arose when France pushed for a

second resolution. The precise language of the resolution is "false statements or omissions in the declarations submitted by Iraq pursuant to this resolution and failure by Iraq at any time to comply with, and cooperate fully in the implementation of, this resolution shall constitute a further material breach of Iraq's obligations and will be reported to the council for assessment."

23. Patrick E. Tyler, "Threats and Responses: The United Nations; U.S. and Britain Drafting Resolution to Impose Deadline on Iraq," *The New York Times*, September 26, 2002, https://www.nytimes.com/2002/09/26/world/threats-responses-united-nations-us-britain-drafting-resolution-impose-deadline.html.

24. "Remarks by the President on the United Nations Security Council Resolution," The Rose Garden, November 8, 2002, https://2001-2009.state.gov/p/nea/rls/rm/15019.htm.

25. *Late Edition with Wolf Blitzer*, CNN, November 10, 2002, http://www.cnn.com/TRANSCRIPTS/0211/10/le.00.html.

26. Michael Dobbs, "Allies Slow US War Plans: British and French Urge Time for Inspectors," *The Washington Post*, January 11, 2003, p. A1.

27. Karen DeYoung, "Powell 'Confident' of Allies' Support for War," *The Washington Post*, January 24, 2002, https://www.washingtonpost.com/archive/politics/2003/01/24/powell-confident-of-allies-support-for-war/5bfd7156-32d0-45f8-99f3-f49b6229df6b/.

28. Quoted in Dobbs, "Allies Slow US War Plans."

29. Craig S. Smith and Richard Bernstein, "3 Members of NATO and Russia Resist U.S. on Iraq Plans," *The New York Times*, February 11, 2003, https://www.nytimes.com/2003/02/11/world/threats-responses-diplomacy-3-members-nato-russia-resist-us-iraq-plans.html.

30. "Threats and Responses; In Their Words: The Security Council," *The New York Times*, February 6, 2003, https://www.nytimes.com/2003/02/06/world/threats-and-responses-in-their-words-the-security-council.html.

31. "President Bush Addresses the Nation," March 19, 2003, https://georgewbush-whitehouse.archives.gov/news/releases/2003/03/20030319-17.html.

32. Gordon and Trainor, pp. 26–28.

33. Quoted in Bob Woodward, *The War Within: A Secret White House History, 2006–08* (New York, NY: Simon and Schuster, 2008), p. 47.

34. Woodward, *The War Within*, p. 21.

35. Gordon and Trainor, p. 464.

36. Packer, p. 133.

37. Quoted in Gordon and Trainor, p. 464.

38. *The National Security Strategy of the United States of America*, The White House, September2002, https://2009-2017.state.gov/documents/organization/63562.pdf.

39. Richard Cheney Interview on *Meet the Press*, September 8, 2002, https://www.leadingtowar.com/PDFsources_claims_aluminum/2002_09_08_NBC.pdf.

40. Colin Powell interview on *Meet the Press*, October 20, 2002.

41. Woodward, *Plan of Attack*, p. 260.

42. French ambassador Jean-David Levitte in conversation with the author, 2005.

43. Quoted in Michael Gordon and Eric Schmitt, "Threats and Responses: Diplomacy; Turkey Saying No to Accepting G.I.'s in Large Numbers," *The New York Times*, December 3, 2002, https://www.nytimes.com/2002/12/04/world/threats-responses-diplomacy-turkey-saying-no-accepting-gi-s-large-numbers.html.

44. James Fallows, "Blind into Baghdad," *Atlantic Monthly*, January/February 2004, https://www.theatlantic.com/magazine/archive/2004/01/blind-into-baghdad/302860/.

45. Packer, pp. 111–112. See Fallows, "Blind into Baghdad."

46. Gordon and Trainor, p. 502.

47. See Gordon and Trainor, p. 119.

48. See, for example, "United We Stand: Eight European Leaders Are as One with President Bush," *The Wall Street Journal*, January 30, 2003, https://www.wsj.com/articles/SB1043875470158445104.

49. Gordon and Trainor, p. 343.

50. "Briefing on Humanitarian Reconstruction Issues," *Office of the Press Secretary*, February 24, 2003, https://georgewbush-whitehouse.archives.gov/news/releases/2003/02/20030224-11.html.

51. Ibid.

52. See Gordon and Trainor, p. 157.

53. John Hughes, "Bush Had Good Reason to Believe There Were WMD in Iraq," *Christian Science Monitor*, April 12, 2006, https://www.csmonitor.com/2006/0412/p09s02-cojh.html.
54. Gordon and Trainor, pp. 155–156.
55. Packer, p. 139.
56. Gordon and Trainor, p. 157.
57. Ibid., p. 155.
58. Ibid., p. 565. The full briefing is provided on pp. 565–569.
59. Ibid., p. 570; excerpts of the National Intelligence Council document appear on pp. 570–571.
60. See, for example, "Reconstructing Iraq: Insights, Challenges, and Missions for Military Forces in a Post-Conflict Scenario," US Army War College's Strategic Studies Institute Report, December 2002, https://press.armywarcollege.edu/cgi/viewcontent.cgi?article=1806&context=monographs.
61. It was difficult in 1991 as well. Public opposition was well pronounced, and the foreign minister, defense minister, and chief of staff resigned in protest. I am indebted to my student Eran Erkan for pointing this out to me.
62. David Petraeus and Andrew Roberts, "The Iraq War, 2003–2011," in *Conflict: The Evolution of Warfare from 1945 to the Russian Invasion of Ukraine* (New York, NY: Harper, 2023).
63. Ibid.
64. Sayle et al., *The Last Card*, p. 5.
65. Cited in "Country Guidance: Iraq," *European Union Agency for Asylum*, updated June 2022, pp. 102–103, https://euaa.europa.eu/sites/default/files/publications/2023-01/2022_Country_Guidance_Iraq_EN.pdf.
66. Quoted in Sayle et al., *The Last Card*, p. 10.
67. Emily Hunt, "Zarqawi's 'Total War' on Iraqi Shiites Exposes a Divide among Sunni Jihadists," Policy Watch 1049, *The Washington Institute for Near East Policy*, November 15, 2005, https://www.washingtoninstitute.org/policy-analysis/zarqawis-total-war-iraqi-shiites-exposes-divide-among-sunni-jihadists.
68. Oral history, *The Last Card*, p. 60.
69. Ibid., p. 47.
70. Ibid., p. 49.
71. Ibid., p. 54.
72. Peter Mansoor, "Designing the Surge," in *Surge: My Journey with General David Petraeus and the Remaking of the Iraq War* (New Haven, CT: Yale University Press, 2013), p. 45.
73. Oral history, *The Last Card*, p. 81.
74. Woodward, *The War Within*, p. 64.
75. Ibid., p. 76.
76. Ibid., p. 69.
77. Ibid.
78. Ibid.
79. Ibid., p. 82.
80. Ibid.
81. Ibid, p. 83.
82. Ibid., p. 98.
83. Ibid.
84. Quoted in Meghan O'Sullivan, "Iraq: Postscript," in *Handoff* (Washington, DC: Brookings Institution Press, 2023), p. 154.
85. David Satterfield, interview with the author, May 17, 2023; Satterfield used very similar language in the Oral History section of *The Last Card*, p. 149.
86. O'Sullivan, "Iraq: Postscript," p. 178.
87. Oral history, *The Last Card*, p. 115.
88. *The Last Card*, p. 214.
89. Oral history, *The Last Card*, pp. 115–116.
90. David Petraeus, interview with the author, March 13, 2023.
91. Zalmay Khalilzad, *The Envoy* (New York, NY: St. Martin's Press, 2012), p. 268
92. Oral History, *The Last Card*, p. 73.
93. Hadley, O'Sullivan, and Feaver, "How the 'Surge' Came to Be," in *The Last Card*, p. 221.
94. Ibid., p. 220.
95. Ibid., p. 221.

96. Ibid.
97. Ibid. p. 222.
98. David Satterfield, interview with the author.
99. Ibid.
100. Hadley, O'Sullivan, and Feaver, "How the 'Surge' Came to Be," p. 223.
101. David Petraeus, interview with the author.
102. O'Sullivan, "Iraq: Postscript," in *Handoff*, p. 172.
103. Ibid.
104. Hadley, O'Sullivan, and Feaver, "How the 'Surge' Came to Be," p. 235.
105. Ibid, p. 236.

Chapter 9

1. Hillary Clinton, *Hard Choices* (New York, NY: Simon & Shuster, 2014), p. 447.
2. Quoted in David Remnick, "Going the Distance," *The New Yorker*, January 19, 2014, https://www.newyorker.com/magazine/2014/01/27/going-the-distance-david-remnick.
3. William J. Burns, *The Back Channel: A Memoir of American Diplomacy and The Case for Its Renewal* (New York, NY: Random House, 2020), pp. 323–324.
4. "GDP, Current Prices: Syria," *International Monetary Fund*, https://www.imf.org/external/datamapper/NGDPD@WEO/SYR?zoom=SYR&highlight=SYR.
5. Joan Juliet Buck, "Asma al-Assad: A Rose in the Desert," *Vogue*, March 2011.
6. Sam Dagher, *Assad or We Burn the Country: How One Family's Lust for Power Destroyed Syria* (New York, NY: Little Brown and Company, 2019), p. 5.
7. Quoted in Frederic Hof, *Reaching for the Heights: The Inside Story of a Secret Attempt to Reach a Syrian-Israel Peace* (Washington, DC: United States Institute of Peace, 2022), p. 45.
8. Jay Solomon and Bill Spindle, "Syrian Strongman: Time for 'Reform,'" *The Wall Street Journal*, January 31, 2011, https://www.wsj.com/articles/SB1000142405274870483270457614340735033236.
9. Christopher Phillips, *The Battle for Syria* (New Haven, CT: Yale University Press, 2020), p. 46.
10. Dagher, *Assad or We Burn the Country*, p. 163.
11. Ibid, p. 173.
12. John Kerry, *Every Day Is Extra* (New York, NY: Simon and Shuster, 2018), p. 392.
13. "Bashar al-Assad's Inner Circle," *BBC*, July 30, 2012, https://www.bbc.com/news/world-middle-east-13216195;
14. "Interview with Bob Schieffer of CBS's Face the Nation," *U.S. Department of State*, March 27, 2011, https://2009-2017.state.gov/secretary/20092013clinton/rm/2011/03/159210.htm.
15. "Statement on the Situation in Syria," *The American Presidency Project*, April 8, 2011, https://www.presidency.ucsb.edu/documents/statement-the-situation-syria-2; "Statement on the Situation in Syria," *The American Presidency Project*, April 22, 2011, https://www.presidency.ucsb.edu/documents/statement-the-situation-syria-3.
16. "Remarks by the President on the Middle East and North Africa," *The White House*, May 19, 2011, https://obamawhitehouse.archives.gov/the-press-office/2011/05/19/remarks-president-middle-east-and-north-africa%20.
17. Hillary Clinton, "Remarks with European Union High Representative for Foreign Affairs and Security Policy Catherine Ashton after Their Meeting," *U.S. Department of State*, July 11, 2011, https://2009-2017.state.gov/secretary/20092013clinton/rm/2011/07/168027.htm.
18. "Speech of Syrian President Bashar Al-Assad at Damascus University on June 20, 2011," *The Syria Report*, June 21, 2022, https://syria-report.com/speech-of-syrian-president-bashar-al-assad-at-damascus-university-on-june-20-2011/.
19. Quoted in Dagher, *Assad or We Burn the Country*, p. 243.
20. Ibid.
21. Walid Jumblatt, interview with Sam Dagher; see Dagher, *Assad or We Burn the Country*, p. 250.
22. Cited in Phillips, *The Battle for Syria*, p. 66.
23. Elizabeth Flock, "Saudi King Abdullah to Syria: 'Stop the killing machine,'" *The Washington Post*, August 8, 2011, https://www.washingtonpost.com/blogs/blogpost/post/saudi-king-abdullah-to-syria-stop-the-killing-machine/2011/08/08/gIQASy3n2I_blog.html?fbclid=IwAR0jmJsdfQI5WcQehlkXH1atkIGlOfm92-K-TrdFy1ZWJ0N3HODXXPEYWBA.

24. Elise Labott, "US Will Call for Syrian Leader to Step Down," *CNN*, August 18, 2011, http://www.cnn.com/2011/POLITICS/08/18/us.syria.call/index.html.
25. Clinton, *Hard Choices*, p. 452.
26. Ibid.
27. Ibid., p. 455.
28. Ibid., p. 454.
29. Phillips, *The Battle for Syria*, pp. 101–102; Clinton, *Hard Choices*, p. 458.
30. Quoted in Clinton, *Hard Choices*, p. 459.
31. "Remarks by the President to the White House Press Corps," *The White House, Office of the Press Secretary*, August 20, 2012, https://obamawhitehouse.archives.gov/the-press-office/2012/08/20/remarks-president-white-house-press-corps/.
32. Clinton, *Hard Choices*, p. 463.
33. Panetta is quoted in Jeffrey Goldberg, "The Obama Doctrine," *The Atlantic*, April 2016.
34. Clinton, *Hard Choices*, p. 462.
35. Ben Rhodes, "Inside the White House during the Syrian 'Red Line' Crisis," *The Atlantic*, June 3, 2018, https://www.theatlantic.com/international/archive/2018/06/inside-the-white-house-during-the-syrian-red-line-crisis/561887/.
36. "Remarks by the President at the Nunn-Lugar Cooperative Threat Reduction Symposium," *The White House*, December 3, 2012, https://obamawhitehouse.archives.gov/the-press-office/2012/12/03/remarks-president-nunn-lugar-cooperative-threat-reduction-symposium.
37. "Statement by Deputy National Security Advisor for Strategic Communications Ben Rhodes on Syrian Chemical Weapons Use," *The White House*, June 13, 2013, https://obamawhitehouse.archives.gov/the-press-office/2013/06/13/statement-deputy-national-security-advisor-strategic-communications-ben-.
38. Samantha Power, *The Education of an Idealist* (New York, NY: Dey St., 2019), pp. 365–367.
39. "Kerry's Remarks on Chemical Weapons in Syria," *The New York Times*, August 30, 2013, https://www.nytimes.com/2013/08/31/world/middleeast/kerrys-remarks-on-chemical-weapons-in-syria.html?ref=middleeast.
40. Rhodes, "Inside the White House during the Syrian 'Red Line' Crisis."
41. Sam Dagher, interview with the author; see Dagher, *Assad or We Burn the Country*, p. 383.
42. Rhodes, "Inside the White House during the Syrian 'Red Line' Crisis."
43. Jeffrey Goldberg, "The Obama Doctrine," *The Atlantic*, April 2016, https://www.theatlantic.com/magazine/archive/2016/04/the-obama-doctrine/471525/.
44. Phillips, *The Battle for Syria*, p. 192; see Dagher, *Assad or We Burn the Country*, p. 389.
45. "Syrian Conflict: Cleric Qaradawi Urges Sunnis to Join Rebels," *BBC*, June 1, 2013, https://www.bbc.com/news/world-middle-east-22741588.
46. Kerry, *Every Day Is Extra*, p. 542.
47. Ibid.
48. Quoted in Remnick, op. cit.
49. See Reuters Staff, "Syrian Rebel Commander Says Nusra Front Seized 'Light Weapons and Ammunition,'" *Reuters*, March 14, 2016, https://www.reuters.com/article/us-mideast-crisis-syria-rebels/syrian-rebel-commander-says-nusra-front-seized-light-weapons-and-ammunition-idUKKCN0WG17D.
50. See Guy Faulconbridge and Jonathan Saul, "Islamic State Is Going to Assad, Some to Turkey, U.S. Official Says," *Reuters*, December 10, 2015, https://www.reuters.com/article/us-mideast-crisis-syria-usa-oil/islamic-state-oil-is-going-to-assad-some-to-turkey-u-s-official-says-idUSKBN0TT2O120151210; Benoit Faucon and Ahmed Al Omran, "Islamic State Steps Up Oil and Gas Sales to Assad Regime," *The Wall Street Journal*, January 19, 2017, https://www.wsj.com/articles/islamic-state-steps-up-oil-and-gas-sales-to-assad-regime-1484835563f.
51. Kerry, *Every Day Is Extra*, p. 548.
52. Ibid, p. 549.
53. Ibid.
54. Ibid., p. 551.
55. Ibid., p. 552.
56. See Evan Hill et al., "Russia Bombed Four Syrian Hospitals: We Have Proof," *The New York Times*, October 13, 2019, https://www.nytimes.com/video/world/middleeast/100000005697485/russia-bombed-syrian-hospitals.html; "Syrian and Russian Forces Targeting Hospitals as a Strategy of War," *Amnesty International*, March 3, 2016, https://www.

amnesty.org/en/latest/press-release/2016/03/syrian-and-russian-forces-targeting-hospitals-as-a-strategy-of-war/.

57. Anne Barnard and Hwaida Saad, "To Freeze Syria War, Russia Proposes Setting Up 'De-Escalation Zones,'" *The New York Times*, May 3, 2017, https://www.nytimes.com/2017/05/03/world/middleeast/russia-syria-de-escalation-zones-astana.html.

58. "Syria: 10 Years of War Has Left at Least 350,000 Dead," *UN News*, September 24, 2021, https://news.un.org/en/story/2021/09/1101162.

59. "Syria Refugee Crisis Explained," *UNHCR*, March 14, 2023, https://www.unrefugees.org/news/syria-refugee-crisis-explained.

60. Clinton, *Hard Choices*, p. 451.

61. Kerry, *Every Day Is Extra*, p. 542.

62. Dagher, *Assad or We Burn the Country*, p. 340.

63. Derek Chollet, *The Long Game: How Obama Defied Washington and Redefined America's Role in the World* (New York, NY: Public Affairs, 2016), p. 128.

64. Ibid, p. 129.

65. Susan Rice, *Tough Love* (New York, NY: Simon and Schuster, 2019), p. 367.

66. See Phillips, *The Battle for Syria*, p. xiii.

67. Ibid., p. 123.

68. Suleiman Al-Khalidi, "Iran Grants $3.6 Billion Credit to Buy Oil Products," *Reuters*, July 31, 2013; Alaa Shahine and Donna Abu-Nasr, "Syria Counts on $1 Billion Iran Fund to Support Pound," *Bloomberg*, June 18, 2013, https://www.bloomberg.com/news/articles/2013-06-18/syria-counts-on-1-billion-iran-fund-to-support-pound#xj4y7vzkg.

69. Quoted in Dagher, *Assad or We Burn the country*, p. 324.

70. "Presidential Executive Office (Russia), "Meeting with Russian Ambassadors and Permanent Representatives in International Organizations," The Kremlin's Official Website, July 9, 2012, http://en.Kremlin.ru/events/president/news/15902.

71. Chollet, *The Long Game*, pp. 140–141.

72. Hof, *Reaching for the Heights*, p. 123.

73. Ibid.

74. Rice, *Tough Love*, p. 367.

75. Dagher, *Assad or We Burn the Country*, p. 340.

76. Clinton, *Hard Choices*, p. 463.

77. Ibid.

78. Kerry, *Every Day Is Extra*, p. 550.

79. Ibid.

80. Clinton, *Hard Choices*, p. 462.

81. Mark Mazzetti, Robert F. Worth, and Michael R. Gordon, "Obama's Uncertain Path Amid Syrian Bloodshed," *The New York Times*, October 22, 2013, https://www.nytimes.com/2013/10/23/world/middleeast/obamas-uncertain-path-amid-syria-bloodshed.html#:~:text=preparation%20for%20use.-,Mr.,said%20at%20a%20news%20conference.

82. Clinton, *Hard Choices*, p. 464.

83. "Press Conference by the President," *The White House*, March 6, 2012, https://obamawhitehouse.archives.gov/the-press-office/2012/03/06/press-conference-president.

84. Goldberg, "The Obama Doctrine."

85. Ibid.

86. "Remarks by the President in a News Conference," *The White House*, November 14, 2012, https://obamawhitehouse.archives.gov/the-press-office/2012/11/14/remarks-president-news-conference.

87. Joel Greenberg, "Israeli Officials Say Syria's Assad Is Doomed," *The Washington Post*, December 14, 2011, https://www.washingtonpost.com/world/middle_east/israeli-officials-say-assad-is-doomed/2011/12/14/gIQAYBuEuO_story.html.

88. Quoted in Robert Gates, *Exercise of Power* (New York, NY: Alfred A. Knopf, 2020), p. 304.

89. Quoted in Joby Warrick, *Red Line* (New York, NY: Doubleday, 2020), p. 251.

90. Dagher, *Assad or We Burn the Country*, p. 293.

91. Fred Hof, interview with the author, February 6, 2023.

92. Ibid.

93. Ibid.

94. General David Petraeus, interview with the author, March 13, 2023.

95. Quoted in Goldberg, "The Obama Doctrine."
96. Goldberg, "The Obama Doctrine."
97. Ibid.
98. Derek Chollet, "Obama's Red Line, Revisited," *Politico*, July 19, 2016, https://www.politico.com/magazine/story/2016/07/obama-syria-foreign-policy-red-line-revisited-214059/.
99. Ibid.
100. Ibid.
101. Chollet, *The Long Game*, p. 21.
102. Quoted in ibid., p. 21, and in Dan De Luce, "Hagel: The White House Tried to 'Destroy' Me," *Foreign Policy*, December 18, 2015, https://foreignpolicy.com/2015/12/18/hagel-the-white-house-tried-to-destroy-me/.
103. Power, *Tough Love*, p. 390.
104. *Corridors of Power*, directed by Dror Moreh. Showtime Documentary Films, 2022.
105. Dagher, *Assad or We Burn the Country*, p. 389.
106. Kerry, *Every Day Is Extra*, p. 541.
107. See *Corridors of Power*.
108. Dagher, *Assad or We Burn the Country*, p. 388.
109. Quoted in Phillips, *The Battle for Syria*, p. 185.
110. Interview with senior Saudi official involved in support of the opposition, April 29, 2023.
111. Cited in Phillips, *The Battle for Syria*, p.187.
112. Rice, *Tough Love*, p. 368.
113. Ibid.
114. Chollet, *The Long Game*, p. 140.
115. Ibid.
116. Ibid.
117. Quoted in Dagher, *Assad or We Burn the Country*, p. 277.
118. General David Petraeus, interview with the author.

Chapter 10

1. "Hearing to Receive Testimony on the Department of Defense Budget Request for Fiscal Year 2024 and the Future Years Defense Program." *United States Senate Committee on Armed Services*, March 28, 2023, p. 51, https://www.armed-services.senate.gov/imo/media/doc/23-18_03-28-2024.pdf.
2. Ibid.
3. The Nunn-Lugar program began as a $1 billion program to safeguard weapons sites in the former Soviet Union and grew over time to include financing scientists, converting nuclear materials to civilian fuel, and other broader measures of nuclear security. "NUNN-LUGAR is said to have helped to deactivate almost 6,000 nuclear warheads," according to the Arms Control Association, at: https://www.armscontrol.org/act/2002-12/features/next-steps-us-nonproliferation-policy
4. See Dennis Ross, *Doomed to Succeed* (New York, NY: Farrar, Straus and Giroux, 2015), pp. 314–317.
5. Joseph Nye, Jr., "Smart Power: In Search of the Balance Between Hard and Soft Power," *Democracy: A Journal of Ideas*, vol. 2 (Fall 2006): 105.

Chapter 11

1. *National Security Strategy*, The White House, October 12, 2022, p. 23.
2. *National Defense Strategy*, U.S. Department of Defense, October 27, 2022, p. 4.
3. "Remarks by President Biden Before the 78th Session of the United Nations General Assembly," *The White House*, September 19, 2023.
4. Hal Brands and John Lewis Gaddis, "The New Cold War: America, China, and the Echoes of History," *Foreign Affairs*, October 19, 2021, https://www.foreignaffairs.com/articles/united-states/2021-10-19/new-cold-war.
5. Lorraine Boissoneault, "The Surprisingly Important Role China Played in WWI," *Smithsonian Magazine*, August 17, 2017.
6. Quoted in Kevin Rudd, *The Avoidable War*, p. 25.
7. Quoted in Rudd, op. cit., p. 27.

8. Michael Beckley, "Delusions of Détente: Why America and China Will Be Enduring Rivals," *Foreign Affairs*, August 22, 2023, https://www.foreignaffairs.com/united-states/china-delusions-detente-rivals.

9. Rudd, op. cit., p. 9.

10. Rudd, op. cit., p. 35.

11. See Cai Xia, "The Party That Failed," *Foreign Affairs*, December 4, 2020, https://www.foreignaffairs.com/articles/china/2020-12-04/chinese-communist-party-failed.

12. Rudd, op. cit., p. 42.

13. Cai Xai, op. cit.

14. Rudd, op. cit., p. 51.

15. Quoted in Joseph Nye, "The Evolution of America's China Strategy," *Project Syndicate*, November 2, 2022, https://www.project-syndicate.org/commentary/us-china-biden-national-security-strategy-by-joseph-s-nye-2022-11.

16. Quoted in Joe Leahy, Kathrin Hille, Andy Lin, and Michael Pooler, "Dare to Fight: Xi Jinping Unveils China's New World Order," *Financial Times*, March 31, 2023, https://www.ft.com/content/0f0b558b-3ca8-4156-82c8-e1825539ee20.

17. Rudd, op. cit., p. 9.

18. Quoted in Graham Allison, "Opportunity for Diplomacy: No Russian Attack Before February 20," *National Interest*, February 4, 2022.

19. James McBride, Andrew Chatzky, and Anshu Siripurapu, "What's Next for the Trans-Pacific Partnership (TPP)?" *Council on Foreign Relations*, September 20, 2021, https://www.cfr.org/backgrounder/what-trans-pacific-partnership-tpp.

20. Chris Buckley, "In a Brother Act with Putin, Xi Reveals China's Fear of Containment," *The New York Times*, March 22, 2023, https://www.nytimes.com/2023/03/22/world/asia/china-xi-putin-ukraine.html.

21. Cai Xia, op. cit.

22. Ibid.

23. Quoted in Keith Fray, Sun Yu, and Joe Leahy, "The Breakdown of China's Social Contract," *Financial Times*, November 2, 2023.

24. Mark Mobius, "China: This Too Shall Pass," https://www.markmobius.com/news-events/china-this-too-shall-pass.

25. Wang Jisi, who heads the Institute of International and Strategic Studies at Peking University, cites the figure of 140. See Wang Jisi, "America and China Are Not Yet in a Cold War," *Foreign Affairs*, November 23, 2023, https://www.foreignaffairs.com/united-states/america-and-china-are-not-yet-cold-war.

26. Xie Feng, "The Chinese Economy Is Doing Better Than You Think," *The Washington Post*, August 30, 2023, https://www.washingtonpost.com/opinions/2023/08/30/china-ambassador-economy-status/.

27. Dale Aluf, "China's Reliance on Middle East Oil and Gas to Rise Sharply," *Asian Times*, December 30, 2021, https://asiatimes.com/2021/12/china-to-rely-more-on-middle-east-for-oil-and-gas/.

28. See US Geological Survey, "Going Critical."

29. Judy Dempsey, "Europe's Dangerous Dependence on China," *Carnegie Endowment for International Peace*, April 4, 2023, https://carnegieeurope.eu/strategiceurope/89448.

30. Matthew P. Funaiole, Brian Hart, and Aiden Power-Riggs, "Mineral Monopoly: China's Control over Gallium Is a National Security Threat," Center for Strategic and International Studies, July 18, 2023, https://features.csis.org/hiddenreach/china-critical-mineral-gallium/.

31. Quoted in Katsuji Nakazawa, "China Never Forgot Night the US Bombed Its Belgrade Embassy," *Nikkei Asia*, April 1, 2021, https://asia.nikkei.com/Editor-s-Picks/China-up-close/Analysis-China-never-forgot-night-the-US-bombed-its-Belgrade-embassy.

32. M. Taylor Fravel, John Ikenberry, et al., *Active Defense: China's Military Strategy Since 1949* (Princeton, NJ: Princeton University Press, 2019), pp. 222–226.

33. M. Taylor Flavel et al., op. cit., p. 223.

34. M. Taylor Flavel et al., op. cit., p. 224.

35. M. Taylor Flavel et al., op. cit., p. 224.

36. M. Taylor Fravel et al., op. cit., pp. 230–231.

37. M. Taylor Fravel et al., op. cit., p. 231.

38. M. Taylor Fravel et al., op. cit., p. 231

39. M. Taylor Fravel et al., op. cit., p. 232.
40. M. Taylor Fravel et al., op. cit., p. 233.
41. Alastair Gale, "China's Military Is Catching Up to the US. Is It Ready for Battle?" *The Wall Street Journal*, October 20, 2022, https://www.wsj.com/articles/china-military-us-taiwan-xi-11666268994.
42. Mackenzie Eaglen, "Setting the Record Straight on Beijing's Actual Military Spending," *American Enterprise Institute*, August 8, 2023, https://www.aei.org/foreign-and-defense-policy/setting-the-record-straight-on-beijings-actual-military-spending/.
43. Karishma Vaswani, "China's Belt and Road Shows the High Price of Beijing's Money," *The Washington Post*, October 2, 2023, https://www.washingtonpost.com/business/2023/10/02/china-s-belt-and-road-shows-the-high-price-of-beijing-s-money/f63adc0e-616a-11ee-b406-3ea724995806_story.html.
44. Vaswani, "China's Belt and Road Shows the High Price of Moving Beijing's Money."
45. See Rudd, op. cit., p. 222.
46. Quoted in Kiran Stacey, "China Signs 99-Year Lease on Sri Lanka's Hambantota Port," *Financial Times*, December 11, 2017, https://www.ft.com/content/e150ef0c-de37-11e7-a8a4-0a1e63a52f9c.
47. Vaswani, op. cit.
48. Kevin Rudd, "Xi Jinping Scrambles as China's Economy Stumbles," *The Wall Street Journal*, May 10, 2022, https://www.wsj.com/articles/xi-scrambles-as-china-economy-stumbles-beijing-economic-prospects-technology-covid-lockdowns-evergrande-president-for-life-re-election-11652190698.
49. Feng Wang, Baochang Gu, and Yong Cai, "The End of China's One-Child Policy," *Brookings Institution*, March 30, 2016, https://www.brookings.edu/articles/the-end-of-chinas-one-child-policy/#:~:text=Starting%20on%20January%201%2C%202016,over%20the%20past%20three%20years.
50. Keith Bradsher and Michael Forsythe, "China Nurtures Make of Electric Car Batteries," *The New York Times*, December 22, 2021, https://www.nytimes.com/2021/12/22/business/china-catl-electric-car-batteries.html.
51. See, for example, Hal Brands, "The Dangers of China's Decline," *Foreign Policy*, April 14, 2022, https://foreignpolicy.com/2022/04/14/china-decline-dangers.
52. Adam Posen, "The End of China's Economic Miracle," *Foreign Affairs*, August 2, 2023, https://www.foreignaffairs.com/china/end-china-economic-miracle-beijing-washington.
53. See Sun Yu and Tom Mitchell, "China's Economy: The Fall-Out from the Evergrande Crisis," *Financial Times*, January 6, 2022, https://www.ft.com/content/13476bf7-a519-427c-afd8-06e5579539d8; Thomas J. Duesterberg, "The Slow Meltdown of the Chinese Economy," *The Wall Street Journal*, December 21, 2023, https://www.wsj.com/articles/slow-meltdown-of-china-economy-evergrande-property-market-collapse-downturn-xi-cewc-11640032283.
54. Yu and Mitchell, "China's Economy."
55. Yu and Mitchell, "China's Economy."
56. Yu and Mitchell, "China's Economy."
57. Lily Kuo, "China's Largest Property Developer at Risk of Default," *The Washington Post*, August 31, 2023, https://www.washingtonpost.com/world/2023/08/31/china-country-garden-default-warning/.
58. Sun Yu Leahy and Chan Ho-him, "Does Xi Jinping Need a Plan B for China's Economy?" *Financial Times*, July 16, 2023, https://www.ft.com/content/00636375-7d47-40ec-9a18-598e3d7faae9.
59. Lingling Wei and Stella Yifan Wie, "China's 40-Year Boom is Over. What Comes Next," *The Wall Street Journal*, August 20, 2023, https://www.wsj.com/world/china/china-economy-debt-slowdown-recession-622a3be4.
60. Mobius, op. cit.
61. Yu and Mitchell, "China's Economy."
62. Quoted in George Will, "Economically Ailing China Suffers from an Incurable Case of Leninism," *The Washington Post*, September 8, 2023, https://www.washingtonpost.com/opinions/2023/09/08/leninism-behind-china-economic-struggles/.
63. Wei and Xie, "China's 40-Year Boom is Over. What Comes Next?"
64. Milton Ezrati, "China's Overwhelming Debt Burden Points to Still Deeper Problems," *Forbes*, January 16, 2023, https://www.forbes.com/sites/miltonezrati/2023/01/16/chinas-overwhelming-debt-burden-points-to-still-deeper-problems/?sh=4a8bb6dc4433.

65. Wei and Xie, op. cit.
66. See C. Textor, "Population Growth in China 2000–2023," *Statista*, January 17, 2024, https://www.statista.com/statistics/270129/population-growth-in-china/.For a discussion of this, see Albee Zhang and Farah Master, "China's First Population Drop in Six Decades Sounds Alarm on Demographic Crisis," *Reuters*, January 18, 2023, https://www.reuters.com/world/china/chinas-population-shrinks-first-time-since-1961-2023-01-17/.
67. Quoted in Steven Lee Meyers and Alexandra Stevenson, "Worries in China that Population May Shrink," *The New York Times*, January 18, 2022, https://static01.nyt.com/images/2022/01/18/nytfrontpage/scan.pdf.
68. Sebastian Mallaby, Catherine Rampell, Lawrence Summers, Max Boot, Josh Rogin, David Ignatius, and Keith B. Richburg, "What Just Happened: Storm Clouds Loom for China's Economy," *The Washington Post*, August 18, 2023, https://www.washingtonpost.com/opinions/2023/08/18/china-economy-deflation-debt-analysis/.
69. Meyers and Stevenson, op. cit.
70. Bruce Stokes, "China May Not Be the Threat We Have Come to Assume," *The Hill*, January 22, 2023; Mallaby, op. cit.
71. Meyers and Stevenson, op. cit.
72. Meyers and Stevenson, op. cit.
73. Keyu Jin, *The New China Playbook: Beyond Socialism and Capitalism* (New York: Viking Press, 2024), p. 4.
74. Quoted in Rudd, *The Avoidable War*, p. 107.
75. See Lavender Au, "Jack Ma Isn't Back," *Wired*, June 15, 2023, https://www.wired.com/story/jack-ma-isnt-back/; Keith Bradsher, "Gloom Is Setting in China's Tech Industry," *The New York Times*, January 8, 2022, p. B3; Rudd, op. cit., p. 110.
76. Keith Richburg, "Xi Will Face a Crisis of Legitimacy, *The Washington Post*, August 18, 2023, https://www.washingtonpost.com/opinions/2023/08/18/china-economy-deflation-debt-analysis/.
77. Eloise Barry, "These Are the Countries Where Twitter, Facebook, and TikTok Are Banned," *TIME*, January 18, 2022, https://time.com/6139988/countries-where-twitter-facebook-tiktok-banned/; Ryan Vlastelica, "Instagram Reportedly Blocked in China amid Hong Kong Prot ests," *Reuters*, September 28, 2014, https://www.reuters.com/article/idUSKCN0HN0VW/.
78. Cited in Li Yuan, "Entrepreneurs Flee China's Heavy Hand: 'You Don't Have to Stay There,'" *The New York Times*, January 19, 2023, https://www.nytimes.com/2023/01/19/business/china-singapore-immigration-entrepreneurs.html.
79. Yuan, "Entrepreneurs Flee China's Heavy Hand."
80. Max J. Zenglein and Jacob Gunter, "The Party Knows Best: Aligning Economic Actors with China's Strategic Goals," Mercator Institute for China Studies, October 2023, https://merics.org/sites/default/files/2023-10/MERICS%20Report%20The%20party%20knows%20best-Aligning%20economic%20actors%20with%20Chinas%20strategic%20goals2_0.pdf.
81. Rudd, op. cit., p. 109.
82. Gavin Bade and Phelim Kine, "Chinese President Xi's 'Siren Call' to US Business Hits Great Wall of Skepticism," *Politico*, November 16, 2023, https://www.politico.com/news/2023/11/16/china-us-xi-biden-california-00127708.
83. Ibid.
84. Cited in Lingling Wei and Stella Yifan Xie, "China's 40-Year Boom Is Over. What Comes Next?" *The Wall Street Journal*, August 20, 2023, https://www.wsj.com/world/china/china-economy-debt-slowdown-recession-622a3be4.
85. Eva Dou, "New Phone Sparks Worry China Has Found a Way around U.S. Tech Limits," *The Washington Post*, September 2, 2023, https://www.washingtonpost.com/technology/2023/09/02/huawei-raimondo-phone-chip-sanctions/.
86. Susan M. Gordon, Michael G. Mullen, and David Sacks, "Independent Task Force Report No. 81, U.S.–Taiwan Relations in a New Era: Responding to a More Assertive China," *Council on Foreign Relations*, June 2023, https://www.cfr.org/task-force-report/us-taiwan-Relations-in-a-new-era/findings.
87. Antony J. Blinken, "A Foreign Policy for the American People," *U.S. Department of State*, March 3, 2021, https://www.state.gov/a-foreign-policy-for-the-american-people/#:~:text=Our%20relationship%20with%20China%20will,from%20a%20position%20of%20strength.
88. Rudd, op. cit., p. 14.
89. Rudd, op. cit., p. 16.

90. Richard Fontaine, "Washington's Missing China Strategy," *Foreign Affairs*, June 14, 2022, https://www.foreignaffairs.com/articles/china/2022-01-14/washingtons-missing-china-strategy.
91. Ibid.
92. Ibid.
93. Ryan Haas, "What America Wants from China," *Foreign Affairs*, October 24, 2023, https://www.foreignaffairs.com/united-states/what-america-wants-china-hass.
94. Robert Zoellick, interview with the author, September 13, 2023.
95. Susan L. Shirk, "The Dangers of Fatalism in US–China Relations," *Globe and Mail*, April 27, 2023, https://www.theglobeandmail.com/opinion/article-the-dangers-of-fatalism-in-us-china-relations.
96. Shirk, "The Dangers of Fatalism in US–China Relations."
97. Shirk, "The Dangers of Fatalism in US–China Relations."
98. Shirk, "The Dangers of Fatalism in US–China Relations."
99. Susan L. Shirk, "Overreach: How China Derailed Its Peaceful Rise," *National Committee on US–China Relations*, https://www.youtube.com/watch?v=qGo8CDP6soI.
100. Leahy, Hille, Lin, and Pooler, "'Dare to Fight': Xi Jinping Unveils China's New World Order."
101. Shirk, "Overreach: How China Derailed Its Peaceful Rise."
102. Quoted in Michael Beckley, "Delusions of Détente."
103. Hal Brands and Zack Cooper, "America Will Only Win When China's Regime Fails," *Foreign Policy*, March 11, 2021, https://foreignpolicy.com/2021/03/11/america-chinas-regime-fails/gime.
104. Joseph S. Nye Jr, "What Killed US–China Engagement," *Project Syndicate*, January 4, 2024, https://www.project-syndicate.org/commentary/us-china-engagement-trump-was-fuel-on-fire-that-china-lit-by-joseph-s-nye-2024-01?barrier=accesspaylog#:~:text=While%20former%20US%20President%20Doald,no%20longer%20bide%20its%20time.
105. Jessica Chen Weiss, "Even China Isn't Convinced It Can Replace the U.S.," *The New York Times*, May 4, 2023, https://www.nytimes.com/2023/05/04/opinion/china-us-world-order.html.
106. Ibid.
107. Jessica Chen Weiss, "The China Trap: U.S. Foreign Policy and the Perilous Logic of Zero-Sum Competition," *Foreign Affairs*, August 18, 2022, https://www.foreignaffairs.com/china/china-trap-us-foreign-policy-zero-sum-competition/.
108. Ibid.
109. Henry Paulson, "A Deep Crisis in China Would Pose a Choice for Two Leading Powers," *The Washington Post*, August 21, 2023, https://www.washingtonpost.com/opinions/2023/08/21/paulson-china-economy-xi-jinping-test/.
110. See Laura Silver, Christina Huang, and Laura Clancy, "China's Approach to Foreign Policy Gets Largely Negative Reviews in 24-Country Survey," *Pew Research Center*, July 27, 2023, https://www.pewresearch.org/global/2023/07/27/chinas-approach-to-foreign-policy-gets-largely-negative-reviews-in-24-country-survey/.
111. Hu Wei, "China Dissent on Ukraine," *US-China Perception Monitor*, March 5, 2022.
112. Carla Freeman and Alex Stephenson, "Xi Ramps Up Campaign for a Post-Pax Americana Security Order," *United States Institute of Peace*, May 4, 2023, https://www.usip.org/publications/2023/05/xi-ramps-campaign-post-pax-americana-security-order.
113. Fontaine, op. cit.
114. Quoted in Rudd, op. cit., p. 186.
115. Tom Donilon, interview with the author, August 28, 2023.
116. Rudd, op. cit., p. 367.
117. Robert D. Blackwill, "Policy Prescriptions for US–China Relations," *Council on Foreign Relations*, January 9, 2023, https://www.cfr.org/blog/policy-prescriptions-us-china-relations.
118. Zoellick, interview, op. cit.
119. Haas, op. cit.

Chapter 12

1. Francois Murphy, "Iran Undoes Slowdown in Enrichment of Uranium to Near Weapons-Grade," *Reuters*, December 26, 2023, https://www.reuters.com/world/middle-east/iran-undoes-slowdown-enrichment-uranium-near-weapons-grade-iaea-2023-12-26/.

2. "Rafael Grossi, interview by Sara Sidner," *CNN*, July 25, 2022, https://www.cnn.com/videos/tv/2022/07/25/rafael-grossi-amanpour-iaea-iran-nuclear-deal.cnn.

3. "Statement of General Mark A. Milley, before the House Armed Services Committee," Senate Armed Services Committee, 2003, p. 5, https://www.armed-services.senate.gov/imo/media/doc/CJCS%20PB24%20Written%20Statement%20FINAL%2025%20MAR%2023.pdf.

4. "Iran Puts Its Nuclear Program beyond the Reach of American Bombs," *The Economist*, May 30, 2023, https://www.economist.com/middle-east-and-africa/2023/05/30/iran-puts-its-nuclear-programme-beyond-the-reach-of-american-bombs.

5. Suzanne Maloney, "After the Iran Deal: A Plan B to Contain the Islamic Republic," *Foreign Affairs*, February 28, 2023, https://www.foreignaffairs.com/middle-east/iran-nuclear-deal-plan-b-contain-islamic-republic.

6. See Dennis Ross, *Doomed to Succeed* (New York, NY: Farrar, Straus and Giroux, 2015) pp. 170–181.

7. Ronald Reagan, *An American Life: The Autobiography* (New York, NY: Simon and Schuster, 1990), pp. 505–506.

8. "Albright's Remarks on Iran: 'Khatami Deserves Respect,'" *The New York Times*, June 18, 1998, https://www.nytimes.com/1998/06/18/world/albright-s-remarks-on-iran-khatami-deserves-respect.html.

9. Office of the Press Secretary, "Videotaped Remarks by the President in Celebration of Nowruz," *The White House*, March 20, 2009, https://obamawhitehouse.archives.gov/the-press-office/videotaped-remarks-president-celebration-nowruz.

10. Alex Lawler, "Hit by Sanctions and Rising Tensions, Iran's Oil Exports Slide in July," *Reuters*, July 30, 2019, https://www.reuters.com/article/idUSKCN1UP1R0/.

11. Joyce Karam, "US envoy Brian Hook: Sanctions are Hurting Iran's $700m Support for Hezbollah," *The National*, March 22, 2019, https://www.thenationalnews.com/world/the-americas/us-envoy-brian-hook-sanctions-are-hurting-iran-s-700m-support-for-hezbollah-1.840133.

12. Vivian Salama, "Trump Calls On Countries to Protect Own Ships in Strait of Hormuz," *The Wall Street Journal*, June 24, 2019, https://www.wsj.com/articles/trump-calls-on-countries-to-protect-own-ships-in-strait-of-hormuz-11561380556.

13. Jon Gambrell, "Iran Starts Enriching Uranium to 60%, Its Highest Level Ever," *Associated Press*, April 16, 2021, https://apnews.com/article/iran-uranium-enrichment-60-percent-ed89e322595004fddc65fd4e31c1131b.

14. Josep Borrell, interview with Televisión Española, August 23, 2022, https://www.rtve.es/play/videos/la-hora-de-la-1/josep-borrell-gasoducto-midcat-energia/6676150/; quoted in "Borrell: Most Countries Part of Nuclear Talks with Iran Agree with EU Proposal," *Asharq Al-Awsat*, August 23, 2022, https://english.aawsat.com/home/article/3832236/borrell-most-countries-part-nuclear-talks-iran-agree-eu-proposal.

15. Also, see David Sanger and Steven Erlanger, "From Lebanon to the Red Sea, a Broader Conflict With Iran Looms," *The New York Times*, January 7, 2024, https://www.nytimes.com/2024/01/07/us/politics/iran-us-israel-conflict.html.

16. Ali Vaez, "Why the War in Gaza Makes a Nuclear Iran More Likely," *Foreign Affairs*, January 25, 2024, https://www.foreignaffairs.com/israel/why-war-gaza-makes-nuclear-iran-more-likely.

17. Felicia Schwartz and Andrew England, "US Held Secret Talks with Iran over Red Sea Attacks," *Financial Times*, March 14, 2024, https://www.ft.com/content/89b01990-7657-45ea-baaa-1f214b40f1cb.

18. Quoted in Schwartz and England, "US Held Secret Talks with Iran over Red Sea Attacks."

19. *Raja News*, February 20, 2007.

20. Radio Farda, "An Alleged Letter to Bush in 2003 Reignites Controversy in Iran," May 27, 2020, https://en.radiofarda.com/a/an-alleged-letter-to-bush-in-2003-reignites-controversy-in-iran/30636870.html.

21. See Courtney Kube and Doha Madani, "Iran Retaliates for Gen. Soleimani's Killing by Firing Missiles at US Forces in Iraq," *NBC News*, January 7, 2020, https://www.nbcnews.com/news/world/u-s-base-iraq-comes-under-attack-missiles-iran-claims-n1112171.

22. Mike Singh, "Policy Watch 3782: Iran's Nuclear Diplomacy: Feint and Advance," *The Washington Institute for Near East Policy*, September 14, 2023, https://www.washingtoninstitute.org/policy-analysis/irans-nuclear-diplomacy-feint-and-advance.

23. Ray Takeyh, *Hidden Iran: Paradox and Power in the Islamic Republic* (New York, NY: Times Books, 2006).

24. Ray Takeyh, discussion with the author, February 23, 2024.
25. Quoted in Ishaan Tharoor, "Iran Stages Dismal Election as Islamic Regime Circles the Wagons," *The Washington Post*, March 3, 2024, https://www.washingtonpost.com/world/2024/03/03/iran-elections-tehran-vote-khamenei-turnout/.
26. Quoted in Islamic Republic of Iran News Network, "Iran Leader Says Next President Mustn't Appoint 'America-Lovers' to Government," *BBC Monitoring*, June 25, 2024, https://monitoring.bbc.co.uk/product/b0001vvv.
27. Karim Sadjadpour, discussion with author, July 8, 2024.
28. See Farnaz Fassihi, "Iran's Foreign Minister in Leaked Tape, Says Revolutionary Guards Set Policy," *The New York Times*, August 25, 2021, https://www.nytimes.com/2021/04/25/world/middleeast/iran-suleimani-zarif.html.
29. See Karim Sadjadpour, "Reading Khamenei: The World View of Iran's Most Powerful Leader," *Carnegie Endowment for International Peace*, 2009, p. 16, https://carnegieendowment.org/files/sadjadpour_iran_final2.pdf.
30. Ali Khamenei, "By Imposing an 8 Year War on Iran, Imperialism Wanted to Put an End to Resistance," *Khamenei.ir*, September 21, 2022, https://english.khamenei.ir/news/9180/By-imposing-an-8-year-war-on-Iran-imperialism-wanted-to-put.
31. Khamenei, "Geopolitics of the Region Is Changing; Not in Favor of the US but to the Benefit of the Resistance," *Khamenei.ir*, November 29, 2023, https://english.khamenei.ir/news/10360/Geopolitics-of-the-region-is-changing-not-in-the-favor-of-the-US.
32. Khamenei, "Leader's Speech to Members of Ahlul Bayt World Assembly and Islamic Radio and TV Union," *Khamenei.ir*, August 17, 2015, https://english.khamenei.ir/news/2109/Leader-s-speech-to-members-of-Ahlul-Bayt-World-Assembly-and-Islamic.
33. Quoted in Maloney, "After the Iran Deal."
34. Patrick Clawson speaking to the Washington Institute's Soref Symposium, May 29, 2008, https://ciaotest.cc.columbia.edu/wps/winep/0002006/f_0002006_1027.pdf.
35. Karim Sadjadpour, *Reading Khamenei: The World View of Iran's Most Powerful Leader*, Carnegie Endowment, p. 18, https://carnegieendowment.org/files/sadjadpour_iran_final2.pdf.
36. Khamenei, "Islamic Democracy in Iran Has Been Able to Disrupt the Domineering Powers' Agenda," *Khamenei.ir*, May 25, 2022, https://english.khamenei.ir/news/9012/Islamic-democracy-in-Iran-has-been-able-to-disrupt-the-Domineering.
37. Khamenei, "Transformation of the World: Arrogant Powers in Decline and New Powers Emerging," *Khamenei.ir*, September 11, 2023, https://english.khamenei.ir/news/10083/Transformation-of-the-world-Arrogant-Powers-in-decline-new.
38. Khamenei, "Transformation of the World."
39. For example, see Khamenei, "We Are Against Both Domination and Submission in International Relations," *Khamenei.ir*, August 30, 2023, https://english.khamenei.ir/news/10062/We-are-against-both-domination-and-submission-in-international.
40. Karim Sadjadpour, "The Question Is No Longer Whether Iranians Will Topple the Ayatollah," *The New York Times*, December 12, 2022, https://www.nytimes.com/2022/12/12/opinion/iran-protests-veil-khamenei.html.
41. "How Is the Iranian Government Responding to Protests?" *PBS Newshour*, January 2, 2018, https://www.pbs.org/newshour/show/how-is-the-iranian-government-responding-to-protests.
42. See Iran Primer, "U.N. Report on Protest Crackdown," *United States Institute of Peace*, March 8, 2024, https://iranprimer.usip.org/blog/2024/mar/08/un-report-protest-crackdown.
43. Quoted in Tharoor, "Iran Stages Dismal Election as Islamic Regime Circles the Wagons."
44. Quoted in Tharoor, "Iran Stages Dismal Election as Islamic Regime Circles the Wagons."
45. See Christian Triebert, Blacki Migliozzi, Neil Bedi, and Alexander Cardia, "The $2.8 Billion Hole in US Sanctions on Iran," *The New York Times*, February 16, 2024, https://www.nytimes.com/interactive/2024/02/16/world/middleeast/iran-oil-tankers-sanctions.html; Henry Rome and Noam Raydan, "Iran's Soaring Oil Exports," *The Washington Institute for Near East Policy*, September 15, 2023, https://www.washingtoninstitute.org/policy-analysis/infographic-visual-guide-irans-soaring-oil-exports.
46. See Bijan Khajehpour, "Deep Data: The Iranian Economy in 2024," *Amwaj*, February 23, 2024, https://amwaj.media/article/deep-data-the-iranian-economy-in-2024.
47. Khajehpour, "Deep Data."

48. Quoted in Khajehpour, "Will Iran's Central Bank Chief Stabilize the Riyal?" *Amwaj*, July 9, 2023, https://amwaj.media/article/will-iran-s-new-central-bank-chief-stabilize-the-rial.

49. Quoted in Karim Sadjadpour, "Mahsa Amini's Death Still Haunts the Iranian Regime," *TIME*, September 12, 2023, https://time.com/6312691/mahsa-amini-death-anniversary-iran/.

50. See Mohammad Mirzavand and Rahim Baghari, "The Water Crisis in Iran: Development or Destruction," *World Water Policy*, vol. 6, no. 1 (May 14, 2020): 89–97.

51. Eliot A. Cohen, "Iran Cannot Be Conciliated," *The Atlantic*, January 29, 2024, https://www.theatlantic.com/ideas/archive/2024/01/iran-problem/677282/.

52. Maloney, "After the Iran Deal."

53. Maloney, "After the Iran Deal."

54. Maloney, "After the Iran Deal."

55. Henry Rome, "Policy Note 135: Arming the Revolution: Trends in Iranian Defense Spending, 2013–2023," *The Washington Institute for Near East Policy*, June 14, 2023, https://www.washingtoninstitute.org/policy-analysis/arming-revolution-trends-iranian-defense-spending-2013-23.

56. Eric Brewer and Henry Rome, "Biden's Iran Gamble: A Risky New Strategy to Keep Tehran From Going Nuclear," *Foreign Affairs*, June 9, 2023, https://www.foreignaffairs.com/iran/bidens-iran-gamble.

57. Parisa Hafezi and Andrew Hayley, "Exclusive: China Presses Iran to Rein in Houthi Attacks in Red Sea, Sources Say," *Reuters*, January 25, 2024, https://www.reuters.com/world/middle-east/china-presses-iran-rein-houthi-attacks-red-sea-sources-say-2024-01-26/.

Chapter 13

1. Condoleezza Rice, *No Higher Honor: A Memoir of My Washington Years* (New York, NY: Crown, 2011), p. 550.

2. "Full Transcript: Prince Bandar bin Sultan's Interview on Israel–Palestine Conflict," *Al Arabiya*, October 5, 2020, https://english.alarabiya.net/features/2020/10/05/Full-transcript-Part-one-of-Prince-Bandar-bin-Sultan-s-interview-with-Al-Arabiya.

3. To read the Clinton parameters, see Dennis Ross, *The Missing Peace*, (New York, NY: FSG, 2004) annex.

4. See Times of Israel Staff, "Surveillance Soldiers Charge Sexism a Factor in Their Oct. 7 Warnings Being Ignored," *Times of Israel*, November 19, 2023, https://www.timesofisrael.com/surveillance-soldiers-say-oct-7-warnings-ignored-charge-sexism-played-a-role/; Ronen Bergman, "Israel Had a Blueprint for the Oct. 7 Attacks a Year Ago. Officials Dismissed It," *The New York Times*, December 1, 2023, https://www.nytimes.com/2023/11/30/world/middleeast/israel-had-a-blueprint-of-the-oct-7-attacks-a-year-ago-officials-dismissed-it.html.

5. Jerusalem Post staff, "Majority of Jewish Israelis Opposed to Demilitarized Palestinian State—Survey," *Jerusalem Post*, February 21, 2024, https://www.jpost.com/israel-news/article-788114#google_vignette.

6. "Public Opinion Poll No (91)," *Palestinian Center for Policy and Survey Research*, March 20, 2024, https://pcpsr.org/en/node/969.

7. "The Strait of Hormuz is the World's Most Important Oil Transit Chokepoint," *U.S. Energy Information Administration*, November 21, 2023; https://www.eia.gov/todayinenergy/detail.php?id=61002; "Red Sea Chokepoints Are Critical for International Oil and Natural Gas Flows," *U.S. Energy Information Administration*, December 4, 2023, https://www.eia.gov/todayinenergy/detail.php?id=61025; Spencer Feingold, "Red Sea Attacks: What Trade Experts Are Saying about Shipping Disruptions," *World Economic Forum*, February 20, 2024, https://www.weforum.org/agenda/2024/02/red-sea-attacks-trade-experts-houthi-shipping-yemen.

8. David Makovsky, "Beyond the Blocs: Jewish Settlement East of Israel's Security Barrier and How to Avert the Slide to a One-State Outcome," *The Washington Institute for Near East Policy*, April 2022, https://www.washingtoninstitute.org/media/5489.

9. David Makovsky, "Beyond the Blocs."

10. Orhan Niksic, Nur Nasser Eddin, and Massimiliano Cali, "Area C of the West Bank and the Future of the Palestinian Economy," *The World Bank*, 2014, p. 5, https://documents1.worldbank.org/curated/en/257131468140639464/pdf/Area-C-and-the-future-of-the-Palestinian-economy.pdf.

Chapter 14

1. Sean Power, "John Kerry Adds Exclamation Point to Climate Change, Intelligence, and Global Security Conference," *Belfer Center for Science and International Affairs*, April 27, 2021, https://www.belfercenter.org/publication/john-kerry-adds-exclamation-point-climate-change-intelligence-and-global-security.
2. Lawrence H. Summers and N. K. Singh, "The World Is Still on Fire," *Project Syndicate*, April 15, 2024, https://www.project-syndicate.org/commentary/imf-world-bank-spring-meetings-need-to-get-four-things-right-by-lawrence-h-summers-and-n-k-singh-2024-04.
3. Summers and Singh, "The World Is Still on Fire."
4. See Ashutosh Pandley, "Is the US Denying China a Bigger Voice at the IMF?" *DW*, October 13, 2023, https://www.dw.com/en/is-the-us-denying-china-a-bigger-voice-at-the-imf/a-67089133.
5. "Remarks as Prepared for John Podesta, Columbia Global Energy Summit," April 16, 2024, https://www.whitehouse.gov/briefing-room/speeches-remarks/2024/04/16/remarks-as-prepared-for-john-podesta-columbia-global-energy-summit.
6. Catherine Clifford, "Hydrogen Power Is Gaining Momentum, but Critics Say It's Neither Efficient Nor Green Enough," *CNBC*, January 14, 2022, https://hydrogen-central.com/hydrogen-momentum-critics-efficient-green-enough/.
7. "Who Gets to Decide to Re-Engineer the Weather?" *The Washington Post*, April 27, 2024, https://www.washingtonpost.com/opinions/2024/04/27/climate-change-geoengineering/.
8. Dalia Najjar, "That Bites: How Climate Change Increases the Spread of Mosquito-Borne Diseases," *The Bard CEP Eco Reader*, May 2, 2016, https://www.bard.edu/cep/blog/?p=8199.
9. Najjar, "That Bites."
10. Francesco Chiappelli and Jaden Penhaskashi, "Permafrost Immunity," *Bioinformation*, September 30, 2022, https://www.ncbi.nlm.nih.gov/pmc/articles/PMC10326340/.
11. See Katherine Dillinger, "Genetic Sequence of the Coronavirus Was Submitted to US Database Two Weeks before China's Official Disclosure Documents Show," *CNN*, January 17, 2024, https://edition.cnn.com/2024/01/17/health/coronavirus-sequence-database/index.html.
12. Dr. Daniel Douek, interview with the author, May 7, 2024.
13. Douek, interview with the author.
14. "WHO Director-General's Remarks to the Standing Committee on Health Emergency Prevention, Preparedness, and Response of the CDC," September 13, 2023, https://www.who.int/director-general/speeches/detail/who-director-general-s-opening-remarks-at-the-standing-committee-on-health-emergency-prevention--preparedness-and-response---13-september-2023 .
15. Computer Security Research Center, "Cyber Attack," *National Institute of Standards and Technology*, https://csrc.nist.gov/glossary/term/cyber_attack.
16. Jacquelyn Schneider, "A World without Trust—The Insidious Cyberthreat," *Foreign Affairs*, January 2022, https://www.foreignaffairs.com/articles/world/2021-12-14/world-without-trust.
17. "National Cybersecurity Strategy," *The White House*, March 2023, https://www.whitehouse.gov/wp-content/uploads/2023/03/National-Cybersecurity-Strategy-2023.pdf.
18. Office of the Spokesperson, "Release of United States' International Cyberspace and Digital Policy Strategy," *U.S. Department of State*, May 6, 2024, https://www.state.gov/release-of-united-states-international-cyberspace-and-digital-policy-strategy/.
19. Sue Gordon and Eric Rosenbach, "America's Cyber-Reckoning—How to Fix a Failing Strategy," *Foreign Affairs*, January/February 2022, https://www.foreignaffairs.com/articles/united-states/2021-12-14/americas-cyber-reckoning.
20. Gordon and Rosenbach, "America's Cyber-Reckoning."
21. Evan Burke, "The Obama–Xi Summit and the Prospects for a Global Norm Against Commercial IP Theft," *Carnegie Endowment for International Peace*, June 14, 2021, https://carnegieendowment.org/posts/2021/06/the-obama-xi-summit-and-the-prospects-for-a-global-norm-against-commercial-ip-theft?lang=en¢er=global.
22. Derek B. Johnson, "Eight Years Since Obama–Xi Agreement, Chinese Hacking Worse Than Ever," *SC Media*, April 24, 2023, https://www.scmagazine.com/news/eight-years-obama-xi-agreement-chinese-hacking-iworse-than-ever.
23. Quoted in Johnson, "Eight Years Since Obama–Xi Agreement."

24. Lucas Kello, *The Virtual Weapon and International Order* (New Haven, CT: Yale University Press, 2017), p. 123.
25. Kello, p. 124.
26. Joseph Nye, "The End of Cyber-Anarchy? How to Build a New Digital Order," *Foreign Affairs*, January/February 2022, https://www.foreignaffairs.com/articles/russian-federation/2021-12-14/end-cyber-anarchy.
27. Markus Maybaum and Jens Tolle, "Arms Control in Cyberspace: Architecture for a Trust-Based Implementation Framework Based on Conventional Arms Methods," *Cyber Power*, 2018, https://ccdcoe.org/uploads/2018/10/Art-11-Arms-Control-in-Cyberspace.pdf.

Index

For the benefit of digital users, indexed terms that span two pages (e.g., 52–53) may, on occasion, appear on only one of those pages.